PORTUGAL GUIDE

YOUR PASSPORT TO GREAT TRAVEL!

RON CHARLES

OPEN ROAD PUBLISHING

Open Road Publishing offers travel guides to American and foreign locales. Our books tell it like it is, often with an opioniated edge, and our experienced authors always give you all the information you need to have the trip of a lifetime. Write for your free catalog of all our titles, including our golf and restaurant guides.
OPEN ROAD PUBLISHING
P.O. Box 11249, Cleveland Park Station, Washington, DC 20008

This book is dedicated to José Rodrigues dos Santos and João Manuel Vieira de Castro Ribeiro, and also to José Almeida, Maria Regina Moreira, Jean Louis de Talance, Jan Willem Bos, Alfredo Jorge Pereira Santos, Martina de Almeida, António Simoes de Almeida, José Portugal Catalão, and Irene Pereira.

These are the people who have developed the business of accommodating tourists in Portugal into an art form. They have deeply inspired me throughout the years, and I certainly hope that my readers will have the privilege of benefiting from the experience and professionalism of these special "hoteliers."

©Copyright 1995 by Ron Charles
ISBN 1-883323-16-9
Librayr of Congress Catalog Card No. 94-69847

Text and Principal Photography by Ron Charles
Additional photography by Harry Swiderski, Harvey Abend, Dorothy Abend, Neil Evans, Shirley Thomas

PORTUGAL GUIDE

YOUR PASSPORT TO GREAT TRAVEL!

ACKNOWLEDGMENTS

I also wish to thank the following people which I have interviewed for this publication. Without their help it would have taken me several more years to complete my work:

Dr. Alexandre Relvas - Secretary of State of Portugal - Tourism Division (Lisbon); Maria do Carmo Sousa Dias - Portuguese National Tourist Board (Toronto); Paulo Loff - I.C.E.P.- Tourism Promotion, North American Division (Lisbon); Pedro Antunes de Almeida - Chairman of Enatur-Pousadas (Lisbon); Nuno Jardim Fernandes - Marketing Manager of Enatur-Pousadas (Lisbon); João Ricardo Alves - Director of Marketing for Europcar (Lisbon); Luís Filipe da Piedade André - Ticketing Supervisor for TAP Air Portugal (Lisbon); Paulo B. Melo - Northeast Regional Manager for TAP Air Portugal (Boston); Gloria Melo - Supervisor - TAP Air Portugal (Newark Headquarters); Artur Mc Millan - Director of Quasar Tours (Lisbon); António Morais - Director of Feriasol Viagens (Cascais); Nina Chung - Director of Public Relations - Hostelling International (Canada); Sandra Quintino da Silva - I.N.P. Interpreter and Guide (Queluz); Pedro Mesquita - Lawyer and Political Advisor (Porto).

And the countless hotel managers, *quinta* owners, museum curators, winery staff, *pousada* workers, taxi drivers, tour guides, airline employees, mayors, civil servants, *Turismo* offices, and especially the kind and informative local residents of Portugal who have provided me with much of the material used for this book.

HIT THE OPEN ROAD - WITH OPEN ROAD PUBLISHING!

Open Road Publishing now has guide books to exciting, fun destinations on four continents, but, oddly enough, some people out there still don't know who we are! We're old college pals and veteran travelers who decided to join forces to bring you the best travel guides available anywhere!

No small task, but here's what we offer:

• All Open Road publications are written by authors, authors with a distinct, opinionated point of view – not some sterile committee or team of writers. Our authors are experts in the areas covered and are polished writers.

• Our guides are geared to people who want great vacations, great value, and great tips for both standard tourist sites *and* fun, unique alternatives.

• We're strong on the basics, but we also provide terrific choices for those looking to get off the beaten path and *experience* the country or city – not just *see* it or pass through it.

• We give you the best, but we also tell you about the worst and what to avoid. Nobody should waste their time and money on their hard-earned vacation because of bad or inadequate travel advice.

• Our guides assume nothing. We tell you everything you need to know to have the trip of a lifetime – presented in a fun, literate, no-nonsense style.

• And, above all, we welcome your input, ideas, and suggestions to help us put out the best travel guides possible.

TABLE OF CONTENTS

1. INTRODUCTION   11

2. OVERVIEW - EXCITING PORTUGAL!   12

3. A SHORT HISTORY   18

4. PLANNING YOUR TRIP   22
Before You Go   22
Portuguese Embassies in North America   23
When to Visit Portugal   23
What to Pack   24
Portuguese National Tourist Offices   25
Travel Emergency, Trip Cancellation, and Medical Insurance   26
Booking Your Vacation and Travel Agencies   27
Tour Operators   28
Flights to Portugal   30
Flights with Connections to Portugal   32
Charter Flights and Discount Ticket Consolidators   33
Courier Flights   34
Traveling By Air Within Portugal   34
Traveling By Car   35
Trains in Portugal   38
Major Train Routes   42
Traveling By Bus   47

5. ITINERARIES FOR THE PERFECT PORTUGAL VACATION   51

6. BASIC INFORMATION   62

7. TYPES OF ACCOMMODATIONS IN PORTUGAL   73
Pousadas   73
Quintas   74
Hotels   75
Villas & Apartamentos   75
Albergarias, Estalagens, Residencials   76
Pensões, Quartos Privativos, Youth Hostels   77
Camping   79

8. THE MOST MEMORABLE PLACES TO STAY   81

9. MAJOR FESTIVALS   99

10. SHOPPING   103

11. SPORTS & RECREATION   111

12. PORTUGUESE CUISINE   120

13. WINES OF PORTUGAL   125

14. LISBON   134
Arrivals & Departures   136
Orientation   138
Getting Around Town   140
Where to Stay   142
Where to Eat   145
Bars, Clubs, & Nightlife   148
Seeing the Sights   150
Shopping   162
Sports   164
Practical Information   164

15. COSTA DE LISBOA   167

16. COSTA DE PRATA   201

17. PORTO   245

18. COSTA VERDE   258

19. THE MONTANHAS   298

20. THE PLANÍCIES   334

21. THE ALGARVE   378

DICTIONARY & USEFUL PHRASES   424

INDEX   431

MAPS

Regional 10
Portugal 13
Cultural Provinces 15
Lisboa 135
Costa de Lisboa 169
Costa de Prata 203
Porto 247
Costa Verde 259
Montanhas 299
Planicies 335
Train Routes 423

SIDEBARS

Where is Portugal? 12
Average Temperatures 24
Travel Insurance Companies in North America 27
Why Use a Travel Professional? 27
Major Car Rental Companies in North America 37
Take a Scenic Train Ride! 39
Converting Dollars to Escudos 62
There & Back Again by Phone 70
Good Numbers to Know 71
Suggested Tips 72
Hotel Price Guidelines 73
Hostel Information & Reservations 78
European Size Conversions 105
A Dictionary of Commonly-Used Wine
& Spirits Notations 133
Some Useful Phone Numbers for
Local & International Calls 166
Discoverer of Brazil 322

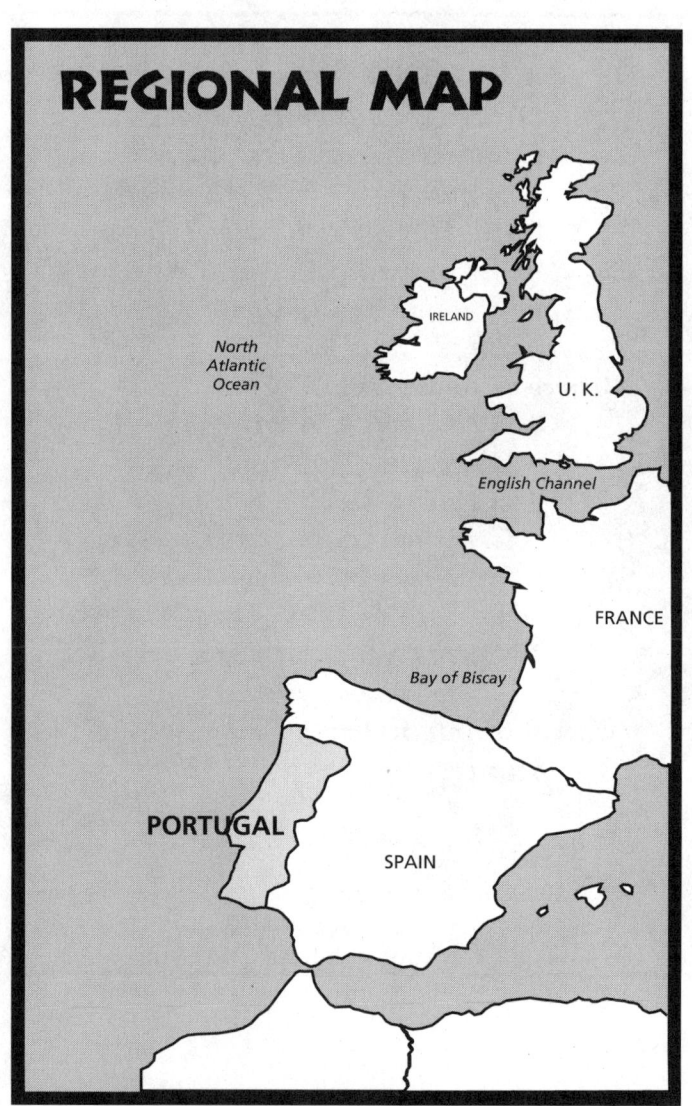

1. INTRODUCTION

Portugal is a warm and mysterious country that has remained all but undiscovered by the vast majority of the North American travelling public.

In today's Europe, it is difficult to imagine a country which is as warm, friendly, and inexpensive to explore. While many tourists have been to the beaches of Portugal's Algarve region, few make the effort necessary to look into the *soul* of Portugal – but I'll show you what this country's really all about: medieval walled villages, Roman temples, prehistoric megaliths, royal palaces, pristine beaches, and traditional fishing villages scattered throughout the entire country. The most important aspect to travelling through any region of Portugal is that you will soon learn to expect the completely unexpected and thoroughly enjoy the adventure.

In Portugal it is possible to spend your vacation in a combination of palaces, castles, romantic bed and breakfast inns, seafront fortresses, opulent villas, turn of the century spas, and resort hotels for much less money than you might imagine. The recent compliance with European Community regulations has lead to the modernization of the once dangerous and archaic transportation and road system. It is now possible to travel from one end of Portugal to the other by superhighway in less than seven hours. A vast amount of the country can be experienced and enjoyed by the casual visitor in the space of just one or two weeks.

During the course of just one vacation you can visit wineries for free tastings, enjoy fine gourmet meals, wander through ancient stone villages, hike through parks filled with wild horses, meet local families, take in several magnificent museums, hunt for handmade local crafts and antiques, play a round of golf on a dramatic seaside course, try your luck at a casino, shop for great bargains, experience a wonderful *Fado* show, and just relax and sunbathe on a magnificent beach.

This book has been designed to give all of the information necessary to create your own unique itinerary. You will find many recommendations included in each chapter to point you in the right direction. With a little research, an open mind, and a taste for adventure, your trip to Portugal will be unforgettable.

2. OVERVIEW - EXCITING PORTUGAL!

Welcome to Portugal! Get ready for the trip of a lifetime!
Prices for accommodations, rental cars, air tickets, trains, and meals are among the lowest in all of Western Europe. The low season is an exceptional value, especially the warmer months of March and October.

> **WHERE IS PORTUGAL?**
> *The mainland of Portugal rests on the westernmost point of the European continent. It is a fairly small country that occupies a little over 91,500 square kilometers (about 34,350 square miles), and has a population base of some 10 million people. The Atlantic Ocean has carved its dramatic coastlines to form the country's southern and western beach-laden borders, while Spain surrounds Portugal to the north and east. The inland sections of the country are covered with remarkable mountains, vast plains, tranquil river valleys, fish stocked lakes, unpolluted rivers, and all but forgotten hamlets.*

Historically, Portugal was divided into 11 seperate provinces – the Minho, Trás-os-Montes, Douro, Beira Alta, Beira Baixa, Beira Litoral, Estremadura, Ribatejo, Alto Alentejo, Baixa Alentejo, and the Algarve. Although these old provincial divisions still remain, these days the government has decided to consolidate these provinces into a series of 6 larger regions which this book will deal with. These regions are thus called, and referred to in this publication as the **Costa Verde**, **Montanhas**, **Costa de Prata**, **Planícies**, **Costa de Lisboa**, and the **Algarve**.

LISBON
Lisbon is a modern, vibrant city, but it is also steeped in history and tradtion. Vendors will stand outside their establishments and chat with passers-by. Fishmongers can be heard in the markets extolling the virtues of today's catch. Children walk to school clutching the bottom of their

OVERVIEW - EXCITING PORTUGAL 13

grandmothers' dresses. It seems that the old village way of life can still be found in some parts of Lisbon.

This blend of old and new permits the casual visitor to experience Lisbon in just one or two long days of wandering around the city. In the space of just a few days, it is entirely possible to do some serious sightseeing, visit impressive art collections, eat inexpensive regional cuisines, shop for bargain-priced fine European goods, walk past hundreds of opulent old houses, and then spend an enjoyable late night out. Lisbon is a rather safe, inexpensive, and welcoming city to explore.

PORTO

The massive city of **Porto**, the second largest city in Portugal, is located on the north bank of the **Douro** river's mouth. Porto's inner beauty will become apparent to all who visit. The magnificent Gothic 14th-century **Igreja de São Fransisco** church and its unforgettable vaulted baroque interior should not be missed.

Shoppers will particularly like Porto; the famed merchant street of *Rua de Santa Catarina* provides the best shopping possibilities for high quality men's and women's clothing, leather goods, jewelry, and antiques.

COSTA DE LISBOA

The **Costa de Lisboa** region contains portions of southern **Estremadura** and northwestern **Baixa Alentejo**, as well as a sliver of southwestern **Ribatejo** province. This beautiful area is comprised mainly of the cities, villages, and seaside resort areas that surround the capital city of Lisbon and its southern suburbs. The majority of this area is in close proximity to the sea and the coast.

COSTA DE PRATA

This relatively peaceful region, north of Lisbon, contains the **Beira Litoral** province, the northern section of **Estremadura**, and a small piece of western **Beira Alta**. Although the **Costa de Prata** boasts some magnificent beaches, most of the region is comprised of forests and countryside. Many small roads wind their way through centuries-old villages and cities, each with their own special charm.

COSTA VERDE

The **Costa Verde** region is located in the extreme northwestern section of Portugal and contains both the **Douro** and **Minho** provinces as well as a tiny slice of northwestern **Trás-os-Montes**. Many mountains, valleys, and rivers surround the Costa Verde's major population areas.

OVERVIEW - EXCITING PORTUGAL 15

The land in this region is very fertile, and much of Portugal's wine production occurs here. Within the last several years, a major increase of industry has resulted in a big increase in population.

THE MONTANHAS

The **Montanhas** – the *mountainous region* – is a remote section in Portugal's northeast corner, seldom visited by tourists. Comprised of large chunks of the **Trás-os-Montes**, **Beira Baixa**, and **Beira Alta** provinces, the **Montanhas** region is full of rugged snow-capped mountains, dense pine forests, and huge boulder spiked valleys which dominate the landscape.

One of the country's oldest rituals is the **Festas dos Rapazes**, where young men dress up in bizzare masks and colorful costumes. The festival is held during the last week of December and first week of January in small villages in the far north of the Montanhas.

CULTURAL PROVINCES

THE PLANÍCIES

The **Planícies** (*the plains*) is the largest region in Portugal and consists of the complete **Alto Alentejo** province, as well as most of the **Ribatejo** and **Baixa Alentejo** provinces, which make up roughly one-third of Portugal's land mass. The majority of this highly agricultural and historic region is covered with cork and olive fields. Prehistoric megaliths, cave drawings, and opulent cathedrals are common sights in this vast area.

The friendly peasants who ride their oxen and donkeys down the small rural highways are happy to stop and talk to locals and tourists alike. Besides the wonderful hand-made ceramics and tapestries created by local artisans, the Planícies produces several varieties of table wines that are quite enjoyable and inexpensive.

THE ALGARVE

The **Algarve** is the southernmost region in mainland Portugal and is drenched with sunshine for almost the entire year. Surrounded by a series of mountain ranges to its north and an abudance of sand dunes and rock cliff beaches on its windswept southern coastline, this area has become the most visited region in all of the country.

Although most of the Algarve's beautiful coast is crammed with one hotel after another, several small fishing villages and inland towns are quite secluded and full of their original historic and traditional character. Most visitors seem determined to spend their days on the vast assortment of sandy beaches (several are topless) and their nights hopping between the many pubs and loud discos in such packed resort areas as **Albufeira**, **Praia da Rocha**, and **Vilamoura**.

BULLFIGHTS

One of the most exciting spectator sports is the Portuguese bullfight (*tourada*). These events have been enjoyed in Portugal since the 14th century, and are a great source of regional pride. Unlike the brutal Spanish form of the sport, in Portugal the bulls are not killed at the end of a fight. Here the sport seems much more like a test of wills rather than a grisly slaughter.

Many cities and towns all over Portugal hold weekly or monthly bullfighting events from April through October in specially designed arena-shaped bullring (*Praça de Touros*).

SHOPPING

Every region in Portugal offers a variety of outdoor bazaar style markets. The wide assortment of goods for sale include local cheeses, meats, live poultry, ceramics, crafts, leather jackets, shoes, clothing,

OVERVIEW - EXCITING PORTUGAL 17

tapestries, furniture, antiques, and an assortment of imported items and trinkets. Fine shoes, shirts, sweaters, dresses, handbags, belts, suits, linens, ceramics, tiles, embroidery, vintage wines, jewelry, and many other items can be found at a fraction of their export price.

FOOD & WINE

Each region of Portugal offers a large selection of unique traditional foods. While wandering through the country it is possible to enjoy sumptuous dishes in small local restaurants and *adegas* at reasonable prices.

Wine in Portugal is superb. Wines are grown in almost every corner of the country. Local residents of small villages and rural hamlets commonly make their own table wines. There are now over 125 different varieties produced in Portugal. Nine special zones have been established as the finest sectors in the country for high quality wine production. These so-called **Demarcated Regions** (*Regioes Demarcadas*) are strictly controlled as to their exact boundaries, types of wines allowed for production, maximum yields, production methods, and length of aging.

ENJOY PORTUGAL!

My hope is that after reading this book, you will be a well-informed and culturally sensitive visitor who can travel throughout Portugal with almost no stress. The best traveler is the well prepared traveler, and that is what I am trying to achieve with this book. I hope that I have been able to assist you in the process of creating the vacation of your dreams – at a price you can afford.

3. A SHORT HISTORY

Little is known about the prehistoric Mediterranean Paloeolithic residents who lived in what is now Portugal as far back as 8,000 years ago. These seemingly tribal people have left little evidence of their existance besides a few scattered burial caves and dolmens. Sometime around 3500 BC the Neolithic Iberians began to settle into the fertile valleys of northern Portugal and were later merged together with invading Celtics who had arrived in northern Portugal by about the 7th century BC.

This skilled Celt-Iberian herding civilization built and lived mainly in fortified hilltop villages (known as **Citânias**) of which several ruins can still be seen throughout the *Montanhas* region where they flourished during the Iron Age. The decendants of these Celt-Iberians came to be known as the Lusitanians and has left us several strange granite pigs (*Berrões*) and phallus shaped fertility symbols (*menhirs*), monoliths, megaliths, and cave drawings which are scattered throughout the **Planícies**, **Costa Verde**, and **Montanhas** regions. It was about this time the the Phoenicians created trading posts on the coast near *Lisbon*, while the Carthaginians traded on the **Algarve**.

After the Second Punic War in the 2nd century BC, the Romans began their annexation of the Iberian peninsula. The local Lusitanian chief Viriatus opposed the advance of the Romans, and was assassinated in 139 BC after many years of defending his territory. The Roman empire now controlled much of the region, and their regional capital became **Lisbon**. The Romans built cities, temples, roads, aqueducts, and cultivated several new crops such as grapes, olives, and almonds to the plains. Swabian farmers settled in what is now Costa Verde and Montanhas.

In the early 5th century AD after increasing violence and social upheaval, the Romans requested the help of the Visigoths to thwart the advance of barbarian tribes and mayhem on the Iberian peninsula. The Visigoths settled in several parts of what is now Spain and Portugal and helped to restore order. When the Roman empire started to decline, the Swabians and Visigoths merged into one culture and accepted Christianity. Now the land was under their control.

A SHORT HISTORY 19

In 711, the Moors began their conquest of Spain and Portugal. It was from their capital in the Algarve that the Moorish people dominated most of Portugal for over 4 centuries. Most of the residents in the south were forced to practice the Muslim religion.

In the late 10th century, the new country of **Portucale** emerges in the Christian-dominated northern reaches of what is now Portugal. This new land was now ruled by a crusader called Henry of Burgundy. Christian forces begin their movement south to defeat the Moors. Afonso Henriques (son of Henry of Burgundy) named himself King Dom Afonso of Portucale in 1139. He promised to free his new country from Moorish rule and reconquers Lisbon in 1147 with the help of thousands of European crusaders.

In the early 13th century, a parliamentary system (*cortes*) is established which administers centralized governmental authority. In 1249, King Dom Afonso III captured the city of Faro in the Algarve, and the Moors are expelled from Portugal forever. In 1290 King Dom Dinis founded the first university in Portugal at Lisbon (the University was moved to Coimbra in 1308), and established Portuguese (A Costa Verde dialect of Spanish) as the country's official language to replace Latin.

In 1385 King Dom João I defeated the Castilians' advancing troops at Aljubarrota and removed the constant threat of their desired occupation of Portugal. Peace reigned in Portugal for over 2 centuries. Now the Portuguese could spend their time and resources in the quest for exploration of the sea and undiscovered territories. In 1386 the Treaty of Windsor forged a long standing Anglo-Portuguese alliance. and was sealed with the marriage of King Dom João I to Phillipa of Lancaster (sister of the soon to be King Henry IV of England).

In the early 15th century, the son of King Dom João I, Prince Henry the Navigator, set up a school of navigation in the town of Sagres in the Algarve to foster what would become Portugal's massive 15th century expansion. Their desire was to put together in one building, the cartographers, cosmographers, and navigators who together could formulate a sea passage from Portugal to India via the South cape of Africa. This was the first school in the world to teach and research the principles which allow for navigation during such transoceanic voyages.

The school at Sagres was responsible for many successful discoveries including the voyages to Cape Bajador in 1434, followed by the rounding of the Cape of Good Hope (the southern tip of Africa) by Bartolomieu Dias in 1487, Vasco da Gama's discovery of a sea route to India in 1498, Pedro Cabral's voyage to Brazil in 1500, and Magellan's circumnavigation of the world in 1522. With discoveries such as these, for several years Portugal became the richest kingdom in Europe. In 1494 after realizing that the Castillian backed Columbus discovery of the Americas would also make Spain a world power, the Portuguese negotiated the Treaty of Tordesillas. This treaty divided the world in to 2 sections, the East would go to Portugal, and the West would go to Spain.

In 1492, the Spanish inquisition forced thousands of Jews to flee Spain and resettle in Portugal. In 1496 King Dom Manuel was forced to accept the expulsion of all Jews in Portugal as a condition to his marriage to the Castillian princess Isabel. The inquisition had come to Portugal. Although many of the Jews were converted into Catholicism, many others fled once again, while some Jews practiced their religion secretly in the more remote provinces of northern Portugal. Since the Jews essentially controlled the banking system in Portugal, the banks lost their ability to manage the kingdom's fortune and invested unwisely. Portugal's wealth began to diminish.

King Dom Sebastião was killed in 1578 during the defeat of the Portuguese troops trying to annex Morocco. This in turn led to the beginning of Spanish rule by King Philip II after the Spanish invasion of Portugal in 1580. In 1640, a rebellion within Portugal allowed the Duke of Bragança to seize power, and crown himself the new Portuguese King Dom João IV. War with the Spanish continued until Spain recognizes Portugal's sovereignty in 1688. In 1703, Portugal signed what was to be known as the Methuen Treaty which would create a defensive agreement with both England and the Dutch. This helps to assure further protection from any Spanish incursion. As the mid-18th century unfolded, gold and gemswere found in Brazil which led to a new source of wealth for Portugal.

On November 1, 1755, a major earthquake all but destroyed Lisbon. Major fires and tidal waves added to the tremendous devastation and loss of life. Immediately King José I ordered his head minister, Marquês de Pombal, to rebuild Lisbon and later Vila Real de Santo António. His forceful tactics and stern attitude make him a feared and powerful man, but he manages to quickly bring Lisbon into the next century and change forever it's appearance which now has many elements of the appropriately named Pombaline style.

In 1807, the Napoleonic war reached Portugal. French troops under the direction of Junot capture Lisbon. The royal family was rescued by British forces, and sailed to Brazil to begin their 14 year exile. British troops commanded by General Wellington land in Portugal in 1808. Wellington's troops are victorious during the bloody battle of Buçaco. France has failed to conquer Portugal and the English General Beresford remains in charge of the Portuguese army.

King Dom João VI returned to Portugal from his exile in Brazil in 1821 to face an army backed coup in *Porto*. The coup leaders created a new parliament and imposed new restrictions on the power and wealth of the

A SHORT HISTORY 21

former feudal lords and religious hierarchy. Brazil gains its independence during this period of civil war. King Dom João dies in 1826 and the throne is passed to King Dom Miguel.

With the assistance of the British, his brother, Dom Pedro, soon returned from Brazil to capture the throne in his name. Dom Pedro became king in 1834, and sent the former King, Dom Miguel, into exile. In 1908, King Dom Carlos and his son were assassinated in *Lisbon*. For the next two years, his other son Dom Manuel II, sat on the throne. In 1910, the monarchy finally ended when Republicans started an uprising. The King was sent into exile.

REPUBLICS, COUPS, & DEMOCRACY

The Proclamation of the Republic was signed by the Republicans on October 5, 1910. This is to be the end of the Portuguese monarchy forever. The republic creates popular discontent by not being able to provide stabilization to the economy and social order. Portugal's limited participation in World War I created additional internal pressures.

In 1928 a new minister of finance, Dr. António de Oliveira Salazar, is appointed to the Portuguese government. Massive budgetary changes allowed Dr. Salazar to reverse the country's deficit, and balance the budget. In 1932, Dr. Salazar becomes Prime Minister, and continued to improve the economic, political, and social conditions while imposing strong arm tactics to suppress his enemies. His leadership soon takes on dictatorial aspects. In his **Nova Estado** (new state) constitution he seized more power, abolishes other political parties, and enforced censorship. Salazar became critically ill in 1968 and passed power to his successor Marcelo Caetano. Dr. Salazar died in 1970. War with the former colonies in Africa start to drain the Governments financial resources.

On April 25, 1974, another coup by the so called **Movimento das Forças Armadas** (Movement of the Armed Forces) toppled the Caetano government. All of the African colonies were given their independence, and over 650,000 Portuguese citizens lost everything they owned in Africa, and became refugees in their own homeland. Many industries were nationalized, and huge tracts of land were seized.

But the country soon began to make its way back to democracy. Currently a new constitution is in place which allows free speech, freedom of the press, multiple political parties, and equal voting rights to all of Portugal's citizens. In 1986, Portugal became a member of the European Economic Community, and began to finally receive the international status and reputation for quality it has deserved for so long. The current president of Portugal, Mário Soares, has remained in power after successive re-elections since 1986.

4. PLANNING YOUR TRIP

BEFORE YOU GO
Visa Regulations

All US and Canadian citizens require only a valid passport to enter Portugal. Visitors who intend to spend over 60 days within Portugal must register with the police to recieve an extension before the end of the first 60 day period.

Customs Regulations upon Arrival

Customs and immigration officials are very relaxed in Portugal. I have very rarely seen anyone be subjected to a luggage search. The following are exerpted from the official Portuguese customs regulations at press time. Please check with the Portuguese consulate if you need further details.

North Americans arriving into Portugal are allowed to bring an unlimited amount of cash for means of payment for tourist or travel expenses.

Adults are each allowed to import into Portugal the following amounts of these products:
- Cigarettes   200
    or
- Cigarillos   100
    or
- Cigars   50
- Perfumes   50 grams
- Liquor   1 liter
- Wine   2 liters

All North American visitors are allowed, for temporary importation, objects for personal use which must leave with them upon departure.

Personal jewelry, cameras and video cameras, a reasonable quantity of film and accessories, binoculars, sports equipment such as tents and camping gear, fishing gear, guns (check with airline for restrictions), non-

PLANNING YOUR TRIP 23

motorized bicycles, tennis rackets, windsurfing boards, delta wings, musical instruments, sound recording equipment, radios and televisions, video recorders, typewriters, calculators, and personal computers.

If you have any additional questions, please contact one of the Portuguese embassies on this side of the ocean before you depart!

PORTUGUESE EMBASSIES
In the US
• *2125 Kalorama Rd, N.W., Washington, D.C. 20008, (202) 328-8610*

In Canada
• *645 Island Park Drive, Ottawa, Ontario K1Y OB8, (613) 729-0883*

WHEN TO VISIT PORTUGAL

For the sake of great sightseeing weather and relatively low cost per day of travel your best bet may be to go during the months of March, April, May, June, September, and October. These spring and fall time periods offer the visitor generally pleasant warm weather. Another benefit to these months is the abundance of available accommodations and airfare at low season rates. Rain falls in low quantities during these months with the possible exception of the northern regions of the country where you may need an umbrella.

If you are interested in visiting beaches to swim in warm ocean waters and sunbathe under the heat of the sun, you may prefer the June through August summer season. During these months all of Portugal becomes burning hot and overcrowded with vacationing tourists from all over the globe. Since most Europeans receive a full month of vacation with pay (typically during August) the airlines and hotels have no problem with increasing their rates by over 100% during these summer months. Although I have enjoyed the summers in Portugal, they are certainly not inexpensive.

The winter season of November through February is a great time to stick to southern Portugal or just visit the major cities throughout the country. Rain, snow, and wind are not uncommon to most regions of Portugal besides the *Algarve* this time of the year. The roads in the northern regions are often closed to traffic, and most of central zone is rather cold each night. The *Algarve* still is drenched with sunlight during the winter, but the climate is just warm.

See the climate chart on the next page for average temperatures in different regions:

AVERAGE TEMPERATURES

	Lisbon	Porto	Faro
January	53F/12C	48F/9C	54F/12C
February	54F/12C	51F/11C	56F/14C
March	57F/14C	53F/12C	58F/15C
April	60F/16C	57F/14C	62F/16C
May	63F/17C	59F/15C	65F/18C
June	67F/20C	63F/17C	72F/22C
July	69F/21C	67F/19C	76F/24C
August	72F/22C	69F/21C	77F/25C
September	70F/21C	65F/18C	73F/23C
October	67F/19C	61F/16C	66F/12C
November	59F/12C	54F/12C	61F/16C
December	54F/12C	49F/9C	55F/13C

WHAT TO PACK

When visiting Portugal there are several items which can come in handy. To begin with, most visitors will not have the need for suits, ties, expensive dresses, and formal clothing. Only a handfull of 5 star gourmet restaurants and snobby nightclubs will enforce a strict dress code. Any hotel will be pleased to welcome guests that are comfortably attired. Even the most important churches will never insist on visitors wearing long pants or long sleeve shirts.

Your main concearn about what to bring to wear should be based on the season which you will be arriving during, and it's typical climatic conditions. Since summers can be quite hot, I suggest lots of thin cotton clothing. In the spring and fall it would be wise to pack for mostly warm days, and chilly nights, with the possibility of rain at any time. In the winter you should be prepared for anything from rain and snow to unexpected heat waves.

In all seasons I suggest that you pack a money belt or sac, an umbrella, bathing suits, a sweater, comfortable walking shoes, sneakers, a waterproof windbreaker, extra glasses or contact lenses, necessary medications with copies of the presciptions, personal hygine items, sunglasses, an empty nylon bag for gifts and shopping, an electric converter, suntan lotion, lots of film and batteries, a waterproof keyholder for swimming, copies of your passport, travel insurance documents, a list of travelers check numbers, good maps, this book, and the phone number of your travel provider in case of emergencies.

PLANNING YOUR TRIP 25

CUSTOMS REGULATIONS
Upon Departure
Upon exiting Portugal, a limit of 100,000$00 Escudos in Portuguese currency and a limit of 1,000,000$00 Escudos worth of foreign currency may be exported without any specific documentation. Additional amounts will require proof of importation of such quantities.

Upon your Return to North America
All US citizens can return to America with up to $400 US without paying duty if you have left the USA for over 48 hours and haven't made another international trip within the last 30 days. Each family member is eligible for the same limits, and these amounts may be pooled together. Normally a 10% duty will be assessed on goods which have exceeded the $400 US value, but are below $1400.00 in total value. Above this point the duty will vary with the specific merchandise being imported.

Each adult may also bring in up to 1 liter of wine or alcohol and either 100 cigars (except from Cuba) or 200 cigarettes. There is no duty on antiquities or works of art which are over 100 years old. Bring all reciepts with the mechandise to customs to avoid additional problems.

All Canadian citizens can return to Canada with up to $300 CDN once each year if you have left Canada for over 7 days, or up to $100 CDN several times each year if you have left Canada for over 48 hours. Each family member is eligible for the same limits per person. Normally a combination of federal and provincial taxes will be assessed on goods which have exceeded the $300 CDN value depending on the specific items involved.

Each adult can also bring in 1.14 liters of alcohol, or 8.5 liters (24 cans or bottles each with 12 onces) of beer. Also allowed for those at least 16 years old are up to 50 cigars, 200 cigarettes, and 400 grams of tobacco. Reciepts will help you avoid additional problems.

PORTUGUESE NATIONAL TOURIST OFFICES IN NORTH AMERICA
Before you begin to plan your vacation in Portugal, it would be a good idea to contact your country's head office of the **Portuguese National Tourist Office**. If you ask a few questions relating to your specific interests, these offices will send you large manilla envelopes full of maps, English language tourist information, artistically designed regional summaries, phrase books, and maybe even a few glossy brochures from the powerful and well connected major tour operators (although these companies are usually not the best).

The receptionists at these offices are usually very informative Portuguese residents who are trying their best to keep up with the tidal wave of daily inquiries. If their line seems constantly busy, or if they don't seem to have the time to answer many questions, it's only because they are so understaffed. These are nice people who have a huge amount of work to do, so you must consider the fact that they just can't spend lots of time with call ins.

On the other hand, a personal visit to one of the Portuguese National Tourist Offices or to a **Portuguese Trade Commission** office, which sometimes share the same office space, can result in a somewhat more intensive discussion and the chance to receive much more specific printed material. The Portuguese government's **I.C.E.P.** (*Instituto Comercio Externo de Portugal*) tourism division prints hundreds of useful documents in several languages which are then eventually sent along to the tourist and trade commissions which they control throughout the world.

Below is a list of Portuguese Tourist Boards in North America:
- Portuguese National Tourist Office
590 Fifth Ave, 4th Floor, New York City, N.Y. 10036, (212) 354 4403
- Portuguese National Tourist Office
60 Bloor St. West - Suite 1005, Toronto, Ontario, Canada M4W 3B8, (416) 921 7376

TRAVEL EMERGENCY & MEDICAL INSURANCE

One of the most important issues of any trip abroad is what to do in an emergency. Since the possibility of a medical problem is always a factor of risk, it is strongly advised that you take out an insurance policy. The best types of travel insurance are in the "Primary Coverage" category. In an emergency, most of these policies will provide 24 hour toll free help desks, lists of approved specialists, the ability to airlift you to a hospital with the proper facilities for your condition, and much more valuable assistance including refunds on additional expenses and unused hotel nights.

TRIP CANCELLATION & INTERRUPTION INSURANCE

Many special policies also cover vacation refunds if a family member gets ill and you must cancel your trip, if the airline you were supposed to be flying on goes out of business, if you must depart early from your trip due to sickness or death in the family, if the airline fails to deliver your baggage on time, if your luggage is stolen from your car, if your stay is extended do to injury, ect.

One element normally not covered are airplane schedule changes, missed connections, and flight cancellations. Please check with your travel agent or tour operator for further details.

TRAVEL INSURANCE COMPANIES IN NORTH AMERICA

Mutual of Omaha (Tele-Trip)
(800) 228-9792 in the USA
(402) 351-8000 in Canada
Travel Guard
(715) 345-0505 in the USA and Canada
Access America
(800) 284-8300 in the USA and Canada

BOOKING YOUR VACATION

Hopefully with the help of this guide book, you will have most of the information and suggestions necessary to begin planning your trip. The next step is to begin to book and paying for the elements which will create a perfect vacation. I strongly advise that you consider prepaying for the airfare, rental car, and some if not all of your accommodations. If you are traveling to Portugal between June and September, do not expect to find availability in many hotels and inns by just showing up. It is best advised to book all summer accommodations well in advance. In the low seasons, I suggest that you book at least the first and last few nights in advance, and then try to find a few places on your own.

WHY USE A TRAVEL PROFESSIONAL?

A good travel agent or specialty tour operator can provide detailed information on hotels, airfare, and car rentals without the need for travelers to spend hundreds of dollars calling overseas and not being able to communicate in Portuguese. They also have access to special prices which are not available to the general public. If anything goes wrong and you need a refund or change to your schedule, a good travel professional with advance notification can often avoid certain penalties that would normally apply.

TRAVEL AGENTS

Travel agents are consultants who usually get paid on a commission basis. If a client desires a normal package tour or bus trip, no additional fee should be charged as the agent's commission of between 8% and 12% is deducted from the package's list price. For special custom vacations (known in the industry as an **F.I.T.**), travel agents may charge as much as $125.00 US in advance to cover the extra hours and long distance calls which will be required. Each advance revision or cancellation may be heavily penalized with stiff fees or just as often may be non-refundable.

28 PORTUGAL GUIDE

Travel agents have access to computer databases which can search out the least expensive regularly scheduled airfares offered by international airlines, and also can look up information about over 7,000 hotels throughout the world. Travel agents also have access to large volume books like the Hotel and Travel Index which gives basic listings on tens of thousands of major hotels.

Unfortunately, most of the best deals on airfare, and most remarkable accommodations in Portugal are not going to appear in a travel agent's computer or hotel book. Since most travel agents have little or no personal knowledge about Portugal, your best bet is to either find an agent who has been to Portugal, or to do most of your own research before booking your trip.

TOUR OPERATORS

These are the wholesale sources for 100% of the packages and 95% of the F.I.T. custom vacations sold in North America. A good tour operator will specialize in just one or a few different countries, and have a staff of experts who have been to almost every hotel and inn located in the countries that they represent. Unfortunately, many tour operators do not sell direct to the public and prefer to deal with agencies to avoid lengthy phone calls.

I have included a list of a few fine tour operators who are quite willing to sell directly to the public. Because the staff of most tour operators do not get paid by commission, their suggestions tend to be honest evaluations of first hand experiences. Most tour operators do not accept credit cards, and will often charge a $50 US fee before booking custom packages.

Unlike travel agencies, these companies will often charge a much more reasonable penalty for each revision or cancellation made in advance. The only drawback with booking through tour operators is that many of them do not have the time to discuss topics at length. I have called many different tour operators and travel agencies to research this guide book. Only the most honest, experienced, and informative tour operators are listed below in order of their helpfulness and accuracy.

Recommended Tour Operators who sell direct to the Public

I have based these recommendations on the results of several cold calls I made to each company as a perspective client. On the first call I pretended to have with minimal knowledge about Portugal. I later called again acting as a former visitor to Portugal which wanted specific information about lesser known spots and accommodations for my next trip over.

The responses I got ranged from detailed answers on the phone with honest and informative follow up information in the mail from the first

PLANNING YOUR TRIP 29

few companies on the list, to no help at all (or totally slanted information) from a dozen or so others that I have deleted from this list.

European Travel Consultants *(800) 585-8085*
Serving all of North America.

An excellent full service custom tour operator which offers discount rates on airplane tickets, car rentals, hotels, *pousadas*, hotels, castles, *quintas*, villas, condos, apartments, bus tours, barge cruises, private guides, transfers, train tickets, golf vacations, totally customized (F.I.T.) fly/drive packages to all regions of Portugal, and long stay vacations. The staff are experts on all aspects of Portuguese travel and have all been to the country several times. The service is top notch.

T.A.P. -Girassol Tours *(800) 361-0699*
Serving Canada.

A large full service package tour operator that is managed in conjunction with TAP airlines which offers airplane tickets, bus tours, hotel reservations, car rentals, long stay vacations, *pousadas*, and a selection of semi customized fly/drive packages which concentrate mostly on major Portuguese resort destinations. The staff have been to Portugal, and the service is pretty good, but the phones can be busy all day.

Perrygolf *(800) 344-5257*
Serving all of North America.

An excellent golf program tour operator which offers a full range of week or longer golf vacations in the *Costa de Lisboa* and *Algarve* regions' finest resorts and courses. They can provide airfare, accommodations, and golf. Excellent service from a staff of dedicated golf enthusiasts, some of which have been to Portugal.

Abreu Tours *(800) 223-1580*
Serving the United States.

A large full service package tour operator which offers airplane tickets, bus tours, hotel reservations, car rentals, long stay vacations, *pousadas*, and a selection of semi customized fly/drive packages which concentrate mostly on major Portuguese resort destinations. Most of the staff have been to Portugal, and the service is pretty good if you don't ask too many questions.

Portuguese Tours *(800) 526-4047*
Serving the United States.

A good full service tour operator which will occasionally allow direct bookings. They can offer airfare, hotels, *pousadas* (minimum of 3 nights), resorts, fly/drive packages, long stay vacations, golf packages, and more. The staff have been to Portugal, and the service is pretty good.

T.A.P.-Discovery Vacations *(800) 247-8686*
Serving the United States.
   A large full service package tour operator managed in conjunction with TAP airlines which offers airplane tickets, bus tours, hotel reservations, car rentals, long stay vacations, *pousadas*, and a selection of semi customized fly/drive packages which concentrate mostly on major Portuguese resort destinations. Most of the staff have been to Portugal, and the service good if you can ever get more than a just a constant busy signal on the line.

Delta Dream Vacations *(800) 872-7786*
Serving all of North America.
   A full service tour operator managed by Delta airlines which offers airfare, hotels, cars, and other services for the Costa de Lisboa area only. They also have the ability to sell vouchers for hotels in some other regions. Some of the staff have been to Portugal, and the service is pretty good for such a big company

Marketing Ahead *(800) 223-1356*
Serving all of North America.
   A small hotel representation company which offers reasonable rates on *pousadas*, a few selected hotels, and rental cars. The staff have all been to Portugal, and service is pretty good if they have what you want.

American Express Vacations *(800) 241-1700*
Serving all of North America.
   A full service tour operator which offers airfare, hotels, cars, and other services for the *Lisbon* area only. Most of the staff have not been in Portugal, and the service is efficient but not informative. A good choice for businessmen going to *Lisbon*.

FLIGHTS TO PORTUGAL FROM NORTH AMERICA
TAP AIR PORTUGAL

> TAP Airlines USA: *1 800 221-7370*
> TAP Airlines Canada: *1 800 361-0699*
> TAP Airlines Lisbon: *(01) 386-1020*

   The best way to get to Portugal from the USA or Canada is to take advantage of the wide variety of non stop flights from the New York area.

PLANNING YOUR TRIP 31

The national carrier of Portugal is called *TAP*, and offers daily non stop flights from the New York area to Lisbon. For the past few years it has been possible to purchase round trip tickets on *TAP* for as little as $398 U.S. during the very limited winter specials, about $599 U.S. during the low season, and about $899 U.S. during the high season.

The airline also offers add on fares from a few major airlines which permit you connect from major North American and European cities onto *TAP's* routes. *TAP* operates a variety of flights from Lisbon to other Portuguese cities which can be added on to your international ticket at discounted rates if booked before you leave North America. Unfortunately, TAP has begun cutting back several of it's gateway cities, starting with the suspension of all service to and from Canada.

In low season, the airline has been known to cancel flights with less than 14 days warning. Make sure that if you are connecting from any other airline, your tickets are changeable in case of international flight rescheduling. Travel insurance does not cover this possibility. Service on *TAP* is quite good, and the planes are usually on time. The food is also good, but I suggest that you consider ordering a special meal (vegetarian, low fat, low salt, fish only, ect.) as these are even better. *TAP* has a frequent flyer program which at this time is not connected to other airlines' programs. Please remember *TAP's* policy of insisting you call them to confirm your flights in both directions at least 72 hours before they depart).

DELTA AIRLINES

> Delta Airlines USA: *1 800 221 1212*
> Delta Airlines Canada: *1 800 221 1212*

To meet the growing demand for additional service to Portugal, *Delta* airlines has now added daily non stop service from New York to Lisbon. This new service allows travellers to benefit from the price competition on this route. The prices for travel on this company usually match the going rate on *TAP*. *Delta* offers a large selection of add on fares for their own flights within North America and Europe, as well as prices with other major European carriers. If you wish to travel by plane to any other city in Portugal, *Delta* usually cannot match the rates which *TAP* offers because they do not operate flights within Portugal.

Service on *Delta* is pretty good, and the planes are usually on time. The food is reasonable, but I still suggest that you consider ordering a special meal (vegetarian, low fat, low salt, fish only, ect.) as these are better. *Delta* has a generous frequent flyer program which at this time is connected to other airline programs such as *Swiss Air*.

TWA AIRLINES

> **TWA Airlines USA:** *1 800 892 4141*
> **TWA Airlines Canada:** *1 800 448 2665*

TWA airlines offers at least 2 non-stop flights to *Lisbon* per week from the New York area. Prices usually match the going rate on *TAP* and *Delta*. *TWA* offers a large selection of add on fares for their own flights within North America and Europe, as well as prices with other major European carriers. If you wish to travel by plane to any other city in Portugal, *TWA* usually cannot match the rates which *T.A.P.* offers because they do not operate flights within Portugal.

Service on *TWA* is good, and the planes are generally on time. The food is reasonable, but I still suggest that you consider ordering a special meal (vegetarian, low fat, low salt, fish only, ect.) as these are better. *TWA* has a generous frequent flyer program.

FLIGHTS WITH CONNECTIONS TO PORTUGAL

Several international airlines offers service to *Lisbon*, *Faro*, and *Porto* from several North American cities. These flights take longer than the above mentioned airlines because the require a change of planes in Europe before continuing on to Portugal. The fares are often the same price as non-stop choices, but sometimes a free stop over in the city where you change planes is allowed.

The following is a partial listing of airlines with service to Portugal via another European gateway:
• **AIR FRANCE** (via Paris)
Air France in the USA *1 800 237-2747*
Air France in Canada *1 800 667-2747*
• **ALITALIA AIRLINES** (via Rome)
Alitalia Airlines in the USA *1 800 221-4745*
Alitalia Airlines in Canada *1 800 361-8336*
• **BRITISH AIR** (via London)
British Air in the USA *1 800 247-9297*
British Air in Canada *1 800 247-9297*
• **IBERIA AIRLINES** (via Madrid)
Iberia Airlines in the USA *1 800 772-4642*
Iberia Airlines in Canada *1 800 363-4534*
• **KLM AIRLINES** (via Amsterdam)
KLM Airlines in the USA *1 800 374-7747*
KLM Airlines in Canada *1 800 361-5073*
• **LUFTHANSA AIRLINES** (via Frankfurt)
Lufthansa Airlines in the USA *1 800 645-3880*

Lufthansa Airlines in Canada *1 800 645-3880*
• **SABENA AIRINESS** (via Brussels)
Sabena Airlines in the USA *1 800 955-2000*
Sabena Airlines in Canada *1 800 955-2000*
• **SWISS AIR** (via Zurich)
Swiss Air in the USA *1 800 221-4750*
Swiss Air in Canada *1 800 267-9477*

CHARTER FLIGHTS

In the high season (July-September) several charter operators offer Portugal airfare from New York, Boston, Toronto, and other North American gateways. Be extra careful whenever booking a charter flight as they are not bound by the same regulations as normal scheduled carriers.

It is not uncommon for these flights to be delayed for hours or days waiting for replacement equipment, while you are stuck at the airport. Charter flight tickets are normally nonchangeable/nonrefundable and are often not covered by travel insurance. For more details, call your travel agent.

Here are two charters I'd recommend:
• **COUNCIL CHARTER**: *1 800 800 8222*
• **AIR TRANSAT CHARTERS**: *1 800 523-0537*

DISCOUNT TICKET CONSOLIDATORS

There are many discount ticket brokers who offer last minute, ad special advance purchase round trip fares for airlines who have not sold enough seats on specific flights. While some of these companies are in the habit of ripping off clients, several large companies have been doing a fairly good job in suppling the traveling public with good deals on very restrictive tickets. First ask your travel agent for their recommendations, or call the local consumer protection agency or Better Business Bureau about any complaints on file about the consolidator you are about to use.

We strongly recommend that you either purchase your tickets from a travel agent, specialty tour operator, or use a major credit card to purchase this type of ticket directly from the consolidators. This way you will be better protected in case of any problems which may occur.

These are a few consolidators with a good reputation:
• **TRAVAC**: *1 212 563 3303*
• **AIR TRAVEL DISCOUNTS**: *1 212 922 1326*
• **UNITRAVEL**: *1 800 325 2222*
• **WORLD TRAVEL**: *1 800 886 4988*
• **TRAVEL CUTS**: *1 416 979 2406*
• **NEW FRONTIERS**: *1 514 526-8444*

COURIER FLIGHTS

In many cases, a large company may need to send documents to Europe on a specific day. Agencies exist that book passengers on flights to Europe and use their luggage allotment to transport several documents to European clients. Since you are giving up your rights to your luggage compartment space, you are only allowed to bring whatever you can carry aboard. Upon arrival, a representative from the courier company will take possession of the stored documents.

These flights can run as low as $199 US roundtrip and usually are valid for only 1 week. This is not the best way to travel because you never know what is really in those suitcases, and you are completely responsible for their contents. Another major disadvantage is that you may be booked on a standby, or next available day basis. Travel agencies do not reserve these types of tickets, so please check the travel section of your local newspaper.

Some reasonably good courier agencies include:
- **D.T.I.:** *1 212 362 3636*
- **NOW VOYAGER:** *1 212 431 1616*

TRAVELING BY AIR WITHIN PORTUGAL

There are several large commuter and tourist airports within Portugal. Most of the air traffic tends to be between Lisbon, Faro, Porto, and the autonomous coastal islands of Madeira and the Azores. Flights are very expensive if booked within Portugal. I have paid over 28,000$00 for a last minute one-way ticket from Lisbon to Faro.

If you intend to fly into one Portuguese airport and fly out of another one it is best to include this segment on your international ticket. Several companies offer inter regional flights on a daily basis, but not all are on jets. Please contact your specialty tour operator or travel agent for prices, reservations, and ticketing.

TAP-Air Portugal
Service between Lisbon and Faro, service between Lisbon and Madeira, service between Lisbon and Porto, service between Lisbon and the Azores, service between Madeira and Porto Santo. Plus other routes.

SATA-Air Azores
Service between most of the islands in the Azores.

Portugalia
Service between Lisbon, Porto, and Faro.

PLANNING YOUR TRIP 35

TRAVELING BY CAR

Other than the fact that driver's seat is still on the left side, driving in Portugal is not an easy task. If you are arriving in *Lisbon*, the hectic rotary exit from the airport is just the tip of the iceberg. It is best to preplan your driving route by using a good map and an outliner. Please ask the rental car company or hotel staff to give you detailed directions to your first location.

Portuguese people often seem to drive like maniacs. Expect other cars to pass on blind curves, pull multiple lane changes at high speeds, and generally disregard any form of manners on the road. If you drive very carefully, and stay in the appropriate lane for your desired velocity, you should be just fine. Be especially careful when driving into the northern reaches of Portugal. Many roads do not have lights or reflectors in small towns and the countryside. I have driven over 25,000 km. within Portugal, and I have never had an accident on the road. Official speed limits (unless otherwise posted) are 60 km/hr in towns and villages, 90 km/hr on normal roads, and 120 km/hr on highways.

Gas is extremely expensive in Portugal. Until very recently, the government had a monopoly on all gas stations, and still controls the pricing. At press time, gas costs approximately 180$00 per liter (about $4.20 US per gallon). Since all of the rental cars are rather small in Europe, fortunately most car's fuel efficiency is very high. Also, many cars in Portugal tend to run with leaded (*Chumbo*) gasoline, while the vast majority of newer rental cars need unleaded (*Sem Chumbo*) gas. Be careful not to use the wrong type of fuel. Over the last few years, many 24 hour 7 days a week gas stations have popped up throughout Portugal. Normal service station hours are from 8am until 7pm Monday – Friday, and are open from 9am – 1pm on Saturday. Some stations still close on Sundays.

It is important for me to explain that most roads in Portugal are named using the prefix of **Estrada Nacional** which means a national route. For the sake of space, I have abbreviated this term as the letter *N*, which is followed by a dash and the road number. In this fashion, you will find that listings for *Estrada Nacional 10* will appear in this book as *route N-10*, but may occasionaly be posted as *E.N. 10* on some maps and older road signs.

With the exception of a few high speed roads including the major *A-1* highway running from Lisbon to Porto (which can cost as much as 3000$00), road and bridge tolls are both rare and quite reasonable. It is a good idea to have a lot of 100$00 ESC coins handy in case you run into the unexpected tolls on the road you are travelling on. The high tech road traffic engineers in Portugal have designed a computerized automatic toll paying system called the *Via Verde* lane for frequent commuters. Please do not use these specially marked lanes (generally located on the extreme left)as your car may be stopped and you will be in big trouble. Now for the good news, there are only a handful of police radar systems in all of Portugal, and speeding tickets are extremely rare.

While crime is not a major issue for tourists in Portugal, a rental car is easy prey anywhere in the world. Please remember not to leave anything in your car when it is parked, and if possible it is advised to lock your gas cap. Since exposed hatchback cars have increased risks for potential pilferage, it is recommended to either cover the hatch, or avoid renting these categories of vehicles (usually the less expensive categories). Many companies (especially Europcar) maintain a very rapid car replacement service in the event that you incur a breakdown or an accident somewhere in Portugal. It is important to find out where the branch offices of your rental car company are located, and their emergency phone numbers.

The official representative in Portugal for members of the AAA and the CAA auto clubs is called the *ACP* (*Automóvel Clube de Portugal*) and if necessary they can be reached at *Rua Rosa Araujo, 24* in *Lisbon*. Please call them for the locations of additional branch offices and towing facilities; *the phone number is (01) 574 732.*

In the event of an accident, contact the police if possible. If you cannot reach the police to come to the scene of the accident, write down the licence plate of the other car(s) involved, and if posible his licence and insurance information. Immediately go to the closest police station and have them give you a copy of the accident report or the report number. Call your car rental company as soon as possible after you have obtained the required documentation.

Car Rentals

All major international airlines arrive to the capital city of Lisbon, the Algarve city of Faro, or the northern commercial city of Porto. In all three of these locations there is an abundance of well known rental car companies which operate both airport kiosks and downtown offices. Avis, Budget, National, Europcar, and several other local and international companies maintain airport hours from early morning until the last flight is scheduled to arrive.

If your flight is extremely late, you may have to camp out at the airport until the next morning to recieve your car. International drivers licences are not required for North Americans driving in Portugal. All that is required for car rental documentation is a major credit card, passport, and your valid US or Canadian drivers license.

If you intend to use a rental car in Portugal, it is advisable to call a specialized tour operator to book and prepay in advance from within North America so you can save up to 45% of the normal rate. If you decide to rent a car only once you have arrived in Portugal, rentals can be

PLANNING YOUR TRIP 37

arrainged from any Portuguese travel ageny or car rental company office. There are rental locations within most major Portuguese cities.

Call your credit card company before you leave for Europe to determine if any insurance is automatically included for car rentals in Portugal. Most forms of insurance (collision damage waiver, liability, personal accident injury insurance, property theft insurance) will be offered upon your pick up of the car and may add up to well over $25.00 US per day additional. Make sure that you are covered one way or another, or else you may wind up with a big problem.

With advance booking and prepayment from the USA or Canada, prices range from below $190 US per week for a small 2 door manual car (Fiat Uno or similiar) to well over $375 US per week for any automatic or 4 door sporty car. Specialty rentals such as Mercedes Benz or Mazeratti are available at rather hefty prices from local Lisbon based comapies like Facil Car. Also, keep in mind that the Lisbon airport has just added a new tax of about 1800$00 to all airport rental car pick ups.

If you so desire, you can pick up a rental car in one major city in Portugal and drop it off in another (usually no drop off charges are added). If you desire to drop off your car outside of Portugal, large drop off surcharges of well over $300 US will apply. Please keep in mind that taking a rental car from Portugal into Spain is only allowed if you inform the rental company that you are doing so in advance, and if they present you with special international insurance papers.

MAJOR CAR RENTAL COMPANIES IN NORTH AMERICA

Avis *in the U.S.A.*	1 800 331 1084
Avis *in Canada*	1 800 879 2847
Budget *in the U.S.A.*	1 800 527 0770
Budget *in Canada*	1 800 268 8900
Hertz *in the U.S.A.*	1 800 654 1101
Hertz *in Canada*	1 800 263 0600

Discount Car Rental Brokers in North America

Why pay full price for a rental car when you can save up to 40% off the above-mentioned rates by calling a full service car rental provider? These companies have deep discount high volume prices with many of the major car rental companies listed above, and offer much better service.

The best of these providers is, without doubt, **AutoEurope**. This organization offers all kinds of special deals on every type of rental car imaginable. On my last visit to Portugal, I saved $73 per week over the next best price quoted by the above companies, and I ended up with a

38 PORTUGAL GUIDE

much better car for no additional charge. The polite and friendly staff here will beat any price on the market, and can provide repeat client discounts, AAA and CAA specials, long stay rates, low season super specials, and inexpensive optional insurance.

Their fully refundable car rental vouchers can be instantly faxed, or sent via mail to your home or office, and only require a small partial prepayment. They tend to use Avis and Europcar rental locations, and lock you into a better exchange rate than even a bank will give you. Other in-house serivces include a worldwide hotel reservation service (free of charge on prepaid bookings), and special departments to handle unusual requests and last minute bookings.

Call the others first, then make your last call here. You'll save money and get much better service:
• **AutoEurope in the US**: *1 800 223-5555*
• **AutoEurope in Canada**: *1 800 223-5555*

TRAINS IN PORTUGAL

The government owns and operates a rail company called **CP** (*Caminhos de Ferro Portugueses*). Although occasionally prone to work stoppage (strikes) the services offered are usually inexpensive when compared with the equivalent bus tariff. There are currently 5 different categories of trains.

The **Rapido** or so called **Alfa** express trains stop less frequently and are an excellent method of longer distance travel between larger cities. The **Inter-cidade** or so called **IC** trains are usually the second fastest train connections between major population bases and are subject to more stops than the express trains. The **Inter-regional** or so called **IR** trains are somewhat slow and tend to stop often. There are also several regional commuter trains known as either a **Suburbano** or a **Regional** which often offer slow service with many stops between smaller cities and villages.

Some trains require advance reservations (especially the first class express or Alfa trains) and some other trains have special facilities such as sleeping compartments and automobile compartments which must be booked in advance with supplemental charges applied to your fare. There are also many trains which offer both the all to often crowded second class seats as well as more expensive and comfortable first class seating.

Most of the trains in Portugal offer reasonably good food and beverages in their dining cars. If you are traveling south of Lisbon, you may have to teke a ferry from the *Praça do Comercio's (Terreiro do Paço)* ferry landing to reach the train station on Barreiro. To purchase train tickets please contact **Rail Europe** before departing North America, or a *CP* station or a travel agency once you are within Portugal. All major train stations in Portugal are open by 9 am.

PLANNING YOUR TRIP 39

Several types of tourist train passes are available directly from the *CP* train offices and stations if presented with proper identification. These Portugal only unlimited **first-class** train passes (**Bilhetes Turisticos**) are available for 7 days (about 17,000$00), 14 days (about 26,000$00), and 21 days (about 36,000$00) and must be purchased within Portugal. Special train discounts are offered for specific cases.

If you are over the age of 65, you may recieve a discount of 30% off any normal fare with a passport. If you are over 65 years old and purchase a special senior citizen card (**Cartão Dourado**) from a major train station, you may be entitled to up to 50% off the normal fares during off peak hours. Children under the age of 4 can travel for free as long as they can sit on the parent's lap. Children between the ages of 4 and 12 years old can recieve up to a 50% discount on their fare. Families with children are also elegible to purchase a special family card (**Cartão de Familia**) which can reduce the price of their tickets when traveling together. Young adults between the ages of 12 and 26 years of age may also be permitted to puchase a special youth card (**Cartão Jovem**) which allows for discounts of up to 50% on long journeys during limited time periods.

> **TAKE A SCENIC TRAIN RIDE!**
> *For those of you interested in scenic train rides, there are a few remaining scenic narrow gauge railways and riverfront lines left in the north of Portugal. Some of these railroads include antique steam engines and railroad cars that date back to the late 1800's. Although the government is in the process of phasing out these lines, you may still find a few which run occasionally. This is a wonderful experience if you have the time. The schedules and routes of the trains have been known to change so a visit to any Turismo, travel agency, or CP station or office will be necessary for more detailed information. I have included listings of some of these lines in the regional chapters, and below in the train route section.*

Official *CP* Rail schedules are available from the *CP* stations in major cities and are called **Guia Horario Official** (about 300$00). If you are intending to use the train system in Portugal, you must get one of these books. Make sure to inquire about the **Suplemento** (supplemental section) of up to date revised schedules which comes with the normal guide. Another good source may be the **Thomas Cook** train timetables which can be found in travel book shops in major cities throughout the world.

Trains don't always run on time, so plan your connections with enough time to still catch the next train. Since the train schedules change quite often, I have not listed most of the them in this guide book. It would be better for you to spend a few minutes planning your trip with the

40 PORTUGAL GUIDE

correct and up to date information. If you have trouble contacting any of the *CP* stations, you may wish to visit any major travel agency in Portugal and they will usually assist you. Please keep in mind that the stations may be several kilometers from the town centers, and transportation may or may not be provided into the heart of town. In the regional chapters of this book I have included many listings train station locations and phone numbers.

Eurail Passes

Eurail passes are accepted on the *CP* train system and must be purchased before your departure from North America, although some services may require a supplemental surcharge. There are several types of youth and adult Eurail passes available for travel within a specific amount of time through 17 different countries in Europe, or soley within one specific country. When using a rail pass you may be allowed to upgrade your journey by reserving seats, couchettes, and sleeping cars for a suplemental charge.

You must purchase Eurail passes before you leave North America, and the best place to do so is from a specialty tour operator, travel agency, or directly from the prompt and reliable staff of **Rail Europe** in both the USA and Canada. Once you have your Eurail pass, any upgrades, specific reservations, or sleeping car requests should be made directly with *CP* at one of their rail stations, or better yet, before you leave with Rail Europe in the USA or Canada. Details of these passes are listed below.

Eurail Portugal–Only Pass

These are **first–class** train passes which are valid to people of all ages. These passes can only be purchased within North America before departure, and are valid from the first day you use it in Portugal. They allow for unlimited travel in Portugal for a maximum number of predetermined days within a given time period:
• *4 days of travel within a 15 day period*: $99 US
• *7 days of travel within a 21 day period*: $155 US

Accompanied children aged 4-11 can recieve a discount of 50% off the above.

Eurail Youthpass

These are **second–class** train passes which are valid to people under 26 years old. These passes can only be purchased within North America before departure, and are valid from the first day you use it in Europe. They allow for unlimited train travel in in 17 European countries (as well as certain bus and ferry routes) within a maximum number of predetermined days:

- *15 day pass*: $398 US
- *1 month pass*: $578 US
- *2 month pass*: $768 US

Eurail Pass

These are **first-class** train passes which are valid for people of all ages. These passes can only be purchased within North America before departure, and are valid from the first day you use it in Europe. They allow for unlimited train travel in 17 European countries (as well as certain bus and ferry routes) within a maximum number of predetermined days:
- *15 day pass*: $498 US
- *21 day pass*: $648 US
- *1 month pass*: $798 US
- *2 month pass*: $1098 US
- *3 month pass*: $1398 US

Accompanied children aged 4-11 can recieve a discount of 50% off the above.

Eurail Saver Pass

These are special **first-class** train passes for people of all ages traveling on the exact same schedule of train travel in 17 European countries (as well as certain bus and ferry routes). They are valid for unlimited travel during a predetermined length of time. Between the months of October through March these passes requires a minimum of 2 people traveling together, between the months of April and September this pass is valid for a minimum of 3 people traveling together:
- *15 day saver pass*: $430 US
- *21 day saver pass*: $550 US
- *1 month saver pass*: $678US

Accompanied children aged 4-11 can recieve a discount of 50% off the above.

Eurail Youth Flexipass

These are **second-class** train passes which are valid to people under 26 years old They must be purchased within North America before departure, and are valid from the first day you use it in Europe. They allow for unlimited train travel in 17 European countries (as well as certain bus and ferry routes) within a maximum number of predetermined days within a given time period:
- *5 days of travel within a 2 month period*: $255 US
- *10 days of travel within a 2 month period*: $398 US
- *15 days of travel within a 2 month period*: $540 US

42 PORTUGAL GUIDE

Eurail Flexipass
These are **first-class** train passes which are valid to people of all ages.They must be purchased within North America before departure, and are valid from the first day you use it in Europe. They allow for unlimited train travel in 17 European countries (as well as certain bus and ferry routes) within a maximum number of predetermined days within a given time period:
• *5 days of travel within a 2 month period*: $348 US
• *10 days of travel within a 2 month period*: $560 US
• *15 days of travel within a 2 month period*: $740 US
Accompanied children aged 4-11 can recieve a discount of 50% off the above.

Rail Europe
This is the best source in North America for Eurail passes, European train tickets, confirmed rail reservations, and special fares on trains in Portugal and throughout Europe. They have also recently added special train/rental car combination packages, and a wholesale hotel booking division which can provide your travel agent with all the necessary elements to book a complete vacation for you.

The staff here is prompt, professional, and well trained to answer all European rail questions, and they will be glad to work directly with the public, or through travel professionals. Advance purchase tickets can be sent by normal mail, or by express mail for a small surcharge.

Rail Europe offices in North America can be reached at:
• **Rail Europe in the US**: *1 800 438-7245*
• **Rail Europe in Canada**: *1 800 361-7245*

MAJOR TRAIN ROUTES

Contact any **CP** office for current schedules and reservations.These train routes are used by many trains with numbers that do not correspond to these route numbers. Some stops may be added or omitted on certain trains and specific days of the week. Transfers to other trains, buses, or ferries are often necessary to complete some portions of these routes.

Route 100
Several times daily in both directions.
Lisbon – Vila Franca de Xira – Santarem – Encontrocamento –Coimbra – Curia – Aveiro – Estarreja – Ovar – Espinho – Vila Nova de Guia – Porto – **Braga**.

Route 100A
Several times daily in both directions.

PLANNING YOUR TRIP 43

Lisbon – Santarem – Entrocamento – Fatima – Seica-Ourem – Pombal – Alfarelos – Coimbra – Pampilhosa – Mealhada – Curia – Aveiro – Ovar – Esmoriz – Espinho – Granja – Valadares – Vila Nova de Guia – **Porto**.

Route 102
Several times daily in both directions.
Lisbon – Vila Franca de Xira – Azambuja – Santana-Cartaxo – Santarem – Entrocamento – Lamarosa – **Tomar**.

Route 110
Several times daily in both directions.
Lisbon – Santarem – Coimbra – Buçaco-Luso – Nelas* – Mangualde – Gouveia – Celorico de Beira – Guarda – Castelo Mendo – **Vilar Formoso**.
*Connections to Viseu.

Route 120
Several times daily in both directions.
Lisbon – Vila Franca de Xira – Santarem – Entroncomento – Almourol – Abrantes – Torre das Vargens* – Castelo de Vide – Marvão – **Valencia de Alcântara**.
Connections to Portalegre – Elvas – **Badajoz, Spain.*

Route 130
Several times daily in both directions.
Lisbon – Vila Franca de Xira – Santarem – Entroncamento* – Almoural – Abrantes – Castelo Branco – Alpedrinha – Penamacor – Fundão – Covilhã – Belmonte-Manteigas – Sabugal – **Guarda**.
*Connections to Porto.

Route 140
Several times daily in both directions.
Lisbon – Queluz-Belas – Mafra – Torres Vedras – Bombarral – Obidos – Caldas da Rainha – São Martinho de Porto – Marinha Grande – Leira – **Figueira da Foz**.

Route 141
Several times daily in both directions.
Lisbon – Queluz-Belas – **Sintra**.

Route 142 (Lisbon Coastal Train)
Several times daily in both directions.
Cais do Sodre – Santos – Alcântara – Belem – Pacos de Arcos – Oeiras – Carcavelos – Parade – São Pedro de Estoril – São João de Estoril – Estoril – Monte Estoril – **Cascais**.

44 PORTUGAL GUIDE

Route 200
Several times daily in both directions.
Porto – Ermesinde – Nine* – Barcelos – Viana do Castelo – Afife – Praia Ancora – Caminha – Vila Nova de Cerveira – **Valença**.
Connections to Braga.

Route 201
Several times daily in both directions.
Porto – Ermesinde – Famalicão – Nine – **Braga**.

Route 203
Several times daily in both directions.
Porto – Pedras Rubras – Vila do Conde – Póvoa de Varzim – **Famalicão**.

Route 205
Several times daily in both directions.
Porto – Maia – Lousado – Santo Tirso – Vizela – **Guimarães**.

Route 210
Several times daily in both directions.
Porto – Penafiel – Livração – Regua – Tua – **Pocihno**.

Route 211 (ask for tickets on the famed scenic **Tâmega** line)_
Several times daily in both directions.
Porto – Livração – Vila Caiz – **Amarante**.

Route 212 (ask for tickets on the famed scenic **Corgo** line)
Several times daily in both directions.
Porto – Regua - Alvacoes – Povocao – Carrazedo – **Vila Real**.

Route 213 (ask for tickets on the famed scenic **Tua** line)
Several times daily in both directions.
Porto – Tua – Vilarinho – Mirandela – Macedo de Cavaleiros – **Bragança**.

Route 300
Several times daily in both directions.
Barreiro* – Casa Branca** – Alvito – Beja – **Tunes***/****.
* *Ferry Connection from Lisbon to Barreiro.*
** *Connections to Tojal – Monte das Flores – Évora.*
*** *Connections to Algoz – Silves – Estombar-Lagoa – Portimão – Lagos.*
**** *Connections to Albufeira – Loule – Almancil – Faro – Olaho – Luz – Tavira – Cacela – Castro Marim – Vila Real de Santo António.*

PLANNING YOUR TRIP 45

Route 302
Several times daily in both directions.
Barreiro* – Pinhal Novo – Casa Branca – Monte das Flores – **Évora****.
*Ferry Connection from Lisbon to Barreiro.
** Bus Connections to Montoito – Reguengos.

Route 303
Several times daily in both directions.
Barreiro* – Pinhal Novo – Casa Branca – Monte das Flores – **Évora****.
*Ferry Connection from Lisbon to Barreiro.
**Bus Connections to Azarja – Estremoz – Borba – Vila Viçosa.

Route 306
Several times daily in both directions.
Lisbon – Entroncamento – Abrantes – **Portalegre***
*Bus Connections to – Cabeço de Vide – Sousel – Estremoz.

Route 307
Several times daily in both directions.
Barreiro* – Beja**
*Ferry Connections from Lisbon to Berreiro.
**Bus Connections to Baleizao – Serpa-Brinches – Pias – Moura.

Route 310
Several times daily in both directions.
Barreiro* – Setúbal – Alcacer do Sal – Grandôla – Ermidas-Sado** – Santa Clara-Saboia – Tunes***/****
*Ferry Connection from Lisbon to Barreiro.
**Connection to Santiago do Cacem – Sines.
***Connection to Algoz – Silves – Estombar-Lagoa – Portimão – Lagos.
****Connection to Albufeira – Loule – Almancil – Faro – Olhão – Luz – Tavira – Castro Marim – Vila Real de Santo António.

Route 311 (Ferry service from Lisbon to Barreiro)
Several times daily in both directions.
Terreiro de Paço (Lisbon) to **Barreiro**.

Route 312
Several times daily in both directions.
Barreiro* – Pinhal Novo – Palmela – **Setúbal****
*Ferry Connection from Lisbon to Barreiro.
**Ferry Connection from Setúbal to the Sado beaches.

46 PORTUGAL GUIDE

Route 314
Several times daily in both directions.
Lagos – Meia Praia – Alvor – Portimão – Estombar-Lagoa – Silves – Tunes – Albufeira – Loule – Almansil – Faro – Olhão – Livramento – Luz – Tavira – Cacela – Castro Marim – Monte Gordo – **Vila Real de Santo António**.

Train Prices and Travel Timesfrom Lisbon to Major Cities
Train, bus, and ferry connections may be necessary for some routes:
• To *Albufeira* (via the *Inter-cidade* train)
3 hour 5 min. trip   2650$00 1st class   1650$00 2nd class
• To *Albufeira* (via the *Inter-regional* train)
4 hour 50 min. trip   2400$00 1st class   1350$00 2nd class
• To *Aveiro* (via the *Inter-regional* train)
3 hour 20 min. trip   2500$00 1st class   1550$00 2nd class
• To *Beja* (via the *Inter-regional* train)
3 hour 10 min. trip   1700$00 1st class   1100$00 2nd class
• To *Cascais* (via the *Suburbano* train)
30 min trip   200$00 1st class   No 2nd class on train
• To *Coimbra* (via the *Inter-regional* train)
2 hour 30 min. trip   2150$00 1st class   1300$00 2nd class
• To *Estoril* (via the *Suburbano* train)
25 min trip   200$00 1st class   No 2nd class on train
• To *Évora* (via the *Inter-regional* train)
2 hour 50 min. trip   1800$00 1st class   1300$00 2nd class
• To *Faro* (via the *Rapido Inter-cidade* train)
4 hour trip   2950$00 1st class   1750$00 2nd class
• To *Fátima* (via the *Regional* train)
4 hour 50 min. trip   1500$00 1st class   950$00 2nd class
• To *Guimarães* (via the *Inter-regional* and *Regional* trains)
7 hour 20 min. trip   3450$00 1st class   1950$00 2nd class
• To *Luso - Buçaco* (via the *Inter-regional* train)
3 hour 30 min. trip   2500$00 1st class   1550$00 2nd class
• To *Oporto* (via the *Alfa* train)
3 hour trip   5100$00 1st class   3100$00 2nd class
• To *Oporto* (via the *Inter-regional* train)
4 hour 25 min. trip   3100$00 1st class   1900$00 2nd class
• To *Setúbal* (via the *Inter-regional* train)
1 hour 25 min, trip   800$00 1st class   500$00 2nd class
• To *Sintra* (via the *Suburbano* train)
50 min. trip   200$00 1st class   No 2nd class on train
• To *Tomar* (via the *Regional* train)
2 hour 25 min. trip   1600$00 1st class   900$00 2nd class

PLANNING YOUR TRIP 47

• To *Viana do Castelo* (via the *Inter-regional* and *Regional* trains)
7 hour 40 min. trip   3750$00 1st class   2100$00 2nd class
• To *Viseu* (via the *Inter-regional* train)
5 hour 5 min. trip   2900$00 1st class   1850$00 2nd class

Main *CP* Rail Information Offices
• **Aveiro**, *(034) 381-632 or (034) 244-85*
• **Coimbra**, *(039) 272-63*
• **Lisbon**, *(01) 888-5101 or (01) 876-025 or (01) 877-509*
• **Porto**, *(02) 201-9517 or (02) 564 141 or (02) 565-670*

TRAVELING BY BUS

Portuguese buses offer a good alternative to driving in Portugal, but is generally much more pricey than the train for the same route. I suggest you stick with the train system unless there is only bus service to the area you wish to go.

The majority of inter-regional and inter-city buses are run by the government owned travel company called *RN* (**Rodoviaria Nacional**) which is undergoing a privatization process. Most major cities have bus stations and are covered by regularly scheduled *RN* express (**Expressos**) bus service. Local and regional busses (**Carreiras**) can get you to smaller towns where there may be a bus stop instead of a bus station. These buses are usually slow since they make many more stops than an express bus would. During weekends and holidays several routes may not operate, so make sure to stop by a bus station to ask for specific information and timetables before planning to travel.

Additional services to various regions of Portugal are provided by dozens of several smaller private bus companies including Empresa Mafrense, Solexpresso, Cabanelas, and Avic which sell their tickets through local travel agents. Many of these buses offer on board videos, while some others play music throughout the journey. If you are traveling south of Lisbon, you occasionally may have to take a ferry from the *Praça do Comercio's* (*Terreiro do Paço*) ferry landing to reach the bus station in *Cacilhas*.

Both *RN* and other private bus companies offer air conditioned deluxe express bus service both directions between the Lisbon and the Algarve (about 2700$00 each way). Several of the private companies' buses depart from the kiosks just behind the Marquêsde Pombal statue in Eduardo VII park in central Lisbon. The *RN* terminal is located just a few blocks away on *Ave. Casal Ribeiro, 18*.

Constantly changing schedules are available directly from the *Turismo* (tourist offices) and the *RN* terminals in several major cities. Remember that many *RN* Bus depots and stops do not publish their phone numbers, and you may have to call a travel agency or a *RN* station for information. In each regional chapter of this book I have included several listings of bus station locations and phone numbers.

Major Bus Routes in Portugal
Please contact any **RN** office for current schedules and reservations. Some routes may be added or omitted on specific buses and specific days. Transfers to other buses, trains, or ferries may be necessary to complete some portions of these routes. These are normal buses and may not be as deluxe or expensive as some of the express services to the same places.

Lisbon to **Agueda**
Several times daily in both directions*.
4 hour trip: 1600$00
*May require a change of buses in Coimbra.

Lisbon to **Albufeira**
Several times daily in both directions.
3 hour 45 min. trip: 1900$00

Lisbon to **Alcobaça**
Several times daily in both directions.
2 hour trip: 1100$00

Lisbon to **Beja**
several times daily in both directions.
3 hour 20 min. trip: 1400$00

Lisbon to **Braga**
Several times daily in both directions.
5 hour 45 min. trip: 2100$00

Lisbon to **Caldas da Rainha**
Several times daily in both directions.
1 hour 30 min. trip: 1100$00

Lisbon to **Chaves**
Several times daily in both directions.
8 hour trip: 2500$00

Lisbon to **Coimbra**
Several times daily in both directions.
3 hour trip: 1400$00

PLANNING YOUR TRIP 49

Lisbon to **Elvas**
Several times daily in both directions.
4 hour 25 min. trip: 1550$00

Lisbon to **Évora**
Several times daily in both directions.
2 hour 50 min. trip: 1350$00

Lisbon to **Faro**
Several times daily in both directions.
4 hour 45 min. trip: 2100$00

Lisbon to **Fatima**
Several times daily in both directions.
1 hour 45 min. trip: 1300$00

Lisbon to **Guarda**
Several times daily in both directions.
6 hour 10 min. trip: 1700$00

Lisbon to **Guimarães**
Once daily (except Saturday) in both directions*.
6 hour trip: 2000$00
May require a change of busses in Vila Nova Famalicão.

Lisbon to **Leira**
Several times daily in both directions.
1 hour 45 min. trip: 1300$00

Lisbon to **Nazare**
Several times daily in both directions.
2 hour 5 min. trip: 1250$00

Lisbon to **Peniche**
Several times daily in both directions.
1 hour 45 min trip: 1000$00

Lisbon to **Porto**
Several times daily in both directions.
4 hour 10 min. trip: 1900$00

Lisbon to **Redondo**
Several times daily in both directions*.

3 hour 25 min. trip: 1350$00
* May require a change of busses in Évora.

Lisbon to Santarem
Several times daily in both directions.
1 hour 20 min. trip: 1000$00

Lisbon to Santiago do Cacem
Several times daily in both directions.
2 hour 30 min trip: 1200$00

Lisbon to Tomar
Several times daily in both directions.
2 hour 20 min trip: 1350$00

Lisbon to Torres Vedras
Several times daily in both directions.
1 hour trip: 800$00

Lisbon to Vila Nova Milfontes
Several times daily in both directions.
4 hour trip: 1450$00

Lisbon to Viseu
Several times daily in both directions.
4 hour trip: 1600$00

5. ITINERARIES FOR THE PERFECT PORTUGAL VACATION

These are just a few of the many possibilities for a great vacation in Portugal. All of this schedules can be altered to suit your specific needs, and unless otherwise noted can be followed by rental car or public transportation. Make sure to check for local markets and regional festivals that might coincide with each area visited.

WEEKEND IN LISBON
(3 days/2nights)
This tour is designed especially for those who have limited time in Lisbon. Travel times are minimal, and flights should be via Lisbon.
Day 1 – Overnight in **Lisbon**.
Take a full day by metro, foot, or bus to sightsee tour in Lisbon.
Day 2 – Overnight in **Lisbon**.
Take a full day by car, train, or bus tour to sightsee in Estoril, Cascais, and Sintra.
Day 3 – No Overnight.
Last minute shopping in Lisbon before departure.

LISBON & SURROUNDINGS
(6 days/5 nights)
This tour is designed especially for those who want to see Lisbon, and would like to visit the nearby sights with minimal travel times. I suggest flights via Lisbon.
Day 1 – Overnight in **Cascais**.
If you like the beach, walk over to Cascais's fine beaches.
Take a full day by foot, car, taxi, or bus to relax and sightsee in Cascais and Estoril.
Day 2 – Overnight in **Cascais**.

52 PORTUGAL GUIDE

If you like the beach, use a car or taxi to get to Guincho.
Take a half day by car, train, or bus to sightsee in Colares and Cabo da Rocha.
Enjoy a fine seafood meal on the Guincho waterfront or in central Cascais.
Day 3 – Overnight in **Sintra**.
If you like the beach, use a car or bus to get to Praia Grande.
Take a full day by car, bus, taxi, or foot to relax and sightsee in Sintra and Queluz.
Day 4 – Overnight in **Lisbon**.
Take a full day by metro, bus, taxi, or bus tour to sightsee throughout Lisbon.
Enjoy a fine *Fado* dinner and drinks in the Bairro Alto.
Day 5 – Overnight in **Lisbon**.
Take a full day by foot, metro, and taxi to relax, wander, and shop throughout Lisbon.
Enjoy a fine casual dinner in the Alfama.
Day 6 – No Overnight.
Last minute shopping in Lisbon before departure.

LISBON & THE NORTH COAST
(7 days/6 nights)
This tour is designed especially for those who want to see Lisbon, and would like to experience a little old world culture, history, and seaside relaxation without having any long distances to travel. Flights should be via Lisbon.
Day 1 – Overnight in **Cascais**.
If you like the beach, walk over to Cascais's fine beaches.
Take a full day by foot, car, taxi, or bus to relax and sightsee in *Cascais*.
Day 2 – Overnight in **Cascais**.
If you like the beach, use a car or taxi to get to Guincho.
Take a full day by car, train, or bus tour to sightsee in Sintra, Queluz, and Mafra.
Enjoy a fine seafood meal on the Guincho waterfront or in central Cascais.
Day 3 – Overnight in **Óbidos**.
Take a full day by foot to relax and sightsee in Óbidos.
Day 4 – Overnight in **Óbidos**.
If you like the beach, use a car or bus to go to Praia de Santa Cruz.
Take a full day by car, train, or bus to sightsee in Peniche and Caldas da Rainha.
Day 5 – Overnight in **Lisbon**.
Take a full day by metro, bus, taxi, bus tour, or foot to relax and

ITINERARIES 53

sightsee in Lisbon.
Enjoy a fine casual dinner in the Alfama.
Day 6 – Overnight in **Lisbon**.
Take a full day by foot, taxi and metro to shop, wander, and eat in Lisbon.
Enjoy a fine Fado dinner and drinks in the Bairro Alto.
Day 7 – No Overnight.
Last minute shopping in Lisbon before departure.

LISBON & THE SOUTH COAST
(7 days/6 Nights)
This tour is designed especially for those who want to see Lisbon, but still would like to experience the dramatic seaside cliffs, beaches, and wine regions of the area. Travel times are minimal, and I suggest flights via Lisbon.
Day 1 – Overnight in **Sesimbra**.
If you like the beach, walk to Sesimbra's fine sandy beach.
Take a half day by foot to relax and sightsee in Sesimbra
Take a half day by car or bus to sightsee around Cabo Espichel.
Enjoy a fine seafood dinner and drinks on Sesimbra's backstreets or seaside.
Day 2 – Overnight in **Sesimbra**.
If you like the beach, use a car or a bus to get to Praia do Meco.
Take a full day by car or bus to sightsee to Azeitão, Palmela, and Setúbal.
Enjoy a tour and wine tasting at the José Maria da Fonseca wine caves in Azeitão.
Day 3 – Overnight in **Estoril**.
If you like the beach, walk over to Estoril's Tamariz beach.
Take a half day by foot to relax and sightsee in Estoril.
Take a half day by car, bus, or taxi to sightsee in Guincho and Cascais.
Day 4 – Overnight in **Estoril**.
If you like the beach, use a car or taxi to get to Guincho.
Take a full day by car, train, or bus tour to sightsee to Sintra, Queluz, and Mafra.
Day 5 – Overnight in **Lisbon**.
Take a half day by metro, bus, taxi, bus tour, or foot to sightsee throughout Lisbon.
Take a half day by foot to relax and sightsee in Lisbon.
Enjoy a fine casual dinner in the Alfama.
Day 6 – Overnight in **Lisbon**.
Enjoy full day by foot, taxi and metro to shop, wander, eat in Lisbon.
Enjoy a fine *Fado* dinner and drinks in the Bairro Alto.

54 PORTUGAL GUIDE

Day 7 – No Overnight.
Last minute shopping in *Lisbon* before departure.

LISBON COAST & MEDIEVAL PORTUGAL
(9 days/8 nights)

This tour is designed especially for those who want to see Lisbon, but are also interested in the rich historic sights in the plains of the country. Travel times are on the moderate side, and I suggest flights via Lisbon.

Day 1 – Overnight in **Cascais**.
If you like the beach, walk over to Cascais's fine beaches.
Take a full day by foot to relax and sightsee in Cascais.

Day 2 – Overnight in **Cascais**.
If you like the beach, use a car or taxi to get to Guincho.
Take a full day by car, train, or bus tour to sightsee in Sintra, Queluz, and Mafra.

Day 3 – Overnight in **Évora**.
Take a half day by foot to relax and sightsee in Évora.

Day 4 – Overnight in **Évora**.
Take a half day by foot to sightsee in Évora.
Take a few hours by car, train, or bus to sightsee in Estremoz.

Day 5 – Overnight in **Monsaraz**.
Take a full day by foot to relax and sightsee in Monsaraz.

Day 6 – Overnight in **Redondo**.
Take a few hours by car, bus or foot to sightsee in Redondo.
Take a few hours by car or bus to visit the Covento de São Paulo.
Take a few hours by car or bus to sightsee in Vila Viçosa and Borba.

Day 7 – Overnight in **Redondo**.
Take a full day by car or bus to sightsee in Elvas, Castelo de Vide, and Marvão.

Day 8 – Overnight in **Lisbon**.
Take a few hours by metro, foot, taxi, or bus to sightsee in Lisbon.
Enjoy a fine Fado dinner and drinks in the Bairro Alto.

Day 9 – No Overnight.
Last minute shopping in Lisbon before departure.

LISBON TO THE ALGARVE
(8 days/7 nights)

This tour is designed especially for those who want to see Lisbon, but are also interested in spending most of their time on the sunny beaches of the Algarve. The travel times are minimal, and I suggest flight arrival into Lisbon and out of Faro.

Day 1 – Overnight in **Lisbon**.

ITINERARIES 55

Take a full day by metro, foot, or bus tour to sightsee in Lisbon.
Enjoy a fine *Fado* dinner and drinks in the Bairro Alto.
Day 2 – Overnight in **Santiago do Cacém**
If you like the beach, use a car or bus to get to Lagoa de Santo André.
Take a few hours by car, bus, or foot to sightsee around Santiago do Cacém.
Take a few hours by car, bus, or train to sightsee in Vila Nova de Milfontes.
Day 3 – Overnight in **Albufeira**.
If you like the beach, use a car, bus, or walk to get to Albufeira's beach.
Take a full day to relax and sightsee by foot around Albufeira.
Day 4 – Overnight in **Albufeira**.
If you like the beach, use a car or bus to get to Praia do Falésia.
Take a full day by car or bus to sightsee in Vilamoura and Loulé.
Day 5 – Overnight in **Praia da Rocha**.
If you like the beach, walk over to get to Praia da Rocha's beach.
Take a half day by foot to relax and sightsee in Praia da Rocha.
Take a few hours by car or bus to sightsee in Lagos.
Enjoy a fine seafood meal on Lagos's seafront.
Day 6 – Overnight in **Praia da Rocha**.
If you like the beach, take a car, bus, or walk to get to *Praia do Vau*.
Take a half day by car or bus to sightsee in *Silves* and *Monchique*.
Day 7 – Overnight in **Vilamoura**.
If you like the beach, walk to get to Vilamoura's beach.
Take a half day by foot to relax and sightsee in Vilamoura.
Take a few hours by car or bus to sightsee in Faro.
Day 8 – No Overnight.
Last minute shopping in Faro before departure.

BEST OF THE ALGARVE
(11 days/10 nights)
This tour is designed especially for those who want to see the sunny beaches, fishing hamlets, country villages, and historical sights of the Algarve. The travel times are in the moderate range. Flights should be via Faro.
Day 1 – Overnight in **Tavira**.
If you like the beach, take a ferry to get to the *Ilha da Tavira*.
Take a full day by foot to relax and sightsee in Tavira.
Day 2 – Overnight in **Tavira**.
If you like the beach, take a car or bus to get to Praia Verde.
Take a half day to sightsee by car, bus, or train in Cacela.
Take a half day to sightsee by car, bus, or train in Vila Real de Santo António.

Enjoy a fine seafood meal on Tavira's riverfront.
Day 3 – Overnight in **Albufeira**.
If you like the beach, use a car, bus, or walk to get to Albufeira's beach.
Take a full day by foot to relax and sightsee in Albufeira.
Day 4 – Overnight in **Albufeira**.
If you like the beach, use a car or bus to get to Praia da Falésia. Take a half day by foot to relax in Albufeira and the beach.
Take a half day by car or bus to sightsee in Loulé.
Day 5 – Overnight in **Carvoeiro**.
If you like the beach, walk to get to Carvoeiro's beach.
Take an hour by car or bus to sightsee in Algar Seco.
Take a half day by car or bus to sightsee in Portimão.
Enjoy a casual fish meal on Portimão's harbourside.
Day 6 – Overnight in **Praia da Rocha**.
If you like the beach, walk over to get to Praia da Rocha's beach.
Take a full day by foot to relax snd sightsee around Praia da Rocha.
Day 7 – Overnight in **Praia da Rocha**.
If you like the beach, take a car, bus, or walk to get to Praia do Vau.
Take a half day by car or bus to sightsee in Silves.
Take a half day by car or bus to sightsee in Lagos.
Day 8 – Overnight in **Monchique**.
Take a half day by car or foot to sightsee in Monchique
Take a half day by car or bus to sightsee in Caldas de Monchique.
Day 9 – Overnight in **Sagres**.
If you like the beach, walk over to get to Praia do Martinhal.
Take a half day by car, bus, or foot to sightsee around Sagres.
Take a half day by car or bus to sightsee in Vila do Bispo.
Day 10 – Overnight in **Vilamoura**.
If you like the beach, walk over to get to Vilamoura's beach.
Take a full day by foot to relax and sightsee in Vilamoura.
Enjoy a fine seafood meal on Vilamoura's marina area.
Day 11 – Overnight in **Vilamoura**.
If you like the beach, walk over to get to Vilamoura's beach.
Take a half day by car or bus to sightsee in Almancil and Vale de Lobo.
Take a half day by car or bus to sightsee in Estoi and Faro.
Enjoy a fine seafood meal on Vilamoura's marina area.
Day 12 – Overnight in **Faro**.
If you like the beach, take a ferry to get to Farol.
Take a full day by car, bus, or foot to relax and sightsee in Faro.
Day 13 – No Overnight.
Last minute shopping in *Faro* before departure.

ITINERARIES 57

NOTHERN WINE REGIONS
(8 days/7 nights)

This tour is designed especially for those who want to see Lisbon, but are also interested in the fine wine producing regions of north and central Portugal. Travel times are moderate, and I suggest flight arrival into Lisbon and out of Faro.

Day 1 – Overnight in **Lisbon**.
  Take a full day by metro, foot, or bus tour into sightsee Lisbon.
Day 2 – Overnight in **Luso** or **Buccaco**.
  Take a half day by car or bus to relax and sightsee in the Buccaco forest.
  Enjoy a great wine from the Palace of Buccaco's caves.
  Take a half day by car or bus to the wineries of the Bairrada wine district.
Day 3 – Overnight in **Luso** or **Buccaco**.
  Take a half day by car or bus to sightsee in Coimbra.
  Take a half day by car or bus to the wineries of the Bairrada wine district.
Day 4 – Overnight in **Viseu**.
  Take a half day by foot to relax and sightsee in Viseu.
  Take a half day by car or bus to the wineries of the Dão wine district.
Day 5 – Overnight in **Lamego**.
  Take a couple of hours by foot to sightsee around Lamego.
  Enjoy the wineries of the Varosa wine district.
  Enjoy a great wine tasting from the Raposeira wine caves just outside of Lamego.
Day 6 – Overnight in **Lamego**.
  Take a full day by car or bus to relax and sightsee in Peso da Régua andVila Real.
  Enjoy the wineries of the Douro (Port) wine district.
  Enjoy a great wine tasting at the Ramos Pinto wine caves in Peso da Régua.
Day 7 – Overnight in **Amarante**.
  Take a half day by foot to relax and sightsee in Amarante.
  Enjoy the wines of the Vinho Verde wine district.
Day 8 – Overnight in **Porto**.
  Take several hours by foot or taxi to sightsee in Porto.
  Take a couple of hours by foot to go wine tasting at the caves of Vila Nova de Gaia.
  Enjoy a great evening wine tasting at the Solar do Vinho do Porto.
Day 9 – No Overnight.
  Last minute shopping in Porto before departure.

BEST OF THE COSTA VERDE
(12 days/11 nights)
This tour is designed especially for those who wish to travel to Porto and the nearby enchanting Costa Verde region. The travel times are somewhat longer, and flights via Porto are strongly suggested.

Day 1 – Overnight in **Porto**.
If you like the beach, take a car or bus to get to Matoshinos.
Take several hours by foot to relax and sightsee in Porto.
Enjoy a glass of vintage Port wine at the Solar do Vinho do Porto.

Day 2 – Overnight in **Amarante**.
Take a full day by foot to relax and sightsee in Amarante.

Day 3 – Overnight in **Amarante**.
Take a half day by car, train, or bus to relax and sightsee in Vila Real.
Take a half day by car, train, or bus to relax and sightsee along the Douro river.

Day 4 – Overnight in **Guimarães**.
Take a full day by foot to relax and sightsee in Guimarães .

Day 5 – Overnight in **Ponte de Lima**.
Take a half day by foot to relax and sightsee in Ponte de Lima.
Take a half day by car or bus to sightsee in Ponte de Barca.

Day 6 – Overnight in **Monção**.
Take a half day by foot to relax and sightsee in Monção .
Take a half day by car or bus to sightsee in the Peneda-Gerês National Park.

Day 7 – Overnight in **Monção**.
Take a half day by car or bus to sightsee in Melgaço.
Take a half day by car or bus to sightsee in Valença and Caminha.

Day 8 – Overnight in **Viana do Castelo**.
If you like the beach, use a car or ferry to get to Praia do Cabedelo.
Take a full day by foot to relax and sightsee in Viana do Castelo.

Day 9 – Overnight in **Viana do Castelo**.
If you like the beach, take a car or bus to get to Praia Moledo.
Take a half day by car or bus to sightsee in Barcelos.
Take a half day by car or bus to sightsee in Braga and Bom Jesus.

Day 10 – Overnight in **Vila do Conde**.
Take a full day by foot to relax and sightsee in Vila do Conde.

Day 11 – Overnight in **Porto**.
Take a half day by foot, bus, taxi, or bus tour to sightsee in Porto.
Enjoy a tour and wine tasting at one of the many wine caves in Vila Nova de Gaia.
Enjoy a fine casual seafood dinner along the Cais de Ribeira.

Day 12 – No Overnight.
Last minute shopping in Porto before departure.

ITINERARIES 59

PORTO & THE MOUNTAINS
(15 days/ 14 nights)
This tour is especially designed for those who wish to see Porto and the seldom visited ancient castle villages and pristine countryside of the far north of Portugal. Travel times are a bit on the long side, and I suggest flights via Porto. I do not advise following this tour during the winter.

Day 1 – Overnight in **Porto**.
If you like the beach, take a car or bus to get to Matoshinos.
Take several hours by foot to relax and sightsee in Porto.
Enjoy a glass of vintage Port wine at the Solar do Vinho do Porto.

Day 2 – Overnight in **Bom Jesus**.
Take a full day by car or bus to relax and sightsee in Braga and Bom Jesus.

Day 3 – Overnight in **Bom Jesus**.
Take a full day by car, train, or bus to sightsee in Barcelos and Viana do Castelo.

Day 4 – Overnight in the **Gerês** area.
Take a half day by car or bus to relax and sightsee in Gerês.
Take a half day by car or bus to sightsee in the Peneda-Gerês National Park.

Day 5 – Overnight in **Chaves**.
Take a full day by foot to relax and sightsee in Chaves.

Day 6 – Overnight in **Bragança**.
Take a full day by foot to relax and sightsee in Bragança.

Day 7 – Overnight in **Bragança**.
Take a full day by car or bus to sightsee in the Montezinho Natural Park.

Day 8 – Overnight in **Vila Real**.
Take a half day by foot to relax and sightsee in Vila Real.
Enjoy a great wine tasting at the Ramos Pinto wine caves in Peso da Régua.
Take a couple of hours by car or bus to sightsee in Mateus.

Day 9 – Overnight in **Viseu**.
Take a full day by foot to relax and sightsee in Viseu.

Day 10 – Overnight in **Guarda**.
Take a few hours by foot to sightsee in Guarda.
Take a several hours by car or bus to sightsee in Monsanto and Sortelha.

Day 11 – Overnight in **Guarda**.
Take a full day by car or bus to sightsee in the Serra da Estrêla.

Day 12 – Overnight in the **Manteigas** area.
Take a full day by car or bus to sightsee in the Serra da Estrêla.

Day 13 – Overnight in **Viseu**.
Take a half day by foot to relax and sightsee in Viseu.
Day 14 – Overnight in **Porto**.
Take several hours by foot to relax and sightsee in Porto.
Enjoy a fine casual seafood dinner along the Cais de Ribeira.
Day 15 – No Overnight.
Last minute shopping in Porto before departure.

DELUXE CASTLES OF PORTUGAL
(12 days/ 11 nights)
This tour is especially designed for the most discriminating travelers who desire accommodations in some of the finest hotels in Portugal and fine gourmet meals. Travel times are moderate, and I suggest that you fly into Lisbon and out of Porto.
This tour is not geared towards those of you who are using public transportation.
Day 1 – Overnight in **Lisbon**.
Take a full day by foot, metro, bus tour, or private sedan tour to sightsee in Lisbon.
Enjoy a fine gourmet dinner at Tavares.
Enjoy a fun late night Fado in the Bairro Alto.
Day 2 – Overnight in **Lisbon**.
Take a full day by foot to relax and sightsee in Lisbon.
Enjoy a fine gourmet dinner at the Hotel da Lapa.
Day 3 – Overnight in **Cascais**.
If you like the beach, use a car or taxi to get to Guincho.
Take a half day by foot to relax and sightsee in Cascais.
Take a half day by car, bus, or taxi to sightsee in Estoril and Guincho.
Enjoy a fine seafood meal at the Hotel Albatroz.
Day 4 – Overnight in **Sintra**.
If you like the beach, use a car or bus to get to Praia Grande.
Take a full day by car, taxi, carraige, or foot to relax and sightsee in Sintra.
Day 5 – Overnight in **Sintra**.
If you like the beach, use a car or bus to get to Praia Adraga.
Take a full day by car, bus, or taxi, to sightsee in Queluz, and Mafra.
Enjoy a fine goumet meal at Cozinha Velha.
Day 6 – Overnight in **Óbidos**.
If you like the beach, use a car, or bus to go to Praia de Santa Cruz.
Take a full day by foot to relax and sightsee in Obidos.
Enjoy a fine goumet meal at the Pousada do Castelo.
Day 7 – Overnight in **Buccaco**.
Take a half day by foot to relax and sightsee in the Buccaco forest.

ITINERARIES 61

Enjoy a great wine from the Palace of Buccaco's caves.
Enjoy a fine goumet meal at the Palace of Buccaco.
Day 8 – Overnight in **Buccaco**.
Take a full day by car to sightsee in Coimbra.
Enjoy a fine meal in at Pompeu.
Day 9 – Overnight in **Águeda**.
Take a couple of hours by car or taxi to relax and sightsee in Águeda.
Take half a day by car or private sedan to sightsee in Caramulo.
Day 10 – Overnight in **Águeda**.
Take half a day by car or private sedan to sightsee in Aveiro.
Enjoy a fine goumet meal at the Palace of Águeda.
Day 11 – Overnight in **Porto**.
Take a full day by foot, metro, bus tour, or private sedan tour to sightsee in Porto.
Enjoy a great vintage Port wine at the Solar do Vinho do Porto.
Day 12 – No Overnight.
Last minute shopping before departing from Porto.

PRAIA DA ROCHA,
IN THE ALGARVE

6. BASIC INFORMATION

BANKS & CURRENCY

The units of Portuguese currency are called the *Escudo* and the *Centavo*. You should know that 1 *Escudo* = 100 *Centavos*. In Portugal, the "$" sign is placed between the *Escudo* and the *Centavo* as a decimal point would be used in our part of the world. Prices are normally listed in the following way 2000$50 (2000 *Escudos* and 50 *Centavos*). Sometimes the *Centavo* value is dropped and the same amount may be shown as 2000$.

> **CONVERTING DOLLARS TO ESCUDOS**
> At press time the value of $1 US is roughly equal to 165 Escudos, while the value of $1 Canadian is roughly 127 Escudos.

Converting your currency and travelers checks into Portuguese *Escudos* is quite simple, and can be done in several ways. Converting foreign currency at international airports is recommended for small amounts only. If you're arriving and need cash for airport tips and taxis, or if you are arriving on a holiday or weekend, you can make your exchange at Lisbon's **Portela** international airport exchange booth (always open). It is advisable to exchange only enough money until you can reach a open bank.

Rates at the many banks in every city are much better. Some banks impose a very small commission or fee for exchanges. When entering a bank (they are open from 8:30am until 3pm Monday - Friday) look for the exchange sign and wait in line. A few banks in very busy areas (especially *Cascais*) will prefer not to exchange your money and pretend they don't offer this service. Private exchange bureaus also exit in the major shopping areas of Cascais and the Algarve although the rate is not always good.

There is no black market in Portugal, so don't even try to look for it. Computerized ATM machines and 24 hour automated currency machines are available in many tourist zones. Hotels also will exchange

BASIC INFORMATION 63

currency for guests, but the rates are not nearly as good as at a bank. Currency in Portugal comes in coins and multicolored banknotes. which range from 1$00 up to 10,000$00.

Credit Cards in Portugal

Credit cards have become a necessary part of most European trips. These days it is necessary in many cases to present a credit card for an imprint to cover any unpaid phone calls, minibar usage, or room service fees charged to your hotel bill. Also, many rental car companies will not let you rent from them without a credit card deposit.

Most 3 and 4 star hotels will accept Visa, Mastercard, and Eurocard but several will not accept American Express or Diners Club because of the high usage fees and commissions they are billed. This situation also exists in many stores and restaurants throughout Portugal. When using your Visa or Mastercard abroad, the rate of exchange is seldom as good as the official bank rates for cash and travellers checks in Europe.

It is a good idea to have a combination of cash, travelers checks and either a Visa Card or a Master card. Another advantage to at least bringing your credit cards is that if you need a cash advance, this may be possible (depending on your specific card).

Travelers Checks

In most places travelers checks are easily accepted. One suggestion is that you should try to keep the denominations fairly small so the cashier will have enough Portuguese cash to give proper change.

While Thomas Cook and Visa travelers checks are usually not a problem, American Express travelers checks are much more widely recognized. Another advantage to American Express is that if you have lost or stolen checks, their refund center in England is available 24 hours per day and can be reached toll free from anywhere in Portugal by dialing *(0505) 44 9080.*

You might also try calling American Express collect at *(919) 333-3211* for a U.S. travelers check refund and replacement office.

BUSINESS HOURS

Most retail stores are open from 9am until 1pm and then 3 pm until 7 pm Monday through Friday, and 9 am until 1 pm on Saturday. There are some shopping centers in the major cities which may also be open until midnight. Banks are open from 8:30 am until 2:45 pm Monday through Friday. Government offices are generally open from 9 am until 5 pm (although many take lunch between 1 pm and 3 pm).

CRIME

After being in Portugal dozens of times, I have not once had the slightest problem with any type of theft in this country, nor have I ever heard of any theft besides that of occasional missing gasoline from unlocked gas tanks. I wish I could say the same thing for Spain!

To begin with, if you're driving around cover any visible items in luggage or hatch area. If possible you should avoid any rental cars with an open uncovered hatchback. Do not leave luggage, cameras, or any type of valuable item within the grasp of unscrupulous people. Be extra careful around gypsies and in bus and train stations. If you have any special items you are traveling around with, leave them at the safety deposit box at your hotel's front desk.

Be careful about walking around deserted city neighborhoods at night. If take these simple precautions you will avoid the possibility of a major problem. In case you run into the one in a million chance of a theft, visit the nearest police station or if you must, call the nationwide emergency hotline (*115*). In Lisbon, the chances of a theft are much higher, but still relatively slim. There is a **special tourist police unit** on *Rua Capela, 13* which may be reached by calling *(01) 346-6141*. To make an insurance claim, assuming you have coverage on either your homeowner's or a special policy, you must have a police report.

ELECTRICITY

Portuguese outlets are designed for 220 Volts AC and 50 Hertz and the plugs are 2 round pins. If you are bringing electrical appliances or components, you should bring a transformer and a plug converter of the appropriate wattage. Many appliances such as hair dryers, razors, and personal computers already have a switchable transformer built in, and may require only an adapter for the plug. Check your owners manual carefully.

EMBASSIES

- **American Embassy**, *Avenida das Forças Armadas, Lisboa (01) 726 6600*
- **Canadian Embassy**, *Avenida Liberdade, 144, Lisboa (01) 347 4892*

FADO

Fado is a unique traditional form of music which expresses the typically Portuguese attitude about how bad luck and tragedy are always just around the corner again. With the help guitar players, a female singer (*Fadista*) belts out a beautiful yet sad story of fate.

Fado originated in 19th-century Lisbon and it is hosted in small restaurants known as *adega tipicas* and *casas de Fado* in Lisbon, Coimbra,

BASIC INFORMATION 65

and several resort areas. Most *adega tipicas* offer traditional dinners and may also have cover charges.

HEALTH & MEDICAL CONCERNS

Portugal currently requires no inoculations or special immunizations for it's visitors from America and Canada. In fact there haven't been any outbreaks of major infectious diseases here in many years. The best thing to do in case you worry about these things is to contact the State Department Information Center in your country and ask if there are any current travel advisories on Portugal. I am sure you will find none.

If you are currently under medication, you should bring a copy of your prescription (with the generic name for the drug) along with your medicine. If necessary a local *Farmácia* (pharmacy) may refill it. To find a 24 hour drug store, or emergency room just call directory assistance (118) or by looking in a local newspaper for listings.

Hospitals are available in most major population areas, and can be found by calling directory assistance (118) or in case of an emergency calling (115) for an ambulance. For a free listing of English speaking doctors in Portugal, please contact **I.A.M.A.T.** in North America at *(716) 754-4883*.

The **British Hospital** on *Rua Saraiva Carvalho, 49 in Lisbon at (01) 606-020* is perhaps the best choice in case of major situations. I have also included listings of a few major medical centers in each regional and major city chapter of this book.

HOLIDAYS

These are the official holidays:

New Year's Day (January 1), Carnival, Good Friday, Liberation Day (25 April), May Day (01 May), Corpus Christi Day, Camões Day (10 June), Assumption Day (15 August), Republic Day (05 October), All Saints' Day (01 November), Independence Day (01 December), Feast of Immaculate Conception Day (08 December), Christmas Eve (24 December), Christmas (25 December).

The government of Portugal occasionally moves holidays around to form long weekends for it's citizens. Many additional regional holidays exist which are not included in this list as they vary with each province. During these days expect many museums, castles, restaurants, banks, government related offices, and several private companies to be closed.

If a holiday falls on a Friday or Monday you can expect many of these places to close for the entire holiday weekend. Trains and buses will tend to run on limited schedules during these time periods.

INSURANCE COVERAGE

Since you are not a Portuguese citizen, health care will not be provided for free. Americans and with private insurance may be covered for reimbursement under their current policy, but that may only help you after months of detailed paper work.

Canadians may find that their provincial health insurance may cover or reimburse certain procedures, but don't count on it. You should check the insurance section later on in this book for advice and available plans for your trip.

LOCAL TIME

Portugal currently follows the same daylight savings system as the US and Canada from April through October. The time difference between the Eastern time zone (New York, Boston, Montreal, Toronto) and Portugal is 5 hours, 6 hours from central time, 7 hours from mountain time, and 8 hours from Pacific time.

NEWSPAPERS & MAGAZINES

There is a vast assortment of Portuguese language dailies and weeklies which can easily be located at any newsstand, hotel lobby, or local tobacco shop (*tabacaria*). Of these, I usually read the informative *Diário de Notícias* and *Público* papers from Lisbon. Excellent weeklies include the serious *Expresso*, and the arts and entertainment laden *Se7e* which is a great source for things to do in Lisbon.

Among the only English language weeklies are the *Portugal Post* and the *Anglo-Portuguese News* (*ANP*) which can be found in most tourist resorts and large cities. If you search around the Costa de Lisboa or the Algarve you may also find current copies of the *International Herald Tribune*, *The European*, and *USA Today*. If you don't mind reading old news, backdated issues of the *New York Times*, *Wall Street Journal*, and the *London Times* may sometimes be collecting dust in hotel-based tobacconists and a few newsstands in the financial districts of Lisbon and Porto.

Special European editions of English-language magazines such as *Time*, *Newsweek*, *Playboy*, and *Penthouse* are also available at leading hotels.

NIGHTLIFE

Each city and town in Portugal has a vast assortment of evening entertainment. There are many establishments which offer fine theater, symphony concerts, jazz bands, rock shows, and even opera. There are also establishments which are not unlike the types of bars, discos, and nightclubs which you are already accustomed to. I have included several lists of local nightlife in each regional and major city chapter, but you

BASIC INFORMATION 67

should always try to find a local resident or hotel worker to fill you in on the best spots.

PASSPORTS - WHAT TO DO IF THEY'RE LOST OR STOLEN

Just in case you happen to somehow misplace your passport, or need the help and advice of your own government, please contact your embassy. They can also provide other services which your tax dollars are paying for, including travel advisories on other nations which you may wish to visit while overseas, lists of local English speaking medical specialists, and other valuable details.

PHYSICALLY-CHALLENGED TRAVELERS

Traveling in Portugal for the physically-challanged person can prove a bit complicated. Getting to the country is the easy part of your journey, as most airlines offer special seating assignments, wheelchair storage, and boarding assistance to anyone who requests so in advance. Upon arrival in Lisbon, additional special airport assistance services are also offered free of charge by the airlines. Now that you have arrived in Lisbon, things get a little more difficult.

Although well marked reserved (so-called "handicapped") parking spaces can be found at the airport and in some cities, none of the major rental car companies offer specially adapted vehicles. With advance notification, the **Association of Rental Car Companies (A.R.A.C.)** on *Rua António Candido,8 - Lisbon at (01) 356-3737* might be able to assit in finding special vehicles with hand controls.

New regulations from the European Economic Community (E.E.C.) are finally starting to have an positive effect on the availability of special services and facilities, especially in the larger cities of *Lisbon, Coimbra*, and *Porto*. The best resource for accessibility information can located at the offices of the **Secretariado Nacional de Reabilitacão** on *Ave. Conde de Valbom, 63 - Lisbon (01) 793-6517*. A special booklet entitled *Guia de Tuirismo para Pessoas com Deficiencias* will provide detailed listings (in Portuguese only) on hotels with minimal obstacles for wheelchairs, customized buses with ramps, taxi companies which are pleased to assist people with special needs, and service station bathrooms that are accessible.

Wheelchair accessable bathrooms, entrance ramps, and well designed elevators with brail and chime features are starting to become more common in the larger 4 and 5 star hotels in resort areas and business centers. Whenever possible I have included a special notation in some hotel listings when special facilities are offered. Each regional *Turismo* office may be able to direct visitors to additional transportation services, accommodations, and restaurants which are properly equipped.

There are also new daily dial a ride door to door bus services in some cities which must be arraigned at least 2 days in advance. A special card might be required from the bus operators. For dial a ride details please call (01) 758-5657 in *Lisbon*, (039) 441-441 in *Coimbra*, and (02) 606-6646 in *Porto*. For groups which need to charter a special accessible bus for private use, contact the **Companhia Carris-Sector de Alugueres** at *Rua 1 de Maio, 101 - Lisbon* at (01) 363-9226.

The following organizations offer special trips and access details:
- **Society for The Advancement of Travel for the Handicapped**, *New York City, USA (212) 447-7284*. A members-only service with basic information about travel needs for the physically challenged. Yearly membership is $45.00 US for adults and $25.00 for students.
- **MossRehab Travel Information Services**, *Philadelphia, Pennsylvania, USA (215) 456-9600*. A free information and referral service with valuable hints and suggestions on companies which offer travel services for the physically challenged.
- **Flying Wheels Travel**, *Owatonna, Minnesota, USA (800) 535-6790*. A great full service travel agency and group tour operator which can provide helpful information and reservations for the physically challenged. Services include all forms of special transportation and accommodation reservations, and guided group tours.

POST OFFICES & MAIL

Throughout the country there is a vast network of post offices (*Correios*) which are open from about 9am until 12:30pm and 2:30pm until 6pm on Monday through Friday. In major cities it is possible to find a few main branch offices which open during lunch time and on Saturday mornings as well. Letters sent via air mail (*por Avião*) from Portugal to North America normally cost aound 130$00 can take up to 2 weeks to arrive. Mail within Portugal itself usually costs about 80$00 and can find their way to the addressee in around 5 days.

Most post offices sell stamps (*selos*) and can help with normal postal needs. You can send and receive mail as well as make phone calls at several of the main branches. If you wish to have a main post office hold mail for you, general delivery can be arranged after a visit a post office to register your name. Incomming letters must be marked "*Posta Restante-Lista do Correios*" and sent to the station where you have registered. When letters arrive they can be picked up at the post office for a 70$00 fee per letter.

You can also receive mail and telegrams via an **American Express** office if you contact them in North America at *(800) 221-7282* before you depart. These client letter services are free to American Express

BASIC INFORMATION 69

cardholders, vacation clients, and traveler's check holders, but can be obtained by others for a small fee. Both **DHL** and **Federal Express** can deliver packages to Portugal from North America within 3 days.

RADIO

Radio in Portugal is a wonderful source free entertainment and most hotel roms and rental cars have the equipment to receive it. There are hundreds of stations broadcasting every type of music and talk show imaginable. One of the funniest things about hearing the radio here is that after several sets of unfamiliar local music, you will then be pelted with tasteless old American songs like Yummy, Yummy, Yummy I've got Love in my Tummy or some all but forgotten Disco era tune.

Stations in large cities and resort areas like Lisbon, Albufeira, Coimbra, and Porto will sometimes offer great rock, blues, or jazz shows. If you want to listen to English language radio, I suggest that you carefully search the dial for the U.S. Armed Forces Radio.

There are also special tourist programs in English which are broadcast in mornings on some stations in the *Algarve* and the *Lisbon* area. If you are lucky enough to have a shortwave set (almost no North Americans do) you can also get the Voice of America and BBC World Service from within most of Portugal.

STUDENT TRAVEL I.D. CARDS

For full time students under the age of 26 who can provide documentation of their current status there is a great card which I strongly suggest. The **International Student Identity Card** (I.S.I.C.) is valid for one year and should be obtained in North America before you depart for about $15 US. It allows it's holder to have discounts on international flights, museums, public transportation, and other services. Included with the cost of these cards is a special emergency medical insurance which can cover $3000 US in medical bills as well as $100 a day in hospital bills for up to 2 months.

To obtain a card, please contact on of the following offices:
• **Council Travel**, *New York (212) 661-1450*
• **Travel Cuts**, *Toronto (416) 979-2406*

TELEPHONES, TELEGRAMS, & FAXES

The phone system in Portugal is not as modern as what you may be used to. To begin with, many pay phones are out of order. The international instructions on some phones prove only moderately helpful. Even worse is the fact the extra digits are always being added to current phone numbers.

70 PORTUGAL GUIDE

The easiest way to place a local call is to go to the front desk of any hotel (even if you are not a guest) and ask to make a pay call. You will be billed a slightly higher rate, but the assistance will be worth it. Another suggestion is to place the call from any post office (*Correios*) telephone department. The standard corner pay phones accept 20$00, 50$00 and sometimes 100$00 coins. Over the last few years the two major phone companies in Portugal now offer prepaid phone cards for use in specially marked phones. The **Crediphone** card is the most common, while the **T.L.P.** card is rare. These cards can be bought in varying denominations at many newsstands and *Correios* (post offices). They are generally useful in the major cities, but not necessarily in the smaller villages and towns.

If you are using a US or Canadian telephone company credit card, be sure to call them before you depart, and get their access numbers and procedures for Portugal.since international calls are very expensive, some regional phone company offices have begun to accept Visa and Mastercard for payments. Please check with the local *Turismo* (tourist office) for the nearest location.

Hotels can also place international but some charge up to 75% mark ups on this service. Hotels also provide the easiest place to send or receive faxes. This service can save a lot of money for the amount of information which is communicated at high speeds. Additional fax facilities may be found at *Correios* which offer the "Corfax" pay fax system. Many post offices offer telegram services at moderate rates.

THERE AND BACK AGAIN BY PHONE

• *To reach the USA and Canada from Portugal, dial 001 and the area code and phone number*

• *To reach Portugal from the USA and Canada, dial 011 351 and then the area code and phone number. If the Portuguese area code shows a zero as a first digit, drop the zero.*

• *To call between two Portuguese cities within the same area code, drop the area code which is listed in parentheses.*

• *To call between two Portuguese cities in different area codes, use the area code (with the zero included) and then the number.*

Pay phones accept 20$00 and 50$00 coins which are inserted into a horizontal slot in the upper right hand corner of the phone. A typical call within one region or city should cost between 20$00 and 40$00 per minute. Calling outside the same city of region can bring the cost up to over 60$00 per minute.

Unfortunately, most of the public phones in Portugal seem to always be broken. If you have bought a *Credifone* or *TLP* phone card from a newsstand or post office, you stand a much better chance in the major

BASIC INFORMATION 71

cities of finding a phone that works. These cards have a predetermined amount of impulses (units) which can allow for multiple uses of the same card. Phone calls can easily be made from most major post offices (pay after you make the call) at low rates, or at much higher prices from any hotel front desk.

If you need to call internationally, you can use MCI and ATT access codes from within Portugal to reach English speaking operators for collect, credit card, and third party calls. It is even possible to use these cards in the hotel's payphone. Calling internationally can cost 100$00 or more per minute.

> **GOOD NUMBERS TO KNOW**
> - *Local Information* 118
> - *International Operator Assistance* 098
> - *USA Country Code* 001
> - *Canada Country Code* 001
> - *U.K. Country Code* 0044
> - *AT&T USA Direct Access Number* 05-017-1288
> - *MCI CALL USA Access Number* 05-017-1234

TELEVISION

While you are traveling within Portugal I urge you to take advantage of the selection of media (some is in English) which is easily available. To begin with, the country offers 2 of their own TV stations which are managed by the *RTP* broadcasting company, as well as couple of private networks. These stations transmit their signal to most parts of the country, and tend to offer a combination of locally produced game shows, Brazilian talk shows, news programs, and poorly dubbed international movies.

The prospect of seeing a Woody Allen movie being shown on the tube in Portuguese may seem unbearable, but I find it rather amusing. Most of the better hotels also offer a selection of other European satellite TV programs from Europe, Germany France, Italy, and in some cases you will find CNN International. Usually at least one of these stations will be the SKY network from England which is quite entertaining. The only word of caution that I should mention is that the German network has a tendency to show soft-core porno flicks on weekend evenings.

TIPPING

There are many situations in which a gratuity may be appropriate. In most cases feel free to use your judgment based on the quality of services rendered. At the top of the next page is a list of the most common people you'll want to tip and suggested amounts.

Many Portuguese do not tip for some services that in our culture may be commonplace. If someone gives you back a tip, do not take it as an insult.

I've put together below a suggested tipping chart for your easy reference:

SUGGESTED TIPS

Taxi Driver	*10% of the meter's rate.*
Hotel Porter	*150$00 per bag.*
Hotel Concierge	*500$00 per favor.*
Room Service	*250$00 per meal.*
Hotel Doorman	*200$00 per taxi.*
Bartender	*100$00 per round.*
Waiter	*10% to 15% of the bill.*
Ushers	*150$00 per event.*
Private Guides	*1700$00 per person per day.*
Private Drivers	*1600$00 per person per day.*
Tour Guides	*1800$00 per person per day.*
Tour Bus Drivers	*1000$00 per person per day.*

TOURIST INFORMATION OFFICES - TURISMOS

Once you have arrived inside of Portugal, there are many places to pick up vital tourist information in several languages. Each major city, tourist destination, and rural town hall (*Cāmara municipal*) operate small offices to assist visitors to their region. These tourist information offices are usually marked with a sign which says *Turismo*.

Many of these offices are open during typical business hours, so during the weekends several may be closed. These *Turismos* are normally staffed by just one or two local residents who have the ability to communicate in multiple languages. *Turismos* are managed by the local government and most of them are extremely friendly and helpful, although I have found a few to be downright nasty and dishonest.

I suggest that when you arrive in a city or town you should pop into the local *Turismo* and find out if they can offer any maps, suggestions, or assistance. If you are nice and specific with a *Turismo's* staff, they will often advise you of totally off the beaten path attractions and unique accommodations that only a lifelong local resident would know about. I have included address and phone listings of many *Turismos* in their corresponding regional chapters.

7. TYPES OF ACCOMMODATIONS

There are over 350 different authorized and government-rated places to overnight in Portugal. Although there is a system of rating which uses from 1 up to 5 stars for many of the properties in the country, the system cannot be fully trusted. I have included brief descriptions in this book's regional chapters of over 200 of the properties throughout Portugal that I have visited and can appropriately review. I have listed these properties in the order of my personal suggestion regardless of price.

You will also find listings of hostels, campsites, apartments, and villas. While the quality and facilities of accommodations may change from season to season, I have given you the most up to date information currently available to help you select the best places to fit your requirements. The price guidelines listed below for all types of accommodations that I have used in my reviews are based on the average high season rate for 2 people staying in a double room for a night including tax (and often breakfast as well).

HOTEL PRICE GUIDELINES
Expensive: 15,500$00 and up.
Moderate: 7,000$00 to 15,500$00
Inexpensive: 1,500$00 to 7,000$00

I also wish to explain the different types of accommodations which you will find all over the country.

POUSADAS

Pousadas are a series of about 30 properties which are part of a government owned company known as *Enatur*. Originally designed as inexpensive inns which hosted Portuguese travelers, these inns have become a favorite of foreign visitors and are now much more expensive. They are often housed in castles, former mansions of civil engineers, or well located traditional homes which have been converted into fashionable hotels with many facilities including private bathrooms. Each *pousada* is unique, and the service quality can range quite substantially from one to the other.

Bookings for these properties can be made from a specialty tour operator, travel agent, directly from each specific *pousada*, or by calling **Enatur** in Lisbon at *(01) 848-1221*. Be advised that prepayment will be requested at the time of booking request, and that penalties may be applied for no shows and cancellations. Many of the *pousadas* are sold out well in advance, and it can take several days to receive a confirmation from any source of these bookings. Sooner or later, Enatur will become a privatized company and the booking situation should become less complicated. I suggest you contact one of the tour operators listed in this book for further details.

QUINTAS

Quintas are typically private estates which offer guests a chance to stay in traditional manor homes and farm houses. Using funds provided by E.E.C. economic development programs, many estate owners have found a low cost way to improve their properties for tourism purposes. These *quintas* can range from wonderfully ornate former palaces to wine producing mansions and rustic mountain lodges. It is common for the host family to greet each client personally and sometimes even offer a glass of wine.

These properties can provide a memorable cultural experience for visitors as they often provide deluxe antique laden guestrooms with private bathrooms in unforgettable settings. Some *quintas* offer apartments and guestrooms with fireplaces, 4 poster beds, scenic patios, and occasionally even kitchens. Other *quintas* can be rented as complete private houses and estates for groups of families or for high end groups and business meetings.

Many of these properties have special features such as horse back riding, bicycles, jeeps, romantic gardens, TV rooms, priceless artwork, farm fresh meals, and their own in house wineries. Be advised that a few of these *quintas* have shared bathrooms in their least expensive rooms.I only have listed the properties which I have either seen or have been a guest in, and can fully recommend.

Most *quintas* are classified by the Portuguese government in 3 different levels of so called **Turismo no Espaco Rural** (Tourism in the Countryside). **Turismo de Habitação (TH)** properties are usually historic manor houses which are of the highest architectural value and comfort

TYPES OF ACCOMMODATIONS

level. The vast majority of *quintas* I have listed fall into this catagory.

Turismo Rural (TR) properties are mostly nice garden-laden mansions and old homes with comfortable accommodations in rural areas near towns. **Agroturismo (AT)** properties are usually basic inns on working farms which offer guests a chance to help with the daily farm work, but it is never mandatory.

Bookings for all types of *quintas* can be made from North America by contacting an expert specialty tour operator such as **European Travel Consultants** at *(800) 585-8085*. It is also possible to call the quintas directly, but not all of the managers speak even a word of English. The last resort could be contacting one of less than helpful *quinta* associations like **Turihab** in Ponte de Lima at *(058) 942-749*. Please keep in mind that full prepayment will be requested at the time of booking request, and that penalties will be applied for revisions, cancellations, or no shows. Many quintas are sold out well in advance during the summer months, so book ahead.

HOTELS

Hotels in Portugal run the full gamut of quality and accommodation levels and are available in several types of classifications. Hotel properties throughout the country which can be housed in everything from multi-story modern buildings to centuries old convents and palaces. Any property which uses the word hotel in its name will be rated by a series of stars.

If a hotel offers **1** or **2 stars**, chances are that it will have private bathrooms and facilities such as a restaurant, bar, and heating. Properties of **3 stars** or more will often be loaded with additional facilities including parking, cable TV, pool, in room phones, minibars, and a breakfast room. Most **4** and **5 star** hotels may have gourmet restaurants, snack bars, lounges, air conditioning, health clubs, sports facilities, marble bathrooms, room service, multilingual staff, a conseirge desk, and bellboys.

Aparthotels are usually full service **2** to **4 star** hotels which offer rooms with kitchens and either 1 or 2 bedrooms for family style use. Bookings for these properties can be made from a specialty tour operator, travel agent, or directly from each specific hotel.

VILLAS & APARTAMENTOS

Villas and **apartamentos** are usually multiple bedroom houses or condo style apartments with all the comforts of home. Since these are usually private and not rated by the government, you must contact a specialist to insure that you get what you pay for. These villas and apartments can range in quality from basic bungalows with 2 bedrooms, a bathroom, and a kitchen to 2 bedroom seaview condos and 12 bedroom castles with dramatic seaviews and private pools.

Usually you must rent these properties for a minimum of 1 week, but in low season a 3 night stay is possible. If you are looking for a long term rental, you will have almost no problems finding one from either a good tour operator in North America, or if necessary from an English speaking Realtor once you arrive in Portugal. If you need long term housing in the *Lisbon* area, you will have big problems as the vacancy rate in this vicinity is about 1%.

To book a villa or apartment in Portugal, contact **European Travel Consultants** in North America at *(800) 585-8085* or check the major travel magazines for rental listings. Be advised that reservations for villas and apartamentos must be prepaid in full in advance, and penalties will apply for cancelations, revisions, and no shows.

ALBERGARIAS

Albergarias are typically properties which are ranked just below a hotel in quality and facilities offered. Many *albergarias* are rather nice and offer most of the facilities of a smaller hotel. Almost all *albergarias* are rated with **4 stars** and will usually offer private bathrooms, restaurant, bar, air conditioning, heating, minibars, in room phones, TV, safe deposit boxes, multilingual staff, heating, parking, and sometimes even a pool. Bookings for these properties can be made from a specialty tour operator, travel agent, or directly with each specific *albergaria*.

ESTALAGENS

Estalagens are typically nice medium to high quality inns which are usually rated by either **4 or 5 stars**. Normally you will find private bathrooms, heating, a restaurant, lounge, breakfast room, TV, parking, safe deposit boxes, and a front desk staff at each *estalagem*. Bookings for these properties can be made from a specialty tour operator, travel agent, or directly with each specific *estalagem*.

RESIDENCIALS

Residencials are basic inns which are usually in or near towns. These inns are rated from **1 to 4 stars** and are not full of as many facilities or services as a *estalagem*. In many *residencials* you will find rooms with private baths, a breakfast room, a restaurant, and sometimes a TV. Since these inns often do not pay commissions to travel agents and tour operators, you can only book most of them by calling directly to the *residencial*.

TYPES OF ACCOMMODATIONS

PENSÕES

Pensões are the lowest rated classification of accommodations in Portugal. These basic and simple inns are rated from **1 to 4 stars** and have minimal facilities. Most *Pensões* offer rooms without private bathrooms, but some of these properties have a few rooms with bathrooms as well.

You may also find some of these inns which have breakfast rooms and attached restaurants. Since these inns often do not pay commissions to travel agents and tour operators, you can only book most of them by calling directly to the *Pensão*.

QUARTOS PRIVATIVOS

Quartos Privativos are essentially rooms for rent in private houses with shared bathrooms. These accommodations are not officially recognized by the government, and are usually part of the underground economy. I have not included listings of these units because they come and go each season and there is no quality assurance. The most common way to find a private room is to either inquire at a *Turismo* office, or go to a local train station and look out for either signs or the hawkers who earn a 15% commission to each tourist they successfully bring in.

YOUTH HOSTELS

For adults and youths alike, the vast network of good Youth Hostels (**Pousadas de Juvenude**) provide a highly economical altenative to budget hotels. Although I have not yet reviewed most of these hostels, I certainly will make sure to do a full inspection and listing in the next printing of this guide. Many of these hostels provide both seperate dormitory style accomodations for each sex, as well as private double rooms for couples and family sized units.

The hostels tend to be located in major resort and population zones and ae usually open from 9am until 12pm and from 6pm until 12 midnight. Many hostels have curfews which are strictly enforced, and lots of rules including an 8 day maximum stay. Each hostel is different, so expect anything from bunk bedded modern buildings with shared bathrooms, to more spacious private bungalows and nice guestrooms with private bathrooms in old converted houses.

The current price range is from about 900$00 to 2200$00 per person each night depending on the season and type of room requested. Many hostels offer inexpensive meals for a small surcharge.

All guests of these hostels must hold a valid hostel membership card which is available for about $25 US per year from any I.F.Y.H. office. These cards also enable their holders to recieve discounts on the hostels themselves, as well as on restaurants and sports rental equipment. Special cards may be available for people under 17 and families at differing prices.

78 PORTUGAL GUIDE

To book reservations, it is best to contact the official member of the **International Federation of Youth Hostels** (I.F.Y.H.) in the country you live in. Some hostels request a 10 day advance booking made via an I.F.Y.H. branch office, but if space is available you can just walk in and stay. A new computer system called the International Booking Network can often be used to reserve and print out confirmations for prepaid bookings in many hostels throughout the world for a mere $2.50 US fee plus the price of the accomodation choosen.

Most Portuguese hostels are open year round, but It is not uncommon for several of them to be sold out well in advance for the summer season, so book early. Please contact one of the following organizations or their many branches for more specific information.

HOSTEL INFORMATION & RESERVATIONS
- *American Youth Hostel Federation*, Washington, DC (202) 783-6161
- *Canadian Hostelling Association*, Ontario (613) 237-7884
- *Portuguese Association of Hostels*, Lisbon (01) 355-9081
- *Council Travel*, New York (212) 661-1450
- *Travel Cuts*, Toronto (416) 979-2406

Listings of Hostels (*Pousadas de Juventude*) by Town
- **Alcoutim** *(Algarve, (081) 460-04)*
- **Praia de Areia Branca** *(Costa de Prata, 061) 422-127)*
- **Braga** *(Costa Verde, (063) 616-163)*
- **Catalazete** *(Costa de Lisboa, (01) 443-0638)*
- **Coimbra** *(Costa de Prata, (039) 229-55)*
- **Fão-Esposende** *(Costa Verde, No Phone Yet)*
- **Lagos** *(Algarve, (082) 761-970)*
- **Leira** *(Costa de Prata, (044) 318-68)*
- **Lisbon** *(Costa de Lisboa, (01) 353-2696)*
- **Ovar** *(Costa de Prata, No Phone Yet)*
- **Penhas da Saude** *(Montanhas, (075) 253-75)*
- **Portalegre** *May be Closed* *(Planícies, (045) 235-68)*
- **Portimão** *(Algarve, (82) 857-04)*
- **Porto** *(Costa Verde, (02) 606-5535)*
- **São Martinho de Porto** *(Costa de Prata, (062) 999-506)*
- **São Pedro** *May be Closed* *(Costa de Prata, (044) 599-236)*
- **Sintra** *(Costa de Lisboa, (01) 924-1210)*
- **Vila Nova de Cerveira** *(Costa Verde, (051) 796-113)*
- **Vila Real de S. António** *(Algarve, (081) 445-65)*
- **Vilarinho das Furnas** *(Costa Verde, (053) 351-339)*

TYPES OF ACCOMMODATIONS 79

CAMPING

With over 150 official public and private campgrounds throughout the country, Portugal is a great place to camp and caravan. If you follow normal precautions and don't leave anything valuable in your tent or caravan you will surely have a wonderful time. One of the most important issues besides security should be where you decide to stay. If you intend to avoid the official campsites and try to stay on private land you may end up with buckshot in your rear end.

If you attempt to illegally camp anywhere in the *Algarve*, you may very well be arrested. To put it simply, the campgrounds are so numerous and cheap that there is almost no reasonable excuse to avoid them. If you happen to find a wonderful secluded rural spot that is not within 1 km. of beaches, cities, or water sources you can always cross your fingers and chances are you will be alright.

Most of the campgrounds and caravan sights are fairly attractive and located in areas which are close to tourism spots, city centers, beach resorts, and beautiful parks. Besides the typical almost hot showers and sanitary facilities, you may often find bungalows, minimarkets, snack bars, tennis courts, rental boats, laundry machines, telephones, on site parking, and swimming pools.

Many sights are open year round and you can expect to pay between 200$00 and 400$00 per night for a 2 person tent site, 300$00 to 600$00 for a 4 person tent site, and 600$00 to 1100$00 for a caravan site. Parking, showers, meals, sports facilities, and electical hook ups may be additional. It would also be a good idea to get an **International Camping Card** from a local camping supply shop or from the **National Campers Association** *(716) 668-6242*.

Before departing for Europe you should make sure that you have bought all the camping supplies that may be needed. Don't forget to bring extra waterproofed tent flys and strong bug repellant as they will most certainly come in handy. If you need to buy camping supplies within Portugal you can expect to pay double or triple of what they cost at home.

If you want specific information on every campsight in Portugal, you can ask in a Portuguese bookshop for a copy of the current *"Roteiro Campista"* guide which costs about 600$00. The local *Turismos* may also offer either a listing of regional campsites, or a copy of the *Guia Official de Parques de Campismo*. You can always ask any Portuguese National Tourist Office if they can send you some information before you depart.

Portuguese Cities and Resort Areas with Campsites

Albufeira, Alcobaça, Alezur, Alpiarça, Alvito, Alvor, Arganil, Azeitão, Beja, braga, Bragança, Caldas da Rainha, Caminha, Caparica, Castelo de Bode,

Castelo Branco, Celorico de Beira, Chaves, Coimbra, Costa Nova, Elvas, Ericeira, Espinho, Évora, Faro, Figueira da Foz, Fundão, Gerês, Golegã , Gouveia, Guarda, Guimarães, Guincho, Ílhavo, Lagoa de Albufeira, Lagoa de Melides, Lagoa de Santo André, Lagos, Lamego, Lisbon, Lourinhã , Lousã , Melgaço, Mira, Miranda do Douro, Mirandela, Monção , Monte Gordo, Nazaré , Oeiras, Olhão, Ovar, Penacova, Peniche, Portalegre, Portimão, Porto, Porto Côvo, Porto de Mós, Praia de Areia Branca, Praia de Galé , Praia Grande, Praia da Luz, Praia da Mira, Praia de Ponte Gordo, Praia de Salema, Praia de Santa Cruz, Quarteira, Sagres, São Pedro de Moel, São Pedro do Sul, Serpa, Sesimbra, Setúbal, Sines, Tavira, TomarVagos, Viana do Castelo, Vila do Conde, Vila Flôr, Vila Nova de Gaia, Vila Praia de Ancora, Vila Real, Viseu, Zambujeira.

8. THE MOST MEMORABLE PLACES TO STAY

After seeing almost 300 different hotels, *estalalagens, albergarias, Pensões, pousadas, quintas,* villas, condos, and resorts throughout Portugal, these are the places that I could never forget. I have based my selections on a combination of aspects, including overall beauty, location, quality of service, value, cuisine, special features, attitude of the staff, and my own sense of what a hotel should offer. Of course there are plenty of other fine hotels throughout the country, but these are the places I feel would help anyone have a great experience.

I have listed these hotels in the order I would suggest them to a friend. Not all of these fine properties are expensive, but most tend to be on the middle to upper end of the price range.

> **PALACE HOTEL DO BUÇACO**
> Buçaco, 3050-Mealhada, Portugal
> (031) 930-101

Without doubt, this is one of the most impressive hotels in all of Europe. Originally built as a royal hunting lodge for King Dom Carlos, this wonderful palace provides the perfect getaway for those seeking a romantic escape from a hectic vacation. The palace's exterior is ornamented with fine stonework and beautiful *azulejos* panels. The inside of this deluxe hotel is even more amazing with it's antique and beautiful art laden grand public rooms.

Each of the 66 air conditioned guest rooms and suites are unique, with antique and handcrafted Deco period furnishings. A recent renovation has added even more comforts to a selected number of modernized rooms. Adjacent to the hotel is a spectacular 17th century Carmelite monastery, a pond filled with swans, sumptuous box gardens, and several historic walking trails which lead through over 250 acres of pristine forest.

The service at this hotel is extraordinary, and guests are invited to dress casually while relaxing. I have even seen both the director and the manager (Sr. Santos and Sr. Castro Ribeiro) roll up their sleeves and help to carry client's baggage and serve dinners during the busiest nights. The unique ambiance here is rather warm and friendly, with a highly professional staff that is eager to please each guest. You may wish to dress up a bit for dinner, but it is not mandatory.

THE MOST MEMORABLE PLACES TO STAY

The gourmet cuisine which is served in the opulent dining room is among the finest in Portugal. To accompany an unforgettable meal at the palace, I strongly suggest a bottle of superb *Buçaco Reserva* wine (*Bairrada* region) made in limited quantities by Sr. Santos in the palace's own caves. For the bravest of guests, I suggest tasting the palace's legendary *Aguardente* (Fire Water) which you will always remember. This hotel is a must for all visitors to Portugal!.

Features: •*Restaurant* •*Air Conditioning* •*Cable TV* •*Tennis* •*Bar/Lounge* •*Winery* •*Concierge* •*Trails* •*Tobacconis* •*Private Bathrooms* •*In-Room Phones* •*Gardens*

HOTEL DA LAPA
Rua do Pau da Bandeira, 4, 1200-Lisbon, Portugal
(01) 395-0005

This is certainly the finest place to stay in Lisbon. This marble-laden converted mansion and adjoining modern wing in the exclusive embassy row district of *Lapa* boasts a clientele base which includes many heads of state and diplomats. The property was recently opened after several years of construction which cost millions of dollars.

With its prime location above the *Tejo* river, guests are surrounded by an ambiance of tranquility which is unique in Lisbon. The fabulous interior boasts large public rooms, airy lounges, and intimate old world salons. This fine 5 star hotel offers over 100 expertly decorated guestrooms and deluxe suites, all with marble bathrooms, and a unique top floor suite with it's own turreted lookout patio.

The service here is quite good, and the front desk can handle almost any special requests from even the most demanding clients. The ambiance at this hotel tends to be formal and serious, with most guests dressed in business attire or designer clothing. Even the porters and doormen here are true professionals, one of them (a former Canadian resident) walked with me for a kilometer to help find an open tobacco store on a Sunday. The funny thing was, he refused to accept a tip since he felt badly that the hotel did not stock my brand of cigarettes.

The hotel offers a beautiful continental restaurant which serves gourmet meals prepared by an extremely talented Swiss chef. I have enjoyed spectacular meals in both the dining room and from room service which seem to always be followed by even more impressive desserts. An extensive wine list is also available at both the restaurant and the relaxing bar.

Features: • *Restaurant* • *Air Conditioning* • *Cable TV* • *Sauna* • *Bar/Lounge* • *Outdoor Pool* • *Concierge* • *Health Club* • *Tobacconist* • *Private Bathrooms* • *In-Room Phones* • *Gardens*

HOTEL ALBATROZ
Rua Frederico Arouca, 100, 2750-Cascais, Portugal
(01) 483-2821

A world famous deluxe hotel built on a cliff overlooking the sea in the jet set resort area of *Cascais*. Housed in a converted royal mansion, this fine 5 star property has a huge repeat clientele base. The wonderful white facade encloses just 40 well-decorated guestrooms and suites, most with unforgettable seaviews. This hotel is so close to the ocean that you can sometimes hear the waves crashing below you at night.

I have spent several nights here, and I found this place hard to leave. Inside the hotel there are several tastefully designed lounges and exclusive boutiques. The one thing that I always appreciated is that each guest receives a complimentary bottle of fine Port wine in their room when they first arrive.

The service here is prompt and courteous, with a small staff which can often remember the guests' names. This hotel has an unusual ambiance due to the fact that the guests can be seen wearing anything from jeans to

Armani suits. Sometimes it is the most casually dressed guests who turn out to be the visiting movie stars and world leaders. One of the best advantages to staying here is it's excellent location for wandering over to *Cascais'* beaches, boutiques, restaurants, and nightlife. For those who are interested in visiting *Lisbon*, the electric train is located just steps behind the hotel.

The hotel's panoramic seaview restaurant offers fine gourmet cuisine which is presented with great care. I have eaten the absolute finest fresh fish here, and I am told that every item on the menu is just as good. Although dinner here can get quite pricey, lunches are often much more reasonable. A vast wine list is available both in the seaview dining room and in the equally impressive bar.

Features: • *Restaurant* • *Air Conditioning* • *Cable TV* • *Sundeck* • *Bar/Lounge* • *Outdoor Pool* • *Concierge* • *Minibars* • *Tobacconist* • *Private Bathrooms* • *In-Room Phones* • *Boutiques*

HOTEL CONVENTO DE SÃO PAULO
Aldeia de Serra, 7170-Redondo, Portugal
(066) 999-100

This fantastic, majestic 14th-century converted convent provides one of the most relaxing and artistically inspiring possibilities for a vacation in Portugal. Situated on over 1,400 acres of fine countryside some 20 minutes northeast of Évora, I couldn't imagine a better place to rest up and explore the historic walled villages of the Planícies region. This deluxe 4 star hotel (it really deserves 5 stars) is housed in a wonderful convent which still contains many original *azulejos* panels and fine frescoes.

Every inch of the convent reveals yet another piece of dramatic art and history. The convent's 21 super luxurious air conditioned rooms are filled with both ancient and modern furnishings, combined with marble bathrooms.

The service at this hotel is extremely warm and typical of the region. One of the most charming aspects of this hotel are the staff who are charming and sensitive local residents. The convent has made a policy of hiring and training people from the general vicinity as a way to benefit both the hotel and the surrounding community.

Breakfast in bed is a truly special event here and includes home made breads and fresh juices and fruits from the convent's own gardens. The convent has a spacious dining room which serves well prepared regional cuisine with warm and personalized service. The ambiance here is completely relaxed, and jeans are quite acceptable. A recently completed outdoor pool and tree lined fountain garden provide a wonderful retreat.

The ever-present Sr. Almeida is among the most delightful and hard working hotel managers in Portugal, and his experiences working at the Ritz during it's heyday shows itself in the quality found here. This hotel is unique in the world, and is without the slightest doubt the finest place to spend a vacation in this region.

Features: •Restaurant •Air Conditioning •Cable TV •Sundeck •Bar/Lounge •Outdoor Pool •Historic Art •Jeep Safaris •Horse Riding •Private Bathrooms •In-Room Phones •Trails

HOTEL PALÁCIO DE ÁGUEDA
Quinta da Borralha, 3750-Águeda, Portugal
(034) 601-977

A dramatic, restored 16th-century palace in the heart of wine country only 25 minutes away from both *Porto* and *Coimbra*. This remarkable 4 star (it deserves to have 5 stars) property is housed in a ornate regal structure which has been lovingly restored by it's current owner, the down to earth world famous French castle designer Mr. Jean Louis de Talance. The hotel is managed by the insightful Mr. Jan Bos, who was formerly in charge of some of London's finest hotels.

The land surrounding the hotel has peaceful gardens, a pond, and a large pool area. Each of the many public rooms and galleries in the hotel contain unusual decorations and art pieces from the owner's private collection. The 48 huge guestrooms and suites offer special touches such as canopied beds, antiques, and oversized bathrooms. Every detail has been well designed to assure the absolute comfort of each guest. The hotel often has scheduled weekend entertainment such as traditional folk dancing groups in it's beautiful bar and lounge. With a location so close to the beaches, wineries, mountains, and historic countryside of both the *Costa Verde* and *Costa de Prata* regions, this is a great hotel and it's price is a bargain.

The service here is especially personalized, with most of the unusually youthful staff always smiling. The owner has the wonderful habit of attempting to greet each of his guests as if to welcome them to his home. The ambiance here is a mixture of casual and also formal, depending what each individual guest prefers.

The hotel has a fine restaurant which offers unusual French/Portuguese cuisine prepared by master chefs from both nations. I can assure you that the specially bottled *Palácio Águeda* reserve wines (*Bairrada* region) are the perfect accompaniment to a wonderful meal here. Ask the waiter if perhaps they still have any 1980 (red) left in the cellar.

Features: • *Restaurant* • *Gardens* • *Cable TV* • *Sundeck* • *Bar/Lounge* • *Outdoor Pool* • *Historic Art* • *Tennis* • *Minibars* • *Private Bathrooms* • *In-Room Phones* • *Minibars*

ALDEAMENTO VILALARA
Alporchinos, 8365-Armação de Pera, Portugal
(082) 314-910

A remarkable, elegant apartment compound on one of the most beautiful private cove beaches in the Algarve region. This small, deluxe, and modern 5 star spa and vacation complex is surrounded by acres of well manicured grounds which boast fine exotic trees and plants, giving this world class resort an isolated and exclusive environment.

The 86 ultra deluxe air conditioned apartments are in modern and vividly designed villa style structures which are on a cliff which ends at the sea. Each apartment has a self contained kitchen, living room, one or more bedrooms, fantastically ornate bathrooms, fine *azulejos*, television, and a lovely patio. The resort offers many special facilities including 3 salt and fresh water pools, jacuzzis, a spa and aquatic therapy program, and well maintained tennis courts. The front desk can help to provide recommendations as well as access to several nearby world class golf courses, local sport fishing outfitters, equestrian centers, sail boats, and all sorts of watersports. With its prime location, and excellent facilities, Vilalara is perhaps the finest place to relax and enjoy all of the best aspects of the Algarve.

Service at the hotel is without doubt the finest in the whole region. The observant front desk staff seem to almost sense that you have a question, and are always ready to assist the guests. The daytime ambiance here is casual yet elegant with a typical clientele of upscale Europeans on vacation, but dinner is a bit more formal. The sumptuous gourmet restaurant and grillroom offer spectacularly prepared cuisine with a special flair towards using local seafoods. A fine wine list is also available for those of you who enjoy vintage bottles. Besides having cool drinks at one of the bars, many clients prefer to sit at one of the oceanview tables on the sundeck and sip the afternoon away.

Features: •*Restaurant* •*Air Conditioning* •*Cable TV* •*Esplanade* •*Bar/Lounge* •*Outdoor Pools* •*Concierge* •*Tennis* •*Kitchens* •*Private Bathrooms* •*In-Room Phones* •*Beach*

POUSADA DO CASTELO
Paço Real, 2510-Óbidos Portugal
(062) 959-105

A fairly tale 16th-century restored royal castle that is perhaps the best known *pousada* in all of Portugal. Its dominating stone block battlements, towers, and walls encircle and loom over the quaint village of Óbidos in the Costa de Prata region. This famous deluxe inn has only nine comfortable guestrooms and suites with private bathrooms, all of which have a typically ancient style. Some of the rooms even have old iron candlesticks (now converted for electricity), solid stone block walls, period furnishings, panoramic windows, and large wooden canopied beds.

Since this fine *pousada* has so few rooms and is well known throughout the world, it is often completely sold out several months in advance for most of the year. The public spaces here have wonderful artwork and beautiful furnishings. Large central lounges and inner courtyards provide a great place to just relax and try to wonder what live must have been like for the former royal inhabitants of this delightful structure.

Service here is pretty good, with a cooperative front desk that is more than willing to provide suggestions on local daytrips and area attractions. The *pousada* also offers a regal dining room which features hearty regional cuisine and Portuguese wines. The ambiance at the *pousada* is rather relaxed and casual, but during dinner it may be best to dress a bit nicely.

Since the location of the inn is picture perfect, all you must do is walk out of the front door and down the stone steps to be in the ancient heart

THE MOST MEMORABLE PLACES TO STAY 89

of an unforgettable walled village. You can just leave your car in the parking area, and explore Obidos completely by foot. Several wonderful beaches, wineries, artisan shops, and historic cities are just minutes away by car, bus, or taxi. I strongly suggest that you at least try to get a reservation here, you never know when a cancellation might just happen to occur.

Features: •Restaurant •Parking •Cable TV •Esplanade •Bar/Lounge •Safe Deposit Boxes •Concierge •Historic Art •Tobacconist •Private Bathrooms •In-Room Phones •Trails

POUSADA DOS LÓIOS
Largo do Conde de Vila Flôr, 7000-Évora, Portugal
(066) 240-51

This large *pousada* has been constructed inside of a 15th-century converted convent's cloister, and is situated in the midst of the most historic sector of central *Évora* in the Planícies region. Its red roof and whitewashed facade give little clue as to the unbelievable beauty which awaits each visitor as you open the door. Inside this impressive structure there are marvelous remnants of the original chapter house, glass enclosed vaulted cloisters, fine public lounges, detailed stone carvings, ancient fountains, imposing arches, massive columns, and a huge grand hall.

Many of the 31 guestrooms (and 1 suite), all with private bathrooms, have been built out of the remains of the convent's original monastic cells and are laden with *Arraiolos* carpets and fine period furnishings.The setting of this remarkable deluxe inn could not possibly be more enchanting. Directly in front of the *pousada's* main entrance you will see the famous Roman temple, and just steps away there are countless fine museums, cathedrals, palaces, mansions, and shops.

The service here is pretty good, with the younger staff being your best source for any specific information. The ambiance here is rather laid back, as most guests tend to spend their days in *Évora* doing lots of walking around. At night things get more formal and sophisticated, and proper attire at dinner is suggested. There is a wonderful regional restaurant within the most romantic part of the inn, and the cuisine is surprisingly good. Make sure that you ask in advance for a table as many non guests have been known to fill up the dining room.

There are many diversions available in the *pousada* itself including a swimming pool and esplanade. I have spent countless hours wandering around this place, and I am equally impressed each time I have stayed here.

Features: •Restaurant •Safe Deposit Boxes •Cable TV •Esplanade •Bar/Lounge •Outdoor Pool •Concierge •Historic Art •Tobacconist •Private Bathrooms •In-Room Phones •Parking

HOTEL INFANTE DE SAGRES
Praça Dona Filipa de Lancastre, 62, 4000-Porto, Portugal
(02) 201-9031

A deluxe converted mansion a central location within the city of Porto. This enchanting 5 star hotel commonly hosts heads of state and corporate chairmen who are in town to conduct official business. As you enter through the elaborate entrance, the hotel's opulent interior is immediately apparent. The hotel boasts several fine public rooms and art laden salons which have an inviting atmosphere. There is also a curious courtyard patio and a unique spiral staircase just off the main lobby. The 80 large air-conditioned and soundproofed guestrooms and suites all have period furnishings and huge bathrooms. If you want to sightsee around *Porto*, all you have to do is walk one block to be on *Ave. dos Aliados*.

The service here is top-notch with a staff to guest ratio of almost one to one. The staff seem quite professional and are multilingual. I have walked in off the street unannounced on several occasions, and the front desk was quite willing to give me advice and directions even though I was not a guest at the time. The ambiance of the hotel is exclusive, serious, and formal, with most guests being wealthy businessmen, but I still feel extremely comfortable walking around the hotel with nice but semi-casual clothes.

The hotel has an amazing main restaurant called the Dona Filipa which has white glove service and some of the most elaborate silverware and china I have ever seen in Portugal. The extensive menu and wine list can be a bit overwhelming at first, but all I had to do was ask the head waiter for some suggestions. In the warmer months the patio is used to offer a less formal outdoor location to enjoy the same gourmet cuisine and wines which are served in the restaurant. A good choice for upscale travelers who demand the finest of everything.

Features: • Restaurant • Air Conditioning • Cable TV • Sundeck • Bar/Lounge • Safe Deposit Boxes • Historic Art • Garage • Patio • Private Bathrooms • In-Room Phones • Minibars

HOTEL PALÁCIO SETEAIS
Rua Barbosa do Bocage, 8, 2710-Sintra, Portugal
(01) 923-3200

A super-deluxe converted nobleman's palace in the historic and enchanted town of Sintra. The magnificent 5 star hotel is among the most respected deluxe properties in the country and has hosted various heads of state, movie stars, royal family members, executives from multinational corporation's, and many of the world's most famous people. The fantastic 18th-century facade is breathtaking, and the opulence and tranquility that awaits you inside is even more impressive.

The hotel has just 30 antique-filled guestrooms and suites which are all unique. A newer wing which was added to the original structure contains several guestrooms which are slightly less impressive, and in my opinion, better rooms in the older and more opulent section of the hotel. The palace contains many antiques, statues, fine tapestries, exotic drawing rooms, grand stairways, chandeliers, opulent lounges, and one of the world's most beautiful antique pianos. Outside of the hotel you will find romantic box gardens, a large outdoor pool, a horse riding center, huge lawns, and great panoramic views of the castles and village of *Sintra*. You will however need to use a car or a taxi to get from this property to any of the major sights in the area.

Service here is prompt, but not particularly friendly. I have never seen anyone working here smile even once. The ambiance is formal and conservative. Young people may find themselves in the vast minority here, as most guests are older rich Europeans. The hotel has a very good restaurant which serves nicely prepared cuisine in a tranquil and luxurious setting just beside the box gardens. This hotel seems like a living museum, only here you can actually touch the items on display. I like this hotel, but only the most refined people may feel comfortable around this type of atmosphere.

Features: •*Restaurant* •*Air Conditioning* •*Cable TV* •*Sundeck* •*Bar/Lounge* •*Outdoor Pool* •*Historic Art* •*Horses* •*Patio* •*Private Bathrooms* •*In-Room Phones* •*Box Gardens*

HOTEL DO GUINCHO
Praia do Guincho, 2750-Cascais, Portugal
(01) 487-0492

A beautifully-converted 17th-century fortress resting on the edge a rocky cliff above a Guincho's fine sandy beach in the Costa de Lisboa region. This inspiring 5 star hotel is a favorite spot for young honeymoon couples who are looking for a romantic seaside getaway. The pastel colored fortress must be entered through a massive doorway which leads past a cute inner courtyard and straight into the hotel. Inside the hotel you will find beautifully designed lounges, antique tapestries, suits of armour, panoramic oceanview picture windows, and mysterious alcoves, cellars, and staircases.

Many of the 36 air conditioned guestrooms, offer fine seaviews, columned terraces, fireplaces, canopy beds, cathedral ceilings with em

THE MOST MEMORABLE PLACES TO STAY

bedded coats of arms, beautiful furnishings, tile floors, and large bathrooms. The location of this hotel makes it a perfect base from which to drive over to *Sintra, Cascais, Estoril, Cabo da Roca,* or even *Lisbon.* This means that excellent golf, tennis, horse riding, restaurants, and nightlife are just minutes away.

Service here is fair at best, but with a little persistence you can get some occasional assistance from the front desk. The international cuisine at the restaurant is extremely good, and fortunately the service here is first rate. I once asked the wine steward for suggestions, and he went on for over an hour explaining the history and production methods of each regional wine. If you have dinner here you should consider having their fantastic Crepes Suzette. The ambiance here is relaxed and casual, with dinner guests not always wearing a jacket or tie.

I like this hotel a lot, but I just wish the some of the staff could be a little more friendly and helpful. I still suggest this beautiful hotel, but don't expect 5 star service.

Features: •*Restaurant* •*Air Conditioning* •*Cable TV* •*Sundeck* •*Bar/Lounge* •*Beach* •*Historic Art* •*Minibars* •*Patio* •*Private Bathrooms* •*In-Room Phones* •*Terraces*

QUINTA DA CORTIÇÃDA
Outeiro da Cortiçãda, 2040-Rio Maior, Portugal
(043) 479-182

A regal old manor house set on several acres of exquisite rural countryside near the tranquil farming community of Rio Maior in the Costa de Prata region. This stately property consists of a lovely pink mansion which is surrounded by a private lake full of fish, stables with fine horses, tennis courts, a huge swimming pool, an esplanade, a sundeck, gardens, a barbecue area, a working farm, and a private grillroom. In the tradition of only the finest *quintas*, this inn keeps a full time staff of professional managers, cooks, and housekeepers.

The charming main house itself is filled with rare iconography, marble and parquet flooring, beautiful antiques, tapestries, lounges, a large dining room, an honor bar, and seven deluxe air-conditioned rooms and suites with private bathrooms. The area of Rio Maior is full of traditionally dressed local residents who can often be seen driving to work in horse drawn wagons.

To get here you will either need to use a rental car, or arrange for a taxi or transfer from the rain or bus stations which several miles away. Your efforts to get this far off the typical tourist path will be well rewarded from the minute you arrive.

The *quinta* can offer delicious home made meals if requested and confirmed in advance, and is commonly used as a retreat and meeting center for small deluxe corporate groups. The staff here are well trained by the owners, the Nobre family, who have spared no expense to convert this unique inn. The ambiance here is casual with a touch of class.

Of the more than 175 *quintas* that I have visited and stayed in, Quinta da Cortiçãda is a fine example of how welcoming and well managed a Portuguese bed and breakfast inn can really be. I strongly advise you to think about a couple of nights in a place like this. A stay in a *quinta* like this will bring you close to experiencing the soul of Portugal.

Features: •*Restaurant* •*Air Conditioning* •*TV* •*Tennis* •*Bar/Lounge* •*Outdoor Pool* •*Historic Art* •*Horses* •*Esplanade* •*Private Bathrooms* •*In-Room Phones* •*Gardens*

THE MOST MEMORABLE PLACES TO STAY 95

> **QUINTA HORTA DA MOURA**
> 7200-Reguengos de Monsaraz, Portugal
> (066) 552-06

    A fabulous new manor house on 40 acres of prime farm land just below the ancient and mysterious walled city of Monsaraz in the Planícies region. This deluxe and artistically designed mansion and estate offers a truly stress-free environment for guests to explore the entire region. The traditional white and blue exterior is surrounded by herds of sheep, fruit trees, prehistoric megaliths, Roman wells, vineyards, tennis courts, an equestrian center and riding academy, winery, patios, and a delightful swimming pool with a sun terrace.

Inside this architectural masterpiece you'll find relaxing lounges, a fine game room with a great billiard table, a bar, and wine cellars. The accommodations consist of 14 air conditioned guestrooms, suites, and a separate little self contained house, all with huge private bathrooms. Most of the units contain fireplaces, patios, living rooms, local artwork and handicrafts, and televisions. The service here is quite good, and the manager, Sra. Calado, greets each client personally. Horta da Moura's ambiance is casual and down to earth, with guests being made to feel as if they are staying in a friend's home.

The inn also offers a fine regional restaurant with special dishes that have been created from a variety of produce and cheese which have been grown on their own farms. The large wine list includes special local wines from their huge cellars and winery which you may never be offered anywhere else.

With a vantage point looking towards the village of Monsaraz, you couldn't ask for a better location to relax and enjoy the living history of this part of the country. The inn can provide wonderful excursions including jeep safaris, horseback and carriage rides, river trips on the nearby *Guadiana* river, and sightseeing. A great place to stay at a remarkably reasonable price.

Features: •Restaurant •Air Conditioning •TV •Tennis •Bar/Lounge •Outdoor Pool •Historic Art •Horses •Esplanade •Private Bathrooms •In-Room Phones •Gardens

QUINTA DO CARACOL
São Pedro, 8800-Tavira, Portugal
(081) 224-75

A cute and welcoming converted farming estate and its 17th-century manor house on the outskirts of the enchanting historic city of Tavira in the sunny Algarve. The typically Algarvian-styled house sits among gorgeous gardens and fruit trees.

Even though you may feel isolated, in reality it is just a short walk from the center of town and the train station. Surrounding the property is a nice swimming pool, tennis courts, a big barbecue area, and a few inquisitive birds which announce your presence. The seven nice apartments all have comfortable bedding, kitchens, dining rooms, private bathrooms, and regional furniture. The last time I stayed here I ended up with a duplex at the same price (quite low) as a normal unit would cost.

Besides peaceful walks into Tavira, the *quinta* also can provide on site diversions including bicycles, tennis, ping pong, as well as access to nearby beaches, horseback riding, golf courses, outdoor markets, and a huge selection of watersports facilities.

THE MOST MEMORABLE PLACES TO STAY 97

The service here is quite good and extremely personalized. The *quinta's* owner, Sr. Viegas, is usually around to assist all of his guests and give them suggestions for worthwhile local activities. Since there is no real restaurant here, you will find several fine seafood establishments close by.

This inn has a down-to-earth ambiance with many return guests coming from Canada, England, and northern European countries. The people who you usually meet here are extremely friendly, and often will offer to give rides to those who arrived by public transportation. At night the inn becomes an inviting social place, with the sounds of hearty laughter extending from the small bar at the edge of the house. This is a great affordable alternative to the many big impersonal hotels in the Algarve.

Features: • *Restaurant* • *Air Conditioning* • *TV* • *Tennis* • *Bar/Lounge* • *Outdoor Pool* • *Historic Art* • *Horses* • *Esplanade* • *Private Bathrooms* • *In-Room Phones* • *Gardens*

QUINTA DA LOMBA
Lomba-Gondomar, 4 km off route N-222
(055) 663-36

This compelling 17th-century restored manor house rests on the peaceful banks of the *Douro* river in the village of Lomba close to the town of Gondomar in the Costa Verde region. The *quinta* has a memorable view over the wide river valley and it's adjacent tree laden hills. As you enter through the stone gateway emblazoned with a coat of arms into the estate, you immediately have the sense that you should feel privledged to be here.

Surrounding the *quinta* you can't help but be drawn into its tranquil riverfront, huge swimming pool, fine lawns, garden side patio and grill area, tennis courts, and boathouse. The majestic main house and it's regal annex contain collections of antique rifles, beautiful artwork, fine tapestries, period furnishings, and wonderful fireside lounges.

The inn is comprised of three deluxe air-conditioned guestrooms with private bathrooms, and an additional three air conditioned apartments (1 and 2 bedroom) with private bathrooms and kitchens, all of which are tastefully decorated. Some of the rooms have magnificent canopy beds, antique cabinets, and fine wooden floors.

The many activities that are part of the inn include swimming, sauna, waterskiing, jet skis, powerboats, tennis, billiards, card room, video room, ping pong, fishing, and beautiful rural roads to wander down. Since it's location is only 42 km from Porto, this is the ideal vacation spot for those who wish to visit the city and still escape the noise and pollution. Several Port wine lodges are nearby in Peso da Régua.

Service here is a special matter, with most of the staff being comprised of local and somewhat shy traditional workers. They seem to just magically appear whenever you need help, and then they vanish again until the next time you need them. The *quinta's* charming owner, Dr. Santos, is a generous and warm hearted host who loves practice his perfect English with guests. The ambiance here is laid back and quite comfortable, with a guest list from all over Europe. The inn provides a hearty homemade breakfast, and additional restaurants can be found in close by.

Features: •*Restaurant* •*Air Conditioning* •*TV* •*Tennis* •*Bar/Lounge* •*Outdoor Pool* •*Watersports* •*Historic Art* •*Horses* •*Esplanade* •*Private Bathrooms* •*In-Room Phones* •*Gardens*

9. MAJOR FESTIVALS

Every region of Portugal hosts several festivals, fairs, religious processions (*romarias*) and special celebrations each year. The following list contains some of the most important religious, cultural, historical, and agricultural festivities.

To receive information on the exact dates of each specific event, please contact either one of the Portuguese National Tourist Offices, or the *Turismo* office in the region you are visiting. Several more fairs and festivals are also listed in each regional chapter.

FEBRUARY
CARNIVAL in *Ovar, Sines, Loulé, Nazaré, Funchal*, and many other cities.

This Mardi Gras type of event in late February is one of the liveliest festivals of the year. Each city has a variety of events which usually include a parade of masked r costumed participants, carnival style floats, and flower battles.

MARCH OR APRIL
HOLY WEEK in *Braga, Ovar*, and *Pavoa de Varzim*.

Many different types of ritual processions with the Ecce Homme.

MAY
FESTIVAL OF THE CROSSES in *Monsanto*

First Sunday in May – girls parade through the streets and up to the ruined castle to throw flowers to commemorate the siege of *Monsanto*.

FESTIVAL OF THE CROSSES in *Barcelos*

A major regional event on the first week of May including concerts, flower covered streets, craft fairs, fireworks, and the Procession of the Holy Cross.

ROSÉ FESTIVAL in *Vila Franca do Lima*

A very unusual parade in which a women wears a massive 80 pound

100 PORTUGAL GUIDE

tray of arraigned flowers (representing a regional coat of arms) on her head during the procession.

PILGRIMAGE TO FÁTIMA in *Fátima*
Over 250,000 Christians from around the globe converge on *Fátima* to honor the anniversary of first apparition of the Virgin Mary by 3 young shepherds on May 13, 1917.

LEIRIA FESTIVAL in *Leiria*
A folkart and traditional dancing festival each Sunday in May.

QUEIMA DAS FITAS in *Coimbra*
Each year in mid may when the school year is finished, the University students of Coimbra burn their graduation gowns and collage ribbons and continue to drink for at least one week. There are concerts and riverfront parties throughout the city.

JUNE
FEAST OF SAINT GONÇALO in *Amarante*.
During the first weekend of June, *Amarante* pays tribute to the Saint of marriage with celebrations and gift exchanges for those in love.

NATIONAL AGRICULTURAL FAIR in *Santarém*
The most famous event in Portuguese agriculture takes place for a week and a half starting on the first Friday of the month. *Santarém*, home to many producers of livestock, hosts a week long celebration which includes bullfights, livestock competitions, and other cultural events. This festival takes on the appearance of a state fair.

ALL SAINTS FESTIVAL in *Lisbon*, *Porto*, and many other cities
Celebrations of massive parades and unusual ritual processions take place in many areas. The St. Anthony festival in *Lisbon* (June 12 and/or 13) is carried out on in the heart of the city when marching bands sing and dance down the *Avenida Liberdade*, and small groups of revelers wander through the *Alfama*. In *Porto*, the St. John festival (June 24) is full of singing, dancing, and bonfires throughout the night. Many other cities and towns join in the festivities with smaller celebrations.

FESTIVAL OF SÃO PEDRO in *Montijo*
Festivals and processions around June 24 are capped off by a release of bulls into the streets.

MAJOR FESTIVALS 101

INTERNATIONAL LUSITANO HORSE SHOW in *Lisbon*
This world class event features exhibitions and competitions of pure bred Lusitanian horses. The exact dates change each year

JULY

COLETE ENCARNADO FESTIVAL in *Vila Franca de Xira*
This festival in the first half of July honors the area's cattlemen, who parade through the streets. Additions festivities include fairs, folk dancing, bullfights, and the releasing of bulls into the streets.

FEIRA DO ARTISANTO in *Estoril*
Estoril's fairgrounds host a nightly array of local handicrafts as well as a sampling of traditional folklore and cuisine. Open 6pm until midnight daily in July and August.

TABULEIROS FESTIVAL in *Tomar*
In every odd numbered year for the first two weeks of July. A harvest festival which includes a strange march of hundreds of supposed virgins wearing huge hats decorated with flowers and other agricultural products (only on the first Sunday)

AUGUST

ST. WALTER FESTIVAL in *Guimarães*
A centuries old festival which includes fairs, bullfights, torch lit processions, and the *Marcha Gualteriana*, a parade of satire with marching bands and strangely costumed participants.

OUR LADY OF SAFE JOURNEY FESTIVAL in *Peniche*
This important festival takes place on the first Sunday in August. Boats of the local fishing fleet carry religious statues in the hopes of another safe year at sea.

OUR LADY OF AGONY FESTIVAL in *Viana do Castelo*
A highly unusual festival on the third weekend of August which includes side shows, magic, fireworks, folklore, a bull run, and a final parade in regional costume, in which Our Lady is carried over a huge tapestry of flowers.

FESTIVAL OF SANTA BARBRA in *Miranda do Douro*
On the 3rd Sunday in August the young men of this isolated border town celebrate by dressing in costumes to perform the stick dance called the *pauliteiros*.

SEPTEMBER

GRAPE HARVEST FESTIVAL in *Palmela*
The harvest of wine grapes is celebrated with a benediction of the grapes, wine tastings, parades, fireworks, folklore, and a bull run. Exact dates change each year.

FOLK MUSIC AND DANSE FESTIVAL in *Praia da Rocha*
A week long event sometime during each September which combines traditional folk singing, folklore, and dancing events throughout the *Algarve*.

THE NEW FAIRS in *Ponte de Lima*.
A huge regional market and festival on the second and third weekend in September when thousands of people gather to watch in dances, concerts, markets, fireworks displays, and processions.

OUR LADY OF GOOD VOYAGES FESTIVAL in *Moita*
The annual blessing of the fishing boats.

OCTOBER

THE FINAL PILGRIMAGE TO FÁTIMA in *Fátima*
This major event honors the final appearance of the Virgin Mary in *Fátima* on October 13, 1917

NATIONAL GASTRONOMY FESTIVAL in *Santarém*
This 10 day event at the end of October celebrates the fine regional cuisines of Portugal. Normally scheduled events include cooking contests, lectures by famous chefs, exhibitions, samplings of traditional dishes from various restaurants, and authentic folklore and music.

NOVEMBER

ST. MARTINS FESTIVAL AND NATIONAL HORSE SHOW in *Golegã*.
A major fair during the first 2 weeks of November is combined with equestrian competitions and parades.

DECEMBER

FESTIVAL OF THE RAPAZES throughout the *Montanhas*.
Starting on the 26 of December, local unmarried boys dress up in multicolored costumes and menacing masks while they run around town terrorizing neighbors.

10. SHOPPING

BOUTIQUES

Shopping in Portugal is a great pleasure. Each region produces different items ranging from hand-painted ceramics to fine tailored designer clothing. I have included information in each regional chapter of the items which should be searched out for their unique qualities. Many of the products which are exported into North America stating "made in Italy" are really made in Portugal.

Fine shoes, shirts, sweaters, dresses, handbags, belts, suits, linens, ceramics, tiles, embroidery, vintage wines, jewelry, and all sorts of additional items can be found at a fraction of their export price. Many larger size items of clothing and footware may not be available (including any North American shoe size over ten and a half). Most jewelry is made with 19 karat gold (*ouro*) or sterling silver (*prata*), but many filigree items are only gold plated.

Remember that most stores are generally open from 9am until 7pm on weekdays (many close for lunch from 1pm until 3pm), and on Saturdays from 9am until 1pm. I have included a selection of my favorite shops and boutiques in several city listings within each regional chapter of this book.

Since Portugal has joined the E.E.C., a program of tax refunds on selected export items has begun. What this **Tax Free for Tourists** program really does is quite simple and worth taking advantage of. Onethousand, six hundred shops in Portugal display the black and blue *Tax Free* sticker on their door.

When you make a purchase of over 10,000$00, you can ask for a *Tax Free* voucher check for your refund. The unsigned check is made out to the tourist (you must have your passport with you) which can only be cashed at the airport upon exiting the country. The value of the check depends on what percentage of tax was placed on the specific item you have purchased. Clothes are usually taxed around 12%, while some luxury items such as gold are taxed at almost 30%. At the airport, go to the

information booth and they will direct you to the cashier (7 days a week) before you reach the gates. My last refund check was for over 23,000$00!
For more specific details either pick up a Tax Free brochure at the airport, or call (01) 418-8703.

ANTIQUE HUNTING

For those of you interested in antiques (*antiguidades*), the best places to find good values are at the outdoor markets. Most major cities have a few select antique shops which can provide a great experience. Bargaining is not uncommon if the proprietor wants to make a sale.

Among the best antique values are old paintings, estate jewelry, rare books, old lamps, ancient door knockers, and wonderful wooden picture frames. Furniture is also a good bargain, but the shipping, insurance, and customs hassles can be discouraging. I have listed some good places to find selected antiques in several city listings within each regional chapter of this book. I must advise all antique hunters that the less reputable shops may display reproductions of antique objects without explaining the true age of the item.

REGIONAL HANDICRAFTS

Each town and village in Portugal offers many unique regional crafts (*artigos regionais*) which can easily be found in the shops, markets, craft fairs, and artisan's (*artesanatos*) kiosks of each area. Several local *Turismo* offices throughout Portugal have copies of a pamphlet called *Feiras de Artesanato* which gives complete listings of all regional craft fairs each year. If you happen to be in *Lisbon*, you can pick up one of these books at the **Associação Industrial Portuguesa** (A.I.P.) on *Praça das Industrias (01) 362-0100*.

The most sought after examples of regional crafts include these fine products:

Alcobaça (Costa de Prata) – Hand and machine painted tiles
Arraiolos (Planícies) – Fine hand made carpets
Barcelos (Costa Verde) – Unusual clay figurines
Caldas da Rainha (Costa de Prata) – Ceramics murals and *azulejos*
Castelo Branco (Montanhas) – Hand embroidered bedspreads
Chaves (Montanhas) – Black pottery
Coimbra (Costa de Prata) – Ceramic crocks
Gondomar (Costa Verde) – Gold and silver filigree jewelry
Illhavo (Costa de Prata) – Vista Alegre porcelain
Lamego (Montanhas) – Hand wooven baskets
Mafra (Costa de Lisboa) – Miniatures
Marinha Grande (Costa de Prata) – Fine Crystal

Nazaré (Costa de Prata) – Hand knit sweaters
Portalegre (Planícies) – Tapesties
Peniche (Costa de Prata) – Hand made lace.
Redondo (Planícies) – Hand painted glazed ceramics.
São Pedro do Corval (Planícies) – Hand painted earthenware.
Tavira (Algarve) – Hand made saddles.
Viana do Castelo (Costa Verde) – Hand made lace.
Vila do Conde (Costa Verde) – Bobben lace.

EUROPEAN SIZE CONVERSIONS

These sizes are an approximate conversion and may not be accurate in certain cases. Please ask for a free measurement or try on items before you purchase them.

Men's Shoes

North America	8	9	10	11	12	13
Europe	40	42	43	44	46	47

Women's Shoes

North America	4	5	6	7	8	9
Europe	34	35	36	37	38	39

Men's Suitings

North America	36	38	40	42	44	46
Europe	46	48	50	52	54	56

Women's Dresses

North America	6	8	10	12	14	16
Europe	32	34	40	42	44	46

Men's Shirts

North America	14	15	16	17	18
Europe	36	38	41	43	45

OUTDOOR MARKETS & FAIRS

Every region in Portugal offers a variety of outdoor bazaar style markets. The wide assortment of goods for sale include local cheeses, meats, live poultry, ceramics, crafts, leather jackets, shoes, clothing, tapestries, furniture, antiques, and an assortment of imported items and trinkets.

Be very careful about purchasing some goods such as shoes or leather goods as they may be synthetic (even if the label says otherwise).

Barganing is somewhat acceptable, especially if you are purchasing in quantity. These local markets provide an excellant excursion.

Many more markets exist, and can be found by simply stopping by the local Turismo or asking the front desk of any hotel in the region.

Here are the main markets by town and city:

Águeda
A rather small yet charming market takes place downtown each Saturday. You can find great bargains on shoes, shirts, and belts.

Albufeira
A market takes place here on the first and third Tuesday of each month.

Almancil
Each first and fourth Sunday, a large and entertaining market comes to Almancil.

Almeirim
On the first Sunday of each month, this quiet town host a wonderful artisan and produce market in the center of town. Look for the fine locally grown melons.

Almoçageme
This small village just west of Sintra offers a cute country market on the third Sunday of each month. Local pottery can be bought at good prices.

Alpedrinha
This mountain view town hosts a nice market on the first Sunday of each month.

Amares
This northern town hosts a weekly market with good handicrafts each Wednesday.

Aveiro
A monthly market known as the Feira dos 28 takes place on the 28th day of most months takes place in this town.

Azeitão
This old market happens only on the 4th Sunday of each month. Look for the hand painted decorative pottery in the shape of small houses and villages.

SHOPPING 107

Another country market takes place on the first Sunday of each month. Specialties include fresh produce and cheeses.

Barcelos
This charming market runs each Thursday to provide the locals and visitors with every imaginable product. Look for the wonderful colorful wood andceramic items.

Benafim
A small local market takes place here on the first Saturday of each month.

Boca do Inferno
A small crafts market (open daily) can be found just off the Boca do Inferno. Prices at this market way too high, while the quality is low.

Braga
This northern city hosts a market known for cheap shoes and shirts on Tuesdays.

Carcavelo
This market opens each Thursday and offers a wide array of household goods, clothing, and seemingly useless items. A daily fish auction takes place at about 4pm at the fish market near the beach.

Celorico de Beira
On the Friday of each fortnight, there's a huge cheese market known for the quality and freshsness of its remarkable *Queijo de Serra* cheeses.

Cascais
The Cascais market behind the town center on Rua Mercado is open on every Wednesday and Saturday. This market is a good source for sweaters and shoes.

Coimbra
On weekdays the old section of the city hosts a small but interesting market. While produce and cheeses are sold in the covered market, gypsys can be seen selling lambswool sweaters and unusual tabecloths on the road above the market.

Elvas
The town hosts a great weekly regional market near the aqueduct on each Monday.

Espinho
A very good weekly market comes into the heart of town every Monday.

Estoi
On the second Sunday of every month an atmospheric local market comes to this historic community. Look for fine leather goods and linens.

Estremoz
On Saturdays, a very good market rolls into town. Furniture, traditional tapestries, unusual foods, woolens, and crafts are all available at reasonable prices.

Évora
On the second Thursday of each month a huge regional market takes place in the Rossio São Brás just outside the town's walls. Keep your eye out for the wonderful tapestries and shepards capes which are found only here.

Figueiro da Foz
An amusing market and fair called the Ferreira a Nova takes place on the 3rd day of each month.

Grandôla
A large market takes place here on the second Monday of each month.

Guarda
The town host a daily market in the southeastern corner of town. Each Wednesday there is also a market in the city's fairgrounds.

Guimarães
Each Friday the town has a local market where you can find nice filagree.

Lagos
Each Saturday morning a local produce market takes place near the bus station. A regional market takes place here on the first Sunday each month.

Lisboa
The Feira da Ladra (Thiefs market) on every Tuesday and Saturday is an excellant source for antiques and flea market type products.

Lourinhã
A cattle market takes place on the first Sunday of each month except September

Loulé
This huge market is one of the best in Portugal. Lasting until midnight on each Saturday, the Loulé market offers more variety than can be imagined. A must for any visitor to the Algarve. The strategy here is to bargain with the vendors.

Melgaço
An outstanding traditional weekly market comes to this border town each Friday.

Moncarapacho
A large market on the first Sunday of each month is hosted in this old Algarve town. My favorite bargains include boots, shoes, and tapestries.

Olhão
A daily (except Sunday) morning seafood and poduce market takes place near the river. This is the best market for fresh shellfish in the Algarve.

Pinhal Novo
A local market takes place here on the second Sunday of each month.

Ponte de Barca
A regional produce and general mechandise market is open each Wednesday.

Ponte de Lima
On every alternating Monday a local market and cattle auction takes place on both sides of the river.

Portimão
A large outdoor market runs here each first Monday of the month.

Porto
This major city offers several daily markets such as the Bolhão market as well as the special Sunday morning bird fair, flower market, and stamp market. A daily artisan fair is held each day in Praça da Batalha.

Quarteira
A weekly handicrafts and produce market takes place each Wednesday off the main street of Rua Vasco da Gama.

São Brás de Alportel
Each Saturday a very nice regional market is held here.

São Pedro de Sintra
This market is located on the main road rom Lisboa to Sintra. Running on the second and forth Sunday of each month, this market is huge. Good buys on folkart, antiques, ceramics, and locally made cheeses are easy to find.

São João das Lampas
This village located about 28 kilometers north of Sintra hosts a market on the first Sunday of each month.

Sines
A large market comes to town on the fourth Monday of each month.

Sobral de Monte Agraco
Each month on the first Monday a small market takes place. Look for the fine clay figures and unusual metalwork.

Terras de Bouro
This small village in the Serra do Gerês offers a charming traditional market on the second Monday of each month.

Valença do Minho
On Wednesdays there is a regional produce and crafts market here.

Viana do Castelo
Friday is market day in this beautiful town. Look for hand made emboidery.

Viseu
Viseu hosts a daily produce market in the heart of town.

Each Thursday the town also hosts a larger regional crafts and produce market in the northern sector of the city near the river.

11. SPORTS & RECREATION

Here are some of the main sports and recreational activities you can enjoy while in Portugal. Please check with each regional chapter for the locations and contact information regarding suppliers, venues, and outfitters for all types of common sports.

BICYCLES

During the last several years the sport of bicycling has become more popular in Portugal. It is now possible to plan either long or shot ange cycle excursions in each egion of the county for those who enjoy on or off road adventures.

Many hotels, *quintas*, and local bike shops offer bicycle rentals for those who are interested in a few hours or days of 2 wheeled fun. You should use the reflectors, flags, and lights for cycling in Portugal as your saftey may depend on them; cars may often not give a bicycle the right of way. I have included a partial listing of places which rent bicycles, but for further information please contact a local *Turismo* office.

For those of you who intend to travel extensively by bicycle in Portugal, these are some points to consider. Most airlines will permit the transportation of bikes, but can charge the passenger for so called extra baggage. Trains in Portugal also permit the tranportation of bikes with a small additional fee. Buses will often not allow for bikes on board due to limited luggage capacity. Most spare parts are quite expensive in Portugal, so bring them with you.

For people interested in group bicycle tours, there are a few companies such as **Cycling Through the Centuries** *at (800) 245-4226* which offer guided cycling tours in Portugal.

CAMPO PEQUENO BULLRING, LISBON

BULLFIGHTS

One of the most exciting spectator sports throughout the country is the typical Portuguese bullfight (*tourada*). These events have been enjoyed in Portugal since the 14th century, and are a great source of regional pride. Unlike the brutal Spanish form of the sport, in Portugal the bulls are not killed at the end of a fight. Here the sport seems much more like a test of wills rather than a grisly slaughter of a helpless animal.

Many cities and towns all over Portugal will hold weekly or monthly bullfighting events from April through October in specially designed arena shaped bullring (*Praça de Touros*). Tickets for these events can range from between 700$00 and 5000$00 per seat depending on the seat's location.

Before the start of the evening's events, there is often a prayer service for the men involved in the fight, followed by small indoor parade of the ornately costumed and highly trained horses with their costumed mounted warriors. When you are first escorted to your seat on the viewing bench, it is customary to give a small tip of around 75$00 per person to the usher. As you are sitting back and enjoying the fight, vendors will walk through the audience offering snacks and drinks.

After a trumpet blast, the participants of the night's events enter the ring to salute both the officials and audience before the action begins. When the ring is cleared, a bull is released from the ringside bullpen. A

SPORTS & RECREATION

gate soon opens and a well trained horse and it's ornately dressed mounted fighter (*cavaleiro*) begin to taunt the bull into action. The object of this sport is for the fighter charge towards the bull in order to plant a series of spears into the bull's body.

After a couple of rounds (about 6 spears) the *cavaleiro* departs the ring and the bull must be restrained and brought back to the pen for the night. To subdue the bull, a strangely dressed team of about eight seemingly suicidal men (*forcados*) line up to torment the bull into charging at them head on in a uniquely Portuguese test of courage known as a *pega*.

The lead *forcado* will attempt to jump on the bull's head and try to avoid being injured while the other seven men grab the bull and remove it from the ring. This is the most dangerous aspect of the bullfight, and many *forcados* have been seriously injured during their relentless attempts to control the animal. The fight will soon continue with more bulls, *cavaleiros*, and *pegas* and an intermission before the night is over.

CAR RACING

Professional car racing is a major attraction in Portugal. I have been to a few grand prix races in this country, and they are serious events. The most widely attended racing event in the country is the **Rallye de Portugal do Vinho de Porto** held each March. This week long event brings professional racers to locations throughout the country and is watched by perhaps millions of Portuguese. People will take their vacation time to coincide with the rally and follow it from location to location.

The more famous event in the racing circuit is the world renowned **Grande Premio de Portugal** formula one grand prix held each September in the **Estoril Autodromo** near *Sintra*. I cannot recommend that you spend the big bucks (10,000$00 or more) for a pass to this weekend event because the track lay out does not permit spectators to know what is really going on.

If you must see this formula one race, get the specially marked *paddock club* gold passes from the ticket offices in Estoril (30,000$00 or more) or else you should bring a portable TV with you to the stands. Ear plugs are definitely a necessity, and traffic is at a standstill anywhere near *Sintra, Cascais, and Estoril* during the race weekend. Every hotel room is booked anywhere within 50 km of either of these races.

FISHING

The rivers, lakes, reservoirs, and seacoast of Portugal contain a vast array of fine fish. No license is required for ocean fishing, but if you intend to fish inland you may need a special permit from either a local town hall or a park ranger. Each season presents opportunities to catch a different assortment of wonderful fresh and salt water fish.

The most common targets for sea fishing include grouper, bass, bream, swordfish, shark, bluefish, tuna, mackerel, rays, and dolphin fish. For those of you who may be more interested in the river and lake fishing throughout the country, you can expect to find trout, salmon, bass, shad, and barbel. Many companies offer excursions by boat into the most famous fishing areas of Portugal.

I have included a listing of fishing clubs and outfitters in each regional chapter of this book, but you should also check with a *Turismo* office for more information and the local rules regarding these activities.

GOLF

Golf is a tremendously popular pastime in Portugal for visiting British, German, and North American visitors. Due to the excellent year round climate, many courses have sprung up throughout the country, and several more are in the planning and construction stages. Many courses have been designed by the world's leading professionals such as Robert Trent Jones and Frank Pennink.

Although golf in Portugal is not particularly inexpensive, the unique conditions and dramatic views make this an unbeatable location for world class facilities. Most clubs offer full range of services including access to opulent clubhouses. A brief description of the 28 major courses is listed below, but please remember to reserve your tee times as far in advance as possible (especially from April-October). The **Portuguese Federation of Golf** (*Federacão Portuguesa de Golfe*) can provide you with specific course maps and green fees; *they can be reached at (01) 674 658.*

Most golf courses (even private clubs) will offer rates for nonmembers to use their facilities. The Algarve and the Costa de Lisboa regions are studded with a vast array of choices for all levels of skill, and there are other courses in most regions of the country with perhaps the exception of the Montanhas.

Just because everything else in Portugal seems like a bargain, don't expect golf to be cheap. I have spent over 11,000$00 for a round of golf on a nice course last year. Electric carts, equipment rental, locker rooms, lessons, and caddies are usually available at additional cost. Many hotels offer discounts and preferred tee times on local courses to their guests, so please at the front desk for details.

Each regional chapter of this book contains the listings of the courses which are available, and I have also included a handy chart of all major golf courses on the following pages. Note: those courses with multiple loops are rated for the longest segment.

SPORTS & RECREATION 115

Major Golf Courses in Portugal
THE ALGARVE
- **Quinta do Lago** *(Almancil, (089)394-782)*, 4 x 9 Holes, 3263 Meters, Par 36
- **Pinheiros Altos** *(Almancil, (089)394-340)*, 18 holes, 6049 Meters, Par 72
- **Pine Cliffs** *(Almancil, (089)501-787)*, 9 Holes, 2324 Meters, Par 33
- **San Lorenzo** *(Almancil, (089)396-534)*, 18 Holes, 6238 Meters, Par 72
- **Alto Golf** *(Alvor, (082)416-913)*, 18 Holes, 6125 Meters, Par 72
- **Vale de Milho Golf** *(Carvoeiro, (082)358-502)*, 9 Holes, 970 Meters, Par 27
- **Carvoeiro Golf** *(Lagoa, (082) 526-10)*, 18 Holes, 5919 Meters, Par 72
- **Vale de Pinto** *(Lagoa, (082) 526-10)*, 18 Holes, 5861 Meters, Par 71
- **Palmares** *(Lagos, (082)762-953)*, 18 Holes, 5961 Meters, Par 71
- **Vale do Lobo** *(Loulé, (089)394-444)*, 3 x 9 Holes, 3334 Meters, Par 36
- **Penina Golf** *(Portimão, (082)415-415)*, 9/18 Holes, 6439 Meters, Par 73
- **Vilamoura 1** *(Vilamoura, (089)313-652)*, 18 Holes, 6331 Meters, Par 73
- **Vilamoura 2** *(Vilamoura, (089)313-652)*, 18 Holes, 6256 Meters, Par 71
- **Vilamoura 3** *(Vilamoura, (089)313-652)*, 3 x 9 Holes, 3180 Meters, Par 36
- **Club do Golfe Vila Sol** *(Vilamoura, (089)302-144)*, 18 Holes, 6183 Meters, Par 72
- **Parque da Floresta** *(Vila do Bispo, (082)653-33)*, 18 Holes, 5888 Meters Par 72

COSTA DE LISBOA
- **Clube de Campo** *(Aroeira, (01)226-1802)*, 18 Holes, 6040 Meters, Par 72
- **Lisbon Sports Club** *(Belas, (01)431-2482)*, 18 Holes, 5278 Meters, Par 69
- **Quinta da Marinha** *(Cascais, (01)486-9881)*, 18 Holes, 6014 Meters, Par 71
- **Tróia Golf Club** *(Setúbal, (065)441-12)*, 18 Holes, 6337 Meters, Par 72
- **Golf Estoril Sol** *(Sintra, (01)923-2461)*, 2 x 9 Holes, 3609 Meters, Par 62
- **Penha Longa** *(Sintra, (01)924-0320)*, 18 Holes, 6228 Meters, Par 72
- **Quinta da Beloroura** *(Sintra, (01)924-0046)*, 18 Holes, 5877 Meters, Par 72
- **Palácio Estoril Golf** *(Sintra, (01)468-0176)*, 18 Holes, 5267 Meters, Par 68
- **Guia Estoril** *(Sintra, (01)486-9881)*, 2 x 9 Holes, 2350 Meters, Par 34

COSTA DA PRATA
- **Vimeiro Golf Club** *(Vimeiro, (061)984-157)*, 2 x 9 Holes, 2431 Meters Par 34

MONTANHAS
• **Vidago Golf Club** *(Vidago, (076)971-06)*, 9 Holes, 2449 Meters, Par 33

COSTA VERDE
• **Miramar Golf** *(Valadares, (02)762-2067)*, 9 Holes, 5146 Meters, Par 34
• **Oporto Golf** *(Espinho, (02)722-008)*, 18 Holes, 5668 Holes, Par 71
• **Estela Golf** *(Estela, (052)685-567)*, 2 x 9 Holes, 3090 Meters, Par 72

HORSEBACK RIDING

With a long equestrian tradition, Portugal offers a wide variety of horseback and carriage riding facilities. Many *quintas*, hotels, resorts, *herdades*, and riding centers can offer hourly riding on wonderful Lusitanian horses for as little as 1200$00 per hour.

Each region contains several different places to access horses, but the *Planícies* region may be the most dramatic area for scenic rides. I have listed a selection of my favorite riding establishments in each regional chapter of this book. If you need further details please contact your hotel's front desk or a local *Turismo* office. There are no horse race tracks in Portugal.

HUNTING

Portugal offers fine hunting for visitors who have obtained a hunting license from the **Instituto Florestal** at *Ave João Crisostomo, 26 in Lisbon*. To receive the license each foreigner must present a passport and a gun license from their country of origin.

If arriving in Portugal with firearms, you must leave a 30,000$00 deposit per gun at customs when you arrive. If you are not bringing your arms, finding equipment is not always an easy ask. The most common game and bird hunting areas are deep within the Planícies and Montanhas regions. In these areas there are several hunting clubs and herdades which offer organized hunting adventures at reasonable prices. Expect to find sanctioned hunting areas for quail, rabbit, partridge, pheasant, duck, and wild boar.

You will find a few listings for these organizations in this book, but your best bet is to visit the main *Turismo* office at *Palácio Foz* in Lisbon for a more complete listing. I have personally attended rather exciting hunts for wild boar, and can assure you that for those interested, the hassle of getting a license is well worth the effort. It would be hard to outdo the hunting outfits Portuguese sportsmen wear. Between the hand-sewn Machado boots and antique engraved rifles commonly used by the locals, a visiting hunter can be easily intimidated.

SPORTS & RECREATION 117

WILD BOAR HUNTING WITH HOTELIER JEAN-LOUIS DE TALANCE

OFF-ROAD VEHICLES

You can rent jeeps by the hour or day from several large car rental agencies in major tourist zones. You may want to see if your insurance will cover you in case of an accident. The best bet is probably to visit one of the outfitters in the Costa de Lisboa, Algarve or Planícies which offer guided excursions into remote areas.

One of the best of these Potuguese jeep safari companies is called **Frescuras** and can be reached in Sintra *at (01) 726-2183*. My favorite source for jeep excursions is at the **Quinta Horta da Moura** in Monsaraz. I have included several listings in this book for companies and properties which offer these services.

SKIING

I don't know anybody who comes to Portugal during the winter especially to ski, but for those of you who need to know, this is the story. In the **Serra da Estrêla** mountains of the Montanhas region there is a ski area at Torre. This slope will certainly not impress all but the most inexperienced downhill skier. Cross-country skiing is a better option with several trails through the parks and villages of the same region. Contact a *Turismo* office for more details.

SOCCER

Like the rest of Europe, soccer *(futebol)* is a major national pastime in Portugal. In the months between September and May there are many serious soccer league matches within the country (especially in *Lisbon* and *Porto*) which can each draw upwards of 80,000 spectators. Since these matches are so faithfully attended, the tickets which can range from 550$00 to 3500$00 per seat are often completely sold out well in advance.

The games that feature the leading teams (*Benfica, Sporting Clube de Portugal, Belém, Porto*) often create huge all night traffic jams due to the tendency of the spectators using the highways as giant parking lots. If you are interested in seeing a match, you can check with the hosting stadium's box office to see if there are any seats available. Be extremely careful not to cheer too loudly for the visiting team, as fans can get a bit rough with their adversaries. Soccer matches are generally accompanied by a series of events not unlike our pro football half time and pre-game festivities.

SWIMMING

Portugal has countless fine beaches, lagoons, rivers, and lakes where you can enjoy a fine swim. Please keep in mind that most swimming areas do not have full time lifeguards, so it is important to take the proper pecautions. When swimming in the ocean there may be strong undertows and cross-currents which must be considered; note are the blue flags which can be seen in many beach resort areas. These blue flags ensure that the area has passed current E.E.C. safe water requirements for purity.

Another option for swimming are the hundreds of municipal swimming pools in the major towns of Portugal. These public pools are normally open during the warmer months of each year and often provide lifeguards, showers, changing rooms, lockers, and poolside lounge chairs which ae available fo locals and visitos alike. Some public pools may charge a small admittance fee. Please check with a local *Turismo* office for hours and locations of public pools and municipal beaches. I have included reviews of my favorite beach areas throughout this book.

SPORTS & RECREATION 119

TENNIS

You can find both private and municipal tennis centers and courts in most major tourist resorts within Portugal. As with golf, there is a higher concentration of these types of facilities in both the Algarve and Costa de Lisboa regions. Many hotels also offer a few courts for their exclusive use of their guests, but sometimes they can be persuaded to welcome others. If you are looking for lessons or court time, you can inquire at either the front desk of your hotel, or at a local *Turismo* office for details and suggestions. I have included a listing several tennis centers in the regional chapters of this book.

WATERSPORTS

With hundreds of miles of superb coastline, Portugal offers many opportunities to swim, sail, windsurf, waterski, jetski, surf, dive, and snorkel. Since there are so many different areas to enjoy watersports in many parts of the country, I have included a listing of the best facilities in each regional chapter.

For the most part, you can expect to find world class windsurfing in the Costa de Lisboa and Algarve, excellant jetskiing and waterskiing on the rivers and lakes of the Costa Verde and Montanhas, fine surfing, sailing, diving, and snorkeling all over the Algarve, and countless spots for either salt or fresh water swimming and sailing in all regions of the country. Check with the local *Turismo* office for details on additional sights and equipment rentals.

12. PORTUGUESE CUISINE

THE REGIONAL CUISINE OF PORTUGAL

Each region of Portugal offers its visitors a huge selection of unique traditional foods. While wandering through the country it is possible to enjoy sumptuous dishes in small local restaurants and *adegas* at reasonable prices.

The following is a listing of the most commonly prepared soups, appetizers, main courses, and desserts from around Portugal. Many of these items have become so popular that they can be found throughout the country. Try a few of these at least once while you are there.

Many more foods and cooking styles are described in the dictionary chapter of this book.

Açorda - A bread and garlic stew with seafood, found in coastal areas.
Alheiras - Hearty veal and bread sausages, found in the *Montanhas*.
Arroz de Marisco - A tomato based rice and seafood stew found everywhere.
Arroz Doce - Thick and creamy rice pudding, found everywhere.
Atum Grelhado - Huge grilled fresh tuna steaks, found in the *Algarve*.
Bacalhau - Dried cod fish which is served in various ways, found everywhere.
Bife à Portuguesa - A grilled steak often cooked with Port wine, found everywhere.
Bola de Sardinhas - Rolls which are filled with sardines, found in the *Costa Verde*.
Cabreiro - Slightly sharp goat's milk cheese, found in the *Planícies*.
Caldeirada - A salty mixed fish and vegatable stew, found in coastal areas.
Caldeirada a Pescador - A spicy stew of mixed fish, found in the *Costa de Prata*.
Caldo Verde - A green cabbage, potatoe, and sausage soup, found everywhere.

PORTUGUESE CUISINE 121

Cataplana - A covered brass pan with fish and vegatables, found in the *Algarve*.
Churrasco - Sticky barbequed chicken, found everywhere.
Chouriço - Smoked spicy pork sausages, found everywhere.
Cozido à Portuguesa - Mixed meat boiled with vegatables, found everywhere.
Espetadas - Grilled kebobs of either fish or meat with vegatables, found everywhere
Frango Piri-Piri - Barbequed chicken with a mild hot sauce, found everywhere.
Frango na Pucara - Stewed chicken with garlic and vegatables, found everywhere.
Leitão Assado - Roast suckling pig, found mainly in the *Costa de Prata*.
Mexilhões de Escabeche - Mussels in vinegar sauce, found in the *Costa de Prata*.
Pão de lo - Light and airey sponge cakes, found everywhere.
Pão de Rala - A pumpkin and almond paste dessert, found in the *Planícies*
Pastéis de Camarões - Delicious shrimp filled fried dumplings, found everywhere.
Pastéis de Nata - Rich little custard tarts with cinnamin on top, found everywhere.
Porco a Alentejana - Pork cooked with clams and peppers, found in the *Planícies*.
Presunto - A full flavored Smoked ham, found in the *Montanhas*.
Queijo da Serra - Sheep's milk cheese that is incredible, found in the *Montanhas*.
Sapateira Gratinada - Oven baked stuffed spider crabs, found in the *Costa Verde*.
Sardinhas Assado - Sardines grilled over charcoal, found mainly in the *Algarve*.
Sopa de Legumes - A thin chicken based vegatable soup, found everywhere.
Sopa de Marisco - A filling soup made with shellfish, found everywhere.
Sopa Dourada - A soup of bread, egg yolks, and sugar, found in the *Costa Verde*.
Torta da Noz - Sweet little baked almond tarts, found everywhere.

BEVERAGES IN PORTUGAL

Throughout Portugal it is common to find the same selection of soon familiar beverages. During breakfast, the most common drink is coffee (*Café*) which can be ordered as either an expresso (*bica*), coffee with warm milk (*Café com leite*), or a rich Café au lait style mixture (*Galão*). Decaffinated instant coffee is available in most larger cities and is called by its brand name (Nescafe). If you end up asking for a juice (*sumo*) just remember that

122 PORTUGAL GUIDE

in the large cities and resort hotels you may often end up with a sugar dowsed drink which tastes like tang. If you want to ensure receiving a fresh juice just ask for a natural juice (*sumo natural*) and the waiter will generally understand what you are asking for.

As the day progresses, a much more varied selection of beverages will be available for consumption. Water from taps in any foreign country can have it's risks, so I suggest always drinking bottled water. In Portugal there are many brands of great tasting spring and mineral mineral waters including my favorite brand called *Luso*. These waters cost about 130$00 per liter in a store and as much as 350$00 in a restaurant.

Most mineral waters and can be ordered with bubbles (*agua com gas*) or without any bubbles (*agua sem gas*) and are always at it's best when served cold (*fresca*). There is also an assortment of carbonated soft drinks like *Coca Cola*, *Sumol* (a citrus flavored soda), and Fanta *Laranja* (orange soda) and they cost about 110$00 per can or bottle in stores, and 180$00 in most restaurants..

Beer

There are also some great brands of Portuguese beer (*cerveja*) including *Super Bock*, *Europa*, and the most common of all, *Sagres*. Beer usually costs about 95$00 per bottle or can with it's refundable deposit included at a store, and can cost between 80$00 and 400$00 per glass at a bar or restaurant. Whenever possible I suggest trying to located your preferred selection on tap as it is much fresher tasting. Other major European brands such as Kronenburg, Heinenken, Bass, and Becks may also be available by the bottle at the more upscale clubs and bars for a premium.

Wine

Of course wine is another major beverage during afternoon and evening meals. There so many different types and brands of white wines (*vinho branco*), red wine (*vinho tinto*), Rosé wines (*Rosé*), sparkling wines (*espumante*), Port wines (*porto*), and desert wines (*mosatel*) that if have included a complete chapter on wines a bit further on in this book. A bottle of good house wine (*vinho de casa*) or table wine (*vinho de mesa*) should cost under 600$00 in a normal restaurant, and about half that much in stores.

For more information about wine, please see the next chapter, *Wines of Portugal*.

RESTAURANTS IN PORTUGAL

Throughout Portugal there are many good eating establishments in all price ranges. In each regional chapter of this book you will see listings

PORTUGUESE CUISINE   123

of several restaurants which I have enjoyed and can fully recommend, but I still suggest that you try to find a few gems of your own. It is easy to find great restaurants serving either regional or various forms of international cuisine by simply asking at your hotel's front desk for a suggestion. Many restaurants accept Visa and Mastercard and will put their logo on the front door, American Express is often not accepted. Many restaurants are rated with a crossed fork symbol on a plaque near front door which has from 1 to 4 stars. I have not found this official rating system to be particularly accurate, so trust your own instints.

Usually a full American style breakfast in a restaurant with eggs, bacon, toast, and coffee costs about 375$00 per person. A typical Portuguese 3 course lunch special can range between 650$00 and 1950$00 per person based on what main dish you select and how fancy a restaurant you select. A Portuguese 5 course dinner with wine can cost from 1800$00 to well over 4500$00 per person depending again on what you choose and where you eat.

Hotels may charge much higher prices (especially 5 star hotels), while little hole in the wall eating establishments may charge a fraction of these prices. If you want to reduce your expenses, you will have no problem in most of Portugal. Also remember that many hotels include in the room price either a continental breakfast (little more than juice, rolls, and coffee), or a buffet American breakfast with all the trimmings.

> **RESTAURANT PRICE SCALE**
>
> *I have divided restaurants into three price categories, reflecting the average cost of a full meal per person without wine:*
> - *Inexpensive:*   *500$00 to 1000$00*
> - *Moderate:*   *1000$00 to 3000$00*
> - *Expensive:*   *3000$00 and up.*

Generally the hours that meals are served are from 7am until 10am for breakfast (*pequeno Almoço*), from 12pm until 3pm for lunch (*Almoço*), and from 7:30 pm until 10pm for dinner (*jantar*). During breakfast most Portuguese people tend to have just bread, cheese, and coffee. Many hotels and restaurants will in big cities and resort areas offer full American style breakfasts with familiar items such as scrambled eggs and bacon to suit the tastes of visitors. Lunch is a major meal here, and many people will take well over an hour to consume multiple courses and wash them down with a fair quantity of wine. Dinner is a late event which can consist of several courses and more wine.

Restaurants come in many types, each with a different typical ambiance. Many cities will have several full service restaurants (*restaurantes*)

124 PORTUGAL GUIDE

with a large selection of either regional or international cuisine. For a little more local atmosphere you may want to visit a quintessential local restaurant (*restaurante Típico*). There are also some wonderful bars which serve great food (*cervejarias*) at moderate prices. For a fine dinner with live *Fado* music you should visit a *fado* house (*adega Típica*). Many cities offer a wide range of simple taverns (*tascas*) where only a few inexpensive selected dishes may be offered. Most seaside towns have fine seafood restaurants (*marisqueiras*) that have large tanks of live shellfish.

In the countryside of northern Portugal you can find places that specialize in roasted meats (*churrascarias*). You can also find snacks and sandwiches (*sandes*) in pastry shops (*pastelarias*), cafes (*cafes*), and assorted fast food joints. When it's time for desserts (*sobremesas*) you can head for the nearest local bakery (*confeitaria*) or tea house (*sala de Chá*). If you need help to translate a menu, please look for the dictionary chapter later on in this book.

In most restaurants you can find selections that are a la carte (*a lista*), daily specials (*lista do dia*), multiple course specials of the day (*prato do dia*), scaled down 3 or 4 course tourist menus (*ementa turistica*), and half size portions of selected items (*meia dose*). Several restaurants offer their shellfish items by the kilogram (2.2 pounds), so you may want to ask for a half of a kilogram (*meia kilo*) at the very most. Also, most restaurants will bill your table a small cover charge (*couvert*) if you indulge in the assortment of bread, cheese, olives, and smoked meats which are presented to you before your meal arrives.

When you have finished your meal recieve the bill (*a conta*) you may notice a 16% charge added in at the end for IVA. This is a government tax, and is not a service charge or gratuity. Consider a 10% tip for good service and a 15% tip for exraordinary service to be left in cash on the table when you depart. If you put a tip on your credit card, I can assure you that your waiter will never get it.

13. WINES OF PORTUGAL

With an average annual production of over 100,000,000 cases, Portugal ranks among the world's largest producers of wines. The history of wine production here can be traced back to the Phoenicians who established the first vineyards in what is now Portugal. The nation's economy now depends heavily on the production of wine, and each year huge revenues are derived from the exportation of well over 17,000,000 cases to destinations throughout the world.

To begin explaining the various types and qualities of Portuguese wines it is first necessary to explain a few facts and details. It is first important that wines are grown in almost every corner of the country. Local residents of small villages and rural hamlets commonly make their own table wines which are often used for their own consumption. At present there are over 125 different varieties of wines in the country, and it would be virtually impossible for anyone to explain all of them to you. All bottles of wine produced for resale in Portugal must carry an official stamp of origin which allows consumers to determine that the wine has been officially analyzed and approved for sale.

The government of Portugal in connection with the I.V.V. (**Instituto da Vinha e do Vinho**) has selected nine special zones which have been painstakingly analyzed as the finest sectors in the country for high quality wine production. These so-called "Demarcated Regions" (*Regioes Demarcadas*) are strictly controlled as to their exact boundaries, types of wines allowed for production, maximum yields, production methods, and length of aging.

For a vineyard or producer to be allowed to bottle wines from within these special regions, the wines must first be subjected to a series of tests and tastings by experts. Once the wine has been approved for sale it will be labeled with a special paper stamp over the cork or on the back of the bottle which shows the producer's code and the serial number of the bottle. The specific demarcated regions in mainland Portugal consist of the *Vinho Verde, Douro, Dão, Bairrada, Colares, Carcavelos, Bucelas, Moscatel de Setúbal*, and *Algarve* production zones.

126 PORTUGAL GUIDE

While the above-mentioned special demarcated regions tend to produce the most famous wines in the country, several other parts of Portugal produce wines which are also quite good. Almost anywhere you travel it is possible to find local wineries which make tasty red, white, Rosé, fortified, and sparkling wines that are rather affordable.

If you are interested in purchasing wine, you have several different ways to find some. The most common place to view a large assortment of wines is at a supermarket (*hypermercado*). A good place to find vintage wines would be at a wine shop (*loja de vinho, garrafeira*) where the proprietors often crack open a bottle to allow you a free sample. You can enjoy wine tastings and tours at many wineries' cellars (*adegas*) by asking a *Turismo* office for nearby wineries that are open to the public. Another way to find wine in Portugal is to look out for a sign in front of a farm or rural house that says (*vende Sé vinho*) which means "wine for sale". These small unofficial producers often enjoy meeting foreigners and selling them hearty and inexpensive homemade table wines.

THE VINHO VERDE DEMARCATED REGION

This huge zone is located in the countryside of the **Costa Verde** region in the northwest corner of Portugal. The refreshing wines of this area are misleadingly called *Vinho Verde* (green wine) but are actually either red or white. You can find good *Vinho Verde* in Portugal for as little as 400$00 per bottle. The grapes are picked and immediately fermented in large vats before being bottled to continue their fermentation process.

The white (*Branco*) wines from this zone appear as mildly yellow in color. They are light, refreshing, a bit fruity, and just slightly sparkling with an alcohol content between 8% and 11.5%. Most of these blended wines do not age well and should be consumed without further aging. Only the fine white wines made from pure *Alvarinho* grapes have a longer shelf life. White *Vinho Verde* is often served chilled, and goes well with seafood.

The red (*Tinto*) wines from this zone appear almost purple in color. These are also a bit fruity, but tend to exhibit a slightly acidic flavor. Red *Vinho Verde* wines go rather well with hearty meat dishes and may be served chilled or at room temparature.

VINHO VERDE LABELS TO LOOK FOR:

Paço d' Anha, Quinta da Franqueira, Palácio da Brejoeira, Quinta de Aderiz, Paço do Cardido, Casa da Tapada, Casa de Sezim, Quinta do Outeiro de Baixa, Adega Cooperativa de Ponte de Barca, Casa do Valle

THE DOURO DEMARCATED REGION

This zone is located along the terraced banks of the **Douro** river and it's surrounding countryside in the *Montanhas* region of north central Portugal. About 60% of the grapes cultivated here are used in the production of hearty red and white *Douro* table wines while the remaining 40% are used for the famous fortified *Port* wines. You can find good *Douro* wines in Portuguese shops for as little as 500$00 per bottle, while the *Port* wines range from 1200$00 to over 5500$00 per bottle.

The white (*Branco*) table wines from this zone appear straw colored. These are dry, smooth, and hearty wines with an alcohol content of at least 11%, and are meant to be enjoyed cold. White *Douro* wines go well together with seafood.

The red (*Tinto*) wines from this zone appear ruby red color. Red *Douro* wines have a fruity rich flavor with an alcohol content of at least 11%, and are served at room temperature. Red *Douro* wines go with meat, fowl, and hearty stews. The blended white wines are aged for a minimum of 9 months and the red wines for a minimum for 18 months before bottling, and can be consumed immediately, or a few years after production.

> **BEST VINTAGES & DOURO LABELS TO LOOK FOR:**
> • *1960, 1980, 1966, 1964, 1965, 1975, 1981, 1984*
> • *Vinha das Madrucas, Casa dos Varais, Sogrape, Borges & Irmão, Quinta do Cotto, Casa Ferreira, Quinta do Confradeiro, Barca Velha, Ramos Pinto*

The *Ports* of Douro

The **Port** wines produced exclusively in this zone are made from a selection of over 20 different grape varieties. After each September's harvest, the crushed grapes are stored in a vat. To facilitate a higher sugar content, an addition of wine brandy equaling 20% of the wine's volume is added to cease the fermentation process and to assure an alcohol content of between 19% and 22%. After being transported to *Vila Nova de Gaia*, the wine remains in vats or wooden casks for at least 2 years before it is ready to be either carefully blended with other *Ports,* or is separated for special use if harvested during a great year.

There are several types of *Port* wine with various different classifications. The young *Port* wine may be blended with other harvest's wines and aged in a cask for 3 to 5 years to produce the sweet red *Ruby Port* which is served at room temperature as a desert drink. A further aging of these *Ruby Ports* in barrels will result in the lighter colored and less sweet *Tawny*

Port. *Tawny Port* is served at room temperature as either an aperitif or a desert wine. In the event that white grapes used for same methods as above, the resulting semi dry, dry, or extra dry wine is known simply as *White Port* and is served chilled as an aperitif. These types of *Port* are not dated, and are immediately ready for consumption.

Some producers of fine *Tawny Ports* are allowed to label bottles as **Ports With an Indication of Age**. On the label of these bottles you will find the date of bottling and either a 10, 20, 30, or Over 40 year indication of the average age of the contents. Other specially marked *Ports* are those from a single harvest during especially good years which are aged in casks for over 7 years. These bottles are known as **Port with the Date of Harvest**, and the label will show the year of harvest and date of bottling. These wines can be consumed immediately, or several years after purchase.

The most prized types of *Port* are the single harvest wines which were produced during the most outstanding years. These so called **Vintage Ports** are aged for 2 or 3 years in casks, and then further aged in the bottle. These bottles are labeled with the vintage year and require at least 10 years in the bottle before consumption. The final type of specially marked *Port* wine are the fine **Late Bottled Vintage Ports**. These are fine bottles of *Vintage Port* which have been allowed to remain in the wooden cask from 4 to 6 years before bottling. These bottles are labeled as *L.B.V.* and include the vintage harvest year and date of bottling. These *L.B.V. Ports* require at least 10 years in the bottle before consumption.

BEST VINTAGES & DOURO PORT LABELS TO LOOK FOR:

• 1908, 1912, 1927, 1945, 1955, 1963, 1966, 1978, 1904, 1917, 1906, 1920, 1924, 1927, 1928, 1934, 1935, 1937, 1947, 1948, 1950, 1955, 1957, 1960, 1963, 1966, 1970, 1975, 1977, 1978, 1980, 1982, 1983, 1985, 1987, 1988, 1989, 1991

• *Fonseca, Casa Ferreira, Taylor, Burmeister, Niepoort, Ramos Pinto, Quinta do Infatado, Quinta da Romaneira, Montez Champalimaud.*

THE DÃO DEMARCATED REGION

Located along the banks of the **Dão** river and their surrounding hilly countryside of the *Montanhas* region in the north of Portugal, this demarcated region produces fine red and white wines. You can find good brands of *Dão* wines in Portugal for as little as 300$00 per bottle.

The white (*Branco*) wines from this zone appear citrus colored. These are dry and quite smooth wines with an alcohol content of at least 11%, and are meant to be enjoyed cold. White *Dão* wines go well with fish and seafood meals.

WINES OF PORTUGAL 129

The red (*Tinto*) wines from this zone appear ruby red in color. The majority of red *Dão* wines tend to develop a velvety rich flavor with an alcohol content of at least 11%, and are meant to be enjoyed at room temperature. Red *Dão* wines go well together with meat, fowl, hearty stews, and cheese. The blended white wines are aged in casks for a minimum of 6 months and the blended red wines for 18 months before bottling, and can be consumed immediately or several years after production.

BEST VINTAGES & DÃO LABELS TO LOOK FOR:

• *1970, 1980, 1983, 1985, 1961, 1964, 1967, 1969, 1971, 1974, 1975, 1987, 1991.*

• *Vinicola do Vale do Dão, Portas dos Cavaleiros, Duque de Viseu, Quinta do Roques, Grão Vasco, Caves Messias, Quinta da Alameda, Quinta dos Carvalhais.*

THE BAIRRADA DEMARCATED REGION

Located amidst the tranquil countryside of the **Costa de Prata** region in the north of Portugal just above Coimbra, this demarcated region produces remarkable red wines, as well as a small quantity of white, Rosé, and sparkling wines. You can find superb brands of *Bairrada* wines in Portuguese wine shops and supermarkets for as little as 700$00 per bottle.

BEST VINTAGES & BAIRRADA LABELS TO LOOK FOR:

• *1960, 1962, 1970, 1975, 1980, 1983, 1963, 1966, 1972, 1974, 1978, 1985.*

• *Bucaco Tinto, Quinta de Pedralvites, Casa de Saima, Quinta do Valdoeiro, Quinta do Carvalhinho, Buçaco Branco, Encostas de Mouos, Luís Pato, Quinta da Rigodeira, Frei João, Adega Cooperativa de Vilarinho do Bairro, Caves Valdarcos, Caves São João, Adega Cooperativa de Souselas, Caves Messias, Quinta do Poco do Lobo, António Cardoso, Caves Alianca*

The white (*Branco*) wines from this zone appear yellow in color. These are dry, fruity, and smooth wines with an alcohol content of at least 11%, and are served chilled. White *Bairrada* wines go well with fish, pasta, salads, and light meals.

The red (*Tinto*) wines from this zone appear garnet in color. These wines develop a deeply rich full flavor with an alcohol content of at least

11%, and are served at room temperature. Red *Bairraida* wines go well with meat and strong cheeses, or can be enjoyed by themselves.

Both the white and red wines are initially aged and fermented in casks before bottling, but the reds must be at least 18 months old be for being marketed. These bottles can be consumed a couple of years, or many years after production, and the red wines get much better with age.

The **Rosé** (*Rosé*) wines are produced in limited quantities. This wine is made from a a blend of red grapes and must which are lightly fermented in an uncrushed form, then further processed and soon bottled with a minimum alcohol content of 11%. These wines are ready for consumption immediately after bottling. These wines can be dry, semi sweet, or sweet and can sometimes have a slight sparkling quality. These are generally served chilled, and are used either as an aperitif, or offered with salads and hors d'oeuvres.

Rosé labels from this region to look for include: *Quinta do Carvalhinho, Nobilis,* and *João Pato.*

The sparkling (*Espumante*) wines are also produced in limited quantities. These wines are made from either red or white grape blends which are either fermented in large vats and transferred into bottles for immediate consumption, or are subjected to fermentation in the bottle itself. These wines can be sweet, medium sweet, medium dry, dry, or extra dry. The specially aged bottles are marked with a classification of how long the wine was allowed to age before degorgement and recorking. These classifications include *Reserva* (1 to 2 years), *Extra Reserva* (2 to 3 years), or *Velha Reserva* (more than 3 years).

Espumante labels from this region to look for include: *Caves Messias, João Pato, Sogrape, Caves Alianca, Caves Borlido, Caves de Solar de São Domingos.*

THE COLARES DEMARCATED REGION

This zone is located on the windswept hills of the **Costa de Lisboa** region near *Sintra*. These sand topped clay based vineyards have been producing fine wines for over 600 years, and were not affected by the Pholloxera epidemic which wiped out most of Europe's grape varieties in 1865. This zone produces small quantities of strong red and white wines of high quality.

The white (*Branco*) wines from this zone citrus in color. These are strong and slightly fruity semi dry wines with an alcohol content of at least 10%, and are meant to be enjoyed quite cold. White *Colares* wines go well with fish, cheese, and seafood meals.

The red (*Tinto*) wines from this zone have a velvety quality and appear reddish brown in color. These robust dry wines reach a minimum alcohol

WINES OF PORTUGAL 131

content of 10%, and are meant to be enjoyed at room temperature. Red *Colares* wines go rather well together with meat, or can be enjoyed by themselves.

The white wines are aged for 6 months and the red wines for 18 months before bottling and can be consumed several years after production. The red wines get much better with age.

> **BEST VINTAGES & COLARES LABELS TO LOOK FOR:**
> • *1964, 1966, 1966, 1975, 1983, 1984, 1960, 1967, 1968, 1969, 1971, 1973, 1979, 1980, 1981, 1982, 1985, 1987*
> • *Caves Visconde de Salreu, Real Vinicola, Tavares & Rodrigues, Adega Regional de Colares, Viuva José Gomes da Silva*

THE CARCAVELOS DEMARCATED REGION

This tiny zone is located near the seaside of the **Costa de Lisboa** region near *Estoril*. A few remaining vineyards still produce a fine topaz colored and somewhat nutty flavored fortified white wine known as *Carcavelos* which is aged in a wooden cask for at least four years.

To boost the sugar content, a small amount of *Moscatel de Setúbal* is usually added to cease fermentation and allow for an alcohol level of about 19%. These wines are quite rare, and come in either sweet or medium dry varieties which are ready for immediate consumption as an aperitif. If you can find a bottle, expect to pay at least 4000$00.

Carcavelos labels to look for include: *Quinta da Bela Vista, Quinta do Barão, Quinta dos Pesos*.

THE BUCELAS DEMARCATED REGION

This small zone is located in the *Trancão* river valley of the **Costa de Lisboa** region close to *Lisbon*. This area's vineyards produce a fine sharp dry white wine known as *Bucelas* which is fermented in open vats and later transferred to age in wood casks for at least 10 months before bottling.

These fine wines have a minimum alcohol content of 10.5% and are ready for immediate consumption. If you can find a bottle, expect to pay at least 1400$00.

> **BEST VINTAGES & BUCELAS LABELS TO LOOK FOR:**
> • *1966, 1971, 1974, 1976, 1979, 1980, 1983, 1985, 1987*
> • *Caves Velhas, Quinta da Romeira, Prova Regia*

THE MOSCATEL DE SETÚBAL DEMARCATED REGION

This small zone is located between the **Tejo** and **Sado** rivers in the southern portion of the **Costa de Lisboa** region around *Setúbal*. The local vineyards produce rather sweet fortified desert wines which are made by adding a small amount of brandy to the must and later adding cut grapes to the mixture. This mixture is then aged for a year in casks before being strained and further aged before bottling. The longer the wine ages, the darker it becomes.

The regular honey colored 5-year old *Muscatel* is available throughout Portugal at prices starting at 1100$00. The darker colored 20-year old *Muscatel Roxo* is rather rare and expensive but offers much deeper flavor. These wines have a minimum alcohol content of 16.5% and are ready for immediate consumption after purchase.

Muscatel labels to look for include: *João Pires, José Maria da Fonseca, Herdade de Rio Frio.*

THE ALGARVE DEMARCATED REGION

This large zone is located in several parts of the **Algarve** region including the areas near *Lagoa, Lagos, Portimão,* and *Tavira*. The refreshing wines of this area are produced in both red or white varieties. Since the region is blessed with lots of sun, the grapes tend to have a higher sugar content which leads to a higher alcohol content of the wines which they are used to produce. Good wines from this region can be found in stores for as little as 400$00 per bottle.

The white (*Branco*) wines from this zone are usually dry and fruity with a pale straw coloring and a minimum alcohol content of 11.5%. These wines are served chilled as either an accompaniment with fish or as an aperitif.

The red (*Tinto*) wines from this zone are full flavored and fruity with a deep red coloring and a minimum alcohol content of 12%. These red wines are served at room temperature and go well with meat dishes. The white wines are fermented in vats and aged for 6 months and the red wines for 8 months before being bottled.

Algarve labels to look for include: *Adega Cooperativa da Lagoa.*

Other Good Wine Producing Areas

Varosa, Chaves, Valpacos, Planalto Mirandes, Lafões, Encostas da Nave, Castelo Rodrigo, Pinhel, Cova da Beira, Encostas de Aire, Tomar, Alcobaça, Obidos, Santarém, Chamusca, Portalegre, Cartaxo, Alenquer, Coruche, Borba, Redondo, Reguengos, Vidigueira, Torres, Arruda, Palmela, Setúbal, Arrábida.

These areas all produce fine wines and spirits in every concievable variety. If you are near any of these zones, you should try to sample some of their local wines.

A DICTIONARY OF COMMONLY-USED WINE & SPIRITS NOTATIONS

Acido – Acidic
Adega – Wine Cellar
Adamado – Sweet
Aguardente – Firewater Brandy
Alcool – Alcohol
Bagaceira – Grape Marc Brandy
Branco – White
Brandimeil – Honey Brandy
Bruto – Extra Dry
Castas – Grapes
Caves – Wine Cave or Cellar
Cerveja – Beer
Colheita – Vintage
Demarcada – Demarcated
Doce – Sweet
Engarrafado – Bottled
Espumante – Sparkling Wine
Garrafa – Bottle
Garrafeira – Cellar Aged Vintage Reserves
Ginja, Ginginha – Cherry Brandy
L.B.V. – Late Bottled Vintage Port Wine
Maduro – Table Wine
Medronha – Berry Brandy
Meio – Medium
Produzido – Produced
Quinta – Estate
Região – Region
Reserva – Reserve Wine
Rosé – Rosé Wine
Seco – Dry
Selo de Origem – Seal of Origin
Tinto – Red
Vinha – Vineyard
Vinho – Wine
Vinho da Casa – House Wine
Vinho de Mesa – Table Wine
Vinicola – Wine Production
Velha – Old

14. LISBON

Lisbon – *Lisboa* – the capital of Portugal, is among the friendliest of European cities. Located about 18 km from the Atlantic Ocean, this bustling city is home to more than 1,300,000 residents. As Portugal's center of politics, finance, commerce, economic power, arts, and entertainment, Lisbon attracts a special breed of big city residents.

The pace of downtown Lisbon is rather hurried and often confusing to first time visitors. Each business day starts with a seemingly endless stream automotive traffic and commuters pounding the pavement near the rail, ferry, and bus stations. The center of town is filled with people of all classes searching for a quick strong coffee before starting work. Many people here are well educated, speak a fair amount of English, and are trying to get ahead in life. The huge banks which dominate the city's skyline are proof that there is serious business and economic growth taking place in this city.

While the busy downtown commercial areas near the **Baixa** seem to run at full speed for most of the day, the older and more traditional districts feel comparatively quiet. The neighboring districts such as the **Alfama**, **Bairro Alto**, **Chiado**, **Belém**, **Alcântara**, and **Lapa** take a more laid back and natural rhythm. Vendors will stand outside their establishments and chat with passers by. Fishmongers can be heard in the markets extolling the virtues of today's catch. Manual laborers still hand-cut and set square cubes of black and white rock into the pavement of the many steep and winding ancient streets. Children walk to school clutching the bottom of their grandmothers' dresses. It seems that the old village way of life can still be found in some parts of Lisbon.

This blend of old and new permits the casual visitor to experience many aspects of Lisbon in just one or two long days of wandering around the city. In the space of just a few days, it is entirely possible to do some very serious sightseeing, visit impressive art collections, eat inexpensive regional cuisines, shop for bargain priced fine European goods, walk past hundreds of opulent old houses, and then spend an enjoyable late night out. Lisbon is a rather safe, inexpensive, and welcoming city to explore.

LISBON 135

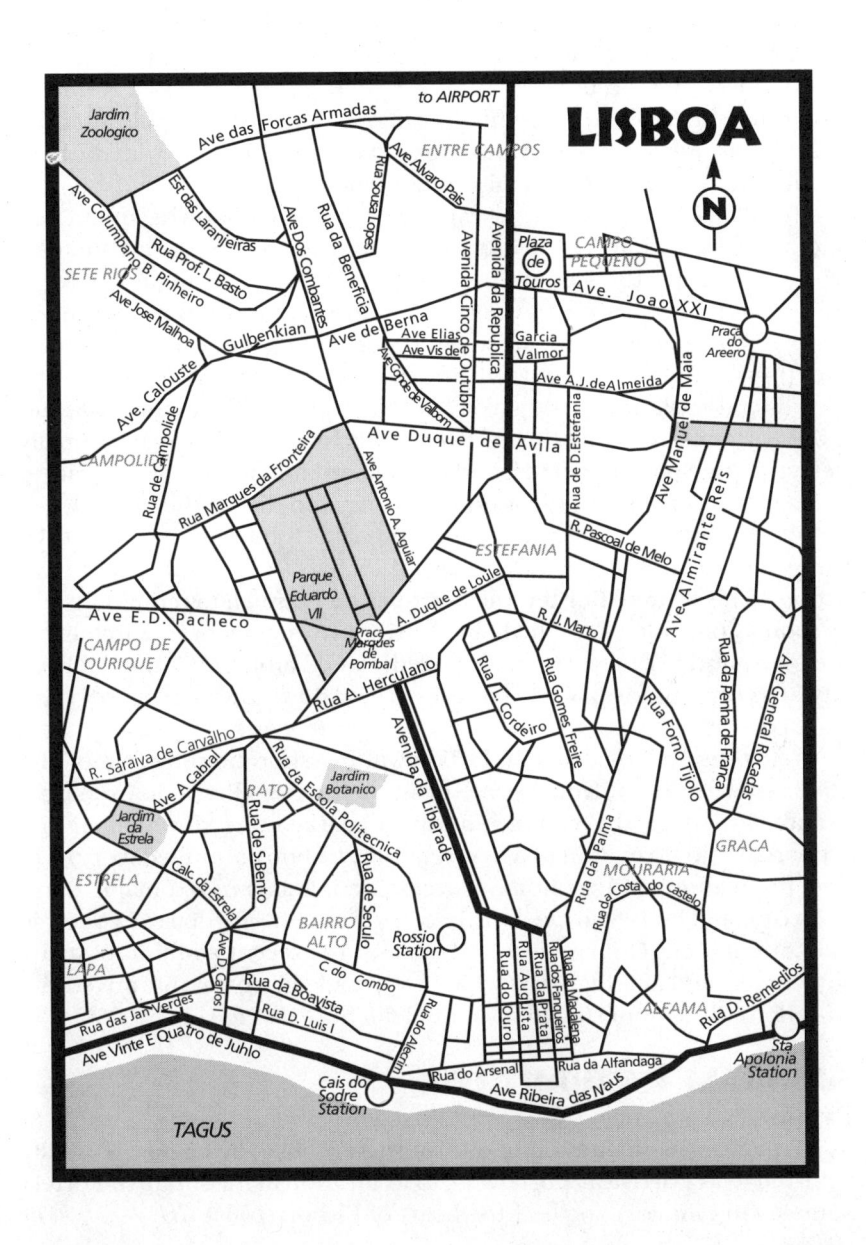

HISTORY

Lisbon was originally founded by the Phoenicians sometime about 1200 B.C. Its strategic location nestled atop seven hills overlooking a safe natural harbor on the **Tejo** (**Tagus**) river has been the source of centuries of conquest and occupation by the Greeks, Carthaginians, Romans, Visigoths, and Moors. Lisbon finally came under Portugal's rule after the defeat of the Moors by King Dom Afonso Henriques in 1147 with the help of English, German, and Flemish crusaders.

In 1255, Lisbon became the capital of what would soon become a rich and powerful nation. The Portuguese empire expanded throughout the world during the 15th-century Age of Discoveries by Portuguese navigators. Lisbon became one of the world's most important trading centers for precious metals, gems, spices, and porcelain products. Throughout the 16th century, Lisbon was thrown into a series of tragic events, including devastating earthquakes, the black plague, the inquisition, and a 60-year annexation by Spain. **King Dom João IV** of Bragança finally defeated the Spanish in 1640 and created an independent Portugal (to this day the Portuguese still tend to distrust and dislike the Spanish).

On November 1, 1755, a major earthquake, followed by massive tidal waves and fires, destroyed over half of the city. King Dom José I gave orders to his Prime Minister, the **Marquês de Pombal**, to rebuild Lisbon as soon as possible. With the help of inventive engineers and architects, the Marquêsde Pombal successfully redesigned and rebuilt much of the city in its present form which features grided downtown street areas and wide central avenues.

Life returned to normal in Lisbon within a short period of time. The 1908 assassination of King Dom Carlos I in the city's Praça do Comércio eventually led to the revolution which marked the downfall of the monarchy and formation of a new republic. Lisbon continued to grow in size, population, and economic development and is now a major European capital. The 1986 inclusion of Portugal into the European Economic Community (E.E.C.) has paved the way for the recent addition of many skyscrapers and new highways which have made Lisbon a truly mixed city with both ultra-modern and ancient elements existing side by side.

ARRIVALS & DEPARTURES
By Air

Portugal's main international airport, **Aeroporto de Lisboa**, is usually referred to as **Portela** airport owing to its location in the subub of Portela some 8 km (5 miles) north of the heart of Lisbon *(phone (01) 802-060 or (01) 848-1101).*

Upon arrival, you will be bused from your plane to the new arrivals wing and immediately pass through an immigration check point. Here you'll present your passport, after which you'll follow the signs to the baggage claim area, grab a free luggage cart if you need one, load up, and clear customs.

After passing through customs, you'll enter a small reception lounge where you can find a 24-hour currency exchange kiosk, a few tourist information booths, and several limo drivers and private guides holding up signs for VIPs. Just past the arrivals lounge is the entrance to the main terminal wing where you will see all the major car rental kiosks, another tourist information booth, and the main taxi stand. If you're supposed to meet someone here and can't locate each other, go to the airport information booth and ask them to page them over the public address system.

Most everybody at the airport speaks English and are happy to assist you. The airport also has a cafeteria, snack shop, cafe, bar, and some small gift shops. There are also duty-free stores for departing passengers only.

From the Airport to the City

You have several choices of transportation from the airport. **Taxis** charge about 2100$00 per ride (plus a 300$00 surcharge for luggage) to most hotels in Lisbon. Make sure you have enough Potuguese currency since taxis cannot exchange money and usually don't accept credit cards.

Buses provide a less expensive way to get downtown. The green-painted **Linha Verde** express bus (#90)costs about 275$00 per person and can take you from the main airport bus stop in fromt of the terminal to *Rossio* and *Santa Apolonia* train station with departures every 20 minutes or so, from 7:30 am until 10 pm. The local bus routes also available here include the #44 and #45 buses departing every 15 minutes or so from 6 am until 1 am at the other bus stop a few steps past the parking lot, and charge about 175$00 person to take you to the *Praca dos Restauradores* or *the Cais de Sodre* station. Make sure you have plenty of coins for your bus.

If you're renting a car at the airport, make sure to ask the staff to provide you with detailed directions to your destination. Lisbon is a confusing city, and its easy to get lost. Most rental companies offer maps and direction sheets that they can mark with the exact streets and turns you'll need to take. If you're not staying in Lisbon, make sure you have enough Potuguese currency to pay for any tolls along the way.

By Bus

Bus services are provided by *RN*, a state-owned bus company that can sell you tickets and explain the current schedule.

You may want to call or visit the following:
• **RN Main Bus Station**, *Avenida Casal Ribeiro, 18 (01) 577-715*
• **RN Bus Main Office**, *Ave. Columbano B. Pinheiro, 86 (01) 726-7123*

138 PORTUGAL GUIDE

By Ferry

Ferry service across the Tejo river to Barreiro, Montijo, Seixal, Cacilhas, Trafaria, and other points made be accessed from several ferry stations thoughout Lisbon which are operated by either **CP** or by a private company called **Transtejo**.

You may want to call or visit the following:
* **CP Ferry Information**, *Terreiro de Paço (01) 877-179*
* **Transtejo Ferry Information**, *Lisbon (01) 879-035*

By Train

CP rail offers extensive train service into and out of Lisbon from most points in Portugal. For tickets and schedules please stop by any travel agency or contact CP Rail. Please be advised that several southern train routes require ferry connections. These ferries to the city of **Barreiro** (just across the river) may be made from the **Terreiro de Paço** fluvial station.

You may want to call or visit the following:
* **CP Rail Head Office**, *Rua de Vitor Cordon, 45 (01) 346-3181*
* **Santa Apolónia Train Station**, *Ave. Infante D. Henrique (01) 876-025.* The main international and intercity station.
* **Cais de Sodré Train Station**, *Cais de Sodré (01) 347-0181*. Trains to Estoril, Cascais, mass transit tickets and passes sold in main building.
* **Rossio Train Station**, *Rossio (01) 346-5022*. Trains to Sintra and other areas.

LISBON HIGHLIGHTS

The **Baixa** district is the lower elevation section of downtown Lisbon which starts at the **Tejo** (Tagus) river and spokes upward to the **Avenida da Liberdade**. Before the destruction of most of the Baixa in the 1755 earthquake, most of the area was built on stilts to avoid flooding by the frequent rises of the river. After the earthquake, the reconstruction of Lisbon by the Marquêsde Pombal left much of the Baixa with a gridded street pattern, wide open avenues and some pedestrian only streets with relaxing sidewalk cafes and tons of boutiques.

Immediately in front of the river is the famed **Praça do Comércio** (Commerce Square) which is locally known as the **Terreiro do Paço** since it was once once home to the Royal Palace before it was destroyed by the earthquake of 1755. These days an assortment of pink colored 18th century government office buildings surround a large bronze statue of King Dom José I on a horse. It was in this very square, right near the parking lot, that in 1908, King Dom Carlos I and his son Prince Luís Filipe were assassinated.

On the northernmost border of the square is the vast **Arco Monumental da Rua Augusta** gateway which leads to the banks, shops, and restaurants of the lower town. Directly across the arch on the southern side of the square is a large marble staircase which leads down to the banks of the Tejo river and shows off the view. Also in this general area you will find the **Terreiro do Paço** ferry terminal with service to the opposite side of the Tejo river and the towns of **Barreiro, Montijo, Seixal,** and **Cacilhas**.

If you pass under the Arco Monumental in Praça Comércio you will be led through the pedestrian only **Rua Augusta** and into the northern section of the Baixa. This small 24 square block area contains several 19th-century stone patterned streets which have descriptive old names like **Rua da Ouro** (Street of Gold) and **Rua da Prata** (Street of Silver). To this day, many of these blocks still contain beautiful shops which sell the items they are named after like fine silver filigree and handcrafted gold jewelry. I have found some of the best values on fine European shoes, suits, and lambs wool sweaters located in the large assortment of shops in this area.

Located at the northern end of these streets is the wonderful public square known simply as the **Rossio** (also called the **Praça de Dom Pedro IV**) with both a fountain and a statue of King Pedro IV in the center. Cafés still line the Rossio and the commuter crowds flock to there for a *café* (espresso) and some *pastéis* (pastries with meat, fish or sweat fillings). A stop for rich *galão* (Café-au-lait) at **Café Suiça** or **Café Nicola** in the Rossio is a great way to experience the local ambiance. The beautiful **Teatro Nacional D. Maria II** (National Theater) rests at the northern end of the Rossio. Across the avenue from the theater you will see the ornate facade of the Rossio train station.

DOWNTOWN LISBON

Just above the Rossio is the beginning of **Avenida da Liberdade** (Liberty Avenue) which leads up through town and into the **Praça dos Restauradores** (Square of the Restorers). This delightful square is named for the men who led the revolt against Spanish annexation in 1640. The square is dominated by the red facade of the **Palácio Foz** whose Italian designed structure now houses the offices Secretary of State for Tourism and his staff. This is the building to go if you need a good *Turismo* office for advice and maps.

If you walk east for one block from the lower section of **Avenida da Liberdade**, you will run into the parallel **Rua das Portas de Santa Antão** with it's vast selection of seafood restaurants and small shops. Although the world famous **Restaurante Gambrinus** is the most deluxe place to eat here, there are many other fine casual restaurants all over the street. As you wander a few blocks further north, Rua Portas de Santa Antão becomes **Rua Alves Correira** which features many fine antique stores.

GETTING AROUND TOWN

Public transportation is rather inexpensive (usually less than 170$00 per ride) and effective. Mass transit is well organized, and with the exception of a few pickpockets, extremely safe at all hours. I suggest you first decide how much you intend to travel by mass transit, and then purchase one of the several discount passes and ticket booths sold at major stations.

Hours of operation for the *Metro, Carris, and Elevadors* are usually from 6:30am until 1am daily, and for the *Electricos* from 6:30am until midnight daily.

Discount books of multiple tickets and special passes can be purchased for the Metro, trolley, and bus services from the appropriate stations. A special tourist pass valid on Metro, bus, and trolley is available for multiple day periods to foreigners only (you must bring a valid passport) and can be bought at most major terminals including the *Cais de Sodré* station for about 1450$00 (4 days) and 1950$00 (7 days).

The Lisbon transportation company produces a map of their mass transit routes which sells for under 300$00 and can be bought where you purchase passes and ticket books. Some private companies also sell maps of Lisbon which include public transportation routes, these are available from newsstands throughout the city.

If you have any further questions about transportation within Lisbon, please visit one of the several *Turismo* offices located throughout the city, ask your hotel's concierge for help, or call one of these numbers:
• **Metro Information**, *Ave. Fonte de Melo, 28 (01) 575-974*
• **Bus, Tram, Elevador Information**, *Rua 1 de Maio, 103 (01) 363-2021*

LISBON 141

By Bus

Buses often known as **carris** also abound in Lisbon, and tickets cost about 150$00 if bought from the bus driver, or a book of 10 one zone tickets can be bought in advance from a bus station (easiest to buy them at the booth at the bottom of the *Elevador de Santa Justa*) for about 350$00.

By Trolley

The electric trolley system called **electricos** is a very effective means of local rapid transit. The trolley stops are marked with a sign which reads *paragem*. Tickets for the *electricos* are the same as bus tickets.

By *Elevador*

Funicular systems called **elevadors** are used to connect the higher elevation districts of Lisbon with the lower lying districts. Tickets on these funiculars cost the same as bus tickets.

By Train

For those of you who are staying in or visiting **Cascais** and **Estoril**, a fast and comfortable electric train runs frequently between these points and the Cais de Sodré train station in Lisbon. These trains cost about 165$00 each way and provide an excellent alternative to getting stuck in terrible commuter automobile traffic.

By Ferry

You can also cross the Tejo river by ferry (**fluvial**) between Lisbon's riverfront and several communities across the river such as **Barreiro** and **Cacilhas**; check at the *Terrio de Paço* ferry station (*Terminal Fluvial*) across from Praça do Comercio for specific details.

By Metro

Stop by any **Metro** (Metropolitano) station, marked with a large "M" above the entrances, and get for a route map at the ticket booths. Metro tickets cost about 75$00 each or can be purchased at *Metro* stations in books of 10 for about 550$00.

By Taxi

Taxis are inexpensive (typically about 650$00 at most) but are well known for overcharging foreigners. On one of my last visits, I was overcharged for more than half of my rides! (watch out for baggage overcharges, a 300$00 charge per ride maximum, and the illegal use of night rates during the day). You can usually identify a vacant taxi if the "Taxi" light on top of the cab is illuminated, and you can flag them in much the same way you would in any North American city, or you can go to one of many taxi lines and wait your turn. Recently a law has been passed which demands all taxis post their price regulations in several languages including English. Good luck trying to read this sign while being bounced around.

By Rental Car

Rental cars can be picked up either at the airport, or at a downtown location. Last minute bookings are subject to heavy surcharges.

You may want to call or visit the following:
- **Avis Rent a Car**, *Ave. Praia da Victoria, 12 (01) 356-1176*
- **Hertz Rent a Car**, *Ave. 5 de Outubro, 10 (01) 579-027*
- **Europcar Rent a Car**, *Ave. António A. de Aguiar, 24 (01) 353-5119*

By Tour

If you are in need of hotel reservations, plane tickets, sightseeing tours, guides, train tickets, or rental cars you should contact one of the following travel agencies:
- **Quasar**, *Rua Artilharia Um, 39, (01) 691-919*. The best travel agency in Portugal. Most of the staff speak perfect English and can book any imaginable hotel, *quinta, pousada,* car rental, guided tour, and tickets.
- **Abreu**, *Ave. da Liberdade, 160, (01) 347-6441.* A large travel agency with offices throughout Portugal. They can book all types of travel arraignments but specialize in packages.
- **Top**, *Ave. Duque de Loulé, 108, (01) 315-5885.* The official American Express agent in *Lisbon*. This office has full ticketing facilities.

WHERE TO STAY

Expensive

HOTEL DA LAPA, *Rua do Pau da Bandeira, 4, (01) 395-0005.*

One of Portugal's most deluxe hotels with 87 beautiful rooms and suites. This hotel has become a second home to heads of state and the jet set. Facilities include bar, restaurant, air conditioning, minibars, pool, sauna, TV, boutiques, and valet garage.

HOTEL TIVOLI LISBOA, *Avenida da Liberdade, 185, (01) 530-181.*

A favoured address among top executives, the Tivoli offers 326 modern rooms in a pleasant central location with good service. The hotel's facilities include air conditioning, bar, resturants, pool, TV, minibars, tennis, barber shop, and parking.

HOTEL ALFA LISBOA, *Ave.Columbano B. Pinheiro, (01) 726-2121.*

A huge 5 star hotel with an impressive quality of service. If your here on business, this is a great choice. The 440 air conditioned rooms are well designed. Facilities include bar, restaurants, pool, sauna, health club, TV, shops, minibars, and parking.

LISBON 143

REAL PARQUE HOTEL, *Ave. Luís Bivar, 67, (01) 570-101.*
A brand new 4 star hotel with excellent service, staff, and facilities near the *Marquêsdo Pombal* area. One of the best bargains in *Lisbon*. Facilities include bar, café, restaurants, air conditioning, newsstand, minibars, room service, TV, and garage.
HOTEL RITZ LISBOA, *Rua Rodrigo da Fonseca, 88, (01) 692-020.*
Formerly the most prestigious hotel in town, the Ritz remains a deluxe business style hotel. The hotel offers 310 renovated rooms and suites and offers good service. Facilities include bar, snackbar, restaurant, air conditioning, TV, and garage.
HOTEL ALTIS, *Rua Castilho, 11, (01) 522-496.*
A serious 5 star business style hotel with good service. The 303 air conditioned rooms are quite comfortable. Facilities include bar, restaurants, air conditioning, pool, sauna, health club, salon, shops, TV, rent a car desk, and parking.
HOTEL MERIDIAN, *Rua Castilho, 149, (01) 690-900.*
A large and pretentious modern French hotel with a lack of charm. The hotel offers 331 nice rooms, but the staff is less than friendly. Facilities include bar, restaurants, air conditioning, minibars, TV, sauna, barber shop, boutiques, and parking.
SHERATON LISBOA, *Rua Latino Coelho, 1, (01) 575-757.*
A piece of America in *Lisbon*. The perfect choice if you are from a big multinational corporation. May not be so good for tourists, as they will be ignored. Facilities include bar, restaurants, air conditioning, pool, sauna, health club, TV, and parking.

Moderate
HOTEL METROPOLE LISBOA, *Praça Dom Pedro IV, 300, (01) 346-9164.*
A newly reopened Deco style boutique hotel with great views of the *Rossio*. This hotel is a great value, and is staffed by true professionals. Facilities include bar, lounge, breakfast room, minibars, TV, air conditioning, and a great location.
HOTEL DOM RODRIGO, *Rua Rodrigo da Fonseca, 44, (01) 386-3800.*
A special all suite hotel owned by the Tivoli company with 39 nice 1 and 2 bedroom suites in the heart of town. Facilities include bar, kitchens, TV, pool, and parking.
HOTEL LISBOA PLAZA, *Rua Duque de Palmela, 32, (01) 576-145.*
A warm and friendly hotel in the heart of downtown. Some of the rooms are a bit small, but the staff treats it's clientele like family. Facilities include bar, restaurant, air conditioning, direct dial phones, minibars, TV, radio, and parking.

HOTEL TIVOLI JARDIM, *Rua Julio Cesar Machado, (01) 539-971.*
A famous 4 star hotel with very good service and nice rooms. Located in the center of downtown, this 119 room hotel is known for great service and good value. Facilities include bar, restaurant, air conditioning, pool, tennis, TV, and parking.

HOTEL BARCELONA, *Rua Laura Alves,10, (01) 795-4273.*
A new and extremely modern high rise hotel near the Gulbenkian museum. Many of the 125 large and comfortable rooms have patios and balconies. Facilities include bar, breakfast room, air conditioning, garage, and ground floor restaurant.

YORK HOUSE, *Rua Janelas Verdes,32, (01) 396-2435.*
A famous 16th-century converted convent located in the *Lapa* district. Some scenes from the movie "The Russia House" were filmed here. The courtyard view rooms are much nicer than the others. Beautiful antiques are scattered throughout the inn. Facilities include bar, restaurant, heating, direct dial phones, and nearby parking.

HOTEL MUNDIAL, *Rua Dom Duarte,4, (01) 879-129.*
A large full service 4 star hotel behind the *Rossio* with 147 renovated rooms with great views. Facilities of this friendly hotel include bar, restaurants, air conditioning, direct dial phones, minibars, TV, parking, and extremely helpful staff.

HOLIDAY INN CROWNE PLAZA, *Campo Grande, 390, (01) 759-9639.*
A huge tower hotel in the absolute wrong part of town unless you wish to have a good view over the airport. The service and rooms are pretty good. Facilities include bar, restaurant, air conditioning, sauna, health club, shops, and parking.

HOTEL EDUARDO VII, *Ave. Fontes Pereira de Melo,5, (01) 530-141.*
A pretty good but basic 3 star hotel near the heart of town with 130 comfortable rooms and a skytop restaurant. Facilities include bar, restaurant, air conditioning, minibars, tour desk, direct dial phones, TV, and parking.

HOTEL LISBOA, *Rua Barata Salgueiro,5, (01) 355-4131.*
A centrally located business style hotel with large, modern, and well equipped rooms. A good place to stay if you need to be near the *Avenida da Liberdade*.Facilities include piano bar, air conditioning, minibar, safes, and TV.

HOTEL ALIF LISBOA, *Campo Pequeno,51, (01) 795-2464.*
A beautiful marble laden hotel with a great view of the bullring. It's 9th floor glass enclosed breakfast room provides an excellent view over *Lisbon*. Facilities include bar, rooftop breakfast room, air conditioning, TV, minibars, and garage.

HOTEL AVENIDA PALACE, *Rua 1 de Dezembro, (01) 346-0151.*
A run down hotel in a great location which should have 3 of it's 5 stars taken away. Not much has changed in this antique 95 room hotel, including the linens and ugly furniture. Facilities include a bar, reastaurant, air conditioning, TV, and parking.

Inexpensive
HOTEL A.S. LISBOA, *Av. Almirante Reis, 188, (01) 847-3045.*
A small and cozy hotel with reasonable service near the airport. Some of the larger rooms are very beautifully designed. This is a good budget choice. Facilities include bar, breakfast room, air conditioning, TV, and nearby parking.
HOTEL BORGES, *Rua Garret, 108, (01) 346-1951.*
A clean and comfortable hotel next to the A Brasileira Café in the *Chaido* section. It's 100 basic rooms with private bathroom offer basic comfort at bargain prices. Facilities include bar, restaurant, phones, and thats about all. Good luck parking!
CASA DE SÃO MAMEDE, *Rua da Escola Politécnica, 159, (01) 396-3166.*
A nice and comfortable converted house which offers 28 guestrooms with and without private bathroom near the Eduardo VII park. Parking on site.
PENSÃO LONDRES, *Rua Dom Pedro V, 53, (01) 346-2203.*
This is perhaps the only very cheap property in *Lisbon* with any class. Located in an old building in the *Bairro Alto* section, this basic and simple establishment offers nice comfortable rooms for budget minded tourists with or without private bathroom.
PENSÃO DUBLIN, *Rua de Santa Maria, 45, (01) 355-5489.*
A clean and basic inn with 34 guestrooms with and without private bathroom. Located a few blocks from the *Ave. de Liberdade*, this establishment offers reasonably nice rooms with minimal facilities at bargain prices.

WHERE TO EAT
Expensive
EMBAIXADA, *Rua Pau da Bandeira, 4, (01) 395-0005).*
Located in the super-luxurious Hotel de Lapa, this opulent restaurant serves incredible continental cuisine. The talented Swiss chef prepares unforgettable international dishes with truly innovative recipes. If you're searching for a fine formal meal, this is the place to go.
AVIS, *Rua Serpa Pinto, 12, (01) 342-8391.*
A deluxe and beautiful old world establishment in the *Baixa* area. The well dressed clientele can choose between French, Portuguese, and other

cuisine. The fine cuisine is very well resented, and the service can be overwhelming.

GAMBRINUS, *Rua das Portas de Santo Antao, 23, (01) 346-8974).*

This formal establishment is without doubt the most famous seafood restaurant in Lisbon. They serve up an amazing selection of excellent shrimp and lobster specialties for those of you prepared to spend some serious money.

ALCÂNTARA-CAFÉ, *Rua Maria Luisa Holstein,15, (01) 363-7176.*

This lively and architecturally unique restaurant is located in a converted warehouse in the *Alcântara* area. Slightly nouveau Portuguese cuisine is pleasantly served. The crowd is casual but elegant. After midnight, the adjoining bar (with a very unusual design and artwork) and club attract hundreds of *Lisbon's* most serious revelers.

CASA DO LEÃO, *Castelo São Jorge, (01) 875-962.*

An excellent restaurant and outdoor terrace in the walls of the *Castelo de São Jorge*. The beautiful interior contains vaulted ceilings and *azulejos* murals. Portuguese meat and seafood dishes are served nightly until 10:30pm.

BACCHUS, *Largo da Trindade,9, (01) 322-828.*

A wonderful wooden walled wine bar and restaurant with 2 different floors. Besides an extensive wine collection, Bacchus creates extraordinary meals. The slightly formal atmosphere is comfortable and the service is excellent.

TAVARES RICO, *Rua Misericórdia , 35.*

An opulent restaurant with tons of gilded wookwork and antique furnishings which served fine continental cuisine to well dressed businessmen and Lisbon's elite.

A GONDOLA, *Ave. de Berna, 62, (01) 770-426.*

This upscale and intimate restaurant faces the Gulbenkian Museum's main entrance and serves the best regional Italian cuisine in town. Well-dressed clients spend hours enjoying fine dinners amd wines in the pretty courtyard.

Moderate

PATIO ALFACINHA, *Rua do Guarda Loias,44, (01) 642-171.*

An excellent restaurant featuring typical Portuguese cuisine and occasionally great fado. Located in *Ajuda*, this famous establishment may require reservations.

LAUTASCO, *Beco do Azinhal, 7, (01) 861-073.*

This great find in the Alfama area near the *Rua de Sao Pedro* has plenty of atmosphere and a wonderful outdoor patio dining section. They prepare unusual fish and meat diehses from all over Portugal and the service is excellent.

PAP'AÇORDA, *Rua da Atalaia,57, (01) 346-4811.*
A nicely designed and popular regional restaurant inside of an old converted bakery in the heart of the *Bairro Alto*. Great food and good ambiance, try the Açorda.

COTAS DAS ARMAS, *Beco São Miguel,7, (01) 868-682.*
A small traditional restaurant in the Alfama area. This two level restaurant has the look of a converted stable. The hearty dishes are served by friendly staff who speak several languages. The owner is on hand to personally greet many of the clients.

PAGINAS TINTAS, *Rua Diario de Noticias, 87, (01) 346-5495.*
A charming two-floor restaurant in the Bairro Alto. The chef's specialties include unusual steak and fish meals. Try their codfish with cream sauce; its delicious!

Inexpensive
CERVEJARIA DA TRINDADE, *Rua Nova da Trindade,20, (01) 342-3506.*
One of my favorite places in *Lisbon*. Very casual restaurant in the *Bairro Alto* area built inside an ancient church encrusted with beautiful tile murals. The relaxed ambiance is only surpassed by the fine seafood (try the stuffed crab). Open until about 2am. One of the truly unpassable attractions in Lisbon.

BARTIS, *Rua Diario de Noticias, 97, (01) 324-795.*
This is one of the *Bairro Alto* hotspots where struggling local artists and musicians can be found after dark. The post-modern industrial interior is rather amusing, and you can find good fish and meat dishes at surprisngly low prices.

RESTAURANTE ALFAIA, *Travessa da Queimada,18, (01) 346-1232.*
This simple and charming local restaurant is in the heart of the *Bairro Alto*. Inexpensive traditional Portuguese food is served to a packed crowd of young families and friends from *Lisbon*. Get there before the line starts at about 9pm.

HUA LI TOU, *Rua da Misericórdia ,93, (01) 346-9478.*
I hate to admit it but after 3 weeks of eating grilled fish, even I need a break from Portuguese food. This small and friendly Chinese restaurant serves surprisingly good food. Excellent noodle and rice dishes are prepared and served by authentic Chinese exchange students who are studying in Lisbon. In the center of *Bairro Alto*.

REI DOS FRANGOS, *Travessa de Bom Jardim, 11 (no phone).*
When you're in the mood for a simple and cheap meal after wandering around the *Baixa* district, stop in here for a great roasted chicken.

See also *Fado* immediately below if you want to combine food, drink, and entertainment.

BARS, CLUBS, & NIGHTLIFE
Fado
   Fado is a traditional Portuguese music mostly about bad luck and tragedy. With the help of one or more guitar players, a female singer (*Fadista*) belts out a beautiful yet sad story of fate. *Fado* originated in 19th century *Lisbon* and it is hosted in small restaurants known as *adega tipicas* and *casas de Fado* in the *Alfama, Mouraria, Lapa,* and especially the *Bairro Alto* districts. Usually the singing starts at 11pm or so, so don't get there too early. Most *adega tipicas* offer traditional dinners and may also have cover charges.
   Here are some good *Fado* houses. Expect to pay a minimum cover charge of 2500$00 in most of these places:
   ARCADAS DO FAIA, *Rua da Barroca,54, (01) 342-1923. Expensive.*
   My personal favorite *Fado* house and restaurant in the *Bairro Alto* area. The music is great, and the food is quite good as well.
   SENHOR VINHO, *Rua Do Meio a Lapa,18, (01) 672-681. Expensive.*
   A larger *fado* restaurant in the *Lapa* area with a mixed crowd of tourists and some Portuguese. The food is pretty good and the *Fado* is compelling.
   A SERVERA, *Rua das Gaveas, 51, (01) 342-8314. Moderate.*
   A famous *Fado* house named after an infamous *Fadista*. This *Bairro Alto* hot spot offers fun *fado* and rather good meals.
   CANTO DO CAMÕES, *Travessa da Espera,38, (01) 346-5464. Moderate.*
   A wonderful little restaurant which serves great seafood specialties. The *Fado* here is a bit more powerful than usual. A good choice.
   PARREIRINHA, *Beco do Espírito Santo,1, (01) 868-209. Moderate.*
   A smaller more intimate *Fado* house in the *Alfama*. Large meals with good *Fado*.
   ADEGA MACHADO, *Rua do Norte,91, (01) 360-095. Moderate.*
   A larger well known establishment where both the *Fado* and the meals are pricey.

Bars & Clubs
   The typical evening out starts after dinner is finished at about 10:30pm. A large percentage of Lisbon's single population begins the inevitable migration to the *Bairro Alto* section. Over 35 small clubs and bars can be found mixed in with quirky little gallery/restaurants on every stone block of the area. The *Barrio Alto* is in full swing from 11pm until 3am behind sometimes unmarked entry doors. When you find the bar you wish to enter for you may need to ring the bell for admission.
   Tourists are not discriminated against in the *Barrio,* and you should have little problem to enter inside any bar you wish. Cover charges are

rare in the *Barrio*, but at a few discos and live music clubs like the wonderful *Café Luso* may ask for a small entrance fee.

After midnight or so, the action switches to the bars and discos in the *Santos* district off *Avenida 24 Julho* near the bridge. Here there is a combination of fun taverns, rock bars, packed dance clubs, and a few more restrictive discos which select their patrons from large line ups (they prefer beautiful women and famous Portuguese clientele). By 1am over a thousand young people are in the street immediately outside the already full clubs.

For the past few years, the *Alcântara* section has become home to a number of large converted warehouses which are now discos. Many of the "in" people who frequent Lisbon's nightlife scene prefer this area. By about 4am, most of these clubs are closing, and the action shifts to private parties or outlaw after hours clubs.

As these bars and clubs are known to change location often, I have included a listing of the names only. Any taxi diver will know the current location of any of these places, as will a good hotel conseirge. Cover charges run about 1,000$00.

Many larger clubs will hand you a drink card upon entry. Each drink you order will be stamped on the card, and you do not usually pay at this point. At time of exit you will be asked for your card so that your bill can be totaled. Don't lose your drink card!

PAVILHÃO CHINES, *Rua Dom Pedro V, 89*
A uniquely designed bar on the edge of the *Bairro Alto*. Complete with unusual collections of Oriental and European items, a pool room, and a very suggestive menu. Prices are steep, but this place is a must-see. Get there before 11pm and watch the action. A very good place to begin your adventure into the night.

GARTEJO, *Rua Cascais*
A huge multilevel club/concert hall/bar in the *Alcântara* section designed and owned by a well known architect. Great live music on some nights. A very fashionable night spot. Ask any taxi driver, they know how to best get you here.

THE HOT CLUB, *Praça da Alegria, 38*
A small jazz bar behind *Ave. da Liberdade* which features the finest live Jazz in *Lisbon*. Very reasonable cover charges and drink prices. Friendly crowd of casual city residents, almost no tourists.

ALCÂNTARA-MAR, *Rua da Cozinha Económica*
A huge industrial club in the *Alcântara* area with a younger crowd who dance all night. Some side rooms contain oversized sofas and candle lit tables. Try a B-52.

KAPITAL, *Ave. 24 de Julho*
One of the hotspots in the *Santos* area with doormen who make

people wait hours to get in. Once inside this multilevel glamour palace you will pay big bucks for drinks.

FRAGIL, *Rua da Atalia, 126*
A trendy medium sized club/bar which caters to the art and music crowd in the *Barrio Alto*. Get here before midnight or you may never get past the doorman.

ESTADIOU, *Rua São Pedro de Alcântara*
A dimely lit bohemian hang out for the local artist and student crowds in *Bairro Alto*. This is the place to drink coffee and feel like your in East Berlin.

KREMLIN, *Escadinhas da Praia, 5*
A cavernous disco in the Santos area located just around the corner from *Ave. 24 de Julho*. The young crowd dances to hip hop and rock mixes. Casual.

PLATEAU, *Escadinhas da Praia, 7*
Located immediately next to the Kremlin in *Santos*. A noisy and impolite dance club with a more aggressive beat. If they know your a tourist, you'll get in quicker.

NOVA, *Rua Rosa, 261*
A smaller more relaxed bar with a high percentage of Nordic clientele. A good place to party all night in the *Barrio Alto*. The darkened back room often smells like hash.

CAFÉ LUSO, *Travessa da Queimada, 10*
An excellent small bar and occasional live music club. Probably the most relaxing place to hang out in the *Barrio Alto*.

ANOS SESSENTA, *Largo do Terreirinho, 21*
A weekend only *Alfama* venue for good rock bands from Portugal and beyond. A great place to check out good local talent for a small cover charge.

SEEING THE SIGHTS

If you're spending at least a few days in Lisbon, you'll find that wondering around the city on your own is the best way to see the city. Make sure to bring this guide book and a good map of the city with you.

Although crime is almost unheard of, I still suggest wearing a money belt, or hideaway wallet pack. To begin wandering through Lisbon it is better to avoid using your car. The traffic, parking, and navigation situation in Lisbon is perhaps the worst of any European capital. I have had no choice but to drive through Lisbon over 35 times, and I still get either lost, or stuck in a traffic jam every time. The best way to see Lisbon is to leave your car in a parking lot, and travel by a combination of foot, taxi, metro, bus, funicular and trolley. Walking on the patterned stone

LISBON 151

sidewalks is a delight, and the reasonable size of the city allows you to view all of downtown by foot.

Private guides can be rented by the half or full day via your travel agent or tour operator, or as a last resort by contacting the *Sindicato National de Actividade Turistica* at *(01) 346-7170*. The typical price for a licensed private guide starts at about 15,000$00 plus expenses per day.

Perhaps the best alternative to the high cost of a private guide is the vast selection of guided city bus tours. These excursions offer tourists both half and full day tours which include admission to a variety of museums and places of interest. The tours are conducted by licensed multilingual local guides and utilize large deluxe air conditioned motorcoaches. Over the years I have taken almost all of these bus tours, and I can suggest the following companies and itineraries. These can be reserved in advance via your travel agent, tour operator, hotel concierge, calling the bus companies directly, or by showing up at the tour company kiosks in front of *Eduardo VII* park and purchasing tickets.

Advance reservations may also allow for a complimentary transfer directly from your hotel in Lisbon, Estoril, and Cascais, please call the bus company directly for more details.

Some of the tour companies and tours I'd recommend include:
CITIRAMA *(01) 355-8569.*
• **3 hour Lisbon City Tour** – *price per person is 4500$00.*

Includes *Marquêsde Pombal* area, panoramic view from top of *Eduardo VII* park, admission and tour of Coach Museum, visit to Jerónimos monastery, visit to Tower of *Belém* and the Monument of Discoveries, stop at St. Jorges castle, a short walk in the *Alfama*, and a drive past the *Rossio*. Tour departs at 9:30 am and again at 2:30 pm.
• **4 hour Lisbon by Night Tour** – *price per person is 10,500$00.*

Includes *Marquêsde Pombal* area, *Ave. da Liberdade, Rossio,* Monument of the Discoveries, Tower of *Belém*, Jerónimos monastery, *Ponte 25 Abril, Alcântara,* and dinner at a *Fado* restaurant with folkloric show. Tour departs at 8:30 pm.

PORTUGAL TOURS *(01) 352-2902*
• **10 hour Lisbon and Estoril Coastal Area Tour** – *price per person is 10,000$00.*

Includes downtown *Lisbon,* St. Jorges castle, walking tour in the *Alfama,* Coach Museum visit, Jerónimos monastery visit, Tower of *Belém,* Monument of Discoveries, free time for lunch at *Marquêsde Pombal,* afternoon visits to *Sintra, Queluz,* palace admissions, visit to *Cabo da Rocha, Guincho, Boca do Inferno, Cascais,* and *Estoril.* Tour departs at 9:30 am.

RN TOURS *(01) 538-846*
• **8 hour Lisbon and Costa Azul Tour** – *price per person is 10,500$00.*
Includes visits throughout downtown *Lisbon*, Jerónimos monastery, Coach museum, Tower of *Belém*, Monument of the discoveries, St. Jorges castle, includes a typical local lunch, visits to the coastal areas of *Sesimbra, Setúbal, Palmela*, and a wine tasting in *Azeitão*. Tour departs at 9:30am and does not run on weekends.
• **8 hour Obidos and Surroundings Tour** – *price per person is 13,500$00.*
Includes visits to *Obidos*, the monastery at *Alcobaça*, a tour and a typical lunch in *Nazaré* , and a visit to the famous religious center of *Fátima* . Tour departs at 8:30 am daily.

A complete listing of other long distance tours (half day, full day, and multiple day) can be secured by calling each of these companies directly.

The Chiado
The **Chiado** district of Lisbon is a wonderful world of its own. The most interesting way to get to this part of town is to take the fabulously strange elevator called the **Elevador de Santa Justa** from it's base on the western edge of the *Baixa* at *Rua da Ouro* which will drop passengers off near the **Largo de Carmo**. This small and exclusive district consists of a handfull of streets which lead westward towards the restaurant and boutique lined *Rua da Misericórdia* which marks the border of this area.
Traditionally Lisbon's most elegant shopping district, much of the Chiado was destroyed by a major fire in 1988. Fortunately the area is currently being restored to it's original beauty but still contains some very upscale stores for jewelry, leather goods, designer clothing, and excellent porcelain. Among the finest sights in the Chiado is the Gothic church called the **Convento do Carmo** located on *Rua do Carmo* just near the exit if the *Elevador Santa Justa*. Constructed in the 15th century, the convent lost it's roof during the earthquake of 1755.
Nowadays the structure is home to the **Museu Arqueológico do Carmo** *(Archaeological Museum)* which is filled with Prehistoric, Roman, Visigothic, Arab, and medieval artifacts. This museum really must be visited when you are in the area (closed on Sundays).
One of the most relaxing attractions of the *Bairro Alto* is the excellent **A Brasileira Café** on *Rua Garrett #120*. This café has a history of literary patrons, and the inside and outside tables provides the best place in *Lisbon* to watch people while enjoying a good café and maybe a small pastéis. It may also be worthwhile to cross over the *Rua da Misericórdia* to look around the shops just off of the bench- filled *Praça Luís de Camões* (named for a great Portuguese writer who frequented this area).

LISBON 153

The Bairro Alto

The **Bairro Alto** section of Lisbon is located on the upper elevations of downtown, to the west of the Baixa. This area contains some of the best boutiques, antique stores, and rare book shops in Lisbon. From the *Praça Luís de Camões* you can walk up the the *Rua da Misericórdia* and then make a left (west) turn on the *Travessa da Espera* to enter inside the small grided enclave of stone roads which make up the heart of the *Bairro Alto*.

After strolling through streets like the atmospheric *Rua da Rosa*, *Rua da Barroca*, and *Rua Diário Notícias*, you should head back eastward on the *Travessa da Queimada* to rejoin the *Rua da Misericórdia*. A few blocks north (up) on *Rua Misericórdia* the street name will change to *Rua de São Pedro de Alcântara* and lead towards an unforgettable panoramic lookout point of Lisbon from the **São Pedro de Alcântara Belvedere** park. An afternoon visit to the **Solar do Vinho do Porto** on *Rua São Pedro de Alcântara # 45* (just across from the park) will allow you to taste many vintage Port wines at very reasonable prices (open till 10pm, closed on Sundays). For those of you who prefer dry white wines, try a glass of *Porto Branco*, a dry white variety all but unknown to North Americans.

A few blocks further up, *Rua de São Pedro de Alcântara* bends towards the west and merges into antique shop heaven: *Rua Dom Pedro V* reveals the wonderful stately homes and shops of the **Praça Principe Real** square. Once again the street changes its name, this time to *Rua Escola Politécnica*, and then leads towards the remarkable **Jardim Botánico** (Botanical Gardens) with its romantic paths.

During the evening, thousands of young revelers disappear into the maze of narrow alleys in the center of the Bairro Alto and frequent a vast assortment of small clubs, bars, *Fado* (typical Portuguese folk music) houses, and restaurants. Many local families and students have dinner in *adega tipicas* (restaurants where traditional *Fado* music is played live) which can be found throughout the *Bairro Alto*. Dinner here is a late event usually starting after 8pm, while the *Fado* music and nightclubs usually start up around 11pm.

If you have some time to kill before dinner, I suggest a drink at the wonderfully ornate **Pavilhão Chines** bar on *Rua Dom Pedro # 89* where an unusual collection of Deco style objects clutter the walls. At the end of your visit, you can either take a taxi back to your hotel, or if it's before midnight you can take the *Elevador da Glória* tram from just south of the *Alcântara* lookout and park to the *Palácio Foz* on *Avenida da Liberdade*, and then walk back into the *Rossio* before getting a bus, metro, or taxi.

Cais de Sodré & the Bica district

Directly south of the Chiado and Bairro Alto districts at the bottom of *Rua do Alecrim* on the banks of the Tejo river, you can wander around the markets in and around the **Cais de Sodré** area. Known primarily as an entrance point to Lisbon for many of its workers, this district has a fluvial station with ferries that criss-cross from here to the southern banks of the Tejo, and an adjacent train station for the packed electric commuter trains to and from the suburban cities of Cascais and Estoril.

On most weekdays Cais de Sodré becomes filled with huge numbers of commuters each morning and afternoon. This noisy hectic little neighborhood is home to a few markets that are stocked each day (except Sunday) with a vast assortment of fish and vegetables. The fish market next to the station itself is open all day, while the early morning wholesale fruit and vegatable market a few blocks further west along the riverfront is busiest around 5am.

Also worth a quick stop inside is the **Ribeira** meat and produce market, housed in an old dome topped building just across from the station just east of the the busy bus and trolley stops of the **Praça Duque da Terceira** square.

The streets just above the Ribeira market and the adjacent **Praça Dom Luís I** square make up the **Bica** district. Filled with small old buildings which house some of the market suppliers, this small area is also worth a stroll through.

The Bairro do Castelo

Atop one of Lisbon's seven famous hills just a handful of blocks east of the Baixa is the remarkable **Bairro do Castelo** district with its wonderful historic sights and ancient enclosed neighborhoods. The most famous and obvious of these atractions is the 5th-century **Castelo de São Jorge** castle (open daily until sunset), visible from almost anywhere in town. Originally built by the Visigoths, this castle has passed through the hands of several different civilizations, and was once the old city's center.

During the Moorish occupation Lisbon was completely surrounded by a defensive wall known as the **Cerca Moura**, and later a palace known as the **Alcazar** was built inside the castle walls. After Lisbon was conquered by King Dom Afonso in 1147, the former Moorish Alcazar palace was replaced with the **Palácio Real de Alcácova** and became home to the Portuguese royal family for a few centuries. Although the castle was seriously damaged by the 1755 earthquake, it was restored in 1938.

Unfortunately, most of the Alcácova palace inside the castle walls still lies in ruins, but a small museum can be visited on its former sight. The garden-laden grounds of the castle itself (open daily until sunset) are still filled with magnificent towers, fortified walls, plazas, pools, and a dramatic parapet walkway called the **Caminho de Ronda**. Within the walls of the castle complex you can stroll along the old enclosed **Santa Cruz** quarter to look at the fine ancient homes, old lanes, and fine restaurants.

LISBON 155

The slightly confusing *Rua da Costa do Castelo* road circles most of the *castelo* and can be taken to reach several other quarters including the old **Mouraria** (Moorish quarter). The Mouraria can be found by walking a block or so north of the castle, and is centered around the streets and lanes which run off of *Rua da Mouraria*.

Although there are not many specific sights I can suggest in this area, a good walk around will be a nice adventure. After visiting the Mouraria, you can head back down to the *Rua da Costa do Castelo* and follow it as winds it's way around to the castle's east side. This street soon leads to the *Largo Rodrigues de Freitas* which then feeds into *Rua São Tome*. If you walk south towards the river on *Rua São Tome*, you will soon pass the an original Arabic-style gateway in the **Largo das Portas do Sol** (you may want to visit one of the many taverns). Just off the south end of the *Largo* is the wonderful **Fundação Ricardo do Espírito Santo e Silva** foundation which is housed in a converted 17th-century palace. The foundation is home to the fantastic **Museu de Artes Decorativas** (Museum of Decorative Arts). This large museum and school offers comprehensive tours (closed on Sundays and Mondays) through its vast collections of antique furnishings, paintings, *Arraiolos* carpets, ceramics, and rare silver.

From the museum, take *Rua do Limoeiro* down a block or so before reaching the **Igreja da Santa Luzia**, near a spectacular lookout point from the café-filled *Miradouro da Santa Luzia*. After a brief rest and panoramic photo opportunity, you are ready to continue down the *Rua do Limoeiro* to reach the **Sé** cathedral and the heart of the neighboring Alfama district.

The Alfama

Nestled below the imposing **Castelo de São Jorge** castle, the **Alfama** district is perhaps the most famous part of Lisbon. The stone-topped maze-like streets have been here since the Moors occupied this area in the 8th century, and the Alfama retains much of its ancient ambiance since it was largely spared from the 1755 earthquake. Streams of laundry are suspended between old whitewashed houses, many with elegent faded tile facades, as young children play soccer below.

Among the many impressive sights worth visiting in the Alfama is the **Sé** cathedral on *Rua Augusto Rosa*. This prominent cathedral dates back to the 12th century and was built on the sight of Lisbon's main mosque as an insult to the newly defeated Moors.

A long and leisurely walk through much of the Alfama is the only way to really see this section. Giving you a route to walk around the Alfama is almost impossible since getting lost in its Arabic labyrinthine lanes is close to inevitable.

Among the most unique and compelling streets in the Alfama is the **Beco do Carneiro** (Alley of Sheep) with it's extremely narrow passages that typify life in this district in the old days. The *Rua da Judiaria* (Street of Jewish quarter) is another interesting attraction in what was once the Jewish quarter and dates back to the 16th century. The tile-covered houses off the **Patio das Flores** plaza are also worthwhile sights. Another interesting stop is the 16th-century *Igreja de São Vicente de Fora* church on *Rua São Vicente* in the eastern section of the Alfama which houses the tombs of several Portuguese kings in it's eerie tiled cloisters (open daily).

A great flea market takes place on Tuesday mornings and all day on Saturday right near the Igreja de São Vicente de Fora church in the **Campo de Santa Clara** square. This unique market is called the **Feira da Ladra** (thieve's market) and is a great place to find excellent antiques at great prices (don't be afraid to bargain) mixed in with lots of junk. At a recent visit to this market I purchased two wonderful 19th-century brass cupid picture frames for less than 5,000$00 each.

After a long day of wandering around the Alfama, you might want to walk to the southern edge of this district near the river. Just off the market-laden *Rua de São Pedro* you can wander around the **Largo do Chafariz de Dentro** fountain square where the locals spend their spare time gossiping. You can also find a vast array of good, inexpensive restaurants and bars throughout this area.

If you happen to be in Lisbon in mid-June, don't miss a chance to see the amazing **St. Anthony Festival**, which makes this part of town really come alive.

Central Lisbon

The central Lisbon district starts somewhere along the northern edge of the *Avenida da Liberdade*, Lisbon's main drag. Here you will see a fine example of the wide open boulevards created by the Marquêsde Pombal after the great earthquake of 1755. Many of Portugal's largest companies have their head offices on this avenue, including the T.A.P. reservations center at the top of the street.

At the end of *Avenida da Liberdade* you will find the busiest and most irritating major intersection in Lisbon, the **Praça Marquês de Pombal**. This giant rotunda and its statue are a monument to the 18th-century restorer of Lisbon and is located immediately in front of the 65 acre **Parque Eduardo VII** park. The park's name commemorates a visit by the former British King and contains ponds, paths, statues, and an outdoor terrace. A wonderful panoramic view of Lisbon and the river can be seen from a vantage point atop the high point of the Eduardo VII park.

A short walk away is the beautiful **Estufa Fria** (cold greenhouses) where an assortment of exotic flowers and plants are displayed beside lakes and waterfalls (open daily). If you are in the mood for some serious shopping, from the southern edge of the Eduardo VII park, follow the

Ave. Joaquim António de Aguiar west for past the side of the Ritz hotel for several blocks until you can't miss the huge *Amoreiras* indoor shopping complex.

Lapa
The **Lapa** district is home to some of the most elaborate residences and embassies in Lisbon. Situated high above the Tejo river about a km. or so west of the Bairro Alto, Lapa has become one of the most desirable districts to live in. Although some smaller and more rustic houses still exist in this area, progress has paved the way for additional development of the area.

Lisbon's most deluxe accommodations at **Hotel da Lapa** have become the home away from home for the many E.E.C. diplomats and world leaders on assignment in Portugal. Several ornate and imposing embassies stand next to regal mansions which are on the verge of collapse. Lapa is a great place to wander through the small alleys and gaze at the massive villas with their pricey river views. The **Museu Nacional de Arte Antiga** (National Museum of Antique Art) *at the Jardim 9 de Abril off Rua das Janelas Verdes* is a must-see for anyone interested in Portuguese and international art from the 11th century and onwards (closed on Mondays). The famous and intimate **York House** hotel is just a short walk away from the museum.

Belém
The **Belém** district is a mainly residential area about 5 km. west of Praça do Comércio. The best way to get here is by taking a taxi or the #15 tram from the Praça do Comércio. It is from this district's riverfront park area that several of Portugal's greatest voyages were launched. On the banks of the river rests the **Torre de Belém** tower, a 16th-century fortress designed to protect Lisbon's harbor (closed on Mondays), with it's adjoining palm tree gardens. Another obvious riverfront attraction is the **Monument of the Discoveries**, completed in 1960 to commemorate the 500th anniversary of the death of Prince Henry the Navigator.

As you move inland from the marinas on the river, the first structure you will see is the **Centro Cultural de Belém** (Belém Cultural Center), which currently houses art exhibitions and an international conference center. On my last visit to Belém, the cultural center hosted a fine exhibit of international photography.

The next vast structure you will see the **Mosterio dos Jerónimos** monastery (closed on Mondays). Damaged by the 1755 earthquake, this monastery dates back to about 1502 when it was commissioned by King Dom Manuel to commemorate the return of Vasco de Gama. Designed by the famous architect Diogo Boitac, this structure has been called the masterpiece of all Manueline architecture. The vaulted double cloister must be visited to experience the true beauty of this impressive architectural achievement. Inside the structure are the tombs of both Vasco de Gama and Luís de Camões.

The monastery and its adjacent **Praça do Império** are home to several different museums including these 3 fine choices: The **Museu de Arquelogico** (Archaeology Museum) contains a collection of Paleolithic and Roman artifacts (closed on Monday); the **Museu da Marinha** (Navy Museum) contains with boats, model boats, seaplanes, a cartography room, and a vast collection of navigational implements (closed on Monday); and the **Gulbenkian Planetarium** offers delightful simulated sky gazing sessions on weekends.

Also worth a visit is the nearby **Museu Nacional de Coches** (National Coach Museum) where fine examples of 16th-19th century coaches, as well as several royal portraits are on display (closed on Mondays). No visit to Belém would be complete without standing in line at the popular **Fabrica dos Pastéis de Belém** (Belém Pastry Factory) *at Rua de Belém 86*, where hundreds of people wait each day and night to buy fresh from the oven custard pastries (Also try their wonderful coconut macaroons).

Ajuda

A short walk north of Belém on the *Calçãda da Ajuda* will bring you into the **Ajuda** district. The first sight the this area reveals is the immense structure of the 19th century **Palácio da Ajuda** palace, which now contains a museum of antique furnishings, books, and silver (closed on Wednesdays and holidays). Very close to the palace is the 9.5 acre **Jardim Botánico de Ajuda** where Portugal's oldest botanical garden (founded in 1768) awaits you with many exotic species of flowers and plants (closed on Mondays).

Alcântara

If you prefer a long walk after visiting Ajuda, follow the river and head east towards the omnipresent **Ponte 25 de Abril** bridge (a copy of San Fransisco's Golden Gate bridge). In about 10 minutes you will pass the many bars and clubs of the **Alcântara** district. At night, many of Lisbon's most notorious clubs have huge lines of revelers awaiting their selection to be admitted inside. Like other major cities in the world, it pays to know the right people to get in the door of some of these clubs. Additional restaurants and nightspots are located in the warehouse laden back streets of Alcântara close to the bridge.

Try a visit to the rather unusual **Alcântara-Mar Café** whose legendary B-52 drinks are made with *absinto* (absynth).

LISBON 159

Northern Lisbon
This expanding area near the international airport contains several interesting sights. From the *Marquêsde Pombal* rotunda turn right (northwest) and follow *Ave. Fontes Pereira de Melo* until you have reached the first rotunda which is called the **Praça Douque de Saldanha**. Besides looking around the fine buildings of this square and rotunda, you should follow the only big street, which is now renamed *Avenida da República*, up as it winds its way up several blocks towards the **Praça de Touros** (bullring) in the **Campo Pequeno** area. The bullring is a beautiful structure which seats over 8000 spectators and is the sight of many seasonal evening bullfights (generally Thursdays and Sundays from April through October) in which the bull is never killed.

If you head a few blocks eastward from the bullring on *Ave. João XXI*, you will soon find *Ave. da Roma*. This delightful street has a large assortment of fine boutiques and designer shops which sell high end goods. If you continue a few blocks south on *Ave de Roma*, you will find additional boutiques at *Praça de Londres*.

A few blocks north of Campo Pequeno is the garden-laden **Campo Grande** area, which contains several attractions including the huge **Biblioteca National** (National Library) with its fine **Museu de Intrumentos Musicais** (Musical Instrument Museum) that has a collection of 16th-20th century instruments (closed on Sundays and Mondays).

Also in the same general area you will find the **Museu da Cidade** (Museum of the City) which is housed in the 18th century **Palácio Pimenta** and contains historical information and iconography about Lisbon (closed on Mondays). Campo Grande also contains a large indoor shopping center called the **Calaidoscopo**.

Traveling west of Campo Pequeno on *Ave. de Berna* towards the **Praça Espanha** (Spanish Square), you will find yourself at the incredible **Museu Calouste Gulbenkian** museums. This fantastic museum complex contains the massive collection of a millionaire from Armenia who resided in Portugal and left his estate of several hundred million dollars worth of western and Oriental art and jewelry to a specially created Portuguese foundation that now bears his name. His endowment created an educational foundation that the general public could benefit from. The result is one of the finest art collections anywhere in the world. Several sections of the museum exhibit different periods and styles of art including everything from ancient Mesopotamian up to modern art masterpieces. The museum occupies several buildings at the **Parque Palhava** and are surrounded by a wonderful park and sculpture garden with a comfortable performance area. There is even a reasonably priced cafeteria on location. Free admission on Sundays (closed on Mondays).

Continuing westward past the Praça Espanha on *Avenida Calouste Gulbenkian* you will wind up at the **Aqueducto das Aguas Livres**, an 11 mile long aqueduct which was constructed in 1728 to supply drinking water to Lisbon. A series of glazed ceramic murals can be seen on the way to the aqueduct. The huge **Parque Florestal de Monsanto** (Monsanto Floral Park) surrounds most of this area with including the beautiful zodiac patterned box gardens at the **Palácio dos Marqueses de Fronteira**. This 17th century Itialian Renaissance style palace contains several remarkable paintings, *azulejo* and delft tile panels, a woderful terrace, and fantastically furnished grand rooms (closed on Sundays).

Nearby the palace, you can also pop into the **Jardim Zoologico** zoo if you want to look at some caged wildlife. The oddest sight in this beautiful park may be the presence of a huge campsite which gets filled during the summer.

Directory of Museums, Palaces, & Monuments
• **Archaeological Museum of Carmo**, *Convento de Carmo, Largo do Carmo, (01) 346-0473.* Contains prehistoric and medieval art, rare medieval coins, ancient epigraphy, sculptures, tiles, and ceramics. Open 10 am until 1 pm and 2 pm until 5 pm Oct. through April; Open 10 am until 5 pm May through Sept.; Closed on Sundays and holidays.
• **Calouste Gulbenkian Museum**, *Avenida de Berna, 45, (01) 795-0236.* Contains a private collection of ancient paintings, fabrics, pottery, glass, brass, sculptures, jewelry, furniture, porcelain, ivory, books, and decorative arts. Open 10 am until 5 pm October through May; Open 2 pm until 7:30 pm Wednesday and Saturday June through Sept.; Open 10 am until 5 pm Tuesday, Thursday, Friday, and Sunday June through Sept. Closed on Mondays and holidays.
• **Castelo de São Jorge**, *Rua da Costa do Castelo*. Contains the former Alcácova royal palace ruins and museum, as several towers and defensive walls which can form a walking path with fine views. Open daily from 9 am to Sunset.
• **City Museum**, *Campo Grande, 245, (01) 795-1617*. Contains documentation regarding the evolution of Lisboa from prehistoric days until the revolution of 1910. Also includes an 18th century Ensemble Epoque. Open 10 am until 1pm and 2 pm until 6 pm year round. Closed on Mondays and holidays.
• **Decorative Arts Museum**, *Espírito Santo e Silva Foundation, Largo das Portas do Sol, 2, (01) 862-183*. Contains collects of antique Portuguese and European fine furniture, ceramics, *Arraiolos* carpets, textiles, silver, and 15th-19th century Portuguese paintings. Open 10 am until 1 pm and 2 pm until 5 pm tear round. Closed on Sundays, Mondays, and holidays.

LISBON 161

- **Modern Art Center of the Gulbenkian Foundation**, *Rua Dr. Nicolay Bettencourt, (01) 795-0241*. Contains Modern paintings, sculpture, and engraving from around the world. Open 10 am until 5 pm from Oct. through May Open 2 pm until 7:30 pm Wednesday and Saturday from June through Sept. Open 10 am until 5 pm all other days from June through Sept. Closed Mondays and holidays.
- **National Museum of Ancient Art**, *Rua das Janelas Verdes, 95, (01) 397-6061*. Contains European sculpture, jewelry, silverware, ceramics, as well as Namban art, textiles, designs, furniture, porcelain, engravings and 16th-century filigree. Open 10 am until 1 pm and 2:30 pm until 5 pm year round. Closed Mondays and holidays.
- **National Museum of Archaeology**, *Praça do Império, (01) 362-0000*. Contains Portuguese archaeological findings from Paleolithic periods and onward. Included ancient jewelry, coins, sculpture, mosaics, and a vast library on the subject. Open 10 am until 1 pm and 2:30 pm until 5 pm year round Closed Mondays and holidays.
- **National Museum of Coaches**, *Praça Afonso de Albuquerque, (01) 363-8022*. Contains a collection of royal coaches from as far back as the 17th-century. Also includes bullfighting costumes and a royal portrait gallery. Open 10 am until 5:30 pm year round. Closed Mondays and holidays.
- **National Museum of Costumes**, *Largo Julio de Castilho - Lumiar, (01) 759-0318*. Contains Coptic fabrics from as far back as the 4th century, clothing from the 17th century and onward, antique toys, and textile weaving and printing documentation. Open 10 am until 1 pm and 2:30 pm until 5 pm year round. Closed on Mondays and holidays.
- **National Palace of Ajuda**, *Largo da Ajuda*. A royal palace from the 19th-century. Open 10 am until 5 pm year round. Closed Wednesdays and holidays.
- **Palace of the Marquises of Fronteira**, *Largo São Domingos de Benfica, 1, (01) 782-023*. A 17th-century regal palace and gardens. Open for a 1 hour tour at 10:45 am year round. Closed Sundays and holidays.
- **Marionette Museum**, *Largo Rodrigues de Freitas, 19A*. Contains a collection of marionettes dating from the 19th century. Open 11 am until 1 pm and 3 pm until 6 pm year round. Closed Mondays and holidays.
- **National Museum of Azulejos** *at the Convento on Rua da Madre de Deus, (01) 814-7747*. Contains a collection of Portuguese and foreign tiles from as far back as the 15th century. Also included a collection of 17th- and 18th-century paintings. Open 10 am until 12:30 pm and 2 pm until 5 pm year round. Closed Mondays and holidays.
- **Monastery of St. Jerónimos**, *Praça do Império, (01) 362-0034*. A Manueline style 16th century monastery with exceptional cloisters. Open 10 am until 1 pm and 2:30 pm until until 5 pm Oct. through May. Open 10

am to 6:30 pm June through Sept. Closed on Mondays and holidays.
- **National Museum of Natural History**, *Rua da Escola Politécnica, 58, (01) 396-0854.* Contains collections of mineralogical, geological, zoological, anthropological, and botanical exhibitions in three separate sections. Contact the museum directly to make a reservation.
- **Tower of Belém**, *Praça do Império, (01) 301-6892.* A 16th century defensive structure on the Rio Tejo. Open 10 am until 6:30 pm June through Sept. Open 10 am until 1 pm and 2:30 pm until 5 pm Oct. through May. Closed on Monday and holidays.

SHOPPING

For the most part, bargains on certain items can be found in differing sections of Lisbon. The **Baixa** streets such as *Rua do Ouro, Rua dos Sapateiros,* and *Rua Augusta* offer visitors an vast array of shops which offer reasonably priced clothing, leather goods, jewelry, and designer goods.

The best place to start looking for good deals on antiques, old books, *azulejos* (tiles), and fine furnishings will be along the *Rua Dom Pedro V* and *Rua do Alecrim* in the Bairro Alto as well as on *Rua Alves Correira* near the central *Avenida da Liberdade* area. For those of you interested in fine hand wooven *Arraiolos* carpets, your best bet is in the Chiado.

For the finest European designer clothing you may be better off looking around the *Avenida da Roma* off the *Praça de Londres* square. For those of you who are more interested in finding real bargains in typical outdoor markets, there are several to choose from. The most interesting markets in Lisbon include the **Feira da Ladra** flea market at *Campo Santa Clara* in the Alfama (Tuesdays mornings and Saturday), the **clothing markets** at *Praça de Chile* (closed on Sunday) and at the **Aeroporto Rotunda** near the airport (Sundays). Additional shopping can be found at the large mall-style shopping complexes which are listed below this section. Don't forget to ask about the Tax Free refund vouchers which are discussed in the shopping section of this book.

Below are just a few of the places I have managed to buy great products at very low prices, and I'll tell you what to expect.

In Baixa
- **Malhas Achega**, *Rua dos Fanqueiros, 30.* A modern and bright store which sees to always have a clearance sale on classic lamb's wool sweaters for about 4,000$00. I have seen these sweaters in New York selling for $95US.
- **Sofia Lavores**, *Rua Augusta, 179.* A great little shop which sells fine hand embroidered tablecloths and fabrics starting at about 10,000$00 which cost much more on this side of the ocean.

- **Esquina da Roupa**, *Rua de S. Nicolau, 44.* This small and crammed shop has several racks of men's and women's pants, shirts, and jackets at very low prices. Last trip I purchased several pairs of pure wool pants (they all say "made in Italy") for 3,800$00 each.
- **Moda Viva**, *Rua dos Fraqueiros, 259.* A busy clothing boutique offering last seasons best fashions at bargain basement prices. I have bought pure wool hand tailored suits for 21,000$00.
- **Barbosa, Esteves**, *Rua da Prata, 295.* Specializing in gold and silver jewelry, this pleasant shop contains several inexpensive gift items. My sterling silver key chain cost only 2,200$00 here.
- **Sapataria Lisbononse**, *Rua Augusta, 202.* A well stocked shoe store with prices starting at 6,900$00 per pair.

In Bairro Alto
Casa Saboia, *Rua Garrett, 66.* A good designer shop which sells fine European mensware at good prices.
- **Fabrica Sant'ana**, *Rua do Alecrim, 95.* A workshop, factory outlet, and shop which sells reproductions of classic Portuguese *azulejos* (tiles). They can also custom manufacture from your design.
- **Antiquario Dom Pedro V**, *Rua Dom. Pedro, V.* One of the better antique shops along this street which offers a large assortment of European furnishings and accesories at good prices.

In Chiado
- **Casa Quintão**, *Rua Ivens, 34.* A great store with a wonderful collection of fine *Arraiolos* capets with hefty prices. They are certainly worth at least looking at while in town.
- **Vista Alegre**, *Largo do Chiado, 18.* This is an elegant shop for the finest porcelain made in Portugal. Their creations start at about 5000$00 per setting, and they are extraordinary.
- **Interio**, *Rua Garrett, 49.* A good source for accesories used in interior decorating. Great stuff!

If you prefer large air-conditioned shopping centers, the following malls are open 7 days a week from 9 am until midnight:
- **Centro Comércio das Amoreiras**, *Ave. Eng. Duarte Pacheco.* Currently the largest mall in Portugal with over 360 shops. Indoor parking.
- **Centro Comércio Alvalade**, *Praça de Alvalade.* A medium sized center with about 80 shops.
- **Centro Comércio Imaviz**, *Ave. Fontes Pereira de Melo (next to the Sheraton).* An upscale shopping center with reasonable prices and about 60 shops.

- **Centro Comércio Fonte Nova**, *Estrada de Benfica*. A large center on the outskirts of town with over 100 shops.

SPORTS
Horseback Riding
- **Sociedade Hipica**, *Campo Grande, (01) 774-881*

Sailing
- **Clube Naval**, *Doca de Belém, (01) 363-0061*
- **Paço de Arcos**, *Paço de Arcos, (01) 443-2238*

Swimming
- **Aqua Park**, *Ave. Descobertas, (01) 617-000*

Tennis
- **Monsanto Parque**, *Parque Florestal, (01) 648-067*

PRACTICAL INFORMATION
Currency Exchange

All banks in Lisbon have currency exchange counters (*cambios*) which are open from 8:30 am until 3 pm (some take a lunch break). Several downtown banks now offer automatic exchange machines which operate 24 hours a day. The airport exchange counter is open until very late each day, although the rate is not great.

Exchange commission fees usually run about 1,000$00 per transaction. Exchange rates can vary from one bank to another. If you need to exchange currency or travelers checks when the banks are closed, most hotels will do a small exchange at rather unreasonable conversion rates.

Cash advances from **Visa** cards are no problem at any large bank. **American Express** travelers checks can be replaced by calling their European headquarters toll free *at 0505-44-9080 or by calling the US office collect at 801-964-6665.*

Embassies
- **US Embassy**, *Avenida das Forças Armadas, (01)726-6600*
- **Canadian Embassy**, *Avenida da Liberdade, 144, (01) 347-4892*
- **UK Embassy**, *Rua S. Domingos a Lapa, 37, (01) 396-1191*

Emergency & Useful Phone Numbers
These are some useful phone numbers:
- **Emergency Services** (S.O.S.), *115*
- **Directory Assistance**, *118*

LISBON 165

- **Lisbon Police**, *(01) 346-6141*
- **Lisbon Fire Dept.**, *(01) 342-2222*
- **Ambulance Service**, *(01) 617-777*
- **The British Hospital**, *(01) 602-020 day, Rua Saraiva Carvalho,49, (01) 603-785 night*. An excellent hospital with English speaking staff.
- **Tourist Police**, *(01) 346-6141, Rua Capelo, 13*. For police theft reports needed for insurance claims
- **TAP Reservations**, *Praça Marquêsde Pombal, 3, (01) 386-1020*
- **Delta Airlines** *in Lisbon, Rua Rodrigues Sampaio,170, (01) 353-7610*
- **TAP** *at Lisbon Airport, (01) 386-0480*
- **Portugalia Airlines**, *(01) 848-6693*
- **A.C.P.**, emergency road services, *(01) 942-5095*. The representative for the AAA and CAA auto clubs in Portugal.
- **Taxi**, *Rossio, (1) 793-2756*
- **Portela Airport**, *(1) 802-060*

Mail

There several post offices (*correios*) in Lisbon which sell stamps (*selos*) and can help with normal postal needs. You can send and receive mail as well as make phone calls at one of the main branches. If you wish to have Lisbon's main *Praça do Comércio -Terreiro do Paço* post office hold mail for you, general delivery can be arrainged after a visit to the post office to register your name (address: **Central Post Office**, *Praça do Comércio, (01) 346-3231*.

Incomming letters must be marked with your full name and in big words it should say *Posta Restante-Lista do Correios* and be sent to *Terreiro do Paço, 1100 Lisboa, Portugal*. They can be picked up at the central post office with proper ID for a 70$00 fee per letter. You can also receive mail via an American Express office if you contact them in the US before you depart. Both DHL and Federal Express can deliver packages to Portugal from North America within 3 days.

Telephones

Pay phones in Lisbon usually accept 20$00 and 50$00 coins which are inserted into a horizontal slot in the upper right hand corner of the phone. Unfortunately, most of the public phones in Lisbon always seem to be broken.

If you have bought a *Credifone* or *TLP* phone card from a newsstand or post office, you stand a much better chance. These cards have a predetermined amount of impulses (units) which can allow for multiple uses of the same card. Phone calls can easily be made from most major post offices (pay after you make the call) at low rates, or at much higher prices from any hotel front desk.

The area code for Lisbon is (01) if calling from within Portugal, (1) if calling from outside Portugal. If you are calling from within the Lisbon area, drop the area code completely. If you need to call internationally, you can use MCI and ATT access codes from within Portugal to reach English-speaking operators for collect, credit card, and third-party calls.

SOME USEFUL PHONE NUMBERS FOR LOCAL & INTERNATIONAL CALLS

- *Emergencies, 115*
- *Local Information, 118*
- *International Operator Assistance, 098*
- *USA Country Code, 001*
- *Canada Country Code, 001*
- *UK Country Code, 0044*
- *ATT USA Direct Access Number, 05-017-1288*
- *MCI CALL USA Access Number, 05-017-1234*

Tourist Information
- **Main Tourist Office (Turismo)**, *Palácio Foz, Praça dos Restauradores, (01) 346-3643*. Located just off *Avenida da Liberdade*, and open 7 days a week, they can provide maps, brochures, suggestions, reservations, and help in English.
- **Airport Tourist Office**, *(01) 848-5974*. Also open daily.

15. COSTA DE LISBOA - THE LISBON COAST

The **Costa de Lisboa** region contains portions of southern **Estremadura** and northwestern **Baixa Alentejo**, as well as a sliver of southwestern **Ribatejo** province. This beautiful area is comprised mainly of the cities, villages, and seaside resort areas that surround the capital city of Lisbon and its southern suburbs. The majority of this area is in close proximity to the sea and the coast.

Since most visitors to Portugal arrive at Lisbon's international airport, the Costa de Lisboa is a perfect base from which to explore many historical villages, mountain top castles, authentic fishing towns, sporting centers, long sandy beaches with dramatic windswept cliffs, and of course the impressive capital city of Lisbon. As the region extends towards the interior of the country, beautiful valleys, hills, and rivers abound. The short distances between the major attractions of this region make it very easy to day trip from a central location. We'll start with the north, and then finish with the region's southern reaches.

Among the most impressive sights here are the fine beaches at **Guincho**, **Estoril**, **Praia Adraga**, **Caparica**, and **Tróia**, the inspiring castles and palaces of the beautiful and mysterious town of **Sintra** and nearby **Queluz**, and the dramatic cliffs at **Cabo da Roca**. The traditional fishing village of **Sesimbra**, the golf courses throughout the **Estoril** area, the fine bullfighting village of Vila Franca de Xira, and the jet-set resort of **Cascais**.

OEIRAS & THE COASTAL BEACHES

The historic city of **Oeiras** lies some 15 km west of Lisbon *off route N-6 west*. Here you can view the former 18th-century **Palácio do Marquês** palace, once home to the Marquês de Pombal. Now part of the Gulbenkian Foundation, this lovely pink palace is generally closed to the public (but nobody stopped me from entering its tranquil gardens).

There is little else to see in the town itself besides the fine 17th-century **Igreja Matriz** church and a few seafront fortress from the 16th-18th century just south of the town.

A few km southwest of town, you will find several sandy beaches including the resort area of **Carcavelos**, which attract a mixture of local and foriegn vacationers. If you happen to be around Carcavelos on Thursday, check out it's weekly **mercado** (market) in the town's center where you can find local produce and cheap leather goods.

Additional beaches can be found along the coast at **Parede**, **São Pedro de Estoril**, and **São João de Estoril** but expect lots of company during the summer.

WHERE TO STAY

HOTEL PRAIA MAR, *Carcavelos, (01) 457-3131. Moderate.*

A nice and friendly resort hotel facing the beach at *Carcavelos* The rooms are quite nice and full of amenities. Facilities include bar, gourmet restaurant, lounge, snackbar, pool, sundeck, TV, beach views, nearby shops, and parking.

QUINTA DAS ENCOSTAS, *Parede, (01) 457-0056. Moderate.*

A beautiful 18th century manor house and estate a few minutes away from the beach which offers 6 fine antique laden guestrooms withn private bathrooms. Facilities include gardens, TV room, pool, library, and parking.

PENSÃO NARISCO, *Praia de Carcavelos, (01) 247-0157. Inexpensive.*

A nice and comfortable inn just near the beach which offers 16 good guestrooms with private bathrooms. Facilities include bar, restaurant, TV, and nearby parking.

WHERE TO EAT

DOM PEPE, *Ave. Marginal-Parede, (01) 247-0636. Expensive.*

A wonderful and sophisticated regional restaurant on the Estrada Marginal which offers superb shellfish and grilled meat and fish specialities in an upscale setting.

A CHOUPANA, *Estrada Marginal-São João de Estoril, (01) 468-3099. Moderate.*

A very good fish and steak restaurant on Estrada Marginal with great seafood, good service, and one of the best views in the entire area. Closed on Mondays.

ESTORIL

Located some 26 km west (down river) from Lisbon on *route N-6* is the cosmopolitan city of **Estoril**. This exclusive resort town is primarily

COSTA DE LISBOA

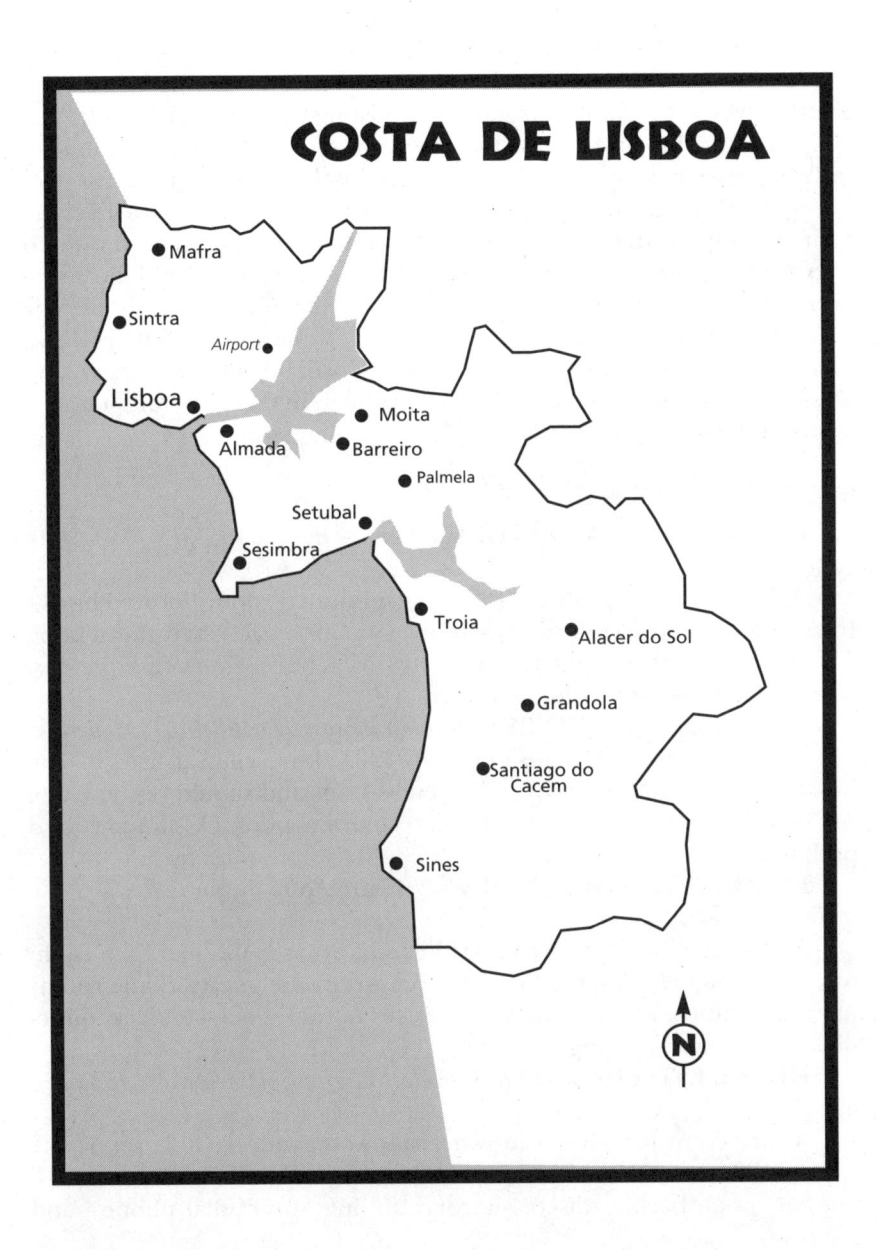

known for it's palm lined avenues, beaches, casino, and mansion sized villas of exiled European royalty. Estoril has become a second home for the rich and famous. Some of the most impressive sights in town are the immense stately houses tucked away on quiet side streets and water-view cul de sacs. Ferraris and Porsches can be seen disappearing behind the gated driveways of well-guarded villas hosting foreign dignitaries. As a visitor to Estoril, I have always had the impression that the most interesting people and places in town are missed by the casual visitor.

Recently Estoril and its neighboring **Monte Estoril** area have become a bit crammed with hotels and condo complexes which seem to pop up over night. Huge events such as the summer concert series, and the yearly evening crafts festival (**Feira do Artesanto**) brings thousands of new visitors to the Estoril area in July and August. A massive Formula 1 **Grand Prix** in September attracts sell-out crowds of over 90,000 spectators in the **Estoril Autodromo**. Traffic is a major problem in this area, and it is best to avoid the roads during morning and evening rush hours.

WHERE TO STAY

HOTEL PALÁCIO ESTORIL, *Parque do Estoril, (01) 468-0400. Expensive.*

A 5 star grand hotel with 162 air conditioned rooms located blocks from the sea. This old world style hotel contains a bar, restaurants, pool, TV, minibars, sauna, golf facilities, nearby tennis, direct dial phones, barber shop, boutiques, and parking.

HOTEL DE INGLATERRA, *Rua do Porto, (01) 468-4461. Moderate.*

A restored former mansion in the hills above central Estoril. The hotel has just undergone extensive renovations and should become one of Estoril's best. Facilities include bar, restaurant, pool, TV, sundeck, and parking.

LENOX COUNTRY CLUB, *Rua Alvaro Pedro de Sousa,5, (01) 468-0424. Moderate.*

A very small inn located a few blocks away from the sea. Each room has been uniquely designed for the comfort of the guests. Some rooms have nice patios. Facilities include bar, restaurant, pool, sundeck, direct dial phones, and parking.

HOTEL ESTORIL PRAIA, *Estrada Marginal, (01) 468-1811. Moderate.*

A nice comfortable downtown 4 star hotel with friendly service. A very good hotel with some good amenities and minimal facilities including bar, pool, barber, disco, air conditioning, direct dial phones, and parking.

HOTEL CLUBE MIMOSA, *Ave. do Lago, (01) 467-0037. Moderate.*

An apartment-hotel complex situated very close to downtown Estoril.

COSTA DE LISBOA   171

A good hotel for those who prefer to cook their own meals. Facilities include bar, snackbar, restaurant, air conditioning, pool, sauna, direct dial phones, shops, TV, and parking.

CASAL DE SÃO ROQUE, *Ave Marginal, (01) 468-0217. Moderate.*

A decent seaview inn near the heart of *Estoril* offering 6 nice guestrooms with and without private bathrooms. Minimal facilities but lots of atmosphere.

HOTEL LIDO, *Rua do Alentejo, 12, (01) 468-4123. Moderate.*

A pretty good hotel about 5 minutes away from the beach. Most rooms have a nice balcony. The Lido offers several facilities including bar, snackbar, restaurant, pool, sundeck, shops, ping pong, and lots of paking.

RESIDENCIAL SMART, *Rua José Viana, 3, (01) 468-2164. Inexpensive.*

One of the better budget properties in the area offering 13 clean guestrooms with private bathrooms. Facilities include bar, garden, TV room, and parking.

PENSÃO CASA LONDRES, *Ave. Fausto Figueiredo, 7, (01) 468-541. Inexpensive.*

The least expensive place to stay in town. This reasonsably comfortable 2 star inn offers 9 clean guestrooms with and without private bathrooms. No facilities.

WHERE TO EAT

FOUR SEASONS GRILL, *Hotel Palácio Estoril, (01) 468-0400. Expensive.*

A fine duplex restaurant serving elegant cuisine to well dressed clientele. You must be properly dressed to feel comfortable in this atmosphere.

FURUSATO, *Rua de Lisboa, 5, (01) 468-4430. Expensive.*

A beautiful Japanese restaurant located at waters edge in a converted mansion. I have only had appetizers here, and they were quite good.

THE ENGLISH BAR, *Ave. Marginal, (01) 468-0413. Moderate.*

A well established nice and simple restaurant with an old English wood and leather interior. Fresh seafood is always available at somewhat reasonable prices.

A MARE, *Ave. Marginal, (01) 468-5570. Inexpensive.*

A small informal restaurant and pub with nice views off the *Ave. Marginal in Monte Estoril*. They specialize in low priced International cuisine with friendly service.

NIGHTLIFE

The nightlife in Estoril centers around a seies of pubs and dance clubs around the center of town, the Monte Estoril area, and the seafront. May people tend to start off at bars along *Ave. Saboia* which runs through both Estoril and Monte Estoril like **Bauhaus** and **Mr. Busby's**. Other people tend to stay around downtown Estoril and go to the cafes and small clubs that line the **Parque do Estoril**. After 1 pm, the crowds gavitate to the hip hop dance clubs like the wonderful **Ruinha** and less attractive **Louvre** on *Ave. Fausto Figueiredo*.

The real late night people tend to dance the night away in *São João de Estoril* at the seafront **Forte Velho** on *Ave. Marginal*. Estoril's older crowd tend to party at the **Casino de Estoril** or the nearby **Frolic Club**.

SPORTS & RECREATION

The Estoril area offers abundant sporting activities. There are several **golf academies** in the area, as well as **tennis, sailing, sea fishing, water skiing**, and **horseback riding**.

In the center of the city is a large public garden with an international **casino** set in the middle. Although small by North American standards, the casino attracts many tourists to its nightly dinner shows featuring topless dancers and orchestrated Hollywood-esque music. To enter any of the gaming rooms you must show your passport, dress fairly well, and pay a small entrance fee. The public garden creates a relaxed and civilized atmosphere to stroll in and is surrounded by several outdoor cafes.

During the warmer months many of the area's young people relax on the sand and the outdoor tables in front of the **Praia do Estoril** and **Praia do Tamariz** beaches. There is a rather attractive **seaview esplanade** that stretches all the way to Cascais.

CASCAIS

Situated 5 km away from Estoril *on route N-6 west*, the former fishing village of **Cascais** has become home to the younger jet set crowd of Europe. Although the mosaic-lined lanes in much of the city are now filled with designer boutiques, Cascais still has managed to maintain an elegant old world atmosphere.

Many European expatriates live in the area and have created a huge English-speaking community. This very pricey little city has evolved from obscurity to become the favored suburb of Lisbon's upper class. Romantic young couples stroll down the beachfront while glowing in the moonlight and being serenaded by the crashing ocean waves.

WHERE TO STAY

HOTEL ALBATROZ, *Rua Frederico Arouca, (01) 483-2821. Expensive.*
Certainly the finest hotel in Cascais. This former mansion is perched on top of a seacliff with dramatic views from several guestrooms and the

COSTA DE LISBOA 173

dining room. Service is top quality, and the food is superb. A wonderful hotel with just 40 rooms. Facilities include bar, restaurant, room service, pool, air conditioning, cable TV, and garage.

SENHORA DA GUIA, *Estrada do Guincho, (01) 486-9239. Expensive.*

A beautiful small inn (28 rooms) which has the ambiance of a rich friend's home. The rooms are decorated with beautiful antiques. Very overpriced for it's category. Facilities include bar, restaurant, air conditioning, pool, TV, and parking.

HOTEL ESTORIL SOL, *Parque Palmela, (01) 483-2832. Expensive.*

A huge and uninspiring deluxe hotel with 404 modern air conditioned rooms. Although the hotel offers friendly service, it's location is not that good. Facilities include bar, restaurants, shops, pool, sauna., health club, minibars, and parking.

VILLAGE CASCAIS, *Rua Frei N. de Oliveira, (01) 483-7044. Moderate.*

A modern seaview apartment-hotel with 233 very comfortable rooms. This hotel is situated directly across from a lighthouse. A great place to stay with facilities such as a bar, restaurant, pool, sundeck, air conditioning, TV, minibars, and parking.

QUINTA DA MARINHA, *Estrada do Guincho, (01) 486-9881.Moderate.*

This complex of townhouse apartments and villas rests on a fine 18 hole golf course. A perfect spot for a family vacation if you love golf and tennis. Facilities include bar, restaurant, pool, golf, tennis, TV, sundeck, and parking.

HOTEL BAIA, *Estrada Marginal, (01) 483-1033. Moderate.*

A simple beachfront 3 star hotel in the heart of old *Cascais*. Most of the rooms have air conditioning, sea views, and a balcony. A good place to save some money. Facilities include bar, restaurants, snackbar, pool, air conditioning, TV, and parking.

CASA PERGOLA, *Avenida Valbom, 13, (01) 484-0040. Moderate.*

A seasonal bed and breakfast inn located 2 blocks from the sea. The rooms are very comfortable although there is no air conditioning. Open April through October. Almost no facilities.

ESTALAGEM DO FAROL, *Estrada Boca do Inferno, (01) 483-0173. Moderate.*

A cute seaside country inn near the *Farol* lighthouse which offers 11 good rooms with private bathrooms. Facilities include bar, restaurant, pool, tennis, and parking.

APARTMENTOS FERIASOL, *throughout the town of Cascais, (01) 486-8232. Moderate.*

A series of studio and 1-3 bedroom apartments and villas scattered throughout the area. Ask the English speaking staff about what may be available.

174 PORTUGAL GUIDE

HOTEL EQUADOR, *Alto da Pampilheira, (01) 484-0524. Inexpensive.*
Perhaps the least expensive reasonably comfortable hotel in Cascais. The location is quite far from downtown, but free shuttle service is included. Facilities include bar, restaurant, shops, TV room, kitchens, pool, sundeck, beach bus, and parking.

SOLAR DOM CARLOS, *Rua Latino Coelho, 8, (01) 486-5154. Inexpensive.*
A converted 16th-century mansion with 17 comfortable guestrooms with private bathooms. Facilities include bar, TV room, breakfast room, and nearby parking.

WHERE TO EAT

HOTEL ALBATROZ, *Rua Frederico Arouca, (01) 483-2821. Expensive.*
The dining room's supurb vantage point above the ocean waves is only outdone by the fine cuisine and wines served at the Albatroz. One of the finest restaurants in all of Portugal. Fresh fish is elegantly prepared and served by very polite staff.

JOÃO PADEIRO, *Rua Visconde da Luz, 12, (01) 483-0232. Expensive.*
This famous seafood restaurant in the heart of town creates delicious Lobster and sole specialties. Although a bit pricey, the dining rooms are full on most nights.

BALUARTE, *Ave. Dom Carlos, (01) 286-547. Expensive.*
A formal and exclusive seafood restaurant with great seaviews from the panoramic seaside prominade near the town's beach. A bit too pricey and upscale for me.

VISCONDE DA LUZ, *Jardim Visconde da Luz, (01) 486-6848. Moderate.*
Hidden behind a small park in downtown *Cascais*, this small and tranquil restaurant serves fine Portuguese food. A very good establishment with great food.

LUCULLUS, *Rua Palmeira, 6, (01) 284-4709. Moderate.*
A great pizzaria and Italllian restaurant with a wonderful hidden outdoor patio section in the heart of *Cascais*. The best pizza in town at reasonable prices.

DUKE OF WELLINGTON, *Rua Direita, (01) 483-0394. Inexpensive.*
An English pub with very good non Portuguese foods. You may find some familiar entrees on the large daily menu. Good food and great beer.

SEEING THE SIGHTS

When arriving in town by car, your first obstacle is to find parking. I suggest that you head directly into the heart of the city and look for either an open parking meter or a space in the municipal parking lots at the end of *Ave. Marginal*. If you have arrived by train into the Cascais station then

COSTA DE LISBOA 175

all you must do is walk along the bending *Ave. Marginal* for a couple of blocks until it merges with the seafront.

Your first stop in Cascais should be the **Praia da Ribeira** town beach which is lined by palm trees, colorful fishing boats, and a romantic seafront mosaic walkway. This area is a great place to stroll along and see the fine regal mansions which line the waterfront. If you walk to the eastern edge of the beach you will find a nice pier which jets outward into the sea. This pier and the buildings at its base are the last remaining vestiges of Cascais' fishing industry. If you walk to this area at about 4:30 pm on most days you can witness the fish auction that takes place at the fish **mercado** (market building) near the pier.

There are also some beautiful *azulejos* decorated mansions hidden from most tourists, which can be found by wandering up the steps at the base of the pier area that lead on to the *Rua Fernandez Tomas*. From this street you can intersect with the *Rua da Saudade* and turn sharply to your right to find the **Largo da Praia da Rainha** plaza and its lovely **Praia da Rainha** beach area. If you wander up this edge of town, you will soon find the luxurious **Hotel Albatroz**, built right on the side of a cliff. Even if you are not staying here, you must take a peek inside of it.

THE SPLENDOR OF CASCAIS' BEAUTIFUL COAST

After a good look around the main beach areas of town, you are now ready to stroll back up the *Ave. Marginal* and this time you will turn right (east) onto *Rua Frederico Arouca*. This street is the heart of the old town, and is where you will find some of Europe's most famous designer shops. The street is also full of restaurants, cafes, and the fabulouus **Panisol** bakery that makes the best coffee and pastries in town. This major tourist street is well worth visiting, but don't expect to find any bargains here.

After you have walked down the entire street, you should return towards the *Ave. Marginal*, and cross it to reach the **Largo Luís Camões** square. Here is where you will find several bars and restaurants that have tables outside in the square. At night, the square is a great place to have a strong beer while being cooled down by a constant gentle wind. If you happen to be in town on Wednesday, visit the regional **mercado** (market). To get there, *follow Ave. Marginal up to Ave. 25 de Abril and take the first right (east) turn onto the Rua do Mercado*.

To reach several additional cultural and historic sights in the west side of town, walk back down to the west end of the beach. Follow the seafront as it turns sharply onto the dramatic mansion-lined *Ave. Dom Carlos*. Keep your eye out for the first street which goes inland at the start of this turn, and follow the *Rua MarquêsLeal Pancada* as it winds its way inland to the **Largo da Assuncão**. This plaza is home to a whitewashed 18th-century baroque church known as the **Igreja de Nossa Senhora da Assuncão**.

Inside the church you will find beautiful *azulejos* as well as several remarkable paintings by famed artists Josefa D'Obidos and José Malhoa. Across from the church you can pop inside the famed **Ceramicarte** shop, which sells high quality ceramics, tapestries, and *azulejos*. If you're in the mood for a little culture, from the Largo da Assuncão follow the *Rua da República* west for a block and turn right (north) into the lovely **Jardim da Parada** gardens. Inside the gardens you can also visit the **Museu do Mar** sea museum (closed on Saturdays, Sundays, and Mondays) to view unusual profane and religious artifacts related to the sea. From here you might want to consider getting your car as many other sights further west of town are a bit far away, but if you don't mind a two hour walk by the sea you can continue by foot.

Return to the *Ave. Dom Carlos* and continue westward as it turns yet again and merges into the *Estrada da Boca do Inferno*. The edge of town is dominated by the seafront **Forte Militar Cidadela** fortress that once served as a royal residence but now houses army training facilities. As you continue on the coastal road you will soon wind up in front of the tranquil **Parque do Marechal Cermona** municipal park, which contains the remarkable **Museu-Biblioteca dos Condes de Castro Guimarães** (Museum-Library of the Counts of Castro Guimarães). This impressive castle-mansion contains a vast collection of rare books, furniture, gold, and ceramics (closed on Mondays).

Almost directly across from the museum is a great little seafront esplanade known as the **Esplanada de Santa Maria**, which offers great panoramic views and a cute snack bar that is built right on seafront cliff and serves inexpensive fresh grilled fish. Further down the same road is the lighthouse called **Farol da Guia**, the huge **Coconuts** nightclub (with its impressive oceanfront terraces), and an assortment hotels and inns situated next to decaying vacated seafront palaces.

If you continue up the *Estrada da Boca do Inferno* for 2 km or so, you will arrive at the famed **Boca do Inferno** (Jaws of Hell), where the ocean's waves crash down into an abyss. Tourist shops, cafes, snack bars, and a small crafts **mercado** (market), located next to the entrance to Boca do Inferno, but the prices are rather high.

There are some interesting diversions in the Cascais area including the Sunday night bullfights at the **Praça de Touros** (bullring) in the suburban northwestern corner of town. Also there is a large complex of movie theaters, fast food joints, and fancy European boutiques called **Cascaishopping**, *located about 10 minutes north on route N-9 towards Sintra*. In the summer there are concerts and festivals held throughout the area.

NIGHTLIFE

The nightlife in Cascais starts fairly early when the after beach crowd crams into the main bars and pubs which can be found throughout the downtown area streets which lead off the pedestrianized **Rua Federico Arouca**. There are also a series of English-style pubs like the famous **John Bull** which surround the **Largo Luís Camões** plaza.

The best place to be after 11 pm is without doubt at the massive **Coconuts** disco and outdoor bar which is next to the lighthouse a few km up the coastal road towards Guincho.

GUINCHO

About 9 km west of Cascais, as you follow the *Estrada da Boca do Inferno* as it turns into *route N-247 north* you will next find yourself at the windswept beaches of **Guincho**. Famed for hosting the **International Windsurfing Championships**, the beach at Guincho seems much like a giant sand dune and is one of my favorites in all of Portugal. If the weather is warm enough, this may be the best beach in the area to take some sun. Beach chairs and umbrellas are available for rent at the seashore beach clubs.

There are several oceanview restaurants in this area serve fine seafood dishes. A former fortress high above the beach is now home to the architectural marvel known as **Hotel do Guincho**, with its wonderful vaulted ceilings and expensive gourmet dining room with live piano serenades and great wines (see Chapter 8, *The Most Memorable Places to Stay*, for more information).

WHERE TO STAY

HOTEL DO GUINCHO, *Praia do Guincho, (01) 487-0491. Expensive.*
A beautifully converted fortress high above *Guincho's* pristine beaches. Most of the 36 rooms feature canopy beds, royal coats of arms, marble fireplaces, and seafront balconies. The only problem with the hotel is the attitude of the not so polite staff. Facilities include piano bar, resaurant, air conditioning, TV, and parking.

ESTALAGEM DO MUCHAXO, *Praia do Guincho, (01) 487-0221. Moderate.*
This 60 room windswept inn offers reasonably comfortable accommodations with several rooms in desperate need of repair. I suggest you see a few different rooms and select the best one. Facilities include bar, restaurant, TV, and parking.

WHERE TO EAT

FAROLEIRO, *Estrada do Guincho, (01) 487-0225. Moderate.*
My personal selection for best affordable seafood in the area. Located just across from the ocean, the friendly service and great food make this place irresistible. The house specialty, *Açorda de lagosta*, is a casserole with lobster, garlic and bread.

PORTO DE SANTA MARIA, *Estrada do Guincho, (01) 487-0240. Moderate.*
This modern seaview Portuguese restaurant offers great grilled Sea Bass and Sole dishes. The waiters are prompt and multilingual. Closed on Mondays.

CABO DA ROCA

On the 14 km ride north on *route N-247* from Guincho, you will pass through the **Serra de Sintra** mountains, sheep pastures, and several abandoned windmills on the way to a small village called **Azoia**. The village offers a glimpse of what life was like in the old days, but offers no specific attractions.

If you follow the signs from Azoia, you will travel on a somewhat scary mountain top road for a little over 4 km to reach the rocky cliff known as **Cabo da Roca**. This cape is Europe's westernmost point and was once though of as the end of the world. The cape itself is scoured by sever winds, and has a barren look. A lighhouse is located on the tip of the cape.

Beautiful hand calligraphied and wax stamped *diplomas* can be purchased (350$00 for white paper, 550$00 for parchment) at the *Turismo* building (open daily until 7 pm) to document your personal exploration of this point.

COSTA DE LISBOA 179

COLARES & THE COASTAL BEACHES

Seven km further up *route N-247 north* from *Cabo da Roca* is the quaint town of **Colares**. This camellia-encrusted village dates back to Roman times. These days an abundance of 300 year-old houses and beautiful flowers surround the village square.

For several centuries Colares has grown and produced a very special red wine from the oldest native grape variety in Europe. Many wine lovers (including myself) consider these wines to be among the finest in Portugal. From Colares it is easy to reach the dramatic coastal beaches of **Praia Adraga**, **Praia Grande**, **Praia Pequena**, **Praia das Maçãs**, and the lovely picturesque cliff perched village of **Azenhas do Mar**. A visit to these wonderful beaches is a must during the summer.

WHERE TO STAY

HOTEL MIRAMONTE, *Praia das Maçãs, (01) 929-1230. Moderate.*
A nice modern 2 star hotel with 72 rooms and a nice garden area. The hotel has several facilities including a very nice pool. A good choice for this area. Facilities include bar, restaurant, pool, sundeck, and parking.

PENSÃO DO CONDE, *Quinta do Conde, (01) 929-1652. Moderate.*
A remote and somewhat rustic manor house with 11 rooms and a few cabanas. The *quinta* is very comfortable and has excellent views. Closed in low season. Facilities include bar, TV room, heating, and parking.

HOTEL DA PISCINA, *Praia das Maçãs, (01) 929-2145. Inexpensive.*
A reasonable 2 star hotel overlooking a rather large pool with comfortable rooms near the beach. Facilities include bar, restaurant, pool, sundeck, TV, and parking.

CASA POR DO SOL, *N-247-Colares, (01) 931-4337. Inexpensive.*
A cute rustic house offering a two-bedroom apartment with kitchen, bathroom, and patio near the tiny village of Ulgueira. Good luck finding it!

SINTRA

Located about 27 km northeast of Cascais on *route N-9 north* is the elegant castle-laden town of **Sintra**. This is one of my favorite towns in all of Europe.

Surrounded by mountains known as the **Serra de Sintra**, this wonderful area really must be seen by all visitors to Portugal. Rich with artistic and royal history, Sintra offers an enchanting getaway for those seeking refuge from the chaos of Lisbon and its suburbs. During the Romantic period of the 18th- and 19th-century several famous writers, artists, and poets came here to work and play including William Beckford, William Burnett, Gil Vicente, Luís Camões, Lord Byron, and Robert Southey.

Many European royal families built their summer residences in this area, often attempting to embarrass their neighbors by constructing an even more glamourous mansion. The **Vila Velha** (old town) is comprised of several ancient houses, many of which contain bars, cafes, and souvenir shops. An abundance of public and private golf, tennis, and equestrian clubs are located throughout Sintra and the surrounding area.

Parking in Sintra is fairly easy, and there is a free parking lot in the town's center.

WHERE TO STAY

PALÁCIO DE SETEAIS, *Rua Barbosa du Bocage, 10, (01) 923-3200. Expensive.*

A very deluxe and formal converted palace in the hills above old Sintra. All 18 rooms contain museum quality antiques and most have beautiful views. The typical clientele here are demanding and usually keep to themselves. Facilities include a bar, fine dinning room, pool, TV, and horse stables. Service here is without a smile.

QUINTA DE SÃO THIAGO, *Estrada de Monserrate, (01) 923-2923. Expensive.*

An expensive and deluxe former convent house which offers 10 beautiful rooms with private bathroom to an older exclusive clientele. They are often sold out in the summer. Facilities include bar, tennis, TV room, gardens, and parking.

QUINTA DA CAPELA, *Estrada de Monserrate, (01) 929-0170. Expensive.*

A 16th-century estate and Manor house offering 10 deluxe guestrooms with private bathrooms and antiques. Facilities include bar, pool, trails, heating, library, gardens, dining room, health club, sauna, TV room, and parking.

QUINTA DAS SEQUÓIAS, *Estrada de Monserrate, (01) 923-0342. Moderate.*

A wonderful old estate and manor house once known as Casa da Tapada which was converted into a great bed and breakfast inn. The owner, a delightful retired doctor, enjoys talking with her guests. A new swimming pool should be completed by now. Facilities include bar, billards, TV room, dining room, library, and parking.

TIVOLI SINTRA, *Praça da República, (01) 923-3505. Moderate.*

This modern hotel is located in the heart of the old town. While it's facade is nothing special, the rooms are very comfortable, and the service here is excellent. Facilities include bar, restaurant, air conditioing, TV, tour desk, and parking.

VILLA DAS ROSAS, *Rua António Cunha, 4, (01) 923-4216. Moderate.*

COSTA DE LISBOA 181

An antique house which is now a small and charming inn. The couple who own and manage the property are very eager to assist every guest. A nice place to stay. Facilities include a lounge, antiques, dinning room, TV room, garden, and parking.
RESIDENCIAL SINTRA, *Travessa dos Avelares, 12, (01) 923-0738*. *Inexpensive*.

A nice old house in the São Pedro de Sintra area offering 9 nice rooms with private bathrooms. Facilities include bar, pool, garden, breakfast room, and parking.
RESIDENCIAL RAPOSA, *Rua Dr. Alfredo Costa, 3, (01) 923-0465*. *Inexpensive*.

This 8 room inn contains simple yet comfortable rooms. A good choice for those of you who are on a tight budget. Almost no facilities, but still a decent place to stay.

A project is currently underway to restore the onetime home to Lord Byron, **Estalagem dos Cavalheiros**. When completed, this inn (situated halfway between the *Turismo* and *Palácio Seteais*) may very well become the best hotel in Sintra.

WHERE TO EAT

CANTINHO DE SÃO PEDRO, *Praça D. Fernando, 18, (01) 923-0267*. *Expensive*.

A combination of French and Portuguese specialties are served in an elegant yet rustic setting. This may be the finest food in all of *Sintra*. Closed on Mondays.

SOLAR DE SÃO PEDRO, *Largo de Feira, 12, (01) 923-1860. Moderate*.

Another French-Portuguese restaurant with very good food. Service is not wonderful, especially during the local market day. Closed Wednesdays.

RESTURANTE REGIONAL DE SINTRA, *Travessa. do Municipio, (01) 923-4444. Inexpensive*.

A good regional restaurant serveing local meat and seafood specialities including great soups and desserts. The prices are quite reasonable.

TULHAS, *Rua Gil Vicente, 4, (01) 923-2378. Inexpensive*.

A very good and unpretentious restaurant and bar in the old town of Sintra. A great place to relax and be casual. Fish is the specialty of the house.

SEEING THE SIGHTS

Several castles and fine museums can be seen in Sintra. You should first start in the heart of the Vila Velha part of downtown at **Largo Rainha**

D. Amelia which is dominated by the **Palácio Nacional de Sintra** (also known as the **Paço Real**). This former home to Portuguese royalty including King Dom João I and King Dom Manuel I can be easily recognized by the two large cone-shaped chimneys that extend upward from the kitchens. The interior is laced with beautiful old Mudéjar *azulejos*, frescoes, and royal coats of arms. There are guided tours of several of the palace's rooms every half hour or so.

Also located in the heart of the old city are the **Museu Ferreira de Castro** art museum (closed on Mondays) on *Rua Consiglieri Pedroso* and the **Museu de Sintra** municipal museum of art and archaeology (closed on Monday) at *Praça da República, 23*.

The *Estrada de Pena* winds its way through the densely wooded hills of the Serra de Sintra mountains above the south zone of the Vila Velha to even more spectacular castles. The reasonably well-preserved 8th-century **Castelo dos Mouros** (Castle of the Moors) can be reached by taking the well-marked path about 3 km up this road.The views over the region from this castle are extraordinary.

A bit further up the *Estrada da Pena* is the outrageously designed **Palácio da Pena**. This remarkable castle was built by the Prussian engineer Baron Ludwig von Eschwege for the Prince of Bavaria who later would become Portugal's King Ferdinand II. The multicolored facade includes several turrets, ornate windows, and a large dome. The palace (closed on Monday) was constructed in 1840 on the ruins of a 16th-century Hieronymite monastery. Although there are generally no guided tours, you can wander around the palace and read the multilingual discription signs in each room. Make sure to take a good look at the 16th-century Manueline cloister which is about all that remains from the site's original monastery. In the cloister you can see a fine *azulejos* covered altar by Nicolas Chanterene.The

The palace is surrounded by the romantic 500 acre **Parque de Pena** park with it's wonderful assortment of exotic trees and beautiful plants, lakes, fountains, and birdlife. A well marked footpath near the statue of Baron Von Eschwege leads up the stone **Cruz Alta** (high cross) which offers stunning panoramic views of the region.

There are fine gardens and breathtaking mansions located on the road towards Colares known as the *Rua Barbosa du Bocage,* which then merges with the *Estrada de Monserrate* that runs through the hills above the old city. Make sure you peek through the gates of the amazing palaces and villas on both sides of this narrow road. Some of these properties are abandoned or not open to the public, but a good zoom lens can help to look deep inside the gateways.

A fine example of perfectly manicured box gardens can be viewed at the 18th-century **Palácio de Seteais**. The name loosely translates to the

COSTA DE LISBOA 183

palace of seven sighs, but the real story is that after the owner recieved the bill for constructing this opulent palace, he muttered something profane seven times. Formerly the residence of a Dutch Consul this grand property has been converted into a rather deluxe hotel where casual visitors are not exactly encouraged, but are typically ignored.

A bit further on you'll pass the 18th-century **Quinta de Monserrate**, once inhabited by William Beckford and later by Sir Francis Cook. The gardens are quite impressive (the mansion itself is not open to the public). Additional fine inns featuring antique furnishings such as **Quinta das Sequóias**, **Quinta da Capela**, and **Quinta de São Thiago** can be found off this wonderful road of hidden palaces and mansions.

SHOPPING

On the second and fourth Sunday of each month, a wonderful large outdoor regional **mercado** (market) takes place in **São Pedro de Sintra** (located about 3 km from the old town). Make sure to look for the wonderful local ceramics and fresh cheeses sold at the market.

AT THE MARKET IN SÃO PEDRO DE SINTRA

QUELUZ

The large suburban city of **Queluz** is *located about 11 km southeast of Sintra just off route IC-19 east*. Although the city itself is not of particular interest, the beautiful 18th-century **Palácio Queluz** is worth the trip. This rococo style royal summer palace and garden was inspired by Versailles and is painted in a deep pink color. The interior includes beautiful crystal chandeliers, gilded woodwork, 18th-century *azulejos*, and fine oil paintings.

The landscaped hedge and flower gardens (created in 1762 by Jean Baptiste Robillon) contain several ponds, statues, and Baroque fountains. Visiting heads of state are often entertained here with the palace staff dressed in period costume. Tours are offered everyday except Tuesday. While at the palace, treat yourself to a fine gourmet lunch or dinner at the wonderful **Cozinha Velha** restaurant.

WHERE TO STAY

Currently there are no recommended hotels in Queluz. In late 1996, a new *pousada* should be completed in the **Palácio Nacional**.

WHERE TO EAT

COZINHA VELHA, *Palácio Nacional, (01) 435-0232. Expensive.*
A fantastic restaurant operates in the kitchens of the **Palácio Nacional de Queluz**. Expect excellent traditional cuisine and fine wines offered in a rustic yet luxurious setting. Service is both warm and efficient.

MAFRA

The historic city of **Mafra** lies some 22 km from Sintra *on route N-9 north*. In 1711 the still childless King Dom João V swore to build a monastery if an heir to his throne would be born. After the long-awaited birth of his first child some six years later, the king commissioned German engineer Friedrich Ludwig to create a **monastery** to house 13 Franciscan monks. After selecting a large tract of land in what has become the town of Mafra, construction started in 1717. The Italian trained German artist Johann Ludwig brought in master tradesmen in from Italy to oversee the estimated 50,000 peasant workers who toiled for the many years of construction.

Upon it's completion in 1735, the monastery had grown significantly in size (over 10 acres) in order to accommodate cells for over 400 monks and trainees, as well as a royal palace, limestone basilica, 37,000 volume baroque library, and over 4500 doors and windows. The world's largest collection of church bells are housed in ornate bell towers at which Sunday morning carillon concerts are presented. A famed school of

COSTA DE LISBOA 185

sculpture flourished here in the 18th century attracting students and teachers such as Joaquim Machado de Castro, Alessandro Guisti, and Giovanni António. The monastery is closed on Tuesdays.

WHERE TO STAY

HOTEL CASTELÃO, *Ave. 25 de Abril, (061) 812-050. Moderate.*
A simple 2 star hotel located near the *Turismo* in the heart of Mafra. The rooms are clean and comfortable, but not very memorable. Facilities include bar, restaurant, air conditioning, direct dial phones, minibars, TV, and parking.

ERICEIRA

About 11 km northwest of Mafra *on route N-116 west* is the former fishing town called **Ericeira**, surrounded by sandy beaches, a few fishing areas, and huge condo developments. Although this area has a reputation for being a relaxing summer resort, I don't find much charm left here.

The town itself is based around the **Praça da República** square which is lined with cafes. From here it is a short walk down *Rua Dr. Eduardo Burnay* to the beach. The most redeeming quality I have found is the reasonable prices for oceanview accommodations and meals. If you're in the area anyway, visit the local beaches – the rocky **Praia do Sul**, and the pretty **Praia do São Sebastião** which is about 6 km up the coast.

WHERE TO STAY

HOTEL PEDRO O PESCADOR, *Rua Dr. E. Burnay,22, (061) 864-302. Moderate.*
A nice 2 star hotel on the way to the beach which offers about 25 good guestrooms with private bathrooms. Facilities include bar, restaurant, radio, and parking.

ESTALAGEM DOM FERNANDO, *N-247-Ericeira, (061) 855-204. Moderate.*
A well located bed and breakfast inn with 12 nice rooms with private bathrooms. A good place to stay with many facilities and a pleasant staff. Facilities include bar, restaurant, TV room, kitchens, and parking.

HOTEL DE TURISMO DA ERICEIRA, *Rua Porto Revez, (061) 864-608. Moderate.*
A large oceanfront hotel with over 150 rooms. The view from many of the guestroom's large balconies are very impressive. Facilities include multiple swimming pools, tennis, and cable TV. The hotel could use some renovations.

HOTEL MORAIS, *Rua Dr. Miguel Bombarda, (061) 864-200. Moderate.*
This 2 star hotel has 40 comfortable and spacious rooms. The service

here is very friendly and prompt. A good place to relax and enjoy the ocean breeze. Facilities include bar, restaurant, pool, sundeck, billards, TV, minibars, and parking.
RESIDENCIAL FORTUNATO, *Rua Dr. E. Burnay, 7, (061) 628-29. Inexpensive.*
A good seaview inn with clean and comfortable guestrooms with private bathrooms.

VILA FRANCA DE XIRA

The bustling industrial city of **Vila Franca de Xira** rests on the Tejo river just at the border of the **Ribatejo** province some 32 km northeast of Lisbon *on the A1 highway*. Since the city has been historically linked to the breeding of bulls for the country's bullfights, Vila Franca de Xira remains a renowned host for many seasonal bullfights at its huge **Praça de Touros de Palha Branca** bullring.

There are also world famous festivals such as the **Colete Encarnardo** (red waistcoat) festival each July which attracts thousands of visitors from all over Europe to participate in the running of the bulls and colorful parades through the city's center. The city itself offers several sights including an atmospheric fishermen's quarter (**Avieiros**) off *Rua Luís de Camões*, the regal **Praça Câmara Municipal** (town hall square) with its adjacent 16th-century pillory, the 17th-century **Igreja da Misericórdia** church with it's *azulejos* and gilt wood interior, and several nearby charming old stone streets such as *Rua Miguel Bombarda* and *Rua Direita*.

The town also contains a few interesting museums, including the **Museu Municipal** museum (closed on Monday) on *Rua Serpa Pinto*, an ethnographic museum near the bullring (closed on Monday), and a local artists gallery.

WHERE TO STAY

QUINTA DO ALTO, *Monte Alto, (063) 268-50. Moderate.*
A great inn just outside of town which offers 10 guestrooms with private bathroom. Facilities include bar, restaurant, pool, sauna, tennis, bicycles, billards, library, walking paths, gardens, horse back riding, ping pong, TV, and parking.
LEZIRIA PARQUE HOTEL, *N-10-Povos, (063) 266-70. Moderate.*
This modern 3 star hotel a few minutes away from town offers 71 comfortable air conditioned rooms. Facilities include bar, restaurant, TV, minibar, and parking.

CAPARICA

The tourist-laden beach and resort area of **Caparica** and the sur-

COSTA DE LISBOA

rounding area known as the **Costa da Caparica** can be reached from Lisbon by following the *A-2 highway south across the bridge and connecting to route IC-20 west for 5 km*. This area has become a favoured vacation spot for residents of Lisbon.

Comprised of large beaches surrounded by condo and apartment complexes, Caparica has turned into a mecca for sun worshippers who take the local narrow gauge train service from one beach community to another. The main drag, *Rua dos Pescadores*, is full of inns and good restaurants. With more than 20 km of almost unspoiled beaches, the area attracts different crowds – Caparica catering to families, the southern beaches attracting singles, nudists, and gays. The fishing village origins of the area have all but vanished in the wake of tourist development.

WHERE TO STAY

HOTEL PRAIA DO SOL, *Rua dos Pescadores, 12, (01) 290-0012. Moderate.*

A medium sized 54 room hotel which barely overlooks the sea. The rooms are somewhat bare but reasonably nice for this area, and the service is good. Facilities include bar, minibars, TV, and parking.

APARTAMENTOS OCEANO, *Rua Mestre Manuel, 26, (01) 290-4253. Inexpensive.*

This large tourist apartment complex with some hotel services. The rooms are fairly comfortable and include kitchen. Facilities include bar, pool, TV room, and parking.

PATIO ALENTAJANA, *Rua Professor. S. de Sousa, (01) 290-0044. Inexpensive.*

A cute little Belgian owned inn which offers several comfortable rooms with private bathrooms which are not far from the beach. They also have a good restaurant.

HOTEL MAIA, *Ave. Dr. A. Branco, 22, (01) 290-4623. Inexpensive.*

This hotel is nothing special, but the prices are reasonable. Rooms are acceptable.

WHERE TO EAT

MANIE'S, *Ave. General H. Delgado, 7, (01) 290-3398. Moderate.*

A cute seafood restaurant with a rustic interior of hanging pots and pans which serves huge portions of well prepared *arroz de marisco* (seafood and rice).

RESTAURANTE CAPOTE, *Rua dos Pescadores, 9, (01) 290-1274. Moderate.*

A casual seafood restaurant which offers reasonably priced freshly caught fish including several local specialities such as *tamboril* (a very tasty but ugly fish).

PALMELA

You'll find the historical town of **Palmela** *31 km southeast of Lisbon just off the A2 highway south*. This castle-encrusted hill is situated on the border of the **Serra do Lurro** mountains. The town itself is made up of several stone lanes and ancient houses which are adjacent to an impressive castle whose ruins date back to the Roman period. In the 15th century, a monastery and church known as the **Igreja Santiago** were built inside the fortified walls of the castle.

The monastery has been converted into the beautiful **Pousada Palmela**. Although very expensive, the pousada contains the area's finest accommodations and cuisine as well as a great view over the sea. While in town you can also visit the lovely 18th-century **Igreja Misericórdia** church and the nearby ancient pillory and fountains.

WHERE TO STAY

POUSADA PALMELA, *Castelo de Palmela, (01) 235-1226. Expensive.*

As mentioned above, this is the best place to stay and eat in the area. The 28 great rooms offer views over the sea. Facilities include a bar, restaurant, TV, and parking.

PALÁCIO DE RIO FRIO, *Rio Frio, (01) 230-3401. Moderate.*

This magnificent azulejos lined palace is really about 21 km. northeast of *Palmela*. The palace is surrounded by trees and offers 4 nice guestrooms with private bathrooms. Facilities include pool, horses, TV, and parking. Worth the extra drive!

RESTHOTEL PALMELA, *N-252-Carrascas, (01) 387-6500. Inexpensive.*

Located just outside of town, this motel style inn offers 60 nice rooms at reasonable rates. Perfect for those who require hotel accomodations at motel prices. Facilities include bar, restaurant, air conditioning, TV, direct dial phones, and parking.

AZEITÃO

The wonderful little wine-producing town of **Vila Nogueira de Azeitão** *is located about 12 km away from Palmela on route N-379 west*. One of the most enjoyable stops in town is the **José Maria de Fonseca** wine cellars.

Visitors can take a tour through the winery and taste several fine *Setúbal* sweet white *Moscatel* wines. Among the best buys in the retail shop are the ancient returned voyage port wines which were brought back to Portugal after years of ocean crossings. A vast collection of antique wine awards and certificates of merit are displayed along with beautiful *azulejos* and a fine garden.

COSTA DE LISBOA 189

Across from the winery is the 16th-century **Tavora Palace**, once home to the disgraced and later executed Duke of Aveiro. Several small streets with beautiful old houses can be found just behind the palace.

A few km away is **Vila Fresca de Azeitão**. In this famous wine-producing town several regal villas and palaces are hidden behind ancient walls and hedges. The **Quinta de Bacalhoa** contains Portugal's oldest *azulejos* and produces an incredible wine from California grape varieties. This former queen's palace is owned by Thomas Scoville, a Washington, DC lobbyist, whose mother rescued its fine beautiful structure, gardens, loggia, and tiles from certain ruin. Visitors can stop by and see the gardens Monday–Saturday, 10 am–1 pm. The *quinta* can be rented for two-week periods as a deluxe family retreat along with its excellent chef and staff. *For reservations, call Mr. Scoville in the US at 202/686-7336 or write him at 3637 Veazey Street, NW, Washington, DC 20008.*

PORTUGUESE GYPSIES ON THE MOVE NEAR AZEITÃO

A 16th-century manor house called **Quinta das Torres** is also located in the area and rents 11 beautiful rooms that overlook impressive gardens and vineyards. The huge wine producing firm of J.P. Vinhos, producers of *Lancers* and *João Pires* brand wines, is also located in this town.

WHERE TO STAY

QUINTA DAS TORRES, *N-10-Azeitão, (01) 208-0001. Moderate.*
This tranquil 15th century manor house offers superb rooms and fine dinning. A very special place for all those who visit. There are also suites and small villas for rent. Facilities include bar, great restaurant, pool, gardens, trails, and parking.

QUINTA DE SANTO AMARO, *Aldeia da Piedade, (01) 218-9230. Moderate.*
A lovely wine producing estate and 18th century manor house 5 minutes south of Azeitão offering 8 guestrooms with private bathrooms, pool, tennis, antiques, an old *azulejos* covered chapel, gardens, TV room, nearby horse riding, and parking.

QUINTA DA PIEDADE, *Aldeia da Piedade, (01) 208-0381. Moderate.*
A relaxing family run country inn about 5 minutes south of Azeitão with 4 guestrooms with private bathrooms. The inn has a pool, mountain view patio, lounge, TV room, gardens, reading room with fireplace, nearby horse riding, and parking.

WHERE TO EAT

QUINTA DAS TORRES, *N-10-Azeitão, (01) 208-0001. Moderate.*
A wonderful inn with an even better restaurant which serves remarkably good international cuisine including fresh meats and vegatables from the area.

SESIMBRA

You can reach the wonderful fishing town and resort area of **Sesimbra** by taking *route N-370 west for about 14 km from Azeitão*. This dramatic fishing beach and resort area rests at the seashore below the cliffs of the **Serra da Arrábida** mountains. Each day, many fishermen line the beach and the narrow downtown streets behind the 17th-century **Santiago** fortress while they hand sew fishing lines and prepare for another day in the open sea. Sesimbra is one of Portugal's last remaining large traditional fishing towns, and must be explored by foot to be fully appreciated.

WHERE TO STAY

HOTEL DO MAR, *Rua General. H. Delgado, 10, (01) 223-3326. Expensive.*

COSTA DE LISBOA 191

An excellent seaview hotel with rooms perched above the sea on a cliff. Each time I visit the hotel there are even more fine facilities and improvements. Facilities include bar, restaurant, pools, sundeck, air conditioning, TV, radio, and parking

ESTALAGEM DOS ZIMBROS, *N-379-Azoia, (01) 223-3954. Moderate.*

A nice 4 star inn near the tip of the penninsula at *Cabo Espischel* which offers 35 nice rooms with private bathrooms, a bar, restaurant, pool, billards, TV, and parking.

CASA NOSSA SENHORA, *Argeis-Sesimbra, (01) 797-1984. Moderate.*

A small bed and breakfast inn owned by an religious Christian women. The rooms are quite comfortable, although not all have a private bathroom. Very relaxing views.

HOTEL ESPADARTE, *Ave. 25 de Abril,11, (01) 223-3189. Moderate.*

A basic and somewhat comfortable 3 star hotel facing the sea with several rooms with private bathrooms. Some rooms are less than acceptable, look at a few.

VARANDAS DA FALÉSIA, *Ponte d'Argeis, (01) 223-3769. Inexpensive.*

Reasonably nice and well located tourist apartments with kitchens outside of the downtown area. A good choice for families who don't mind having few facilities.

PENSÃO NAUTICO, *Bairro Infante Dom Henrique,3, (01) 223-3233. Inexpensive.*

A well located 3 star inn with about a dozen good rooms with pivate bathrooms. Facilities include bar, telephones, safe deposit boxes, garden, and TV room.

A vast amount of new condo units can be rented by the night or week at reasonable rates. *Check with the Turismo at (01) 223-5743 on Largo da Marinha for details.*

WHERE TO EAT

PEDRA ALTA, *Largo Bombaldes, (01) 223-1791. Moderate.*

A good informal seafood restaurant whch serves huge portions of freshly caught seafoods and local meat specialities. Great home style service and ambiance.

ESCONDIDINHO, *Rua Industriais ,(01) 223-3480. Inexpensive.*

A wonderful little seafood restaurant on the back streets of downtown *Sesimbra* offering some of the best reasonably priced fresh fish lunches and dinners in town.

SEEING THE SIGHTS

At night the area's seaview cafes and restaurants are brimming with both locals and tourists who come here to enjoy some of the finest inexpensive seafood in Portugal. If you look out towards the ocean you can still see the many row boats which carry out ancient methods of net fishing. A harbour area known as the **Porte de Abrigo** is located on the western edge of town which contains the more modernized fishing fleet and hosts an interesting daily fish auction. Just behind the harbour entrance is another well preserved 17th-century fortress. A Moorish **castelo** (castle) is located some 2 km high above of the western flank of the old town and provides a great panoramic view of the area.

If you would like a nice excursion, try taking a bus or car ride over to the haunting and almost desolate area known as **Cabo Espichel** about 12 km west of Sesimbra at the southwestern tip of the peninsula. This cape has been a well known pilgrimage area for over seven centuries and contains the simple 18th-century **Santuario de Nossa Senhora do Cabo** church.The church was built to commemorate the glowing image of the Virgin Mary which helped to direct a local fisherman to saftey after almost being lost at sea. The cliffs and windstruck lighthouse of this cape offer superb views over the ocean and beaches below.

If you follow the northern coastline you can visit several fine beaches such as **Praia do Meco**, which is located on the southern end of the long **Lagoa de Albufeira** lagoon.

SETÚBAL

The large city of **Setúbal** *lies some 10 km from Palmela on the A2 highway south on the banks of the Sado estuary.* Setúbal is one of Portugal's largest ports, and is still an important fishing harbor. The new industrial zone of the city has several large factories and is becoming increasingly polluted.

WHERE TO STAY

POUSADA DE SÃO FILIPE, *Castelo de São Filipe, (065) 523-844. Expensive.*

The best place to stay in the area if money is no object and you reserve a long time in advance. The 14 nice guestrooms are very comfortable and have great views. Facilities include bar, restaurant, TV, and parking.

QUINTA DO PATRICIO, *Encosta de São Filipe, (065) 522-088. Moderate.*

A beautiful manor house with 2 double rooms and an apartment (in a converted windmill). The quinta is well decorated and the service is very friendly. Facilities include bar, dinning room, pool, sundeck, gardens, and parking.

HOTEL IBIS, *N-10-Vale de Rosa, (065) 772-200. Moderate.*

A typical chain motel located outside of downtown. The rooms are very clean and the service is very good. Not very memorable, but a good place to sleep. Facilities include bar, restaurant, air conditioning, TV, and parking.

COSTA DE LISBOA 193

ALBERGARIA LAITAU, *Ave. General de Sousa, 89, (065) 370-31. Moderate.*
This nice little inn has 41 respectable guestrooms with telephones and minibars. Facilities include bar, restaurant, air conditioning, TV, and parking.

PENSÃO BOCAGE, *Rua de São Cristóvão, 14, (065) 215-99. Inexpensive.*
This medium sized bed and breakfast inn and added annex has a total of 38 rooms. Service is very good, and the rooms are reasonably nice. A good budget choice.

WHERE TO EAT

CACTUS, *Rua Vasco da Gama, (065) 346-87. Moderate.*
A nice steak an seafood restaurant with great service and very good food. There is also a fairly popular bar scene here during the evenings.

GALANTINO, *Rua Ocidental do Mercado, 8, (065) 319-24. Inexpensive.*
This packed local seafood restaurant serves the freshest fish in Setúbal. Great atmosphere in a casual setting which appeals to everybody.

SEEING THE SIGHTS

The old section of town is bordered by the **Praça Almirante Reis** and the **Largo Defensores da República**. In this ancient part of town you can wander along several stone alleys full of beautifully preserved old houses and other vestiges of the way things used to be.

Just off the **Miguel Bombarda** plaza is the 15th-century marble **Igreja de Jesus** church with its interesting early Manueline design and remarkable vaulted Gothic interior designed by Diogo Boitac. A municipal museum called the **Museu da Cidade** is housed in the Gothic cloister of the church, and contains several collections of antique azulejos and oil paintings. Nearby on *Rua de Dr. Paulo Borba* is the 18th-century **Igreja de São Julião** church, covered with *azulejos*.

A Spanish-built **castelo** (castle) and tile-covered chapel is located just above the city and has an excellent panoramic view of the area. This 16th-century structure has been converted into the deluxe **Pousada de São Filipe** with 14 beautiful rooms and a very good restaurant serving regional specialties.

Recently a large shopping center has been constructed on the main road from Setúbal to Lisbon. Open from 9am until midnight, the mall contains some very large stores and boutiques which constantly have clearance sales.

TRÓIA

Tróia is a long and sandy peninsula *located some 4 km south of Setúbal*. Separated from the mainland by a bay and a river, you must either drive a long distance to access the area, or take a 250$00, 19 minute ferry ride from Setúbal's Doca do Comércio dock and take your car along for about 500$00 extra. Although the fine sand dune beaches are quite clean, major tourist development has created a city-like atmosphere with towering modern buildings. The only historic element in Tróia are the Roman ruins at **Cetobriga**, which are quite limited. Local fun includes golf, tennis, and beach-hopping.

WHERE TO STAY

COMPLEXO TURISTICO, *Ponte do Adoxe, (065) 44-151. Moderate.*
This is the central reservations number for the huge high rise apartment and condo complex which dominates most of Tróia including the Rosa Mar and Magnolia Mar.

ALCÁCER DO SAL

The lovely town of **Alcácer do Sal** is *situated some 51 km southeast of Setúbal on route IP-1 south (also called route E-01)*. First inhabited during the Iron Age thousands of years ago, this area was of primary importance to the Romans who created a major road system that ran through this town.

At one time the village was a Moorish stronghold used as a market town with access to the nearby **Sado** river estuary. The ruins of the Moorish **castelo** (castle) still remains but is now home to several storks' nests.

Three beautiful churches are worth visiting in Alcácer do Sal. The oldest church is the 12th-century **Igreja de Santa Maria** up by the castle, whose chapel has beautiful *azulejos*. The 15th-century **Convento de Santo António** is located below the castle and contains some rather impressive Renaissance artwork. The third church is called **Igreja do Espírito Santo** on *Largo Pedro Nunes*, now home to the **Museu Pedro Nunes** municipal museum of archaeology (closed on Saturdays and Sundays).

This area is famed for handicrafts, including ceramics and hand-woven baskets, which can be found in local shops. A stroll along the town's riverview esplanade is a relaxing way to end your visit.

WHERE TO STAY

HERDADE DA BARROSINHA, *N-5-Barroshina, (065) 623-63. Inexpensive.*
A clean and comfortable inn located about 5 km outside of town in the village of Barroshina with 11 good double rooms and a restaurant.

COSTA DE LISBOA 195

SANTIAGO DO CACÉM
& THE COASTAL BEACHES

The historic town of **Santiago do Cacém** can be reached *from Alcácer do Sal by taking route N-120 south (also called route IP-1 or route E-01) for 21 km, connecting onto route IP-8 south for another 33 km, and then bearing right (east) onto route N-261 for another 4 km or so.*

WHERE TO STAY

POUSADA DE SÃO TIAGO, *Estrada Nacional, (069) 224-59. Moderate.*

A pretty comfortable government run inn with acceptable rooms on the outskirts of town. The pousada features 7 guestrooms, a pool, and a restaurant.

QUINTA DA ORTIGA, *Santiago do Cacém, (069) 228-71. Moderate.*

A nice country home converted and operated as a *pousada* a few minutes out of town on a peaceful farming estate. The inn offers 12 rooms with private bathrooms, a bar, a restaurant, a pool, watersports facilities, TV, horses, gardens, and parking. Moderate.

QUINTA DA CERCA VELHA, *Cercal do Alentejo, (069) 944-04. Inexpensive.*

A nice small inn with two nice guestrooms and a pool in the small hamlet of **Cercal** some 28 km south of Santiago do Cacém off route N-120 south.

ALBERGARIA DOM NUNO, *Ave. Dom Nuno Alveres Pereira, 92, (069) 233-25. Inexpensive.*

A bland but well equipped 4 star inn with 77 rooms which have private bathooms. Facilities include bar, restaurant, TV room, safe deposit boxes, and parking.

PENSÃO GABRIEL, *Rua Prof. Egas Moniz, 24, (069) 233-45. Inexpensive.*

A nice 3 star inn near the town center, with a few dozen comfortable rooms. Private bathooms, breakfast room, TV room, and nearby parking.

SEEING THE SIGHTS

Located in the **Serra de Grandôla** mountains, the town contains the restored defensive walls of a Moorish **castelo** (castle), now protecting a cemetery. Several regal mansions still grace the zig-zag stone lanes of the old town and windmills can be seen dotting the landscape. The **Museu Municipal** on **Praça do Municipo** is located in a 19th-century former prison (closed on Fridays, Saturdays, and Mondays) used by the infamous leader Salazar to house his undesirables. Today it exhibits several decorated cells and various local artifacts.

The most interesting sight are the Roman ruins, known as **Mirobriga**, which can be reached by following the *Rua de Lisboa* for about 1 km before turning right at the signposted access road. These excavated ruins (closed on Sundays and Mondays) of a temple, baths, and market area provide a glimpse into the Roman era. Some experts have suggested that this area was first settled by the Celts.

My favorite reason for visiting Santiago do Cacém is its proximity to several breathtaking lagoon beaches (dotted with plenty of cafés and pubs) such as **Lagoa de Santo André** and **Lagoa de Melides** some 20 km northwest of town. There are also beautiful cave beaches at **Porto Côvo** about 28 km southwest of Santiago do Cacém, and a little further south are more wonderful coastal beaches like those across from the almost deserted island known **Ilha do Pessegueiro** – which can only be reached by paying area fisherman to take you there (and back). Hotels in these areas are terrible, so staying in Santiago do Cacém and taking a day trip to the sea may be your best bet

VILA NOVA DE MILFONTES & THE COASTAL BEACHES

The charming beachfront community of **Vila Nova de Milfontes** can be reached *from Santiago do Cacém by taking route N-120 south for 29 km before reaching the village of Cercal and turning right onto route N-390 south for 15 km.*

The town's position on both the sea and the **Mira** river has made this place a favored summer resort for northern Europeans and Portuguese families alike. The windswept sand dune beaches can become saturated with sun worshipers in the high season, and accomodations become extremely scarce.

The town boasts a beautiful 16th-century castle that has been converted into a deluxe inn, owned by a woman who screens her guests (she has been known to tell people the inn is full when in fact it is not). Try to at least persuade her to let you inside to see the unusual interior.

The town seems to always be in a good mood, and in low season you can still enjoy the views of the beaches and water, without paying too much for the privilege. From here you can also visit the dramatic beach areas of **Almograve** and **Zambujeira do Mar**.

WHERE TO STAY

CASTELO MILFONTES, *V.N. Milfontes, (083) 961-08. Expensive.*

A deluxe and highly atmospheric castle who's unusually picky owner offers selected guests the ability to stay in one of 7 seaview rooms. Meals are mandatory.

COSTA DE LISBOA 197

QUINTA DO MOINHO DE VENTO, *V.N. Milfontes, (083) 963-83.* Moderate.
A welcoming country inn near town which offers 6 comfortable guestrooms and apartments with privae bathrooms. Facilities include restaurant, pool, sauna, tennis, minibars, and parking. The owners are extremely nice and speak English.
CASA DOS ARCOS, *V.N. Milfontes, (083) 962-64. Inexpensive.*
A clean and comfortable modern inn which offers rooms with private bath.

PRACTICAL INFORMATION FOR THE LISBON COAST

CASINOS
• **Estoril Casino**, *Parque do Estoril, (01) 468-4521*

CURRENCY EXCHANGE
Most of the banks on the Lisbon Coast will exchange foreign currency and traveler's checks without hesitation. On my past few visits to Cascais, I was stunned to learn that several banks claim to not offer this service. If a bank refuses to help you exchange, ask to speak with the manager.
   Private exchange booths, and hotel front desks will offer you a rather poor exchange rate. Remember that banking hours are from 8am until 3pm on Monday through Friday only.

EMERGENCY PHONE NUMBERS
• **Emergency Services** (S.O.S.), *115*
• **Director Assistance**, *118*
• **District Hospital- Cascais**, *(01) 484-4071*
• **Sintra Health Center**, *Rua Visconde de Monsarrete, (01) 923-3400*
• **Automobile Club of Portugal** *(Lisbon), (01) 942-5095*
• **Lisbon's Portela Airport**, *(01) 802-060*
• **TAP at Lisbon Airport**, *(01) 386-0480*

MUSEUMS, PALACES, & MONUMENTS
• **Archaeological and Ethnographic Museum**, *Ave. Luisa Todi, 162, Setúbal, (065) 393-65.* Contains collections of archaeological and ethnographic items and findings from the Paleolithic through Roman eras. Open 9:30 am until 12:30 pm and 2 pm until 5:30 pm Tuesday through Saturday. Open 9:30 am until 12:30 pm on Sundays. Closed Monday and holidays.
• **Ethnographic Museum of Vila Franca de Xira**, *Praça de Touros de Palha*

Blanco, Vila Franca de Xira, (063) 230-57. Contains collections of paintings and sculptures from the region. Open 10 am until 12:30 pm and 2 pm until 6 pm Tuesday through Sunday. Closed on Mondays and holidays.
- **Municipal Museum and Sea Museum of Sesimbra**, *Largo Luís de Camões, Sesimbra, (01) 223-3885.* Contains collections of archaeological findings, and information about fishing. Open 10 am until 12:30 pm and 2 pm until 5:30 pm Tuesday through Friday. Closed on Weekends and Mondays
- **Municipal Museum of Vila Franca de Xira**, *Rua Serpa Pinto, 65, Vila Franca de Xira, (063) 220-31.* Contains collections of archaeological findings, sculpture, paintings, and medals. Open 9:30 am until 12:30 pm and 2 pm until 5:30 pm Tuesday through Sunday. Closed on Mondays and holidays.
- **Museum-Library of the Counts of Castro Guimarães**, *Palácio dos Condes de Castro Guimarães, Ave. Rei Humberto de Ialia, Cascais, (01) 284-0861.* Contains collections of 18th century books, oil paintings, antique furniture, jewelry, ceramics, silver, gold, archaeological artifacts, and rare documents and manuscripts. Open 10 am until 5 pm Monday through Friday. Open 10 am until 1 pm Saturday. Closed Sundays and holidays.
- **National Palace**, *Sintra, (01) 923-4118.* Open 10 am until 1 pm and 2 pm until 5 pm Thursday through Tuesday. Closed on Wednesdays.
- **National Palace of Mafra**, *Casa do Adro-Rio Fria-Mafra, (061) 523-32.* Open 10 am until 1 pm and 2 pm until 5 pm Wednesday through Monday. Closed on Tuesdays and holidays.
- **National Palace of Queluz**, *Queluz, (01) 435-0039.* Open 10am until 1 pm and 2 pm until 5 pm Wednesday through Monday. Closed Tuesdays and holidays.
- **Pena Palace**, *Sintra, (01) 923-0227.* Open 10 am until 5 pm Monday through Friday. Open 10 am until 1 pm and 2 pm until 5 pm on Weekends. Closed Mondays and holidays.
- **Municipal Museum of Santiago do Cacém**, *Town Hall, Praça do Município, Santiago do Cacém, (069) 224-11.* Contains a collection of local artifacts and crafts. Open 10 am until 12 pm and 2 pm until 5:30 pm Sunday through Thursday. Closed on Fridays, Saturdays, and holidays.
- **Regional Museum of Sintra**, *Praça da República,2 3, Sintra, (01) 923-4121.* Contains collections of archaeological and ethnographical artifacts and documents. Open 9:30 am until 12 pm and 2 pm until 6 pm Tuesday through Friday. Open 2 pm until 6 pm on Weekends. Closed on Mondays.
- **Setúbal Museum (Museu da Cidade)**, *Igreja de Jesus-Largo de Jesus, Setúbal, (065) 524-772.* Contains collections of 16th-century Euro-

COSTA DE LISBOA 199

pean oil paintings, jewelry, azulejos, ceramics, rare coins, sacred art, and historic archives. Open 9 am until 12 pm and 2 pm until 5 pm Tuesday through Sunday. Closed on Mondays and holidays.
• **Toy Museum**, *Largo Latino Coelho, 9, Sintra, (01) 923-5079.* Contains a collection of toys from as far back as the 16th century. Open 10 am until 12:30 pm and 2 pm until 6 pm Tuesday through Sunday. Closed on Mondays and holidays.

SPORTS & RECREATION
• **Caparica Equestrian Center**, *Caparica, (01) 295-5581*
• **Areia Horse Center**, *Cascais, (01) 289-284*
• **Quinta da Marinha Golf Club**, *Cascais, (01) 486-0881*
• **Quinta da Marinha Horse Riding**, *Cascais, (01) 486-9084*
• **Tip Tours** (bicycle rentals), *Cascais, (01) 486-5150*
• **Yacht and Fishing Club**, *Cascais, (01) 486-8712*
• **Estoril Golf Club**, *Estoril, (01) 468-0175*
• **Estoril Tennis Club**, *Estoril, (01) 466-2770*
• **Oeiras Tennis Club**, *Oeiras, (01) 443-6699*
• **Buzio Tennis Center**, *Praia da Maçãs, (01) 929-2172*
• **Quinta da Ortiga Horse Center**, *Santiago do Cacém, (069) 228-71*
• **Bazano Horse Center**, *Sintra, (01) 929-1324*
• **Estoril Sol Golf**, *Sintra, (01) 293-2461*
• **Liberdade Park Tennis**, *Sintra, (01) 924-1139*
• **Penha Longa Golf**, *Sintra, (01) 924-9022*
• **Palácio Seteais Horse Center**, *Sintra, (01) 923-3200*
• **Sintra Equestrian Center**, *Sintra, (01) 923-3778*
• **Hotel do Mar Watersports**, *Sesimbra, (01) 223-3666*
• **Ernesto Carapinha Fishing**, *Sesimbra, (01) 223-0260*
• **Sesimbra Yacht Club**, *Sesimbra, (01) 223-3451*
• **Quinta do Rio Horse Center**, *Sesimbra, (01) 208-1043*
• **Setúbal Yacht Club**, *Setúbal, (085) 523-915*
• **Setúbal Tennis Club**, *Setúbal, (085) 270-38*
• **Tróia Golf**, *Tróia, (065) 441-12*
• **Torralta Tennis**, *Tróia, (065) 442-21*
• **Quinta do Alto Horse Center**, *Vila Franca de Xira, (063) 268-50*

TOURIST OFFICES (TURISMOS)
• **Cabo da Roca Tourist Office**, *Cabo da Roca, (01) 928-0081*
• **Cascais Tourist Office**, *Rua Visconde da Luz, 14, (01) 486-8204*
• **Colares Tourist Office**, *Alamada C.L. de Lima, (01) 929-2638*
• **Ericeira Tourist Office**, *Rua Dr. E. Burnay, 33, (061) 631-22*
• **Estoril Tourist Office**, *Arcadas do Parque, (01) 468-0113*
• **Mafra Tourist Office**, *Ave. 25 de Abril, (061) 812-023*

- **Sesimbra Tourist Office**, *Cãmara Municipal, (01) 223-1926*
- **Setúbal Tourist Office**, *Travessa Frei Gaspar, (065) 524-284*
- **Sintra Tourist Office**, *Praça da República, 3, (01) 923-1157*
- **Queluz Tourist Office**, *Palácio Nacional, (01) 436-4315*

TRANSPORTATION

Most of the towns and villages of this area are linked by train, bus, ferry, and tram service. For specific routes and schedules, contact the local *Turismo* office, visit a local travel agency, or contact the transportation companies directly:
- **RN Bus Office – Estoril**, *Ave. Marginal, (01) 468-2293*
- **RN Main Bus Station – Lisboa**, *Ave Casal Ribeiro, 18, (01) 726-7123*
- **RN Bus Office – Setúbal**, *Ave. 5 de Outubro, (065) 525-051*
- **RN Bus Office – Sintra**, *Largo D. Manuel I, (01) 923-0662*
- **CP Rail – Estoril**, *Ave. Marginal, (01) 468-0113*
- **CP Rail Lisboa – Cais de Sodré**, *Cais de Sodré, (01) 347-0181*
- **CP Rail Lisboa – Rossio**, *Rossio, (01) 346-5022*
- **CP Rail Station – Sintra**, *Largo D. Manuel I, (01) 923-2605*
- **CP Rail – Setúbal**, *Ave. da Portela, (065) 571-458*
- **Estoril Taxi**, *(01) 468-0067*
- **Sintra Taxi**, *(01) 923-0067*
- **Avis Rent a Car in Estoril**, *Estrada Marginal, (01) 468-5728*
- **Hertz Rent a Car in Sintra**, *Quinta da Penha Longa, (01) 924-9011*
- **Europcar Rent a Car in Cascais**, *Ave. Marginal, (01) 486-4419*

TRAVEL AGENCIES

- **Feriasol Viagens**, *Ave. Gonçalo V. Cabral, 194-#7C, (01) 486-8232.* This small and personalized Cascais-based agency specializes in booking unusual accommodations throughout Portugal. The helpful staff speak perfect English, French, and German. Perhaps the best agency for adventurous travelers.
- **Abreu**, *Ave. 25 de Abril, 79, (01) 483-5282.* The Cascais branch office of the huge Abreu organization. Come here for all types of transportation or large hotel bookings.
- **Wagon-Lits**, *Galerias do Parque, (01) 268-0264.* This Estoril branch office of a major company can reserve tickets for bus tours, airplanes, trains, rental cars, resort hotels and some other services.

16. COSTA DE PRATA - THE SILVER COAST

This relatively peaceful region, which begins about 46 km north of Lisbon, contains the **Beira Litoral** province, the northern section of **Estremadura**, and a small piece of western **Beira Alta**. Although the **Costa de Prata** contains some magnificent beaches, most of the region is comprised of forests and countryside. Many small roads wind their way through centuries old villages and cities, each with their own special charm.

Among the many worthwhile visits in this area include the walled medieval village of **Óbidos**, the fishing port of **Peniche**, the enchanted forest and **Palace of Buçaco**, the canalled city of **Aveiro**, the seaside resort city of **Nazaré**, the turn-of-the-century spa town of **Curia**, the ceramic producing towns of **Alcobaça** and **Caldas de Rainha**, the bed and breakfast-filled countryside around **Tomar**, the historic university city of **Coimbra**, the market of **Águeda**, many fine wineries, and, for the truly adventurous, the **Berlenga Islands**.

The towns and sights in this chapter are arranged from south to north.

TORRES VEDRAS

From Lisbon, *take the A-8 highway north for 30 km or so and connect to route N-8 north for another 29 km* to reach the wine-producing city of **Torres Vedras**. The town charter dates back to the 12th century when King Dom Afonso Henriques captured the area from the Moors. Ruins of a medieval castle still be seen perched above the highest point in town.

In 1809 a secret system of defensive trenches and forts was designed by Britian's General Wellington to defend Lisbon from the invading Napoleonic army. This strategic defensive system know as the **Linhas Torres Vedras** led to the retreat of the Napoleonic troops, and a fine example of this system can still be seen at the **Forte de São Vicente** fortress. An ancient mile and a half long aqueduct also runs through the city. On the outskirts of town you can still find functioning windmills.

The small **Museu Municipal** museum is located in part of the 17th-century *azulejos*-filled **Convento Graça** convent *at Rua Serpa Pinto* near the central **Praça 25 de Abril** square and contains examples of 17th-century coins, weapons, and crowns. Also in the town center is a Gothic fountain from 1331 called the **Chafariz dos Canos**, and several interesting churches to visit including the 12th-century Romanesque **Igreja de Santa Maria do Castelo**, and the Manueline **Igreja de São Pedro**.

About 13 km from Torres Vedras off route N-9 west, there are wonderful wide beaches at the village of **Santa Cruz** that are well worth the side trip. During the warm season you can rent chairs and cabana sized tents at Santa Cruz's **Praia Norte** north beach. Also in the area is a famous health spa called **Termas do Vale dos Cucos** (closed October-April), *located about 3 km east in the town of Cucos* and is known for it's healing thermal springs.

Before leaving the area, try one of the special reserve wines produced by the *Adega Cooperativa de Torres Vedras*.

WHERE TO STAY

HOTEL IMPÉRIO JARDIM, *Praça 25 Abril, (061) 314-232. Moderate.*
A modern 2 star business style hotel in the heart of town. The hotel offers 47 rooms with small twin beds, TV, and private bathroom. Facilities include bar, sidewalk café , snack bar, restaurant, barber, direct dial phones, and parking.

APARTHOTEL SÃO JOÃO, *Rua Dr. Afonso Costas, (061) 240-03. Moderate.*
A nice and modern apartment complex in the heart of town. The hotel has 37 comfortable 1 bedroom apartments with kitchen, a bar, disco, tennis, and parking.

RESIDENCIAL DOS ARCOS, *Praça Rua Norte,1, (061) 312-489. Moderate.*
A simple and modest inn with 28 single and double rooms with private bathrooms, direct dial phone, and heating. Located in the atmospheric Bairro Arenes section.

HOTEL DAS TERMAS, *Cucos, (061) 231-27. Moderate.*
A grand pink mansion which contains a health spa (Open May 1 until September 30) a relaxing garden, a good restaurant and about 21 guestrooms with private bathroom and TV.

HOTEL SANTA CRUZ, *Praia de Santa Cruz, (061) 971-99. Moderate.*
A 2 star hotel right near the beach with 32 comfortable double guestrooms with private bathroom. Facilities include bar, restaurant, disco, TV room and parking. Perhaps the most modern place to stay in Santa Cruz.

COSTA DE PRATA 203

PENSÃO MAR LINDO, *Praia de Santa Cruz, (061) 972-97. Inexpensive.*
Basic accommodations can be rented from the office in the Restaurante Mar Lindo on Travessa Jorge Cardoso. Nothing fancy, but reasonable rates.

WHERE TO EAT

RESTAURANTE BARRETO PRETO, *Rua Praia de Andrada, (061) 220-63. Moderate.*
A good and reasonably priced local restaurant near the train station which serves fine meat dishes in a casual setting with friendly service.

VIMEIRO & THE COASTAL BEACHES

The little town of **Vimeiro** is known for its thermal waters, historical battles, and its proximity to several great beaches. *Situated 12 km northwest of Torres Vedras off of route N-8-2 north*, Vimeiro is home to the historical (the Romans used to come here) springs known as **Termas do Vimeiro**.

In 1808, the British forces under Wellington's command dominated the invading Napoleonic troops here and sent them on their way back to France. Most vacationers visit Vimeiro for the excellent spa-hotel with several curative and sports based programs including thermal baths, massage, golf, and horse riding activities. I had an extremely relaxing visit to the spa just a year or so ago.

The other reason for going to Vimeiro is to have easy access to some of the finest sandy beaches in Portugal. *If you head just 7 km or so to the west towards the ocean*, you'll reach the relatively quiet beach towns of **Porto Novo** and **Santa Rita**. In this coastal area you can find nice beaches, large swimming pools, tennis, golf, lots of water sports, excellent local fish restaurants, and good nightlife. People here really know how to party!

WHERE TO STAY

HOTEL DAS TERMAS, *Rua Joaquim Belchor, (061) 984-496. Moderate.*
A comfortable 2 star hotel known for its spa and sports programs. There are 88 double guestrooms with private bathroom, bar, restaurant, a nice pool, golf, and tennis. Open only in high season.

HOTEL GOLF MAR, *Praia do Porto Novo, (061) 984-157. Moderate.*
A huge 300 room 3 star hotel complex with balconies overlooking the sea. The full service hotel has 2 pools, tennis, ping pong, restaurants, and a nice beach area.

RESIDENCIAL RAINHA SANTA, *Quinta da Piedade-Vimeiro, (061) 984-234. Inexpensive.*
A nice inexpensive inn with 18 good rooms with private bathroom in

COSTA DE PRATA 205

a nice part of town. Closed from mid October until January 1 each year. A good budget choice.

PENSÃO PROMAR, *Praia do Porto Novo, (061) 984-220. Inexpensive.*

A clean and comfortable 2 star inn with 29 rooms with pprivate bathrooms just across from the sea. Facilities include restaurant, TV room, and nearby parking.

LOURINHÃ

Founded in 1160 after many years of Arab occupation, the city of **Lourinhã** *can be found 19 km northwest of Torres Vedras on route N-8-2 north.* This small city contains several ancient buildings, beautiful churches, and a slightly confusing maze of stone streets which create a medieval atmosphere. While strolling through the old part of the city, make sure to stop in at Gothic 14th-century **Igreja de Nossa Senhora do Castelo** parish church.

After a brief stop in Lourinhã , you may wish to visit the coastal area a few km to the west of town. Of all the area's fine beaches, I suggest a visit to the almost undiscovered beaches, cliffs, and fine shellfish restaurants at **Porto das Barcas**. On my last summer visit to this pristine beach there were no other people within sight. The beaches at **Praia da Areia Branca** and **Porto Dinheiro** have become a little developed and maintain a small resort town ambiance. You must try some of the local fish chowders (*caldeiras*) served in the small local seafront restaurants and cafés.

WHERE TO STAY

QUINTA DA MOITA LONGA, *Toxofal de Cima, (061) 422-385. Moderate.*

A beautiful traditional manor house with a large pool, gardens, and 4 beautiful rooms with private bathroom, TV, and heating. The complete house can also be rented by the week with advance booking.

QUINTA DA SANTA CATARINA, *Rua Visconde de Palma, (061) 422-313. Moderate.*

A family owned and managed 16th century manor house in *Lourinhã* . The inn contains 5 deluxe guestrooms and has a pool, tennis, breakfast room, and garden.

ESTALAGEM BELA VISTA, *Rua Dom Sancho I, (061) 412-713. Moderate.*

A peaceful, comfortable and very secure inn with 29 rooms. The many hotel facilities include pool, tennis, gardens, restaurant, bar, TV room, and free parking.

ESTALAGEM AREIA BRANCA, *Praia da Areia Branca, (061) 412-491. Moderate.*

A good 4 star inn on a cliff above the sea. The inn has 29 comfortable rooms, several with great views. Facilities include a pool, bar, TV room, and restaurant.

APARTAMENTOS SÃO JOÃO, *Praia da Areia Branca, (061) 422-491. Inexpensive.*

A good place for couples and families that desire reasonable accommodations with kitchen facilities. Lots of facilities including pools and a great location.

PENSÃO SÃO JOSÉ, *Porto das Barcas, (061) 420-95. Inexpensive.*

Decent rooms can be rented near the beach from the offices of this restaurant.

CADAVAL

The tranquil valley village of **Cadaval** rests at the foot of the beautiful **Serra de Montejunto** mountains, *about 29 km east of Lourinhã on route N-361 east*. Wines are the main product in this area but local artisans can still be found producing wicker and ceramic pieces by hand. Many visitors to this picturesque village come for the many religious festivals, including the annual festival of **Our Lady of Snow** held on August 5 at the beautiful **Igreja de Nosa Senhora de Neves** church.

In the general area of Cadaval there are several interesting sights, including the neolithic cave dwellings 9 km southeast in **Pragança**, and the beautiful gardens at the **Palácio de Gorjões** about 10 km northwest in pretty town of **Bombarral**. Also worth a dare are the available hang-gliding excursions from the top of the Serra de Montejunto mountains.

WHERE TO STAY

QUINTA DA NOGUEIRA, *Portela-Bombarral, (062) 624-48. Moderate.*

A nice rustic estate which operates as a bed and breakfast inn off *route N-361*. There are only 2 double guestrooms and a 2 bedroom apartment with private bath.

RESIDENCIAL LOURENÇO, *Rua H, 10-Cadaval, (062) 664-76. Inexpensive.*

You'll find 22 cheap and reasonably comfortable guestrooms with private bathrooms here, in the center of town. A good budget choice for those who require few facilities.

PENICHE & THE BERLENGA ISLANDS

The seafront city of **Peniche** can be found *jutting out towards the sea, some 19 km northwest of Lourinhã just past the end of route N-247 north*. Located on a rocky peninsula which was at one time a separate island, Peniche has become an important fishing harbor and processing center.

Each year on the first Sunday of August, Peniche hosts the festival of **Nossa Senhora de Boa Viagem** (Our Lady of Safe Voyages), when great fireworks and dancing follow the celebration when the boats of the fishing fleet carry religious statues and are blessed by the local parish priest.

WHERE TO STAY

HOTEL PRAIA NORTE, *Ave. Monsenhor Bastos, (062) 711-66. Moderate.*

A large modern sea view resort hotel with 92 comfortable rooms. The full service hotel has air conditioning, child and adult pools, restaurants, bar, and other facilities.

QUINTA DAS TRIPAS, *Atouguia da Baleia, (062) 757-33. Moderate.*

A simple and rustic private farm estate house about 2 km from the ocean which rents 11 rooms with private bath. Facilities include bar, pool, horses, and parking.

FORTE DE S. J. BAPTISTA, *Berlenga Grande Island, (062) 789-571. Inexpensive.*

You can book rooms at the fort by calling the above number at the *Turismo* on *Rua Alexandre Herculano*. You must arrainge your own transportation. Quite rustic.

RESIDENCIAL FELITA, *Largo Prof.F. Friere,12, (062) 721-190. Inexpensive.*

A small 8 room inn with reasonably comfortable rooms. Nothing special.

WHERE TO STAY

RESTAURANTE NAU DOS CORVOS, *Cabo Carvoeiro, (062) 724-10. Moderate.*

An excellant seaview fish and seafood restaurant with a wonderful menu of reasonably priced grilled fish specialities. Get a table near the windows.

RESTAURANTE ANCORA, *Ave. do Mar,78, (062) 714-56. Inexpensive.*

One of several fine inexpensive and casual fish restaurants near the seafront on *Avenida do Mar*. Try anything grilled especially the sardines when available.

SEEING THE SIGHTS

Next to the large harbor is a 16th-century **Fortaleza** (fortress), which was formerly used as a maximum security prison and now contains a local museum (closed on Mondays) displaying crafts and former prison cells.

The harbor itself contains a promenade called **Largo da Ribeira** where each afternoon the fishing fleet returns with the impressive daily catch of sardines and other fish. In town you may wish to view 16th-century church known as the **Igreja de Nossa Senhora da Ajuda**. The local artisans of Peniche produce fine lace work which can be found in the better shops around downtown's waterfront.

At the tip of the peninsula is the **Cabo Carvoeiro** cape where you can visit the **Forte da Luzo** fortress, a windmill, and paths which will take you to see strange rock formations in the sea such as the stone called the **Nau dos Corvos** (Stone of the Crows) as well as a great panoramic view. If you drive just a bit further on the winding northbound coastal road you can visit the colored tile encrusted church called **Igreja de Nossa Senhora dos Remédios** in the small village of **Remédios**.

About 5 km east of Peniche is a small town called **Atouguia da Baleia** which contains a medieval castle and several nice churches including the 13th-century **Igreja de São Leonardo** with its beautiful nativity scene. A few km further east is the 14th century royal palace of King Dom Pedro I and a beautiful windmill in the peaceful hamlet of **Serra de El-Rei**.

Several nice beaches grace the Peniche area including the town's own **Praia de Peniche** which is getting a bit dirty. The southern coast beaches like **Praia de Consolacão** and **Praia São Bernadino** are much nicer and are only a few more km away. The beach just north of Peniche at **Praia do Baleal** is also quite nice but the undertow can be a bit difficult.

A series of almost deserted granite islands known as the **Ilhas Berlengas** are located 11 km out to sea west of Peniche. Only the largest of the islands, **Berlenga Grande**, is accessible to visitors. During the summer a ferry runs to and from Peniche two or three times each day (if the weather is good) and costs about 1100$00 round trip. You can also catch a ride in one of the resident's fish-filled boats if you don't mind being knee deep in sardines for an hour or so. The island is inhabited by a few fishermen families and thousands of wild seabirds. The island can be visited on a day trip, and if you are in the mood for something very unique you can overnight there as well.

On the island, which is an official National Bird Reserve, there is an ancient fortress, a lighthouse, and several sea caves including the memorable **Blue Grotto**. Some of the fishermen's wives sell fantastic homemade fish cakes for 95$00 each. A local supply store and restaurant also sells very basic provisions and reasonable food. A fortress called **Forte de São João Baptista** was built on the island in the 17th century and has been converted into a sort of hostel with extremely minimal facilities and a cooperative kitchen. A small camping area has also been set up for those with tents.

On my first visit to the fort at Berlenga Grande some 12 years ago, my oceanfront room had no windows causing an ocean spray to hit my face every few minutes. Bring warm blankets as there is no heating system at the fort. If you wish to explore the sea caves and tunnels around the island you can take a boat tour from the island's pier for about 400$00. Berlenga is for the truly adventurous.

ÓBIDOS

If you follow *route N-114 east from Peniche for about 20 km and connect to route N-8 north for another km or so*, you will find the access road to the remarkable medieval town of **Óbidos**. Although hundreds of international tourists are bused into this tiny town daily, it has somehow managed to retain its medieval image and ambiance.

The original castle was built in this strategic location by Celts about 300 B.C. Later transformed by the Romans, the Visigoths, and then the Moors, Óbidos and its ancient castle were captured by King Dom Afonso Henriques in 1148. In the 13th century the town was given by King Dom Manuel to his new Queen Isabel, and in the 16th century a royal palace was constructed at the sight of the original castle. For several centuries the town remained the property of the Portuguese royal family.

WHERE TO STAY

POUSADA DO CASTELO, *Paço Real, (062) 959-146. Expensive.*

This former royal palace is perhaps the only deluxe inn within the walls of Obidos. Facilities include bar, restaurant, TV, heating, and parking. Try a dinner here as well.

CASA DE RELOGIO, *Rua da Graça, (062) 959-282. Moderate.*

A wonderful authentic village house which rents 6 double rooms with private bathrooms in the heart of the walled city. Comfortable but few facilities are offered.

ALBERGARIA JOSEFA D'ÓBIDOS, *Rua Dom João d'Ornelas, (062) 959-228. Moderate.*

Don't be fooled by the antique exterior, this inn offers modern air conditioned rooms with great bedding. Facilities include bar, restaurant disco, TV, and parking.

CASA DO POCO, *Travessa da Rua Nova, (062) 959-358. Moderate.*

A traditional little townhouse in the heart of old *Óbidos* which rents 4 twin rooms with private bathrooms to guests. Look for the Moorish well in the patio.

CASAL DO PINHÃO, *Barrio Senhora da Luz, (062) 959-078. Moderate.*

A cute country estate about 3 km northeast of town which offers 6 nice guestrooms with private bathrooms. Facilities include fireplace lounge and dining room.

ALBERGARIA RAINHA SANTA ISABEL, *Rua Direita, (062) 959-115. Moderate.*

A decent inn located in the heart of Obidos. The rooms are simple and need a bit of renovation. Facilities include bar, breakfast room, and TV. The staff here is not very nice sometimes.

CASA DE CARLOS PARADA, *Bairro da Raposeira, (062) 959-744. Inexpensive.*

This house is located a few km. outside of town and rents 3 guestrooms which offer clean and reasonable accommodations for budget minded tourists.

PENSÃO MARTIM DE FREITAS, *N-8-Obidos, (062) 959-185. Inexpensive.*

A clean and basic 2 star inn a few minutes north of town on *route N-8* which offers a selection of decent guestrooms with and without private bathrooms.

WHERE TO EAT

POUSADA DA CASTELO, *Paço Real, (062) 959-146. Expensive.*

Without a doubt this is the best place in town for fine cuisine in a romantic storybook setting. Try the incredible *ensopado de borrego* (lamb stew) if it's offered.

RESTAURANTE ALCAIDE, *Rua Direita, (062) 959-220. Moderate.*

An atmospheric little bar and restaurant in the heart of town which offers fine grilled meats and seafood dishes. The main dining area is upstairs from the noisey bar.

RESTAURANTE DAS MURALHAS, *Rua Dom João d'Ornelas, (062) 959-816. Moderate.*

A great regional restaurant whic offers fine local cuisine at moderate prices in a relaxed and comfortable setting. The friendly staff even speak a bit of English.

SEEING THE SIGHTS

The town still is dominated by the huge surrounding walls and arched entrances. The narrow **Porta da Vila** town gate is the main entrance to Óbidos, and has damaged hundreds of cars, including my own.

Once inside the town you are bombarded by beauty in every direction. The small village houses are beautifully maintained and usually display large clay pots filled with flowers. Each door knocker, window sill, archway, stone lane, terra cotta roof, and whitewashed ancient house is worth a picture. Around town you can still see remnants of the 16th-century **Usseira** aqueducts and Moorish ramparts. Each step in Obidos discloses yet another architectural jewel.

An important 17th-century female artist named Josefa d'Ayala artist (now called Josefa D'Obidos) was responsible for beautiful panels which can be seen in the *azulejos* filled 14th-century **Igreja de Santa Maria** church. In the town square you can also find a royal crested whipping post and behind the Igreja de Santa Maria you can visit the **Museu da Cidade** municipal museum with it's interesting collections of Josefa D'Obidos works, archaeological finds, and weapons from the Napoleonic battles (closed on Mondays). The Gothic 13th-century **Capela de São Martinho** is also worth a brief look.

Walking through Obidos is quite and adventure. Even though there are only about 6 parallel streets in town, I have spent 10 hours at a time just walking around and taking photos here. At the end of the day you may wish to try a glass of the locally brewed *Ginja* which is an incredible cherry liqueur. Also worth a visit while in the Obidos area is the **Obidos Lagoon** (**Lagoa de Óbidos**) where you can rent windsurfing and fishing equipment, and the beaches of **Praia do Cortico** and **Praia d'el Rei** which are located at the mouth of the lagoon.

THE TOWN OF ÓBIDOS

RIO MAIOR

The town of **Rio Maior** is *located about 21 km away from Óbidos on route N-114 east*. Although most tourists never make to this area, I believe that a side trip to a normal and peaceful village like this can be quite interesting.

The Rio Maior area has many vestiges of prehistoric and pre Roman civilizations which can be seen in several archeological digs at **Arruda das Pisões** and **Quinta da Rosa**. In the northern sector of the municipality there is an amazing dolmen located at **Alcobertas**. There are also several other sights worth looking at including the ruined castle of São Martinho and the 16th century church called the Igreja de Misericórdia .

These days the production of livestock, agricultural items such as onions, and extraction of rock salt are the area's main source of income. To this day the residents celebrate the annual onion festival in the first week of September. The traditional connected white and blue bordered farm houses around the **Outeiro da Cortiçada** section of the town are among the prettiest in all of Portugal.

WHERE TO STAY

QUINTA DA CORTIÇÁDA, *Outerio da Cortiçãda, (043) 479-182. Moderate.*

One of the most elegant manor houses in Portugal. The 7 unforgettable guestrooms contain fine furnishings and beautiful antiques. Facilities include private lake, lounge, gardens, a farm, a nice swimming pool, outdoor grill room, and horses.

RESIDENCIAL RIO MAIOR, *Rua Dr. F. Barbosa, (043) 920-87. Inexpensive.*

A clean and well maintained inn with few facilities. Nothing special but a good value.

CALDAS DA RAINHA

The artist spa town of **Caldas da Rainha** *is located some 6 km up from Obidos on route N-8 north*. Its royal history dates back to 1484, when Queen Leonor took her first bath in the town's healing waters. In fact the name of the city translates to the *baths of the queen*.

These days besides the spa, Caldas da Rainha is known for it's production of porcelain and ceramic wares which can be found in shops around the town's central **Praça da República** square. There is also a daily fruit and vegtable **mercado** (market) in this square.

WHERE TO STAY

CASA DOS PLATANOS, *Rua Rafael B. Pinheiro, 24, (062) 841-810. Moderate.*

A whitewashed 18th-century house near the park which offers 8 nice rooms with private bathrooms. Facilites include fireplace lounge, dining room, and parking.

QUINTA DA FOZ, *Foz do Arelho, (062) 979-369. Moderate.*

A pretty and historic 16th-century manor house 7 km west of town (near the beach) offering 5 rooms with private bathrooms. Facilities include bar, fireplace lounge, dining room, horses, gardens, TV room, chapel, gardens, and parking.

QUINTA DOS BUGALHOS, *Matoeira, (062) 930-517. Moderate.*

A charming farm house located a few km. southeast of town. The house rents a few 2 bedroom apartments with pool access and nice views in a peaceful location.

CALDAS INTERNATIONAL HOTEL, *Rua Dr. F. Rego, 45, (062) 832-307. Moderate.*

A large central 83 room hotel with many facilities including bar, restaurant, pool, sundeck, air conditioning, TV, and parking. The rooms are a bit bland but are comfortable. The front desk staff can be a little uncooperative at times.

HOTEL MALHOA, *Rua António Sergio, 31, (062) 842-180. Inexpensive.*

A simple 3 star city center hotel with 113 rooms with private bathroom. Facilities include a bar, restaurant, pool, sauna, mini bars and cable TV, and nearby parking.

PENSÃO ESTRAMADURA, *Rua Dr. J. Barbosa, 23, (062) 823-313. Inexpensive.*

A clean and comfortable 2 star inn with 22 guestrooms both with and without private bathrooms. No real facilities, but close to everything you might want.

WHERE TO EAT

ADEGA DO BORLÃO, *Rua Eng. C. de Abreu, (062) 842-690. Moderate.*

A wonderful little wine cellar style restaurant on a quiet sidestreet which offers unusual local game and beef dishes at reasonable prices from its open kitchen.

PATEO DA RAINHA, *Rua de Camões, 39, (062) 246-72. Moderate.*

A warm and friendly casual restaurant which serves well prepared Portuguese food and fondues. Try the arroz de tamboril (rice and tamboril fish), it's great!

RESTAURANTE ZÉ DO BARRETE, *Travessa Cova da Onca, 18, (062) 832-787. Moderate.*

A great local restaurant which serves fine roasted meats preparred to order in an unassuming atmosphere. I notice more locals than tourists here, so call for a table.

SEEING THE SIGHTS

Across the square you can visit the famous spa at the **Hospital Termal Rainha Dona Leonor**, which specializes in treatments using the heavy mineral infused waters of the thermal springs. Adjacent to the spa area is the wonderful 15th-century **Igreja de Nossa Senhora do Populo** church with it's fine azulejos and Josefa D'Obidos painting.

Just behind the termal hospital you should make a point to walk through the relaxing **Parque Dom Carlos I** municipal park. This wonderful park has a nice lake with boats for rent and tennis facilities. My favorite reason for walking around the park is that it is lined with several fine artistic museums: the modern **Museu de José Malhoa** museum of contemporary art (closed on Monday), the remarkable house which contains the **Museu de Ceramica** ceramics museum (closed on Monday), and the adjacent **Altier Museu António Duarte** museum of sculpture (open daily).

Another fine museum known as the **Museu-Casa de São Rafeal** can be visited on *Rua Rafael Bordalo Pinheiro* to see fine ceramics made by this local ceramics master who's name stll graces a large ceramics plant in town.

After leaving the park area, you should walk back to the **Praça da República** square and follow the *Rua Diário de Notícias* for a block further to see the lovely 18th-century **Chafariz das 5 Bicas** fountain. Now you can make your way to the bottom of the square and take the *Rua Herois de Grande Guerra* east for about 4 blocks until you arrive at the **Praça 25 de Abril** plaza. Here you can see several ornate buildings including the fine **Igreja de Nossa Senhora da Conceição** church with it's vaulted azulejos laden interior and the nearby bullring.

That's about all there is to see in this great city, but more great sights await you a few km northwest at the **Foz do Arelho** seafront and adjacent **Lagoa de Óbidos** lagoon.

NIGHTLIFE

This city has a lively night scene which tends to be most active in the seaside area of **Foz de Arelho** just northwest of town. The major attractions are the **Foz Praia**, **Big Apple**, **Green Hill**, and **Dreamers**.

ALCOBAÇA

The church-dominated city of **Alcobaça** *can be reached by taking route IC-1 north for some 22 km from Caldas da Rainha.* In 1153, the first king of Portugal (Dom Afonso Henriques) decided to build the wonderful Gothic **Mosteiro de Alcobaça** church and monastery in the center of what has become the city of Alcobaça.

A massive 25 year construction project resulted in what is still Portugal's largest church. The understated abbey has huge open spaces and sparse ornamentation. Inside you will find the tombs of King Dom

COSTA DE PRATA 215

Pedro and his forbidden, and later assassinated, wife Queen Dona Inês de Castro. Also inside the church you can visit several fine **claustros** (cloisters) which contain fine statues of early Portuguese kings, and a massive kitchen.

The town itself offers few attractions other than the many ceramic stores across from the church, where I have found several large *azulejos* murals at good prices (after some creative negotiation). High above town you can visit the ruins of an ancient **castelo** (castle).

A couple of km northwest is a spa town at **Piedade** known mostly for rheumatic and digestive relief. From Alcobaça it is an easy 11 km drive south and then east to the wonderful seaview cafes and sun-drenched shallow beaches of **São Martinho do Porto**.

WHERE TO STAY

CASA DA PADEIRA, *N-8-Aljubarrota, (062) 482-72. Moderate.*

A great bed and breakfast inn with 10 great rooms and apartments with private bathrooms. It is located about 6 km northeast of Alcobaça in Aljubarrota. The house has a pool, billards, breakfast room, and parking.

HOTEL SANTA MARIA, *Rua Dr. Francisco Zagalo, (062) 597-395. Moderate.*

A small 2 star in town hotel with some church views. The 31 rooms are comfortable and have TV, phones, and private bathrooms. The only decent hotel in town.

RESIDENCIAL MOSTERIO, *Ave. João de Dues, 1, (062) 421-83. Inexpensive.*

A good 3 star basic and centrally located inn with some 12 guestrooms both with and without private bathrooms. Facilities include restaurant and TV room.

HOTEL TERMAL DA PIEDADE, *Piedade, (062) 420-65. Inexpensive.*

A decent 1 star hotel in the spa area which offers 63 basic rooms with private bathrooms Facilities include bar, restaurant, TV, and parking. Closed in winter.

PENSÃO CARVALHO, *São Martinho de Pedro, (062) 989-605. Inexpensive.*

A clean and comfortable 3 star inn near the beach which offers several rooms both with and without private bathroom. Facilities include restaurant, and TV room.

WHERE TO EAT

RESTAURANTE CAFÉ TRINDADE, *Praça Dom A. Henriques, 22, (062) 423-97. Moderate.*

A good regional meat and seafood restaurant and Café with an

outdoor dining area during the warmer months and a casual but atmospheric dining room.
RESTAURANTE A CURVA, *N-8*-Ponte Jardim, (062) 431-33. *Moderate.*
A nice and simple little restaurant near the wine museum with good basic food.

NAZARÉ

The former quaint fishing village of **Nazaré** has grown into a major seafront tourist resort. *Located about 11 km northwest of Alcobaça on route N-8-4 west at the foothills of the **Serra da Pederneira** mountains*, the city has lost most of its traditional fishing methods that used to lure tourism here.

Nazaré is sandwiched between the mountains and the sea, but the wide sand beach in front of town has lost much of its appeal since the oxen dragged fishing boats were replaced by motorized craft. Occasionally you can find some fishermen or their widows (dressed in black skirts) sifting through sand on the beach. During the high season, every imaginable square inch of beach is packed with tents and beach towels. The city recently installed a public address system which blasts out terrible music all day.

If you're looking for a less packed beach around Nazaré, try the **North Beach** (**Praia Norte**) just a few minutes away, or the southern beaches at **Praia Nova**. Although Nazaré is famed for fine lacework, I have never found a good deal on any here. Above town is the peaceful **Sitio** cliff, reached in high season via funicular. The panoramic sea views from this upper cliff and the **Fortaleza de São Miguel** fortress are wonderful, and on Saturdays the local bullring gets packed.

WHERE TO STAY

HOTEL MARE, *Rua Mouzinho de Albuquerque, (062) 561-226. Moderate.*
A modern 36 room hotel with lots of facilities including a snack bar, restaurant, bar, pool room, baby sitting services, minibars and cable TV in the rooms.

HOTEL DA PRAIA, *Ave. Vieira Guimarães , 39, (062) 561-375. Moderate.*
A good 3 star hotel with 36 good rooms with private bathroom. Facilities include bar, restaurant, shops, billards, TV, minibars, and parking.

HOTEL DA NAZARÉ, *Largo Afonso Zuquete, (062) 561-311. Moderate.*
A modern 3 star hotel with 52 comfortable rooms (some with views) near the beach. Facilities include bar, restaurant, disco, minibars, TV, and some air conditioning.

COSTA DE PRATA 217

PENSÃO RIBAMAR, *Rua Gomes Freire, 9, (062) 551-158. Moderate.*
A reasonably comfortable seaside inn with 23 small rooms with private bathrooms. Facilities include bar, restaurant, and nearby parking.
PENSÃO MADEIRA, *Praça Sousa Oliveira, 71, (062) 551-180. Inexpensive.*
This small and slightly cramped inn offers decent rooms in the heart of town.

WHERE TO EAT

ARTE XAVEGA, *Calçãda do Sitio, (062) 552-136. Expensive.*
A wonderful international restaurant for the true connaisseur of fine cuisine. This classy retreat is set at the very edge of town with wonderful food and ambiance.
O CASALINHO, *Praça Sousa Oliveira, (062) 551-328. Moderate.*
A great underated seafood restaurant in the heart of town which offers large portions of grilled local fish and seafood. Try whatever they suggest.
RESTAURANTE RIBAMAR, *Rua Gomes Freire,9, (062) 551-158. Moderate.*
One of the better reasonably priced local seafood restaurants specializing in grilled fish dinners served with fries and salad. Try the giagantic *caldeirada* (fish stew).

THE COAST AT NAZARÉ

BATALHA

Located some 20 km northeast of Alcobaça on route N-8 north is another church-dominated town called **Batalha**.

To commemorate his overwhelming victory over the Spanish in 1385, King Dom João ordered a beautiful Gothic **monastery** to be built here. It took 45 years, over a dozen architects, and thousands of overworked peasants to finally finish this opulent 15th-century church called **Igreja de Santa Maria da Victoria**.

The church's architectural mixture of both Gothic and Manueline styles is supported by a series of massive flying buttresses, etched arches, and wide pillars. The interior of the church contains several fine *claustros* (cloisters), sculptures, a huge nave, and straight wooden pews. The tombs of King Dom João, his queen, and their children (including Prince Henry the Navigator) rests in the **Capela do Funidor** chapel. Part of the structure consists of a bizzare seperate structure known as the **Capelas Imperfeitas** (unfinished chapels), which for some reason (possibly a lack of funds) were never completed. The town itself offers very little of interest besides some souvenir shops.

About 8 km south of town on route N-362 south, you can visit the castle town of **Porto de Mós**. The 13th-century **castelo** (castle) and its strange tower-laden ramparts are not open to the public, but they are stll worth a quick look at. Below the town you will find the **Serra dos Candeeiros** and **Serra de Aire** mountain ranges that form the boundaries of the lovely **Parque Natural das Serras de Aire e Candeeiros** regional park. The park offers many tranquil villages and rivers which seem to have been lost in time. There are also a series of underground caves in the eastern sector of the park such as the eerie stalagmite and stalactite laden **Grutas de Mira de Aire**, **Grutas de Alvados**, and the **Grutas de Santo António** (all open daily) near the town of **Mira de Aire**.

WHERE TO STAY

POUSADA DO M.A. DOMINGUES, *Largo M.A Domingues, (044) 962-60. Expensive.*

A nice and modern 21 room 2 story pousada with nice rooms and an excellent view of the monastery. The bedrooms are pretty nice and very spacious. Facilities include bar, restaurant, air conditioning, minibar, and TV room.

QUINTA DA RIO ALCAIDE, *Porto de Mós, (044) 402-124. Moderate.*

A charming little group of old rustic houses in the park which offer rooms and apartments (1-3 bedrooms) with pool, fireplaces, kitchens, and private bathrooms.

QUINTA DA FIDALGO, *Batalha, (044) 961-14. Moderate.*
A nice centrally located 17th century inn just steps away from the monastery with 4 comfortable rooms with private bath in the house's annex. A nice home style inn.
MOTEL SÃO JORGE, *N 1-Amiera, (44) 962-10. Inexpensive.*
A modern 58 roommotel just outside of town. The simple and small rooms are about the least expensive accomodations in this tourist area.

FÁTIMA

The constantly growing town of **Fátima** is *located about 17 km southeast of Batalha on route N-356 east.* Here you will find Christian pilgrims from around the world trying to escape the grips of the sharklike souvenir peddlers and pick pocketing gypsies.

The world famous apparitions of the Virgin Mary where first witnessed by 3 shepherds on May 13, 1917, during a walk through a nearby field called **Cova de Iria**. After the sightings reoccurred on the 13th day of the next 6 months, the apparition of the Virgin told the shepherds three secrets. The first two secrets were later revealed to predict World War II and the spread of both Communism and atheism. The third secret remains locked in a drawer in the Pope's chamber of the Vatican, and has never been revealed. After several years of debate between religious scholars, the Bishop finally declared the authenticity of the visions.

The city has many commemorative shrines, chapels, a large **Basilica** which houses the tombs of two of the shepards who originally saw the vision. The area adjacent to the basilica contains the large grounds where pilgrams gather during the 12th and 13th day of each month. On the anniversary of the first and last sightings (May 13 and October 13) the town swells with up to 1,300,000 faithful visitors who stand on the sanctuary grounds for masses, candlelight processions, and the passage of the statue of Virgin Mary through the crowd.

Nearby Fátima in the small village of **Aljustrel** many tourists visit the cottages of the of the three shepherds and the **Chapel of Apparitions**.

The best way to deal with visiting Fátima during the middle of any month is to overnight out of town (perhaps **Tomar** or **Ourém**), then get in and out of town as early as possible. I don't go near Fátima during these pilgrimage days as it tends to be a zoo.

WHERE TO STAY

HOTEL DE FÁTIMA, *Rua João Paulo II, (049) 533-351. Expensive.*
A large modern hotel near the sanctuary with 133 simple rooms and many facilities including bar, restaurat, air conditioning, TV, direct dial phones, and parking.

220 PORTUGAL GUIDE

HOTEL ALECRIM, *Rua Fransisco Marto, (049) 531-376. Moderate.*
A centrally located 2 star hotel with 54 air conditioned rooms with private bathroom, bar, restaurant, TV room, and parking.
ESTALAGEM DOM GONÇALO, *Rua Jacinto Marto,100, (049) 533-062. Moderate.*
A nice inn located close to the heart of Fátima with 43 air conditioned rooms, bar, restaurant, TV, direct dial phones, and parking.
HOTEL CINQUETENARIO, *Rua Fransisco Marto, (049) 532-141. Moderate.*
A nice 3 star hotel with comfortable rooms that are steps away from the sanctuary. Facilities include bar, restaurant, air conditioning, TV, phones, and parking.
CASA BEATO NUNO, *Ave. Beano Nuno,51, (049) 531-522. Inexpensive.*
A large boarding house with 132 simple rooms with private bath and telephone. A good budget property that is actually managed by Carmelite fathers.

WHERE TO EAT

RESTAURANTE O ZÉ GRANDE, *Rua Jacinto Marto,32, (049) 531-367. Moderate.*
A simple and basic regional restaurant in the heart of town offering reasonably priced meat and fish dishes. The polite staff speak some English.

TOMAR & THE SURROUNDING AREA

From Fátima, *take route N-356 north for 6 km and connect to route N-113 east for another 26 km or so* to reach the historic city of **Tomar**. Located at the base of a castle topped hill on the banks of the **Rio Nabão** river, Tomar is a wonderful place to visit. Unlike other convent and monastery dominated towns like Fátima and Batalha,Tomar has a life of its own. The city is divided by the river with an old stone bridge and a waterwheel, but almost all of the best sights lie on the western bank.

WHERE TO STAY

QUINTA DA ALCAIDARIA MOR, *Vila Nova de Ourém, (049) 422-31. Moderate.*
A beautiful 17th century manor house and estate managed by a wonderful older man who's family has owned this property for generations. Seven beautiful double rooms and 2 apartments with private bathrooms, a nice pool, TV room, library, gardens, a working farm, and a host that will be glad to offer advice on day trips in the area.

HOTEL DOS TEMPLARIOS, *Largo Candido dos Reis, (049) 321-730. Moderate.*
A large modern air conditioned hotel with good service and 88 nice guestrooms with balconies. Facilities include swimming pool, tennis, restaurant, and a bar.

QUINTA DO VALLE, *Santa Cita, (049) 381-165. Moderate.*
A deluxe inn located 7 km south of *Tomar* in *Santa Cita*. 7 nice apartments are located across from a 16th century manor house with horses and a nice pool.

QUINTA DA ANUNCIADA VELHA, *Tomar, (049) 345-218. Moderate.*
A beautiful manor house which offers it's guests 4 double rooms and a 2 bedroom apartment with private bathroom, bar, pool, trails, gardens, TV room, and parking.

POUSADA DE SÃO PEDRO, *São Pedro de Tomar, (049) 381-175. Moderate.*
A nice small lake view inn 11 km. southeast of *Tomar*. This was the home of engineers who built the *Zêzere* dam. 15 simple guestrooms and lots of watersports.

ESTALAGEM VALE DE URSA, *N-238-Cernache, (074) 995-11. Moderate.*
A nice and relaxing modern 4 star inn on the northern bank of the *Zêzere* river across from *Dornes*, some 26 km. northeast of *Tomar*. Facilities include bar, restaurant, pool, tennis, gardens, trails, radio, TV, direct dial phones, and parking.

HOTEL DOS CAVALHEIROS, *Praça 5 de Outubro, (049) 812-420. Moderate.*
A nice 3 star hotel with 60 comfortable double rooms in the heart of *Torres Novas*. Facilities include bar, restaurant, TV, and ample parking.

ESTALAGEM ILHA DO LOMBA, *Ilha do Lomba, (049) 371-108. Moderate.*
A nice and simple inn on a peaceful island in the *Zêzere* river about 14 km. east of *Tomar*. This relaxing retreat can be reached via ferry (call hotel for schedules). Facilities include bar, restaurant, pool, TV room, tennis, garden, and watersports.

RESIDENCIAL SINAGOGA, *Rua Gil Avô,31, (049) 316-783. Inexpensive.*
A modern and centrally located 3 star inn with 24 nice rooms with private bathroom. Facilities include bar, air condtioning, elevators, radio, TV, and nearby parking.

RESIDENCIAL UNIÃO, *Rua Serpa Pinto, 94, (049) 312-831. Inexpensive.*
A clean and comfortable well located 3 star inn with over 20 good

rooms with private bathrooms. Facilities include bar, restaurant, TV room, and nearby parking.

WHERE TO EAT

A BELA VISTA, *Travessa Fonte Choupo,3, (049) 312-870. Moderate.*
This unusual little restaurant next to the old bridge of town offers reasonably priced regional cuisine and strong local wines in a friendly casual environment.
RESTAURANTE NUNO ALVARES, *Ave. Dr. Nuno Pereira,3, (049) 312-873. Moderate.*
A modest regional restaurant which prepares some splendid roasted meats and grilled fish dinners at extremeny afforable prices. A good choice.

SEEING THE SIGHTS

The old part of town contains flower lined stone streets and mosaic paved plazas which are a delight to walk upon. To begin with, you may wish to park your car somewhere off the central **Praça da República** square. From the square you can see and visit the 16th-century church known as **Igreja de São João Baptista** with it's wonderful Gregório Lopes panels. Two blocks south on *Rua Dr. Joaquim Jacinto* is the 15th-century **Abraham Zacuto Sinogoga** temple in the heart of the old **Judiaria** (Jewish quarter).

A few blocks further south you can turn right (west) up the *Ave. Dr. Candido Madureira* and pass the *Turismo* office in **Praça Infante Dom Henrique** to reach and the **Parque Sete Montes** park where I usually stop for a quick rest. Every two years (1996, 1998, 2000, etc.) a wonderful festival called the **Festa dos Tabuleiros** is held in Tomar culminating in a strange and beautiful procession on the first Sunday of July. During the event, hundreds of young women dressed in white wear giant hats made of loafs of bread and flowers while they walk through town. The festival also includes a fair, folklore, fireworks displays, and the generous donation of food and wine to many less fortunate area families.

Imposing itself over the western side of town is the huge **Castelo dos Templarios** (Castle of the Templars) which protects the **Convento de Cristo** (Convent of Christ) whose construction started in1162 and took over 150 years to finish. This fortified convent was the home and operations center of the Knights of Templar. Upon entering the church take note of the doorway designed by Spaniard João de Castilho with its ornate carvings. The cloisters inside the fortified walls have been built around the octagonal arch surrounded 12th-century **Charola** (Templars' Rotunda) which contains the high alter. Two opposing passages lead from the 16th-century Manueline nave inside the Charola to several *claustros* (cloisters) including the bare and simplistic Renaissance style main cloister. While you are in the cloisters you should view the famous Manueline chapter house window. Known throughout the world, this rather ornate sculptured window contains several sea and sea vessel motifs topped by the royal crest of King Dom Manuel I. It is considered the finest example of the Manueline style.

The area surrounding Tomar is filled with picturesque traditional farming communities and riverfront resort areas which are full of fine country inns. The wonderful castle topped town of **Vila Nova de Ourém** is *about 21 km northwest of Tomar* on *route N-113 west*. Here you can stay in a number of fine country inns and visit the beautiful 15th-century **Igreja Matriz** church and view the royal 15th century Gothic **castelo** (castle).

About 10 km east of Tomar you can access the dammed-up **Zêzere** river valley where you can swim, fish, trek, rent boats, and stay at a number of good bed and breakfast inns which line the river and the **Castelo de Bode** dam. In the middle of the river is a remote and tranquil island called **Ilha de Lomba** which can be reached via ferry service. If you are looking for serenity, nature, and rustic accommodations in a natural setting this area is for you. I haven't been there for several years, but my last visit was wonderful. *For ferry schedule details please contact the Turismo office in Tomar.*

Further north, the Zêzere becomes even more beautiful, and the area around **Dornes** also contains some interesting sights including a 12th century tower. The city of **Torres Novas** can also be visited by taking *IC-3 south for 18 km. from Tomar*. The city offers a beautiful 14th-century castle. From Torres Novas, a splendid trip can be made to **Constância** and on to the dream like castle on the island of **Almourol** (see the Planícies section).

LEIRIA & THE NEARBY COASTAL BEACHES

The city of **Leiria** is *located some 46 km. northwest of Tomar off route N-113 west on the banks of the Liz river*. Above the town on a hill is an ancient Moorish **castelo** (castle) which contains a beautiful loggia, a former royal **Palácio** (palace), and the ruined Gothic 15th century **Igreja de Nossa Senhora da Pena** church.

The town has a nice old section which starts below the castle near the 16th-century **Sé** cathedral and continues across *Rua Barão de Viamonte* where the old Jewish quarter once was. From here you can walk down towards the center of the old town to find the **Praça Rodrigues Lobo** square, where you'll find plenty of cafés and restaurants. Near the square you will find several regal old homes and overhanging arches on streets like *Rua Afonso Albuquerque* and *Rua Dom Diniz*.

About 9 km out of town you can visit the glass workshops and stores of nearby **Marinha Grande** to look at some of the finest decorated glassware in Portugal. There are also a few beautiful forest-bordered beaches just west and northwest of Marinha Grande, especially those at **São Pedro de Muel, Praia Velha, Pedras Negras**, and **Praia de Vieira**.

WHERE TO STAY

HOTEL EUROSOL, *Rua D. José A. da Silva, (044) 811-205. Moderate.*
A large modern highrise with 135 air comditioned rooms. Facilities include bar, restaurant, pool, sauna, health club, barber, disco, TV, garden, shops, and parking.

HOTEL DOM JOÃO III, *Ave Dom João III, (044) 812-500. Moderate.*
A modern 3 star air conditioned business style hotel with 64 good rooms. Facilities include bar, restaurant, minibars, TV, direct dial phones, and parking.

HOTEL MAR E SOL, *São Pedro de Muel, (044) 599-182. Moderate.*
A comfortable resort area hotel near the beach with 42 air conditioned rooms and lots of facilities including bar, restaurant, TV, minibars, and parking.

HOTEL SÃO PEDRO, *São Pedro de Muel, (044) 599-120. Moderate.*
A good 3 star hotel near the beach with 53 nice rooms with private bathrooms. Facilities include bar, restaurant, air conditioning, TV, minibars, and parking.

HOTEL SÃO LUÍS, *Rua Henrique Sommer, (044) 813-197. Inexpensive.*
A medium sized modern 2 star hotel within walking distance to the center of town. Facilities include bar, air conditioning, TV, direct dial phones, and parking.

PENSÃO LEIRIENSE, *Rua A. de Albuquerque, 6, (044) 320-61. Inexpensive.*
A nice and clean 3 star inn located in the heart of the old town with 16 good guestrooms with private bathrooms. Facilities include bar and TV room.

FIGUEIRA DA FOZ

Situated some 55 km up from Leiria on route N-109 north is the resort area of **Figueira da Foz**. Nowadays huge industrial harbors surround the city and have polluted the waters a little, but many families still spend their summer vacations here. The city faces a series of wide sandy beaches bordered by a rather busy road.

WHERE TO STAY

CLUB VALE DE LEÃO, *Vais-Buarcos, (033) 230-57. Expensive.*

A small apartment complex a bit up in the mountains overlooking Buarcos and the sea. They offer 24 studio, 1 and 2 bedroom apartments with kitchens and TV. Facilities include bar, restaurant, pool, squash, sauna, and parking.

GRANDE HOTEL DA FIGUEIRA, *Ave. 25 de Abril, (033) 221-47. Expensive.*

A large 4 star beach view hotel with 91 comfortable rooms, some of which have balconies over the sea. Facilities include a bar, good restaurant, pool access, direct dial phones, barber, TV, and a video room.

HOTEL INTERNACIONAL, *Rua da Liberdade, 20, (033) 220-51. Moderate.*

A mid sized hotel located next to the casino and about 5 minutes walk to the beach. The hotel has 50 air conditioned rooms with minibars, direct dial phones and television. A nice simple hotel.

APARTHOTEL ATLÂNTICO, *Ave. 25 de Abril, (033) 202-45. Moderate.*

A large tower across from the beach with 70 small but comfortable 1 and 2 bedroom units with kitchenettes. The building also contains a small shopping center.

HOTEL TAMARGUEIRA, *Marginal-Buarcos, (033) 325-14. Moderate.*

A full service 3 star hotel with 88 air conditioned rooms on a great beach. The rooms are acceptable but not very impressive. The hotel has a bar, restaurant, air conditioning, minibars, direct dial phones, and parking.

RESIDENCIAL CENTRAL, *Rua Bernardes Lopes, 36, (033) 223-08. Inexpensive.*

A good 3 star inn near the casino which offers 15 large rooms both with and without private bathroom. Minimal facilities, but near everything in town.

RESIDENCIAL MODERNA, *Praça 8 de Maio, 61, (033) 227-01. Inexpensive.*

Your basic no frills inn with small but clean rooms in the heart of Figueira da Foz.

WHERE TO EAT

SEREIA DO MAR, *Ave. do Brasil-Buarcos, (033) 261-90. Moderate.*

An excellant seafood restaurant in *Buarcos* which offers several house specials which are all worth ordering including their famous *espetadas* (fish kabob).

ESCONDIDINHO, *Rua Dr. F. Diniz, 60, (033) 224-94. Moderate.*

A remarkably good Goan restaurant which serves fine fish and meat dishes with an unusual flavor (be careful, some items are spicy!). A great value with good service.

SEEING THE SIGHTS

Wandering around this old city is quite interesting. Try a walk around **Largo Luís de Camões** and the artistic townhouses which are across from the ancient pillory and whipping post. I usually start my journey through town at the lovely fountains in **Praça 8 de Maio**. From the old town center casually stroll down the old streets and pay special attention to the villas and mansions which can be found practically everywhere. Several nice parks are located throughout the city including my favorite relaxation stop at the café/restaurant and swimming pool in **Parque Santa Catarina** park.

Worth a brief look is the 18th-century seafront museum-house known as **Casa do Paço** on *Largo Professor Victor Guerra* in which several rooms are covered in Dutch tiles rescued from a local shipwreck (closed weekdays). The **Palácio Sotto Mayor** on *Rua Joaquim Sotto Mayor* is also open to the public and contains some beautiful period paintings (closed weekdays).

There is another museum called **Museu Municipal do Santos Rocha** with interesting photographs and ceramics on *Rua Caloste Gulbenkian*. The unique 17th-century fortress called **Fortaleza da Santa Catarina** and its chapel can be visited at the eastern end of the main beach area.

SPORTS & RECREATION

As far as activities go, Figueira da Foz still maintains a wide variety of resort facilities. A fairly large **casino** complex on *Ave. Bernado Lopes* contains a beautiful 19th-century gaming room as well as a dinner theater called *Le Belle Epoque* with tacky revue shows.

There are also beachfront tennis courts, a yacht club, bicycle and windsurfing rental shops, fishing excursions, a bullring, and of course several large beaches and pools which rent chairs and umbrellas in the summer. The cleanest beaches are located just north of town at the former pirate heaven and onetime fishing village of **Buarcos**. A little further up the road from Buarcos you should stop at the **Cabo Mondego** lighthouse for the panoramic view.

NIGHTLIFE

The nightlife in this resort area starts off at about 9 pm when the younger set hops towards the **Beach Club** on the *Esplanada Silva Guimarães*, the **Perfumaria Pub** on *Rua Dr. Calado*, or the **Branco e Negro** bistro on *Rua da Fonte*.

The late night action takes place over at the **Amnistia Disco** on *Rua de Coimbra* as well as in the **Silver Dreams** on *Rua Maestro David de Sousa*, **Solário** in *Buaracos*, and **Flashen** at the *Praia de Quiaios*. The older folks party at the **Casino** complex that houses a disco and a piano bar.

COSTA DE PRATA 227

MONTEMOR-O-VELHO

Some 16 km from Figueira da Foz off route N-111 east is the village of **Montemor-o-Velho**. On a hill above town is an impressive ancient fortress constructed first by the Romans, and later rebuilt to help defend nearby Coimbra after the expulsion of the Moors.

The double perimeter walls contain several towers and surround the **Igreja de Santa Maria de Alcácova** church with it's unusual twisted arch columns. A beautiful view can be seen from the ramparts of the castle.

CONIMBRIGA

The important Roman city of **Conimbriga** has been excavated about 17 km southeast of Montemor-o-Velha on route N-347 east. The original walled settlement dates back to the Iron Age when it was a Celtic city. Before the 1st century, the Romans founded a city on this spot which was located on the ancient road from Braga to Lisbon. Despite the eventual fortification of the ramparts, the city was destroyed by Swabian warriors in the 5th century.

The ruins are part of the **Museu Monographico de Conimbriga** complex which is open to the public daily and costs 350$00 to enter. Among the most interesting sights here are the beautiful mosaic floors made with tiny colored rocks. There is a fully excavated noble house called the **Casa do Cantaber** which contains remnants of warm air ventilation systems, private baths, plumbing systems, and indoor hot and cold water indoor baths.

There is also a public bath house with steam baths, a few ancient stores, ruins of an aqueduct, a palatial dwelling, an inn, and the famous **House of Fountains** adorned with beautiful painting and awesome mosaics. Be sure to either take a guided tour, or buy one of the English guide books and maps.

COIMBRA

The enchanting old university city of **Coimbra** is *situated some 16 km northeast of Conimbriga off route N-1 north on the banks of the **Mondego** river*. Coimbra is a wonderful city to explore, especially if you are in the mood for lots of walking. In every corner of town there is a youthful element which seems to blend in well with the Medieval character of the city. There are beautiful sections of the city which are full of ancient history, but function at full 20th century speed.

While the site of present day Coimbra has been inhabited since prehistoric times, this former Roman village greatly enlarged in both population and importance just after the Saubians conquered the nearby city of **Conimbriga**. After Dom Afonso Henriques I moved the royal court from Guimarães, he chose the Christian stronghold of Coimbra as nation's next capitol. Coimbra continued to prosper as Portugal's capitol until King Dom Afonso III moved the royal court to Lisbon in the mid 13th century. In 1537 Coimbra's royal palace became the home to Portugal's oldest university which was first established in Lisbon over 200 years earlier. To this day the city has maintained strong links to it's traditions and history. Many students can still be seen walking around town dressed in traditional black robes with colored ribbons indicating which college they belong to.

Parking remains a bit difficult in town but there are several public lots along the river at *Ave. Marginal* and *Ave. Emidio Navarro*.

WHERE TO STAY

HOTEL ASTÓRIA, *Ave. Emidio Navarro,21, (039) 220-55. Moderate.*
A deco era hotel with large and comfortable guestrooms. The service is top quality, and many of it's 64 air conditioned period rooms look out onto the *Mondego* river. Facilities include bar, restaurant, direct dial phones, cable TV, and nearby parking.

HOTEL TIVOLI, *Rua João Machado, (039) 239-34. Moderate.*
A modern business style hotel in the commercial district of town. The 100 air conditioned rooms are rather large. The hotel has a bar, restaurant, pool, sauna, health club, minibars, direct dial phones, TV, and parking.

HOTEL DOM LUÍS, *N-1-Santa Clara, (039) 442-510. Moderate.*
A new tower style 3 star hotel across the bridge from *Coimbra* with good city views, 100 big air conditioned rooms with cable TV, and often terrible service.

RESIDENCIAL PARQUE, *Ave. Emidio Navarro,42, (039) 292-02. Inexpensive.*
A nice and simple inn with 29 clean and comfortable rooms with private bathrooms. A good budget choice.

PENSÃO MODENA, *Rua Adelino Veiga,9, (039) 254-13. Inexpensive.*
A fairly nice 3 star inn near the *Praça de Comércio* which offers 30 small but comfortable rooms with private bathrooms. Facilities include TV room and phones.

HOTEL MONDEGO, *Largo das Ameias,4, (039) 290-87. Inexpensive.*
A simple 1 star hotel in the commercial district with almost acceptable small rooms with and without private bathroom.

WHERE TO EAT

TROVADOR, *Largo da Sé Velha, (039) 254-75. Moderate.*
An almost fancy restaurant right near the old cathedral with great

service, excellent meat dishes, a casual atmosphere, and *Fado* on weekends. Closed on Mondays.

ZÉ MANUEL, *Beco do Forno, 12, (039) 237-90. Inexpensive.*

This packed well known *Coimbra* hotspot is adorned with rustic furniture and walls full of old poems. The cuisine here are amazing, and the portions are huge.

ADEGA PAÇO DO CONDE, *Rua Paço do Conde, 1, (039) 256-05. Inexpensive.*

A simple barbecue restaurant which caters to mostly students. Nothing fancy.

SEEING THE SIGHTS

The **Largo da Portagem** is the best place to start your first excursion into the heart of Coimbra. This delta-shaped public plaza directly across from the **Ponte de Santa Clara** bridge marks the beginning of the **Baixa** (lower) section of town. The *Largo da Portagem* funnels down onto the *Rua Ferreira Borges*, featuring several cafés full of students and local blue collar workers loudly gossiping each morning.

After a stop for a good coffee, you should continue up boutique-laden *Rua Ferreira Borges* for a few hundred yards and turn left to descend a set of stairs towards the **Praça do Comércio**. This square is the crossroads of downtown. Besides the fine shops, bakeries, and cafés that line the plaza, you can't help but notice the dramatic **Igreja da São Tiago** off to the far right side. This 13th-century church is usually covered with pigeons, but you can still see it's arched spiral columned doorway.and bold facade.

Almost all of the streets commencing at the Praça do Comércio contain small shops that sell everything from high quality shoes and fabrics to horse meat. An occasional Mormon from Utah can be found stalking the plaza looking for today's catch.

After a good look around Praça do Comércio, head back down the *Rua Ferreira Borges* for a block or so until you reach the 12th century **Porta Almedina** gate with its adjacent medieval tower. If you walk through the gate you will soon find the *Rua Quebra Costas,* which leads several stairs to the **Largo de Sé Velha** square in which stands the 12th-century Romanesque **Sé Velha** (old cathedral) dating back to the time when Coimbra was the new capital of Portugal. The fortress-like design of the Sé Velha was created by Frenchmen Robert of Auverne. Although the facade is not particularly unusual, the interior contains a beautiful Gothic altarpiece designed by Flemish artists Gand and Y'pres, several Jean de Rouen carvings from the early 16th century, and a 13th century cloister.

A few blocks away from the Sé Velha up *Rua de Borges Carneiro* you will find the **Museu Nacional Machado de Castro** located inside the ornate former archbishop's palace (closed on Mondays) The museum contains many ancient artworks including statues, sculptures, gold, silver, pottery, altarpieces, and paintings from as far back as the 12th century. The museum also exhibits prehistoric artifacts, Roman ruins, and a magnificent courtyard with a 2 level panoramic loggia and terrace. Just outside of the museum you will notice the 12th century **Igreja de São Salvador** church as well as the 17th century **Sé Nova** (New Cathedral) which are both worth a short tour.

From the Sé Nova you will walk down (south) for a block to reach the **Velha Universidade** (old university) via the 17th-century **Porta Ferrea** (The Iron Gate). This arch opens onto a three sided courtyard called the **Patio das Escolas** (student's patio) containing several regal buildings, a 18th century clock tower, the former royal palace, and a large statue of King Dom Pedro III.

From here use the stairs to get to the **Sala dos Capelos**, now contains paintings of former kings. A chapel known as the **Capela de São Miguel** is entered via a regal Manueline doorway encrusted with royal symbolism and upon entering you can't miss it's wonderful azulejos, frescoes, and ancient pipe organ. Just off to the left is the 18th-century library known as the **Biblioteca Joanina** with its three huge rooms with gilded shelves loaded with leather and gold bound antique volumes, fine antique furniture, and Baroque trimmings everywhere. I have never seen a library like this anywhere else in the world. From behind the university you can access the **Jardim Botánico** gardens which contain the **Aqueducto de São Sebastian** aqueduct.

After a restful stop at the botanical gardens you can walk back along the Mondego river until you are once again at the *Largo da Portagem* plaza. This time you will continue up *Rua Ferreia Borges* and again pass through the **Almedina** gate. This time you will turn left (north) on *Rua de Sobre Ripas* until you reach the **Palácio de Sub Ripas** palace. The beautiful tower was once part of the city's wall fortifications but was subsequently converted into a private mansion and remains closed to the public.

You can however enter the **Torre de Anto** tower just a bit further up *Rua de Sobre-Ripas*, which is now home to an artist's cooperative and store (closed most Saturdays and Sundays). From here you should double back through the Almedina gate and can turn right (north) up *Rua Rua Ferreira Borges* which soon turn into the *Rua Visconde Visconde da Luz*.

Several hundred yards up *Rua Visconde da Luz* you will run into the **Praça 8 de Maio**. I suggest a brief rest and relaxation stop in the converted chapel which now is home to the impressive **Café Santa Cruz** (closed on Sunday). From the café's outside tables you can stare at the 12th century **Mosteiro de Santa Cruz** which is perhaps the most dramatic church in all of Coimbra. The monastery was almost completely rebuilt in the 16th century, but the facade has been severely eroded by pollution. Inside this

COSTA DE PRATA 231

massive structure you will marvel at the beautiful Manueline ceiling, 16th and 17th century master paintings, fantastically carved choir chairs, haunting royal tombs, a azulejos lined nave, and a remarkable Renaissance pulpit. At the back of the church are the pretty **Jardim de Manga** gardens and fountain which you will pass along the way to town's covered daily **mercado** (market) and gypsy fair just a block or so behind the garden.

Now that you have seen most of the sights in Coimbra itself, you may want to return to the riverfront area and get your car. If you cross the Ponte de Santa Clara bridge to the other bank of the river, you can visit a few additional sights in **Santa Clara**. Just off the *Ave. João das Regras* you will find the ruins of the gothic 14th-century **Convento de Santa Clara a Velha**. The tombs of Inês de Castro (the murdered wife of king Dom Pedro) and and the queen St. Isabel were once located here, but were moved after several floods began to destroy this old convent.

A few blocks behind this convent stands the newer 17th-century **Convento de Santa Clara a Nova** which contains both the original stone tomb of queen St. Isabel and the 17th century silver tomb which she was moved into, as well as a variety of fine paintings and gilted woodwork. The small and uninteresting **Museu Militar** military museum is located in part of this convent (open daily).

Also in the same vicinity of these convents is the **Portugal dos Pequenitos** children's park which contains scale models of various Portuguese buildings and other minature structures.

The other remaining sight on this side of the river is the eerie **Quinta das Lagrimas** manor house and park off *Rua António Goncalves*. This private estate is where Dona Inês de Castro, the forbidden wife of then prince Pedro was assisinated under orders of his father (King Afonso IV). Although the quinta is not in great shape, you can still see much of it from the roadside. Entrance is strictly forbidden to the public.

NIGHTLIFE

Since the majority of nightlife is centered around the students, most of the better cafes and bars are near the university and the *Parque de Santa Cruz*. Try walking around the **Praça da República** and pick your favorite café or dance club. The best spot in town forr late night drinking may be at the **Noites Longas** on *Rua Garrett, 9*, which is an architectural masterpiece with great jazz.

Otherwise your best bet is to find an English-speaking student and ask for a recommendation.

BUÇACO, LUSO, & MEALHADA

The magical forest and castle of **Buçaco** (also spelt *Bussaco* or *Buccaco*) is one of the most picturesque areas in all of Portugal. This 248-acre national forest can be reached *from Coimbra by taking route IC-2 or the A-1 highway north for about 19 km to the Mealhada exit, and following route N-234 east for another 7 km through Luso where you will find signs to Buçaco.*

The **Mata do Buçaco** forest was originally inhabited by Benedictine monks over 1200 years ago. Upon the arrival of the Carmelite monks in the 17th century, a monastery was constructed and the forest was surrounded by a stone wall about a yard tall with several gated entrances and women were forbidden to enter. As these barefooted monks wandered through their forest they constructed simple hermitages throughout the forest to exist in complete isolation for long periods of time, 11 of which can still be seen.

The Carmelites were obsessed with the preservation of this area, and started to plant hundreds of exotic species of trees from all over the world including Australian Bunya-buyna Pine, Tasmanian Eucalyptus, Californian Sequóias, Moroccan Cedars, and many other species. In order to protect Europe's most unique forest, Pope Urban VIII signed an edict in 1643 to excommunicate any person harming a tree in Buçaco.

Things were relatively quiet at Buçaco until September 1810 when the Napoleonic troops under Massena challenged Wellington's English and Portuguese forces in what would be remembered as the Battle of *Buçaco*. The French troops attacked up a foggy hill and were repeatedly repelled back down. Wellington was victorious and left Buçaco to regroup his troops behind the secret Torres Vedras lines which would eventually lead to the final victory and repulsion of the invading French forces.

After the dismantlement of all religious orders in 1834, the Carmelites were evicted from Buçaco, and the property was passed on to the state. The preservation still continues, and the forest is one of my favorite places to visit in Europe. The Department of Waters and Forests has administered the land and has since planted many more varieties of plants.

A project was started in the 18th century to convert the monastery grounds into a royal hunting lodge. Parts of the original monastery still exist including the mosaic covered chapel and some monastic cells. The royal hunting lodge was designed in 1888 by Italian architect Luigi Manini with a neo Manueline style. Now known simply as **Palácio Buçaco**, it's fantastic facade is adjacent to the remaining parts of the monastery. Beautiful *azulejos* cover both the interior walls and covered exterior perimeters. The public spaces are filled with fine antique furniture, beautiful paintings, terra cotta trimmings, ornate patios, and many amusing artifacts of an age long gone. The huge red carpeted main staircase is surrounded by historical *azulejos*, a large stained glass window, and a suit of armour which guides you up to what are now the deluxe guestrooms.

The project was completed in 1907, but the royal family never officially used the palace before King Dom Manuel II abdicated the throne and the royal family was banished from power. In 1910, the palace became a deluxe hotel with its own excellent winery and one of the most elegant restaurants in the world. In my opinion, this is the best hotel in Portugal.

The grounds at Buçaco are well maintained and include beautiful gardens which surround a large pond with friendly swans. There are several trails which wind through the forest and can provide a wonderful afternoon of trekking past streams, waterfalls, and historical monuments.

You can wander through the forest on the well-marked paths and visit some of the hermitages, the **Fonte Fria** spring with its 144 stone stairs, the 17th-century chapels along the **Via Sacra** (sacred way) the **Rua dos Fetos** (Fern Alley), several of the original gates such as the **Portas de Coimbra**, and the beautiful view of the whole region from the *Cruz Alta* cross. Outside the wall there is an Obelisk monument to the Battle of Buçaco as well as the **Museu Militar** military museum (closed on Mondays).

Just below the forest is the pretty little spa town of **Luso** with its famous curative thermal springs. Here visitors from around the world come to bath in the warm mineral rich slightly radioactive waters are piped into the town's famous spa. To compliment its well known healing facilities, the town of Luso boasts tennis, swimming pools, walking trails, and boating. Luso also bottles a less potent mineral water which in my opinion is the best tasting water in Portugal.

A bit further east from Luso is the traditional town of **Mealhada**, whose route N-1 has the region's finest *churrascaria* (roasted suckling pig) restaurants. Ask at your hotel for reservations at a special restaurant and former stage coach stop known as **Pompeu**, in the village of **Malaposta**.

WHERE TO STAY

PALÁCIO HOTEL DO BUÇACO, *Palácio Buçaco, (031) 930-204. Expensive.*

The finest hotel in all of Portugal, the Palácio offers 66 rooms in both modern and deco styles. The hotel has its own winery, huge gardens, fine furnishings, *azulejos*-covered walls, a peaceful lounge, an excellent restaurant, air conditioning, tennis, direct dial phones, cable TV, gardens, trails, and lots of parking.

VILLA DUPARCHY, *Mealhada, (031) 939-120. Moderate.*

A delightful 19th-century manor house and estate just off *route N-234* some 6 km above Mealhada which offers 6 great guestrooms with private bathroms. Facilities include dining room, fireside lounges, pool, gardens, TV room, and fine furnishings.

GRANDE HOTEL DAS TERMAS, *Rua dos Banhos-Luso, (031) 930-450. Moderate.*

A nice large 173 room hotel next to a park in the heart of *Luso*. The spa and *Fonte de São João* spring is located steps away. Lots of facilities including bar, restaurant, pool, tennis, squash, billards, disco, direct dial phones, TV, and parking.

HOTEL EDEN, *Rua Emidio Navarro-Luso, (031) 939-171. Moderate.*

A full service hotel with 56 good rooms. Facilities include bar, restaurant, minibars, TV, and parking. Very close to the spa.

PENSÃO ALEGRE, *Rua Emidio Navarro-Luso, (031) 939-251. Inexpensive.*

A nice 3 star antique inn with large and comfortable rooms with private bathroom and lots of charm.

WHERE TO EAT

PALÁCIO HOTEL DO BUÇACO, *Palácio Buçaco, (031) 930-204. Expensive.*

The best food in the region is served in this amazing dining room. Specials change daily, but each item is a gem. The wines and desserts are also unbelievably good.

PEDRO DOS LEITOS, *N-1-Mealhada, (031) 220-62. Moderate.*

A large and well known *churrascaria* (roasted suckling pig) restaurant which serves great food. The large dining room is usually full and the service is good.

CURIA

The once grand old world spa town know as **Curia** can be reached *from Luso by taking route N-234 west for 7 km and connecting to route IC-2 north for another 8 km or so*. In its heyday, Curia attracted the upper class of Europe's social elite to its **Termas do Curia** spa area, filled with thermal baths and ritzy hotels.

Nowadays it still evokes the feeling of a resort town with a tree-lined main entrance from the main road, but many of the old houses are falling to bits. The hotels here are still worthy of note, including the **Grand Hotel de Curia** with it's advanced medically supervised spa programs, and the **Palace Hotel** which has maintained many original turn of the century aspects.

WHERE TO STAY

GRAND HOTEL DA CURIA, *Curia, (031) 515-720. Moderate.*

COSTA DE PRATA 235

A beautiful large hotel with nicely decorated rooms and a fully supervised spa. Facilities include bar, restaurant, indoor pool, sauna, library/lounge, air conditioning, TV, minibar, and great room service.
PALACE HOTEL DA CURIA, *Curia, (031) 512-131. Moderate.*
A seasonally open grand hotel located next to the *Curia* springs. The hotel offers 114 rooms, bar, restaurant, tennis, pool, billards, gardens, spa access, and parking.

ÁGUEDA

Situated halfway between Coimbra and Porto, the small city of Águeda can be found *by taking route IC-2 north from Coimbra for about 47 km*. This great little town, originally settled by the Celtics, rests on the banks of the **Rio Águeda** river and is rarely visited by tourists.

The charming downtown area has a small enchanting commercial district with unusual raised tile facades on many of the shops. The weekly Saturday market off of *Ave. 25 de Abril* is one of the best in the region. An interesting house and museum called the **Foundation of Dionisio Pinheirho** on *Praça Dr. António Breda* contains great examples of 19th-century oil paintings and furnishings.

You can also take a quick look at the ancient 16th-century renaissance **Capela do Sacramento** chapel with its fine *azulejos* and altar. The town is located very close to excellent wineries such as the **Caves São João** (5 km away) and provides an excellent base from which to explore Coimbra, Aveiro, Porto, and the fine coastal beaches.

The historic **Quinta da Borralha** has been lovingly converted into one of Portugal's most beautiful historic hotels known as **Palácio Águeda**. This remarkable manor house has been recently restored by master designer Jean Louis Talance, and is now one of the finest hotels in Portugal. I wish that all the hotels in Portugal were even half as comfortable as this one.

WHERE TO STAY

HOTEL PALÁCIO ÁGUEDA, *Quinta da Borralha, (034) 601-977. Moderate.*
One of the finest hotels in Portugal. A beautiful converted 16th-century manor house with 48 huge luxurious rooms. Facilities include bar and lounge, fine restaurant, swimming pool, satellite TV, a beautiful garden, trails, horse back riding nearby, special events, antiques everywhere, and great service. Affordably priced!

POUSADA DE SANTO ANTÓNIO, *Serem, (034) 523-192. Moderate.*
A small government owned inn a few km. outside of Águeda with 13 nice rooms and a staff of unhappy workers. Facilities include bar, restaurant, pool, and parking.

WHERE TO EAT

HOTEL PALÁCIO ÁGUEDA, *Quinta da Borralha, (034) 601-977. Moderate.*

The French and Portuguese chefs here create some of the most delicious food in all of Portugal. The menu includes many exotic dishes like the souffle de queijo, spectacular seafood, fresh local and imported game, and amazingly delicious desserts.

AVEIRO & THE COASTAL BEACHES

The beautiful city of **Aveiro** is *located about 27 km northwest of Águeda on route N-230 west in the heart of the* **Ria de Aveiro** *estuary*. Known primarily for its canals and the salt pans which pile up on the edge of town, Aveiro is a wonderful city to explore by foot with it's main streets covered in patterned mosaics of sea creatures. Several brightly painted fishing boats (they are actually used to collect seaweed) are moored to the sides of the canals which run through the center of town. I first visited *Aveiro* over a decade ago, and I wouldn't even think of a trip to Portugal without a stop here. I also recommend that you take one of the Ria ferries or boat tours that run from the Aveiro canals during the summer.

WHERE TO STAY

HOTEL IMPERIAL, *Rua Dr. N. Leitão, (034) 221-41. Moderate.*

A large 3 star hotel one block from the monastery. The 107 rooms offer good views and soft bedding. Facilities include a bar, restaurant, and cable TV.

POUSADA DA RIA, *Bico do Muranzel-Murtosa, (034) 483-32. Moderate.*

A modern motel style pousada right on the Ria estuary north of Aveiro in Murtosa. Facilities include waterview bar, restaurant, TV, watersports, and parking.

PALOMA BLANCA, *Rua Luís de Carvalho, 23, (034) 225-29. Moderate.*

A nice converted house which rents clean and well stocked rooms with private bathrooms to tourists. Facilities include bar, TV, gardens, and parking.

HOTEL QUINTA DA LOGOA, *Mira, (031) 458-620. Moderate.*

A hotel and apartment complex not to far from the beaches. They have 49 nice rooms and 20 or so 2 bedroom fully stocked apartments. Facilities include bar, restaurant, disco, pool, tennis, watersports, direct dial phones, and ample parking.

HOTEL ARCADA, *Rua Viana do Castelo, 4, (034) 230-01. Inexpensive.*

A 2 star canal view hotel with 49 comfortable rooms with private bathroom in the center of town. A good value for this location, the Arcada offers pleasant service.

COSTA DE PRATA 237

PENSÃO SANTA JOANA, *Ave. Dr. L. Peixinho, 27, (03) 286-04.*
Inexpensive.
A modern and clean inn close to the train station with 16 good rooms with private bathrooms. Problably the best cheap place to stay in Aveiro.

WHERE TO EAT

TAVERNA DOM CARLOS, *Rua Dr. N. Leitão, 46, (034) 220-61.*
Moderate.
A traditional restaurant in a nice old mansion located in the center of town. Specialties include fresh roasted meats and grilled seafoods. Very good service.

PIZZARTE, *Rua Eng. Von Hafe, 27, (034) 271-03. Inexpensive.*
Surprising good pizza in an ultra modern restaurant and bar. Lots of students.

SEEING THE SIGHTS

To fully appreciate Aveiro, you should start you excursion from the centrally located **Praça Humberto Delgado**. From this spot you can see the canals and the historic houses which line *Rua João Mendonca* including the *Turismo* office of the **Rota da Luz** subregion. Don't trust any of this office's hotel recommendations as I have been told that the staff receive kickbacks from the hotels they divert you towards.

This part of town contains the bustling fish market on *Rua Marnotos*, and several old streets with traditional houses. a nice park area called **Largo do Rossio**, the solemn chapel of **São Goncalinho**, and several boutiques. After a brief exploration of this section, wander back to the **Praça Humberto Delgado** and cross the bridge over the canal. If you look to you left you will see a tile mural of the seaweed collectors at work.

On this side of the canal you should visit Baroque 15th-century **Mosterio de Jesus** convent on *Rua de Santa Joana Princesa* where Portugal's princess Joana once lived and now lies in a marble tomb. In the 18th century, the interior of the convent's church was redesigned by António Gomes and José Correia to include beautiful frescoes and *azulejos* murals showing scenes from the live of Joana, lots of gilded woodwork, and a fantastic altar. Now the convent houses the **Museu de Aveiro** museum which contains various paintings, porcelains from the nearby **Vista Alegre** factory, statues, coaches, rare books, religious articles, and an unforgettable portrait of Joana from the 15th century (closed on Mondays).

South of Aveiro are some of the most peaceful coastal towns and beaches in all of Portugal. Traveling south you will come to the fishing town of **Costa Nova**, with its striped houses and an amusing weekend fish market. Here you can eat cheap seafood meals in any one of the several outdoor restaurants and cafes. The town also has a stand which sells "American Cookies" which are actually very good crepes with a waffled exterior that can be filled with chocolate.

If you continue south on the coastal road you'll reach **Vagueira** and the wide sand dune beach at **Praia de Vagueira** with it's traditional oxen pulled fish nets. Try a piece of local sardine filled bread at the small stand named **Casa Rocha** on the road towards the beach. Also in the area are the traditional fishing villages at **Praia de Mira** beach, some 21 km south of *Aveiro*. Here you can watch the fishermen and oxen at work in the summer months surrounded by a series of house on stilts.

There is also seasonal ferry service from Aveiro to the port and beach some 7 km north at **São Jacinto** where the singles go to mingle in the bars and cafes. If you wish to visit a fine porcelain museum, head south of Aveiro for some 7 km until you reach the signs for **Vista Alegre** just south of **Ílhavo**. This is the finest factory for high quality porcelain in Portugal, and ships it's products all over the world (closed on Saturday and Sunday).

OVAR

Some 29 km up from Aveiro off route N-109 north you will soon come to the city of **Ovar**. This cute market city rests near the northern edge of the **Ria de Aveiro** waterway and has several nice *azulejos*-covered homes and buildings, including the 17th-century **Igreja Matriz** church.

The town also offers visitors a chance to stop by at the interesting **Museu Regional e Etnografica de Ovar** on *Rua Helidoro Salgado, 11*, which is full of local costumes, paintings, ceramics, and other exhibits (closed on Fridays). You should make it a point to try the local *Pão de lo* sponge cakes sold in the local cafes and bakeries.

Near the town itself, you can head to the wonderful pine-bordered beaches at **Furadouro**.

WHERE TO STAY

HOTEL MEIA LUA, *Rua das Luzes, (056) 575-031. Moderate.*
A nice 4 star hotel in a great location which offes 54 large rooms with private bathrooms, a bar, pool, solarium, air conditioning, minibars, TV, and parking.

ALBERGARIA SÃO CRISTÓVÃO, *Rua Aquilino Ribeiro, 1, (056) 575-105. Moderate.*
A great 4 star inn which has 57 nice rooms with private bathrooms, a bar, restaurant, air conditioning, direct dial phones, minibars, TV, and nearby parking.

PRACTICAL INFORMATION FOR THE COSTA DE PRATA

CASINOS
- **Casino de Figueira da Foz**, *Rua Bernardo Lopes, (033) 220-41*

CURRENCY EXCHANGE
Most of the banks in the *Costa de Prata* area will exchange foreign currency and traveler's checks without hesitation. Private exchange booths, shops, restaurants, and hotel front desks will offer you a rather poor exchange rate. Remember that banking hours are from 8am until 3pm on Monday through Friday.

In places like some of the more tourism related areas and big towns you may find a 24 hour ATM or currency exchange machine.

EMERGENCY & USEFUL PHONE NUMBERS
- **Emergency assistance** (S.O.S.), *115*
- **Directory Assistance**, *118*
- **Águeda Hospital**, *Rua C. José Coutinho, (034) 622-075*
- **Caldas da Rainha Hospital**, *Parque Rainha D. Leonor, (062) 832-133*
- **Coimbra University Hospital**, *Praça Pr. Mota Pinto, (039) 722-116*
- **Leira Hospital**, *Largo D. M. Aguiar, (044) 321-33*
- **Tomar District Hospital**, *Ave. Dr. C. Mandueira, (049) 313-074*
- **Automobile Club of Portugal**, *Porto, (02) 830-1127*
- **Automobile Club of Portugal**, *Lisbon, (01) 942-5095*
- **Lisbon's Portela Airport**, *(01) 802-060*
- **TAP Reservations in Lisbon**, *(01) 386-1020*

MUSEUMS, PALACES, & MONUMENTS
- **Wine Museum**, *Institute da Vinha e Vinho, Alcobaça, (062) 422-22*. Contains examples of wine making and a collection of wines from around Portugal. Open 9 am until 12 pm and 2 pm until 5 pm Monday through Friday. Closed on Saturdays, Sundays, and holidays.
- **House Museum of the Pinheiro Foundation**, *Praça Dr. António Breda, Águeda, (034) 623-720*. Contains a collection of 19th century porcelain, ceramics, ivory, tapestries, silverware, furniture, and fine oil paintings. Open 3 pm until 6 pm Tuesday, Thursday, Saturday, and Sunday. Closed Mondays, Wednesdays, Fridays, and holidays.
- **Aveiro Museum** (**Museu de Cidade**), *Igreja de Jesus-Rua de Santa Joana Princesa, Aveiro, (034) 232-97*. Contains a collection of antique paintings, clothing, ceramics, sculpture, and jewelry. Open 10 am until

12:30 pm and 2 pm until 5 pm Tuesday through Sunday. Closed on Mondays and holidays.
- **Military Museum of Buçaco,** *Buçaco, (031) 939-310.* Contains collections of weapons and artifacts from the Battle of Buccaco. Open 10 am until 5 pm Tuesday through Sunday. Closed Mondays and holidays.
- **House Museum São Rafael,** *Rua Rafael Bordalo Pinheiro, Caldas da Rainha, (062) 231-57.* Contains a collection of ceramics and equipment which once belonged to Pinheiro. Open 9am until 12:30pm and 2:30pm until 5:30pm Monday through Friday. Closed Saturdays, Sundays, and holidays.
- **José Malhoa Museum,** *Parque Rainha Leonor, Caldas da Rainha, (062) 831-984.* Contains a collection of paintings from José Malhoa and several other Portuguese artists. The museum also contains several sculptures. Open 10am until 12:30pm and 2pm until 5pm Tuesday through Sunday. Closed on Mondays and holidays.
- **Biblioteca Joanina Library,** *Velha Universidade de Coimbra, Coimbra.* Open 9:30 am until 12:30 pm and 2 pm until 5 pm Monday through Saturday. Closed on Sundays and holidays.
- **Bissaya Barreto Museum,** *Rua da Infantaria, 23, Coimbra, (039) 224-68.* Contains collections of antique furniture, azulejos, rare books, paintings, and china. Open 3 pm until 5 pm Tuesday through Friday. Open 10 am until 12 pm and 3 pm until 5 pm on Saturday and Sunday. Closed Mondays and holidays.
- **Machado de Castro National Museum,** *Largo Dr. José Rodrigues, Coimbra, (039) 237-27.* Contains collections of 16th century oil paintings, Renaissance sculptures, ceramics, azulejos, baroque sculptures, tapestries, and oriental art. Open 9:30 am until 12:30 pm and 2 pm until 5:30 pm Tuesday through Sunday. Closed on Mondays and holidays.
- **Mosterio de Santa Cruz,** *Praça 8 de Maio, Coimbra, (039) 229-41.* Open 9 am until 12 pm and 2 pm until 6 pm daily.
- **National Museum of Science,** *Rua dos Coutinhos, 23, Coimbra, (039) 249-22.* Contains collections of models from Leonardo da Vinci inventions, equipment from Madame Curie experiments, and other exhibits in various buildings of the museum. Open 9 am until 12:30 pm and 2 pm until 5:30 pm Monday through Friday. Open 2 pm until 6:30 pm on Saturday.Closed Sundays and holidays.
- **Sacred Art Museum of Coimbra University,** *Capela da Universidade, Coimbra, (039) 354-48.* Contains collections of ecclesiastical items and religious books. Open 9:30 am 12:30 pm and 2 pm until 5 pm. Closed during Christmas.
- **Sé Velha,** *Largo de Sé Velha, Coimbra, (039) 252-73.* Open 9:30 am until 12:30 pm and 2 pm until 5:30 pm daily.
- **Monographic Museum of Conimbriga,** *Condeixa-a-Nova-Conimbriga,*

(039) 941-1177. The archaeological excavations of Roman village. A museum also displays collections of Roman coins, artwork, and artifacts from the site. Open 10 am until 5 pm Tuesday through Sunday. Closed on Mondays.
- **Fátima Museum**, *Rua Jacinto Marta-Edificão João Paulo II, Fátima, (049) 532-858*. Contains statues and a multimedia show about the Fátima miracle. Open 9 am until 6 pm daily.
- **Wax Museum of Fátima**, *Rua Jacinto Marto, Fátima, (049) 532-102*. Contains wax figurines based on the the apparitions in Fátima. Open 10 am until 5 pm daily
- **Dr. Santos Rocha Museum**, *Ave. Calouste Gulbenkian, Figueira da Foz, (033) 245-09*. Contains collections of Roman stamps, antique furniture, and archaeological items. Open 9 am until 12:30 pm and 2 pm until 5:30 pm Tuesday through Sunday. Closed on Mondays and holidays.
- **Vista Alegre Ceramic Museum**, *Vista Alegre Factory, Ílhavo, (034) 322-365*. Contains a collection of rare Vista Alegre porcelain including some Royal pieces. Open 9 am until 12:30 pm and 2 pm until 4:30 pm Tuesday through Sunday. Closed on Mondays and holidays.
- **Leira Museum (Museu de Cidade)**, *Castelo de Leiria, Leiria, (044) 813-982*. Contains a collection of paintings, sculptures, porcelain, tapestries, rugs, coins, furniture, medals, and glassware dating back over 5 centuries. Open 10 am until 12:30 pm and 2 pm until 5 pm Tuesday through Sunday. Closed on Mondays and holidays.
- **Archaeological Museum of Nazaré**, *Rua D. Fuas Roupinho, Sito da Nazaré -Nazaré, (062) 551-687*. Contains collections of archaeological artifacts, fishing implements, paintings, sculptures, and ceramics. Open 10 am until 12 pm and 2 pm until 5 pm Tuesday through Sunday. Closed on Mondays and holidays.
- **Óbidos Museum (Museu da Cidade)**, *Praça Santa Maria, Óbidos, (062) 959-263*. Contains a collection of Josefa D'Obidos works, oil paintings, weapons from local battles, furniture, sacred art, and some artifacts. Open 9 am until 1 pm and 2 pm until 6 pm daily.
- **Ovar Museum (Museu Etnografica)**, *Rua Heliodoro Salgado, 11, Ovar, (056) 572-822*. Contains antique paintings, ceramics, and local costumes. Open 10 am until 12 pm and 2 pm until 6 pm daily. Closed on Fridays and holidays.
- **Peniche Museum (Museu da Cidade)**, *Campo da República, Peniche, (062) 781-848*. Contains collections of handicrafts, paintings, sea shells, azulejos, and artifacts. Open 10 am until 12 pm and 2 pm until 6 pm Tuesday through Monday. Closed Mondays and holidays.
- **Portugal dos Pequenitos Children's Park (Jardim do Portugal dos Pequenito**s), *Santa Clara-Coimbra, (039) 441-215*. A garden theme

park with a display of miniature buildings and castles from all over Portugal and it's colonies. The museum contains miniature furnishings and toys. Open 9:30 am until 12:30 pm and 2 pm until 5 pm each day.
- **Aquiles de Mota Match Box Museum**, *Convento de São Fransisco, Tomar, (049) 322-601*. Contains a huge collection of match books and boxes. Open 2 pm until 5 pm Sunday through Friday. Closed on Saturdays and holidays.
- **Convent of Christ of Tomar**, *Tomar, (049) 313-481*. Open 9:30 am until 12:30 pm and 2 pm until 5 pm Monday through Friday. Closed on Saturdays, Sundays, and holidays.
- **Abraham Zacuto Synagogue and Museum**, *Rua da Judiaria, 73, Tomar, (049) 322-601*. Open 9 am until 12:30 pm and 2:30 pm until 6 pm daily
- **Torres Vedras Museum**, *Rua Serpa Pinto, 7, Torres Vedras*. Contains collections of 16th century paintings, stamps, azulejos, and artifacts. Open 10 am until 12 pm and 2 pm until 5 pm Tuesday through Sunday. Closed on Mondays and holidays.

SPORTS & RECREATION
- **Alcobaça Tennis Club**, *Alcobaça, (062) 596-745*
- **Quinta das Tripas Horse Center**, *Atouguia da Baleia, (062) 757-33*
- **Aviero Equestrian Center**, *Vilarinho, (034) 912-108*
- **Vale do Leão Squash Club**, *Buarcos, (033) 230-57*
- **Caldas de Rainha Horse Center**, *Quinta da Rainha, (062) 358-51*
- **Coimbra AAC Fishing Club**, *Coimbra, (039) 280-72*
- **Coimbra Hipico Horse Center**, *Mata do Choupal, (039) 376-95*
- **Coimbra Tennis Club**, *University Stadium, (039) 441-384*
- **Afga Travel** (bicycle & moped rentals), *Figueira da Foz, (033) 277-77*
- **Amadores Fishing Club**, *Figueira da Foz, (033) 294-34*
- **Figueira da Foz Tennis Club**, *Ave. 25 de Abril, (033) 222-87*
- **Leiria Tennis School**, *Leiria, (044) 315-06*
- **Amadores Fishing Club**, *Marinha Grande, (044) 504-516*
- **Neptuno Boating Club**, *Obidos, (062) 950-271*
- **Peniche Tennis Club**, *Baluarte-Peniche, (062) 789-500*
- **Tenisplash Tennis Club**, *Peniche, (062) 759-667*
- **Golf Mar Golf and Horse Center**, *Porto Novo, (061) 984-157*
- **Rio Maior Tennis Club**, *Jardim Municipal, (043) 921-04*
- **Quinta da Cortiçãda Horse Riding**, *Rio Maior, (043) 479-182*
- **Zêzere Boating Club**, *Sertã, (074) 997-45*
- **Tomar Tennis**, *Park Desportivo, (049) 322-604*
- **Picadeiro Paio Correia Horse Center**, *Torres Vedras, (061) 981-218*
- **Vimeiro Golf Club**, *Vidago, (076) 971-06*

COSTA DE PRATA 243

TRANSPORTATION
Most of the towns and villages of this area are linked by train, bus, and ferry service. For specific routes and schedules, contact the local *Turismo* office, a local travel agency, or call the transportation companies directly:
- **Aveiro RN Bus Depot**, *Ave. Dr. L. Peixinho, (062) 217-55*
- **Caldas da Rainha RN Bus Depot**, *Rua C. S. Brito, (062) 220-67*
- **Coimbra RN Bus Depot**, *Ave. F. de Magalhaes, (039) 270-81*
- **Fátima RN Bus Depot**, *Ave. Correia da Silva, (049) 531-651*
- **Figueira da Foz RN Bus Depot**, *Rua J. da Silva Fonseca, (033) 230-95*
- **Leiria RN Bus Depot**, *Jardim Municipal, (044) 220-49*
- **Nazaré RN Bus Depot**, *Ave. Vieira Guimares, no phone*
- **Obidos RN Bus Depot**, *Porta da Vilha bus stop, no office*
- **Tomar RN Bus Depot**, *Ave Combatentes, (049) 312-738*
- **Aveiro CP Rail Station**, *Ave Dr. L. Piexinho, (062) 244-85*
- **Caldas da Rainha CP Rail Station**, *Ave. Indepencia Nacional, (062) 236-93*
- **Coimbra CP Rail Station A**, *Largo das Amenias, (039) 272-63*
- **Coimbra CP Rail Station B**, *3 km north of town, (039) 246-32*
- **Figueira da Foz CP Rail Station**, *Largo de Estação, (033) 243-56*
- **Leiria CP Rail Station**, *3 km northeast of town, (044) 882-027*
- **Obidos CP Rail Train Station**, *at the foot of the town, (062) 959-186*
- **Tomar CP Rail Station**, *Ave. Combatentes, (049) 312-815*
- **Avis Rent a Car in Nazaré**, *Hotel Mare, (062) 519-28*
- **Hertz Rent a Car in Figueira da Foz**, *Rua M. D. Sousa, 103, (033) 251-80*
- **Europcar Rent a Car in Coimbra**, *Rua da Sota, 2, (039) 270-11*

TOURISM OFFICES (TURISMOS)
- **Águeda Tourism Office**, *Rua 5 de Outubro, (034) 601-42*
- **Alcobaça Tourism Office**, *Praça 25 de Abril, (062) 423-77*
- **Aveiro Tourism Office**, *Rua João Mendonca, 8, (062) 236-80*
- **Batalha Tourism Office**, *Largo Paulo VI, (044) 961-80*
- **Caldas da Rainha Tourism Office**, *Rua E. D. Pacheco, (062) 831-003*
- **Coimbra Tourism Office**, *Largo da Portagem, (039) 238-76*
- **Costa Nova Tourism Office**, *Praia Costa Nova, (034) 369-560*
- **Fátima Tourism Office**, *Ave. Correia da Silva, (049) 531-139*
- **Figueira da Foz Tourism Office**, *Ave. 25 de Abril, (033) 226-10*
- **Leiria Tourism Office**, *Jardim Luís de Camões, (044) 237-73*
- **Nazaré Tourism Office**, *Ave. Viera Guimares, (062) 561-154*
- **Obidos Tourism Office**, *Rua Direita, (062) 959-231*
- **Peniche Tourism Office**, *Rua Alexandre Herculano, (062) 789-571*
- **Rio Maior Tourism Office**, *Praça da República, (061) 941-154*
- **Torres Vedras Tourism Office**, *Rua 9 de Abril, (061) 314-094*

TRAVEL AGENCIES
- **Afga Travel**, *Rua Miguel Bombarda, 79, (033) 27-777*. A full service travel agency in the heart of Figueiro da Foz which also rents bicycles.
- **Viajens Melia**, *Rua da Sofia, 33, (039) 205-71*. The Coimbra-based office of a travel agency for all types of reservations and tickets.
- **RN Tours**, *Rua Coronel Sampaio Rio, 3, (044) 324-13*. A Leira branch office of a large government owned full service travel company.

MAGNIFICENT WAVES BREAKING ALONG THE COSTA DE PRATA

17. PORTO (OPORTO)

The massive city of **Porto** (also called **Oporto**) is located on the north bank of the **Douro** river's mouth. With a population of over 470,000 people, Porto is the second largest city in Portugal. Upon first sight the city may not seem particularly pretty, but with a fair amount of patience, Porto's inner beauty will become apparent to all who visit. Constantly under construction, this major cosmopolitan area is typically noisy, somewhat polluted, and always difficult to drive around (avoid rush hour completely, or better yet arrive in town on Saturday).

HISTORY

Porto's history can be traced back well before it's origins as the Lusitanian village once known as Portus. During Roman times the city was an important trading zone on the Douro river which was connected to its sister city across the **Douro** river, **Cale** (now called **Vila Nova de Gaia**), by boats operating as ferries.

By the 8th century, the area had been occupied by both the Saubians and the Moors but the local Christian forces managed to take back control of the area. Soon the city had become know by a combination of its two original names and began to be known as Portucale. As the Christian dominated territory grew in size, the entire region under their control became known as Portucale. In 1139 when Afonso Henriques declared himself king of this new nation, Portucale became the country's official name. Over time the named changed slightly to the current spelling of Portugal. In the late 14th century Porto became a major European trading harbor. It was in this city that Prince Henry the Navigator was born, raised, and began his love of the sea which resulted in his naval capture of Cuerta, Morocco and the beginning of the age of discoveries.

In 1703 the English and Portuguese signed the **Treaty of Metheun**, which lowered taxes on several products including Portuguese wines which were already beginning to find a small market in the United Kingdom. Later in the 17th century, a trade dispute stopped the flow of

French wines into England, and the British turned to Portugal as it's major supplier of wine products. While seeking larger quantities of wine, British merchants set up shipping companies and syndicates which despite efforts by the Marquêsde Pombal, still control much of Port wine's international distribution.

In 1809, the Napoleonic troops led by Soult captured Porto but were subsequently routed by Wellington's British troops. The English occupation of Porto lasted 11 years before a popular uprising removed them from power, and was followed in time by several anti-monarchial revolts which may have been the catalyst for the eventual abdication of King Dom Manuel II and the proclamation of the republic in Lisbon in 1910.

ORIENTATION

To begin exploring the city of Porto, start in the heart of the city. After several visits here, I tend to favor an early start at the narrow park in the middle of *Avenida dos Aliados*. On this avenue you can find parking meters and nearby parking lots (marked with a big P) which are quite rare in *Porto*. If you're staying in town for the night, leave your car at the hotel's parking lot and take a taxi or a bus to this point. From the *Avenida dos Aliados* you can't help but notice the bell tower topped **City Hall (Câmara Municipal)** which is worth a short visit (closed on weekends).

You may want to head into the *Turismo* office just to the left (west) of City Hall on *Rua Clube dos Feniados, 25* (opens at 9 am except Sunday when it opens at 10 am). At the *Turismo*, be sure to get a copy of the Porto map, list of events, and tourist guide. As you look down the avenue you will see several 19th century buildings which work their way down towards the **Praça da Liberdade**.

WHERE TO STAY

Expensive
HOTEL INFANTE DE SAGRES, *Praça D. Filipa de Lancastre, (02) 201-9031.*

Without doubt, the finest hotel in *Porto*. This extravagantly decorated deluxe hotel offers great service, 117 nice rooms, inner courtyard, antiques everywhere, a fine restaurant, amazing public spaces, and a great location. Very quiet and reserved.

HOTEL SHERATON PORTO, *Ave. Boavista, 1269, (02) 606-8822.*

An excellent American style business hotel in the heart of downtown. The hotel offers 253 large rooms with many amenities. Also has health club, indoor pool, meals.

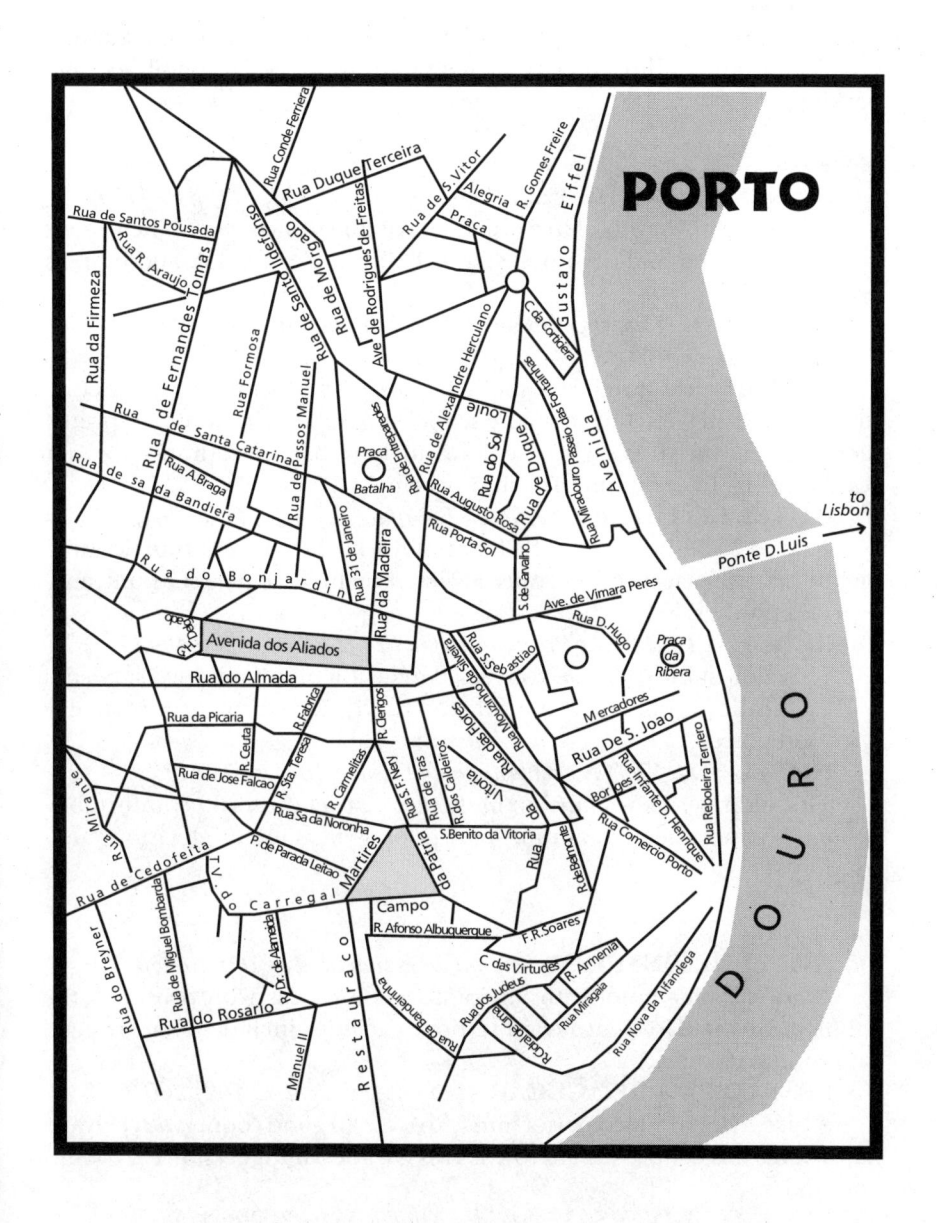

PORTO

HOTEL TIVOLI PORTO ATLÂNTICO, *Rua Afonso Lopes Vieira, 148, (02) 649-941.*

A good business class hotel located in a part of town which makes it hard to find. This 5 star property offers 58 nice rooms, a bar, restaurant, health club, air conditioning, pool, sauna, shops, cable TV, minibars, and parking.

Moderate

IPANEMA PARK HOTEL, *Rua de Serralves, 124, (02) 810-4174.*

A modern tower hotel in a quiet part of downtown *Porto*. The rooms are well designed and the hotel staff is helpful. Health club and indoor pool access.

GRANDE HOTEL DO PORTO, *Rua de Santa Catarina, 197, (02) 200-8176.*

This old world hotel is in the best walking and shopping district in town. Although it is a bit worn, the service is great, most rooms are pretty nice, and the price is right. Facilities include bar, restaurant, TV, air conditioning, in room phones, and parking.

HOTEL DO IMPÉRIO, *Rua da Batalha, 127, (02) 200-6861.*

A good 3 star hotel near the heart of town which offers 100 nice and big rooms with private bathrooms. Facilities include a bar, restaurant, and in room phones.

RESIDENCIAL REX, *Praça da República, 177, (02) 200-4548.*

This almost inexpensive converted mansion offers minimal services. A great location and 21 or so unusual rooms with private bathrooms make it a good place.

HOTEL BOA VISTA, *Esplanada do Castelo, (02) 617-3818.*

This old river view mansion in the *Foz* district offers 39 comfortable rooms, a panoramic restaurant, bar, pool, gym, sauna, television, and friendly service.

Inexpensive

HOTEL PENINSULAR, *Rua Sá da Bandeira, 21, (02) 200-3012.*

A good 2 star hotel with 59 comfortable rooms with private bathrooms near the São Bento train station. Facilities include a bar, restaurant, minibars, and TV.

PENSÃO PÃO DE AÇÚCAR, *Rua do Almada, 262, (02) 200-2425.*

A nice 3 star art deco period inn with over 40 good rooms with private bathrooms in a central part of town. This is a good budget choice if rooms are available.

PENSÃO UNIVERSAL, *Ave. dos Aliados, 38, (02) 200-6758.*

Inexpensive budget accommodations with some great views in a great location.

WHERE TO EAT

PORTUCALE, *Rua da Alegria, 598, (02) 570-717. Expensive.*

An excellent formal restaurant with great food, excellent service, an impressive wine list, and the best views of *Porto* imaginable. You must call for a reservation.

DONA FILIPA RESTAURANT, *Praça D. Filipa. de Lancastre, (02) 200-8101. Expensive.*

This beautiful and formal restaurant in the Infante de Sagres Hotel serves some of the finest cuisine in the city. Specialties from both Portuguese and French cuisine.

CASA FILHA MAE PRETA, *Cais da Ribeira, 39, (02) 315-515. Moderate.*

A good local seafood restaurant which serves excellent fried fillets. The location is just off the river in the old part of town. Food is good and the service is friendly.

O BECO PUB AND RESTAURANTE, *Rua Padre L. Cabral, 974, (02) 618-5601. Moderate.*

A charming old converted house in the *Foz* area has several different rustic dining rooms and a terraced patio serving traditional cuisine. Good food and service.

TAVERNA DE BEBOBOS, *Cais da Ribeira, 21, (02) 313-565. Inexpensive.*

This very dim lit antique tavern is full of charm and good fish meals. Located in the old part of town, it is perhaps the most atmospheric restaurant on the riverfront.

CHEZ LAPIN, *Rua dos Canatreiros, 40, (02) 310-291. Inexpensive.*

This one of the more popular *Ribeira* establishments which serve good food in a nautical environment. The tiny restaurant is rustically decorated. A good value.

CONFEITARIA DE BOLHÃO, *Rua Formosa, 339, (02) 200-9291. Inexpensive.*

This wonderful bakery also has a downstairs restaurant with a rustic and traditional ambience. Lunch here is a real delight, and the bill is even more attractive.

SEEING THE SIGHTS

Facing the front of city hall, you should turn right (east) onto *Rua Formosa* and a block or so ahead is the lively market called the **Bolhão**. This marketplace (closed Saturday afternoon and Sunday) sells mostly seafood, meats, and produce, but there are some small boutiques with fine jewelry as well. If you wish, you can find excellent breads, olives, cold *Vinho Verde* wine, and fresh cheeses which can provide a great picnic meal for a bit later.

Nearby the Bolhão market is the wonderful **Confeitaria de Bolhão** bakery on *Rua Formosa, 339* where you can find strong coffee and great pastries. A couple of blocks further west is the famed merchant street of *Rua de Santa Catarina* with its fascinating assortment of fine shops. This street provides the best shopping possibilities for high quality men's and women's clothing, leather goods, jewelry, and antiques. I buy all of my European made ties and scarves on this street at about half of what they cost at home.

After a nice stroll around *Rua Santa Catarina* you should head back to the city hall area. You might want to drop by the **Casa Januario** shop on *Rua do Bonjardim, 352* which sells many vintage local wines. From the *Avenida dos Aliados* and head towards the statues in the **Praça da Liberdade** square. From the plaza you can walk 1 block down (south) into the *azulejos* covered interior of the **Estação de São Bento** train station and across through the **Praça Almeida Garret onto Rua das Flores**.

As you walk down *Rua das Flores* you will be in front of the 16th-century **Misericórdia** church which is worth a quick look. While in the church, make sure to see its next door offices which contain a beautiful Renaissance painting of the royal family with Jesus. From the station, cross the *Largo de São Domingos* and head down (south) onto the *Rua Ferreira Borges* will take you next to the **Mercado Ferreira Borges** marketplace with its enclosed kiosk stalls that are packed on the 2nd and 4th Saturday morning of each month with the **Vandoma** fair.

At the end of the street is the **Praça do Infante Dom Henrique**, with its Gothic 14th-century **Igreja de São Fransisco** church and unforgettable vaulted baroque interior. Adjacent to the church you will find **Palácio da Bolsa**, which is now home of the **Porto Stock Exchange**. The 19th-century structure of the Bolsa contains a few grand rooms which can be visited including the richly decorated Arabian hall.

For most people, it's now time for a break. Head south to *Rua Nova da Afândega* until you reach the riverfront area known as the **Ribeira**. The stone streets and maze-like alleys of the *Ribeira* haven't changed much in centuries. Nearby on *Rua da Reboleira, 37,* you can and pop inside the **Center of Traditional Arts and Crafts** which sells several different artistic items at reasonable prices.

On the way to the riverfront, take a seat on the benches near the rotating cube statue in **Praça da Ribeira** plaza. The sight of children chasing stray cats against the old buildings' colored ceramic facades create an amusing environment to relax in. From here it's just steps away to both the esplanade and the lower level of the **Cais da Ribeira**. Here you can also see the bridges leading over to the Port wine caves in **Vila Nova de Guia** including the iron bridge designed by Eiffel which is called the **Ponte Maria Pia**.

PORTO'S WATERFRONT

The Ribeira contains several great inexpensive fish restaurants which serve the largest portions you could imagine. There are also several stalls in front of the river which sell assorted tourist items. Make sure to wander around the ancient streets like *Rua Lada* and *Rua de Cima do Muro* just behind the Cais de Ribeira. If you brought your pic-nic, you can carefully cross the upper level of the **Ponte Dom Luís** bridge and sit on a bench in front of the panoramic view out over the Douro and old Porto. After lunch I suggest a stop or two in the Port wine caves. Several world famous Port Wine producers such as Sandeman, Calem, and Taylor offer free tours and wine tasting (see *Vila Nova de Gaia* section).

After you've had a good lunch, a couple of glasses of assorted Port wines, and a good rest, you will be ready to return across the bridge. When you come off the bridge and head up to the *Ave. de Vimera Peres* you will soon find the **Sé** cathedral This 12th-century former fortress church was considerably modified in the 17th- and 18th-centuries by Manuel Teixeira, Manuel Guedes, and Nicolau Nasoni respectively. Its interior boasts a Gothic cloister and several baroque elements while it's main entrance includes both a pink Romanesque window and a baroque entrance. Just around the corner from the church's exit you will find Nasoni designed building which is now home to the **Museu Guerra Junqueiro** museum which exhibits rare 15th and 16th century tapestries, pottery, furniture, gold and silver.

After a good morning and afternoon of sightseeing, you may wish to get a good view over the town. If you head back to the base of **Praça da Liberdade** you should now turn left (west) onto the *Rua dos Clérigos* which will lead you to the church and tower of **Torre de Clérigos**. This highly unusual Baroque and rococo church was designed by Italian Nicolau Nasoni in the mid-17th century. The church itself is renowned for it's highly detailed carved granite facade. The 249 foot tower (closed on Wednesdays) was built during the same period, and contains a long stairway which leads out to a superb panoramic view of the city and it's surrounding areas.

For those of you that really want a special treat, take a taxi over to the **Solar do Vinho do Porto** (closed on Sundays). Located in a riverfront mansion known as **Quinta da Macieirinha** on *Rua de Entre Quintas, 220,* this beautiful exposed beam and granite bar is a great place to relax after a long day of sightseeing. Most of the staff are a bit shy to speak in English, but the menu of wines is easy to understand. Here you have a chance to sample over 105 vintage Ports by the glass in a truly remarkable atmosphere. The beautiful riverfront *Quinta* was once the residence of King Carlos Alberto of Sardinia, and also contains a so called Romantic Museum exhibiting his unusual household items

From here you may wish to take a taxi over to the extreme western sector of town, known as the **Foz** district, around the **Praça de Zarco Goncalves**. Besides being next to the **Foz de Douro** beaches, you can take a look at the **Castelo de Queijo** (Castle of Cheese) and slowly stroll down the *Ave. de Montevideu* towards the beautiful **Esplanada de 28 de Maio** which overlooks the rocky seafront. There are several blocks of huge mansions just a block or so inland from the coastal avenues between the here and the beautiful **Jardim do Passeio Alegre** gardens which contain the old **Forte de São João de Foz**.

You may also wish to walk a few more blocks toward the bridges to the historic **Farol de São Miguel** lighthouse. Now it's time to either eat dinner and wait for the rush hour to end (about 8pm) or to return to your hotel and rest before a late dinner.

Directory of Museums & Monuments
- **Eng. António de Almeida Museum**, *Rua Tenente Valadim, 231, (02) 667-481.* Contains collections of ancient coins, 17th- and 18th-century Portuguese and French furniture, 17th-century paintings, antique porcelain from China, Persian tapestries. Open 2:30 pm until 5:30 pm. Closed on Sundaysand holidays.
- **Botany Institute, and Botanical Garden of Dr. Gonçalo Sampaio**, *Rua de Campo Alegre, 1191, (02) 698-134.* Contains a museum, library, laboratory, and huge botanical garden. Open 9 am until 12 am

Monday through Saturday by appointment only. Closed on Sundays and holidays.
- **Cãmara Municipal (City Hall)**, *Praça Gen. Humberto Delgado, (02) 200-9871.* Open 8:30 am until 12 pm and 2 pm until 5 pm Monday through Friday. Closed Saturdays, Sundays, and holidays.
- **António Carneiro House & Museum,** *Rua de António Carneiro, 363, (02) 579-668.* Contains collections of António Carneiro paintings and drawings. Open 10 am until 12 pm and 2 pm until 5:30 pm Tuesday through Friday. Open 2 pm until 6 pm on Saturday. Closed on Sundays, Mondays, and holidays.
- **Ethnological Museum of Porto**, *Palácio de São João Novo, (02) 200-2010.* Contains collections of ethnological and archeological objects from the region including wine making equipment, costumes, handicrafts, and litho instruments. Open 10 am until 12 pm and 2 pm until 5 pm Closed on Sundays, Mondays, and holidays.
- **Casa do Infante**, *Rua da Afândega, (02) 316-025.* The restored birthplace of Prince Henry the Navigator. Open sporadically with special temporary exhibits.
- **Guerra Junqueiro House & Museum**, *Rua D. Hugo, 12, (02) 213-644.* Contains collections of art collected by this famous poet including ceramics, jewelry, paintings, furniture, textiles, pottery, and carvings. Open 10 am until 12 pm and 2 pm until 5 pm Tuesday through Saturday. Closed on Sundays, Mondays, and holidays.
- **Military Museum of Porto**, *Rua do Heroismo, 329, (02) 565-514.* Contains collections of military equipment from the past up until World War 1. Open 2 pm until 5 pm Wednesdays through Monday. Closed on Tuesdays and holidays.
- **Modern Art Museum**, *Rua de Serralves, 977, (02) 680-057.* Contains collections of paintings, sculpture, jewelry, and photography. Open 2 pm until 8 pm Tuesday through Sunday. Closed on Mondays and holidays.
- **Palácio da Bolsa**, *Rua Ferreira Borges, (02) 200-4497.* Contains several gilded halls and a collection of fine jewelry. Open 9 am until 12 pm and 2 pm until 5:30 pm Monday through Friday. Closed on Saturdays and Sundays.
- **Romantic Museum**, *Rua Entre-Quintas, 220.* Contains a collections of 19th century furniture and unusual household items. Open 10 am until 12 pm and 2 pm until 5 pm Tuesday through Saturday. Closed on Sundays, Mondays, and holidays.
- **Sé Cathedral**, *Terreiro da Sé, (02) 314-837.* Open 9 am until 12 pm and 3 pm until 6 pm daily.
- **Museum Soares dos Reis**, *Rua de Dom Manuel II, (02) 200-7110.* Contains collections of António Soares dos Reis sculptures, interna-

tional paintings from the 16-19th century, ceramics, gold, silver, furniture, and ceramics. Open 10 am until 12 pm and 2 pm until 5 pm Closed on Sundays, Mondays, and Holidays
- **Torre dos Clérigos**, *Rua dos Clérigos, (02) 200-1729*. Contains a 225 step staircase which leads to a vast panoramic view of Porto. Open 10 am until 12 pm and 2 pm until 5 pm Thursday to Tuesday. Closed on Wednesdays and holidays.

BARS, CLUBS, & NIGHTLIFE

As you might expect from any large city, Porto has a fair amount of evening activities. The many students in town tend to either go to the small and crowded bars and clubs a block or so behind the **Cais da Ribeira** like **Postigo do Carvão**. Several other clubs are located across the river in **Vila Nova de Guia** just off *Largo Miguel Bombarda*.

The section of town known as the **Foz** is also home to several larger clubs and pubs such as **Bonaparte** and **Twins**. Ask your hotel's concierge or a local student to tell you about the newest "in" place.

SHOPPING

Porto is full of shopping possibilities. The streets just east of *Avenida dos Aliados* contain lots of great stores. *Rua de Santa Catarina* is perhaps the most centralized shopping street in all of Porto. In the past I have been able to purchase several pairs of fine shoes for about 6800$00 a pair, although finding any size over 10 (European size 43) is almost impossible.

I have bought excellent gold and silver work in some of the fine stores listed below. There are a few shopping centers which are open until midnight, but bargains there take a lot of work to find. Since the fine filigree of Portugal comes from nearby **Gondomar**, you can get great deals on these items in Porto's shops. I also have found unique calfskin wallets with unusual linings for as little as 3200$00.

Overall I suggest a lot of comparison shopping before you make a final decision on any large ticket item. Don't forget to inquire about the **Tax Free** refund voucher discussed in the shopping section of this book.

These are just a few of my favorite shops in *Porto* which offer great products at good prices:
- **Dom Manuel Joias**, *Store 53-Centro Brasília*. The best values in fine gold and precious stone jewelry. Have a look at the women's 19 karat gold rings with real diamonds and emeralds for under 50,000$00 after the tax free rebate. Very helpful English speaking staff who cut deals.
- **Vista Alegre**, *Rua Candido dos Reis, 18*. If you like fine porcelain, this is the best place in town. The original Vista Alegre pieces are among the finest in Europe. Good for special gifts, but not cheap.

- **Joias Rolando**, *Praça Mouzinho Albuqurque, 83*. A great place to find filigree silver and gold pieces including sterling filigree encrusted perfume bottles for 3400$00 each. No pressure tactics here.
- **Amazenes MarquêsSoares**, *Rua de Santa Catarina, 21*. Lots of discounted men's and women's wear and accessories at great prices.

Shopping Centers
Some stores are open on Sundays as well, especially in the Brasília and Dallas shopping centers. These centers are usually open from 10am until midnight Monday through Saturday:
- **Brasília**, *Praça Mouzinho Albuqurque*
- **Dallas**, *Ave. Boavista, 1616*
- **Clérigos**, *Rua dos Clérigos*
- **Foz**, *Ave. Brazil*
- **Aviz**, *Ave. Boavista*

PRACTICAL INFORMATION
Emergency & Useful Phone Numbers
- **Emergency Assistance** (S.O.S.), *115*
- **Directory Assistance**, *118*
- **Porto Police**, *(02) 200-6821*
- **Porto Fire Dept.**, *(02) 484-121*
- **São João Hospital**, *Alamada Prof. H. Monteiro, (02) 487-151*
- **Santo António Hospital**, *Largo Prof. Abel Salazar, (02) 200-7354*
- **A.C.P. in Porto** (Emergency road services), *(02) 830-1127*
- **Pedros Rubras Airport** (15 km out of town), *(02) 948-2141*
- **T.A.P.Airlines Porto**, *Praça Mouz. Albuqurque, 105, (02) 600-5555*
- **T.W.A. Airlines Porto**, *Rua Julio Dinis, 585, (02) 600-0873*
- **US Embassy in Porto**, *Rua Julio Dinis, 826, (02) 690-008*
- **Main Post Office**, *Praça Gen. H. Delgado, (02) 208-0251*

Tourist Informaton & Tour Options
If you have any tourist questions, contact the **Porto Tourist Office**, *Rua Clube dos Feniano, 25, (02) 312-470*.

There is also an assortment of half, full, and multiple day guided motorcoach and barge tours are offered by several leading companies and offer a good first look at Porto. The following is a selection of tours which I have enjoyed over several visits to Porto.

Reservations should be booked directly with the tour operator, by contacting your travel agent, or by visiting a local Portuguese agency in the city you are visiting.
- **RN Tours**, *(02) 382-303* – **4 hour Porto Panoramico Tour**, *about 4800$00 per person*. Includes visits to the Cais da Ribeira, Foz

beachfront, Crystal Palace, Palácio da Bolsa, Sé cathedral, and Vila Nova de Guia with a wine cave visit. Departs at 9:30am every day.
• **Endouro Cruise Lines**, *(02) 324-236* – **1 hour Four Bridges Tour**. *About 1900$00 per person.* The ferry departs from Cais da Ribeira and takes you around the Douro river to see great panoramic views of old Porto, and Vila Nova de Guia. Departs several times daily. There's also the **12 hour Marvelous Douro Tour**, *about 18,000$00 per person*. The vessel departs from Cais da Ribeira and serves breakfast on the way to Régua, then a tour of the Crestuma dam, wine tasting, lunch on board, tour of Carrapatelo area, disembark in Peso da Régua and first class train to Porto. Departs several times each month.

Endouro offers several overnight Douro barge style cruises that are quite good and include a river view cabin and all meals. Please contact Endouro for more info.

Transportation

Bus and tram service connect just about every point in Porto. When you enter the vehicle you must tell the driver what your destination is, and he will inform you of the exact tariff. The average downtown ride is about 170$00. Discount bus fare can be bought at some newsstands, or at kiosks which are located next to major bus stops. You can purchase either books of 20 fares for about 1350$00, 4 day tourist passes for about 1400$00 per person, or 7 day passes for about 1850$00. The company which controls the bus and tram system is called **STCP** and currently does not print a route map.

I recommend using taxis to avoid frustration. Taxis are cheap (about 475$00 per average ride) and can be flagged down or found at the taxi line at **Praça da Liberdade**. During rush hour, all forms of transportation are absolutely full.
• **Porto Taxi**, *Praça da Liberdade, (02) 676-093*
• **Campanha CP Rail Station**, *Rua da Estação, (02) 564-141*. Most long distance and international trains come to this large station.
• **São Bento CP Rail Station**, *Praça Almeida Garret, (02) 200-2722*. Some regional and commuter trains come here in the center of town.
• **Trindade CP Rail Station**, *Rua. Alferes Malheiro, (02) 200-5224*. Trains from the northern cities enter Porto at this station.
• **RN North Bus Depot**, *Praça D. F. de Lancastre   (02) 200-3152*
• **RN South Bus Depot**, *Rua Alexandre Hurculano, (02) 200-6954*
• **Internorte Bus Depot**, *Praça Galiza, 96, (02) 693-220*
• **Caima Bus Depot**, *Rua das Carmelitas, 32, (02) 318-668*
• **Cabanelas Bus Depot**, *Rua da Alegria, (02) 200-2870*
• **Avis Rent a Car Porto**, *Rua Guedes Azevedo, 125, (02) 315-947*
• **Hertz Rent a Car Porto**, *Rua Santa Catarina, 899, (02) 312-387*

• **Europcar Rent a Car**, *Rua Santa Catarina,1158, (02) 318-398*

Travel Agencies
• **Star Travel**, *Ave. dos Aliases, 210, (02) 200-3637.* A large travel company with nice staff which can be helpful in all types of bookings.
• **Mapa Mundo**, *Rua Sá de Bandeira, 784, (02) 310-129.* A well established tour operator and travel agency with full service capabilities.
• **ACP-Porto**, *Rua da Santa Catarina, 848, (02) 200-2499.* A large full service agency with special rates for better hotels, cars, and city tours.

18. THE COSTA VERDE (THE GREEN COAST)

The **Costa Verde** region is located in the extreme northwestern section of Portugal and contains both the **Douro** and **Minho** provinces as well as a tiny slice of northwestern **Trás-os-Montes**. Many mountains, valleys, and rivers surround the Costa Verde's major population areas. The land in this region is very fertile, and much of Portugal's wine production occurs here. Within the last several years, a major increase of industry has caused this area to become more densely populated.

Many of Portugal's oldest and most established families originated in the Costa Verde and maintain magnificent estates and quintas (manor houses), many of which are know bed and breakfast style inns. Steam engined narrow gauge railroads still occasionally run near the banks of the wide **Duoro** river and its adjacent valley. It is on the banks of this river that the famous Port wine vineyards are cultivated, crushed, aged, and later transported to Porto for worldwide export.

Among the many interesting places to visit are the rich and regal cities of **Ponte de Lima** and **Viana do Castelo**, the former capital city of **Guimarães**, the quaint and tranquil village of **Amarante**, the bizarre and mystical church of **Bom Jesus** near **Braga**, the historic market town of **Barcelos**, the northern fortified border towns of **Monção** and **Melgaço**, the unforgettable **Peneda-Gerês Parque Nacional**, the wonderful city of **Porto**, and of course a mandatory wine tasting at one of the Port wine "caves" on the **Vila Nova de Guia** riverfront.

ESPINHO

The seaside resort area of **Espinho** sits right on the edge of the Costa Verde, *about 19 km from Porto off the A-1 highway south*. The city is divided by a grid of parallel odd numbered streets which run from east to west and intersect the north to south even numbered streets. For several decades

THE COSTA VERDE 259

Espinho has become the summer getaway for huge numbers of tourists from Portugal and northern Europe. A long strip of white sandy beaches stretches out over the western edge of town and becomes completely packed in the warmer months.

Besides being home to Portugal's oldest golf course, Espinho contains several attractions including a large municipal swimming pool, several tennis facilities, a **casino** (bring your passport), and some fairly nice bench lined cobblestone lanes. The busy outdoor **mercado** (market) is right in the center of town *on Rua 16* every Monday, and there are seasonal bullfights at the **Praça de Touros** *on Rua 41* in the southern sector of the city.

The best beaches in the area can be found at **Praia da Granja** *about 4 km north of Espinho* and at **Praia de Esmoriz**, *6 km south of town*. Make sure that the blue flag for clean water is up on any area beach you may wish to swim in, the general area is notorious for pollution. Espinho offers very little charm, but that hasn't stopped the hordes of Dutch and German tourists from filling almost all its hotels during July and August.

When you have had your fill of beaches and want some cultural diversion, I suggest a nice daytrip to the historic **castelo** (castle) at old Roman town of **Santa Maria da Feira**. From Espinho, *follow route N-109-4 south for about 19 km or so* to reach this amazing town. When you finally arrive in town you can't help but notice the dramatic 11th-century Gothic **Castelo da Feira** castle which looms above. A wonderful walkway can take you around the castle grounds to see its several towers, a great panoramic view of the rgion, and the massive **Torre de Menagem** keep. In the keep itself there's a remarkable grand hall which was rebuilt in the 15th century.

WHERE TO STAY

HOTEL SOLVERDE, *N-109-Praia da Granja, (02) 726-111. Expensive.*
A nice 5 star seafront hotel just a few km. north of crowded Espinho on Praia da Granja. Facilities include 3 pools, tennis, squash, golf, restaurants, and a disco.

HOTEL PRAIAGOLFE, *Rua 6-Espinho, (02) 720-630. Expensive.*
A large modern 4 star hotel near the sea. The hotel offers nice rooms (many with ocean views), a large health club, pool, sauna, restaurant, disco and golf discounts.

HOTEL APARTAMENTO SOLVERDE, *Rua 21-Espinho, (02) 722-819. Moderate.*
This beachfront property contains 83 apartments (many with sea views) with kitchens. Although facilities are fairly limited, this is a good choice for families.

VILA MARIA, *Rua 62, Espinho, (02) 720-353. Inexpensive.*

This red 19th-century mansion rents 5 comfortable rooms with private bathrooms for visiting tourists. The house is in a garden setting just 5 blocks from the beach.

WHERE TO EAT

BAIA MAR, *Rua 4, #565, (02) 725-415. Expensive.*
A large well known restaurant right near the casino, with views. The menu is a bit pricey, but the meals are impressive. Try the excellent fresh caught seafood.

PIPOLIM, *Rua 19, #768, (02) 725-305. Moderate.*
A tile covered narrow restaurant which serves excellent fish and meat dishes prepared with great care. I had an incredible cod fish dinner here last year.

LAREIRA RESTAURANTE, *Rua 62, #592, (02) 727-980. Moderate.*
Small and traditional, with very good daily seafood specials, live *Fado* music on weekends, excellent house wine, and friendly staff.

VILA NOVA DE GAIA

The suburban industrial city of **Vila Nova de Gaia** rests on the southern bank of the **Douro** river, just across from Porto. Known primarily for its world famous Port wine **caves** and lodges (warehouses), this city has played an important role in the production and distribution of Port wines since the 17th century.

Here you can visit one of several riverfront warehouses (closed on Sundays) and go on a 20 minute guided tour in your language of choice of the Port wine casks and bottling facilities. After the tour you will be invited to taste a few small glasses of complimentary red and white Port wines. I have spent entire afternoons sipping from one cave to the next down the river bank. If you are a true connoisseur of these fortified wines, you can purchase vintage bottles directly from the caves at reasonable prices. Make sure to taste at least one dry white Port wine.

Besides the wine trade, there are only a few other attractions in **Vila Nova de Gaia**. There is a 16th-century beautiful structure known as the **Convento da Serra do Pillar** church on a hill above the city. Although its grounds offer a great panoramic view over Porto, I have never seen the church itself open to the general public.

For art lovers, a quick stop at the the **Museu de Teixeira Lopes** museum can top off your visit to this side of the bridge. The collection of sculptures contains works from both it' namesake as well as Diogo de Macedo can be visited at *Rua Teixeira Lopes, 32* (closed on Mondays). There are also several small bars and clubs just behind the riverfront wine caves as well as on **Largo Miguel Bombarda** that become full in the evening with hundreds of the area's singles.

There are a few reasonably attractive beach areas just south of town at **Madalena**, **Valadares**, and **Praia de Lavadores**. Here you can find inexpensive meals by the sea, and good nightlife.

WHERE TO STAY

GAIAHOTEL, *Ave. da República, 2038, (02) 396-051. Expensive.*

An ultramodern 4 star hotel with 92 deluxe rooms in the center of the city. Facilities include a fancy health club, restaurant, minibars, shopping center, and a garage.

HOTEL CASA BRANCA PRAIA, *Rua da Belgica-Afurada, (02) 781-3691. Expensive.*

A modern 4 star 56 room resort hotel near the beach at *Praia de Lavadores*, 5 km south of Vila Nova de Guia. Facilities include health club, pool, tennis, restaurant.

QUINTA SÃO SALVADOR, *Oliveira do Douro, (02) 309-222. Moderate.*

A beautiful manor house a bit out of town with 7 beautiful guestrooms that have private bathrooms, minibars, and cable TV. Horse riding facilities for guests.

HOTEL IBIS, *Lugar de Chas-Afurada, (02) 781-4242. Moderate.*

A French owned 2 star chain motel with comfortable and well equipped modern rooms and an indoor pool. Located just outside of town in the Afurada district.

RESIDENCIAL ORLA MARATIMA, *Praia da Madelena, (02) 711-6080. Inexpensive.*

A restaurant which offers a few simple and comfortable rooms with private bath. Besides good rooms, the dinners are also very reasonable and hearty.

WHERE TO EAT

RESTAURANTE CARPA, *Ave. da República, 1731, (02) 397-129. Moderate.*

A simple restaurant with good seafood and meat dishes in the center of downtown. Specialties include fresh shrimp and grilled meats.

THE DOURO RIVER TOWNS

Most tourists never get to the small towns and wine producing villages which line the banks of the **Douro** river. If you have the time for a day trip or an overnight, this is one of the most tranquil and beautiful areas you can imagine.

In the old days, many small wooden vessels would sail up and down this river to bring fresh Port wines to **Vila Nova de Gaia** for further

THE COSTA VERDE 263

fermentation and eventual bottling. Now the river has been dammed up, and has created several man made lakes and beaches in the process.

For those of you who wish to take a day trip by car through the area, you can leave Porto via route N-209 east through **Gondomar**. Continue for about 7 km and you will end up in front of the Douro river on the memorable route 108, which continues up the Duoro towards the lovely countryside near **Mesão Frio** and onward to **Peso da Régua** (see Montanhas chapter). You can take this beautiful route up the river until you are ready to cross one of the several bridged dams to the almost forgotten southern bank and its route N-222, which winds its way back to the Port wine vineyards of **Lamego** and onward back towards Porto via Vila Nova de Guia.

On the southern bank of the Douro, some 20 minutes southeast Porto, is the lovely town of **Lomba**. This sleepy peasant town is home to many traditional townsfolk who will are not used to seeing many tourists. This general area is home to several dams and reservoirs including the **Barragem de Crestuma** which allows visitors to waterski and sail in this part of the river. Just in front of the river banks at Lomba is a fantastic manor house called **Quinta da Lomba** which rents opulent rooms and grand apartments.

As you pass by the dams on the river, you can see many people enjoying watersports like windsufing, jet skiing, water skiing, sailing, and swimming in the calm waters. The small villages contain original stone houses and many of the traditional local residents use mules and oxen as transportation. I strongly recommend the Lomba area for those who wish to visit Porto, but prefer to be a bit away from the noise, pollution, traffic, and over priced accommodations of the city itself.

If you prefer to avoid driving, there is a great train line which runs from **Porto's** *São Bento station* east to **Livração**, then south to head up the Douro river's northern bank to **Peso da Régua** and points further east. The three hour ride to **Peso da Régua** is quite interesting as it passes through wine country, but there are also seasonal connections from Livração to Amarante via historic narrow gauge railroads whose future is somewhat in doubt.

Please contact the **São Bento CP Rail station** in Porto *at (02) 200-2722 for further details, or visit any Turismo in the north.* **Endouro** cruise lines also offers excursions upriver from Porto to Peso de Régua. These ferry cruises are a relaxing alternative to the car and train routes, but do not allow for much in the way of local wine tasting and watersport activities. *Endouro can be reached in Porto by calling (02) 324-236 or (02) 208-4161.*

WHERE TO STAY

QUINTA DA LOMBA, *N-222-Lomba, (055) 663-36. Their main number is (02) 482-714. Moderate.*

A fantastic 18th-century riverfront manor house on the south bank of the Douro owned by a charming English speaking retired doctor. Facilities include tennis, jet skis, waterskiing, pool, sauna, grill area, and 6 luxury rooms and apartments. The staff is comprised by local peasant women.

CASA DAS TORRES DE OLIVEIRA, *Oliveira, (054) 237-43. Moderate.*

An opulent wine producing estate and 18th century regal manor house about 9 km northeast of Mesão Frio which has 4 rooms with private bathrooms. Facilities include bar, dining room, pool, bicycles, gardens, TV room, and parking.

CASA DO LARANJAL, *N-108-Porto Manso, (055) 551-232. Moderate.*

A riverfront wine and olive oil producing estate on the north bank of the Douro near Penha Longa which has 5 rooms with semi private bathrooms. Facilities include lounge, gardens, winery, boats, fishing, TV room, ping pong, and parking.

QUINTA DO PAÇO, *N-600-Vila Marim, (054) 699-346. Moderate.*

A historic 18th-century manor house 4 km. north of Mesão Frio which rents 4 rooms with private bathrooms. Facilities include bar, gardens, pool, billards, and TV room.

CASA DOS VARAIS, *N-2-Lamego, (054) 232-51. Moderate.*

A relaxing 18th century manor house and wine growing estate near town with views over the southern bank of the Douro which offers 3 rooms with private bathrooms.

CASA DE SÃO PEDRO, *N-108-Santa Marinha, (054) 981-14. Moderate.*

A 17th-century stone house near the river which offers 5 rooms with private bathrooms. Facilities include lounge, dining room, gardens, TV room, and parking.

HOTEL PANORAMA, *Mesão Frio, (054) 992-36. Moderate.*

A nice modern 31 room hotel in the heart of town with a bar, restaurant, and parking.

ESTALAGEM SANTIAGO, *Aboinha-Gondomar, (02) 984-0034. Moderate.*

A reasonable 4 star inn with 14 guestrooms in the village of Aboinha. Facilities include a good restaurant, bar, TV room, Disco, parking, and direct dial phones.

CASA DEFRONTE, *N-108-Entre Os Rios, (055) 634-84. Moderate.*

A granite manor house near the Crestuma-Lever dam which rents one large 3 bedroom and a comfortable 2 bedroom apartments to visiting tourists.

WHERE TO EAT

PORTA DO RIO, *Marginal-Gondomar, (02) 964-3032. Moderate.*
This unassuming riverfront restaurant off Ave. Clube Cacadores in Gondomar offers great views, good service, and reasonably priced fresh fish and seafood.

AMARANTE

Located just off the **Tâmega** river *about 67 km northeast of Porto on route IP-4 east* is the charming ancient town of **Amarante**. The peaceful town is divided by the river over which passes the 18th-century granite Ponte de São Gonçalo bridge. This riverfront is one of my favorite pic-nic sights in the region. Surrounded by the **Serra do Marão** mountains, every view from Amarante is impressive.

Several 16th- and 17th-century terraced houses line the one riverbank, while the other bank leads directly to the **Convento de São Gonçalo** monastery and the heart of the old town. From the foot of the bridge you can walk to the quaint **Praça da República** square and it's atmospheric side streets lined with local merchants and old plazas, or cross over the bridge to the riverfront *Rua 31 de Janeiro* with its many cafes. The town is a great place to wander through and shop, especially on the weekly Wednesday morning **mercado** (market) right near the bridge.

There are several remarkable attractions worth a good look, including the 16th-century **Convento de São Gonçalo** with its fine interior gilding, amazing 17th-century organ, Renaissance cloisters, statue-laden loggia, and tomb of St. Gonçalo who lived in Amarante during the 13th century. Many singles touch the tomb of Saint Gonçalo, the match maker, in the hopes of being blessed with a spouse.

Each year on the first Saturday in June, Amarante hosts the colorful **Romaria São Gonçalo** festival in honor of this popular saint of love and marriage. Amarante is lucky to be home to a great little museum. Known both as the **Museu de Amadeo de Sousa Cardosa** (closed on Mondays) this unique collection is located next to the town hall in part of the Convento de São Gonçalo complex. Here there are paintings by cubist artist Amadeo de Sousa-Cardoso as well as paintings by António Carneiro, Eduardo Viana, and Resende. There are also displays of fine sculptures as well as archeological finds from the area. If you walk up the *Rua 5 de Outubro* you will soon find the baroque 18th-century **Igreja de São Pedro** church contains unusual azulejos and a beautifully carved wooden ceiling.

WHERE TO STAY

POUSADA DE SÃO GONÇALO, *Curva do Lancete-Ansiaes, (055) 461-113. Moderate.*

Situated about 17 km east of town, this pousada offers 15 rustic rooms with dramatic views of the Serra de Marão mountains. A peaceful place to stay.

CASA DE PASCOAES, *São João de Gatão, (055) 422-595. Moderate.*

A fine historic manor house in front of the Tâmega river off route N-210 some 3 km north of Amarante which offers 4 antique laden guestrooms with private bathrooms. Facilities include dining room, lounge, library. museum, billards, TV, and parking.

HOTEL NAVARRAS, *Rua António Carneiro, (055) 424-036. Moderate.*

A modern 3 star hotel in the heart of town with 63 good sized air conditioned rooms, a restaurant, bar, roof top pool, garage, cable TV, and direct dial phones.

HOTEL SILVA, *Rua Candido do Reis, 53, (055) 423-110. Inexpensive.*

A small 1 star hotel in the town's center with comfortable rooms that have scenic patios. The hotel offers very few facilities besides a great outdoor breakfast area.

WHERE TO EAT

RESTAURANTE ZÉ DA CALÇADA, *Rua 31 de Janeiro, 83, (055) 422-023. Expensive.*

A pretty good local restaurant which specializes in meat and fish dishes from the region. The restaurant's fireplace, terrace, and down home ambiance are wonderful.

RESTAURANTE SÃO GONÇALO, *Largo de São Gonçalo, (055) 422-707. Moderate.*

A pretty good but somewhat overpriced regional restaurant and snackbar next to the church which serves everything from sandwiches to full dinners to mostly tourists.

CELORICO DE BASTO

The peaceful wine producing town of **Celorico de Basto** lies *some 27 km. northeast of Amarante on route N-210 north just off the* **Tâmega** *river.* Set within the **Serra do Marão** mountain range, this lovely town is the perfect base from which to hike, fish, or just enjoy the countryside while sampling fine local *Vinho Verde* (a slightly sparkling fruity white wine) and staying in historic country inns and manor houses.

WHERE TO STAY

CASA DO CAMPO, *N-210-Celorico de Basto, (055) 361-231. Moderate.*

A dramatic 18th century manor house 4 km. north of town which offers 8 incredible rooms with private bathroom. Facilities include bar, dining room, pool, and gardens.

THE COSTA VERDE 267

QUINTA DE VILA POUCA, *N-210-Codecoso, (055) 321-766. Inexpensive.*

A rustic 18th century house 7 km south of town offering 4 guestrooms with private bathrooms for hikers and tourists. Facilities include bar, bicycles, and TV room.

MATOSINHOS

Just north of Porto on the coastal road is the beachfront suburban city of **Matosinhos**. This city attracts mostly Portuguese to its coastal resort area.

Although quite developed with modern structures, there are small pockets of seafront which remain tranquil and appealing. Most people come here to use the ocean or one of three large swimming pools. The harbor is one of the largest fishing ports in the country, and hosts a daily auction of fish which is quite a scene.

If you are in the mood for some culture, visit the aggressively fortified Gothic 13th-century **Mosterio de Leça do Balio** church just outside of town. I usually stay in Matosinhos when I need to visit to Porto during the summer, but desire budget accommodations just a few minutes away.

WHERE TO STAY

HOTEL PORTO MAR, *Rua Brito Capelo, 167, (02) 938-2104. Moderate.*

A simple 2 star hotel with 32 well furnished comfortable rooms in town's center. The hotel offers it's guests a bar, restaurant, private bathrooms, TV, and good service.

ESTALAGEM DA VIA NORTE, *Via Norte-Leça do Balio, (02) 948-0294. Moderate.*

A full service 12 room inn with lots of facilities including bar, restaurant, room service, laundry services, air conditioning, TV, parking, and a friendly helpful staff.

PENSÃO CENTRAL, *Rua Brito Capelo, 599, (02) 937-2590. Inexpensive.*

Centrally located, modest, some hotel services. Most of the basic rooms have private bathrooms. The hotel offers only breakfast.

WHERE TO EAT

OS LVISADAS, *Rua Tomas Ribeiro, 257, (02) 937-8242. Expensive.*

A beautiful and intimate restaurant with a romantic atmosphere and exceptional service. The chefs here serve top quality fine cuisine to well dressed clientele.

LAGOSTA REAL, *Rua Lo Ferreira, 239, (02) 937-1363. Moderate.*

A traditional lobster and fish house with a busy downtown location

next to city hall. I suggest an order of the house specialty seafood dish called Sortido de Marisco.
O GAVETO, *Rua Roberto Ivens,826, (02) 937-8796. Moderate.*

This excellent seafood house specializes in whatever just arrived from the docks. The service here is wonderful, and the huge portions are enough for 2 to share.

VILA DO CONDE

The town of **Vila do Conde** is *located about 28 km. north of Porto on route N-13 north at the mouth of the Ave river.* In the past, Vila do Conde was a famous wooden boat building center, but recently the demand for such vessels has decreased. Although the town has a nice beach, it has not yet been over-developed.

I much prefer the small town atmosphere here to the larger seaside resorts of Espinho and Póvoa de Varzim, because the town maintained some authentic medieval flavor. The rich tradition and royal heritage of this town can still be witnessed in the wonderful old part of town with a vast assortment of 16th-century houses, unusual religious buildings, and museums to visit. A quick visit to the *Turismo on Rua 25 de Abril* can provide you with a free local map of the area's sights.

The Gothic 16th-century **Igreja Matriz** church in the town's center has a beautiful Manueline portico, a 17th-century bell tower, beautiful paintings by artists such as Francisco Machado, and hand made azulejos from the 18th century. Part of the church houses the **Museu de Arte Sacra** museum with it's fine collection of gold and silver ecclesiastical artifacts. Nearby on the north bank of the river is the massive 14th-century **Convento de Santa Clara** church which contains the heavily ornamented stone tombs of King Dom Afonso Sanches and several of his relatives. Connected to the church is an 18th-century aqueduct with over 900 arches. Also worth a visit is the 16th-century city hall building which contains an impressive gilded tribune. Near the docks you can view the ruined polygonal 16th century **Castelo de São João Baptista** fortress.

Vila do Conde is also famous for its fine bobbin lace production. This unique lace has been produced here for over 5 centuries by local young girls. If you wish to see how the bobbin lace is made, stop by the **Escola de Rendas** school on *Rua do Lidador.* There is also an interesting **Centro Artisanato** handicrafts center on *Rua 5 de Outubro* that sells local bobbin lace, heavy hand knitted sweaters, wood carvings, and some leather items. For a fortnight beginning on the last weel of July, town hosts an impressive regional andicrafts fair. Also of interest is the **Museu José Régio** *on Rua José Régio, 138* which is a house that contains the private art collection of this well known local poet.

THE COSTA VERDE 269

Vila do Conde hosts a nice weekly **mercado** (market) and fair on each Friday in the center of town, as well as a daily produce market. This religious community is well known for several big festivals including the **Festa do Corpus Christi** festival held every fourth year in June (the next one is 1996) where carpets of beautiful flowers are placed on the streets of town as a silver and precious stone monstrance makes its way down the procession.

WHERE TO STAY

ESTALAGEM DO BRASÃO, *Ave. Dr. José Canavarro, (052) 642-016. Moderate.*

This converted mansion now contains a full service 4 star inn with good rooms, a bar, restaurant, disco, air conditioning, private bathrooms, and TV. A good place.

SOPETE SANT'ANA, *Azurara, (052) 641-767. Moderate.*

A waterfront aparthotel complex across the river from town. The 35 pleasant 1,2, and 3 bedroom apartments have access to a pool, restaurant, and hotel services. An especially affordable property for families or couples traveling together.

QUINTA DAS ALFAIAS, *Fajozes, (052) 662-146. Moderate.*

A nice 19th century house some 5 km east of town in the village of *Fajozes* which offers 5 large guestrooms with semi private bathrooms, bar, pool, and gardens.

RESIDENCIAL PRINCESA DO AVE, *Ave. Dr. A. S. Pereira, 261, (052) 642-482. Inexpensive.*

A basic and comfortable inn above a restaurant with minimal services and facilities.

WHERE TO EAT

RESTAURANTE PRAIA MAR, *Ave. Infante Dom Henrique, 58, (052) 685-723. Moderate.*

A simple seafood and beef restaurant which has a large menu with good prices.

MAR A VISTA, *Praia do Mindelo, (052) 671-197. Moderate.*

A large restaurant with huge seaview picture windows and great service. The menu changes often, but there are always seafood specialties.

PÓVOA DE VARZIM

The resort town of **Póvoa de Varzim** *sits up the coast some 4 km from Vila do Conde up route N-13 north.* It's now a large tourist mecca for vacationing northern Portuguese families, and has become quite developed with high-rise condos, apartment buildings, and hotels facing the sea.

In the summer months, the beachfront is lined with rows of cabana tents which are full of screaming children and sun weary parents. Besides the beaches and watersports, many other visitors come here to gamble or see a tacky revue of half-naked women in the city's pink **casino** (bring your passport). The fishing industry still maintains its presence here, although the traditional methods are no longer profitable. The entertaining weekday fish auction still takes place near the docks, and it is work a look if you need a break from the beach.

There are some traditional handicrafts produced in the area including hand embroidered sweaters, lace, weaving, and silver filigree. The nearby town of **Rates** contains the well preserved 13th-century Romanesque **Igreja de São Pedro** church.

WHERE TO STAY

HOTEL VERMAR, *Rua Alto Martin Vaz, (52) 615-566. Expensive.*

A seafront 4 star resort hotel with 208 air conditioned rooms (some deluxe rooms have patios) 2 pools, bar, restaurant, health club, tennis, and a nearby golf course.

GRANDE HOTEL DA PAVOA, *Largo Passeio Alegre, (52) 615-464. Expensive.*

This 3 star hotel in the heart of town near the casino offers 96 air conditioned rooms (some with sea views), café, restaurant, bar, TV, and nearby golf course and tennis.

ESTALAGEM SANTO ANDRÉ, *Praia da Agucadouro, (52) 615-766. Moderate.*

A very good seafront inn located just outside of town on a quiet beach. The property offers 49 sea view rooms, a bar, restaurant, TV, squash, and a nearby golf course.

HOTEL TORRE MAR, *Lugar da Fonte Nova, (52) 613-677. Moderate.*

A charming little 31 room hotel in a residential section of town with excellent service, nice rooms, private bathrooms, heating, minibar, TV, parking, and laundry services.

RESIDENCIAL GETT, *Ave. Mouzinho Albuquerque, 54, (52) 683-206. Inexpensive.*

A basic inn with 20 simple rooms containing private bathroom, TV, and telephones.

WHERE TO EAT

O CHEF, *Ave. dos Banhos, 318, (052) 684-126. Moderate.*

A nice and friendly seafood restaurant right near the beach which serves the best steaks in town. The large menu offers huge portions of well prepared regional food.

BELO HORIZANTE, *Rua Tenete Valadim, 63, (052) 624-787. Moderate.*
An unassuming restaurant specializing in assorted fresh seafoods at good prices.

GUIMARÃES

The medieval city of **Guimarães** is *located about 37 km northeast from Póvoa de Varzim on route N-206 east.* This city was the first official capital of Portugal and is home to the 10th-century towered castle in which the first king of Portugal, Dom Afonso Henriques, was born and raised. This was also the birthplace of Gil Vicente, the 15th-century writer and creator of Portugal's national theater.

The city has managed to maintain much of its tradition and original ambiance. Many old houses are built directly into the original walls of the city. To this day, Guimarães produces fine linens and fabrics which can be purchased in several shops throughout the city.

There is plenty to do here. See *Seeing the Sights* a few pages ahead.

WHERE TO STAY

POUSADA S MARINHA DA COSTA, *Lugar da Costa, (053) 514-453. Expensive.*
A vast *pousada* with 51 rooms in a converted 12th century Augustine cloister a few km. out of town at *Pena*. The rooms were monastic cells and tend to be small, but the atmosphere is quite unusual and worth the slight squeeze. A great place to stay. Facilities include bar, restaurant, minibars, TV, and parking.

POUSADA DE N.S. DA OLIVEIRA, *Rua Santa Maria, (053) 514-204. Expensive.*
A charming *pousada* with the best location in town. The 16 guestrooms are quite comfortable, the service is good, and the food is a real treat. Facilities include bar, restaurant, direct dial phones, and parking. A nice place to stay.

CASA DE POMBAIS, *Ave. de Londres, (053) 412-917. Moderate.*
A great 18th century manor house in the east side of town which offers only 2 fine guestrooms with private bathrooms. Call, you may get lucky and they have space.

HOTEL DE GUIMARÃES , *Rua Eduardo de Almeida, (053) 516-234. Moderate.*
A modern 4 star hotel with 70 air conditioned large rooms. Facilities include indoor pool, health club, squash, sauna, garage, a bar, and a large restaurant.

CASA CONDE DE PAÇO VIEIRA, *Paço Vieira-Mesão Frio, (053) 532-881. Moderate.*

A beautiful 19th century manor house with a 17th century chapel that rents 4 pretty rooms with private bathroom to deluxe travellers. The property is about 4 km east of town off *route N 101*. Facilities include bar, dining room, library, TV, and parking.

CASA DE SEZIM, *Santo Amaro, (053) 523-196. Moderate.*

This old manor house 5 km. outside of *Guimarães* looks just like the *Palácio Seteais*. The property is owned by 2 former diplomats who produce fine *Vinho Verde* and rent 6 rooms. Ask to see the painting of New York in the Indian days. Facilities include bar, dining room, gardens, horse back riding, winery, and parking.

HOTEL DO TOURAL, *Largo do Toural, (053) 411-250. Inexpensive.*

Your basic cheap 1 star city hotel with decent rooms that have private bathrooms.

SEEING THE SIGHTS

The *Turismo is located at the southern tip of the oval shaped city on Alameda da Resistencia Fascismo, 83* and is a good place pick up a free map. If you have arrived by car, one of the few municipal parking lots happens to be just two blocks west of the *Turismo* near the corner of the **Largo da República do Brasil**. From the Largo, you can wander up into the old city via the passage at the end of the town's wall. Once you have passed through the wall, walk straight up the short winding street and you will soon find yourself at the **Largo do Oliveira** plaza.

Inside the **Largo do Oliveira** you will first notice the 14th-century **Pedrão do Salado** portico which commemorates a victory over the Moors. Behind the portico is the **Igreja de Nossa Senhora da Oliveira** church which was built in the 14th century, on the site of a 10th century monastery. The church contains a 16th-century Manueline tower and a humble 14th-century Gothic chapel, as well as beautiful cloisters and a chapter house which are home to the **Museu Alberto Sampaio** museum. The museum (closed Monday) contains a collection of azulejos, ceramics, sculptures, a beautiful silver bible, António Vaz paintings, artifacts from the structure's origins as a 10th century monastery, and a wide assortment of ecclesiastical items including a silver triptych altarpiece said to have been captured during a Castillian battle.

Also in the Largo area there are cafes, a few shops, the beautiful **Paços do Concehlo**, and the charming Pousada da Oliveira.

From the Largo da Oliveira you should turn left (north) and head up the cobblestone *Rua de Santa Maria*, one of the city's oldest and most interesting streets. While walking up the *Rua de Santa Maria* you will notice several ornate 14th-century homes which have unusual wood balconies and artistic iron grillwork. As you continue further up (north) you will pass next to an old stone structure called the **Casa dos Arco** (arch house) which is connected to an overhead medieval granite arch. A few steps later you can enter the **Largo Conego José Gomes** and have a look at the facade and the inner courtyard of the former **Convento de Santa Clara** whose 17th-century baroque structure now houses the town hall of Guimarães.

If you continue up *Rua de Santa Maria* towards the north end of town, you will pass the tree-lined park called the **Largo Martins Sarmento**, surrounded on both sides by the 17th-century **Igreja de Carmo** church on the right (east) side, and the house of archaeologist Martins Sarmento on the left (west) side.

A bit further up the street to the right (east) is the massive French designed 15th-century **Paço dos Duques** (also known as **Ducal Palace**). Originally built for the duke of Bragança, this palace was abandoned and then later restored as the official presidential residence in the north. The palace is also a museum (open daily) which can be visited to see it's beautiful tapestries, sculptures, hand crafted wooden ceilings, furniture, and paintings (3 of which are by Josefa D'Obidos), but it certainly does not have a very typically Portuguese design. In front of the palace is a 19th-century statue of King Dom Afonso Henriques by famed Porto artist Soares dos Reis.

From the palace, you can't help but be drawn towards the massive 10th-century **castelo** castle (closed Mondays) which rests on the northeast corner of town and allows it's visitors a great view over the city. It's original structure was reenforced by Count Henriques, the father of Portugal's first king. It contains seven towers and a large defensive wall that surrounds the keep. Just below the castle lies the tiny Romanesque **Igreja São Miguel do Castelo** church where King Dom Afonso Henriques is said to have been baptized.

After visiting the castle and church, you may wish to return to the southern end of town via a different set of streets. Bear right (west) when you reach the fork in the road at the top of **Largo Martins Sarmento**. This street called Rua das Trinas leads into the **Largo Dr. Prego** plaza, and if you go straight through the plaza and onto Rua de Valdonas you will soon reach the large square known as **Largo João Franco**.

At the bottom (south) end of this large square you will find the beautiful 16th-century renaissance **Igreja da Misericórdia** church with a beautiful organ. Roughly behind the church on *Rua Sapateira* is one of prettiest houses in the city. The regal white walled and granite structure was the opulent home of the Lobo Machado family back in the 18th century, and is not open to the public.

From the front of the Misericórdia church you should keep walking west about two blocks until you have left the old town by crossing the top (north) side of the tranquil **Largo do Toural** plaza. From this corner you can see the vast 14th-century Gothic **Convento de São Domingos** church whose cloister is now home to the **Museu de Martins Sarmento** museum. The museum (closed on Mondays) hosts a collection of archaeological and ethnological items ranging from Prehistoric and Celtic artifacts to medieval weaponry.

To visit yet another impressive *azulejos* and marbled church, walk down (south) on the **Largo do Toural** plaza. From here you can pass the *Turismo* office again on *Alameda da Resistencia Fascismo,* and cross over to the 15th-century **Igreja de São Fransisco**.

BRAGA

The large commercial city of **Braga** is *situated about 23 km northwest of Guimarães on route N-101 north.* The history of the city goes back to at least the time of it's Celtic settlement which was first known as Bracari, and was later conquered by the Romans at about 250 B.C. At that time, it became an important Roman merchant city and was known as Bracara Augusta. Since it was situated at the intersection of five important Roman roads, the city became a major merchant trading area with many goods like ceramics and glassware imported here from Egypt, Greece, and other parts of Europe.

Braga was later captured by Suebian troops in the 5th century and became their capital. After three centuries conquer and occupation by the Visigoths and Moors, Braga finally reemerged as a Christian stronghold by 1040. As a major religious center and seat of the archbishop, Braga has became known as *The Rome of Portugal.* In the 16th century, Bishop Diogo de Sousa started to urbanize the city, and was responsible for many of the churches and other structures which adorn the city to this day.

Today, Braga is a major industrial city. Most of the more than 75,000 residents of the city live in large unimpressive concrete block apartments that seem to spring up everywhere. Most are hard working middle-class factory employees from the leather, electronics, and garment industries which surround most of the city.

Braga offers fine museums, religious buildings, and some good shopping possibilities, including a daily market in **Praça Comércio** and a Tuesday **mercado** (market) at **Largo da Feira** which offers a great selection of factory imperfect shoes at low prices. Other than a few ancient streets and the pretty gardens in the **Praça da República**, Braga is not a very pretty place.

WHERE TO STAY

CASA DA PEDRA CAVALGADA, *N-101-Braga, (053) 245-96. Moderate.*

THE COSTA VERDE 275

A pretty and traditional stone Minho house, offering 2 very private guestrooms with their own bathrooms, living room, fireplace and sitting room, and parking.

HOTEL CARANDA, *Ave. da Liberdade, 96, (053) 614-500. Moderate.*

A modern 3 star hotel with 100 air conditioned spacious rooms overlooking the main street in town. Facilities include restaurant, bar, cable TV, pool, and garage.

HOTEL TURISMO, *Pracenta João XXI, (053) 612-220. Moderate.*

This 4 star centrally located hotel offers 132 air conditioned comfortable rooms. The hotel staff is friendly, and facilities include a rooftop pool, restaurant, Café , bar,TV.

RESTHOTEL BRAGA, *N-14-Celeiros, (053) 673-865. Inexpensive.*

A modern motel style 2 star hotel a few minutes away from town which offers 72 nice rooms with private bathrooms and TV, a bar, restaurant, and air conditioning.

PENSÃO SÃO JOÃO BAPTISTA, *Rua Monsenhor Airosa, 66, (053) 752-04. Inexpensive.*

A pretty good small in with about a dozen small but comfortable rooms that have TV.

WHERE TO EAT

RESTAURANTE INACIO, *Campo das Hortas, 4, (053) 613-235. Expensive.*

A small and charming stone walled 2 story restaurant which serves excellent regional and international cuisine with spotty service and plenty of atmosphere.

CHURRASQUEIRA ANGOLANA, *Alameda do Fujacal, 96, (053) 612-127. Moderate.*

A pretty little restaurant with fine meat and seafood specialties, excellent house wine, and impressive service. Try the veal dish called *lombinhos de vitela*.

MAR E TERRE, *Rua Congregados, 105, (053) 730-79. Inexpensive.*

An unassuming little combination restaurant and snack bar which serves huge portions of meat and seafood dishes at great prices. Very good local food.

SEEING THE SIGHTS

Among the sights worth seeing in Braga is the giant 11th-century **Sé Primaz** cathedral. Situated on the site of the **Igreja de Santa Maria de Braga** church that was destroyed by the Moors some four centuries earlier, construction started in 1070 which makes this the oldest cathedral in Portugal. Since it has been rebuilt several times over the years, it has a varied mixture of Romanesque, Gothic, Renaissance, Baroque, and Manueline elements. The church still contains several Romanesque features including some windows, the naves, and the cloister's apse. Most of the other features were either altered or added in the later centuries.

While inside the church don't overlook the fine high altar made from *Anca stone*, the gilded bronze Flemish tomb of Prince Afonso, the double 18th-century pipe organs, the beautiful *azulejos* in the **Chapel of São Pedro de Rates**, and the impressive altars around the exterior cloister. Adjoining the Sé Primaz cathedral are several other chapels which have impressive contents, such as the tombs in the Gothic **Capelo dos Reis** and **Capela da Glória**, as well as the impressive 16th-century altar and ceiling in the **Capela de Nossa Senhora da Piedade**.

Inside the Sé Primaz's treasury is the **Museu de Arte Sacra de Sé Primaz** museum (closed Mondays), which houses a fine collection of sacred art objects including a 10th century ivory casket, 14th-century Gothic chalice, items made of precious metals encrusted wit rare gems, and some beautiful *azulejos*.

Across the street from the Sé Primaz cathedral is the **Antigo Paço Episcopal** palace which is home to the 300,000 volume public library, the municipal archives, and the currently closed Museu do Dom Diego de Sousa museum which will be the future home of the city museum. The palace is comprised of several substructures which were built in the 14th, 16th, and 18th centuries. In the courtyard of the palace is the **Largo do Paço**, which surrounds the 17th-century **Chafariz do Largo do Paço** fountain.

If you walk one block west of the palace, you can take a peek in the 18th-century baroque **Câmara Municipal** (town hall) with its beautiful facade and interior collection of paintings and *azulejos*. In front of the town hall is an 18th century baroque fountain in the form of a pelican. A couple of streets further west on the *Rua dos Biscainhos* is the 17th century **Palácio dos Biscainhos** palace and gardens.

The palace grounds contain the **Biscainhos Museu de Etnografia, Historia, e Arte** museum. Inside this converted 17th century mansion (closed on Monday) you can see artifacts, artwork, azulejos, and furniture from the 17th-19th centuries. The mansion overlooks a tranquil well groomed garden. There is also the **Museu Pio XII** in the eastern sector of town, off the **Campo de São Tiago**. This interesting little collection of Roman and Visigoth artifacts, as well as ecclesiastical items can be found in the **Seminario de São Tiago** nearby.

BOM JESUS

Located 4 km up the hilly route N-103-3 east from Braga is the baroque hilltop church of **Bom Jesus do Monte**. The 18th-century church was

THE COSTA VERDE 277

constructed in neo-classical style by architect Carlos Amarante and its simple interior has been designed in the form of a Latin cross. The side of the church is surrounded by a peaceful park with benches, fountains, small chapels, and a man made lake. In front of the church itself are a set of unusual stairways and terraces which proceed down the hill (you can take a funicular back up).

Immediately in front of the church you can start your descent from the **Terreiro de Moises**, which begins the strange and mysterious granite **Stairway of the Three Virtues** (faith, hope, and charity) and continues downward through the amazing baroque Stairs of the Five Senses. One of these stairways has statues that pour water from different body parts and are known as the fountains of touch, taste, smell, hearing, and sight. On each level of stairs are shrines and chapels referring to differing scenes from the Passion of Christ. As you walk down each set of stairs, you can't help but feel a mysterious power is present. In fact, there is a small road near the church on which locals can show you a strange phenomenon. If you put your car in neutral, it will roll up a hill.

If you continue further up the mountain road called N103-3, you will soon find a beautiful view of the Braga region from atop **Monte Sameiro** mountain, and its church's lantern tower. *Another 3 km further up the mountain road you can take route N-309 south* to the excavated ruins of a Celt-Iberian walled city of **Citânia de Briteiros**, which dates back to before the 24th century B.C.

WHERE TO STAY

CASTELO DO BOM JESUS, *Bom Jesus, (053) 676-566. Expensive.*
A privately owned ornate nobleman's mansion with 10 nice guestrooms, a large pool, jacuzzi, farm, on site prehistoric megaliths, a winery, and beautiful azulejos.

HOTEL DO ELEVADOR, *Bom Jesus, (053) 676-611. Moderate.*
A 4 star quiet and friendly hotel with 25 large and quiet rooms which have antique furnishings. Facilities include restaurant, lounge, cable TV, and room service.

HOTEL DO PARQUE, *Bom Jesus, (053) 676-606. Moderate.*
A beautiful converted mansion which is now home to a 4 star hotel with 50 deluxe rooms. Facilities include bar, park, TV, air conditioning, and handicapped access.

CASA DOS LAGOS, *Bom Jesus, (053) 676-738. Moderate.*
A converted 18th century manor house in a peaceful setting with fine views over *Braga*. They offer 4 large 2 bedroom apartments and 1 nice double room with private bathroom. Facilities include bar, library, gardens, TV room, and parking.

APARTHOTEL MAE D'AGUA, *Bom Jesus, (053) 676-581. Moderate.*
A bright and cheery modern hotel with 30 large and comfortable 1 and 2 bedroom air conditioned apartments with hotel facilities including bar, restaurant, disco, barber, billards, TV, direct dial phones, and parking. A great place for families.

BARCELOS

The beautiful hilltop market town of **Barcelos** rests at the foot of a 14th-century arched bridge *over the Rio Cávado river some 19 km southeast of Braga on route N-205 east*. With its history of being the 13th-century home to the Bragança royal dynasty, this town of 9500 people contains beautiful old houses, palaces, museums, churches, and lots of friendly people to point you in the right direction.

Barcelos is known as one of the major centers for the production of colorful hand painted pottery and crafts. On Thursdays, the huge **Feira de Barcelos mercado** (market) takes over the **Campo da República** fairgrounds and offers it's shoppers items ranging from the famous local pottery to hand sewn leather saddles and live poultry. Here you can negotiate with the country artisans who dress in regional peasant clothes.

One of the most common symbols on items sold here is the famed Barcelos rooster which commemorates the story of an unjustly accused thief. The prisoner was about to be hung when he proclaimed his innocence by miraculously transforming the judge's roasted chicken lunch into a live crowing rooster.

From the central plaza of **Campo da República** you can see dramatic churches, stately buildings, and several streets such as *Rua Dom António Barroso* which full of pottery shops, cafes, monuments, and medieval atmosphere. The 18th-century **Igreja do Terco** church is just above the fairgrounds and is not to be missed. The church's interior is covered with original azulejo murals hand created by António de Oliveira Bernardes which are adorned with incredible paintings, gold leaf woodwork, and unique painted vaulting. Also surrounding the fairgrounds are the lovely 18th-century **Templo do Nosso Senhor da Cruz** and the solemn **Igreja da Misericórdia** church.

The town's original keep, called the **Torre de Menagem**, is on *Largo do Porto Novo* and houses both the *Turismo* and a small local crafts center. Nearby in the **Largo do Municipal** plaza you can find the 13th-century **Igreja Matriz** church with its *azulejo* and baroque interior. In the **Câmara Municipal** (city hall) you can visit a small regional museum of ceramics (closed on Mondays).

If you walk towards the medieval bridge, you can visit the **Museu Archeological** (museum of archaeology), located within the ruins of the former 15th-century residence of the Duke of Bragança, known as the **Paço dos Condos**.

WHERE TO STAY

QUINTA DE SANTA COMBA, *Lugar de Crujaes, (053) 832-101. Moderate.*

A regal manor house and wine producing estate off *route N-204* in the village of *Varzea* some 5 km. south of *Barcelos* with 6 good rooms with private bathroom. Facilities include winery, TV, horses, bikes, tennis, horses, and swimming pool.

ALBERGARIA CONDE DE BARCELOS, *Ave. Alcaides de Faria, (053) 811-602. Moderate.*

A nice 4 star inn with 30 comfortable rooms. Facilities include restaurant, heating, radio, a TV room, bar, direct dial phones, and handicapped access.

CASA DO MONTE, *N103-Barcelos, (053) 811-519. Moderate.*

A charming country house surrounded by lots of trees and flowers a few minutes west of town which offers 3 guestrooms, a 1 bedroom, and a 2 bedroom apartment with private bathrooms, TV, bar, and other facilities.

PENSÃO DOM NUNO, *Ave. Dom A. Periera, 76, (053) 815-084. Inexpensive.*

A nice inn with comfortable rooms with private bathrooms and minimal services.

PENSÃO BAGOEIRA, *Ave. Dr. Sidonio Pais, 495, (053) 811-236. Inexpensive.*

A clean and comfortable basic inn near the fairgrounds which offers 6 rooms without private bathroom. Facilities include a bar and restaurant. Packed on market days.

WHERE TO EAT

CEIA RESTAURANTE, *Rua Dr. F. Torres, 94, (053) 815-270. Moderate.*

A nice clean family style restaurant which offers pretty good fish and meat dishes in a friendly environment. The veal and lamb here are fresh and well prepared.

RESTAURANTE BAGOEIRA, *Ave. Sidonio Pais, 495, (053) 811-236. Inexpensive.*

A funky little restaurant with great regional northern Portuguese simple cuisine presented by a cast of merry staff who love to be busy. A great place to have lunch.

ESPOSENDE & OFIR

The cities of **Esposende** and **Ofir** are separated by an estuary of the **Cávado** river's mouth, *some 14 km away from Barcelos on route N-103-1 east.*

Esposende was once a Roman port called *Aquis Celnis*. These days the quiet fishing village still has a small old town and an understated beach area. While wandering around *Esposende* you can still find typical scenes from the daily life of a medieval small town. In town there are a few old churches including the beautiful baroque Chapel of Our Lord of the Navigators with it's beautiful arched ceiling of gold leaf and medieval paintings. The **Praia de Sauve Mar** beach area is a stones throw away and can be reached by regular shuttle service from the center of town.

Ofir is on a small peninsula which is surrounded by the ocean on one side and the river on the other. Ofir has become a major beach resort area with several sports facilities, hotels, beach clubs, and restaurants. Here you will find very little of the traditional village feeling that is so obvious across the water in Esposende. Most of the vacationers in Ofir stay in large hotels which offer pools, watersports, nightclubs, fancy restaurants, tennis, and other full service facilities.

For the most part, Ofir offers little of cultural interest, but the nearby excavations at the Roman city of **Fão** are worth a look on an overcast day. The beach is the main reason people visit Ofir, and there is plenty of it to go around. Prices here tend to be a bit more reasonable than at the other regional resort areas such as **Póvoa de Varzim** and **Espinho**.

WHERE TO STAY

HOTEL OFIR, *Ave. Sousa Martins-Ofir, (053) 981-383. Expensive.*

This large 4 star hotel is situated right near the beach and offers 200 air conditioned rooms. Facilities include pool, tennis, disco, restaurant, sauna, and nearby golf.

ESTALAGEM ZENDE, *N-13-Esposende, (053) 965-018. Moderate.*

A good 4 star inn with 25 great air conditioned rooms with private bath. Services include a good staff, bar, restaurant, cable TV, room service, handicapped access.

HOTEL NELIA, *Ave. Ribeiro-Esposende, (053) 961-244. Moderate.*

A modern 3 star full service modern hotel with 42 small but good rooms with private bathroom. Facilities include bar, restaurant, pool, squash, ping pong, and billiards.

HOTEL SAUVE MAR, *Ave Oliveira-Esposende, (053) 965-445. Moderate.*

A reasonably nice 3 star sea view hotel with 66 air conditioned comfortable rooms, all with private bath. Facilities include bar, restaurant, pool, tennis, and parking.

THE COSTA VERDE 281

CASA DO MATINHO, *N-546-Forjaes, (053) 871-167. Inexpensive.*
An 18th century country house which rents out 2 rooms with private bathroom in a relaxing area about 11 km east of Esposende. Minimal facilities, but a nice place.

WHERE TO EAT

RESTAURANTE DO RIO, *Ave. Dr. Manuel Pais-Fão, (053) 981-651. Inexpensive.*
Small cornerside restaurant and snack bar – cozy, casual atmosphere, large portions of local fish and meat dishes.

VIANA DO CASTELO & THE COASTAL BEACHES

The port city of **Viana do Castelo** *rests at the mouth of the Rio Lima river about 23 km north of Esposende on route N-13 north.* The rich history of Viana do Castelo is closely linked to the sea which has provided town with a rich industry of international trade and shipbuilding since the 13th century.

By the middle of the 16th century, local merchants and tradesman grew more prosperous and the built many fine palaces and mansions which still grace the city and it's outlying areas. Fortunately, many of these original structures still exist, and can be enjoyed by tourists and locals alike. Here you can find several shops which sell fine locally embroidered table cloths and aprons.

WHERE TO STAY

HOTEL SANTA LUZIA, *Monte de Santa Luzia, (058) 828-889. Expensive.*
A 4 star converted mansion style *pousada* with 55 deco style rooms with great panoramic views. Facilities include terraced gardens, pool, tennis, bar, restaurant.

CASA DOS COSTA BARROS, *Rua de São Pedro, 28, (058) 823-705. Moderate.*
This 16th century converted manor house in the heart of the old town with 10 superior guestrooms with private bath, TV, heating, radio, and lots of antiques.

QUINTA DA BOA VIAGEM, *Além do Rio-Areosa, (058) 835-835. Moderate.*
A wonderful yellow castle like manor house and estate some 3 km northeast of Viana do Castelo. The manor offers 5 seperate 1 and 2 bedroom apartments with kitchens and bathrooms, a pool, billards, bicycles, gardens, TV room, and parking.

QUINTA DO PAÇO D'ANHA, *Vila Nova de Anha, (058) 322-459. Moderate.*

A wonderful 16th century manor house and wine producing estate some 3 km outside Viana do Castello off route N-13 south which offers 4 two bedroom apartments with kitchen, Horse riding, gardens, bicycles, tennis, and parking.

CASA SANTA FILOMENA, *Estrada de Cabanas-Afife, (058) 981-619. Moderate.*

A typical stone farm house about 15 km northeast from Viana which rents 5 spacious guestrooms (some with private bathrooms) in a rustic rural setting.

ALBERGARIA QUIM BARREIROS, *Vila Praia de Ancora, (058) 951-220. Moderate.*

A good 4 star inn with 28 comfortable air conditioned rooms with private bathrooms. Facilities include bar, snack bar, TV, mini bar, and access to nice nearby beaches.

CASA DO PENEDO, *Lugar da Gaiteira-Afife, (058) 981-474. Inexpensive.*

A traditional Minho stone farmhouse which rents 4 rustic double rooms with semi private bathrooms on a hillside location about 9 km northeast of Viana do Castelo.

RESIDENCIAL LARANJEIRA, *Rua General Luís Rego, 45, (058) 822-261. Inexpensive.*

A nice 3 star basic inn located in the heart of town with 26 comfortable rooms with private bathrooms. Facilities include breakfast room, TV room, and parking.

PENSÃO MAGALHAES, *Rua M. Espregueira, 62, (058) 823-293. Inexpensive.*

A pretty decent 2 star inn with double rooms that are reasonably comfortable. You can get rooms with or without a private bathroom. Nothing special but very cheap.

WHERE TO EAT

RESTAURANTE TÍPICO OS 3 PORTES, *Beco dos Fornos, 7, (058) 829-928. Moderate.*

This cozy and charming little restaurant is located near the Praça da República in a stone arched former 16th century bakery. Local folk dancing on summer weekends.

RESTAURANTE DARQUEVILA, *Rua das Rosas-Darque, (058) 322-032. Moderate.*

An excellent local seafood restaurant just south of Viana do Castelo in the town of Darque. This is the place for the grilled fresh fish dinners and good service.

RESTAURANTE MINHO, *Rua G. Coutinho, 107, (058) 823-261. Inexpensive.*

A simple and small restaurant specializing in regional fish and meat dishes.

SEEING THE SIGHTS

The center of town is the 15th-century **Chafariz** fountain in **Praça da República**, surrounded by fine examples of 16th century architecture. Here you can view the elaborate 16th-century **Casa da Misericórdia** and its adjacent church. The Misericordia's facade of balconies is supported by arches and columns sculpted into statues of women and was originally designed by João Lopes. The interior contains beautiful azulejos scenes from the bible which were made in 1721 by António de Oliveira Bernardes.

Next to the Misericórdia is the restored Renaissance 16th-century granite block **Antiga Cãmara Municipal** (old town hall) with it's triple arched doors and the local coat of arms above the middle window. On Friday's, a charming local **mercado** (market) takes place a couple of blocks east of the old town hall off Rua da Palha.

If you follow the *Rua Sacadura Cabral* towards the river you will soon find the Gothic 15th-century **Igreja Matriz** church with fine examples of 16th- and 17th-century wood carvings and paintings. Another block further towards the river and you will find the charming *Rua de São Pedro*, with an abundance of impressive old houses.

If you double back to the **Praça da República** and turn left (west) onto *Rua Manuel Espregueira*, you will soon find the **Largo de São Domingos** with its 18th-century converted palace which is home to the **Museu Municipal** museum. The interior of the palace (closed on Mondays) has azulejo murals by Policarpo de Oliveira Bernardes (son of António) as well as 17th-century ivory inlaid furniture, drawings by Soares dos Reis, 18th-century pottery, fine oil paintings, neolithic vases, massive Celtic and prehistoric statues, Roman coins, and amazing ceilings.

A few blocks up at the north edge of town on *Ave. 25 de Abril* you will find a funicular, which can take you up the hill of **Santa Luzia** to see the 19th-century **Igreja de Santa Luzia**. The church itself contains a few frescoes and is of little interest, the view from atop it's huge white main dome is spectacular. Be advised that the walk up the 142 step narrow staircase to the small viewing platform is a bit scary, but well worth the view.

One of the most exciting times to arrive in town is about the third weekend of August when the **Romaria de Nossa Senhoa da Agonia** festival takes place for a few days. This fun weekend event includes parades, folklore, fireworks, and a great carnival atmosphere.

Many people also come to Viana do Castelo for its nearby beaches and sports facilities. There are beautiful beaches south of town at **Praia do Cabedelo**, accessible by ferry from Viana do Castelo's riverfront dock or via town's bridge. If you desire more isolated beaches you can take a nice drive up the coast to **Montedor, Afife, Moledo,** and **Vila Praia de Ancora.**

These towns offer modest accommodations and restaurants near beaches which are sometimes deserted. Since few non-Portuguese tourists know about these towns, the prices are reasonable and rooms are usually available without advance booking.

PONTE DE LIMA

Situated across an old Roman bridge on the **Lima** river, *some 23 km northeast of Viana do Castelo on route N-202 east* is the beautiful town of **Ponte de Lima.** Although the area was inhabited by Celts, this former Roman fortified village became an important center for trade.

These days the town still maintains its historical ambiance. Although the number of specific attractions may seem few, the town possesses a unique old world charm which, in my opinion, is the main attraction of a relaxing visit here. If you start at the foot of the arched Roman bridge you will enter a unique old town full of majestic streets and riverside avenues which were surrounded by the city's Roman walls.

Just off the Roman bridge you can visit the town's keep which is home to the 18th-century **Biblioteca Municipal** library. From here you can walk to the **Largo Camões** and sit by the fountain or one of the nearby cafes to get a feel for the town. If you wish to see Ponte de Lima from an interesting perspective, you can walk on the pathway above parts of the Roman wall which once encircled the old town.

Among the sights to see in town are the 15th-century converted palace which is now the **Câmara Municipal** (town hall), and the 16th-century **Igreja Matriz** church which has Romanesque, Renaissance, and Manueline elements. Besides wandering around the small stone lanes in the old town, I suggest a leisurely picnic on one of the benches below the trees on the unforgettable riverfront. Naearby you can wander up to the ruins of the old **Torre de Menagem** keep which was once a prison.

After a short rest, you can continue up the riverfront to visit the **Igreja Santo António dos Frades** which is rather captivating. On every fortnight, a Monday market rolls onto the banks of the river. Make sure to try one of the locally produced white wines before you leave this romantic little town. You will notice that most of the area's best accommodations are in converted manor houses (quintas) which are a few km. out of town.

If you happen to be around this area on the third weekend of September, you can witness the **Feiras Novas** festivals. This so called new fair consists of a market, live music in the streets, folklore, and fireworks.

THE COSTA VERDE

WHERE TO STAY

PAÇO DE CALHEIROS, *N-202-Calheiros, (058) 947-164. Expensive.*
A wonderful converted 18th century mansion 7 km northeast of town with 10 rooms with private bathroom. Facilities include bar, dining room, TV, pool, and horses.

CASA DO BAGANHEIRO, *N-201-Queijada, (058) 941-612. Moderate.*
This fine manor house some 7 km southeast of town off route N-201 offers 3 deluxe rooms plus a 2 bedroom apartment, all with private bath. The quinta is owned by a charming English speaking couple. Facilities include pool, lounge, TV, and library.

CONVENTO VAL DE PEREIRAS, *Arcozelo, (058) 742-161. Moderate.*
A beautiful 14th century convent and manor house about 2 km. northwest of town which offers 10 rooms with private bathrooms. Facilities include bar, dining room, pool, tennis, billards, gardens, and lots of wonderful views into the mountains.

CASA DE MARTIN, *N-306-Calheiros, (058) 941-677. Moderate.*
A nice manor house and estate some 4 km north of town with 11 comfortable rooms in the main house and annex. Facilities include pool, tennis, and restaurant.

IMPÉRIO DO MINHO, *Ave. 5 de Outubro, (058) 943-654. Moderate.*
The best otel in the town itself, this 4 star property has 50 rooms with private bathrooms, restaurant, shops, pool, air conditioning, TV, and nearby parking.

CASA DO TAMANQUEIRO, *Lugar das Penas, (058) 941-432. Inexpensive.*
A charming little 18th-century stone Minho house about 8 km. northwest of town with 2 bedrooms and a wood burning hearth. Perhaps the best small house available for families or 2 couples wanting a rustic setting near a small brook. A great place!

PENSÃO SÃO JOÃO, *Rua do Rosario, (058) 941-288. Inexpensive.*
The best inexpensive place to stay in town offering about a dozen rooms with and without private bathrooms. Facilities include a bar, restaurant, and nearby parking.

WHERE TO EAT

RESTAURANTE MADALENA, *Monte St. Madalena, (058) 941-239. Expensive.*
This opulent mountain top restaurant offers fine regional cuisine with great service and an excellent panoramic view of the area. The clientele are well dressed.

RESTAURANTE ENCANADA, *Ave. 25 de Abril, (058) 941-189. Moderate.*

A good local restaurant which is near the river bank. They prepare grilled regional shellfish and hearty local cuisine. The friendly staff speak some English.

RESTAURANTE TULHA, *Rua Formosa, (058) 942-879. Inexpensive.*

This friendly local eating establishment serves several fish and meat dishes, but they specialize in roasted meats. The portions are huge, and the service is good.

PONTE DE BARCA

The quiet little town of **Ponte de Barca** is s*ituated about 17 km northwest of Ponte de Lima off route N-202 east on the banks of the* **Lima** *river.* The town itself begins at the foot of a 15th-century arched stone bridge. The river is the main attraction of this town and is fronted by a lovely riverside park called the **Jardim das Poetas**.

Further along the Lima river, there are many functioning antique watermills along its tranquil banks. The town contains a few interesting churches you may want to visit such as the **Igreja Matriz** with its fine *azulejos* and wood work, the 18th-century **Igreja da Misericórdia**, and the 17th-century **Capela de Santo António**.

Also in the center of the city is a beautiful pillory and public square dating back to the 16th century. This is a very peaceful agricultural area that produces fine *Vinho Verde* white wines. A small local **mercado** (market) takes place in the town on most Wednesdays..

WHERE TO STAY

QUINTA DA PROVA, *N-202-Prova, (058) 421-63. Moderate.*

This pretty little house is located just above the *Lima* river across from town. The quinta rents 3 nice 2 bedroom apartments with kitchen. A very peaceful inn.

TORRE DE QUINTELA, *N-101-Nogueira, (058) 422-38. Moderate.*

A nice old manor house with a 16th century tower just about 4 km. southeast of town off *route N-101* which offers 3 nice guestrooms with private bathrooms.

PAÇO VEDRO, *Paço Vedro, (058) 421-17. Moderate.*

An 18th-century manor house a bit south of town in the hamlet of *Paço Vedro* offering 5 good rooms with semi private bathrooms. Facilities include bar, and parking.

PENSÃO SÃO FERNANDO, *Rua de Santo António, (058) 425-80. Inexpensive.*

A clean and comfortable 2 star in near the heart of town with 22 rooms with private bathrooms and several facilities including telephones and TV in the rooms.

RESIDENCIAL OS POETAS, *Rua Dr. A. Cruz, (058) 435-78. Inexpensive.*

A nice little inn with 10 heated comfortable rooms with private bathroom. Facilities include cable TV, bar, breakfast room, telephone, and great local ambiance.

CAMINHA

The lovely border fishing town of **Caminha** is *located some 28 km. up the coast from Viana do Castelo on route N-13 north and is surrounded by both the Minho and Coura rivers*. This former Roman village was once a major medieval fortified town right in the path of the Spanish armies. These days the town attracts mainly Spanish tourists on day trips to its local beaches, as well as the old town itself.

Here you should wander past the beautiful old buildings which line the town's medieval main plaza called the **Praça do Conselheiro Silva Torres**. Besides the central 16th-century Chafariz fountain, you can view the beautiful 14th-century **Torre do Relogio** clock tower which was part of the original town fortifications. The gate of the clock tower is embossed with the royal coat of arms of King Dom Afonso V.

Also in the plaza are the 17th-century **Paços do Concelho** town chambers with its arcade and boxed wooden ceilings, and the Gothic 15th-century **Casa dos Pitas** whose facade is adorned with battlements. Near the main plaza you can also view a 17th-century prison, the *azulejos* filled 16th-century **Capela dos Mareantes**, the 16th-century carvings and ex-votos in the renaissance **Igreja da Misericórdia** church, and the 15th-century Gothic and renaissance **Igreja Matriz** church with it's unusual carved Mudéjar wooden ceiling and fortified bell tower.

Make sure to keep your eyes open for the great handcrafted copper cookware produced and sold in small shops along *Rua Ricardo Joaquim de Sousa*. The town is quite interesting, and I suggest at least a half day here if you are within striking distance. If you have a little more time, you really should visit the impressive little windmill and watermill-laden town of **Vilar de Mouros** which is only 6 km northeast of town.

WHERE TO STAY

QUINTA DA GRAÇA, *Vilarelho, (058) 921-157. Moderate.*

A 17th century seaview house just outside of town offering 7 nice rooms with private bathrooms. Facilities include lounge, dining room, pool, gardens, and parking.

HOTEL PORTA DA SOL, *Ave. Marginal, (051) 795-377. Moderate.*

A good 3 star resort hotel with 93 air conditioned rooms with private bath. Facilities include restaurant, pool, sauna, tennis, squash, billiards, disco, TV, and minibar.

CASA DE ESTERIO, *Lugar de Esterio, (058) 921-356. Moderate.*
A nice 18th century house surounded by gardens with forest views which rents 1 apartment to travelers who call in advance. Facilities include kitchen and fireplace.
RESIDENCIAL ARCA NOVA, *Largo Sidonio Pais, (058) 922-780. Moderate.*
A 3 star inn with 15 attractive modern rooms with private bathroom near the river bank. Facilities include heating, TV, telephone, breakfast room, and parking.
CASA DA ANTA, *Lugar da Anta-Lanhelas, (058) 921-434. Inexpensive.*
A rustic 17th-century stone Minho house 6 km northeast of town which rents 4 nice rooms with private bathroom, a bar, TV, heating, restaurant, and wine cellar.

WHERE TO EAT

RESTAURANTE REMO, *Sporting Clube, (058) 921-459. Expensive.*
An impressive waterfront restaurant with an extensive wine list and a variety of regional Minho style fish and meat dishes. Both the food and the views are special.
VERSALHES, *Rua São João, 114, (058) 921-199. Moderate.*
A great little fish and meat restaurant just off the *Minho* river with a stone arched interior. The restaurant offers the best rock bass (*Robalo*) I have ever had.
ADEGA DO CHICO, *Rua Visconde de S. Rego, (058) 921-781. Moderate.*
A small informal eating establishment. Serves huge portions of the house codfish specialty (*Bacalhau a Chico*). Good local atmosphere.

VILA NOVA DE CERVEIRA

The small settlement of **Vila Nova de Cerveira** rests *on the Minho river some 9 km northeast of Caminha on route N-13 north*. The history of the small town goes back to the 13th century when it was fortified to ward off any Spanish incursions. These days a small ferry shuttles back and forth across the river to bring the Spainards and their cars across the border for day trips and shopping excursions into Portugal.

There is a lovely is 14th-century fortress here that has been converted into a nice pousada. The only other real sights worth mentioning are the baroque 18th-century **Igreja Matriz** church, the 16th-century **Capelas de São Roque** chapels, and the 17th-century **Igreja de Nossa Senhorha da Ajuda**. There are also a couple of small islands in the middle of the river which may be visited by boat, but finding someone to take you to them is quite difficult.

Vila Nova de Cerveira is a fairly nice stop, but other than the **pousada** there is no real reason to spend more than an hour or two here.

WHERE TO STAY

POUSADA DE DOM DINIS, *Praça da Liberdade, (051) 795-604. Expensive.*

This opulent converted riverfront fortress is definitely the best place to stay in town. The 29 rooms are pretty comfortable and the public spaces are unforgettable. Facilities include bar, restaurant, TV, direct dial phones, and parking.

ESTALAGEM DA BOEGA, *Gondarem, (051) 795-231. Moderate.*

Full service 4 star inn; 30 large, comfortable rooms 3 km south of town. Bar, restaurant, pool, cable TV, river view park, and tennis.

RESIDENCIAL MARINEL, *Ave. 25 de Abril, (051) 795-114. Inexpensive.*

A clean and basic 10 room inn; minimal facilities. A good budget selection.

VALENÇA DO MINHO

The fortress-dominated walled border city of **Valença do Minho** (Valença) is l*ocated 20 km further up route N-13 north from Vila Nova de Cerveira on a hill overlooking the* **Minho** *river.* The city was first founded in the 12th century as a defense post on the Spanish border and was originally known as Contrasta.

The old city of Valença is set on a hill and is completely surrounded by a huge walled enclosure which has 5 stone gates and 2 connected 17th-century forts which remain intact. Within the walls of the old city there are still cannons and watchtowers facing the Spanish city of **Tuy**.

This city of 2700 residents is full of small pebbled lanes and old houses with *azulejos-* covered glass enclosed verandas. As you wander through town, make an effort to see the medieval **Casa do Eirado**, the Romanesque 12th-century **Igreja Matriz** church, the beautiful altar and naves in the **Igreja de Santo Estavão** church that also contains an original Roman mile marker in its courtyard.

For the best panoramic view of the area, you can walk to the vantage points above the ramparts. As with many of the northern towns, fine locally-produced handicrafts can be found in the small shops and at the local Wednesday **mercardo** (market).

WHERE TO STAY

POUSADA DE SÃO TEOTÓNIO, *Valença do Minho, (051) 824-020. Expensive.*

This relatively new structure was built inside the fortress walls of the old town. It has 16 good double rooms with private bathroom, bar, restaurant, TV, and parking.

LARA HOTEL, *Lugar de São Sebastião, (051) 824-348. Moderate.*
A modern 3 star hotel with 53 good rooms with private bathroom, swimming pool, bar, laundry, cable TV, breakfast room, direct dial phones, and lots of parking.
HOTEL VALENÇA DO MINHO, *Ave. Miguel Dantes-Troias, (051) 824-211. Moderate.*
A good 3 star hotel which offers 36 air conditioned rooms with private bathroom. Facilities include bar, restaurant, pool, TV, minibar, and handicapped access.
RESIDENCIAL PONTE SECA, *Ave. Tito Fontes, (051) 225-80. Inexpensive.*
A basic inn with simple heated rooms with or without private bathroom.

MONÇÃO

The small hamlet of **Monção** *sits on the banks of the Minho river some 19 km northeast of Valença do Minho on route N-101.* A ferry now crosses the river into Spain, but a bridge will be finished any time now. This border town was inhabited well before the Roman occupation, which still shows vestiges of the original fortifications. In the 14th century, after Monção's years of continued sieges and war, a local woman named Deu-la-Deu Martins single-handedly expelled the occupying Spanish troops by pelting them with small rolls of bread. You can still find these rolls on sale throughout the old town, and in fact the town erected a fountain and named **Praça Deu-la-Deu** in her honor.

The people of Monção (several are of Jewish descent) are traditional by nature, and can be seen in the small stone streets like *Rua Direita* on their way to the Thursday **mercado** (market). The town has several interesting sights to visit, including the Romanesque **Igreja Matriz** church with its beautiful monstrance, the 17th-century **Igreja da Misericórdia** church, the riverview **Miradouro dos Nerys** lookout, and the local hot springs. The town is located in a wine producing zone which is well known for it's *Alvarinho* wine varieties which must be tasted before leaving Monção.

WHERE TO STAY

QUINTA DO HOSPITAL, *N-202-Valinha, (051) 544-58. Moderate.*
An impressive historic 18th century manor house 8 km east of *Monção* with 5 nice rooms with private bathroom. The facilities include bar, dining room, bikes, and TV.
CASA DE RODAS, *Lugar de Rodas, (051) 652-105. Moderate.*
A pleasant converted 16th century manor house 1 km. south of town

off *route N-101* which offers 3 nice rooms and a 1 bedroom apartment, all with private bathroom.

ALBERGARIA ATLÂNTICO, *Rua General P. de Castro, 15, (051) 652-355. Moderate.*

A good 4 star in town hotel with 24 comfortable rooms with private bathroom and friendly service. Facilities include bar, restaurant, cable TV, minibars, and parking.

PENSÃO MANE, *Rua General P. de Castro, 5, (051) 652-490. Inexpensive.*

A nice 3 star inn located in the heart of town with 8 rooms with private bathrooms. Facilities include a restaurant, TV room, in room telephones, and nearby parking.

MELGAÇO

Melgaço is a wonderful little border town, *just up the **Minho** river some 33 km northeast of Monção on route N-202 east.* This somewhat forgotten town is loaded with character.

In 1170, King Dom Afonso I ordered the construction of a heavily fortified watchtower to be built on the site of a former Moorish look out post. For the past 900 years the impressive castle and massive circular wall have loomed high above a hill above the old town. The streets that unfold beneath the castle are full of merchants, shepherds, and the traditionally dressed local residents which can best be seen during the town's Friday **mercado** (market).

The village itself is a wonder to walk through. Just leave the castle and cross the **Alameda Inês Negra** and follow any of the small lanes ahead. While you are strolling along, take a peek inside the Romanesque 13th-century **Igreja Matriz** church, the beautiful porch on the 15th century **Igreja da Misericórdia**, and the many ancient alleys and walls which can be noticed throughout the old town.

While around Melgaço you can take a beautiful half day ride to the small villages and remote country roads just south of town. A spa area called **Termas do Peso** is located about 4 km southwest of Melgaço in the town of **Peso**, and attracts many people for its curative waters and fine spa facilities. A km or so to the east of town is the fine 13th-century **Igreja de Nossa Senhora da Orada** church.

WHERE TO STAY

QUINTA DA CALÇADA, *Melgaço, (051) 425-47. Moderate.*

A 17th century manor house which rents only one large 1 bedroom apartment with private bathroom and kitchen from July 15 until September 30 each year.

PENSÃO BOAVISTA, *N-202-Peso, (051) 424-64. Moderate.*
A better than average 3 star inn with 41 air conditioned guestrooms with private bathroom, pool, bar, restaurant, laundry, room service, cable TV, and telephone.
PENSÃO FLÔR DO MINHO, *Rua Velha, (051) 429-05. Inexpensive.*
A reasonably basic and clean 1 star inn with 7 rooms and a good restaurant.

PENEDA-GERÊS NATIONAL PARK

The mountain ranges of **Serra da Peneda**, **Serra do Soajo**, **Serra do Amarela**, and **Serra do Gerês** have been classified as the **Parque Nacional da Peneda-Gerês**. Founded in 1970 to protect the delicate ecosystem of the 178,000 acres of pristine forests and rounded peaks, the park contains several towns within its borders. The rustic and minimally-developed park can be accessed via roads from Melgaço, Arcos de Valdevez, Ponte de Barca, Braga, and Montalegre.

The history of the valleys and towns with the park is rather rich. In prehistoric times, several settlements were located in this area. There are several 5,000 year old *dolmens* which can still be seen near **Soajo**, **Portos**, and **Tourém**. During the Roman era, a military road was constructed through the park which linked Braga to Rome and is clearly demarcated by a vast amount of Roman mile markers. Today only about 17,000 residents live in the towns and rural farming communities which are scattered throughout the park.

WHERE TO STAY

POUSADA DE SÃO BENTO, *Caniçada, (053) 647-190. Expensive.*
A hunting lodge-style *pousada* with incredible views and 18 air conditioned rooms. Facilities include a pool, bar, fireplace, restaurant, tennis, and minibars.
QUINTA DE GESTACOS, *Gerês, (053) 391-491. Moderate.*
A rustic house in the heart of the park which offers 6 nice rooms with private bathrooms. Facilities include bar, heating, TV room, and a great scenic location.
QUINTA DAS GLICINIAS, *Vieira do Minho, (053) 648-436. Moderate.*
A nice old stone *Minho* house off route N-304 just a few minutes south of the park entrance near Gerês, offering 2 traditional rooms with private bathrooms.
HOTEL DAS TERMAS, *Caldas do Gerês, (053) 391-143. Moderate.*
A good 2 star 31 room hotel for those who wish to use the spa. Facilities include spa access, bar, restaurant, pool, mini golf, tennis, solarium, and parking.

ESTALAGEM SÃO BENTO, *São Bento da Porta Aberta, (053) 391-106. Moderate.*
A great little 4 star inn located just off the *Caldo* river near *Gerês*. They offer 25 good rooms with private bathroom, bar, restaurant, TV, garage, and good service.

PENSÃO ABRIGO, *Castro Laboreiro, (051) 451-26. Moderate.*
A comfortable and clean inn with 19 modest guestrooms with private bathroom.

HOTEL DO PARQUE, *Caldas do Gerês, (053) 675-548. Inexpensive.*
A nice 2 star hotel right near the spa with 60 comfortable rooms and spa access. Facilities include bar, restaurant, pool, mini golf course, tennis, and a garage.

PENSÃO DA PONTE, *Rua da Boavista-Gerês, (053) 391-121. Inexpensive.*
A basic no-frills inn with a restaurant and rooms with or without private bathroom.

SEEING THE PARK

While it is possible to drive through several parts of the park, roads here range from acceptable to downright dangerous. The park is best enjoyed by horseback or by trekking through it's paths and roads. Those who come here to view the magnificent scenery also have a good chance of sighting wild horses, boars, eagles, owls, deer, mountain goats, and several other elusive creatures.

The park's oak forests are also home to many rare indigenous species of flora and fauna, some of which cannot be found anywhere else on Earth. There are also several waterfalls, vistas, iris lined paths, and rivers which offers spectacular photo opportunities. Several dams were built on the rivers in the park which have created a series of man made trout laden lakes and lagoons. Fishing, swimming, and non-motorized watersports are permitted in some areas of the park. There are also facilities for mountaineers who wish to test their skills.

Among the other interesting sights within the park are the 17th-century spa at **Caldas do Gerês**, the **Bela Vista** lookout, the **Pedra Bela** look out, the **Ponte do Arado** waterfall, the high peak at **Carris**, the panoramic **Miradouro da Junceda** lookout, the ancient village of **Soajo**, the impressive 13th century castle of **Lindoso**, and massive castle at **Castro Laboreiro**.

PRACTICAL INFORMATION FOR THE COSTA VERDE

CASINOS
- Espinho Solverde Casino, *Rua 19, (02) 720-238*
- Póvoa Do Varzim Sopete Casino, *Avenida Braga, (052) 615-151*

CURRENCY EXCHANGE

Most of the banks in the Costa Verde will exchange foreign currency and traveller's checks. Some shops, restaurants, and hotel front desks will offer you a rather poor exchange rate. Remember that banking hours are from 8 am until 3 pm on Monday through Friday.

Currency exchange machines are almost impossible to find this far north but you can still locate 24 hour ATM machines in the larger cities.

EMERGENCY & USEFUL PHONE NUMBERS
- **Directory Assistance**, *118*
- Emergency Assistance (S.O.S.), *115*
- **Braga's São Marcos Hospital**, *Largo Carlos Amarante, (053) 240-42*
- **Espinho Hospital**, *Corner of Ruas 35 & 28, (02) 721-141*
- **Guimarães Hospital**, *Ave. de Londres, (053) 512-612*
- **Vila do Conde Hospital**, *Praça Dr. A.J. d'Ameida, (052) 624-525*
- **Automobile Club of Portugal** (Emergency road services), *(02) 830-1127*
- **Porto's Pedras Rubas Airport**, *14 km. out of Porto, (02) 948-2141*
- **T.A.P.Airlines Porto**, *Praça M. Albuqurque, 105, (02) 600-5555*

MUSEUMS, PALACES, & MONUMENTS
- **Amadeo Cardoso Museum/Albano Sardoeira Library**, *Convento de São Gonçalo, Amarante, (055) 423-663*. Contains collections of Cardoso, Carneiro, Resende, Viana, and other famous artist's work. The museum also displays a collection of regional sculpture. Open 10 am until 12:30 pm and 2 pm until 5 pm Tuesday through Sunday. Closed on Mondays and holidays.
- **Archaeological Museum of Barcelos**, *Largo do Municipal-Paço dos Condos, Barcelos, (053) 821-251*. Contains archaeological findings from the ruins of the medieval Ducal Palace. Open 10 am until 12 pm and 2 pm until 5:30 pm daily October through March. Open 10 am until 7 pm daily April through September.
- **Biscainhos Museum**, *Palácio dos Biscainhos-Rua dos Biscainhos, Braga, (053) 276-45*. Open 10 am until 12:30 pm and 2 pm until 5:30 pm Tuesday through Sunday. Closed on Mondays and holidays.

- **Pio XII Museum**, *Seminario de São Tiago-Largo de Sant'Iago, Braga, (053) 233-70.* Contains collections of religious sculptures, Roman artifacts, and Visigoth artwork. Open 10 am until 12 pm and 3 pm until 5 pm Tuesday through Sunday. Closed Mondays and holidays.
- **Sacred Art Museum (Museu de Sé Primaz)**,*S Primaz Cathedral, Braga, (053) 233-17.* Contains collections of jewelry, ancient ecclesiastical items, and paintings. Open 8:30 am until 12:30 pm and 1:30 pm until 5:30 pm October through May. Open 8:30 am until 6:30 pm June through September.
- **Ducal Palace-Paço dos Duques**, *Guimarães, (053) 412-273.* Contains a vast collection of 16th-18th century decorative and ornamental art. Open 10am until 5:30pm daily. Closed on holidays.
- **Alberto Sampaio Museum**, *Igreja N.S. da Oliveira-Largo de Oliveira, Guimarães, (053) 412-465.* Contains oil paintings by António Vaz as well as other Portuguese painters, ceramics, *azulejos*, Royal clothing, sculptures, and baroque wooden items. Open 10am until 12:30pm and 2pm until 5:30pm Tuesday through Sunday. Closed Mondays and holidays.
- **Martins Sarmento Museum**, *Rua de Paio Galvão, Guimarães, (053) 415-969.* Contains collections of artifacts from local excavations of Celtic settlements. Open 10 am until 12 pm and 2 pm until 5 pm Tuesday through Sunday. Closed Mondays and holidays.
- **Póvoa de Varzim Museum of Ethnography**, *Rua Visconde de Azevedo, Póvoa de Varzim, (052) 622-200.* Contains collections of sacred art, ceramics, azulejos, and ethnographic items. Open 10 am until 12:30 pm and 2:30 pm until 6 pm Tuesday through Sunday. Closed Mondays and holidays.
- **Viana do Castelo Museum (Museu da Cidade)**, *Largo de São Domingos, Viana do Castelo, (058) 242-23.* Contains a collection of local artifacts, paintings, and furniture. Open 9:30 am until 12:30 pm and 2 pm until 5:30 pm Tuesday through Sunday. Closed Mondays and holidays.
- **Vila do Conde Sacred Art Museum**, *Igreja Matriz-Rua da Igreja, Vila do Conde, (052) 631-327.* Contains collections of ecclesiastical items, silverware, and rare books. Open 10 am until 12 pm and 4 pm until 6 pm September through May. Open 3 pm until 5 pm June through August.
- **House Museum of Teixeira Lopes**, *Rua Teixeira Lopes, 32, Vila Nova de Guia, (02) 301-224.* Contains collections of Teixeira Lopes and Diogo de Macedo sculptures, as well as paintings, stamps, porcelain, and tapestries from all over Portugal. Open 9 am until 12:30 pm and 2 pm until 5:30 pm Tuesday through Saturday. Closed on Sundays, Mondays, and holidays.

SPORTS & RECREATION
- **Quinta Santa Comba** (Horses), *Barcelos, (053) 832-101*
- **Braga Tennis Club**, *Rodovia Sports Complex, (053) 611-753*
- **Braga Fishing Club**, *Rua dos Chaos,112, (053) 260-60*
- **Cacadores Hunting Club**, *Braga, (053) 684-503*
- **Hipico Horse Club of Braga**, *Rua de Santo André, 8, (053) 722-61*
- **Porto Golf Club**, *Espinho, (02) 722-008*
- **Casa de Sezim Horse Center**, *Guimarães, (053) 523-196*
- **Naval Club of Leça**, *Leixoes-Matsosinhos, (02) 995-1700*
- **Oporto Sports Club**, *Matsosinhos, (02) 995-2225*
- **Quinta São Salvador** (Horses), *Oliveira do Douro, (02) 309-222*
- **Ovarense Sports Association**, *Ovar, (056) 512-36*
- **Naval Club Povonese**, *Póvoa de Varzim, (052) 624-617*
- **Estela Golf Club**, *Póvoa de Varzim, (052) 685-567*
- Miramar Golf Club, Valadares, (02) 762-2067
- **Vela Club of Viana do Castelo**, *Viana do Castelo, (058) 276-52*

TRANSPORTATION
- **Braga RN Bus Depot**, *Central de Camionagem, (053) 234-33*
- **Guimarães RN Bus Depot**, *Ave. Conde de Margaride, (053) 411-222*
- **Monção RN Bus Depot**, *Antiga Estação, (051) 536-20*
- **Amarante CP Rail station**, *Rua Candido dos Reis, (055) 422-608*
- **Barcelos CP Rail station**, *Ave. Alcaide de Faria, (053) 811-234*
- **Espinho CP Rail station**, *Ave. 8, (02) 720-087*
- **Guimarães CP Rail station**, *Ave. D. João IV, (053) 412-351*
- **Póvoa de Varzim CP Rail station**, *Rua Almirantes Reis, (052) 624-698*
- **Viana do Castelo CP Rail station**, *Ave. dos Combatentes, (058) 822-296*
- **Vila Nova de Gaia CP Rail station**, *Rua de Estação, (02) 304-961*
- **Avis Rent a Car – Braga**, *Largo de Estação, (053) 725-20*
- **Hertz Rent a Car – Viana do Castelo**, *Ave. Conde de Carrera, (058) 822-250*

TOURIST OFFICES (TURISMOS)
- **Amarante Tourist Office**, *Rua Candido dos Reis, (058) 424-259*
- **Barcelos Tourist Office**, *Largo de Porto Nova, (053) 811-882*
- **Braga Tourist Office**, *Ave. da Liberdade, 1, (053) 225-50*
- **Caminha Tourist Office**, *Rua R.J. Sousa, (058) 921-952*
- **Espinho Tourist Office**, *Corner of Ruas 6 & 23, (02) 720-911*
- **Esposende Tourist Office**, *Ave. Marginal, (053) 961-354*
- **Gerês Tourist Office**, *Ave. Alfonso da Costa, (053) 391-133*
- **Gondomar Tourist Office**, *São Cosme, (02) 083-0079*
- **Guimarães Tourist Office**, *Alameda da Resitencia, (053) 412-450*
- **Monção Tourist Office**, *Largo do Loreto, (051) 652-757*

- **Peneda-Gerês Park Information**, *Arcos de Valdevez, (058) 653-38*
- **Peneda-Gerês Park Information**, *Braga, (053) 613-166*
- **Peneda-Gerês Park Information**, *Caldas do Gerês, (053) 391-181*
- **Ponte de Lima Tourist Office**, *Praça da República, (058) 942-335*
- **Ponte de Barca Tourist Office**, *Largo da Misericórdia, (058) 428-99*
- **Póvoa de Varzim Tourist Office**, *Ave. M. de Albuquerque, (052) 614-609*
- **Viana do Castelo Tourist Office**, *Rua Hospital Velha, (058) 822-620*
- **Vila do Conde Tourist Office**, *Rua 25 de Abril, 103, (052) 642-700*
- **Vila Nova de Guia Tourist Office**, *Rua. A. Cabral, (02) 370-2559*
- **Valença Tourist Office**, Ave. de Espanha, (051) 233-74

TRAVEL AGENCIES
- **Avic Travel,** *Rua G. P. de Castro, 28, (053) 251-66.* The Braga branch office of a good full service travel company which can book tickets, reserve hotel rooms, and suggest guided tours of the region.
- **Star**, *Ave. D. Henriques, 638, (053) 415-750.* A good full service *Guimarães* branch office of a Portuguese travel agency and tour operator with both reservation and ticketing capabilities.
- **Costa Verde Travel**, *Ave. da Liberdade, 44, (053) 815-155.* A friendly local Barcelos travel agency which will be glad to assist you in all types of hotel, bus, train, airplane, resort, *pousada*, and car rental requirements.

19. THE MONTANHAS

The **Montanhas** – the *mountainous region* – is a remote section in Portugal's northeast corner, seldom visited by tourists. Comprised of large chunks of the **Trás-os-Montes**, **Beira Baixa**, and **Beira Alta** provinces, the **Montanhas** region is full of rugged snow-capped mountains, dense pine forests, and huge boulder spiked valleys which dominate the landscape.

The harsh geoligical and climatic conditions create a huge temperature fluctuation which can range from well below freezing during the long winter nights up to searingly hot summer days. The area's traditional farmers struggle with terribly difficult conditions to grow the livestock which produce some of Portugal's finest meats and cheeses. Many of the inhabitants still practice a lifestyle which dates back to the middle ages continue to produce most of their own wines, vegatables, and smoked meats.

Several of the villages in the Montanhas are full of centuries-old granite houses which contain small barns in their basements, 3 legged iron cauldrons above raging fireplaces in their livingrooms, and almost no modern convieniences. It is not uncommon to witness traditional festivals and ritual slaughters carried out in the village squares of the many ancient mountain top communities. Besides being home to the largest mountains in Portugal, the **Serra da Estrêla**, travelers can find beautiful parks, rustic villages, pristine lakes, and many prehistoric vestiges scattered aroung the Montanhas.

Among the most impressive of the Montanhas's ancient and mysterious villages is **Monsanto** where traditional descendants of the original ancient residents continue to live in small homes which have been built inside of, underneath, and between huge rocks. One of the country's oldest rituals is the **Festas dos Rapazes** in which young men dress up in bizzare masks and colorful costumes can be witnessed during the last week of December and first week of January in small villages in the extreme north of the Montanhas.

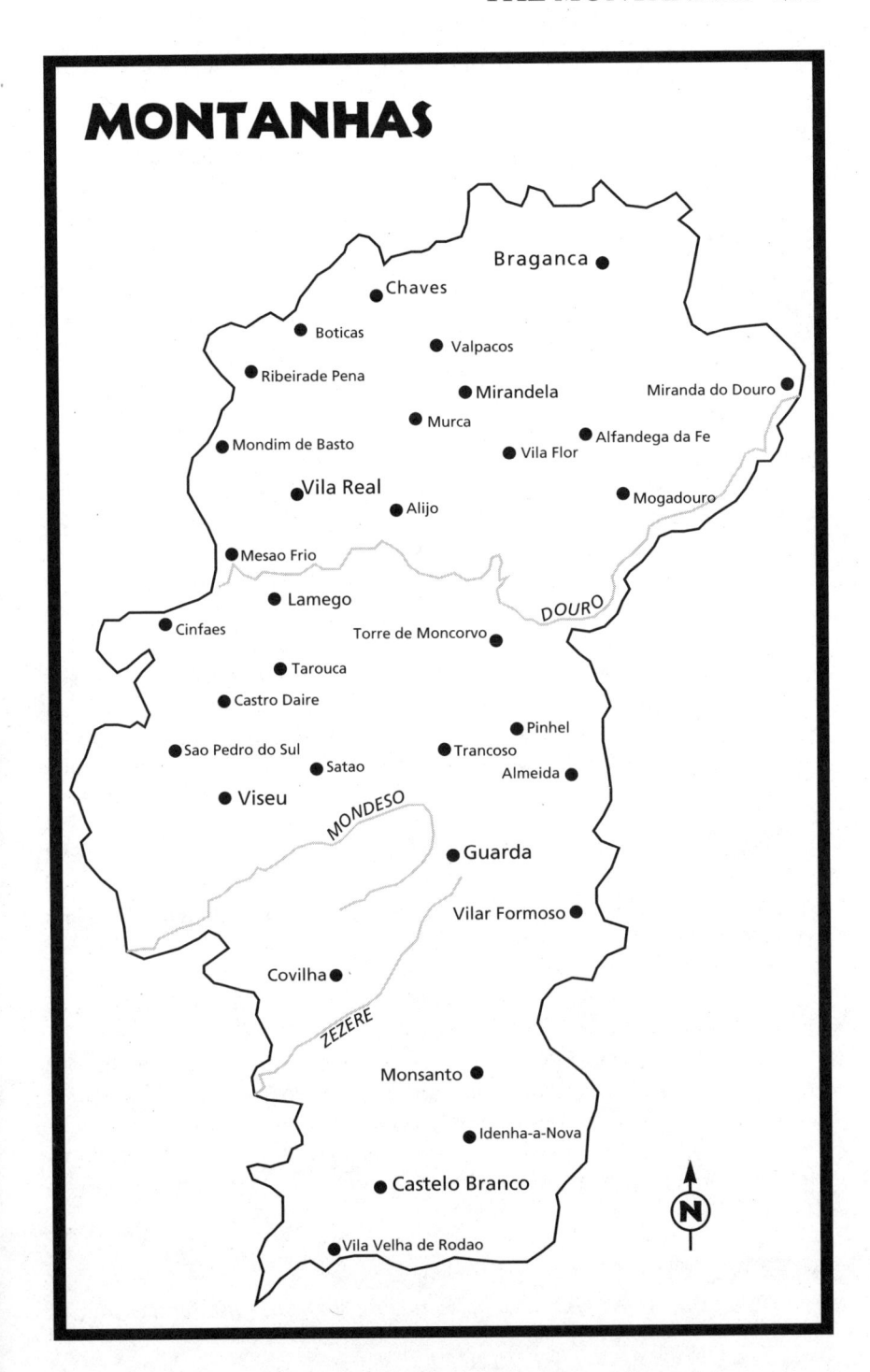

THE MONTANHAS 299

MONTANHAS

- Bragança
- Chaves
- Boticas
- Valpaços
- Ribeirade Pena
- Mirandela
- Miranda do Douro
- Murca
- Mondim de Basto
- Alfandega da Fe
- Vila Flor
- Vila Real
- Alijo
- Mogadouro
- Mesao Frio
- DOURO
- Lamego
- Cinfaes
- Torre de Moncorvo
- Tarouca
- Castro Daire
- Sao Pedro do Sul
- Pinhel
- Trancoso
- Satao
- Almeida
- Viseu
- MONDESO
- Guarda
- Vilar Formoso
- Covilha
- ZEZERE
- Monsanto
- Idenha-a-Nova
- Castelo Branco
- Vila Velha de Rodao

N

Other important sights include the medieval walled village of **Sortelha**, the rustic villages of the **Serra da Estrêla** mountains, the tiny city of **Mirando do Douro** which has its own dialect, the castle and church-topped city of **Lamego**, the historic wine cities of **Viseu** and **Vila Real**, and the vast array of walled and castle-filled towns surrounding **Guarda**.

MONTELEGRE

The small town of **Montelegre** *rests some 13 km east from the easternmost entry point, at Covelães, for the Parque Nacional da Peneda-Gerês on route N-308 west.* This sleepy town just south of the Spanish border is home to some 1900 inhabitants who live in granite and whitewashed houses topped by red clay and tile roofs.

The large turreted castle which dominates the north end of town was built by King Dom Dinis in the 13th century, while it's large keep was later added by King Dom Afonso III. The castle grounds are open to the public, and on a clear day provide a good panoramic view of the surrounding mountain ranges.

As you walk down into town from the circular castle walls, several winding lanes make their way towards the main plaza of town called the **Largo do Municipio**. You should make a point to stroll down the *Rua Direita* during shopping hours and keep your eye out for locally-made hand wooven baskets, and unique capes (capas) which are worn by the local residents during the colder months. Montelegre is a great place to spend a couple of hours but besides the castle and a nice Romanesque church known as the **Igreja de Santa Maria do Castelo**, town offers very few specific sights.

The countryside near town is filled with nice walking paths that lead to small hamlets and prehistoric dolmens. Nearby in the **Serra do Barroso** mountains about 26 km. south of town (across the **Barragem de Paradela** dam and its manmade lake) there are several small primitive ancient villages which are quite unusual and well worth the excursion.

The area produces a hearty wine known as *Vinho dos Mortos* (Wine of the Dead) which is fermented in bottles buried underground. Towns such as **Vila da Ponte**, **Vilarinho Seco**, **Viveiro**, and **Dornelas** offer a glimpse into the old way of life in the mountains. If you are lucky, you may notice a crowd of local spectators watching an oxen fight known as a *Chega de Bois*. Also worth a quick visit are the prehistoric fortress ruins of **Castro de Carvalhelhos**, near the sight of a thermal water spa station in **Carvalhelhos**.

WHERE TO STAY

PENSÃO FIDALGO, *Rua da Corujeira, (076) 524-62. Inexpensive.*

A nice and comfortable 2 star inn in the heart of town offering several nice rooms both with and without private bathrooms. The views from some rooms are great!

CHAVES

The historic and beautiful spa city of **Chaves** *lies about 45 km. southeast of Montalegre on route N- 103.* This area was once home to prehistoric settlements which have left fine examples of Neolithic and Iron Age art throughout Chaves and the surrounding **Trás-O-Montes** subregion, including the many 2000 year old granite pig sculptures (*Berrões*).

In the 1st century, the Romans built the wonderful stone arched Trajan bridge and created a city called *Aquae Flaviae* on the sight of a hot thermal water spring near the intersection of their 2 most important roads. Its strategic location on the banks of the Tâmega river only 13 km. south of the Spanish border then led a vast history of conquer and occupation by the Suebians, Visigoths, Moors, and the Spanish. After it's capture from the Moors in the 12th century, King Dom Afonso Henriques ordered the contstruction of defensive walls to help secure the area. The town was further strenghened in the 14th century with the additional fortifications of a massive turreted **castelo** (castle).

To begin your walking tour of this fine city you should first try to find parking near the large **Praça Luís de Camões** square. The center of this remarkable square contains a beautiful Manueline pillory which is surrounded by several sights which are worth a good look. Behind the pillory is the oldest monument remaing in Chaves, the Romanesque **Igreja Matriz** church.

Adjacent to the Igreja Matriz is the 17th-century baroque **Igreja da Misericórdia** with entrancing 18th-century azulejos by Oliveira Bernardes and a gourgeous ceiling painted by Jerónimo Rocha Braga. Also in the same square you can visit the **Museu de Região Flaviense** regional museum (closed on Monday), which contains a great assortment of prehistoric phallic sculptures and menhirs, Roman artifacts, and ancient coins. Just behind these buildings near the old walls you can view the 14th-century **castelo** (castle) of which little besides a nice garden and the spike topped **Torre de Menagem** keep remains. The keep was used as the official residense of the first Duke of Bragança and now is home to the **Museu Militar** (Military Museum), which contains an assortment of weapons from ancient periods as well as more modern conflicts (closed on Monday). A short trip to the terrace on top of the keep can provide an excellent view over the beautiful houses and winding streets of the city.

The large spa complex just west of the **Praça Luís de Camões** is known as the **Estancia Termal** and is open from June through October.

The hot thermal waters of the spa baths are known to help the treatment of internal organs, rheumatism, and nutritional disorders.

The rest of the old town contains several other fine sights worth walking to. First I suggest a walk to the riverside at the south edge of town to see the wonderful 1st century **Ponte Trajano** Roman bridge with it's 16 arches and Roman mile markers. If you cross the bridge you can take a quick peek at the octangonal 18th-century **Igreja da Madelena** church and cross back again.

Walking from the bridge towards the center of town via the *Rua de Santo António*, turn right (east) at the **mercado** (market). A block down you will find the 17th-century **Forte de São Fransisco** fortress. While walking through the charming streets in this old town, make sure to keep your eye out for the area's black pottery which is unique to this area.

You may also wish to sample the strong smoked ham (*presunto*), sausages (*enchidos*), and firewater (*aquardente*), which can be found in the shops and snack bars on *Rua Direita* as well as near **Praça do Brasil**. About 3 km northwest of Chaves are the unforgettable examples of prehistoric rupestre art inbedded into a large boulder in the area known as the **Outeiro Machado**.

WHERE TO STAY

HOTEL AQUAE FLAVIAE, *Praça do Brasil, (076) 267-11. Expensive.*

A modern 4 star hotel with nice air conditioned rooms in central *Chaves*. Facilities include restaurant, pool, sauna, tennis, room service, TV, and handicapped access.

QUINTA DA MATA, *N-213-Chaves, (076) 233-85. Moderate.*

A wonderful 17th century manor house 3 km. southeast of town offering 5 great rooms with private bathrooms. Facilities include lounge, dining room, winery, sauna, horses, tennis, bicycles, nearby thermal springs, library, TV room, and parking.

QUINTA DE SANTA ISABEL, *Santo Estevão, (076) 218-18. Moderate.*

A beautiful manor house on a wine producing estate 7 km. northeast of *Chaves* off *route N-103*. The house offers 6 fine rooms as well as 1 and 2 bedroom apartments with private bathrooms (some with kitchens) Facilities include TV room and parking.

ESTALAGEM SANTIAGO, *Rua do Olival, (076) 225-45. Moderate.*

A nice and friendly 4 star inn with 28 large and comfortable double rooms with private bathroom. Facilities include restaurant, bar, TV, and parking.

HOTEL TRAJANO, *Rua Candido dos Reis, (076) 332-415. Moderate.*

A good 2 star hotel with 39 regionally styled rooms with private bathroom. Facilities include restaurant, bar, laundry, air conditioning, room service, and cable TV.

THE MONTANHAS 303

GRANDE HOTEL DE CHAVES, *Rua 25 de Abril,25, (076) 211-18. Inexpensive.*

A friendly and reasonable 1 star hotel with 36 basic but comfortable rooms wih and without private bathrooms. Facilities include a decent restaurant, bar, and TV room.

WHERE TO EAT

RESTAURANTE LEONEL, *Campo da Roda, (076) 231-99. Moderate.*

A nicely designed seafood and steak restaurante near the Aerodromo which serves some of the best rice and seafood (*arroz de marisco*) in northern Portugal.

DIONISIOS, *Praça do Municipio, (076) 237-51. Moderate.*

A simple little restaurant near the castle which serves great fish and meat meals for reasonable prices either indoors in the dining room, or on outdoor tables.

O POTE, *Ave. Eng. Duarte Pacheco,10, (076) 212-26. Inexpensive.*

This nice regional resturant across the bridge offers great meat dishes and huge daily specials. Try the wonderful roasted kid (*cabrito a padeiro*) if its available.

BRAGANÇA

The royal city of **Bragança** *lies 98 km northeast of Chaves on route N-103 east, which can take up to three hours through this rugged mountain route.* The city is located on the banks of the **Fervenca** river and is dominated by a large citadel which encircles the picturesque medieval old town and contains a massive 12th century castle.

Originally a Spanish city, Bragança has been altenatively controlled by Romans, Moors, and finally the Portuguese Dukes of Bragança whose dynasty ruled Portugal until the proclaimation of the republic in 1910. To this day the ansestors of the royal family live in the area producing fine wines and hoping (in private) to one day regain both their throne and their vast fortune which was confiscated during the revolution.

WHERE TO STAY

POUSADA DE SÃO BARTOLOMEU, *Estrada de Turismo, (073) 331-493. Moderate.*

A nice *pousada* just out of town with 16 rustic rooms and great views of the castle. Facilities include a good restaurant, lounge with fireplace, tennis, and parking.

HOTEL BRAGANÇA, *Ave. Dr. Fancisco Sá Carneiro, (073) 331-579. Moderate.*

A nice modern 3 star hotel with 42 clean and comfortable guestrooms with private bathroom. Facilities include restaurant, bar, Cable TV, laundry, and parking.

MOINHO DO CANICO, *N-103-Castrelos, (073) 235-77. Inexpensive.*

A nice rustic stone house with a watermill on the bank of the Baceiro river about 12 km west of town. The house rents 2 nice guestrooms with private bathroom.

PENSÃO SÃO ROQUE, *Zona da Estacada,26, (073) 381-481. Inexpensive.*

A clean and simple inn with 30 or so comfortable guestrooms with private bathroom.

WHERE TO EAT

POUSADA DE SÃO BARTOLOMEU, *Estrada de Turismo, (073) 331-493. Expensive.*

Excellent regional cuisine served in a relaxing environment with surprisingly good service. The chef creates sevaral meat and fish specialities including an unforgettable trout dish called *truta em escabeche*.

SOL NEVE, *Rua Loreto, (073) 244-13. Moderate.*

A pretty good local restaurant and snackbar which serves huge portions of daily meat and fish specials with great salads. They serve the coldest beer in town.

SEEING THE SIGHTS

The citadel is located on the extreme southeastern edge of downtown and can be entered via the **Porta de Santo António** gate which passes through the crenellated granite walls. Once inside the citadel you have entered a medieval town which has not changed much in several centuries. Small farmer's houses can be seen with an assortment of livestock roaming the premisis.

The dominant structure in the old town is the **castelo** (castle) itself (open daily), where you can explore its towers, dungeon, cistern, battlements, drawbridge, and **Torre de Menagem** keep. This keep, once used to imprison Queen Dona Leonor, is home to the **Museu Militar** (Military Museum) with a permanent exhibition of 19th century weapons and artifacts (closed on Thursday). The top of the keep can be visited to access a beautiful panoramic view over Bragança's old and new sections.

Also inside the citadel is the wonderful 13th century Romanesque **Domus Municipalis** building which was used as a sort of town hall and meeting place which contains a large cistern on the ground floor which stored the town's water during several major sieges. The next structure you will find in the citadel is columned facade of the 18th-century **Igreja de Santa Maria** church which contains an ornatly painted vaulted ceiling.

Be sure to look at the Iron Age granite boar (**porca da vila**) which has been used as a support for a Gothic pillory.

The small lanes south of the citadel near the riverfront like *Rua dos Fornos* were once home to town's Jewish community (known as *Marranos*) who were trying to flee the Inquisition in neighboring Spain. To the west of the citadel, follow *Rua Serpa Pinto* east down towards the heart of town, to the peaceful and relaxing square known as the **Praça São Vicente** where you'll see the dramatic 17th-century **Igreja da São Vicente** church. Originally a Romanesque-style church, the facade and adjacent portico were added during it's first complete renovation in the 17th century. The interior of the church is richly decorated with 17th- century golden carvings and a strange 19th century depiticion of Christ's ascension.

If you walk back towards the citadel and follow *Rua Santo Condestavel* north and you will soon come to the impressive Renaissance portal of the **Igreja de São Bento** church. The church's fine interior boasts beautiful ceiling work including rare *Mudéjar* woodwork above the chancel. All of these churches are difficult to gain access to. If you cannot find an open door, go over to the *Turismo* office on *Ave. Cidade de Zamora* and ask for the location of the keys.

From the **Praça São Vicente** you can head down the *Rua do Conselheiro Abilio Beco* until you reach the old Episcopal Palace (**Antigo Paço Episcopal**). This 16th-century palace is now home to the **Museu Regional do Abade de Baçal** museum. Inside the walls of this building (closed on Monday) you will find an amazing array of paintings, goldsmithery, decorative artwork, furniture, coins, antique clothing, ecclessiastical items, prehistoric stone pigs, and other important archeological and ethnographical items which were collected by Abade de Baçal, the town's priest. A bit further down the same road and you will arrive at the **Praça da Sé** which is dominated by the large 16th-century **Sé** cathedral which is worth a quick look at. Behind the cathedral you can relax in the tranquil **Jardim António José Almeida** public gardens.

Parque Natural de Montezinho

Just above Bragança is the wonderful **Parque Natural de Montezinho**, with over 200,000 acres of prime parkland within the **Serra de Coroa** and **Serra de Montezinho** mountain ranges. The park is disected by several small roads (several are dirt roads) as well as the beautiful Onor and Tuela rivers which provide much of the fresh fish used in the area's best restaurants, and have recently been used for occasional kayac adventures.

Used mostly by local residents for weekend picnics and family hikes, the park contains a loose network of walking trails, trout-filled streams, and small peasant villages like **Zeive** and **Labiados** which seem frozen in the middle ages. For details about hiking trails, camping, fishing, cabin rentals, stone home rentals (**Casas Abrigo**), and hunting, *please contact the park's office in Bragança at (073) 287-34.*

MIRANDA DO DOURO

The unusual little village of **Miranda do Douro** rests below a huge cathedral, *some 102 km southeast of Bragança on route N- 218 south.* Dating back to the Roman era, this fortified town above the Douro river was finally liberated in 1385 by King Dom João I. Since Miranda do Douro is such an isolated town, many of the local residents still speak an unusual dialect called *Mirandes.*

This small city unfolds below a 16th-century cathedral set on the grounds of the citadel which was blown up in the 18th century. Now about all that remains of the original castle is the **Torre de Menagem** keep, the **Porta da Traicão** (traitor's gate), and a few pieces of the fortified wall. The **Sé** cathedral is open to the public and contains vaulted ceilings, the beloved glass protected hilarious 19th-century statue of **Menino Jesus da Cartolinha** by artist Gregório Hernandez, a wonderful carved organ, beautiful gilded and carved alterpieces, and wooden stalls which are ornemented with beautiful 17th-century paintings.

From the citadel area, you should stroll down the old medieval streets such as the **Rua Costanhila** which have beautiful 15th- and 16th-century houses. While walking through town, be sure to look in the small shops which sell the locally produced dark woolen carpets. When you reach the main square of town, **Praça Dom João III**, you can visit the **Museu da Terra de Miranda** town museum in the old town hall (antiga casa da Câmara) building. Here you can see a good collection of beautiful sacred art, prehistoric artifacts, unusual local costumes, and bizzare antique household items.

If you intend to dine in the area, make sure to try the fantastically tender braised meat known as posta a mirandesa. A good place to find locally made goods and meats is at the daily market on *Rua do Mercado.*

For those of you who would like to explore this unusual little corner of the world, I suggest an early morning start. If you are a good driver, you may wish to take route N- 221 south to see the castle and town of **Mogodouro** amidst the fabulous **Serra de Mogadouro** mountains. You can also cross the border by car into Spain just past the **Barragem de Miranda** dam. Since this part of the world is quite remote, you may wish to return to Miranda do Douro for your overnight.

WHERE TO STAY

POUSADA DE SANTA CATARINA, *Estrada da Barragem, (073) 422-55. Moderate.*

A good little *pousada* with 12 comfortable rooms, most of which have balconies which look out over a large man made lake. The best place to stay in the area.

PENSÃO SANTA CRUZ, *Rua Abade de Baçal,61, (073) 424-74. Inexpensive.*

An nice 2 star inn and restaurant in the heart of the old town with a dozen or so comfortable rooms with and without private bathrooms. A nice place to stay.

RESIDENCIAL PLANALTO, *Rua 1 de Maio, (073) 423-62. Inexpensive.*

A surprisingly good basic inn which offers over 40 clean and comfortable rooms with private bathroom. Almost no facilities but close to everything.

WHERE TO EAT

RESTAURANTE SANTA CRUZ, *Rua Abade de Baçal,61, (073) 424-74. Moderate.*

A great little family run restaurant which serves the hearty regional meats and stews which are only available in this area. The house wines are quite good as well.

MIRANDELA

The wonderful little walled town of **Mirandela** rests at the banks of the **Tua** river, *some 76 km southwest of Bragança on route IP-4 west.* This charming little secluded town offers several fine sights, including the **Porta de Dom Dinis** gate in the old walls, and town's stricking medieval 17 arch **Ponte** (bridge), which was rebuilt atop the foundations of an older Roman bridge.

The town's original fortress and castle are mostly in ruins, but you can still visit the fine 17th-century **Câmara Municipal** which was formerly the Palácio dos Tavoras manor house, and the 17th-century **Igreja Matriz** church. The town also contains the fine **Museu de Arte Moderna** museum (closed on Saturdays and Sundays) which contains a rich collection of works by selected 20th century Portuguese artists as well as by local painter Armindo Texeira Lopes. The town is noted for producing fine woolen blankets which can be found in several small shops.

WHERE TO STAY

HOTEL MIRA TUA, *Rua da República,20, (078) 224-04. Moderate.*

A good 2 star hotel with 31 rooms with private bathrooms. Facilities include bar, restaurant, direct dial phones, TV rooom, safe deposit boxes, and nearby parking.

PENSÃO PRAIA, *Largo 1 de Janeiro, 4, (078) 224-97. Inexpensive.*
A rather cheap 1 star inn which offers a dozen or so basic rooms with and without private bathrooms. Besides a breakfast room, there are few facilities.

VILA REAL

The university city of **Vila Real** rests at the foot of both the **Serra do Marão** and **Serra do Alvão** mountain ranges, *about 65 km. southwest from Mirandela on route IP-4 west*. Originally part of the Roman region once called *Panóias*, Vila Real became an important administrative town in the 15th century and is now home to 32,000 inhabitants which live just off the Corgo river.

Although the city has grown to include industry and some modern suburbs, it still has a small town ambiance. The city has several buildings and churches worth looking at, and your best bet is to park as close as possible to the centrally located *Avenida Carvalho Araujo*, home to several of the most interesting sights here. On the avenue itself you can visit the 15th-century Gothic **Sé** cathedral (sometimes referred to as the **Igreja de São Domingos**), the 15th-century **Casa de Diogo Cão** (the house of a famous Portuguese explorer), the battlement and Manueline window-encrusted **Casa dos Marqueses de Vila Real**, and the Manueline *Turismo* building that is several centuries old.

Nearby, on the busy *Rua 31 de Janeiro* you can visit the beautiful tiles of the baroque 18th-century **Igreja dos Clérigos** church which has become known as the Capela Nova. Throughout the old part of town on streets such as *Rua Serpa Pinto, Rua António de Azevedo*, and *Rua Teixeira de Sousa* you can find many fine examples of 17th-century houses and impressive regal buildings.

The massive 18th-century **Solar de Mateus** palace (open daily) can be reached by driving just 3 km east of the city to the village of **Mateus**. This Nicolau Nasoni designed baroque masterpiece includes several unusual towers, huge statues, impressive granite window moldings, a bold white-washed and granite block facade. The main section of the palace is set back behind two imposing side wings, and is entered by a huge grand staircase. The facade of the palace is fronted by a shallow pool which contains a statue of a drowning naked lady. Connected to the left wing of the palace is the more impressive facade of a Nasoni designed baroque chapel. The interior includes fine 18th-century furniture, remarkable wooden ceilings, a library full of rare editions, and several period paintings. The palace's formal gardens can also be viewed. You may recognize the palace as it adorns the label of **Mateus Rosé** wines.

Also worth a half-day trip from Vila Real is the **Parque Natural do Alvão** park. This wonderful protected area contains waterfalls, trails, and local villages such as **Lamas de Olo**, **Galegos de Serra**, **Amal**, and **Ermelo** which produce beautiful handcrafted wooden clogs and woolen capes.

For further details and trail maps, *contact the park's main information offices in Vila Real on Rua Alves Torgo, 22 at (059) 241-38 or in Amarante area at (055) 382-09.*

WHERE TO STAY

CASA AGRÍCOLA DA LEVADA, *Estrada do Circuito, (059) 322-190. Moderate.*

A quiet farming house just north of town near the river which makes its own provisions from the animals and fruits they raise. They offer 4 rooms with private bathrooms, a lounge, dining room, horses, boating, bicycles, and TV room.

HOTEL MIRACORGO, *Ave 1 de Maio, 76, (059) 250-01. Moderate.*

A large modern 3 star riverview hotel with 76 large air conditioned rooms. Facilities include restaurant, bar, room service, pool, sauna, TV, and handicappped access.

CASA DA CRUZ, *N-304-Campea, (059) 979-422. Inexpensive.*

A typical stone block 18th century house in the mountains about 12 km. northwest of Vila Real. The house rents 3 nice double rooms with bathrooms and kitchens.

HOTEL CABANELAS, *Rua D. Pedro de Castro, (059) 323-154. Moderate.*

A reasonably good 2 star hotel with 24 small double rooms. Facilities include bar, restaurant, heating, TV, direct dial phones, and parking.

QUINTA DE SÃO MARTINHO, *Estrada do Circuito, (059) 239-86. Moderate.*

A rustic country house on a farming area close to the *Solar de Mateus*. The house offers a 2 bedroom apartment with kitchen, sitting room and private bathroom.

PENSÃO O VIZINHO, *Ave. Aureliano Barrigas, (059) 322-881. Inexpensive.*

A decent,basic inn with 13 double rooms with and without private bathroom. Although there are few facilities, this is a good budget choice.

WHERE TO EAT

RESTAURANTE ESPADEIRO, *Ave. Almeida Lucena, (059) 322-302. Moderate.*

An impressive and cheerful restaurant which prepares fine regional fish and meat dishes in front of the clients. Try the fine fresh local river trout served here.

CHURRASCO, *Rua António Azevedo,24, (059) 322-313. Moderate.*
A good little snackbar and restaurant which specializes in roasted meats. The place is far from fancy, but with a little patience you will be rewarded with great food.

PESO DA RÉGUA (RÉGUA)

Régua is a major Port wine producing and transportation city on the northern bank of the **Douro** river, *some 24 km down from Vila Real on route IP-3 south (also called route N-2)*. This town is at the western border of the demarcated Port wine region, and has several wine tasting lodges which are open to the public for tastings and guided tours.

My favorite Port wine tours and tastings in town are held at the **Ramos Pinto** lodges (closed on Sundays). There is little else to do in town besides getting a bit smashed, and waiting until you are sober to take a car, boat, bus, or train to your next stop.

LAMEGO

The wealthy wine producing city of **Lamego** rests a few minutes below the **Douro** river, at the banks of the smaller **Balsemão** river, *some 11 km south of Peso da Régua on route IP-3 south (also called route N-2)*. Now surrounded by terraced agricultural areas, the city was once occupied by Roman, Suebian, Visigoth, and Moorish settlements.

Scattered throughout the city are several interesting granite mansions, small typical neighborhoods, and several beautiful historic buildings on wide avenues such as *Avenida Dr. Alfredo de Sousa* and the more commercial *Rua Alexandre Hurculano*.

The city rests at the base of two large hills. One of these hills is home to the ruins of a 13th-century **castelo** (castle) and some stone houses, while the other hill is covered by the huge pinnacle and azulejos covered 686 step staircase that leads up to the imposing 19th-century baroque **Santuario de Nossa Senhora dos Remidos** church. While the church's interior is nothing special, a stroll down the staircase is a great way to start your visit into the center of town. From the bottom of the staircase you will walk straight down *Ave. Dr.A. de Sousa* and continue past the turnabout until you reach *Ave. Visconde de Sousa*. A brief stop at this street's *Turismo* office may help you to get a local walking map.

A few more steps down *Ave. Visconde de Sousa* you will soon find the **Largo do Camões** plaza which is dominated by the 12th-century **Sé** cathedral. Almost nothing is left from its Romanesque beginnings, but the lovely triple portico, 18th-century organs, and beautifully carved choir chairs are worth noting.

Across the plaza from the Sé is the **Antigo Paço Episcopal** (old Episcopal palace) which houses the **Museu Regional de Lamego** museum. The museum (closed on Mondays) contains over 30 rooms filled with fine examples of baroque chaples, furniture, 16th century Belgian tapestries, statues, azulejos, sacred art, and many paintings including works by 16th-century artist Vasco Fernandes.

Starting the last week of August, the **Festa de Nossa Senhora dos Remidos** festival takes over town for three weeks. Events range from oxen pulled processions to folklore expositions and huge rock concerts. Before leaving town, I suggest you visit the **Caves Raposeira** winery, *a couple of km south of town off route N-2*. Here you can take a guided 20 minute tour of the facilities and sample some great sparkling wines for free.

WHERE TO STAY

QUINTA DA TIMPEIRA, *N-2 -Lugar da Timpeira, (054) 628-11. Moderate.*

A charming wine producing estate some 3 km south of town of *route N-2* which offers 5 nice rooms with private bathrooms. Facilities include piano bar, fireside lounge, dining room, pool, billards, tennis, bicycles, garden, TV, and wine cellar.

HOTEL PARQUE, *Parque N.S. de Remédios, (054) 621-06. Moderate.*

A nice 2 star 33 room hotel with great views over the church and the city. Facilities include a panoramic restaurant, bar, garden, TV, laundry, and handicapped access.

ALBERGARIA DO CERRADO, *Lugar do Cerrado, (054) 631-64. Moderate.*

A modern comfortable inn with 30 air conditioned rooms (some with balconies) just east of town. Facilities include bar, restaurant, and handicapped access.

VILA HOSTILINA, *N-2-Lamego, (054) 623-947. Moderate.*

A cold hilltop spa style estate and 19th century house which offers 8 rooms with private bathrooms, a fireside lounge, dining room, card room, sauna, tennis, pool, bicycles, health club, gardens, TV room, wine cellar, gardens, and a great view.

PENSÃO SOLAR DO ESPÍRITO SANTO, *Rua Alexandre Hurculano, (054) 643-86. Inexpensive.*

A pretty good centrally located inn with 31 double and twin rooms with private bathroom. Facilities include bar, heating, garage, TV, and handicapped access.

PENSÃO SOLAR, *Largo de Sé, (054) 620-60. Inexpensive.*

A clean and comfortable 2 star inn near the cathedral which offers 25 clean rooms with private bathrooms but few other facilities. Close to everything.

WHERE TO EAT

A MINHA, *Rua Alexendre Hurculano,5, (054) 633-53. Moderate.*
A very cozy and rustic typical resturant which serves fine locally produced meats in it's unusual dining rooms. The service is excellant, and the ambiance is great.

COMBINADO, *Rua da Olaria,89, (054) 629-02. Inexpensive.*
A pretty good local fish and meat restaurant which serves up large portions of locally caught trout and other regional specialities at reasonable prices in a casual setting.

VISEU

The enchanting city of **Viseu** stands at the bank of the **Pavia** river, *some 70 km down from Lamego on route IP-3 south (also called route N-2)*. With its roots going back to at least the Roman era, Viseu provides an excellent atmosphere to wander back through time. The city became home to several masters of Portuguese art such as Vasco Fernandes and Gaspar Vaz who have left their mark throughout this city and all of Portugal.

This is a city with so much to see that I stayed more days here than I was expecting to. Viseu has been an important commercial city as far back as in the 14th century when it's *Marranos* (local Jewish merchants) forged the development of its trade methods. The local economy of Viseu and its 22,000 residents is heavily dependant on the *Dão* wine industry. These light and fruity wines are a staple of the country's diet, and excellent bottles are sold for as little as 250$00.

WHERE TO STAY

HOTEL GRÃO VASCO, *Rua Gaspar Barreiros, (032) 423-512. Moderate.*
This 4 star full service hotel near the Rossio offers 88 nice air conditioned rooms with nice interiors. Facilities include bar, restaurant, pool, garden, and good service.

CASA DE REBORDINHO, *Rebordinho, (032) 461-258. Moderate.*
This beautiful 17th century manor house and estate 6 km. south of Viseu off N-231 offers 4 rooms with private bathrooms, lounge, TV room, a farm, and parking.

CASA DOS GOMES, *São João de Lourosa, (032) 461-341. Moderate.*
An attractive 18th-century granite house and farming estate some 5 km southcast of Viseu off route N-231 offering 7 nice rooms with private bathrooms, lounge, dining room, vineyards, pool, tennis, billiards, bicycles, library, TV room, and parking.

HOTEL MANA, *N-16-Via Cacador, (032) 479-243. Moderate.*
A modern 3 star hotel with 73 comfortable rooms about 3 km from

Viseu. Facilties include bar, restaurant, pool, gym, TV, billards, tennis, squash, and parking.

RESTHOTEL VISEU, *Vernum-Campo, (032) 451-258. Inexpensive.*

A nice new 2 star motel style inn a few km. out of town with 60 comfortable air conditioned rooms with private bathroom, bar, restaurant, TV, and parking.

RESIDENCAL DOM DUARTE, *Rua Alexandre Hurculano,214, (032) 257-81. Inexpensive.*

A pleasant centrally located basic inn with 18 comfortable but tacky rooms with private bathroom. The inn has a breakfast room and a TV room. Nothing special.

WHERE TO EAT

RESTAURANTE TÍPICO O CORTICO, *Rua Agusta Hilario,47, (032) 461-278. Moderate.*

This excellent regional restaurant offers it's clients fine local meat dishes served in the relaxing atmosphere of an old granite building in the heart of the old town.

RESTAURANTE A PARREIRA, *Ave. de Belgica,2, (032) 417-94. Moderate.*

An informal meat and seafood restaurant located in an old stone house in the center of *Viseu*. The ambiance, service, and hearty dishes are among the best in town.

RESTAURANTE CACIMBO, *Rua Alexandre Hurculano,95, (032) 422-894. Inexpensive.*

A down to earth eating establishment with a limited selection of roasted meats and fried fish specialities. This basic restaurant serves large portions of good food.

SEEING THE SIGHTS

To begin your journey by foot through this amazing city, you must first find parking around the **Praça de República** square in the city's center (also called the **Rossio**). From the Rossio's statue of Prince Henry the Navigator, the first Duke of Viseu, you may wish to pop into the *Turismo* office which can be reached by walking one block south on *Avenida 25 de Abril* and then half a block to the left (east) on *Avenida Caloute Gulbenkian*. While in the *Turismo* ask for one of the great free town street maps in English.

As you walk back up the *Ave. 25 de Abril* towards the Rossio, you will first find the baroque 18th-century **Igresa dos Terceiros de São Francisco** church. This church's solemn interior contains beautiful azulejos and carefully carved and gilded pulpits. Upon exiting the church and walking a few steps north into the Rossio you will have no problem noticing the large *azulejos* mural of regional life by Joaquim Lopes. The 19th-century **Câmara Municipal** (town hall) with it's imaginative tile interior and the granite staircased mastestic courtyard.can be visited across from the mural.

The Rossio extends up (northward) until it reaches the **Largo Major Teles** where you will find the lovely **Jardim das Maes** gardens, adjacent to the **Casa-Museu de Almeida Moreira** house and museum. The museum (closed on Mondays) contains the private collections of furniture, ceramics, armour, and paintings.

From the museum, head up (north) on *Rua Soar de Cima* for a block or so until you have reached the massive 16th-century **Porta do Soar de Cima** gate, built as the main entrance to the old town wall by King Alfonso V. As soon as you cross into the old town you are bombarded with immensely powerful facades and churches in every direction. As you make your way towards the heart of the old town, the **Praça da Sé** plaza, you will find yourself next to the whitewahed and granite facade of the beautiful 18th-century **Igreja da Misericórdia** church. The exterior of this church contains two large bell towers and a large portal which rests below a higely decorated baroque patio.

Directly across from the entrance to the Igreja de Misericórdia is the fantastic 12th-century Romanesque **Sé** cathedral. Rebuilt several times since its initial construction, the cathedral contains an odd assortment of elements including Gothic pillars, a vaulted stone block ceiling which is adorned with 16th-century knot shaped tracery, a gilded 16th century barouque altarpiece, beautiful azulejos, and Renaissance cloisters. You can visit the chapterhouse of the cloisters that contains the **Museu de Arte Sacra** museum (closed on Sundays) which contains several several rare treasures and ecclesiastical items dating as far back as the 12th century.

Next to the **Sé** cathedral you will find yet another remarkable building known as the **Antigo Paço Episcopal dos Três Escaloes**.This granite 16th century former bishop's palace is now home to the unforgettable **Museu de Grão Vasco** museum. Inside the three-floor museum (closed on Monday) you will find several rooms full of 16th century masterpieces by local artists such as Vasco Fernandes (Grão Vasco) and Gaspar Vaz including the paintings moved here from the adjacent Sé cathedral's original retable. Other rooms contain a selection of beautiful 13th through19th century works including paintings, ceramics, sculptures, azulejos, carved ivory. furniture, and tapestries.

From the left (west) side of the **Praça da Sé** plaza, take *Rua Silva Caio* up past the northern edge of old town. After you have crossed the *Ave. Emidio Navarro,* you will soon find the beautiful **Porta dos Cavaleiros** gate which passes through the old town walls. Just west of the gate there is the ancient town well which may also be visited. Double back to the **Praça da**

Sé and this time head south from the middle of the square and pass through the **Praça Dom Duarte** onto *Rua Dom Duarte*. On this street you can view the 14th century birthplace of King Dom Duarte, the medieval **Casa da Torre**, adorned with an unusual twin Manueline window.

From here you can follow *Rua Dom Duarte* south as it merges with *Rua Direita* and turn right (west) onto **Rua Formosa** which leads you back past town's daily **mercado** (market). From the eastern edge of the market you can also take a small walk up *Rua Dr. Luís Ferreira* to see some fine shops.

Return to the market, and turn right (west) onto *Rua Formosa* and follow it back to the Rossio. Before departing the city, make sure to stop by the tranquil **Parque Aquilino Ribeiro** park just below the Rossio for a nice restful stop or picnic. On Thursdays, the town hosts a large weekly **mercado** (market) in the north part of town below the riverside.

CARAMULO

The gorgeous spa town of **Caramulo** rests on a hill deep in the windswept **Serra de Caramulo** mountains, *58 km southwest of Viseu. Although there are several scenic mountain approaches to the city, it is easiest to arrive by taking IP3 south from Viseu and carefully connecting to route N-230 west near Tondela.*

Surrounded by mountains, parks, gardens, pine forests, and hiking trails in every direction, Caramulo is extensively visited by local families in search of peaceful weekend outings. The quiet city is home to the **Fundação Abel de Lacerda** foundation (named for its benefactor, a local doctor), which maintains the city's two interesting museums (closed on Mondays). The foundation's art museum boasts several collections wonderful art. The most impressive of the museum's paintings consist of Portuguese masterworks by Vasco Fernandes (Grão Vasco), Eduardo Nery, Frei Carlos, and Amadeu de Sousa Cardoso, while it's European collection includes modern paintings by Dali, Picasso, Miro, Chagall and Leger. Also included in the foudation's collection is a vast array of ceramics, tapestries, statues, jewelry, and furniture. The adjacent musem contains an assortment several dozen classic cars and motorcycles including a rare vintage 1911 Rolls Royce, a mint 1898 Hurtu, and the world's only remaing Pegaso.

Many of the visitors who picnic through this wonderfully peaceful area take a short drive or hike to the panoramic plateaus and small mountaintop villages nearby. *The most accessible of these fine vistas can be reached by taking route N-230-3 south for about 3 km, and take the signposted left side turn off which takes you to the dramatic* **Cabeço da Neve** *lookout.* If you prefer a 45 minute hike, *go back to route N-230-3 south and continue another half mile or so to the marked path for* **Caramulinho**, which leads to an impressive view over several mountain ranges.

WHERE TO STAY

POUSADA DE SÃO JERÓNIMO, *Caramulo, (032) 861-291. Moderate.*

A small and cozy *pousada* with 6 nice balconied guestrooms that have nice views, a relaxing fireplace lounge, a good regional resturant, good service, and a pool.

PENSÃO SÃO CRISTÓVÃO, *Caramulo, (032) 861-394. Inexpensive.*

A reasonable and simple 2 star inn with good rooms with and without private bathrooms in the heart of town, The inn is often closed during winter months.

MANGUALDE

The quaint town of **Mangualde** *lies 17 km southeast of Viseu on route IP-5 east*. This lively commercial town of 9000 residents has managed to preserve its small but delightful old section full of stone lanes and tiny granite houses which seem to be lost in time.

Mangualde boasts several beautiful churches including the medieval 13th-century **Igreja Matriz** with its fine paintings and eery courtyard, and the 18th-century **Igreja das Almas** which contains a rather ornate altar. The most impressive structure in town is the wonderful 18th-century noble residence known as the **Palácio dos Condes de Anadia** – still privately owned. The opulent house (closed on Mondays) contains a vast assortment of bizzare scenic azulejos as well beautiful period furnishings, portraits of the Count of Anadia and his family, beautiful ceilings, and several regal rooms.

There are also several smaller houses in the old quarter that are emblazoned with bold coats of arms. Mangualde provides an excellent base from which to explore the wonderful **Serra da Estrêla** mountain range just 21 km away.

WHERE TO STAY

CASA DAS MESQUITELA, *Mesquitela, (032) 614-210. Moderate.*

A wonderful 16th-century manor house with 6 luxuriously furnished guestrooms with private bathroom some 4 km southeast of Mangualde near route N-16. This truely remarkable inn also contains a period dining room which serves regional cuisine.

CASA DE QUINTELA, *Quinta de Azzura, (032) 622-936. Moderate.*

A large granite 16th century manor house 5 km northeast of Mangualde off IP-5 with 5 nice guestrooms with private bathroom. Facilities include dining room, lounge, pool, tennis, trails, TV room, gardens, library, and parking.

HOTEL SENHORA DO CASTELO, *Monte Senhora do Castelo, (032) 611-608. Moderate.*

A large 3 star hotel with 85 air conditioned rooms not far from *Mangualde's* center. Facilities include bar, grillroom, restaurant, pools, sauna, cable TV, and billards.

ESTALAGEM CASA DE AZURARA, *Rua Nova, 78, (032) 612-010.* Moderate.

A nice 4 star inn located near the heart of *Mangualde* with 15 comfortable rooms with private bathroom, bar, restaurant, air conditioning, TV, and kitchen facilities.

ESTALAGEM CRUZ DA MATA, *Lugar da Cruz da Mata, (032) 611-945.* Inexpensive.

A reasonably good inn with 19 basic twin and double guestrooms with private bathroom, bar, restaurant, room service, heating, laundry, and good service.

THE SERRA DA ESTRÊLA

The remarkable **Parque Nacional da Serra da Estrêla** mountain range, Portugal's highest, *can be reached by taking route N-232 south from Mangualde for 21 km.* The rugged glacier-carved valleys, mountain peaks, pristine lakes, and watermill-laden rivers make this area an irresistable attraction for anyone interested in challenging its winding, windswept roads (often closed during winter).

Although seldom seen by non-Portuguese tourists, the Serra da Estrêla offers visitors a vast array of activities and sights including downhill skiing, fishing, trekking, thermal water spas, regional country fairs, and peaceful villages dotted with historical monuments. Many of the local inhabitants are engaged in the traditional tending of large goat and sheep herds which provide the area with an abundance of excellent wool as well as the raw materials which are magically transformed into the soft and tasty *Queijo da Serra*, which you should not leave the region before sampling.

As you enter the Serra da Estrêla area from the quaint city of **Gouveia**, you will be immersed in the beauty of the mountains. The peaceful town of Gouveia is one of the Serra's bases of production for woolen clothing, and contains the beautiful azulejos covered **Igreja de Matriz** church.

Nearby, *at Rua Direita, 45,* is the small **Museu Municipal de Arte Moderno Abel Manta** museum (closed on Mondays), exhibiting several paintings from its namesake as well as ceramics, weapons, and local artifacts. The town also contains the **park information office** *on Rua dos Bombeiros Voluntarios, 8,* which can give you free park maps and help with trail and hiking information. *You can call them at (038) 242-11.*

From Gouveia, route N-232 twists and turns south and then east past the Mondego river and the huge **Penhas Douradas** peak during its dramatic 39 km journey towards the most famous city in the area,

Manteigas. This stunning city of 3500 people is filled with beautiful 17th century whitewashed and granite houses with hand carved wooden balconies. After a stroll through town you can take route N-338 south about 5 km to the spa complex at **Caldas de Manteigas** whose hot sulphur thermal springs are known to ease the pain of those suffering from rheumatism, respiratory and muscular diseases.

From the bridge spanning the **Zêzere** river at Caldas de Manteigas, you can take a small and curvy dirt side road east for 7 km or so to view the **Poco do Inferno** waterfall. You may wish to have a brief rest near the waterfall, and then backtrack to route N-338 south and follow it about 14 km south along the glacier-formed Zêzere river basin until you have reached the intersection at Nave de Santo António. From here you can either exit the mountains via **Covilhã**, or if you have a few more hours before sunset (do not attempt to drive in the Serra da Estrêla at night!), you may decide to see more of the area by turning right (west) onto route N-339.

After about 4 km on route N-339 west you can stop at **Covão do Boi** to view some wonderful granite sculptures whose origins remain a mystery. A few more km further up route N-339 you will find the left side access road to the snow-capped **Torre**, the largest of the peaks in the range with its ski area and panoramic views over the melted snow pools which feed the Zêzere river.

After you have returned to route N-339 you can continue past the beautiful **Lagoa Comprida** lake and down into the valley past the quaint traditional villages of **Sabugueiro**, **Aldeia da Serra**, and **Seia**. At this point it is time to consider ending your first day on the Serra de Estrêla roads and check into your hotel (you should pre-reserve your room far as in advance as possible). If you enjoy the area, on your next day you might consider taking route N-231 south from Seia to Pedras Lavradas which in turn connects to route N-230 east past the lovely spa town of **Unhais de Serra** and on to the city of **Covilhã**.

WHERE TO STAY

POUSADA DE SÃO LOURENÇO, *Penhas Douradas, (075) 982-450. Expensive.*

A lovely chalet style *pousada* 14 km west of Manteigas with 22 rooms with private bathroom and great views. Facilities include a fireplace lounge and restaurant.

POUSADA DE SANTA BÁRBARA, *Oliveira do Hosipital, (038) 522-52. Expensive.*

A nice 16 room (some with balcony) pousada just west of the Serra da Estrêla range in Oliveira do Hospital. Facilities include bar, restaurant, pool, tennis.

CASA DA CAPELA, *Rio Torto, (038) 464-23. Moderate.*
An ornate 18th century mansion and chaple off route N-17 some 7 km west of Gouveia which offers a great 2 bedroom apartment with kitchen and fireplace.

QUINTA DA PONTE, *Faia-Guarda, (071) 961-26. Moderate.*
A nice 18th century manor house near the Mondego river a few km. northwest of Guarda near the village of Faia. They offer 5 rooms and 5 one bedroom apartments with private bathrooms, fireside lounge, dining room, pool, billards, and parking.

CASA DAS TILIAS, *São Romano-Seia, (038) 200-55. Moderate.*
A peaceful estate and 19th century manor house next to a stream some 2 km south of Seia off route N-231 in the hamlet of São Romão. This pleaseant house offers 6 nice rooms with private bathrooms, lounge, breakfast room, bicycles, and gardens.

QUINTA DO PINHEIRO, *Cavadoude, (071) 961-62. Moderate.*
A dramatic 17th century stone manor house some 15 km. northwest of Guarda off route N-16 near the town of Porto da Carne. The house offers 6 great rooms with antiques and private bathrooms, lounge, TV room, bicycles, billards, and parking.

CASA DE SÃO ROQUE, *Rua de Santo António,63, (075) 981-125. Moderate.*
A charming house in the center of Manteigas which rents 6 nice guestrooms with private bathroom. The owners are quite friendly and speak some English.

CASA GRANDE, *Paços de Serra, (038) 433-41. Moderate.*
An impressive 18th century manor house about 9 km. north of Gouveia off route N-17 which rents 2 rooms and 3 rustic apartments with kitchen and private bathroom.

HOTEL TURISMO DA COVILHÃ, *Covilhã, (075) 323-843. Moderate.*
One of the brand new hotels in this city, it has 60 large air conditioned rooms. Facilities include bar, restaurant, squash, TV, disco, sauna, and minibars.

ESTALAGEM DE SEIA, *Ave. Dr. A. Costa-Seia, (038) 226-66. Moderate.*
A nice 3 star inn with 35 comfortable guestrooms not far from the city's center with private bath. Facilities include bar, restaurant, pool, billards, heating, and TV room.

HOTEL CAMELO, *Rua 1 de Maio-Seia, (038) 225-10. Moderate.*
A nice 3 star hotel with 66 double rooms with private bathrooms in the heart of town. Facilities include bar, restaurant, tennis, billards, TV, mini bars, and parking.

HOTEL DE MANTEIGAS, *Caldas de Manteigas, (075) 982-400. Moderate.*
A reasonably good full service hotel near the spa with 26 barren

rooms with private bathroom. Facilities include bar, restaurant, tennis, sauna, gym, and garage.
HOTEL DE GOUVEIA, *Ave. 1 de Maio-Gouveia, (038) 428-90. Moderate.*
A clean and basic 2 star hotel with 31 clean rooms with private bathroom. Facilities include bar, snackbar, resturant, heating, direct dial phones, TV, and good service.
CASA DO PONTE, *Alvoco de Serra, (038) 933-51. Inexpensive.*
A granite house in front of the Alvoco stream some 24 km from Seia off route N-231 with 6 rustic rooms with private bathroom to travellers. Minimal facilities.

GUARDA

The historic city of **Guarda** rests at the eastern foot of the **Serra da Estrêla** mountains, *96 km southeast of Viseu off route IP-5 east.* Since its settlement by the Romans, this strategic city has been the guardian of the mountains since it was first fortified by the Visigoths, captured by the Moors, and finally liberated and further strengthened by the Portuguese in the 12th century. Although the town lacks any real beauty, there are a few worthwhile sights to see if you decide to stop here.

WHERE TO STAY

SOLAR DE ALARCÃO, *Rua Dr. Miguel de Alarcao,25, (071) 243-92. Moderate.*
A nice centrallly located 17th century manor house which rents 3 rooms with private bathroom. Facilities include bar, TV and Video room, garden, library, and parking.
HOTEL TURISMO, *Ave. Coronel O. de Carvalho, (071) 222-05. Moderate.*
A pleasant large hotel with 105 comfortable rooms in a relatively peaceful area of town. Facilities include bar, restaurant, pool, disco, TV, parking, and some shops.
RESIDENCIAL FILIPE, *Rua Vasco de Gama,9, (071) 212-659. Moderate.*
A pretty good 25 room establishment near in the heart of town with friendly service and basic services. Facilities include bar, restaurant, direct dial phones, and TV.
PENSÃO ALIANCA, *Rua Vasco de Gama,8, (071) 212-135. Inexpensive.*
A nice and comfortable 3 star inn located in the heart of town which offers 29 rooms with private bathroom, a restaurant, bar, TV room, direct dial phones, and parking.

SEEING THE SIGHTS

The 12th-century **Torre de Menagem** keep, and a few remaining gates which pass through wall segments known as the **Torre dos Ferreiros**, **Porta de Erva**, and the **Porta d'el Rei** are about all that remains of city's ruined castle. Below the ruined castle you willl find the **Praça Luís de Camões** square which is home to several bold 16th- and 18th-century noblemen's house emblazoned with coats of arms.

Also in the square is the massive **Sé** cathedral. The cathedral's construction began in 1390 and it's original Gothic design was considerably altered by Diogo Boitac with Manueline finishings by the time of it's completion in 1541. Besides its dominant Gothic and Manueline portals and beautiful granite Manueline window, the tower and butress laden exterior of the Sé is a bit overbearing. The solemn vaulted interior includes 16th century statues and an altarpeice which were created by Jean de Roen, as well as fine Renaissance portals which lead to the Pinas family chapel and its Gothic family tomb carved of solid granite. Next door to the Sé, *on Rua D. Miguel de Alarcão, 25*, is a beautiful facade and tile courtyard of the 17th-century manor house known as the **Solar de Alarcao**.

Also worth visiting are the nearby 18th-century **Chafariz de Santo António** fountain, the 17th-century baroque **Igreja da Misericórdia** church across from the Torre dos Ferreiros tower, and next door at the **Museu Regional de Viseu** museum (closed on Mondays) in a 17th-century mansion *at Rua General Alves Rocadas, 30*, which showcases a collection of 16th-20th century paintings, sculptures, armory, and assorted artifacts. A short walk in the small streets like *Rua Direita, Rua Fransisco de Passos,* and *Rua dos Clérigos* will reveal even more fine 15th-18th century houses with unusual doors and windows.

The town host a daily **mercado** (market) in the southeastern corner of town just off *Rua Dom Nuno Alvares Pereira* and a huge Wednesday **mercardo** (market) in the fairgrounds by *Ave. Monsenhor Mendes do Carmo*.

THE CASTLE TOWNS AROUND GUARDA

Being of prime defensive importance, the area surrounding Guarda is filled with several fortified cities which are well worth visiting. A full day of village hopping from one of these impressive castles to another is an experience that I strongly reccommend. There are two seperate circles that will take a full day each to truly experience. If you don't have two full days to spend looking at the remarkable walled villages and castles of this area, I suggest you select the southern circle. I have also included the northern circle for those who are interested.

THE SOUTHERN CASTLE CIRCLE

To see the wonderful villages of the **southern circle of castles**, *you must first depart from Guarda on route N-18 south for just about 18 km until you can turn left on a small road towards* **Comeal da Torre**. A minute or two down the road you can see the bizzare Roman structure known as **Centum Cellas**. This unusual pink granite tower with several openings has been a matter of controversy with leading archeaologists, and the upcoming excavation of the surrounding area should better explain it's exact age and purpose.

From the tower you should head back to route N-18 south for another 4 km or so until you can turn left on route N-345 east for half a mile, to **Belmonte**. This wonderful small city is dominated by the impressive walls (which contain a beautiful Manueline window) and keep of a **castelo** (castle), which dates back to the King Dom Dinis I reign of the 13th century.

> ### DISCOVERER OF BRAZIL
> *Belmonte was the birthplace of Pedro Alvares Cabral, the discoverer of Brazil. In fact the town has named its main square,* **Praça Pedro Alvares Cabral**, *in his honor. He brought back with him a large 15th-century cross which now rests just outside the town walls.*

Adjacent to the castle is the remarkable 14th-century Romanesque **Igreja de São Tiago** church whose beautiful interior contains the remnants of it's original frescoes, and the stone tombs of local hero Cabral and his mother. Although a new modern city has emerged here, the medieval old town has keep most of its original charm.

Belmonte is also home to the ancestors of Jewish settlers who were forced to flee from Spain during large anti-semetic riots in the 14th century. Although they were resigned to live in a seperate area called the *Judiara* (Jewish quarter), they integrated into the social and commercial society of Belmonte. When the Inquisition was brought to Portugal in 1496, the king ordered the forceful conversion of these Jews to Christianity. Many of these so-called *Marranos* secretly practised their faith even though they seemed to be attending regular services in the Igreja de São Tiago church. The Jewish community today has its own synagogue, but *Marranos* still live within the old Judiaria section of town beside the castle.

From Belmonte you can go back to route N-18 south for about 27 km until reaching Fundão. Keep going on route N-18 south for 9 km until you can make a left turn onto route N-239 east; go another 37 km to the signposted turn-off to see the incredible mountaintop village of **Monsanto**. Of all the villages and castles in this region of Portugal, Monsanto is bar far the loveliest. The winding approach through town brings you past the post office and the newly built ultra-modern *pousada*. Park here as the road becomes perilously narrow beyond this point. The village has not changed very much in the centuries since its pre-Roman occupation.

The shy and traditional residents of Monsanto live in granite houses which are under, on top of, and between huge boulders. Most of these unusual folks still practice a way of life which has all but vanished from western Europe. The small stone patio on the main road just before the pousada is the sight of monthly communal pig slaughters that are horrific.

There are also several more ornate residences with small window gardens and patios, and a beautiful Romanasque belltower. As you walk through the stone lanes you can notice that the older peasant population maintain working barns in the basements of their houses and gated chicken coups using the boulders as ceilings. If you're lucky enough to befriend one of the locals, they may show you the way they use the region's famous three-legged iron fire blasted cauldrons to prepare the heartiest meals I have ever seen.

High atop the rocky mountain perch at he end of town lies the fog-enshrouded ruins of a once important defensive castle. The exhilirating walk up the rugged path is best enjoyed on sunny days as the view is dramatic.

A TYPICAL STREET SCENE IN MONSANTO

After your memorable visit to Monsanto, *take route N-239 west for some 7 km until you can turn right onto route N-332 north for about 16 km* until you reach the ruined castle of **Penamacor**. The town has been home to a castle

324 PORTUGAL GUIDE

since the 9th century, but it was sacked several times since. Most of the current wall fragments and Torre de Menagem tower dates back to the 16th century. The town contains several fine 16th- and 17th-century granite houses concentrated around the streets radiating from the peaceful main square known as the **Praça 25 de Abril**. Also worth noting is the beautiful 18th-century **Câmara Municipal** (town hall), and the imposing 16th-century **Igreja da Misericórdia** church. The nearby **Serra da Malcata** mountain park is a great place to watch wildlife.

From Penamacor, continue up route N-332 north which is now merged with route N-233 north for about 6 km, until you can bear left onto route N-233 north, when the road again divides, for about 27 km until you come to the town of **Sabugal**. Dominating the small town is the large restored 13th-century pentagon shaped keep with it's massive fortified walls. The sleepy town offers little else worth noting with the exception of the vast panoramic views from the ramparts over the nearby **Côa** river.

After a brief stopover at Sabugal, *take route N-233 south for 12 km until you reach Terreiro das Bruxas, and turn right onto route N-18-3 west for 8 km until you reach the town of Santo Amaro*, where you will find the signposted road to the haunting walled city of **Sortelha**. After Monsanto, this is the second most impressive castle villages in the region. Although seemingly deserted, several people still live in the 20 or so granite houses of the old part of town which are entered via a massive Gothic portal through the large fortified wall which also surrounds the partially ruined 12th century castle. A beautiful old church and pillory remain close to the castle, while several gardens strech between the ivy covered rustic village houses. Not much really happens here anymore, as the majority of town's inhabitants have moved into more comfortable dwellings in the newer section of town outside the walls.

Upon returning to **Santo Amaro**, you should visit the large ruins of a spa hotel once known as **Aguas Radium**. This once grand hotel is scheduled to become a major golf and spa resort, but the stone cutters and woodcrafters have not done much in the past two years to rebuild the bizzare structure. I won't hold my breath.

From Santo Amaro, take route N-18-3 west for about 20 km until you can bear right onto IP-2 north and return to Guarda by dinnertime.

WHERE TO STAY

POUSADA DE MONSANTO, *Monsanto, (077) 344-71. Moderate.*
A brand new *pousada* with 10 designer double rooms with bizzare modern furnishings. Facilities include a nice bar, good restaurant, and some parking.

ESTALAGEM VILA RICA, *Penamacor, (077) 343-11. Inexpensive.*
A nice little old farmhouse which offers 10 spacious and comfortable

rooms with private bathroom. Facilities include bar, regional restaurant, library, and parking.
HOTEL BELSOL, *N-18-Belmonte, (075) 912-207. Inexpensive.*
A good 2 star hotel with 39 clean and comfortable rooms a few km. out of town at Quinta do Rio. Facilities include bar, restaurant, TV, direct dial phones, and parking.
CASA DO PATIO, *Sortelha, (071) 681-13. Inexpensive.*
A nice rustic house outside of the town walls whichs rents 1 nice room and a huge 2 bedroom apartment with kitchen, sitting room, TV, and fireplace. Minimal facilities.
CASA DO VENTO QUE SOA, *Sortelha, (071) 681-82. Inexpensive.*
An old basic granite house within the old city walls. The house can be rented by the day or week with a several basic and traditional bedrooms as well as a kitchen.

THE NORTHERN CASTLE CIRCLE

To view the villages of the northern circle, you must start out early in the morning. *Your best bet is to start again from Guarda on route N-16 north for some 23 km to the cheese producing city of* **Celorico da Beira**. This small city contains a wonderful walled castle, a beautiful Mannerist church, and a peaceful main square which is home to the large cheese market each fortnight on Friday. *From Celorico de Beira you can take the small unnamed road leading south for some 11 km. (past the quaint village of Cortico de Serra) until you reach* **Linhares**. This wonderful 15th-century walled village is located high in the mountains and is a great place to wander through. The town contains several straw covered lanes, an ancient pillory, beautiful period houses, two remaining Gothic and Romanesque keeps, and massive fortified walls which once surrounded the original castle.

After visiting Linhares, *take the same small road back up for a couple of km or so until you reach the left side turn-off, which leads 5 km west to route N-17 north. From there you can go back through Celorico de Beira on your way to route N-102 north. After roughly 18 km along route N-102 north you should take a left at the intersection onto route N-226 north and drive for 4 km, until your see the massive castle which rests above the village of* **Trancoso**. It was in this lovely village during the 13th century that King Dom Dinis met and soon after married his 12 year old bride, Queen Isabel. The town became one of Queen Isabel's wedding presents and is watched over by a massive citadel and strong fortified walls.

From Transcoso, continue up route N-226 north for some 7 km until you can bear right onto route N-229-1 north for about 32 km to the small town of **Penedono**. Herc the town's 1000 residents live on a hilltop beneath the shadow of the remarkable 15th century triangle shaped castle of knight

326 PORTUGAL GUIDE

Alvaro Coutinho. The wondefully-preserved turreted walls and towers provide a great panoramic views over the mountains.

From Penedono, you bear right onto route N-331 west for some 25 km until you turn right onto route N-102 south, and follow it 8 km south to the abandoned village and ruined castle at **Marialva**. Altough nobody lives here anymore, you can still stroll down the unpaved lanes to see the 15th-century Manueline **Igreja Matriz**, the remaining towers from the 13th-century castle, and several empty houses. This is a great place to relax and perhaps take a rest.

From Marialva, head back to route N-102 and this time head north for about 20 km until you can bear right onto route N-222 east; go for 14 km until you find another ruined castle amidst the village of **Castelo Melhor**. Only a couple of hundred residents remain in this small hilltop village which contains a dramatic medieval wall. *From Castelo Melhor, drive down route N-222 south as it merges with (and is renamed) route N-332 south for 21 km.or so to get to* **Castelo Rodrigo**. This fortified village with its shrinking population of about 240 traditional dwellers conains the ruins of a once grand castle. The castle was destroyed by angry town residents who did not approve of the Count of Castelo Rodrigo's decision to side with Philip of Spain during his efforts to conquer Portugal.

After you have visited Castelo Rodrigo, *continue on route N-332 south for about 22 km,* until you reach the wonderful border town of **Almeida**. Although the site of several conficts throughout the centuries, the town still stands within the six sided star shaped walls of a frontier castle last modified in the 18th century.

The town itself is quite lively, and contains is three original entry gates, several ornate houses, the original 18th-century barracks which at one point held over 250,000 troops, several small gardens, and the area's only *pousada*. After walking trough the town, *head back on route N-332 south for another 13 km until you can turn west onto route N-16 west (the service road of IP-5) for some 17 km or so until you have found* **Castelo Mendo**. This small hilltop settlement of stone houses is surrounded by it's partially ruined defensive wall. The town itself contains the fine 17th-century **Igreja Matriz** and its unusual pillory. The town is crowned by the ruins of a castle and a church.

From here you can return to Guarda via route N-16 west for 30 km to rest or spend the night.

WHERE TO STAY

POUSADA DA S. DAS NEVES, *Almeida, (071) 542-83. Expensive.*

A new pousada with great views over the old town and castle. The *pousada* offers 21 good air conditioned rooms and a bar, restaurant, TV, heating, and parking.

HOTEL MIRA SERRA, *IP-5-Celorico de Basto, (071) 733-82. Moderate.*
A nicely furnished and welcoming 3 star hotel with 42 comfortable rooms with private bathroom. Facilities include bar, restaurant, disco, TV, and a garage.

PENSÃO FIGUEIRENSE, *Castelo Rodrigo, (071) 325-17. Inexpensive.*
A nice inn with 16 comfortable rooms a few km. away from town at Figueira da Castelo Rodrigo. Facilities include bar, restaurant, TV room, garden, and parking.

FUNDÃO & ALPEDRINHA

The charming city of **Fundão** is full of fruit trees and flowers. *It lies at the starting point of the wonderful* **Serra da Gardunha** *mountains some 59 km down from Guarda on route N-18 south.* The heart of town, **Praça do Municipo**, is lined by the main streets of *Ave. da Liberdade* and *Rua 5 de Outubro* where you can find good shopping and dinning. Make sure to view the extraordinary *azulejos*-covered **Igreja Matriz** church. Be sure to try the wonderful fresh fruits that are grown locally.

About 11 km further south on route N-18 south, you will soon ome to another quaint local town know as **Alpedrinha**. This wonderful little agricultural community offers several old *palácios* (mansions) and a variety of great manor houses and fine inns to stay in. The mountainview lanes off the central **Largo da Misericórdia** in the center of town offer several sights worth seeing, including the 18th-century **Chafariz de Dom João** fountain, the simple **Igreja Matriz** church, the **Paços do Concelho** town hall and museum, a fine furniture workshop, and a few nice lanes with curious inhabitants. On the first Sunday of each month, the town hosts a **mercado** (market).

WHERE TO STAY

CASA DOS MAIS, *Fundão, (075) 521-23. Moderate.*
A beautiful 18th century manor house and gardens set in the Praça da Municipio of peaceful Fundão with 6 great rooms with private bathroom, a TV room, and library.

ESTALAGEM DA NEVE, *Fundão, (075) 522-15. Moderate.*
A good 4 star inn on Rua de São Sebastião which offers rooms with private bathrooms, air conditioning, pool, bar, resturant, cable TV, minibars, and parking.

HOTEL SAMASA, *Fundão, (075) 712-99. Moderate.*
A modern multilevel hotel on Rua Vasco de Gama which offers 50 air conditioned rooms with private bath. Facilities include lounge, minbas, TV, and parking.

CASA DA COMENDA, *Alpedrinha, (075) 571-61. Moderate.*

A fortified 17th century stone house in the center of town which offers 4 rooms with private bathrooms, a garden, lounge, TV room, pool, billards, and parking

CASA DE BERREIRO, *Alpedrinha, (075) 571-20. Moderate.*

A uniquely designed manor house on Ave. Paço Vieira with great views which offers 6 rooms with private bathroom, lounge, dining room, bicycles, and TV room.

ESTALAGEM SÃO JORGE, *Alpedrinha, (075) 571-54. Inexpensive.*

A nice 4 star inn located in the heart of town at Largo da Misericórdia which offers rooms with private bathroom, a bar, restaurant, TV room, and parking.

PENSÃO TAROUCA, *Fundão, (075) 521-68. Inexpensive.*

A clean and basic 2 star inn located in Rua 25 de Abril which offers rooms with and without private bathroom. Very few facilities, but close to everything.

CASTELO BRANCO

The city of **Castelo Branco** can be reached *by taking route N-18 south for about 48 km from Fundão.* Once a grand border town crowned by a massive **castelo** (castle), this city has grown into a more modern commericial center full of broad avenues, good shopping and dinning possibilities, and a few interesting attractions. Unfortunetly there is little left of its ruined castle and origins, which date back to Roman times. During the Napoleonic war of the early 18th century, the French invaded, occupied, and looted much of the city and it's treasures.

The most impressive sight in town is the **Museu Fransisco Tavares Proenca** museum housed in the old Episcopal Palace (*Antigo Paço Episcopal*) *on Rua de Frei Bartolomeu da Costa.* Inside the museum (closed on Mondays), you can view a vast collection of Roman artifacts, ancient coins, weaponry, 16th-century Flemish tapestries, 17th-century Portuguese furniture, sacred art, 16th century paintings, weaving implements, and a beautiful collection of locally-made colchas (linen bedspreads hand embroidered with silk designs). Next to the museum are the **Jardim do Antigo Paço Episcopal** gardens, with 18th-century sculptures, carefully pruned trees, and several small ponds.

A nice walk through the old town via the quaint *Rua dos Ferreiros* and onward past the old town's quaint main **Praça Luís de Camões**, with its remarkable 16th-century **Câmara Municipal** (town hall) and several other ornate mansions. From here you can stroll past several shops and restaurants on the *Rua de Santa Maria.* At the end of the street, bear right and follow the *Rua do Arressario* up and around to the grounds of the **Igreja de Santa Maria do Castelo** church.

THE MONTANHAS 329

From here you can view the scant remains of the former castle, and walk up the staircase to the lovely **Miradouro de São Gens** promenade to see the beautiful panoramic views over both the old and the new city. On your way back through town you can window-shop for a fine bedspread to take home with you.

WHERE TO STAY

HOTEL RAINHA D. AMELIA, *Rua de Santiago, 15, (072) 326-315.* Moderate.

This modern and comfortable 64 room air conditioned hotel is in the new part of the city. Facilities include bar, restaurant, cable TV, minibar, and lots of parking.

RESIDENCIAL ARRAIANA, *Ave. 1 de Maio, 18, (072) 216-34.* Moderate.

A clean and centrally located inn with several basic and comfortable rooms with private bathroom. Facilities include a bar, TV, direct dial phone, and minibar.

PENSÃO MARTINHO, *Alameda da Liberdade, 41, (072) 217-06.* Inexpensive.

A basic and clean inn which offers cheap accomodations in somewhat comfortable rooms which are either with or without private bathroom. Minimal facilities.

WHERE TO EAT

RESTAURANTE PRAÇA VELHA, *Praça Luís de Camões, (072) 286-330.* Moderate.

A charming eating establishment with exposed beam and granite interiors that serves it's upscale clientelle a vast selection of local meat dishes with fine service.

PRACTICAL INFORMATION FOR THE MONTANHAS

CURRENCY EXCHANGE

Many of the banks in the Montanhas will exchange foreign currency and traveler's checks. Some tourist shops, restaurants, and hotel front desks will offer you a rather poor exchange rate. Remember that banking hours are from 8 am until 3 pm on Monday through Friday.

Currency exchange machines are almost impossible to find this far north but you can still locate 24-hour ATM machines in large cities.

EMERGENCY & USEFUL PHONE NUMBERS
- **Emergency Assistance** (S.O.S.), *115*
- **Directory Assistance**, *118*
- **Castelo Branco Hospital**, Ave. Pedro Cabral, *(072) 322-133*
- **Guarda Hospital**, Rua Dr. F. Prazeres, *(071) 222-133*
- **Automobile Club of Portugal** (Emergency road services), *(02) 830-1127*
- **Porto's Pedras Rubas Airport** (14 km out of Porto), *(02) 948-2141*
- **T.A.P.Airlines Porto**, Praça M. Albuqurque, 105, *(02) 600-5555*

MUSEUMS, PALACES, & MONUMENTS
- **Abade de Baçal Museum**, Rua do Conselheiro Abilio Beca, 27, Bragança, *(073) 232-42*. Contains a collection of scared art, furniture, archaeological findings, tapestry, and 17th-18th century paintings. Open 9 am until 12 pm and 2 pm until 5 pm from Tuesday through Sunday. Closed on Mondays and holidays.
- **Abel de Lacerda Foundation Art Museum**, Caramulo, *(032) 861-270*. Contains collections of paintings by Portugues masters including Sousa-Cardosa, Vasco Fernandes, Eduardo Nery, and Eduardo Viana as well as works by Cgagall, Dali, Leger, and Miro. There are also exampes of tapestries, jewelry, and ceramics. Open 10 am until 1 pm and 2 pm until 6 pm daily.
- **Abel de Lacerda Foundation Automobile Museum**, Caramulo, *(032) 861-493*. Contains collections of several dozen classical cars from the 19th and 20th century. Open 10 am until 1 pm and 2 pm until 6 pm daily.
- **Fransisco Tavares Proenca Museum**, Rua de Frei Bartolomeu da Costa, Castelo Branco, *(072) 242-77*. Contains a collection of Roman artifacts, coins, 16th century Flemish tapestries, 16th century Portuguese paintings, and a display of local *colchas* bedspreads. Open 10 am until 12 pm and 2:30 pm until 5 pm Tuesday through Sunday. Closed on Mondays and holidays.
- **Castle Tower and Miltary Museum of Bragança**, Torre de Menagem, Bragança, *(073) 223-78*. The original keep of Bragança's castle which also contains a collection of weapons and artifacts from previous centuries. Open 10 am until 12 pm and 2 pm until 5 pm daily.
- **Francisco Tavares Proenca Museum**, Paço Episcopal, Rua Bartolomeu Costa, Castelo Branco, *(072) 242-77*. Contains collections of 16th-century Flemish tapestries, 17th century Portuguese furniture, locally embroidered bedspreads, antique coins, ceramics, and artifacts. Open 10 am until 12 pm and 2:30 pm until 5 pm Tuesday through Sunday. Closed on Mondays and holidays.
- **Regional Museum of Chaves**, Praça de Camões, Chaves, *(076) 219-66*. Contains a vast collection of archeaological findings from pre-Roman

up through modern eras, 19th and 20th century paintings, and locally made handicrafts. Open 9:30 am until 12:30 pm and 2 pm until 5 pm Tuesday through Friday. Open 2 pm until 4:30 pm Saturday and Sunday. Closed on Mondays and holidays.
- **Castle Keep and Military Museum of Chaves**, *Praça de Camões, Chaves, (076) 219-66*. Contains a vast collection of military objects including weapons from the 12th century and more recent military displays. Open 9:30 am until 12:30 pm and 2 pm until 5 pm Tuesday through Friday. Open 2 pm until 4:30 pm Saturday and Sunday. Closed on Mondays and holidays.
- **Abel Manta Modern Art Museum**, *Rua Direita, 45, Gouveia, (038) 431-55*. Contains collections of Abel Manta paintings as well as ceramics, modern art, some antique weappons, and local archeaoligical items. Open 10 am until 12:30 pm and 2 pm until 5 pm Tuesday through Sunday. Closed on Mondays and holidays.
- **Guarda Regional Museum**, *Rua Gen. Alves Rocadas, 30, Guarda, (071) 213-460*. Contains a collection of 16th-20th centry paintings, sculptures, weapons, and archeaological finds from all over the region. Open 10 am until 12:30 pm and 2 pm until 5:30 pm Tuesday through Sunday. Closed Mondays and holidays.
- **Lamego Town Museum**, *Largo de Camões, Lamego, (054) 620-08*. Contains collections of 16th-century Flemish tapestries, antique jewelry, metal sculptures, scared art, furniture, and 16th-20th century Portuguese paintings. Open 10 am until 12:30 pm and 2 pm until 5 pm Tuesday through Sunday. Closed on Mondays and holidays.
- **Terra de Miranda Museum**, *Praça Dom João III, Miranda do Douro, (073) 421-64*. Contains collections of local festival costumes, arceaological findings, furniture, ceramics, weapons, handicrafts, and other regional artifacts. Open 10 am until 12 pm and 2 pm until 5 pm Tuesday through Sunday. Closed on Mondays and holidays.
- **Mateus Manor House Museum**, *Solar de Mateus, Mateus-Vila Real, (059) 323-121*. A regal 18th century manor house and chapel which contains vast collections of antique furniture, paintings, dicuments, sculpture, jewelry, porcelain, and gardens. Open 10 am until 1 pm and 2 pm until 5 pm daily from October through April. Open 9 am until 1 pm and 2 pm until 8 pm daily from May through September.
- **Almeida Moreira House & Museum**, *Rua Soar de Cima, Viseu, (032) 423-769*. Open 10 am until 12:30 pm and 2 pm untl 5:30 pm Tuesday through Sunday. Closed on Mondays and holidays.
- **Grão Vasco Museum**, *Paço dos 3 Escaloes, Viseu, (032) 422-049*. Contains a large collection of paintings from Vasco Fernandes (Grão Vasco) as well as other 16th-20th century paintings, furniture, ceramics, and sacred art. Open 9:30 am until 12:30 pm and 2 pm until 5 pm Tuesday

through Sunday. Closed on Mondays and holidays.
- **Sacred Art Museum of Viseu**, *Sé Cathedral-Adro da Sé, Viseu, (032) 422-984*. Contains a collection of paintings, jewelry, and assorted sacred art items. Open 10 am until 12 pm an 2 pm until 5 pm Monday through Saturday. Closed on Sundays and holidays.

SPORTS & RECREATION

Most of the sporting activities in the Montanhas are available in either the **Serra da Estrêla** mountains, or at hotel-run sporting facilities.

Please contact a *Turismo* for more specific information on hunting and fishing licences, horse riding, bicycle rentals, trail maps, and municipal swimming areas. Try the following:
- **Quinta da Mata Horse Riding**, *Chaves, (076) 233-85*
- **Casa Agrícola Levada Horse Riding**, *Vila Real, (059) 322-190*
- **Vidago Golf Club**, *Vidago, (076) 971-06*

TRANSPORTATION

Traveling by public transportation is not too easy in the *Montanhas* due to the limited quantity of services and stations in the region. Since the train and bus lines in this area are in constant flux, I have included only a few station locations.

Please call any of the below *CP* and *RN* offices, or any *Turismo* office for more detailed locations and further information.
- **Bragança RN Bus Depot**, *Largo de Estação, (073) 228-70*
- **Guarda RN Bus depot**, *Ave. Coronel Caravalho, (071) 227-20*
- **Viseu RN Bus depot**, *Ave. Dr. António Almeida, (032) 412-337*
- **Bragança CP Rail station**, *Largo de Estação, (073) 223-97*
- **Castelo Branco CP Rail station**, *Ave. D. Nuno Alvares, (072) 222-83*
- **Guarda CP Rail station**, *5 km out of town, (071) 211-565*
- **Vila Real CP Rail station**, *Rua Miguel Bombarda, (059) 322-193*
- **Viseu CP Rail station**, *Ave. Capitão H. Ribeiro, (032) 423-100*
- **Avis Rent a Car in Viseu**, *Hotel Grão Vasco, (032) 257-50*
- **Hertz Rent a Car in Viseu**, *Rua da Paz, 21, (032) 421-846*
- **Europcar in Castelo Branco**, *Praça R. da Leonor, 13, (072) 262-04*

TOURIST OFFICES (TURISMOS)

- **Belmonte Tourist Office**, *Praça Pedro Cabral, (075) 911-48*
- **Bragança Tourist Office**, *Ave. Cidade de Zamora, (073) 282-73*
- **Castelo Branco Tourist Office**, *Alameda da Librdade, (072) 210-02*
- **Covilhã Tourist Office**, *Praça do Municipo, (075) 221-70*
- **Chaves Tourist Office**, *Rua de Santo António, (076) 210-29*
- **Fundão Tourist Office**, *Ave. de Liberdade, (075) 527-70*
- **Gouveia Tourist Office**, *Ave. dos Bombeiros, (038) 421-85*

THE MONTANHAS 333

- **Guarda Tourist Office**, *Praça de Luís Camões, (071) 222-51*
- **Lamego Tourist Office**, *Ave. Visconde Teixeira, (054) 620-05*
- **Manteigas Tourist Office**, *Rua Dr. G. de Carvalho, (075) 981-129*
- **Miranda do Douro Tourist Office**, *Largo do Men. Jesus, (073) 421-32*
- **Moncovo Tourist Office**, *Rua Manuel Seixas, (079) 222-89*
- **Penamacor Tourist Office**, *Praça 25 de Abril, (090) 341-06*
- **Seia Tourist Office**, *Praça do Mercado, (038) 222-72*
- **Vila Real Tourist Office**, *Ave. Carvalho Araujo, (059) 322-819*
- **Viseu Tourist Office**, *Ave. Calouste Gulbenkian, (032) 279-94*
- **Serra da Estrêla Park Info-Viseu**, *Rua dos B. Voluntarios, (038) 242-11*

TRAVEL AGENCIES

Novo Mundo Travel, *Ave. João da Cruz, 5, (073) 226-36*. A full service branch travel agency in central Bragança with expertise in booking accomodations, tickets, and specialty excursions throughout Portugal.

- **Intercontinental Travel and Tours**, *Rua Direita, 150, (076) 214-83*. A friendly and reliable Chaves branch travel agency and tour operator with full service booking and ticketing facilities for all sorts of travel services.
- **Abreu Tours**, *Ave. Calouste Gulbenkian, (032) 423-545*. A Viseu office of a major tour company and travel agent with computerized central reservations systems and good rates at a large assortment of resorts.

20. THE PLANÍCIES

The **Planícies** (*the plains*) is the largest region in Portugal and consists of the complete **Alto Alentejo** province, as well as most of the **Ribatejo** and **Baixa Alentejo** provinces, which comprise roughly one-third of Portugal's land mass. The majority of this highly agricultural and historic region is covered with cork and olive fields. Prehistoric megaliths, cave drawings, and opulent cathedrals are common sights in this vast region.

Due to the extremely long growing season, the plains produce most of the country's food supply. Although the region has some fine Atlantic coastline and many fish laden rivers, it is primarily a dry and somewhat arid region which receives very little rainfall each year. A controversial project is currently underway to create a massive man made lake-reservoir near the Spanish border to solve the water supply problems, while submerging thousands of acres full of historic sights.

The Planícies is known for raising Lusitanian horses and purebred bulls for Portugal's non-lethal bullfights.The landscape of the plains also includes mountain ranges, including the unspoiled beauty of the **Serra dos Ossa**, and a small strip of seafront just north of the Algarve. This region is very rich in history and culture. The friendly peasants who ride their oxen and donkeys down the region's small rural highways are happy to stop and talk to locals and tourists alike. Besides the wonderful handmade ceramics and tapestries created by local artisans, the Planícies produces several varieties of table wines which are quite enjoyable and inexpensive.

While all of this region is worth exploring, the most impressive stops include the perfectly preserved mountaintop walled village of **Monsaraz**, the endless wonders in the incredible city of **Évora**, the 15th-century **Convento de São Paulo** in **Redondo**, the ancient fortress towns of **Marvão** and **Elvas**, the world famous artisans of **São Pedro do Corval**, **Portalegre**, and **Arraiolos**, the wine producing villages around **Cartaxo**, the quaint traditional fishing settlement of **Escaropim**, the historic old sections of **Castelo de Vide**, the beaches of **Milfontes**, **Porto Corvo**, and **Santo André**. And don't forget to take in a bullfight!

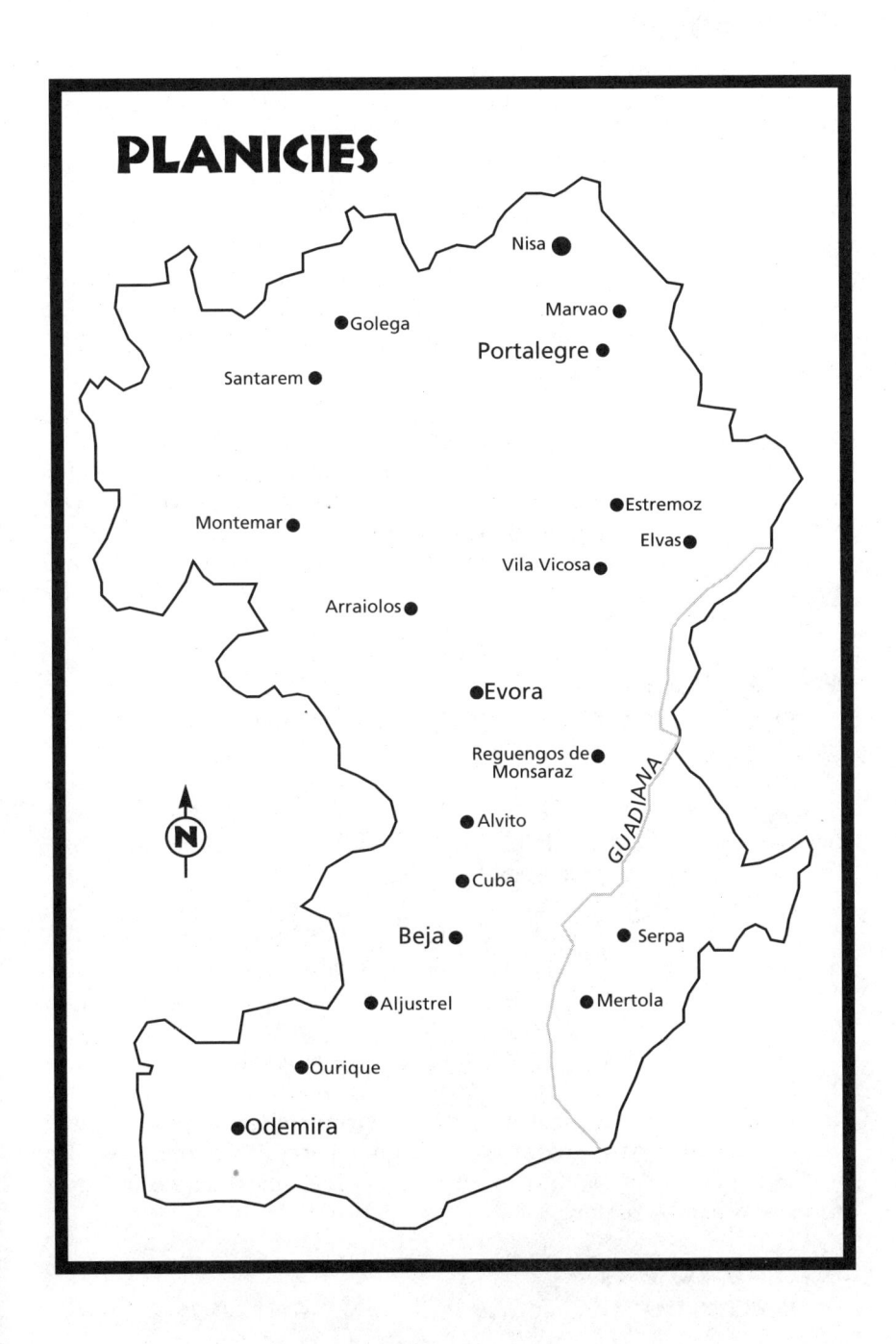

THE PLANÍCIES 335

SANTARÉM

The hilltop city of **Santarém** rests above the **Tejo** river and the fertile plains that make up much of the Planícies region. *The city can be reached by taking the A-1 highway northward from Lisbon for 72 km.*

The history of Santarém goes back to the days when barbarians roamed through Europe. After the city was captured from the Moors in 1147 by King Dom Afonoso Henriques, Santarém remained an importante agricultural and commercial city that has been home to several royal parliments (cortes) and historical events. During the Napoleonic wars, Santarém was occupied by the French troops who destroyed and pillaged several of town's most important structures, but fortunetely several fine sights still remain fairly intact.

Nowadays, Santarém has become the district capital of the Ribatejo and its 21,000 inhabitants are typically preoccupied with the vast number of agricultural, gastronomic, bullfighting, and horsemanship events for which the city has become famous. If you are lucky enough to be in town when a bullfight is scheduled, don't miss the opportunity.

Each October the city is the host of a huge 10 day gastronomic festival where visitors and residets alike can stroll from one booth to another tasting all sorts of regional cuisine from all over Portugal.

WHERE TO STAY

QUINTA DE VALE DE LOBOS, *Azoia de Baixo-Santarém, (043) 429-264. Expensive.*

A lovely 19th century manor house and estate some 6 km. north just of town off route N-3. The historic inn offers 4 nice rooms and two 1 bedroom apartments with private bathrooms. Facilities include bar, library, pool, hunting, trails, and parking.

QUINTA DE SOBREIA, *Vale de Figueira, (043) 420-221. Moderate.*

An inviting manor house on a farm located about 16 km. north of Santarém on route N-365 near the peaceful village of Vale de Figueiro. The inn offers 3 nice guestrooms with private bathroom, bar, pool, bicycles, library, TV, and parking.

RESIDENCIAL VICTORIA, *Rua Visconde de Santarém, 21, (043) 225-73. Inexpensive.*

A nice and friendly small inn with a dozen or so clean and comfortable guestrooms with private bathrooms in a good part of Santarém. If you're willing to pay a bit extra, you can get a balcony. Facilities include breakfast room and nearby parking.

WHERE TO EAT

PORTAS DO SOL, *Jardim de Portas do Sol, (043) 295-20. Moderate.*

A beautiful and casual little resturant near the castle's belvedere that has a patio area surrounded by the gardens. The friendly and helpful staff provide some insight on which regional dish is the best of the day. A great place to eat and relax.

SEEING THE SIGHTS

The best way to start you trip through Santarém is to look for the municipal parking area on the city's centrally located *Rua Serpa Pinto*. After securing your car, you can walk up *Rua Serpa Pinto* a couple of blocks until you find yourself at the beautiful **Praça Sá da Bandeira** plaza. The imposing 17th-century **Nossa Senhorha da Conceição** Jesuit seminary church with its bold baroque whitewashed and granite block exterior is your first stop.

Inside this wonderful building, once the site of a royal palace, you will find impressive azulejos covered hallways, 18th-century frescoes, niches filled with interesting statues of Jesuits, several gilted wood altars, and a large 18th-century marble incrusted high altar. From the mosaic paved plaza in front of the church, continue up through the **Largo Piedade** and turn right onto *Rua 31 de Janeiro* to stroll through the tranquil **Jardim do República** gardens.

From here you can continue up the *Rua 31 de Janeiro* to view the Gothic 13th century **Igreja de Santa Clara** and the nearby panoramic **São Bento Miradouro** lookout. If you double back to the western edge of the garden, you can turn up *Rua Cidade da Covilhã* for a block or so and visit the *azulejos*-covered public **mercado** (market), which is the perfect place to buy small quantities of local produce, meats, bread, and cheeses that can be used for a fine picnic a bit later on through your visit. Head back to the **Praça Sá da Bandeira** and this time follow shop lined *Rua Capelo Ivens* down through town. You may want to pop in to the *Turismo* office at # 63 for a free local map.

From *Rua Capelo Ivens* you should turn left (east) onto *Rua 1 de Dezembro* for a couple of blocks until you can turn left into the quaint **Praça Visconde Serra Pillar** square and bear right to visit the 16th-century **Igreja da Marvila** church. The church, whose original construction actually dates back to the 12th century, contains an impressive Manueline portal, and has 17th century *azulejos* covering it's walls.

From the Marvila church, bear right for a block or so to *Rua Coselheiro Figueiredo Leal* where you'll find the 13th-century Romanesque **São João de Alporão** church which is now home to the city's archaeological museum (closed on Mondays). Here you can find a somewhat disorganized clutter of ancient pottery, coats of arms, coins, *azulejos*, sculptures, and the tomb of Duarte de Menses whose tooth is all that remained of him after he was killed battling the Moors in the 15th century. Across from the church you can see the **Torre das Cabacas** bell tower built in the 15th century which is adorned by several large clay pots known as cabacas.

From the tower, you can head back to the *Rua 1 de Dezembro* and take a left turn to reach the **Largo Pedro Alvares Cabral**. Here you will find the 14th-century Gothic **Igreja de Nossa Senhora da Graça** which has a large Rosé window carved of a single block of stone, a beautiful interior containing ornate tombs, and fine azulejos panels. From the church, you can head back to the Torre das Cabacas and turn right onto *Ave 5 de Outobro*, which ends at the old citadel's walls and the **Portas do Sol** gardens. The gardens provide a beautiful place to sit on a bench and enjoy a picnic while looking down onto the Tejo river and the plains which unfold before you. If you didn't stop at the market for picnic supplies, try lunch on the patio of the lovely **Portas do Sol** restaurant.

There are several cities along both the western and eastern banks of the Tejo river which can all be visited in the space of one long day. I have included an easy to follow circular itinerary in the following pages that will take you to **Cartuxa**, **Azambuja**, and then back up the other bank of the river through **Benavente**, **Salverra de Magos**, **Almeirim** and back into Santarém.

I strongly suggest you consider using one of your free days in the area to see some of these great little traditional towns. Accomodations are almost non-existant in these towns, so staying in Santarém is your best bet. I should also mention that there are also fine outdoor **mercados** (markets) held in town during the 2nd and 4th Sunday of each summer month. Please check with the *Turismo* for details about exact market schedules and ask them about additional festivals which may also be worth seeing.

CARTAXO

About 15 km southwest of Santarém on route N-3 south is the pretty little agricultural town of **Cartaxo**. This peaceful town produces some of my favorite white wines in all of Portugal, which are premiered yearly at the area's famed **Feira do Santos** festival in November.

With its rich history and beautiful traditional houses, this town is especially of interest to wine lovers. The town itself offers visitors a few interesting sights located within easy walking distance from the **Largo Vasco de Gama** plaza in the town's center.

Among my favorite sights are the arts and crafts exhibits at the small town museum in the Largo Vasco de Gama, and a 15th-century Manueline cross at the portico of town's **Igreja Matriz** at **Largo João Baptista**. On the outskirts of town off *Rua José Ribeiro da Costa* you will find the **Quinta das Pratas**, home to the beautiful wonderful **Museu Rural e do VInho** rural life and wine museum. The exhibits are located in buidings which are part of a beautiful 50 acre farm with impressive traditional buildings (closed on Mondays).

Several wineries are based around the town, most notably the **Quinta da Fonte Bela** cellars a few minutes east. I reccommend a stop in to the **Câmara Municipal** on the **Praça 15 de Dezembro** to ask for a wine route map and more detailed tourist information. Cartuxa is also close to a traditional fishing village called **Palhota** which is just a few km south of town on the Tejo river.

AZAMBUJA

The once sleepy agricultural town of **Azambuja** *lies about 13 km further down route N-3 south from Cartuxa.* These days the town has become a base for industries such as automobile manufacturing, but it still offers some interesting sights.

The town is home to the festive and colorful **Feira de Maio** fair at the end of each May. During the fair, the yard which surrounds the fine Manueline pillory of the **Igreja Matriz** on **Largo do Adro** becomes a makeshift bullring, and the streets of town are full of young people trying to out run the bulls. The small streets such as *Rua do Espírito Santo* and *Rua Eng. Moniz da Maia* are full of old world ambiance and a few shops that sell the locally-produced wines and baskets made from corn husks.

A small museum of African art is here (closed on weekends) on *Rua Victor Cordon, 69.* If you stroll down to the **Largo dos Combatentes da Grade Guerra**, you should go inside the train station to view some wonderful *azulejos* panels. A few minutes east of town, you can visit the quaint riverfront fishing village of **Lezirão**, while a short drive north of town will lead you to **Manique do Intendente** and its outrageous 18th-century **Palácio Pina Manique** palace.

SANTO ESTEVÃO & BENAVENTE

The bull breeding town of **Benavente** *can be reached from Azambuja by following route N-3 south for about 11 km, then take the A-1 highway south to cross the bridge from Vila Franca de Xira to route N-10 east. From route N-10 you should continue for 26 km or so until you can exit for route N-119 north, where you'll turn off in 2 km or so to the left* for the cute settlement at **Santo Estevão**.

The scenic bull-raising hamlet of **Santo Estevão** contains many colorfully dressed *campinos* (herdsmen) who live a traditional way of life (the Portuguese equivilant to our cowboys). You can visit a working farm estate in this area called **Monte dos Condes** where time seems to have stood still. The drive on route N-118-1 north from Santo Estavão to Benavente is a bit rough, but the sights are worth the bumps for the 15 km drive. Most of the land along the way belongs to familiy-owned stud farms as well as a few melon plantations.

In **Benavente**, stroll down the open streets and stop to view the 17th-century **Igreja da Misericórdia** with its unique azulejos on the lovely *Rua da Misericórdia* , walk up past the **Largo do Municipio** to take a peek at a rebuilt 16th-century pillory, continue to the beautiful Sorraia riverfront, and then back through town until you reach *Rua Luís de Camões,* home to the **Museu Municipal de Dr. António Gabriel** museum. The museum contains an assortment of unusual items including 19th- century photography, antique postcards, and lots of items which relate to life in the region. While walking around the streets of town, keep your eye out for shops which sell the linen stockings which are worn by many townspeople. The town is at its bestt during the annual **Fiera do Sardinhas** in June, when free grilled sardines and wine is served to all who arrive.

SALVATERRA DE MAGOS

The former royal hunting village of **Salvaterra de Magos** is *located some 6 km north of Benavente on route N-118 north.* Agriculture and livestock production are still the dominant economic base of this town, and the local acorn-fed pork is the best in the country. From the 13th through19th centuries, the town was inhabited by several members of the royal family who built several massive structures in town and practiced the art of hunting and Falconry.

Although most of the original royal palace was destroyed by the 1755 earthquake, you can still visit the multiple arched falconry, the fine **capela** (chapel) and parts of it's kitchens just off the **Largo dos Combatentes**. In the 18th century, a new palace was built, and can still be seen at the edge of town. Also woth a visit is the 18th century **Igreja da Misericórdia** with a beautiful *azulejos-*covered interior. The town hosts a few yearly bullfights at its large bullring, and each year in June there are bullruns and folklore displays during the local **Fandango** festival.

For me, the highlight of a visit here is a stop at the riverfront settlement of **Escaropim**, about 3 km north of town where wildly painted fishermens' houses rest on stilts at the water's edge. Nearby at the beach of **Praia Doce**, you can enjoy a nice summer swim.

WHERE TO STAY

CASA DO GRANHO, *Granho Novo, (063) 585-16. Moderate.*

A cute little house off route N-114-east near the Magos reservoir which offers a nice apartment with 2 beds and 2 sofa beds with a kitchen and private bathroom.

ALMEIRIM

Located some 28 km away from Salvaterra de Magos on route N-118 north is the lovely garden laden village of **Almeirim**. Situated just across the **Tejo** river bridge from Santarém, this town contains a rich tradition of royalty, artisans and folklore.

The town produces a fruity white wine often served with slices of the fabled *Almeirim* melon. The center of town is the lovely **Praça da República** square, a great place to start a short walking tour of town. Make sure to stop in at the 16th century whitewashed and granite **Igreja Matriz** on *Rua Conde de Tiapa*, the Moorish **Fonte de São Roque** on *Rua de São Roque*, and the **Casa do Povo** which houses a small ethnological museum on Rua de Coruche. Just out of town off route N-118 south you can visit the lovely 19th-century **Quinta da Alorna** horse farm and manor house, which produces great local wines. They'll be happy to sell you their wine directly from the caves.

ALPIARÇA

The quiet town of **Alpiarça** *lies near the eastern bank of the Tejo river across the Tejo river and some 10 km east of Santarém*. The surrounding area is loaded with archaeological findings that date back to prehistoric times.

Primarily a wine producing town, Alpiarça hosts an enchanting **Feira do Vinho** wine festival on the last weekend of every March. On the edge of town you can visit the wonderful **Casa dos Patudos** museum (closed on Mondays and Tuesdays) housed in the elegent former mansion of local art collector, diplomat and philantropist José Relvas on the appropriately named *Rua José Relvas*. The beautiful museum contains a fine collection of 16th-century paintings, ceramics, sculptures, azulejos, *Arraiolos* rugs, pottery, and other rare items. The town also has a beautiful 19th-century church called **Igreja de Santo Eustaquio** that has some unusual paintings.

An old fishing village known as the **Porto do Patacão de Cima** can be found just northwest of town at the Tejo riverfront.

CHAMUSCA

The tranquil village of **Chamusca** *lies at the foot of the eastern bank of the Tejo river some 16 km up from Alpiarça on route N-118 north*. A short stop in this town will allow you to visit several intersting sites, and purchase beautful hand made leather goods and beautifully painted ceramics.

The town features several pretty little plazas, including the **Largo Sacadura Cabral** which contains a mosaic-filled park and bandstand, the **Largo da Misericórdia**, home to the 17th-century **Igreja da Misericórdia** full of gilted woodwork and *azulejos*, the **Largo Vasco de Gama** which is dominated by the 16th century Gothic **Igreja Matriz**, and the **Largo 25 de Abril** and the adjacent **Parque Municipal** park and gardens, which contains the **Traditional Rural House** and **Museu Municpal** archaeological museums.

Above all, the town presents a good opportunity to hunt for unusual handicrafts. During the town's wonderful **Festa da Ascensão** (Ascension Day Festival), you can witness several bullfights and the running of the bulls which goes on for about a week.

GOLEGÃ

The famous horse breeding town of **Golegã** is *situated directly across the Tejo river bridge from Chamusca on the western side of the Tejo river some 31 km northeast of Santarém*. Known primarily for the yearly **Feira Nacional da Cavalo** (National Horse Fair), consisting of races, parades, feasts, and bullruns during the first two weeks of November.

While in town, make sure to visit the 16th-century Manueline **Igreja Matriz** at the top of *Rua do Campo* which has an incredible doorway. Also well worth a stop is the fantastic **Museu de Carlos Relvas** photography museum in the ornate palatial mansion of this 19th century photographer on *Rua José Farinha Relvas*. Nearby on the **Largo da Imaculada Conceição** is the wonderful **Museu de Mestre Martins Correia** museum of this artist's modern sculpture and painting (closed on Mondays).

The nearby village of **Azinhaga**, *about 8 km away on route N-365 south just off the Almonda river,* is a great place to see traditional rural life. Few tourists ever get here, but your efforts will be rewarded with excellent ancient mansions, churches, manor houses, and beautiful farms.

WHERE TO STAY

CASA DA AZINHAGA, *Azinhaga, (049) 951-46. Moderate.*

A beautiful 18th century nobleman's manor house on *Rua da Misericórdia* in the village of *Azinhaga* which offers 7 rooms and suites with private bathrooms, lounge, dining room, billards, bicycles, boating, fishing, TV room, and parking.

CASA DE S.ANTÓNIO DE AZINHAGA, *Azinhaga, (049) 951-62. Moderate.*

A relaxing manor house on *Rua Nova de Santo António* in the peaceful village of *Azinhaga* which offers travellers 3 nice guestrooms with private bathrooms . Facilities include libtaty, fireside lounge, dining room, TV room, and parking.

CONSTÂNCIA

The historic town of **Constância** sits on a small hill, *at the confluence* *of the Tejo and Zêzere rivers just northeast of Golegã. It is best reached by taking route N-365 north from Golegã for about 7 km and then transfering on to route N-3 east for another 11 km.* The heart of the town can be found among the ornate facades and central pillory which can be found at the lovely **Praça Alexandre Herculano** square.

From the square I recommend a walk up the *Rua Luís de Camões* towards the **Galeria** that contains a restored traditional house that you can visit. Just off the Galeria you can turn on to *Rua da Barca* and see the remains of the old city walls and a house where poet Luís de Camões once lived. Throughout town there are great parks and gardens which are some of Constância's most delightful sights including the **Jardim de Horta Camoniano** off *Ave. das Forças Armadas* at the edge of town, and the nearby riverfront **Parque de Merendas** where you can enjoy a nice picnic or ust sit and watch the rivers collide.

The town also has a great reputation for locally-made handicrafts including dolls and wooden models of the traditional river boats which can be found in small shops throughout town. The town offers several nice churches to visit, including the 17th-century **Igreja Matriz** with its José Malhoa frescoe and the **Igreja da Misericórdia** with its beautiful *azulejos* and gilted wood altar. On Easter Monday, the fishermen of Constância gather to celebrate the **Festa do Senhora da Boa Viagem** festival when the boats are blessed and the residents parade down the old town streets with marching bands.

WHERE TO STAY

QUINTA DE SANTA BÁRBARA, *Constância, (049) 992-14. Moderate.*
A beautiful 17th century manor house 1 km east of town with 6 great rooms with private bathroom, bar, billards, pool, dining room, library, trails, and horse riding.

CASA O PALÁCIO, *Rua F. Falcão, (049) 992-24. Moderate.*
A nice antique noble mansion on the *Tejo* river in the old part of town. The inn offers 4 double rooms with private bathroom, bar, gardens, TV room, and parking.

ALMOUROL

The romantic **Castelo do Almourol** is the most amazing castles in all of Portugal, *perched atop a small island in the* **Tejo** *river about 4 km. southwest of Constância.* Built in 1171 on the grounds of an even older Roman fortress, this massively fortified 11 tower castle can be reached by ferry row boat (in high season) from the northern bank of the river for about 350$00. *Check with the people at Constância's Câmara Municipal (town hall) at (049) 992-05 for more specific ferry information.*

Although abandoned since the 14th century, Almourol is in surprisingly good condition, and the view from above the towering square keep is impressive. Every person that I have told to visit this castle has returned home and thanked me!

ABRANTES

The quint town of **Abrantes** *rests on a hill above the banks of the Tejo river some 13 km away from Constância on route N-3 east.* The ruins of a 14th-century **castelo** (castle) – of which little remains except the keep – overlooks the town . Inside the castle walls (closed on Mondays) you can view the 15th-century **Igreja de Santa Maria do Castelo** that now houses the **Museu de Lope de Almeida** museum (closed on Mondays) and contains collections of Roman statues, Spanish-Arab tiles, ceramics, old manuscripts, 16th century paintings, and ornate tombs. From the top of the keep you can look out over the town and the beautiful olive trees which line the banks of the river. The town can be reached by leaving the castle keep and strolling past the ancient maze like alleys.

With much of its economy coming from agriculture, Abrantes is home to the **Victor Guedes** company which produces a limited qantity of traditionally harvested fine extra, extra virgin olive oil under the Gallo brand name. If you love cooking, you'll want to bring home some of their amazing *Azeite Novo* olive oil which can match any famous Italian brand at a quarter of the price.

One place well worth visiting in Abrantes is the 16th-century **Igreja da Misericórdia** church with its Gregório Lopes paintings. The town's most interesting attractions include the streets, gardens, and residents themselves who seem to show great interest and curiosity in vistors.

WHERE TO STAY

QUINTA DOS VALES, *N-118-Tramagal, (041) 073-63. Moderate.*

A nice country inn and horse stable which offers 6 nice rooms with private bathrooms 10 km. west of town across the river. Facilities include lounge, dining room, TV room, library, gardens, horse back riding, and parking.

HOTEL TURISMO, *Largo de Santo António, (041) 212-71. Moderate.*

A good 3 star hotel above the river with 41 good rooms with private bathroom. Facilities include bar, restaurant, air conditioning, tennis, pool, TV, and parking.

PENSÃO CENTRAL, *Praça Raimundo Soares,15, (041) 224-22. Inexpensive.*

A clean and basic inn with 14 reasonably comfortable rooms with and without private bathrooms. Almost no facilities, but it is the only budget choice.

WHERE TO EAT

RESTAURANTE CRISTINA, *N-3-Rio de Moinhos, (041) 981-77. Inexpensive.*

A homey and simple restaurant a few km. west of town which serves huge portions of locally raised meat and fish dishes with friendly service. The ambiance is great.

RESTAURANTE LIRIOS, *Praça da Batalha,31, (41) 221-42. Inexpensive.*

A nice family owned restaurant near the center of town which offers several regional meat and fish specialties at very good prices. The desserts are great.

CASTELO DE VIDE

The Gothic spa town of **Castelo de Vide** rests on a hill in the Serra de **São Mamede** mountains. *The best way to arrive here from Abrantes is to cross the river's bridge and follow the route N-118 east for some 68 km until you reach the town of Alpalhão and can turn off onto route N-246 east for about another 16 km.* This cute little town with rows of whitewashed houses rests below a 12th-century fortified **castelo** (castle) whose original tower looms above its defensive walls. Besides visiting the tower for a good view of the town's flower-lined alleys, the 17th-century **Igreja de Nossa Senhora da Alegria** church with impressive *azulejos* can be visted inside the compound.

Below the castle, the town's lovely streets and plazas await your visit. The town's medieval Jewish section known as the **Judiaria** is where local Jewish residents (known as *Marranos*) were forced to live apart from the neighboring Christians before the time of the Inquisition when they were forced to convert. There is a small and unassuming 14th century rabbi's house and temple on *Rua da Judiaria* that can be visited here as well as a small handicrafts shop and studio located in the former town jail.

Just below the Judiaria is the town's famed 16th century baroque **Fonte da Vila** (town fountain) spews a constant stream of unfiltered mineral water which is said to cure several internal ailments. From the fountain, you can proceed towards the heart of town, the **Praça Dom Pedro V** square, which is surrounded by fine examples of 17th and 18th century structures. Among the buildings worth viewing in this square are the 17th-century **Torre Palácio** , the 17th-century **Cãmara Municipal** (town hall), and the lovely **Igreja de Santa Maria** church.

WHERE TO STAY

QUINTA DA BELA VISTA, *Póvoa-Meadas, (045) 981-25. Moderate.*

A charming 19th-century country inn on a farm about 14 km north of town with 4 great guestrooms with private bathroom, bar, restaurant,

pool, tennis, billards, air conditioning, TV room, billards, bicycles, trails, and parking. A great little inn!
ALBERGARIA JARDIM, *Rua Sequeira Sameiro,6, (045) 912-17. Moderate.*
An attracive and beautifully furnished 4 star inn with 43 guestrooms with private bathroom in a great part of town. Facilities include a bar, restaurant, and TV room.
HOTEL SOL E SERRA, *Estrada São Vicente, (045) 913-37. Moderate.*
A large and comfortable 3 star hotel near a park with 50 air conditioned rooms, all with private bathroom. Facilities include bar, restaurant, pool, TV room, and parking.
CASAL DOS LILASES, *Castelo de Vide, (045) 912-50. Inexpensive.*
A fairly comfortable country house which offers 5 rustic rooms with semi private bathrooms on a small farm about a 2 km. south of town. Almost no facilities.
PENSÃO CASA DO PARQUE, *Ave. de Aramenha,37, (045) 912-50. Inexpensive.*
A well furnished and comfortable inn with good rooms that have private bathroom.

MARVÃO

The medieval walled village of **Marvão** *lies some 13 km southeast of Castelo de Vide on a hairpin curved access road off route N-246-1.* The tiny village located atop a cliff in the **Serra de São Mamede** mountain range near the Spanish border is one of the most dramatic fortified towns in Portugal.

Once you have left your car in the demarcated parking area, follow *Rua do Espírito Santo* past an assortment of Renaissance and Gothic era balconied whitewashed houses and on to the bold **castelo** (castle). After passing through a series of gates you can walk up the staircase to enter the 13th century keep. From atop the castle it is easy to view all of tiny Marvão and its massive defensive capabilities which include watchtowers that seem to barely cling to the top of cliffs.

Besides the castle and several picturesque lanes, town offers few specific attractions. You can visit the **Igreja de Santa Maria** church just below the castle at the **Largo do Municipio** which contains the small **Museu Municipal** museum with a few interesting exhibits of traditional life in town including costumes and local artifacts. While you're wandering around, make sure to stop in at the **Pousada de Santa Maria** *on Rua 24 de Janeiro* for a great meal or a nice cold beer.

After walking down all of the half dozen or so lanes which disect the village, you may follow the access road back down the hill for a hundred yards or so to stop at the Gothic 15th century **Igreja de Nossa Senhora da Estrêla** church which contains unusual azulejos and a nice altar.

WHERE TO STAY

POUSADA DE SANTA MARIA, *Rua 24 de Janeiro, (045) 932-02.* *Expensive.*

A beautiful *pousada* converted from 2 adjoining typical homes. The inn offers 28 rooms and 1 suite which are well appointed with traditional furnishings. Faclities include fireside lounges, bar, restaurant, air conditioning, cable TV, and parking.

ESTALAGEM DOM DINIS, *Rua Dr. António M. Magalhaes, (45) 932-36. Inexpensive.*

A nice and rustic traditional inn which offers 15 comfortable rooms (some with views) with and without private bathrooms, a bar, and a restaurant.

Inexpensive and moderately priced nice local rustic apartments and houses can be rented by the night or by the week by contacting the *Turismo* office on *Rua Dr. António Matos Magalhaes at (045) 932-26.* The quality varies greatly from one house to another.

WHERE TO EAT

POUSADA DE SANTA MARIA, *Rua 24 de Janeiro, (045) 932-02.* *Moderate.*

Although I don't usually recommend hotel restaurants, this *pousada* offers great regional cusine in a wonderfully relaxing setting. The rabbit (*coelho*) is amazing.

PORTALEGRE

The bustling city of **Portalegre** *rests at the western foot of the Serra de São Mamede mountains, about 21 km away from Marvão on route N-359 south, which then intersects with route N-246 south and leads into town.* Known primarily for its tapestries and silk weaving, Portalegre can seem to be somewhat of a disappointing sight after visting the beautiful small villages of the area.

WHERE TO STAY

QUINTA DAS VARANDAS, *Serra de São Mamede, (045) 288-83.* *Moderate.*

A tranquil amnor house and estate some 5 km. from town off route N-246-2 which offers 5 rooms with private bathrooms, a lounge, dining room, pool, TV room, beautiful formal gardens, horse riding, fountains, fine antiques, and parking.

QUINTA DA FONTE FRIA, *Serra-Portalegre, (045) 275-75. Moderate.*
A nice country inn located 3 km out of town of the Estrada do Monte Carvalho. The inn rents 3 large and comfortable 3 bedroom apartments with kitchens and private bathrooms. Facilities include bar, pool, trails, library, TV room, and parking.
HOTEL DOM JOÃO III, *Ave. de Liberdade, (045) 211-92. Moderate.*
A large and functional 3 star hotel in the heart of town with 56 comfortable rooms (some with park views), bar, restaurant, pool, disco, TV room, and parking.
PENSÃO ALTO ALENTEJO, *Rua 19 de Junho, 59, (045) 222-90. Inexpensive.*
A nice and comfortable inn located in the heart of the old town with 15 guestrooms with and without private bathroom. Almost no facilities, but close to everything.

WHERE TO EAT

O ABRIGO, *Rua de Elvas, 74, (45) 227-78. Inexpensive.*
A charming and quite little cork lined restaurant in the heart of the old town which serves hearty regional cuisine with nice and friendly service. A casual place.

SEEING THE SIGHTS

The best way to wander through the city is to park your car in the municipal parking areas off *Rua 1 de Maio* in the southwestern part of town. From here you can walk through the old town walls and over to the **Largo de Sé** plaza. Here you can't help but be drawn towards the bold marble columns and strange pinnacles of the 16th-century **Sé** cathedral that contains some beautiful chapels filled with fine altarpieces, 16th-century *azulejos*, and paintings. The plaza is also home to **Museu Municipal** museum, housed in a former 16th century seminary (closed on Tuesdays). The museum contains a vast assortment of sacred art including a beautiful 16th century gold and silver church plates, a 15th-century gilded wood Spanish *Pieta*, a wonderful 17th century silver and ebony tabernacle, altarpieces, ivory statues, and other ecclesiastical art. The museum also contains collections of ceramics, silver sniff boxes, furniture, 17th-century china, *Arraiolos* rugs, and paintings by Abel Santos.

From the **Largo de Sé** plaza, head up *Rua de São Vicente* for a block or so until you find the beautiful 17th-century **Abrancalhas** (Yellow Palace) that has an elaborate facade complete with highly decorative wrough iron grillwork. From the palace, continue uptown on *Rua da Figueira* for a block or so until bearing right (east) to connect to *Rua Luís de Camões* and stroll past some wonderful houses and shops. From here

THE PLANÍCIES 349

you can continue in the same direction through the old town walls and find more good shopping along *Rua 5 de Outubro*. A few blocks further up you can turn right (east) to reach a former 17th-century Jesuit seminary on *Rua Guilherme Gomes Fernandes, 26*, where you can take a 20 minute guided tour (10am and 4pm weekdays) of the famous **Fabrica Real de Tapisseria** tapestry workshop. If you have a several thousand extra dollars, you can commision a beautiful tapestry here, but it may take a few years to complete.

From the tapestry factory, you can continue east along the same street until you come to the beautiful **Parque Miguel Bombarda** park and gardens. After a brief stroll through the park, you should make your way back downtown to the old part of the city. This time from the **Sé** cathedral head left (east) down the charming *Rua 19 de Junho* to view some unforgettable old houses. From here turn left (north) onto *Rua Luís Barahona* to view the unremarkable ruins of a former 13th-century castle.

After a brief stop at the ruins, head back to the *Rua 19 de Junho* and turn left (east) which will lead you out of the town walls and down to the **Praça da República** square. At the end of the square, bear right (south) onto *Rua José Régio*. Here you can visit the 18th-century mansion of this famed early 20th century poet and novelist which houses the **Museu de José Régio**. The museum (closed on Mondays) contains many pieces of religious art and local artifacts collected by it's famous namesake.

A nice side trip from Portalegre is the drive *on route N-119 west for 20 km or so* to the town of **Crato**. This beautiful little town offers several fine examples of 16th-century mansions and churches which surround the main square, including the remarkable **Varanda do Grão Prior**. You may want to stop by its small **Museu Municipal** museum *on Rua 5 de Outubro* (closed on Mondays) to see some interesting local art and handicrafts.

From Crato, *you can take route N-363 west for about 6 km* to reach a large prehistoric dolmen near **Aldeia da Mata**. *From the dolmen, return to Crato and turn south onto route N-245 south for some 12 km*, before reaching the wonderful equestrian breeding town of **Alter do Chão**. The heart of town is undoubtedly the mosaic-lined **Praça da República** square, centered around a pentangonal 14th-century **castelo** (castle). The castle's **Torre de Menagem** keep leads visitors upward for a great panoramic view. The square also contains a regal 16th-century marble columned fountain. Just a few km out of town on the unnamed road towards **Reguengo** you can visit the 18th-century royal stud farms and equestrian museum of the **Coudelaria de Alter Real**. The beautiful and well-disciplined horses that are trained and bred here are highly prized and bring huge prices at the annual **Couldelaria horse auction** on April 25th, which is followed the next day by the town's wonderfully amusing **Festa da Nossa Senhora da Alegria** festival.

ELVAS

The intriguing fortified border city of **Elvas** is *located some 58 km southeast of Portalegre on route N-246 south*. As the perimeter road turns toward the southern sector of the old town, you will pass the beautiful 16th-century **Aqueducto da Amoreiras**. The massive aqueduct system of 3 and 4 story arches still brings fresh water into the town's fountains from a source some 7 km away.

The area around this aqueduct hosts the town's large weekly regional **mercado** (market), which is held each Monday and is well worth the visit. After passing under the aqueduct, bear left and pass the *pousada* to access the **Portas de Olivenca** town gates from which *Rua de Olivenca* proceeds into the mosaic-lined **Praça da República** square in heart of town. After you have found parking (not always such an easy task), your first stop should be at the local *Turismo* office on the southern side of the square for a large and rather detailed walking map.

If you walk a block or so west on *Rua de Cadeia*, which is just behind the *Turismo*, you can view the massive **Torre de Fernandina** tower. Walk back to the Praça da República, and as you cross the square, the Cãmara Municipal (town hall) will be on your left and in front of you on the northern side, you can visit the **Igreja de Nossa Senhora da Assuncão** cathedral. This Manueline 16th-century structure was built on the sight of town's ruined 13th-century Gothic **Sé** cathedral and it's exterior contains a beautiful Manueline main portal topped by a Rosé colored window, a pyrimid shaped bell tower, and some nice iron grillwork. Inside the vaulted interior you will see several examples of 18th century azulejos, a fine 18th-century organ, and lots of marble.

Behind the cathedral, you will find the medieval **Largo do Dr.Santa Clara** plaza, home to the octagonal shaped 16th-century Renaissance **Igreja de Nossa Senhora da Consolacão** church. Here you'll see an inspiring dome-topped interior, covered with unique *azulejos* bearing lace and flower motifs and several nice paintings above the altars.

The plaza itself is a great sight as it is loaded with attractions. The plaza's central 16th-century Manueline **pelourinho** (pillory) is spiked with iron hangman's hooks and is surrounded by the church, several regal homes, and two massive towers from the town's old defensive walls. The towers are bridged by a wonderful gate which rests below an ornate Moorish *loggia*. As you pass under the gate and onto **Largo da Alacova** bear left and then right onto the charming *Rua das Beatas* that will take you towards the old **castelo** (castle). The castle grounds (closed on Thursdays) dates back to Moorish times and contains a small exhibit inside of the former governor's house. If you walk the ramparts, you will see a wonderful view of the city. Follow the old town walls back down in either direction to reach the **Porta de Olivenca** gate.

THE PLANÍCIES

If you happen to be in Portugal during the third week of September, you may want to visit this city during it's annual **Festa do Senhora da Piedade** and **Feira de São Mateus** festivals.

WHERE TO STAY

POUSADA DE SANTA LUZIA, *Ave. de Badajoz, (068) 622-194. Expensive.*

This pleasant country inn style *pousada* is just outside of the town walls. It's 16 rooms and 1 suite offer typical regional furniture and private bathrooms. Facilities include a good restaurant, bar, air conditioning, garden, and parking.

HOTEL D. LUÍS, *Ave. de Badajoz, (068) 622-757. Moderate.*

A good 3 star hotel facing the aqueduct outside of the walls of *Elvas* with 70 rooms with private bathroom. Facilities include bar, restaurant, TV, and parking.

ESTALAGEM DON SANCHO II, *Praça da República,20, (068) 622-686. Moderate.*

A well located and comfortable 4 star inn near the *Turismo* with 26 comfortable rooms with private bathroom, a bar, restaurant, TV room, and nearby parking.

MONTE DA AMOREIRA, *São Brás, (068) 624-687. Moderate.*

A quaint farm house and estate off *route N-514* some 7 km west of town offering 7 rooms with semi private bathrooms, lounge, hunting, TV room, and parking.

PENSÃO QUINTA DAS AGUIAS, *Ave. de Badajoz, (068) 622-340. Inexpensive.*

A clean and basic inn which offers guestrooms with and without private bathrooms.

WHERE TO EAT

O AQUEDUTO, *Ave. da Piedade, (068) 623-676. Moderate.*

A nice and friendly regional restaurant which serves great meat and seafood specialities. The food is rather good and the service is prompt and effeciant.

CHURRASQUEIRA ALENTEJANA, *Rua da Cadeia, (068) 622-471. Moderate.*

A nice and simple barbeque and roasted meat restaurant near the *Praça da República* which serves huge portions of tasty meat dishes in a casual atmosphere.

BORBA

The marble laden town of **Borba** *lies some 28 km southwest of Elvas on* *route IP-7 east*. Every inch of the area surrounding this town seems to be filled with huge quarries that produce fine marble that ends up being sold in North America as so-called Italian Carrera marble. Every house, office building, and bathroom in the area is crammed full of the stuff.

The town once was dominated by a medieval castle, but almost nothing remains of it. While passing through the town you should visit the **Praça da República**, the town's main square, and walk around from there to visit the modest 15th-century **Igreja de Nossa Senhora das Neves** church with its fine paintings, the frescoes and marble-laden interior of the vaulted 17th-century Renaissance **Igreja de São Bartolomeu** church, the 17th-century **Câmara Municipal** (town hall), the 18th-century marble **Fonte das Bicas** fountain, and a quick drive over to see the **Museu de Ceramica** museum (closed on Mondays) at **Quinta dos Lobos**. Before leaving town, try to taste an old bottle of hearty red *Borba* wine. The best bottles have a label made of real cork.

VILA VIÇOSA

The former royal town of **Vila Viçosa** rests on the side of a hill, *about 5 km southeast of Borba on route N-255 south*. In the 15th century, the town grew in prominence as it became residence to the dukes of Bragança and so became home to the kings of Portugal. Now that the kings are gone, Vila Viçosa remains as a living museum.

As you enter town you are drawn to the huge 16th-century **Paço Ducal** palace which is entered from behind the large statue of of King João IV on his horse in the **Terreiro do Paço** square. Here you can visit over 50 beautifully furnished rooms located in both wings (closed on Sundays and Mondays) of the royal residence constructed by Dom Jaime I, the 4th duke of Bragança. The 45 minute tour of exhibits include *Arraiolos* carpets, frescoed ceilings, *azulejos*, armor, massive kitchens, 19th-century royal portraits by Malhoa and Sousa Pinto, classical furniture, ceramics, a gallery full of paintings by King Carlos, jewelry, a 17th century holy cross studded with thousands of diamonds and rubies, and over 75 royal coaches from the 17th-19th centuries.

The plaza also contains several somber, beautiful churches including the 16th-century **Convento das Chagas** which has some royal tombs, and the 17th century **Igreja de Santo Agostinho** which also contains royal tombs made from solid marble. A bit further up *Rua de Duque D. Jaime* above the northern edge of the plaza are the medieval **Porta da Vila** old town gate and the 16th-century Manueline **Porta dos Nos** town gate with its sculptured knot motif.

The first local residence of the dukes of Bragança was the moated 13th-century **castelo** (castle) which can be reached by walking south on the *Avenida Duque de Bragança* through the heart of town until you can see the large 16th-century pillory. The castle, entered via a drawbridge, housed the royal family members until the Paço Ducal was completed.

Inside the castle (closed on Mondays) you can visit the keep, home to a collection of artifacts from the prehistoric through the Roman eras. There is also a tour which leads visitors through the ramparts, dungeon, and living quarters of the castle. A cluster of old houses and the 15th-century **Igreja da Nossa Senhora da Conceição** church are also within the castle compound.

WHERE TO STAY

CASA DE PEIXINHOS, *Vila Viçosa, (068) 984-72. Expensive.*

A delightful miniature 17th century castle located on a farming esate just a few minutes walk from the castle which offers it's guests 6 great rooms with private bathrooms, bar, restaurant, gardens, bicycles, TV room, trails, library, and parking.

CASA DOS ARCOS, *Vila Viçosa, (068) 985-18. Moderate.*

An 18th century manor house in the heart of town which rents 4 guestrooms and 2 studio apartments with private bathrooms, kitchens, bar, TV room, and parking.

WHERE TO EAT

RESTAURANTE FRAMAR, *Praça da República, (068) 988-82. Inexpensive.*

A pretty good regional restaurant in the heart of town which serves reasonably prices large portions of local specialities in a nice dining room.

REDONDO

The friendly and typical rural town of **Redondo** rests near the foot of the peaceful **Serra de Ossa** mountain range, *about 18 km southwest of Vila Viçosa on route N-254*. Redondo is located directly in the middle of the region's most important tourist sights. I choose to stay here because it is just 20 minutes away from **Évora**, **Estremoz**, **Vila Viçosa**, **Monsaraz**, and several other great towns.

Redondo is the perfect base from which to take day trips throughout the entire area. This quiet town is based around a beautiful central plaza known as the **Praça da República**, where local farmers can be seen chatting with businessmen dressed in full length wool capes in front of the lovely 18th-century **Câmara Municipal** (town hall) – which is also the town's *Turismo* office. Parking in this town is no problem as most tourists don't seem to know of that any parking exists.

A walk through the town's central streets will lead you through several ancient gates and towers which were part of Redondo's defensive walls and ruined castle including the **Porta da Ravessa** gate, the **Porta do Sol** gate, the **Postigo de Relogigo** clock and belltower gate, and the towering **Torre de Menagem** keep. Nearby you can wander through several beautiful ancient lanes and stone-paved streets such as the *Rua do Castelo* to view the town's impressive whitewashed and blue bordered homes. There are also a couple of wonderfully decorated churches in the heart of town including the fine 16th-century whitewashed and granite **Igreja de Nossa Senhora da Anunciacão**, and the nearby 16th-century somber **Igreja da Misericórdia** .

At the edge of town there is the wonderful little **Pirraca** earthenware shop and studio (follow the blue **Artisanato** sign), which has some of the finest and least expensive hand-painted casserole dishes and pitchers in all of Portugal. The town is also well known for its fine wines, including the inexpensive *Porta da Ravessa* brand (produced by the **Cooperativa de Redondo** winery, which may be visited on the outskirts of town).

Looking out over the wonderful sights in and around Redondo is the magnificent 16th-century **Convento de São Paulo** about 8 km up route N-381 north just after the village of **Aldeia de Serra** at the base of the majestic **Serra de Ossa** mountains. This wonderful convent situated on hundreds of acres of beautiful land has been restored into what has become the most impressive hotel in Portugal. Its original *azulejos*-lined walls, marble floors, ceiling frescoes, fine furniture, and amazingly deluxe public rooms, opulent guestrooms, and fine regional restaurant are among the finest in all of Europe. Even if you are not a guest, ask for the friendly English speaking manager (Mr. José Almeida) and he will be glad to show you around. I strongly recommend you stay here a few days, as it is an experience you will never forget. Off season rates are extremely reasonable.

WHERE TO STAY

HOTEL CONVENTO DE SÃO PAULO, *Aldeia de Serra-Redondo, (066) 999-100. Expensive.*

A wonderful converted convent on a huge estate which offers 21 super deluxe guestrooms with air conditioning and marble bathrooms. Facilities include a bar, Café , pool, gardens, restaurant, breakfast in bed, room service, historic *azulejos*, pool, patio, gardens, cable TV, tons of antiques, and parking. A great place to relax.

QUINTA DA TALHA, *N-524-Redondo, (066) 999-468. Moderate.*

A rustic farming estate in the *Serra de Ossa* area which offers houses with 4 good rooms with private bathrooms, a lounge, dining room, and vineyards.

PENSÃO BASTIÃO, *Rua Manuel J. da Silva, (066) 991-02. Inexpensive.*

A clean and basic small 2 star establishment offering several basic rooms with private bathroom. Almost no facilities in the inn except for a bar.

ESTREMOZ

The castle-topped historical town of **Estremoz** sits on a hill, *26 km northwest of Redondo on route N-381 north*. Home to several Portuguese kings and queens, Estremoz has seen much of the country's history unfold within it's defensive walls.

WHERE TO STAY

POUSADA RAINHA SANTA ISABEL, *Largo Dom Dinis, (068) 226-18. Expensive.*

Newly renovated, this historic part of the 13th century royal palace contains 23 great rooms with private bathrooms and nice furnishings. Facilities include a bar, great restaurant, wonderful views, TV room, direct dial phones, and parking.

MONTE DOS PENSAMENTOS, *Estrada Estação do Ameixal, (068) 223-75. Moderate.*

A nice 19th century country style inn 2 km. out of town owned by a charming older English women. The inn offers 4 nice rooms ith private bathrooms, a bar, pool, TV room, library, traditional regional furnishings, garden, bicycles, and parking.

POUSADA DE SÃO MIGUEL, *Sousel, (068) 551-155. Moderate.*

A modern pousada about 16 km. northwest of *Estremoz* near the hunting area of *Sousel*. This hilltop 28 room inn offers special services for sportsmen as well as tourists. Facilities include bar, restaurant, air conditioning, TV, kennels, and parking.

PENSÃO CARVALHO, *Largo da República, 27, (068) 227-12. Inexpensive.*

A clean and basic 2 star inn located in the heart of the lower town with 15 clean guestrooms with and without private bathrooms. Amost no facilities.

WHERE TO EAT

POUSADA RAINHA SANTA ISABEL, *Largo Dom Dinis, (068) 226-18. Expensive.*

This attractivly decorated and somewhat formal fine restaurant is a must for those of you who wish to splurge on dishes like lamb chops with fresh mint sauce.

RESTAURANTE ARLEQUIM, *Rua Dr. G. Resende, 15, (068) 237-26. Inexpensive.*

A friendly and simple restaurant near the Rossio which offers hearty regional cuisine prepared with extremely fresh local produce and presented by nice staff.

SEEING THE SIGHTS

To begin exploring the upper portion of town, drive up through the massive 14th-century gateway to the castle area known as the **Largo Dom Dinis** plaza and leave your car near the *pousada* in the parking lot. The first stop on your walking tour is the 13th-century **Torre de Menagem** keep which is topped by a ring of pointed merlons. Inside the keep you can visit the octagonal room and the rooftop observation deck.

The adjacent former royal armory of the ruined palace is home to the delightful **Pousada da Rainha Santa Isabel**, which must be visited to view the elegant decor and fine stairways. Steps away from the *pousada* is the 17th-century **Capela da Rainha Santa** chapel which is covered in lovely *azulejos* panels sowing various scenes from the life of the late queen Isabel who died in Estremoz in 1336. Also worth a peek inside is the 16th-century **Igreja dae Santa Maria** church which is filled with locally mined marble and unusual primative paintings.

Other impressive sights in this plaza include the Gothic vaulted loggia of the 13th-century **Paços de Audiencia** which was the former audience gallery of King Dom Dinis, and the **Museu Municipal** museum (closed on Mondays) located in a 17th-century alms house which contains traditional furniture, ceramics, clay dolls, *azulejos*, and 20th century paintings.

Below the Largo Dom Dinis plaza rests the lower and somewhat more modern part of town. A small road winds its way down to the town's central **Rossio do Marquis de Pombal** square. The square contains a nice Manueline pillory, the *Turismo* office, the 18th-century former **Convento de Congregados de São Filipe de Nery** whose wonderful *azulejos*-covered interior houses the **Câmara Municipal** (town hall), and the **Museu Rural de Casa do Povo de Santa Maria** museum (closed on Mondays) which houses a strange collection of local handicrafts and artifacts.

Each Saturday morning, a large regional produce **mercado** (market) takes place in this square. Estremoz is well know for its wonderful clay figurines, water pitchers, and pottery which can be found in small shops near the central square.

ÉVORA MONTE (ÉVORA MONTE)

The tiny typical sleepy village of **Évora Monte** rests peacefully below a castle on a large hill, *12 km southwest of Estremoz on route N-18 south*. Its one and only main road is filled with charming village houses painted in traditional whitewash with blue borders. A large reconstructed **castelo**

THE PLANÍCIES 357

(castle) has been on this spot since Roman times, although the current structure bears little resemblance to its original design.

The current castle, its tower-topped ramparts, and its 16th-century **Torre de Menagem** tower loom high above the surrounding plains of olive and orange trees. At night the castle is brightly lit up and can be seen from far away. The beautiful 16th-century **Igreja da Misericórdia** church can be seen on the main street.

WHERE TO STAY

MONTE DA FAZENDA, *Évora Monte, (068) 951-72. Inexpensve.*

A very rustic farm house just outside of town on a difficult dirt road. The family which operates the house as an inn offer 2 basic rooms with private bathroom. Facilities include a bar, pool, TV room, billards, library, hunting, horse riding, and parking.

ÉVORA

The incredibly beautiful walled city of **Évora** rests on a hill in the heart of a vast plain, *some 44 km southwest of Estremoz on route N-18 south*. Of all the wonderful sights in Portugal, Évora is the one place which I find myself returning to on every trip to Portugal. After more than 20 visits to this exceedingly active and historical city of 45,000 inhabitants, I always find new sights to explore. The area around Évora has been inhabited since prehistoric times, as is evident by the megaliths located a few minutes out of town in places like **Guadalupe**.

The city itself retains several reminders of the Roman occupaton since the 1st century B.C, after which the Visigoths and then the Moors controlled the ancient city and left their mark as well. The city came under Christian control in 1165 after a bold attack by local hero Geraldo Sem-Pavor (Gerald the Fearless) and his local outlaw forces, and was given its first official charter by King Dom Afonso Henriques. Évora became home to several kings and royal families in the 12th–16th centuries, and they filled the town with many ornate palaces and churches that still grace every corner of the city.

As numerous politicians, artists, poets, religious leaders and scholars poured into Évora, its 16th-century university was established and the city flourished to become an important center of Portugal's Renaissance. With the Spanish occupation of Portugal in 1580, Évora lost much of its prominence and slowly faded out of the limelight.

WHERE TO STAY

POUSADA DOS LOIS, *Largo Conde de Vila Flôr, (066) 240-51. Expensive.*

A beautiful, deluxe, and historic 32 room inn located amidst the cloisters of a 15th century monastery. The well furnished and antique laden pousada is sold out on many nights. Facilities include bar, restaurant, pool, direct dial phones, and parking.

O'EBORNESE, *Largo da Misericórdia , (066) 220-31. Moderate.*

A pleasant and well located 16th century manor house which has been converted into a good 3 star bed and breakfast inn with 25 comfortable rooms with private bathrooms. The inn offers a lounge, breakfast room, terrace, TV, and parking.

MONTE DAS FLORES, *Estrada das Alcacovas, (066) 254-90. Moderate.*

A charming farm house and stables which offer several traditionally decorated guestrooms with private bathrooms a few minutes outside of town. This great little inn offers bar, lounge, dining room, TV room, gardens, horse riding, and parking.

ÉVORAHOTEL, *N-114-Évora, (066) 734-800. Moderate.*

A new modern business style hotel a few minutes west of town which lacks any real charm or good service. The property offers a multitude of air conditioned American style rooms with private bathrooms, a bar, restaurant, pool, TV, and parking.

CASA DE SAM PEDRO, *Quinta de Sam Pedro, (066) 277-31. Moderate.*

A charming 18th century manor house some 5 km north of town near the hamlet of *Monte de Oliveirinha* which offers 3 fine bedrooms with private bathrooms, lounge, dining room, antique laden public rooms, library, bicycles, and parking.

CASA DE SÃO TIAGO, *Largo Alexandre Hurculano,2, (066) 226-86. Moderate.*

A typical whitewashed old house in the heart of town which offers 6 good rooms with private bathrooms, a fireside lounge, dining room, TV room, library, and parking.

ESTALAGEM POKER, *N-114-Évora, (066) 337-21. Moderate.*

A cute and modern little 4 star inn located a couple of minutes west of town which offers 15 nice and comfortable double guestrooms with private bathrooms, bar, restaurant, snack bar, TV, air conditioning, pool, tennis, and parking.

HOTEL PLANACIE, *Rua Miguel Bombarda,40, (066) 240-26. Moderate.*

An older 3 star hotel in the heart of *Évora* which offers 33 basic and somewhat comfortable guestrooms with private bathrooms. The hotel is in need of some renovations, but its ever friendly staff make it a good place to stay. Facilities include a bar, restaurant, TV, air conditioning, and direct dial phones.

RESIDENCIAL DIANA, *Rua Diogo Cao, 2, (066) 220-08. Inexpensive.*

A nice old house in the heart of town which has been converted into

a pleasant inn. The dozen or so rooms offer private bathoom and are comfortably furnished. Facilities include bar, restaurant, TV room, and safe deposit boxes.
PENSÃO POLICARPO, *Rua Freiria de Baixo,16, (066) 224-24. Inexpensive.*
A quaint family owned inn located in a great part of town which offers 24 guestrooms both with and without private bathrooms. See a few rooms before selecting yours as they are not all alike. Very few facilities except a breakfast room.
QUINTA DA NORA, *Estrada dos Canaviais, (066) 298-10. Inexpensive.*
A rustic farm house who's absentee owners offer 5 traditionally furnished guestrooms with private bathrooms. The house is just a few minutes northwest of town on a farming estate. Facilities include pool, bicycles, TV room, and parking.

WHERE TO EAT
POUSADA DOS LÓIOS, *Largo Conde de Vila Flôr, (066) 240-51. Expensive.*
Simply the most elegant place to eat in all of *Évora*! Although rather expensive and somewhat formall, this amazingly ornate restaurant serves fine regional cuisine with a special flare. Try the unforgettable *borrego assado no forno* (oven roasted lamb).
COZINHA DE SANTO HUMBERTO, *Rua da Moeda, 39, (066) 242-51. Expensive.*
A wonderfull restaurant located just off the *Praça do Giraldo* in a converted wine cellar which offers superb regional cuisine in a great setting with fine service. The excellent food here has won several gold medals. Try anything the staff suggest.
RESTAURANTE FIALHO, *Travessa das Mascarenhas,16, (066) 230-79. Expensive.*
A well known and long established family owned regional restaurant with exposed beam ceilings and lots of atmosphere. The fine chefs specialize in locally raised porc, lamb, and fish specialities which are prepared with great flair.
RESTAURANT TÍPICO GUIÃO, *Rua da República,81, (066) 230-71. Moderate.*
This small and charming little restaurant near the bottom of the *Praça do Giraldo* offers great food at reasonable prices. If you are ready for some of the best affordable regional cuisine in *Évora*, this is the place to go. Try the great trout here.

SEEING THE SIGHTS

As you come into Évora you will notice a road known as the *Estrada da Circunvalacão* that fully circles the walled town. The easiest way to find parking is to take a left at that circular road and another left to enter town at the signposted pousada exit. After going up the small street for a block, you will intersect with the *Rua de Colegio*, where can find a municipal parking lot beside you and another parking lot next to the university. With your back to the edge of town, walk right down the *Rua do Colegio* and continue for a block as it bends towards the left to meet with **Largo Duques de Cadaval**. The large structure you will see on your left is the 14th-century **Palácio dos Duques de Cadaval** palace. This former royal residence is flanked by two large towers, one of which was originally part of Évora's defensive walls. The palace's **Torre das Cinco Quinas** tower houses a small museum (closed on Mondays) that has Flemish bronze tombs, paintings, sculptures, and historical documents.

A small road leads uphill from the palace past a quaint sculpture garden and onto the wonderful **Largo do Conde de Vila Flôr** square. The most obvious attraction in the square is the mystical granite and marble columned **Templo Romano** temple which dates back to the 2nd century during Évora's Roman occupation. Surrounding the temple are several impressive buildings.

Just across from the temple is the magnificent 15th-century Gothic **Igreja de São João Evangelista** church (also known as the **Igreja dos Lois**), which was built on the site of a former Moorish castle. As you pass through the church's original Gothic portal (closed on Mondays) you will be lead into a beautiful vaulted interior which boasts fine 18th-century *azulejos* by famed master craftsman António de Oliveira Bernardes and the eery tombs of the noble Melo family.

The church's adjacent cloisters now contain the elaborate **Pousada dos Lois**, by far the most impressive place to stay in town. The *pousada* must be visited to view it's lovely chapterhouse doorway, Renaissance gallery, Manueline columns, and fine furnishings. On the end of the square is the former 17th-century bishop's palace which houses the **Museu de Évora** museum. This wonderful museum (closed on Mondays) contains a vast assortment of Roman, medieval, Manueline, and Moorish-Portuguese sculptures. There are also several exhibits of 16th-century Portuguese and Flemish paintings, archaeological findings, furniture, ceramics, jewelry, and fine azulejos.

As you pass the museum you will find yourself on the **Largo do Marquêsde Marialva**, which is dominated by the huge Gothic 12th-century **Sé** cathedral (closed on Mondays). The octagonal dome topped cathedral's facade contains massive granite block towers under which a Gothic portal supported by marble columns sculpted with figures of the

TAKING A BREAK

Apostles leads you inside. While walking within the vaulted interior, take notice of the fine Gothic Rosé windows, the baroque chapel, the hand carved choir stalls in the *coro alto*, and the Renaissance chapel portal designed by Nicolas Chanterene. If you buy tickets, you can also visit the fantastic 14th-century sculpture- and tomb-filled cloisters, as well as the **Museu de Arte Sacra** museum that features several fine religious pieces, including a bizzare 13th-century ivory Virgin which opens up to show scenes from her life. There are also exhibits such as a 17th-century reliquary cross, studded with over a thousand precious stones, a piece of wood from the cross which Jesus died on, jewelry, furniture, sculpture, and more.

After visiting the cathedral you should tourist shop and café-laden *Rua 5 de Octubro* down towards the city's central square known as the **Praça de Giraldo**. Besides being home to Évora's helpful *Turismo* office, the plaza's fountain is also the gathering place for local students and workers alike. Several shops, cafés, and banks line the square but don't expect the 24 hour currency conversion machine to be working.

At this point of the day I suggest a stop at the square's **Café Arcadia** for a great *torta* with a café or *galão*. At the top of the square is the whitewashed facade of the 16th-century **Igreja de Santo Antão** church. If you're in town for shopping, you may wish to head up past the church and browse in the widows along *Rua João de Dues* where lace, clothing, and shoe shops are in abundance. From the Praça de Giraldo's opposite end, continue your tour by taking *Rua da República* a few blocks down to the 15th-century Gothic **Igreja de São Fransisco.** This unusual church contains a huge vaulted interior with both baroque and Renaissance elements including an unforgettable gilted wood baroque altar in it's lateral chapel. The most unusual sight of this fine church is the adjacent **Capela dos Ossos** (chapel of bones), lined with a collection of neatly arranged bones and skulls belonging to former monks. Its rather amusing welcoming epitath loosely translates to "our bones are waiting for your bones." Entrance to the chapel of bones is extra, and photographers must pay a small fee to take pictures inside. If you're lucky, the **Museu do Artesanato** handicrafts museum and shop just across the street may be open.

As you exit the church, the city's bustling covered **mercados** (markets) await your visit just steps away across the **Praça 1 de Maio.** Its two seperate buildings house several dozen vendors which sell fine cheeses, fresh produce, fish, and my personal favorite item, the hot peppers and *piri-piri* hot sauce sold by a man with a huge red nose (problably the effect of too much *piri-piri*). Why not buy some bread, *queijo de cabra* (goat cheese), and tomatoes for a great picnic lunch?

A few ceramics merchants sell colorful but not so tastefull items directly in front of the marketplace. Behind the markets you can stop for your picnic in the lovely bench, pond, tree, and sculpture filled **Jardim Público** gardens. At the edge of the gardens stands the impressive 15th-century **Palácio de Dom Manuel** palace, which boasts a series of Mudéjar arcways and beautiful windows.

From the gardens, walk up the *Rua da República* thatpasses the back of the Igreja de São Fransisco, and turn right onto the **Largo da Graça**. The plaza is home to the 16th-century Renaissance **Igreja da Nossa Senhora da Graça** church. The structure's unusual columned granite facade is topped by spear carring statues that seem ready to leap up and chase you away.

ROMAN TEMPLE AT ÉVORA

From the front of the church, walk up the narrow steps of the small **Travessa da Caraca** and turn right onto the **Largo de Alvaro Velho** plaza, which contains a great blacksmith shop and is surrounded by shops with cheap shoes and clothing. From the left side of the end of the plaza, go up the *Rua da Misericórdia* to view the 16th-century **Igreja da Misericórdia** church containing fine 18th-century *azulejos*. On the same street you will also find the 15th-century Manueline **Casa Sor** mansion, adorned with arches and a large spire. At the end of the street, a right turn onto the peaceful **Largo das Portas de Moura** square and its spherical Renaissance fountain will lead you to several beautiful old whitewashed and yellow bordered houses including the wonderful 16th-century cone topped and arched facade of the elegent **Casa Cordovil** house.

Return back up the plaza and make a wide right turn onto *Rua Conde de Serra da Tourega* that can be found near the front of the two large stone towers from the medieval town walls. This street will take you to the **Largo do Colegio** university area where you can view the 15th-century **Paço des Condes de Basto** palace and the 16th century azulejos and painting lined **Igreja de Espírito Santo** church. At this point you have seen the vast majority of Évora's sights and beautiful streets. You can proceed to your car which is just steps away, or enjoy a fine dinner at one of several great restaurants.

If you are departing town, make sure to turn left on the *Estrada da Circunvalacão* to view the 16th-century arched **Aqueduto da Agua da Prata** aqueduct just moments away. If you're lucky eough to be in town on the second Thursday of the month, a huge regional **mercado** (market) takes over several acres of land just outside the walls in the **Rossio São Brás** square.

In the general area of Évora, you can visit several prehistoric monuments which are worth while. The *Turismo* sells a useful pamphlet on this subject called *Roteiro do Megalitismo* at their office in the Praça do Giraldo square. The most famous of these sights is called the **Menhir Os Almendres**, *located near the town of* **Guadalupe** *some 9 km west of Évora off route N-114 west*. Other impressive sights include the **Zambujeiro** dolmen, *located near the village of* **Valverde** *some 11 km southwest of Évora off route N-380 south*, and the **Anta do Silval** stones *located near the town of* **Valeira** *some 11 km northwest of Évora on route N-114-4 north*.

For details of these and other prehistoic sights, please contact the *Turismo* offices in Évora and Montemor-O-Novo.

NIGHTLIFE

Since Évora is home to several thousand university students, there are many fine bars, pubs, and dance clubs located throughout the city. The best place to get up to date information on the club scene is to ask any of the younger staff at the *pousada*. I usually get a drink at the bar of the *pousada*, and after leaving a good tip, I ask the bartender to suggest a few spots. Bring your map and ask about **Amas do Cardeal**, **Xeque Mate**, and **Club 16**, and see what else they suggest.

ARRAIOLOS

A nice side trip from Évora can be enjoyed *by taking route N-114-4 west for 11 km and connecting to route N-370 north for another 11 km or so to the wonderful little town of **Arraiolos**.* Above town you can visit the fortified walls of a 13th-century **castelo** (castle) built by King Dom Dinis which circles around the 16th century whitewashed and *azulejos*-laden **Convento dos Lóios** convent.

The small town below the convent and castle ruins has been the center of production for beautiful hand-embroidered carpets. Many traditionally dressed local women can be seen on the porches of their homes weaving these colorful carpets. During the Age of Discoveries, the Portuguese began returning from India and Arabia with elaborate rugs. At some point in the 17th century, the local residents of this town began imitating several patterns and weaving techniques that eventually evolved into today's unique styles. Several local companies now offer these fine carpets at somewhat reasonable prices (about 25,000$00 per square meter).

An exhibit of these carpets can be viewed at the town hall on **Praça Lima de Brito**, the main square of town. Make sure to see the 16th century **Antigo Paços do Concelho** (town hall and prison), the spiralled 16th-century pillory with hangman's hooks, the old ruined **castelo** (castle), and the lovely stone fountain known as the **Fonte de Pedra**.

MONSARAZ

Situated on a hilltop about a half hour's drive southeast of Évora, the wonderful mountaintop walled city of **Monsaraz** is certainly one of the best sights in the entire region. To get here from Évora, *take route N-18 east for some 16 km until it you can connect to route N-256 east for another 21 km to the city of Reguengos de Monsaraz. From here follow the signposted road to Monsaraz known locally as the Estrada de Monsaraz through several small hamlets before the twisting access road turns past numerous cork and olive trees, then upward towards the towering medieval walls that completely surround Monsaraz.*

The tiny town has not changed much for several centuries and its population of traditional inhabitants live-in houses which were built by their ancestors. Even the door locks, hinges, and knockers are hundreds of years old. Other than electricity and TV, the only other modern convience Monsaraz has accepted is a traveling salesman who each fortnight drives his minivan to the center of town and offers selection of household goods to the village women. The town itself is strictly off limits to cars, and several locals use oxen and donkeys as their preffered mode of transportation.

WHERE TO STAY

QUINTA HORTA DA MOURA, *Monsaraz, (066) 552-41. Moderate.*

A charming and luxurious refined country inn and farming estate just below the mountain. This great inn offers a dozen beautifully decorated suites, deluxe rooms, and a 3 bedroom cottage all with air conditioning, fireplaces, private bathrooms, cable TV, and minibar. The inn offers fine regional cusine, fireside lounge, billards, winery, bicycles, jeeps, horse rides, tennis, pool, sundeck, excursions, and parking.

ESTALAGEM DE MONSARAZ, *Monsaraz, (066) 551-12. Moderate.*

A quaint old inn just outside the walls of town owned by a young couple who offer 8 well decorated and comfortable guestrooms and suites with private bathrooms. Facilities include rustic lounge, a good restaurant, pool, excursions, and parking.

CASA DE DOM NUNO, *Rua Direita, (066) 551-46. Inexpensive.*

A typical rustic village house with exposed beams and regional furniture which has 6 rooms with semi-private bathrooms in the heart of town. No facilities except a bar.

WHERE TO EAT

QUINTA HORTA DA MOURA, *Monsaraz, (066) 552-41. Expensive.*

This fine inn's beautiful dining room serves the freshest possible local game and produce including their own home made cheese, olives, and jams. Ludi, the English speaking owner, will enchant you with her highly professional staff's delightful meals.

ESTALAGEM DE MONSARAZ, *Largo de São Bartolomeu, (066) 551-12. Moderate.*

The favored spot for visiting Spanish day trippers, the inn's dining room offers a daily selection of well prepared regional dishes served in an ambiance loaded with charm. Even the salads are great here, but the daily speials are the way to go.

CASA DO FORNO, *Travessa da Sanabrosa, (066) 551-90. Moderate.*

A somewhat elegant restaurant in the midst of this medieval village with a wonderful window laden dining room which shows off the splendid countryside. The selection of regional specialties includes fine roasted lamb, pork, and occasionally rabbit.

SEEING THE SIGHTS

The best way to tour Monsaraz is by foot; leave your car at the parking lot in front of the **Estalagem de Monsaraz** inn at the right border of the village. From here you can walk through the town's walls and up *Rua Direita*, the village's main street. There are about four streets that run the length of town (only 6 blocks long) and they all offer great photo opportunities and historical sights. Every whitewashed and iron grilled house offers a different glimpse into why the local residents prefer to keep medieval ways of life in their small corner of the world.

As you walk through the stone lanes of town, you will pass by dozens of 16th-century homes with delicate iron grilled patios. At the **Largo Dom Nuno Alveres Pereira** (the only square in town) you will find the beautiful 18th-century sphere topped pillory. Surrounding the square you can visit several buildings including the 16th-century former prison and town hall known as the **Paços do Concelho** (closed on Tuesday), which houses a wonderful ancient frescoe depicting the judgment of good and evil. There are also several other churches and chapels that can be entered.

At the end of the plaza you can walk to the ruins of a 13th-century **Castelo** (castle), which includes the massive **Torre de Menagem** keep and a small bullring that may date back to Roman times. The views from the castle's walls out over the plains are amazing, with vistas of clay, vineyards, cork trees, sheep, and olive trees.

If you want a truly unforgettable experience, call the **Quinta Horta da Moura** a few days in advance and arrange a horseback or carraige ride up the mountain to the castle. Just tie up your horse to the castle walls and have a nice walk through town. A few minutes from the base of town you can see several Roman wells, megaliths and monoliths including the **Menhir do Outeiro**, the **Menhir da Bulhoa**, the **Cromlech do Xerez**, and the **Antas do Olival da Pega**. Although these prehistoric sights are just minutes away, you may wish to ask the *Turismo* office at the pillory square in Monsaraz for specific instuctions on how to reach their dirt access roads – which are not always marked.

On the way out of town on the *Estrada de Monsaraz* towards **Reguengos de Monsaraz**, you will pass three important stops. First there are the local pottery artisans whose colorful hand-painted bowls and pitchers are found inside the rustic studio/showrooms in the village of **São Pedro do Corval** some 9 km west of Monsaraz. A few km further west is the wonderful artist cooperative known as T.E.A.R. which sells and exhibits fine iron work, traditional ceramics, wood work, tapestries, miniatures, and other fine handicrafts. The artists can be found throughout the building in the process of creating their unique crafts. Do not miss this place! Also along this same road you will find the **Cooperativa de**

Reguengos wine company, which makes a good local wine known as *Terras del Rei*.

PORTEL

The castle-dominated town of **Portel** can be reached *by taking route N-256 west for 21 km from Reguengos de Monsaraz and connecting to IP-2 south for about another 22 km*. This agricultural town produces excellent fresh goat and sheeps milk cheeses which are sold throughout the region.

Of particular interest to visitors are the huge walls and **Torre de Menagem** keep at the medieval **Castelo** (castle), the 16th-century **Igreja de Espírito Santo** church, the old public **Chafriz** fountains, and several azulejo laden churches such as and 18th-century **Igreja da Misericórdia** which can be found a short walk away from the town's central **Praça D. Nuno Alvares Pereira** square. Near the entrance to town you can also visit the ancient **Convento de Capuchos** convent.

Horseback riding is available in several neighboring farm houses which are referred to as **Herdades** and the *Turismo* office at the **Câmara Municipal** on the central square will provide you with a free list.

VIANA DO ALENTEJO

The sleepy fortified town of **Viana do Alentejo** *lies on the plains some 28 km from Portel on route N-384 west*. This remarkable town is dominated by the defensive walls and towers of it's 14th-century **castelo** (castle) that provide a great path atop the walls.

In the 15th century, several structures including a pillory and the buttress and turret laden facade of the gothic **Igreja Matriz** church were added within the fortifications. The church was designed by Diogo de Arruda and among it's many spledid elements are a large Manueline portal, *azulejos*-covered walls, carved columns, and an elaborate crucifix.

ALVITO

The remarkably peaceful fortified town of **Alvito** *lies about 10 km. down from Viana do Alentejo on route N-257 south*. Until recently, Alvito has been a stop-over point for supplies before continuing to the swimming, fishing, and watersports access of the beautiful **Odivelas** and **Alvito Barragems** (dams that create lakes) just minutes out of town.

Recently, the town's wonderful turreted 15th-century Gothic, Manueline, and Mudéjar styled **castelo** (castle) along with it's fine gardens and square **Torre de Menagem** keep has been remarkably transformed into a deluxe *pousada*, which will undoubtedly bring more foreigners within the town's lanes lined with ancient rustic homes that have fine Manueline windows and doorways, adorned by incredible door knockers.

THE PLANÍCIES 369

The town also has a 13th century **Igreja Matriz** church, a well-used pillory, and some small gardens. This is a great place which has yet to see many tourists – get here soon!

WHERE TO STAY

POUSADA DO CASTELO ALVITO, *Castelo de Alvito, (084) 483-83. Expensive.*

A wonderfully deluxe *pousada* which offers 20 great rooms with private bathrooms and a hard working staff. Facilities include a bar, regional restaurant, pool, air conditioning, hunting excursions, garden, chapel, TV, and parking.

QUINTA DOS PRAZERES, *Largo das Alcacarias, (084) 481-70. Moderate.*

A cute and comfortable rustic country inn which sometimes serves as a sort of base lodge for the sportsmen who frequent the area. The inn offers 6 nice rooms with semi private bathrooms. Facilities include fishing and hunting excursions, boats, bar, dining room, barbeque, pool, bicycles, gardens, and lots of parking.

MOURA

The regal former spa town of **Moura** rests amidst the ruins of a 13th-century **castelo** (castle), *57 km southeast of Alvito on route N-258 east.* According to local legend, a 12th-century Moorish princess named Saluquia jumped off the castle after mistakenly opening the doors of town to advancing Christian troops disguised as her future husband and his friends. Below the castle you can visit the 13th-century **Convento do Carmo** with its amazing frescoed chancel ceiling, and then walk around and down past the famed hot springs next to the **Jardim Santiago** gardens into the heart of the old town.

The old town is made up of several sections including the beautiful **Mouraria** (Moorish quarter) that contains many original Moorish houses with Arab chimneys and unusual *azulejos*. The town's central **Largo de Santa Clara** plaza contains the wonderful Gothic and Manueline **Igreja de São João** church with its amazing portal and 17th-century *azulejos*.

WHERE TO STAY

HOTEL DE MOURA, *Praça Gago Coutinho, 1, (085) 224-95. Moderate.*

An old world style hotel which is in the process of restoring it's 37 grand rooms. The hotel is laden with gardens, terraces, *azulejos*, and turn of te century furnishings. Facilities include bar, snackbar, restaurant, TV, disco, and parking.

SERPA

The old Moorish walled city of **Serpa** can be found *28 km southwest of Moura on route N-255 south*. The most dramatic attraction in town may very well be the **Castelo de Serpa** castle whose keep (closed on Mondays) is home to the **Museu de Arqueologia** museum, which holds collections of local prehistoric and Roman artifacts.

Near the castle you can visit the 13th-century Gothic **Igreja da Santa Maria** church, and a beautiful clock tower. The only other sights I found of interest are the old town's lovely winding lanes like the *Rua da Parreira*, the small but imaginative **Jardim Botánico** gardens, the impressive 11th-century aqueduct, and the **Museu de Etnologia** ethnological museum (closed on Mondays) on the **Largo do Corro** plaza which contains a series of exhibitions dedicated to the methods of production of Serpa's local handicrafts.

A wonderful waterfall called **Pulo do Lobo** is l*ocated some 17 km south of town on the road which goes past São Brás*. Ask directions from someone in town, though, as it is easy to get lost along the dirt stretch of this road.

WHERE TO STAY

POUSADA DE SÃO GENS, *Alto de São Gens, (084) 537-24. Moderate.*

A cute little hill top *pousada* a few minutes south of town which offers 16 nice air conditioned rooms with private bathrooms, bar, restaurant, pool, and parking.

CASA DE SÃO BRÁS, *São Brás, (084) 902-72. Inexpensive.*

A relaxing rustic farm house a few minutes south of town near the village of São Brás which offers a few nice guestrooms with private bathrooms. Facilities include bar, TV room, Video room, pool, tennis, trails, gardens, horse riding, and parking.

BEJA

The historic city of **Beja** can be reached *by taking route N-260 west for 29 km from Serpa*. Originally the Roman city of *Pax Julia*, Beja continued to flourish under Visigoth and Moorish civilization.

Today Beja is an important agricultural trade center for the area's vast supply of wheat and olive oil and offers several interesting attractions to those of you in need of a stop over point from Évora to the Algarve. The old section of the city is dominated by a large **castelo** (castle) rebuilt by King Dom Dinis in the 13th century on the sight of a Roman struture. This eloboraelt deorated castle is surrounded by a crenellated defensive wall incorperating several towers. Inside the castle's merlon topped **Torre de Menagem** keep you can climb up a winding stairway to reach its Gothic windows and lookout which present a great view over the area. Additional buildings within the compound have been converted into a military museum containing several weapons ranging from spears to shotguns. Near the castle you can aslo visit the 15th-century Visigothic **Igreja de Santo Amaro** which contains a museum of Visigoth artifacts (closed on Mondays).

From the castle you can walk a block down and bear left to get to the **Praça da República** square. While strolling through the square you will notice the 16th-century **Igreja da Misericórdia** church which is worth a quick visit, and take *Rua dos Infantes* down a couple of blocks until reaching the heart of the old town at the central **Largo dos Duques de Beja** square.

Here you will find the former 15th-century **Convento de Nossa Senhora de Conceição** convent. The convent was once home to the infamous 17th century nun named Mariana Alcoforado who supposedly wrote the **Cartas Portuguesas** (Five Love Letters of a Portuguese Nun) to a French knight named Chamilly whom she fell in love with during his posting to Beja. Although the letters were widely published in France, they have never been authenticated and some doubts remain as to their true origins. The convent itself is quite beautiful as it contains marble and gilted chapels, Moorish *azulejos* covered cloisters, an unforgettable chapter house, and many paintings which are all enclosed under an elaborate pinnacled roof.

The convent now contains the **Rainha Leonor Museu Regional de Beja** museum (closed on Mondays), which has vast collections of Roman artifacts, 17th-century *azulejos*, and fine Spanish and Portuguese paintings from the 15th-18th centuries. Across the from the museum you will see the beautiful facade and bell tower of the Gothic 16th-century **Igreja de Santa Maria** who's azulejos covered interior is rather impressive.

About 9 km southwest of Beja off route N-18 west are the ruins of a 1st century Roman villa at **Pisões**. Recently, excavation has uncovered a fine mosaic floor of tiny green stones which form unusual patterns.

WHERE TO STAY

Any day now, the city of *Beja* will finally have a wonderful deluxe *pousada*. The cement is still drying at press time, but by the time you read this the new **POUSADA DO CONVENTO DE SÃO FRANSISCO** should be ready to host tourists. The inn will offer 37 rooms with facilities including bar, restaurant, pool, tennis, TV, massive gardens, and original chapel. Ask the local *Turismo* for the phone number or better yet ask your travel agent to book you well in advance as it may be sold out.

RESIDENCIAL CRISTINA, *Rua de Merttola, 71, (084) 323-036. Moderate.*

A clean and comfortable modern hotel with 31 large guestrooms with private bathrooms. Facilities include bar, direct dial phones, TV, and nearby parking.

MÉRTOLA

The quiet riverfront town of **Mértola** rests above western bank of the Guadiana river some 53 km. southeast of Beja on route N-122 south. Most of this border town's visitors come to see the ruins of it's Moorish 13th century **Castelo** (castle), the vaulting and ancient marble columns of the 11th century **Igreja Matriz** church which has retained some of the features from it's Moorish Alhomad mosque origins, the **Museu Arqueológico** on Rua da República which contains fine examples of Moorish pottery and local artifacts, and the famous endangered black storks which reside around the river. I personally come to Mértola for the river fishing and boat excursions which are offered on the beautiful Guadiana river valley.

WHERE TO STAY

CASA JANELAS VERDES, *Rua Dr. Manuel F. Gomes, (086) 621-45. Inexpensive.*

A rustic house in the old part of town near the river which offers 3 double rooms with private bathrooms. Facilities include lounge, patio, TV room, and parking.

PENSÃO BEIRA RIO, *Rua Dr. Afonso Costa, 18, (086) 623-40. Inexpensive.*

A nice and basic inn with guestrooms which share bathrooms. Nothing fancy.

PRACTICAL INFORMATION FOR THE PLANÍCIES

CURRENCY EXCHANGE

Most of the banks in the main towns of the Planícies will exchange foreign currency and traveller's checks without hesitation. In most cities, restaurants and hotel front desks will offer you a rather poor exchange rate. Remember that banking hours are from 8 am until 3 pm on Monday through Friday only.

Electronic 24 hour exchange booths can be found in **Évora**, but they tend to be out of order.

EMERGENCY & USEFUL PHONE NUMBERS
• **Emergency Services** (S.O.S.), *115*
• **Directory Assistance**, *118*

- **Arraiolos Hospital**, *Largo do Matadouro Velho, (066) 422-70*
- **Estremoz Health Center**, *Rossio Marquis de Pombal, (068) 222-27*
- **Évora Hospital**, *Largo Senhor da Pobreza, (066) 250-01*
- **Golegã Hospital**, *Rua José Relvas, (049) 943-69*
- **Redondo Health Center**, *Rua do Castelo, 17, (066) 991-68*
- **Vila Viçosa Hospital**, *Rua Câmara Pereira, (068) 981-86*
- **Automobile Club of Portugal – Lisbon**, *(01) 942-5095*
- **Lisbon's Portela Airport**, *(01) 802-060*
- **TAP at Lisbon Airport**, *(01) 386-0480*

MUSEUMS & CASTLES

- **D. Lope de Almeida Museum**, *Igreja de Santa Maria do Castelo, Abrantes, (042) 223-26*. Contains collections of local Roman artifacts, Moorish tiles, sculptures, paintings, ceramics, and other ethnographical items such as histoic books and documents. Open 10 am until 12 pm and 2 pm until 5 pm Tuesday through Sunday. Closed on Mondays and holidays.
- **Casa dos Patudos Museum**, *Town Hall, Alpiarça, (043) 543-90*. Contains the coolection of local politician José Relvas which includes 16th century Portuguese paintings, ceramics, *Arraiolos* carpets, *azulejos*, and furniture. Open 10 am until 12:30 pm and 2 pm until 5 pm Wednesday through Sunday. Closed on Mondays and Tursdays.
- **Museum of Azambuja**, *Rua Victor Cordon, 69, Azamuja, (063) 422-58*. Contains a collection of African art from the former Portuguese colonies. Open 10 am until 12 pm and 2 pm until 5 pm Monday through Friday. Closed on Saturdays, Sundays, and holidays.
- **Beja Castle and the Military Museum of the Baixo Alentejo**, *Castelo de Beja, Beja, (084) 221-52*. The castle contains a tower and several other old buildings which contain collections of various military weapons, uniforms, flags, and devices. Open 10 am until 1 pm and 2 pm until 6 pm daily from April through September. Open 9 am until 12 pm and 1 pm until 4 pm daily from October through May. Closed on holidays.
- **Municipal Museum (of Queen Leonor) of Beja, Convento de Nossa Senhora da Conceição**, *Largo da Conceição, Beja, (084) 233-51*. Contains a vast colection of Roman artifacts, 16th century Chinese porcelain, 15th-17th century paintings, marble statues, and *azulejos*. Open 10 am until 1 pm and 2 pm until 5 pm Tuesday through Sunday. Closed on Mondays and Holidays.
- **Municipal Museum (of Queen Leonor) of Beja- Visigothic Section, Igreja de Santo Amaro**, *Castelo de Beja, Beja, (084) 233-51*. Contains a collection of 7th-9th century Visigothic artifacts. Open 10 am until 1 pm and 2 pm until 5 pm Tuesday through Sunday.. Closed on

Mondays and Holidays.
- **Dr. António Lourenço Municipal Museum**, *Rua Luís de Camões, Benavente, (063) 524-66*. Contains a collection of 19th-century photography, antique postcards, regional clothing, weapons, African art, ceramics, and local artifacts. Open 9 am until 12:30 pm and 2 pm until 5 pm Tuesday through Friday. Open 2 pm until 6 pm Satuday and Sunday. Closed on Mondays and holidays.
- **Rural Museum and Wine Museum of Cartaxo**, *Quinta das Pratas, Cartaxo, (043) 702-372*. A large historic farming estate which contains exihibits on rural life and agricultural products such as wines, grains, olive oil, horses, and bulls. Open 10:30 am until 12:30 pm and 3:30 pm until 5:30 pm Tuesday through Sunday. Closed on Mondays and holidays.
- **The Museums of Chamusca**, *Chamusca, (049) 760-176*. A series of 5 seperate museums which consist of the following: A Traditional Rural House in the Parque Municipal, An Ethnology section at Carregueira, An Archelogy section in the Parque Municipal, A Music section at the Coreto da Vila, and A Funerary section at the Cemetario Municipal. Open from 9 am until 12:30 pm and 2 pm until 5:3 0pm daily.
- **Municipal Musem of Crato**, *Rua 5 de Outubro, Crato, (045) 971-61*. Contains collections of local artifacts, ceramics, furniture, sacred art, and crafts. Open 10am until 12 pm and 3 pm until 7 pm Tuesday through Sunday. Open 3 pm until 6 pm on Sunday. Closed on Mondays and holidays.
- **António Pires Ethnological Museum**, *Rua dos Apostolos, Elvas, (068) 624-02*. Contains collections of pre-historic through Moorish era artifacts, ceramics, painting, crafts, sacred art, and other regional items. Open9 am until 12:30 pm and 2 pm until 5:30 pm Tuesday through Sunday. Closed on Mondays and holidays.
- **Municipal Museum of Estremoz**, *Largo Dom Dinis, Estremoz, (068) 227-83*. Contains collections of local artifacts, crafts, ceramics, local clay dolls, and furniture. Open 10 am until 12 pm and 2 pm until 6 pm Tuesday through Sunday. Closed on Mondays and holidays.
- **Casa do Povo Rural Museum**, *Rossio de Marquêsde Pombal,89, Estremoz, (068) 225-38*. Contains collections of local and regional crafts. Open 10 am until 1 pm and 3 pm until 5 pm Tuesday through Sunday. Closed on Mondays and holidays.
- **Évora Sacred Art Museum**, *Igreja das Merces, Rua Raimundo, Évora, (066) 226-04*. Contains collections of religious objects, 17th century jewelry, and paintings. Open 10 am until 12:30 pm and 2 pm until 5 pm Tuesday through Sunday. Closed on Mondays and holidays.
- **Sé Cathedral Sacred Art Museum**, *Sé Cathedral, Largo de Sé, Évora, (066) 269-10*. Contains the cathedral's treasures including a 13th century

folding ivory Virgin, a presious stone studded reliquary, a piece of the True Cross, furniture, and jewelry, Open 9 am until 12 pm and 2 pm until 4:30 pm Tuesday through Sunday. Closed on Mondays.
- **Town Museum of Évora**, *Largo do Conde de Vila Flôr, Évora, (066) 226-04.* Contains a large selection of Roman through Manueline era sculptures, 16th and 17th century paintings, local artifacts, jewelry, ceramics, *azulejos,* and furniture. Open 10 am until 12:30 pm and 2 pm until 5:30 pm Tuesday through Sunday. Closed on Mondays and holidays.
- **Évora Toy Museum**, *Jardim Público-Parque Infantil, Évora, (066) 217-89.* Contains a historical collection of antique and more recent toys. Open 10 am until 12 pm and 2 pm until 5 pm Monday through Friday. Closed on Saturdays, Sundays, and holidays.
- **Mestre Martins Correira Museum**, *Largo da Imaculada Conceição, Golegã , (049) 94387.* Contains paintings and sculptures of the museum's namesake. Open 11 am until 12:30 pm and 3 pm until 6 pm Tuesday through Sunday. Closed on Mondays.
- **Municipal Museum of Marvão**, *Igreja de Santa Maria, Largo do Municipio, Marvão, (045) 932-26.* Contains collections of local artifacts, documents, sacred art, and weapons. Open 9 am until 12:30 pm and 2 pm until 5:30 pm daily.
- **José Régio Museum**, *Rua José Régio , Portalegre, (045) 236-25.* Contains a collection of local sacred art and regional crafts. Open 9:30 am until 12:30 pm and 2 pm until 6 pm Tuesday through Sunday. Closed on Mondays and holidays.
- **Museum of Portalegre**, *Rua José Maria da Rosa, Portalegre, (045) 216-16.* Contains collections of ceramics, sacred art, *Arraiolos* carpets, and furniture. Open 9:30 am until 12:30 pm and 2 pm until 6 pm Wednesday through Monday. Closed on Tuesdays and holidays.
- **Santarém Archaeologicl Museum**, *Igreja de São João de Alporão, Largo Eng. Zeferino Sarmento, Santerém, (043) 226-45.* Contains a collection of local archaeological items from many eras. Open 9 am until 12 pm and 2 pm until 5 pm Tuesday through Sunday. Closed on Mondays and holidays.
- **Castle Keep and Serpa Archaeological Museum**, *Castelo de Serpa, Serpa, (084) 903-51.* Contains archaeological findings from prehistoric through Roman eras. Open 9 am until 12:30 pm and 2 pm until 5:30 pm Tuesday through Sunday. Closed on Mondays and holidays.
- **Serpa Ethnological Museum**, *Largo do Corro, Serpa, (084) 903-51.* Contains workshops dedicated to local crafts and ethnological items. Open 9 am until 12:30 pm and 2 pm until 5:30 pm Tuesday through Sunday. Closed on Mondays and holidays.
- **Castle of Vila Viçosa**, *Castelo de Vila Viçosa, Vila Viçosa, (068) 981-28.* Contains a colection of furniture, painting, and artifacts from prehis-

toric through Roman eras. The facility also houses royal family archives. Open 9:30 am until 1 pm and 2 pm until 5 pm Tuesday through Sunday. Closed on Mondays and holidays.
- **Museum of the Bragança Family Ducal Palace**, *Paço Ducal, Vila Viçosa, (068) 986-59*. Contains a huge assortment of *Arraiolos* carpets, paintings, ceramics, a 17th-century diamonnd and ruby laden holy cross, *azulejos*, jewelry, weapons, rare books, musical archives, classical furniture, and the royal coach collection. Open 9:30 am until 1 pm and 2 pm until 5 pm Tuesday through Sunday. Closed on Mondays and holidays.

SPORTS & RECREATION

There are dozens of horse riding, fishing, and hunting establishments throughout the region which may be found by asking at your hotel or any regional *Turismo* office. These are just a few of the best facilities:
- **Herdade de Porches** (Hunting), *Alcácer do Sal, (066) 622-42*
- **Herdade dos Coelheiros** (Hunting), *Arraiolos, (066) 471-31*
- **Herdade das Lages** (Horses, Fishing), *Arraiolos, (066) 462-21*
- **Quinta Santa Bárbara** (Horse riding), *Constância, (049) 992-14*
- **Constância Sports Training Center**, *Constância, (049) 941-79*
- **Monte das Flores** (Horse riding), *Évora, (066) 254-90*
- **Évora Bicycle Rentals**, *Évora, (066) 761-453*
- **Monte da Fazenda** (Hunting, Horses), *Évora Monte, (068) 951-72*
- **Horta da Moura** (Horses, Jeep safaris), *Monsaraz, (066) 552-06*
- **Herdade do Carrascal** (Hunting), *Portalegre, (045) 228-56*
- **Casa de São Brás** (Horses), *Serpa, (084) 902-72*
- **Pousada São Miguel** (Hunting, Fishing), *Sousel, (068) 551-160*

TRANSPORTATION

Most of the towns and villages of this area are linked by trains and buses. For specific routes and schedules, please contact the local *Turismo* office, visit a local travel agency, or contact the transportation companies directly.
- **Beja RN Bus Depot**, *Rua Cidade de São Paulo, (084) 240-44*
- **Castelo de Vide RN Bus stop**, *Rua de Bartolomeu Santa, no phone*
- **Elvas RN Bus Depot**, *Praça da Republica, (068) 622-144*
- **Estremoz RN Bus Depot**, *Rossio, (068) 222-82*
- **Évora RN Bus Depot**, *Rua da República, (066) 221-21*
- **Portalegre RN Bus Depot**, *Rua N. Alvares Pereira, (045) 227-23*
- **Santarém RN Bus Depot**, *Rua Duarte Periera, (043) 220-01*
- **Serpa RN Bus stop**, *Rua Soldado, no phone*
- **Vila Viçosa RN Bus stop**, *Rua André Pereira, no phone*
- **Azambuja CP Rail station**, *Largo dos Combatentes, (063) 431-57*

- **Beja CP Rail station**, *2 km northeast of town, (084) 325-056*
- **Castelo de Vide CP Rail station**,*4 km northeast of town, (045) 916-63*
- **Elvas CP Rail station**, *Rua de Campo Maior,, (068) 622-816*
- **Évora CP Rail station**, *Rua da República, (066) 221-25*
- **Portalegre CP Rail station**, *11 km south of town, (045) 961-21*
- **Santarém CP Rail station**, *2 km northwest of town, (043) 333-180*
- **Hertz Rent a Car in Évora**, *Rua de Isabel, 7, (066) 217-67*
- **Europcar Rent a Car in Beja**, *Rua Angola, Centro Carmo, (084) 328-128*

TOURIST OFFICES (TURISMOS)
- **Arraiolos Tourist Office**, *Praça Lima e Brito, (066) 42-105*
- **Borba Tourist Office**, *Praça de República, (068) 941-13*
- **Chamusca Tourist Office**, *Largo 25 de Abril, (049) 760-566*
- **Constância Tourist Office**, *Rua Eng. Vicente Castro, (049) 992-05*
- **Estremoz Tourist Office**, *Largo da República, (068) 225-38*
- **Évora Tourist Office**, *Praça do Giraldo, (066) 226-71*
- **Monsaraz Tourist Office**, *Largo D. Nunes Pereira, (066) 551-36*
- **Portel Tourist Office**, *Praça D. Nuno A. Pereira, (066) 623-35*
- **Redondo Tourist Office**, *Praça da República, (066) 996-60*
- **Santarém Tourist Office**, *Rua Pedro de Santarém, (043) 263-18*
- **Vila Viçosa Tourist Office**, *Praça da República, (068) 983-06*

Travel Agencies
- **Turalentejo**, *Rua Miguel Bombarda, 78, (066) 227-17.* A good travel agency in **Évora** which·books excursions, hotels, cars and tickets.
- **Alegretur**, *Rua do Comércio,43, (045) 242-40.* A **Portalegre** based travel agency which offers all types of reservtion servies.
- **Omnitur**, *Rua Serpa Pinto, 77, (043) 264-89.* A full service travel agency in **Santarém** which can also exchange currency.

21. THE ALGARVE

The **Algarve** is the southernmost region in mainland Portugal and is drenched with sunshine for almost the entire year. Surrounded by a series of mountain ranges to its north and an abudance of sand dunes and rock cliff beaches on its windswept southern coastline, this are has become the most visited region in all of the country.

The Algarve contains hundreds of hotels, seaside apartments, deluxe villas, golf courses, tennis schools, watersport facilities, casinos, restaurants, and night clubs which have been a huge tourism magnet for Portugal for the last 20 years or so. Vacationing English, German, Scandinavian, and Dutch tourists have swamped many of the area's beaches, resulting in a huge amount of oceanfront development.

Although most of the Algarve's beautiful coastline is crammed with one hotel after the other, several small fishing villages and inland towns are quite secluded and full of their original historic and traditional character. Most visitors seem determined to spend their days on the vast assortment of sandy beaches (several are topless) and their nights hopping between the many pubs and loud discotechs in the packed resort areas such as **Albufeira**, **Praia da Rocha**, and **Vilamoura**.

When you have had enough time on the beaches, you might want to visit a few less commercialized areas, such as the fishing village of **Olhão**, the charming towns of **Silves** and **Tavira**, the photogenic cliffs near **Praia do Vau**, the beach islands off **Faro** and **Olhão**, the giant Saturday outdoor market in **Loulé** (open until midnight), and the historic village of **Sagres**.

In this chapter I'll begin with the western Algarve and continue eastward, extending towards the Spanish border.

ODECEIXE

The Algarve region begins on the southern bank of the **Ribeira de Seixe** river, *about 19 km southwest of the Alentejan town of* **Odemira** *on route N-120 south.* As you cross the river and enter the Algarve's western coast area, you will come to the first of several charming little beachfront

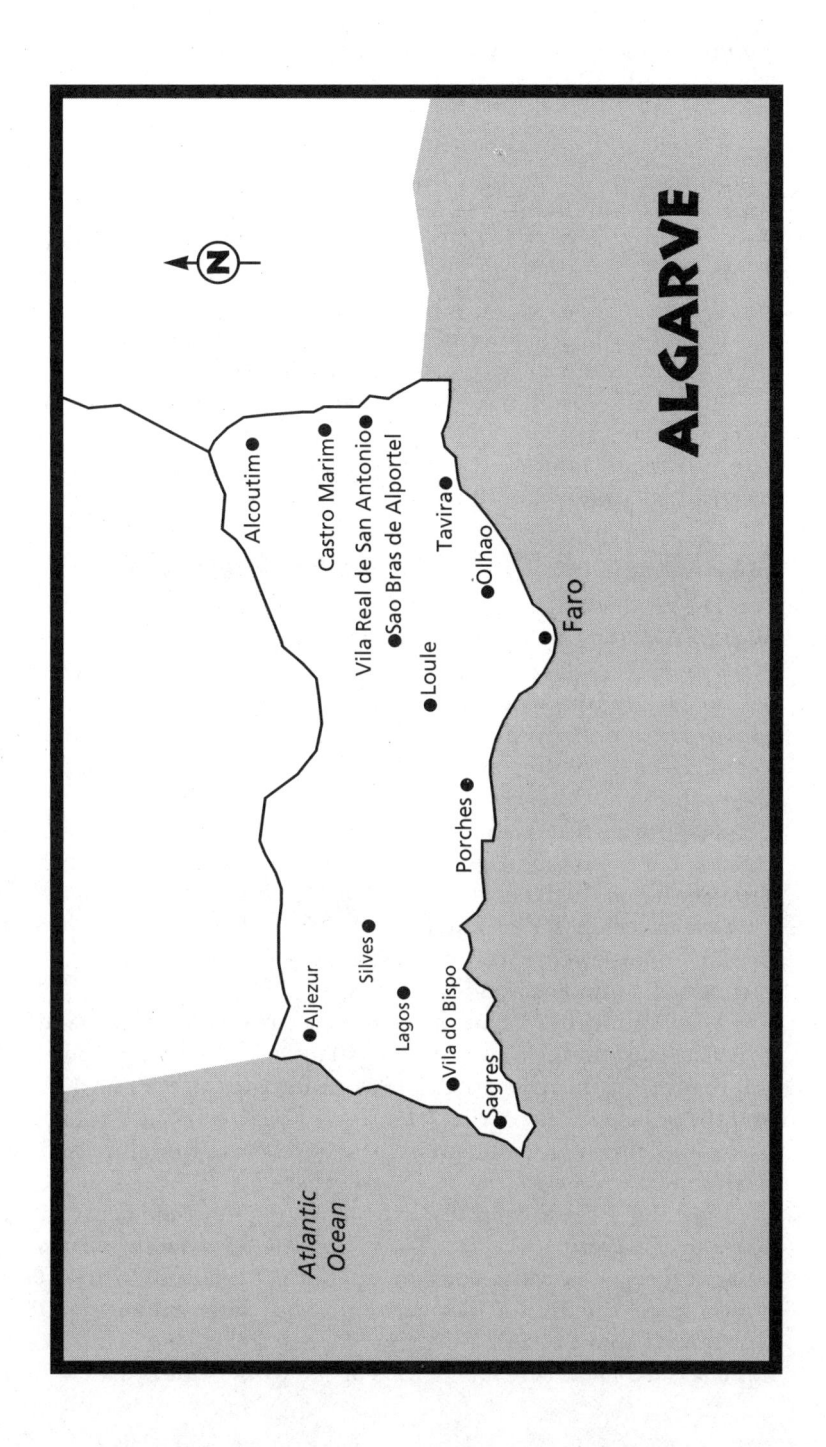

THE ALGARVE

communities known as **Odeceixe**. The town consists of a few hundred whitewashed and red roofed houses which are surrounded by farms and pine forests.

The village itself rests on the riverside and retains a sleepy and inviting atmosphere in the months before and after summer. As the summer approaches, hundreds of younger Dutch and German tourists trampel through town on the way to the beautiful sandy **Praia de Odeceixe** beach a mile or so out of town. During these months, you can see a huge assortment of VW vans with peace sign bumper stickers blasting reggae music near the beach. Several locals have told me they actually depart the town in July and August, presumably in disgust.

In the off season, the town becomes quiet once again, and is a fine place to relax. Accomodations in town and around the beach consist of several private houses which offer guestrooms without private bathrooms, and a campsite which gets full during the summer.

ALJEZUR & THE COASTAL BEACHES

The castle-topped town of **Aljezur** *lies some 14 km away from Odeceixe on route N-120 south.* The town rests below a ruined hilltop 10th-century Moorish **castelo** (castle), on a small plain off the **Ribeira de Aljezur** river within the **Espinhaco de Cao** foothills. Since much of the Moorish section of town was destroyed by the infamous 1755 earthquake that rocked Portugal, many of the town's structures are more modern but still retain the traditional whitewashed and blue bordered facade style.

The town's fine 17th-century **Igreja Matriz** church is about the only other specific attraction worth noting besides a pretty windmill known as the **Moinho do Rogil** *about 8 km north of town in the hamlet of* **Rogil**. Aljezur's *Turismo* office on the central **Largo do Mercado** plaza can provide lists of private homes offering rooms, campsites (still full of Germans and Dutch during the summer), and local maps.

Most visitors to Aljezur come here to access several dramatic beaches which are just minutes away on the Atlantic's coastline. Among the most impressive local beaches are the nearby wide and sandy **Praia da Amoreira** and the adjacent **Praia de Monte Clerigo** beaches *about 7 km northwest of town*, and the huge windswept beaches below the cliffs at **Praia da Arrifana** beach *some 11 km southwest of town*.

Another beautiful day trip I strongly suggest would be to drive *30 km down route N-268 south to the village of* **Carrapateira**. Here you can visit the ancient **Igreja e Fortalcza da Carrapateira** church and fortress and then continue to the fishing havens and sand dune beaches at **Praia da Bordeira**. From Praia da Bordeira, *you can take a small coastal road south a few minutes to the cliffs and beaches* at the wonderful **Praia do Amado**.

WHERE TO STAY

HOTEL VALE DA TELHA, *Vale de Telha-Aljezur, (082) 981-80. Inexpensive.*

A good 2 star air conditioned hotel a few minutes south of Aljezur which offers 26 comfortable double rooms with private bathrooms. Facilities include bar, snackbar, restaurant, pool, tennis, disco, direct dial phones, and plenty of parking.

VILA DO BISPO & THE COASTAL BEACHES

Some 30 km down from Aljezur on route N-268 south (bear right off route N-120 south at Alfambras) is the small village of **Vila do Bispo**. This cute little town offers few attractions besides it's famed 18th-century **Igreja Matriz** church, heavily decorated with fine *azulejos* and contains a small **Museu de Atre Sacra** sacred art museum.

Vila do Bispo is problably best known as an access point for a few nice beaches for swimming, surfing, and fishing. The finest beaches are about 5 km northwest of town at **Praia do Castelejo** and **Praia de Barriga**, reached by small roads from town that are not well maintained. Accomodations here include a couple of basic small inns, houses which rent rooms, and a huge campground.

WHERE TO STAY

PENSÃO MIRA SAGRES, *Rua do Hospital, 3, (082) 661-60. Inexpensive.*

A basic 2 star inn; 4 rooms with shared bathroom. Not many facilities.

SAGRES & THE COASTAL BEACHES

As you follow route N-258 south from Vila do Bispo for some 8 km, the road will pass by the historic fishing village of **Sagres**. It was in this town that Prince Henry the Navigator founded his famous School of Navigation in the 15th century. The school became a major center for the study of navigation, cartography, and astronomy thus enabling it's members to begin a series of expeditions to Africa and beyond which would become known as the Age of Discoveries.

Among the most famous students at this institute were Christopher Columbus, Vasco de Gama, Pedro Alvares Cabral, and Fernão de Megellan. The school was also responsible for the design and construction of a new type of sailing vessel known as caravels which allowed the ships to tack very tightly (sail almost towards the direction of the wind). Most of the school was unfortunately destroyed by Sir Francis Drake in the 16th century.

The town itself rests on cliffs above the sea and offers little of historical significance as the 1755 earthquake destroyed most of it's original structures. Sagres has become popular with younger European vacationers who tend to be on tight budgets. The village is made up of few streets full of small restaurants and bars which run between town's small main square and a fishing harbour which brings in most of the Algarve's highly prized lobsters.

Outside of town there are many new condo, villa, and resort developments which are beginning to chip away at the once charming atmosphere which Sagres was once known for. From the village, you can take a road leading just south of town onto a small peninsula. Here you can go through the tunnel to enter the plateau topped **Fortaleza** (fortress) which contains the 15th-century **Rosa dos Ventos** wind compass and restored 14th century **Capelo da Nossa Senhora da Graça** chapel.

Besides the fortress, the only other attractions in Sagres are the fine beaches such as **Praia da Mareta** which is just across from the village. Other nice beaches for windsurfing, fishing, and sunbathing include **Praia da Baleeira**, **Praia do Martinal**, and **Praia do Ingrina** which are a bit east of town's harbour. The undertow at any of these area beaches is quite strong, so I recommend extreme caution.

About 6 km west of Sagres is another peninsula called the **Cabo de São Vicente**. This rugged area is Europe's southwesternmost point and was once thought of as O Fim do Mundo (the end of the Earth). The Romans had believed that this was the oint where the sun sank into the sea. The cape was later named for Saint Vincent who's body arrived here by ship in the 8th century. The saint became the focal point for a Christian shrine and a 16th-century monastery which now lies in ruins.

Atop the cape's sparscly vegetated cliffs is the large **Farol** (lighthouse) which may be toured on the site of Prince Henry's former residence. The long windy isolated beach of **Praia de Beliche** is located just west of the cape and offers a great place to take some sun or do some fishing.

WHERE TO STAY

POUSADA DO INFANTE, *Sagres, (082) 642-22. Expensive.*

A seaview villa style pousada which offers 38 nice rooms (many with balconies). Facilities include bar, restaurant, air conditioning, pool, tennis, TV, and parking.

HOTEL O NAVEGANTE, *Sitio da Baleeira-Sagres, (084) 643-54. Moderate.*

A modern hotel complex above Praia da Baleeira beach which offers 55 small but comfortable 1 bedroom apartments. Facilities include bar, restaurant, pool, air conditioning, squash, direct dial phones, TV, and parking.

RESIDENCIAL DOM HENRIQUE, *Sitio da Mareta-Sagres, (082) 641-33. Moderate.*

A nice and friendly inn located above *Mareta* beach in the village of *Sagres* which offers 16 good guestrooms with semi-private bathrooms, a bar, and a restaurant.

APARTAMENTOS TONEL, *Sagres, (082) 644-71. Moderate.*

A nice and modern complex near the beach which offers 2 bedroom apartments with kitchens. Facilities include a pool and parking.

RESIDENCIA DOM HENRIQUE, *Sitio da Mareta-Sagres, (082) 641-33. Moderate.*

A nice seaview 4 star inn above *Mareta* beach which offers 16 rooms with private bathrooms. a bar, restaurant, TV room, patio, and parking.

MOTEL OS GAMBOZINOS, *Praia do Martinhal-Sagres, (082) 643-18.Moderate.*

A nice 3 star motel near the beach which offers 26 large and comfortable rooms with seaviews. Facilities include a bar, restaurant, TV room, and lots of parking.

HOTEL DA BALEEIRA, *Sitio da Baleeira-Sagres, (082) 642-12. Moderate.*

A large and adequate 3 star air conditioned hotel with 117 double rooms (some with nice views). Facilities include bar, restaurant, pool, tennis, disco, and parking.

FORTALEZA DO BELICHE ,*Sitio do Beliche, (082) 641-24. Moderate.*

The annex to Sagre's pousada which offers 4 basic double rooms at much lower prices than the pousada in a converted clifftop fortress with a bar and restaurant.

WHERE TO EAT

A TASCA, *Sagres, (082) 641-77. Moderate.*

A typical local fish restaurant which offers fresh seafood served amidst increadable views of the sea. Try the increadable *Caldeira* fish stew it's enough for 2 persons.

TELHEIRO DO INFANTE, *Praia de Mareta-Sagres, (082) 641-79. Moderate.*

An excellant beachfront regional restaurant which specializes in daily caught fresh shellfish. I had the most delicious broiled *lagosta* (lobster) in the universe here.

FORTALEZA DO BELICHE, *Sitio do Beliche, (082) 641-24. Moderate.*

This small annex to the local pousada offers fine regional cuisine served in a rather unusual rustic seting above the sea. Try the grilled *Robalo* (bass) if it's available.

NIGHTLIFE

Since the town attracts a younger blend of international tourists, the small village offers several fun cafes, bars, and clubs to visit in the summer season. I recommend you try walking through the village and peek inside the seafront **Last Chance Saloon** and the **Rosa dos Ventos** bar near the main square. For those of you who want to party all night, try the **Clube Caravelo** disco located a few minutes north of town.

SALEMA

The small small fishing village of **Salema** *lies some 8 km southeast of Vila do Bispo just south of route N-125 east*. The town has recently developed into a small resort community of villas and apartments which rest on the slopes of cliffs and hills which meet the sea at the fine **Praia do Salema** beach.

Although several foreigners inhabit this area, the seafront village seems to have kept it's original ambiance. On any given day, several local fishermen still work hard to get the day's catch. There are no specific attractions in the village, but it is a great place to relax and not feel like you have entered a tourist trap. I am sure that the future of this village is not particularly traditional, so get here fast. A nice 18 hole golf course called **Parque da Floresta Golf** is just minutes away from town.

WHERE TO STAY

ESTALAGEM INFANTE DO MAR,*Salema, (082) 654-43. Moderate.*

A nice 4 star local inn above the sea on a cliff which offers 30 comfortable cdouble rooms (many with balconies to the sea) that have private bathrooms. Facilities include a bar, restaurant, pool, TV room, direct dial phones, and parking.

SALEMA PRAIA CLUB, *Salema, (082) 652-52. Moderate.*

A modern English managed resort community with villas, apartments, and townhouses for rent. Facilities include a bar, restaurant, pool, tennis, and parking.

BURGAU

Some 8 km away from Salema off route N-125 east is a former fishing village known as **Burgau**. While the town is fairly tranquil, it has already started to undergo a transformation into a resort community and is well on it's way to losing much of its original atmosphere.

The village lies below shrub-laden hills and is made up of a few stone paved streets which ramble past a small main square. English tourists tend to select Burgau as one of their tourism bases in the Algarve and have built many villa and condo properties surrounding the village area. The beach area remains the main attraction of town and contains several little bars and watersports rental facilities, including the **Beach Bar** where you can arrainge water skiing, windsurfing boat rentals, and rent chairs.

THE ALGARVE

WHERE TO STAY
CASA GRANDE, *Burgau, (082) 651-68. Moderate.*
An amusing inn converted from an old house on the way to Luz, run an English women. Some guestrooms have semi-private bathrooms.

WHERE TO EAT
RESTAURANTE ANCORA, *Burgau, (082) 691-02. Moderate.*
A seaview fish and regional cuisine restaurant near the town which offers huge portions of freshly caught local fish prepared to order.

LUZ

Some 5 km from Burgau off route N-125 east is the beachfront tourist trap resort area of **Luz**. I once liked this area, but now I am disgusted by what massive development by English and Portuguese construction companies has done here. The beach is still fairly nice, but the town itself offers litle of interest besides shops, pub-style bars, and some decent restaurants.

Other than the nearby scuba, golf, and windsurfing facilities, I don't see the attraction of staying here. Many of the villa and timeshare properties are not up to par with the rest of the resorts on the Algarve. If you get stuck staying here, you may wish to head east to the more peaceful beaches of **Porto do Mós** which tend to attract a more local crowd.

WHERE TO STAY
THE OCEAN CLUB, *Praia da Luz, (082) 789-763. Moderate.*
One of the better villa and apartment complexes in Luz. They rent nicely furnished inland as well as seaview villas and apartments with hotel facilities and nearby pools.

RESIDENCIAL VILAMAR, *Estrada de Burgau-Luz, (082) 789-541. Moderate.*
A nice 3 star 15 room inn not far from the beach which offers good guestrooms with private bathrooms, bar, restaurant, tennis, gardens, TV room, and parking.

LUZ BAY CLUB, *Praia da Luz, (082) 789-640. Moderate.*
A huge villa complex where most units are crammed next to each other. They rent decent apartments and fairly comfortable villas that are not far from the sea.

WHERE TO EAT
RESTAURANTE O ANTÓNIO, *Porto de Mós, (082) 763-560.*
A nice beachfront grillroom and restaurant with a great outdoor dining area a few km. east of Luz at the beach of Porto de Mós. They serve great *linguado* (sole).

LAGOS & THE COASTAL BEACHES

The historic walled city of **Lagos** rests on the seafront *some 10 km away from Luz on route N-125 east*. Unlike many seafront areas, Lagos does not depend soley on tourists for its economy, and there are many sights worth visiting while you are here.

The city was first founded by the Carthaginians sometime before the 3rd century B.C. and was home to later Roman and Moorish trading settlements. After the Christians took control of the area in the 13th century, Lagos became a prominant commercial city and it's wide harbour became a martime base for exploration during the 15th century Age of Discoveries. In 1576, the city became the capital of the Algarve and remained prosperous until 1755 when the massive earthquake destroyed most of the city and it's historical structures. Fortunately, several ancient remnants of this delightful city can still be found in both the old quarter of town and in assorted other locations.

WHERE TO STAY

HOTEL DE LAGOS, *Rua Nova da Aldeia, (082) 769-970. Expensive.*

A large 4 star modern hotel with beautiful gardens above the center of town which offers 318 nice air conditioned rooms. Facilities include bar, restaurant, snackbar, shops, pools, nearby golf, tennis, TV, shuttle buses to a beach club, and parking.

HOTEL GOLFINHO, *Praia de Dona Ana, (082) 769-900. Expensive.*

A good seaview 4 star hotel with 262 comfortable rooms (many are waterview) just outside of town. Facilities include bar, restaurant, snackbar, pool, bowling, nearby golf, air conditioning, shops, billards, TV, disco, babysitting, beach, and parking.

QUINTA DA ALFARROBEIRA, *Meia Praia, (082) 798-424. Moderate.*

A lovely stone and whitewash country inn and estate close to the ocean which offers 2 large guestrooms and a nice apartment, all with private bathrooms. Facilities include bar, terraces, gardens, pool, nearby golf and horses, and parking.

MEIA PRAIA BEACH CLUB, *Meia Praia, (082) 769-980. Moderate.*

A nice family style apartment-hotel complex just east of town which offers 77 comfortable apartments with kitchen and TV near the sea. Facilities include bar, pool, billards, game room, direct dial phones, nearby golf, and lots of parking.

CASA DO PINHÃO, *Praia do Pinhão, (082) 762-371. Moderate.*

A charming cliffside house slightly west of town which rents 3 nice rooms with private bathrooms just above the sea. Facilities include bar, terrace, TV room, and parking.

HOTEL MARINA SÃO ROQUE, *Meia Praia, (082) 763-761. Moderate.*

THE ALGARVE 387

A good value 3 star hotel not far from the beach area which offers 27 double rooms at lower rates than most area hotels. Facilities include bar, restaurant, pool, squash, billards, TV, air conditioning, direct dial phones, nearby golf, and parking.

ALBERGARIA MARINA RIO, *Ave. dos Descobrimentos, (082) 769-859. Moderate.*

A clean and comfortable seafront inn near the heart of Lagos which offers 36 air conditioned double rooms with private bathrooms, bar, TV room, radio, and parking.

PENSÃO RUBI MAR, *Rua da Barroca, 70, (082) 763-165. Inexpensive.*

A nice small centrally located inn with 9 rooms (some with views) with and without private bathroom. Almost no facilities besides the complimentary breakfast.

PENSÃO DONA ANA, *Praia de Dona Ana, (082) 762-322. Inexpensive.*

A clean and comfortable inn located above a great beach which offers 11 rooms with and without private bathrooms. Almost no facilities except a breakfast room.

WHERE TO EAT

RESTAURANTE ALPRENDE, *Rua António B. Viana, 17, (082) 762-05. Expensive.*

A luxurious seafood restuarant which offers a huge menu of Portuguese cuisine mixed with continental flare. The intimate setting provides a great ambiance.

DOM SEBASTIÃO, *Rua 25 de Abril, 22, (082) 762-795. Expensive.*

A wonderful relaxing establishment whic offers fine seafood and regional meat dishes served in either it's atmospheric dining rooms, or outside on the terrase. Try the grilled fish here, it is the finest in the Algarve. Reservations are necessary.

O GALEÃO, *Rua da Laranjeira, 1, (082) 763-909. Moderate.*

A remarkably good restaurant which offers continental and regional cuisine served from it's amazingly active open kitchen. This place is a lot of fun to people watch in.

RESTAURANTE PIRI-PIRI, *Rua Afonso D'Almeida, 10, (082) 763-803. Inexpensive.*

A narrow little restaurant which serves an assortment of well prepared regional meals at quite reasonable prices. This is one of the best casual places to eat in town.

SEEING THE SIGHTS

The best way to explore the many sights in the city itself is to park your car somewhere off the picturesque seafront *Ave. dos Descobrimentos,* perhaps near the **Praça da República** square. Just off the east side of the plaza's edge on *Rua da Senhora da Graça* you can visit the remaining arcades of the former **Casa de Afândega** custom's house which hosted a **Mercado de Escravos** (slave market) where ships returning from 15th century African expeditions sold their cargo of captured humans.

On the other side of the plaza you can view the solemn interior and Manueline windows of the 15th-century **Igreja da Santa Maria** church. From the front of the church you should walk up the *Rua Henriques Correira Silva* (which then becomes *Rua de São Gonçalo*) until the next corner where you will see the beautiful baroque 18th-century **Igreja de Santo António**. The inside of this church is filled with fantastic wooden animals and cherubs covered in pure Brazilian gold, vaulted ceilings, and fine azulejos. Adjacent to the church you really should visit the **Museu Municipal de José Formosinho** museum (closed on Mondays), which contains a vast assortment of local artifacts including Roman mosaics, 16th-century ceramics, replias of Algarve style chimneys, the 16th century charter of Lagos, and lots of other unusual paintings, embroideries, and sculptures.

From the museum you can walk a bit further up *Rua de São Gonçalo* until you can make the next right (east) turn which leads you across town on *Rua Candido dos Reis* past several interesting shops. At the end of this street you will find the **Praça Luís de Camões** plaza, and a right turn from this plaza onto *Rua Garrett* will lead you directly onto the main **Praça Gil Eanes** square with it's somewhat tasteless statue of King Dom Sebastião. From the front of the Cãmara Municipal (town hall) you can turn left (east) onto *Rua das Portas de Portugal* which leads you back to the seafront.

If you happen to be in town on Saturday morning, you may wish to pop into the **Mercado** (market) just to your left (east) on this part of *Ave. dos Descobrimentos*. In any case, you can head back west along the seafront for several blocks to reach the harbour and it's 17th-century **Forte Ponta da Bandeira** fortress (closed on Mondays) and the old town walls across the street.

Of course, many people visiting Lagos are not at all interested in historical sights and fine architecture. Most tourists come here to visit the beautiful local beaches and coves which are just outside of town, while others arrive in town to use famed Frank Pennink designed 18 hole **Palmares Golf** course on **Meia Praia** beach.

Just south of Lagos you can follow the coastal road towards Sagres starting from the fortress across several cliffs to and down the carved stone stair paths to reach some impressive beaches starting with the rather small **Praia do Pinhão** just west of town. The most dramatic sandy beaches are the beautiful rock coves at **Praia de Dona Ana** and **Praia do Camilo** which offer extremely photogenic swimming areas.

At the nearby seaside resort of **Ponta da Piedade** you can walk down

THE ALGARVE 389

near the lighthouse to view some beautiful sea caves and boulders which have been formed by the ocean's waves. If you prefer a larger and less dramatic sandy beach, you can go in the opposite direction to find **Meia Praia** just to the southeast of town.

NIGHTLIFE

A resort city this large tends to have lots of nightlife, and Lagos is certainly no exception. To start off your night you may wish to go to a good bar like **Roskos** on *Rua Candido dos Reis*, **Lords Tavern** on *Rua Antonio C. Santos*, or **Zanzibar** on *Rua 25 de Abril*.

After 11pm rolls around, you should head to one of the larger clubs like **Mullens** on *Rua Candido dos Reis*, or **Pheonix** on *Rua 5 de Outubro*.

ALVOR & THE COASTAL BEACHES

The hotel-packed resort area of **Alvor** l*ies some 17 km past Lagos off of route N-125 east*. Alvor itself is a nice little port town on the banks of the Alvor river estuary which contains the Manueline 16th century **Igreja Matriz** church, several old houses, a few cute streets, and a mixture of bars and restaurants serving the nearby tourist developments.

There is little else of interest here besides the nearby sports facilities including several fishing, waterskiing, and tennis facilities as well as the 9 and 18 hole Henry Cotton designed courses at the **Penina Golf Clube** and nearby **Alto Golf** complex. The hotels of the Alvor area attracts mostly bus groups to the massive hotels owned by the Salvor company, situated near the beaches of **Praia de Alvor** and **Praia dos Três Irmãos**, as well as several modern tower hotels, infamous timeshare properties, and massive English villa complexes of nearby **Praia Torralta**. Although these are nice beaches, you can certainly find nicer spots in other parts of the Algarve.

WHERE TO STAY

HOTEL ALVOR PRAIA, *Praia dos Três Irmãos, (082) 458-900. Expensive.*

A nice seaview 5 star resort hotel with 201 comfortable air conditioned rooms. Facilities include bar, restaurant, snackbar, pools, shops, nearby golf, tennis, billards, disco, sauna, TV, minibars, direct dial phones, and parking.

PENINA GOLF HOTEL, *Penina-Alvor, (082) 411-093. Expensive.*

A great 5 star golf resort and hotel a few km. away from town which offers 192 nice air conditione rooms, a bar, restaurant, shops, pool, golf courses, tennis, billards, children's park, babysitting, sauna, TV, minibars, gardens, and parking.

QUINTA NOVA, *Alvor, (082) 458-812. Moderate.*

One of the better large apartment and villa complexes which contains over 400 units with kitchens and TV. Facilities include market, car rental, pools, tennis, nearby golf.

HOTEL DOM JOÃO III, *Praia de Alvor, (082) 459-135. Moderate.*

A pretty good 4 star air conditioned family style hotel with 220 air conditioned rooms (many facing the sea). Facilities include bar, restaurant, snackbar, pools, billards, TV, nearby golf and tennis, direct dial phones, and parking.

CLUB ALVOR FERIAS, *Praia do Alvor, (082) 459-230. Moderate.*

A small complex of 1,2,and 3 bedroom apartments with kitchens. Facilities include bar, restaurant, pool, air conditioning, sauna, tennis, shops, billards, and parking.

TORRALTA APARTMENT TOWERS, *Praia do Alvor, (082) 459-211. Moderate.*

A massive complex of several unimpressive towers which offer hundreds of tourist apartments near the beach. Facilities include market, pools, and nearby golf.

HOTEL DELFIM, *Praia dos Três Irmãos, (082) 458-970. Moderate.*

A huge and somewhat tasteless group hotel which is just behind the Alvor Praia. I don't like this place but many people get stuck here. Facilities include bar, restaurant, pool, air conditioning, nearby golf and tennis, and parking.

PRAIA DA ROCHA

The long sandy beach and bustling resort area of **Praia da Rocha** *is situated about 7 km east of Alvor along the small unnamed coastline road at the edge of the bay of* **Portimão**. The heavily-developed town is centered on the wide beach and it's many colorful dramatic cliffs and searocks which are the most famous in the Algarve.

The town has become quite developed, and contains many hotels, clubs, and restaurants which line the *Ave. Tomas Cabreira* which seperates the town from the beach area. A nice walkway runs the width of town starting from the **Forteleza de Santa Catarina** fortress (now home to a Café and restaurant) and is laden with bars and small seaview cafes. The town maintains a steady year round flow of tourists of all ages from all over the world, many of which go to the **Casino de Alvor** which is actually here in Praia da Rocha.

The least crowded and most impressive beaches lies just west of town at **Praia do Vau**. This is a great place to relax, sunbath, and enjoy fine cuisine in all price ranges. If you are looking for a buzy and attractive resort area where all types of people gather, this is the place for you.

WHERE TO STAY

HOTEL ORIENTAL, *Ave. Tomas Cabreira, (082) 413-000. Expensive.*

A beautiful Moorish palace style 4 star hotel which offers 85 beautiful deluxe air conditioned apartments on a cliff just off the beach. Facilities include a bar, café, pool, billards, sauna, direct dial phones, and parking. Great service and views!

HOTEL BELA VISTA, *Ave. Tomas Cabreira, (082) 240-55. Expensive.*

A wonderful Moorish style mansion hotel just off the sea which is laden with fine antiques and azulejos. The hotel has 25 nice double rooms, a bar, and restaurant.

HOTEL ALGARVE, *Ave. Tomas Cabreira, (082) 415-001. Expensive.*

This deluxe seaview hotel hosts an older crowd in it's 220 balconied air conditioned rooms. Once the best hotel in town, it still offers great service. Facilities include bar, restaurant, minibars, pool, shops, beach, sauna, health club, tennis, and parking.

CASA TRÊS PALMEIRAS, *Praia do Vau, (082) 401-275. Moderate.*

A nice seaview country inn on a cliff which offers it's guests 5 comfortable guestrooms with private bathrooms, a bar, TV room, pool, garden, and parking.

HOTEL AVENIDA PRAIA, *Ave. Tomas Cabreira, (082) 417-740. Moderate.*

A comfortable and reasonably priced 3 star hotel across from the sea which offers 61 air conditioned double rooms with private bathrooms. Facilities include bar, disco, sun deck, and direct dial phones. Nothing special, but a good value.

APARTHOTEL PRESIDENTE, *Praia do Vau, (082) 417-507. Moderate.*

One of the best apartment-hotel complexes in the area. This modern hotel offers 107 seaview balconied 1 and 2 bedroom apartments with kitchens and TV next to a great beach. Facilities include bar, restaurant, shops, pool, tour desk, and parking.

PENSÃO SOLAR PENGUIM, *Rua António Feu, (082) 243-08. Inexpensive.*

A nice converted mansion on a cliff near the sea which offers 13 comfortable rooms with private bathrooms. Almost no facilities, but still a good choice.

CLUB PRAIA DA ROCHA, *Ave. das Com. Lusiadas, (082) 412-912. Moderate.*

A huge and relatively unappealing apartment complex which offers 600 or so 1 and 2 bedroom units with kitchens just outside of downtown. Facilities include bar, restaurant, shops, pool, tennis, squash, billards, babysitting, gym, and parking.

PENSÃO PRAIA DO VAU, *Praia do Vau, (082) 253-12. Inexpensive.*
A clean and comfortable 2 star basic inn not far from the sea with 21 double rooms with private bathrooms and minimal facilities. Nothing special, but good for budgets.

WHERE TO EAT

SAFARI, *Rua António Feu, (082) 235-40. Moderate.*
A great little seaview restaurant which specializes in fresh fish and regional cuisine with a somewhat African atmosphere. The outdoor terrace is the best in town.

DON PEPE, *Rua Eng. Fransisco Bivar, (082) 414-721. Moderate.*
This great Spanish restaurant in the Club Vila Rosa complex serves the best *paella* (Spanish rice and seafood) in all of the *Algarve*. A great place with good service!

FORTALEZA DE SANTA CATARINA, *Ave. Tomas Cabreira, (082) 220-66. Moderate.*
Located inside the walls of this old fort you will find a nice little seaview restaurant serving excellant seafood dishes at good prices. The ambiance is remarkable.

FU HUA, *Ave. Tomas Cabreira, (082) 852-05. Inexpensive.*
A small casual chinese restaurant in the Pimenta building which prepares pretty good Hunan style dishes with surprisingly friendly service.

RIO A VISTA, *Rua António Feu, (082) 251-95. Inexpensive.*
A pretty good casual Italian restaurant and pizzaria which prepares the best pizza in in town. I should mention that Portuguese pizza is a bit unusual, but it is still good.

NIGHTLIFE

The night starts off with drinks on the seafront cafes and bars, and then the crowds move on to **Bacchus** *off Ave. Marginal* and finally on to **Coconuts** *on Rua Bartolomeu* Diaz.

PORTIMÃO

A few km up from Praia da Rocha on route N-124 north is the huge city of **Portimão**. This bustling dynamic city rests at the mouth of a large bay formed by the **Arade** river and can trace its history as a fishing port to before the Roman era. The town is reliant on the its worldwide export of locally caught and canned sardine indusry, and has grown to become the largest city in the Algarve.

Signs of the city's origins are quite difficult to find since it was destroyed by the 1755 earthquake. The most picturesque part of town is it's harbourside off *Ave. Louis de Camões* where fishing boats unload their daily catch which is then transported the frantic **Lota** fish market. Several casual and inexpensive restaurants line the harbour and serve great grilled sandines to hungry residents and visitors alike on small outdoor tables.

There are a few other sights in town worth a quick peek at including the mosiac lined **Praça 1 de Dezembro** plaza, the 18th-century **Câmara Municipal** (town hall), and a couple of marble and gold laden churches. The only other activity I can recommend is the vast shopping possibilities here. The prices of most items are rather reasonable compared to stores in nearby resort areas. Portimão is home to many boutiques, shopping centers, antique shops, and a large monthly outdoor **mercado** (market) on the first Monday. Across the bay you can see the 16th-century **Fortaleza de São João** fort standing guard over the small sister city of **Ferragudo**.

WHERE TO STAY

HOTEL GLOBO, *Rua 5 de Outubro, 26, (082) 416-350. Moderate.*

A nice and friendly 3 star hotel a few blocks from the harbour offering 71 rooms with private bathrooms, a bar, restaurant, billards, disco, babysitting, TV, and parking.

VILA ROSA DE LIMA, *Portimão, (082) 411-097. Moderate.*

A nice rustic inn a few km. northwest of town off the *N-125* which offers 4 good guestrooms with private bathrooms, TV room, pool, gardens, and parking.

RESIDENCIAL MIRA-FOIA, *Rua V. Vaz de Vacas, 33, (082) 417-852. Moderate.*

A clean and comfortable inn located in the heart of town with 32 rooms with private bathrooms. Facilities include bar, minibars, TV, direct dial phones, and parking.

RESIDENCIAL O PATIO, *Rua Dr. J. V. Mealha, 3, (082) 242-88. Inexpensive.*

A cute little 2 star inn near the *Turismo* offering 17 guestrooms with private bathroom in a tranquil atmosphere. A great budget selection with few facilities.

WHERE TO EAT

AVOZINHA, *Rua do Capote, 7, (082) 229-22. Moderate.*

An excellant award winning seafood restaurant serving the finest *cataplana* (seafood stew) I have ever had in the area. Reservations are recommended.

FLÔR DE SARDINHA, *Cais de Lota, (082) 248-62. Inexpensive.*

A nice and simple outdoor fish restaurant near the harbour and fish market which serves some of the best grilled sardines you can imagine. Very casual atmosphere.

MONCHIQUE

Set within the rainy wooded **Serra de Monchique** volcanic mountains *23 km up from Portimão on route N-266 north* is the busy market town of **Monchique**. This pretty little camilla-laden town is well known for it's spicy *presunto* hams and the strong eucalyptus oils which are locally pressed.

In the town itself there are few sights worth noting besides the beautiful portal and azulejos covered interior of the 16th century Manueline **Igreja Matriz** church and the crumbling ruins of the 17th century **Mosterio de Nossa Senhora do Desterro** monastery. The most impressive sights around town are the views from nearby mountain peaks from which you can see all the way down the western Algarve coastline. The best of these dramatic lookouts is the 2960 foot high peak at **Monte Foia** mountain, *reached by taking route N-266-3 west for a few km past cork, pine, and eucalyptus forests.*

On the way back to the coast you will first pass through the old spa town of **Caldas de Monchique**. It is here that the hot volcanic nascentes termais (thermal waters) from the mountains spring up and are utilized and bottled by the local **Termas das Caldas de Monchique** spa (open June through October). Many people including former kings have bathed in the heavy mineral waters of this town to relieve rheumatism and digestive tract problems. The town's main square is dominated by several old buildings including a former casino, now home to a wonderful handicrafts center which sells everything from pottery and hand made fabrics to the strong locally made brandy. The town is quite pleasant, and long walks around the flower covered outskirts of town can be quite enjoyable.

WHERE TO STAY

ESTALAGEM ABRIGO DA MONTANHA, *Estrada da Foia, (082) 921-31. Moderate.*

A great little 4 star inn on the *Foia* road which offers several nice rooms with private bathroom and views. Facilities include bar, restaurant, pool, gardens, and parking.

ALBERGAIA DO LAGEADO, *Caldas de Monchique, (082) 926-16. Moderate.*

A comfortable inn near the center of town which offers 20 good rooms with private bathrooms. Facilities include bar, restaurant, gardens, pool, and parking.

ESTALAGEM MON-CICUS, *Estrada de Foia, (082) 926-50. Moderate.*

THE ALGARVE 395

A pretty and pleasant 3 star inn which has 10 comfortable rooms with private bathroom. Facilities include bar, restaurant, sauna, gardens, and parking.

PENSÃO BICA-BOA, *Rua da Saboia-Foia, (082) 922-71. Inexpensive.*

A friendly little inn and restaurant which has 6 rooms both with and without private bathroom. Facilities include TV room, splash pool, gardens, and parking.

WHERE TO EAT

TERESHINA, *Estrada da Foia, (082) 923-92. Moderate.*

A wonderful regional restaurant offering supurb meat and fish specialities served both in their dining room and on a nice patio. The views are also great here!

RESTAURANTE CENTRAL, *Caldas de Monchique, (082) 922-03. Moderate.*

An atmospheric restaurant which serves several good regional dishes including the locally made *presunto* ham. The prices are good, but don't expect great service.

RESTAURANTE CHARETTE, *Rua Samora Gil, no phone. Inexpensive.*

A simple and unpretentious restaurant in the heart of town which offers large portions of pretty good local dishes at remarkably affordable prices.

PARAISO DA MONTAHA, *Estrada da Foia, (082) 921-50. Inexpensive.*

A large regional restaurant serving roasted meat and chicken specials. Try the spicy piri-piri chicken with a half bottle of house wine. Expect a short line on weekends.

SILVES

The beautiful and historic walled city of **Silves** *can be reached from Monchique by taking route N-266 south for about 15 km and connecting to route N-124 east for another 10 km or so.* The town stands at the confluence of the Odelouca and Arade rivers and was once the important Moorish stronghold and rich region capital called Xelb until it was savagely attacted by the the Crusaders in 1189 and finally conquered in the 13th century.

The town is dominated by a wonderfully restored Moorish **castelo** (castle) surrounded by a ring of massive crenellated sandstone towers and defensive walls. Now the walls have been converted into a wonderful panoramic walkway and incircle a tranquil garden which rests above 2 large cisterns.

Below the castle you can enter the town to view the Gothic 13th century **Sé da Santa Maria** cathedral which was constructed on the sight of an important Moorish mosque. The interior of the cathedral still contains a few original Mosque vestiges as well as several tombs of the Crusaders, while its exterior is laden with Gothic towers and gargoyles. At one point the body of King Dom João II was buried here as well, but was later moved to the monastery at Batalha. Silves is also home to the **Museu Arqueológico** museum (closed on Sundays) on *Rua das Portas de Loulé* which offers visitors a great collection of prehistoric, Arabic, and early Portuguese artifacts.

The town also contains a busy little daily produce **mercado** (market) just off the riverfront a few blocks west of the ancient bridge which is a great place to pick up supplies for local picnics (closed on Sundays). On the riverfront itself you will find several small outdoor restaurants offering grilled fish.

As you depart the city *you can head towards the edge of town on route N-124 east* and take a peek at the 16th century carved **Cruz de Portugal** cross. Each June the amusing **Festa do Cerveja do Silves** national beer festival takes over the castle and can be heard from miles around. It is a great chance to experience the microbreweries' products which are hard to find in normal shops.

WHERE TO STAY

QUINTA DA FIUEIRINHA, *Silves, (082) 442-671. Moderate.*

A nice rustic farming estate and country inn a few km. east of town which offers it's guests 3 comfortable apartments (a 1 bedroom and two 3 bedroom) with kitchens in a tranquil setting of fruit trees and flowers. Facilities include pool, and parking.

ALBERGARIA SOLAR DOS MOUROS, *Horta do Porchino Santo, (082) 443-106. Moderate.*

A clean and comfortable inn with 22 guestrooms with private bathrooms. Facilities include a bar, restaurant, air conditioning, direct dial phones, TV, and parking.

RESIDENCIAL SOUSA, *Rua Samora Barros, 17, (082) 442-502. Inexpensive.*

A clean and basic inn near the heart of town which offers several decent rooms with private bathrooms, heating, TV room, breakfast room, and nearby parking.

WHERE TO EAT

MARISQUEIRA RUI, *Rua Com. Vilarhino, (082) 442-682. Moderate.*

The most famous seafood restaurant in this part of the *Algarve*. Altough this simple restaurant becomes packed during lunch and dinner, it's worth the wait.

THE ALGARVE 397

CARVOEIRO

The heavily developed cliffside beach town of **Carvoeiro** rests on the seafront *some 10 km south of Silves on route N-124 -1 south via the wine producing town of* **Lagoa**. Carvoeiro has somehow managed to save a small amount of its former fishing village ambiance despite continual overbuilding of villas, condos, timeshare complexes, and resorts. It is the small sandy **Praia do Carvoeiro** beach and the adjacent cliffs and sea cave-laden beaches around the town that attract hundreds of tourists here daily to sunbath, swim, and start fishing excursions.

The town itself fans out from it's relaxing beachfront **Largo da Praia** plaza and leads up several streets lined with cafes, bars, and ice cream parlors. I really like the laid-back ambiance here, and I come here often in the months of May and June before the beach becomes a zoo. The town also boasts two great golf areas including the Ron Fream designed **Quinta do Gramacho** 18 hole golf course at the **Carvoeiro Country Club**, and the Dave Thomas designed 18 hole course at **Vale de Milho**.

Just 2 km east of town off the coastal road you can visit the beautiful **Algar Seco** sea rock formations and rock carved step pathway to it's caverns and wave pounded caves which are truely dramatic. The area is the sight of lots of boat excursions to beaches which are inaccesible by land, so the police suspect drug smugglers operate here often. Your car may very well be stopped by heavily armed police with drug sniffing dogs on your way out of town.

WHERE TO STAY

HOTEL ALMANSOR, *Vale Corvo-Carvoeiro, (082) 358-026. Expensive.*

A huge seaview 4 star resort hotel which was built on the side of a cliff just outside of town. This big modern hotel offers 293 nice air conditioned rooms (many with seaviews and balconies) . Facilities include bar, restaurants, coffee shops, pool, beach, billards, game room, minibars, TV, tennis, nearby golf, and parking.

APARTMENTOS CRISTAL, *Carvoeiro, (082) 358-601. Expensive.*

One of the best apartment hotel complexes in the area offering 100 air conditioned apartments near the sea with kitchens and TV. Facilities include bar, restaurant, shops, pool, tennis, billards, sauna, babysitting, minibars, nearby golf, and parking.

HOTEL DOM SANCHO, *Largo da Praia Carvoeiro, (082) 357-301. Moderate.*

A friendly 4 star beachview hotel in the main square of town. The 51 comfortable air conditioned rooms make this small hotel a real winner. Facilities include bar, restaurant, pools, terrace, minibars, TV, beach, nearby golf, and lots of parking.

APARTMENTOS SOLFERIAS, *Sitio do Mato Serrão, (082) 357-403. Moderate.*

A good 4 star apartment hotel near both the beach and town. Seveal dozen comfortable air-conditioned apartments (some can accommodate up to 8 people). Bar, restaurant, pools, terrace, minibars, TV, beach, tennis, billiards, safe deposit boxes, gardens, nearby golf, parking.

WHERE TO EAT

RESTAURANTE TEODOROS, *Rampa da Encarnado, (082) 357-864. Moderate.*

A beautiful seaview restaurant which offers fine seafood dishes and great service in an artistic air conditioned setting above the sea. Ask for a table on the patio.

ARMAÇÃO DE PERA

The resort town and fishing village of **Armação de Pêra** lies *15 km away from Carvoeiro just off route N-125 east.* The long sandy beach here is said to be the largest in the Algarve and has a nice walkway. Unfortunately, every inch of seafront seems to have a resort or villa built above it.

The best advice I can offer is to travel to the less crowded beaches west of town like **Praia Senhora da Rocha** near the village of **Alporchinos**, or a bit further west at **Praia Marinha**.

WHERE TO STAY

VILA LARA, *Praia Senhora da Rocha, (082) 314-910. Expensive.*

This is without any doubt the most deluxe resort in the *Algarve.* The hotel offers 86 luxury air conditioned suites high above the sea. Facilities include bar, gourmet restaurant, spa, pools, private beach, tennis, gardens, and the finest service around.

VILA VITA PARC, *Alporchinos, (082) 313-068. Expensive.*

A deluxe German owned luxury resort community of villas and apartments near the sea. Facilities include bar, restaurants, pool, tennis, TV, nearby golf, and parking.

HOTEL VIKING, *Praia Senhora da Rocha, (082) 314-876. Expensive.*

A modern seafront 4 star resort hotel with 184 large and comfortable air conditioned rooms (many with seaview and balconies). Facilities include bar, restaurant, pools, sauna, health club, beach, billards, TV, minibars, direct dial phones, and parking.

HOTEL GARBE, *Ave. Marginal, (082) 312-187. Expensive.*

Once the best hotel in the area, this large 140 air conditioned room hotel attracts an older crowd. Facilities include bar, restaurant, pool, beach, TV, and parking.

CASA DE BELA MOURA, *Alporchinos, (082) 313-422. Moderate.*
A country inn style hotel which offers 8 nice rooms with private bathrooms. Facilities include bar, patio with barbeque, TV room, pool, sundeck, gardens, and parking.

VILA SENHORA DA ROCHA, *Praia Senhora da Rocha, (082) 312-349. Moderate.*
A pretty nice clifftop complex which rents 1,2, and 3 bedroom apartments and villas near the sea. Facilities include bar, restaurant, pools, tennis, and parking.

PENSÃO CIMAR, *Rua das Redes, 10, (082) 312-171. Inexpensive.*
A clean and comfortable inn which rents 22 double guestrooms with private bathrooms. Facilities include bar, TV room, direct dial phones, and parking.

ALBUFEIRA

The beachfront resort city and party town of **Albufeira** is nestled within several small hills *about 16 km away from Armação de Pêra off route N-125 east*. When my single friends ask me for the most outrageous place in Europe to spend their summer vacation, I send them here.

The town was first inhabited by the Romans who called the town Baltum, soon after the Moors arrived here and built defensive fortresses it was renamed to *Al-Buhena* (the castle of the sea) and finally it was captured by the Christians in 1191 and renamed slightly to Albufeira. Most of town's historical buildings were devastated by the 1755 earthquake and the huge tidal waves which followed it. The city still contains many winding mosaic lined roads, whitewashed buildings, and stone cut stairways who's design can certainly be attributed to the city's former Moorish roots.

In the early 1960's, Albufeira was discovered again, this time by English and German tourists in search of an inexpensive resort area to develop in southern Europe. This was the beginning of what eventually would turn the Algarve into the major destination for tourism in Portugal

WHERE TO STAY

PINE CLIFFS RESORT, *Praia da Falésia , (089) 501-999. Expensive.*
A uniquely deluxe and friendly large 5 star seaside Sheraton resort hotel near *Albufeira* offering 215 luxurious air conditioned rooms (many with seaviews). Facilities include bars, restaurants, pools, golf, tennis, health club, and parking.

VILA JOYA, *Praia da Galé , (089) 591-839. Expensive.*
A wonderful deluxe German operated exclusive seaview inn with 13 of the most increadable rooms you can imagine. Facilities include bar,

gourmet restaurant, air conditioning, pool, sundeck, nearby golf and horses, terraces, beach, and parking.

HOTEL SOL E MAR, *Rua José B. de Sousa, (089) 586-721. Expensive.*

The only hotel right above the town beach. This 4 star property may be the finest downtown property with views from many of it's 74 rooms. Facilities include bar, restaurant, babysitting, air conditioning, TV direct dial phones, and parking.

HOTEL CERRO ALAGOA, *Via Rapida, (089) 588-261. Moderate.*

A large and modern 4 star hotel minutes from the beach with 310 comfortable air conditioned rooms with balconies. Facilities include bar, restaurants, pool, sauna, beach bus, billards, cable TV, minibars, safe, shops, health club, and parking.

CLUB MED (DA BALAIA), *Praia Maria Luisa, (089) 586-681. Expensive.*

This all inclusive resort offers it's combination of single and married clients 320 air conditioned rooms near the sea. No minimum length of stay is required. Facilities include bars, restaurants, pool, golf, tennis, archery, windsurfing, and parking.

FALESIAHOTEL, *Praia da Falésia, (089) 501-237. Moderate.*

A modern 4 star hotel near the sea with 169 air conditioned rooms with balconies. Facilities include bar, restaurant, pools, sauna, tennis, beach bus, TV, and parking.

HOTEL MONTECHORO, *Rua Dr. F. S. Carneiro, (089) 589-423. Moderate.*

A huge 4 star resort hotel with 362 large air conditioned rooms (many with balconies) just a few minutes inland from the heart of town in the *Montechoro* area. Facilities include bars, restaurants, pools, sauna, squash, tennis, TV, and parking.

ESTALAGEM DO CERRO, *Rua B-Cerro da Piedade, (089) 586-191. Moderate.*

A nice inn a few minutes from town in the *Cerro da Piedade* with 85 clean and comfortable rooms with private bathrooms. Facilities include bar, restaurant, pool, sauna, health club, TV, kitchens, and parking.

APARTAMENTOS PATIO DA ALDEIA, *Areias de São João, (089) 589-231. Moderate.*

One of the best small apartment complexes in town. The hotel offers 70 garden apartments and villas with kitchens in a quiet location not far from the beach. Facilities include bar, pool, gym, air conditioning, direct dial phones, and parking.

APARTHOTEL ALMAR, *Cerro de Alagoa, (089) 586-265. Moderate.*

A comfortable apartment complex near the edge of town with 44 studio and 1 bedroom terrace apartments with kitchens, bar, watersports, pools, and parking.

ALFAGAR, *Semina, (089) 514-960. Inexpensive.*
This 210 room apartment complex a few minutes out of town near *Praia do Santo Elalia* beach offers comfortable accomodations above the seacliffs. Facilities include bar, restaurant, pools, market, billards, tennis, TV, beach bus, and parking.
  CLUB PRAIA DA OURA, *Praia da Oura, (089) 589-135. Moderate.*
A massive and ugly 579 room time share apartment hotel near the beach that is filled to the brim with English tourists. I don't really like this place very much.
  PENSÃO ALBUFEIRENSE, *Rua da Liberdade,18, (089) 512-079. Inexpensive.*
A modern and clean 2 star inn with 20 or so guestrooms with private bathrooms. One of the few decent cheap establishment in the center town. Nothing special.
  RESIDENCIAL LIMAS, *Rua da Liberdade, 27, (089) 514-025. Inexpensive.*
A reasonably nice and well located 3 star inn near the heart of town. The 11 rooms come either with or without private bathrooms and are a real bargain. No facilities.
  PENSÃO RESTAURANTE SILVA, *Travessa 5 de Outubro,18, (089) 512-669. Inexpensive.*
A 6 room inn with clean and basic rooms with and without private bathroom.

WHERE TO EAT

  A RUINHA, *Largo Cais Herculano, (089) 512-094. Expensive.*
A multilevel regional seafood restaurant in an old atmospheric building near the sea with several dining areas both indoors and outside. Excellant fresh fish dishes.
  CABAZ DA PRAIA, *Praça Miguel Bombarda, (089) 512-173. Expensive.*
A nice Portuguese restaurant serving regional cuisine with a wonderful patio above the beach. The large menu includes many unusual meat and seafood dishes.
  RESTAURANTE O TÚNEL, *Rua 5 de Outubro, 6, (089) 514-184. Moderate.*
A nice little casual restaurant near the *Turismo* which serves seafood and meat specials in a friendly setting. Try the *cataplana* here, it's enough for 2 people.
  MINAR, *Travessa Cais Herculano, (089) 513-196. Moderate.*
A great little Indian tandoori restaurant near the fisherman's beach which offers a vast assortment of traditional Indian food which ranges from mild to extremely hot.

SEEING THE SIGHTS

To begin with, the town centers around a large and active square known as the **Largo Eng. Duarte Pacheco** which is surrounded by cafes, pubs, gift shops, and restuarants. A series of little arched lanes and atmospheric streets merge off this square and are all worth strolling along. From the edge of this square you can walk two blocks west to intersect with the main street through the town called *Rua 5 de Outubro* which boasts several eating establishments, gift shops, boutiques, bars, and the *Turismo*.

As you walk south on this main street you will come to a tunnel which leads directly under the **Praça da República** square and on to the large cliff bordered **Praia de Albufeira** town beach. On hot summer days, as many as 15,000 people can be seen packed closely together (many are half naked) in persuit of each other's attention at this beach. There are a few dozen motorized fishing boats that continue to utilize the **Praia dos Barcos** and **Praia dos Pescadores** fishermen's beaches off the **Largo Cais Herculano** plaza on the eastern end of the town for their landings.

While the fishing industry still makes a contribution to the local economy via the large fish **mercado** (market) just above their beach, I would hesitate to describe this city as a fishing village. The town offers a few specific sights worth peeking at including ruins of its Moorish **castelo** (castle) behind the city, the lovely 16th century Manueline **Igreja Matriz** church off the *Rua Miguel Bombarda*, the seemingly fortified **Câmara Municipal** (town hall) near the beach off *Rua Bernardo de Sousa*, and the remaining sections of the **Vila Velha** (old town) which can be seen off the *Rua do Cemiteiro Velha*. I should warn you about the obnoxious hard selling time share salesmen who hawk their free gift offers around town if you spend an hour at one of those presentations. Don't fall into their trap!

Since the municipality of Albufeira extends for several km along the coastline and inland, many local beaches and hotels are actually not in the town center itself. The closest sub-sections of town are just minutes away and consist of areas such as **Areias de São João, Cerro de Alagoa, Montechoro, Paia da Oura, Sesmarias, Semina,** and **Cerro da Piedade**. To the west of town you can visit the less crowded rock cove beach areas of **Praia de São Rafael, Praia do Castelo,** and **Praia da Galé**. To the east of town you can visit several other beaches such as the over developed **Praia da Oura, Praia Maria Luisa,** and **Praia do Balaia**, the quaint fishing beach at **Olhos d'Agua**, or the long sandy beach of **Praia da Falésia** . In this general area you will find several sports and family activitiy facilities including water parks, tennis complexes, and the Pine Cliffs' 9 hole golf course designed by Martin Hawtree.

THE ALGARVE 403

NIGHTLIFE

Since Albufeira is the biggest party town in the Algarve, its aggresive nightlife scene is rather varied and a big part of the town's appeal to younger tourists. The drinking starts at the beginning of sunset when several of the bars on the main **Largo Eng. Duarte Pacheco** like the famous **Sir Harry's** offer live music and happy hours.

As the night wears on, several more downtown bars such as the **Zanzibar** *on Rua Miguel Bombarda*, the **Classic Bar** *on Rua Candido dos Reis*, and **Steps Bar** *on Rua J.P. Samora* are also worth a try. The action really picks up after 11pm when thousands of well-dressed nightcrawlers hop over to the multifloored **Kiss Disco** in the Montechoro area, **Silvia's Disco** on **Rua São Gonçalo de Lagos**, and **Club 7 1/2** *off Largo Cais Herculano*. All offer drinking and dancing with somewhat reasonble cover charges until 4am.

VILAMOURA

The modern sporting resort of **Vilamoura** *located about 24 km away from Albufeira off route N-125 east*. This impressive small city is centered around its golf courses and extensive marina which is lined with waterview cafes, boutiques, and restaurants which tend to cater to a more upscale and middle aged clientelle.

Designed in the 1970's and financed by rich multinational oil companies, Vilamoura contains several large 9 and 18 hole golf courses designed by Frank Pennink, Robert Trent Jones, and Joseph Lee. The town boasts several other entertainment and sports attractions including the **Vilamoura Casino**, tennis courts, a horse riding center, fishing outfitters, cinemas, and nightclubs. Here you can find a full range of accomodations which look out over the golf courses or the yachts and adjacent long sandy beaches.

On the northeast edge of town a Roman village known as **Cerro da Vial** has been excavated. The ruins can be viewed on site, and at the local **Museu de Cerro da Vial** museum. I like this town alot, but it is completely artificial by nature. This is a good place to spend your vacation in a civilized resort, and is located close enough to day trip to every part of the Algarve. The nearby overbuilt city of **Quarteira** offers little of interest besides it's Wednesday regional **mercado** (market) off Rua Vasco da Gama, and the seaview prominade adjacent to Ave. Infante Sagres.

WHERE TO STAY

VILAMOURA MARINOTEL, *Vilamoura Marina, (089) 389-988. Expensive.*

A serious marble laden 5 star deluxe business style 5 star hotel in front of the town's marina. The 385 air conditioned rooms (many are sea view) offer superb comfort. Facilities include bars, gourmet restaurants, shops, pool, sauna, sundeck, health club, nearby tennis and golf, minibars, direct dial phones, TV, and lots of parking.

HOTEL ATLANTIS, *Vilamoura Beach, (089) 389-977. Expensive.*

A good resort hotel near the beach which offers 313 comfortable rooms, bars, restaurants, air conditioning, pools, sundeck, beach, health club, nearby golf and tennis, sauna, shops, TV, handicapped facilities, diect dial phones, and parking.

HOTEL DOM PEDRO, *Vilamoura, (089) 389-650. Expensive.*

A pretty good 4 star hotel not far from the beach which is starting to show signs of aging. Facilities in this 261 room hotel include bar, restaurants, air conditioning, pools, sundeck, nearby golf and tennis, sauna, billards, squash, TV, and parking.

HOTEL AMPALIUS, *Vilamoura Beach, (089) 388-008. Moderate.*

A wonderfully friendly family style 4 star hotel on the beach which offers 357 large air conditioned seaview rooms. Facilities include bar, restaurants, pools, health club, nearby golf and tennis, beach, childrens park, shops, TV, minibars, and parking.

ALDEIA DO MAR, *Vilamoura, (089) 302-635. Moderate.*

A nice villa and apartment complex in the heart of town which offers 70 villas and 192 apartments with kitchens which sleep up to 6.. Facilities include bar, restaurant, pools, shops, nearby golf and tennis, TV, handicapped facilities, and parking.

ESTALAGEM DA CEGONHA, *Vilamoura, (089) 302-577. Moderate.*

A nice old 4 star inn near the horse riding center with 10 comfortable rooms. Facilities include bar, restaurant, pool, horse riding, nearby golf, and parking.

MOTEL DO GOLF, *Vilamoura Golf Course, (089) 302-092. Moderate.*

A warm and friendly motel on the golf course which can use a bit of renovation. Facilities include bar, restaurant, pool, sundeck, air conditioning, and parking.

PENSÃO MIRAMAR, *Rua G. Velho, 8-Quarteira, (089) 315-225. Inexpensive.*

A resonably good 3 star inn near the heart of *Quarteira* which offers 18 guestrooms with private bathrooms. No real facilities besides it's breakfast room.

WHERE TO EAT

A MARGARIDA, *Vilamoura Marina, (089) 312-168. Moderate.*

A great marina view restaurant serving fine fresh meat and seafood dishes by a staff of friendly English speaking waiters. Try the grilled espadarte (swordfish).

RESTAURANTE CANTON, *Vilamoura, (089) 314-772. Moderate.*
This casual Chinese restaurant near the cinema offers good Cantonese cuisine at great prices. Lets face it, we all need a break from local cuisine sometimes.

VILAMOURA

LOULÉ

The fascinating market town of **Loulé** *lies some 13 km northeast of Vilamoura on route N-396 north.* The town offers several enchanting sights to visit including the defensive walls and towers of a large medieval Moorish **castelo** (castle).

These days the castle walls have been converted into a great panoramic walking path which surrounds the small **Museu Municipal** museum of local art and artifacts (closed on Mondays). Nearby the castle you should visit the 12th-century Gothic **Igreja Matriz** church which contains wonderful altars, and fine azulejos. There are also several charming streets throughout town which are full of cafes and local craftsmen semmingly hard at work.

The best time to visit Loulé is during the huge weekly regional **mercado** (market) on Saturdays until midnight. Although you may get stuck in some serious traffic, a trip to the Algarve is simply incomplete without an excursion here on Saturday. Loulé celebrates the annual **Carnival** in late February with a variety of parades and costume parties.

WHERE TO STAY

QUINTA DA VAREZA, *Querenca-Loulé , (089) 414-443. Moderate.*

A charming country inn on a tranquil farming estate about 10 km. north of Loulé which offers 9 nice guestrooms with private bathrooms. Facilities include bar, pool, tennis, billards, horse riding, gardens, library, winery, jeep safaris, and parking.

HOTEL LOULÉ JARDIM, *Praça Manuel Arriaga, (089) 413-096. Moderate.*

A nice and well located 3 star hotel with 52 comfortable rooms. Facilities include bar, pool, air conditioning, TV, direct dial phones, and parking.

PENSÃO IBERICA, *Ave. Marcal Pacheco, 157, (089) 414-100. Inexpensive.*

A clean and comfortable 3 star basic inn with over 40 good guestrooms with private bathrooms. Facilities include breakfast room, TV room, and parking.

WHERE TO EAT

O AVENIDA, *Ave. J. da Costa Mealha, (089) 621-06. Moderate.*

A great little regional restaurant in the heart of town, offering simple but delicious meat and fish plates at reasonable prices. The place gets packed on market days.

ALMANCIL & THE GOLF RESORTS

The quiet town of **Almancil** *can be reached from Loulé by taking route N-125-4 south for about 7 km before connecting to route N-125 west for another 4 km.* The town itself offers little of interest besides a few charming crafts shops and good restaurants. Just east of the town you can visit the remarkable Romanesque **Igreja de São Lourenço** church, which features incredibly ornate 18th-century *azulejos* created by Policarpo de Oliviera Bernardes, son of the master craftsman António de Oliveira Bernardes whose famous work adorns the churches of Évora and Barcelos.

The reason most people come through this village is to gain access to several major resort areas which are nearby. The most famous of these local hotspots are the **Vale do Lobo** and **Quinta do Lago** golf and tennis resorts just south of town near the seashore. These well-marketed areas are packed with upscale British, German, and Scandinavian vacationers who wish to be among other older and wealthy tourists and sports enthusiasts.

Golfing here is serious business, and most of these oceanview courses are more expensive than their equivilant would be back at home. Among the most famous of theses courses are the seaview 9 hole courses at **Vale** de Lobo Golf which were designed by Henry Cotton, and the several tranquil 9 hole William Mitchell and Joe Lee desinged courses at **Quinta do Lago Golf** and **San Lorenzo Golf.**

There are also several sand dune beaches, a large tennis center, and a horse riding complex in the vacinity. The hotels, villas, and apartment complexes in these resorts are almost all deluxe and extremely exclusive. Many seasonal inhabitants own their own villas, and you can see the Porches and Ferraris slipping past heavily secured driveways.

WHERE TO STAY

HOTEL QUINTA DO LAGO, *Quinta do Lago, (089) 396-666. Expensive.*

A deluxe 141 room 5 star hotel and golf resort which attracts a middle aged upscale clientelle who want serious accomodations with golf facilities near the beach. Facilities include bars, restaurants, pool, sauna, terrace, nearby private beach, golf, health club, air conditioning, shops, minibars, billards, TV, and lots of parking.

HOTEL DONA FILIPA, *Vale do Lobo, (089) 394-141. Expensive.*

An exclusive 5 star golf and tennis resort just off the beach. This is another deluxe property which offers 147 balconied and air conditioned rooms, bar, restaurants, pool, terrace, golf, tennis, beach, shops, babysitting, TV, minibars, and parking.

VALE DO LOBO VILLAS, *Vale do Lobo, (089) 393-939. Expensive.*

An impressive resort community of 1000 apartments and private villas with kitchens and TV set among the hills near the area golf courses. Facilities include maid service, bar, restaurants, pools, sauna, tennis, golf, health club, shops, and parking.

QUINTA DAS ROCHAS, *Almancil, (089) 393-165. Moderate.*

A wonderful bed and breakfast inn with 6 spacious rooms with private bathrooms and cable TV not far from the sea. Facilities include bar, bicycles, and parking.

DUNAS DOURADAS VILLAS, *Almancil, (089) 396-297. Moderate.*

A deluxe and tranquil small complex of luxury 2 and 3 bedroom townhouse apartments and independant villas. Facilities include bar, restaurant, pools, tennis, nearby health club and golf, shops, private beach, front desk, TV, and parking.

VILAR DO GOLF, *Quinta do Lago, (089) 396-615. Moderate.*

An English operated villa and apartment complex; 180 apartments and villas.Bar, restaurant, pools, tennis, golf, shops, and parking.

VALE DE GARRÃO, *Almancil, (089) 394-593. Moderate.*

A 4 star apartment and villa complex near the golfing areas which offers 103 apartments and villas. Facilities include bar, restaurant, pool, tennis, and parking.

PENSÃO SANTA TERESA, *Rua do Comércio,13, (089) 395-525. Inexpensive.*

This clean and comfortable downtown *Almancil* 3 star inn has just about the only budget accomodations in the area. They have 22 rooms with private bathroom.

WHERE TO EAT

O TRADICIONAL, *Almancil, (089) 399-093. Moderate.*

A converted old farmhouse which now offers great French-Portuguese cuisine in a casual country setting. A great spot to have dinner after a long day of golf.

PEQUENO MUNDO, *Almancil, (089) 399-866. Moderate.*

A cute and highly atmospheric restaurant serving international cuisine in an antique laden old house. The English and Portuguese chefs prepare fine dinners.

FARO

Faro, the waterfront capital city of the Algarve region, *is located 13 km away from Almancil on route N-125 east.* As the home of southern Portugal's international airport, this remarkable city is seldom visited by the thousands of daily arrivals which tend to immediately depart towards the more fashioable resort areas.

This large city was in Moorish hands until its capture in 1249 by King Dom Afonso III and his Christian forces. Many of Faro's original structures were destroyed by the massive earthquake in 1755 but several historic sights are still standing throughout the old sections of town.

WHERE TO STAY

LA RESERVE, *Santa Bárbara de Nexe, (089) 904-74. Expensive.*

An exclusive and extremely deluxe apartment hotel about 15 km. northwest of *Faro* off *route N-125 west* which offers 20 double air conditioned seaview suites, bar, gourmet restaurant, pool, tennis, shops, minibars, TV, and parking.

HOTEL EVA, *Ave. de República, (089) 803-354. Moderate.*

A modern seaview air conditioned 4 star hotel with 150 rooms. Facilities include disco, piano bar, restaurant, rooftop pools, TV, direct dial phones, and parking.

CASA DE LUMENA, *Praça Alexandre Hurculano, (089) 801-990. Moderate.*

A charming old mansion which offers 12 nice guestrooms with private bathrooms in the heart of town. Facilities include bar, restaurant, and nearby parking.

THE ALGARVE 409

HOTEL FARO, *Praça Francisco Gomes, (089) 803-276. Moderate.*
A large 3 star harbourfront hotel which offers 52 reasonable rooms. Facilities include bar, restaurant, terrace, air conditioning, direct dial phones, and parking.

ESTALAGEM AEROMAR, *Praia de Faro, (089) 817-542. Moderate.*
A nice seaview 4 star inn with 23 good rooms on *Faro's* beach island. Facilities include bar, restaurant, shops, billards, TV room, direct dial phones, and parking.

PENSÃO O FARÃO, *Largo da Madelena, 4, (089) 823-356. Inexpensive.*
A nice and centrally located 3 star inn with 30 rooms with private bathrooms. Bar, restaurant, TV room, terrace, and telephones.

APARTMENTOS VITORIA, *Rua Serpa Pinto, 58, (089) 806-583. Inexpensive.*
A nice and modest apartment building in the heart of the city which offers 12 clean and basic 1 bedroom apartments with kitchens. No facilities but close to everything.

PENSÃO MADELENA, *Rua Consel. Bivar, 109, (089) 805-806. Inexpensive.*
A clean and basic 2 star inn located in the heart of town with 20 or so guestrooms with and without private bathroom. Not a bad choice but nothing special.

WHERE TO EAT

CIDADE VELHA, *Rua Domingos Guiero, (089) 271-45. Expensive.*
A wonderful French influenced Portuguese resturant in a historic building in the old section of town. The meat and fish dishes here are among the best in the Algarve.

DOS IRMÃOS, *Largo Terrio do Bispo, 13, (089) 823-337. Moderate.*
A well established seafood restaurant specializing in regional fish meals cooked to perfection. The ambiance here is old world, and they have a massive menu.

SEEING THE SIGHTS

Upon arriving in the city you will find that parking near the **Doca de Recreio** (docks) is an easy task. To begin your walking tour of Faro, I suggest starting at the dockfront and garden bordered **Praça D. Fransisco Gomes** plaza. As you walk through the **Jardim Manuel Bivar** gardens, you can have a quick refresing drink at one of the small outdoor cafes. As you leave the southern end of the garden you should first stop off at the *Turismo* just off the corner of *Rua da Misericórdia* and pick up a free city map of attractions.

A few steps back down from the *Turismo* is the 18th-century **Arco da Vila** town gate which leads to the *Rua do Municipo* and into the **Cidade**

Velha (old town) section of Faro. As you enter the old walled area you will soon find yourself at the **Largo da Sé** plaza which is dominated by the ancient **Sé** cathedral. This beautiful *azulejos*-filled cathedral was built on the sight of the city's former mosque and rebuilt once again after the 1755 earthquake damaged it severely.

Directly across the plaza you can also view the ornate 18th-century **Paço Episcopal** (bishop's palace) which backs onto the medieval ramparts of the old town. Behind the Sé you can walk down *Rua Dominingos Guieiro* to reach the **Praça Afonso III** where the 16th century **Convento de Nossa Senhora da Assuncão** whose cloisters have become home to the town's **Museu Arqueológico e Lapidar Infante Dom Henrique** museum. This rather unusual archaeology museum (closed on Saturdays and Sundays) contains local Roman and Moorish artifacts, as well as fine paintings and azulejos. In the convent's chapel there are additional collections of sculptures and antique furnishings. After strolling down the stone lanes of this part of the city you can depart via the waterview **Arco da Porta Nova** town gate and follow the *Rua Com. Francisco Manuel* back to the dockside gardens.

There are several more worthwhile sights scattered around the city. Follow the *Rua D. Francisco Gomes* from the northern end of the garden until it merges with the boutique laden *Rua de Santo António*, the city's main commercial street. From this street you should turn right onto *Rua Pe da Cruz* to enter the **Museu de Etnografia Regional** museum of ethnography. Inside this museum (closed on Saturdays and Sundays) you will find collections of paintings, photographs, models of traditional cottages, handicrafts and fishing methods.

From the museum you can continue down the same street until it ends at the **Largo do Pe da Cruz** plaza. Here you can view the magnificent 17th-century **Igreja de Pe da Cruz** church that contains impressive frescoes and fine paintings. At this point you should head back to the **Praça D. Francisco Gomes'** northern edge and follow the *Rua Conselheiro Bivar* up for a few blocks before turning right onto the *Rua de São Pedro*. At the end of this street you will be lead into the **Largo de São Pedro** plaza and its finely decorated 16th century **Igreja de São Pedro** church.

A block straight ahead from the front of the church is another large plaza known as the **Largo do Carmo**. From this plaza you can't help but notice the massive bell towers of the baroque 18th-century **Igreja de Nossa Senhora da Carmo**. The church has a strange **Capela dos Ossas** (chapel of bones) which is covered with skeletal remains of former monks (closed on Saturdays and Sundays). Once again it is time to head back to the dock area. This time I suggest a final stop at the city's famous **Museu Maratimo de Admiral Ortigão** maritime museum at the northern edge of the docks behind the Hotel Eva in the port captian's offices. Here you can see a vast collection of miniture scale models of historic and traditional Portuguese sea vessels.

The beaches around Faro also are worth some considration. Altough I am somewhat doubtful about the quality of the water here, you can at least get a nice tan. The closest beach to town is an island called **Praia de Faro** which is packed during the summer. It can be reached by ferry from the terminal in front of the Cidade Velha area, where you can also catch high season ferry service to the better and somewhat developed **Ilha da Culatra** and **Ilha Deserta** island baches in the Ria Formosa natural park area (see Olhão).

NIGHTLIFE

Most of Faro's best nightspots can be found along the *Rua do Prior*. Here there are several different types of bars, pubs, and clubs which fill up on weekend nights. I suggest you start at the infamous **Adega dos Argos** where the patrons sing along to old songs, from here you can peek inside the more agressive hotspots such as the **Chaplin Bar** and **Megahertz**, but expect to pay a cover charge for entry. The more upscale tourists tend to go to the Hotel Eva and dance in their **Sheherazade Club**.

OLHÃO & THE COASTAL ISLANDS

The picturesque town of **Olhão** *rests about 9 km away from Faro on route N-125 east*. The town is situated on a river estuary, seperated from the ocean by a series of seabird-filled salt marshes and small islands known officially as the **Parque Natural da Ria Formosa**. This old Moorish city still makes much of its livelihood from the fishing industry.

The Moorish design of the town's many whitewashed cube-shaped houses is based on the typical style of North African coastal communities which local merchants have trading with since the 16th century. There are few specific attractions in the town itself, with the possible exception of its nice harbor, the tranquil riverside **Parque de Joaquim Lopes** municipal gardens with its pleasant cafes, the nearby riverfront morning seafood and produce **mercado** (market– daily except Sunday), the small **Museu Municipal** museum (closed on Sundays) with a few local artifacts and fossils on the **Largo da Lagoa**, and several meandering stone streets off the Ave. da República.

The finest view of town can be seen from atop the towers of Olhão's delightful 17th-century **Igreja Matriz** in the heart of town. The reason for most visitors to come here is to catch the local ferry service which runs from the dock near the gardens to a couple of long sandy beach islands at the seaside edge of the Parque Natural da Ria Formosa. The ferry ride to the beaches, cafes, and rental cottages on **Ilha da Armona** takes 20 minutes and costs only about 380$00 roundtrip, with service several times daily year round. The longer 50 minute ride to the fishing villages and beaches on the **Ilha da Culatra** costs about 500$00 roundtrip with service several times each day. Remember that your best bet is to wait until you have reached the more promising beach area of **Farol** to disembark.

Accomodations on these islands are extremely limited, so expect to return to the mainland by sundown.

WHERE TO STAY

HOTEL RIA SOL, *Rua General H. Delgado,37, (089) 705-276. Moderate.*

A modern and comfortable 2 star hotel which offers 52 nice double rooms in the heart of town. Facilities include bar, breakfast room, TV room, and nearby parking.

PENSÃO BELA VISTA, *Rua Teofilo Braga,65, (089) 702-538. Inexpensive.*

A fairly nice little 2 star inn with a tranquil courtyard in the heart of town offering about 9 guestrooms with and withoout private bathrooms. Almost no facilities except a TV.

ESTOI & THE COUNTRYSIDE

The historic town of **Estoi** can be found *by taking route N-2-6 north from Olhão for about 10 km*. This sleepy town contains the wonderfully ornate 18th-century **Palácio do Visconde de Estoi**. Visitors can walk through its formal gardens while the palace's beautiful interior is in the process of being renovated. The town offers little in the way of specific attractions besides pleasant little squares and parks and its regional **mercado** (market) on the second Sunday of each month.

A mile or so west of town you should stop at the remarkable Roman ruins of **Milreu**. Originally this 2nd century hamlet was known as *Ossonoba*. The site was first found in 1876 and minimal excavation has lead to the uncovering of a Roman villa, courtyard, mosaics, baths, columns, mausoleums, and a converted temple which may be the oldest Christian church in the world. The ruins are closed on Mondays; *call their office at (089) 916-20* to guarentee a visit to the sight.

The quaint countryside market towns to the north and east of Estoi are also well worth a visit. *I strongly suggest an 8 km trip up route N-2 north to visit the pleasant valley village of **São Brás de Alportel***. Here you can visit the beautiful old **Igreja Matriz** church and the stately home which houses **Museu Etnografico** museum of traditional Algarvian costumes (closed on Mondays). There is also a regional **mercado** (market) in the town's center on every Saturday.

Another old fashioned local town called **Moncarapacho** *lies some 13 km. away from Estoi on route IP-1 east*. Here you can stroll through the quaint streets and, if you're lucky enough to arrive on the first Sunday of the month, you can follow the hordes of local country folk down towards the huge produce, handicrafts, and livestock **mercado** (market). The town is quite relaxing and contains several nice bed and breakfast inns.

WHERE TO STAY

POUSADA DE SÃO BRÁS, *São Brás de Alportel, (089) 842-306. Moderate.*

A hilltop country inn located above town offering 24 rooms with private bathrooms. and nice views. Facilities include bar, restaurant, pool, tennis, and parking.

MONTE DO CASAL, *Estoi, (089) 915-03. Moderate.*

A nice English owned bed and breakfast inn with seaviews and 12 comfortable double rooms. Facilities include bar, gourmet restaurant, pool, terrace, and parking.

ESTALAGEM MOLEIRO, *Estoi, (089) 916-43. Moderate.*

A good 4 star inn with 36 rooms with private bathrooms a few minutes out of town. The property offers bar, restaurant, pool, tennis, gardens, TV, radio, and parking.

TAVIRA

The elegant fishing town of **Tavira** *lies some 29 km away from Olhão on route N-125 east*. This delightful small city has a rich history that dates back thousands of years before successive Greek, Roman, and Moorish occupations. The Moors were finally conquered in 1242 by Christian forces under the command of Dom Paio Peres Correia as revenge for the murders of 7 knights of the St. James order.

During the 1755 earthquake several of the mosr important structures in town including the castle and old 7 arch Roman bridge were heavly damaged. Nowadays Tavira's economy depends on a combination of local fishing and nearby beachfront resort development which has thus far spared the historic parts of town.Tavira is based on both sides of the **Sequa** and **Gilão** rivers that merge under its lovely bridges, lined by beautiful balconied homes. Many ornate churches, palaces, regal pastel colored homes, and ramparts still can be viewed along many of the old winding streets on both sides of town.

WHERE TO STAY

QUINTA DO CARACOL, *Tavira, (081) 224-75. Moderate.*

A wonderful former farming estate which has been converted into a fabulous bed and breakfast inn with 7 apartments with kitchens. Facilities include bar, pool, gardens, tennis, bicycles, and a great barbeque area. Near the train station.

EUROTEL TAVIRA, *Tavira, (081) 324-324. Moderate.*

A modern 3 star hotel with 80 air conditioned and balconied rooms just outside of town. Facilities include bar, restaurant, pool, tennis, billards, TV room, and parking.

HOTEL GOLDEN DUNA, *Cabanas, (081) 204-81. Moderate.*

A nice hotel and villa complex near the beach which offers 147 rooms in either it's main hotel or in the several cabana style villas at land's edge. Facilities include pool.

PEDRAS DEL RAINHA, *Cabanas, (081) 201-81. Moderate.*

A large cabana complex with hundreds of adjacent 1 to 4 bedroom cabanas with kitchens which surround a central recreation complex. Facilities include bar, restaurant, shops, pool, bicycles, tennis, disco, babysitting, and phones.

ESTALAGEM OASIS, *Manta Rota, (081) 951-660. Moderate.*

A nice and friendly 4 star inn near the beach which offers 20 rooms with private bathroom. Facilities include bar, restaurant, gardens, sundeck, TV, and parking.

PEDRAS D'EL REI, *Santa Luzia, (081) 325-352. Moderate.*

A huge low end cabana complex which has hundreds of adjacent cabanas with kitchens and small beds for rent to famililies on tight budgets. The complex is not very appealing to people wanting any form of luxury or peace. Facilities include bar, restaurant, shops, pool, barbeque, bicycles, tennis, babysitting, and phones.

RESIDENCIAL PRINCESSA DO GILÃO, *Tavira, (081) 226-65. Inexpensive.*

A nice 2 star inn on the *Rua Borda da Agua de Aguiar* just across the river from the mercado which offers 22 rooms with and without private bathrooms. Nice views.

RESIDENCIAL LAGOA, *Tavira, (081) 222-52. Inexpensive.*

A nice and basic 2 star inn on *Rua Almirante Candido dos Reis, 34* with 16 guestrooms with and without private bathrooms. A good budget choice.

WHERE TO EAT

O CANECÃO, *Rua José P. Padinha, 162, (081) 819-21. Moderate.*

A wonderful harbour front restaurant with huge picture windows serving the finest *cataplana* (seafood stew) in the *Algarve*. One order is enough for 3 people.

RESTAURANTE IMPERIAL, *Rua José P. Padinha, 24, (081) 222-34. Moderate.*

A fine harbourfront seafood and meat restaurant which offers well prepared fresh caught grilled anf fried fish including Tavira'a famed *bife de atum* (tuna steak).

RESTAURANTE BICA, *Rua A. Can. dos Reis,24, (081) 222-82. Inexpensive.*

A good and reasonably priced casual seafood restaurant in the Residencial Lagoa which offers huge portions of the day's catch. A great budget choice.

SEEING THE SIGHTS

Upon arriving in the downtown area, your best bet is to park in the central riverside **Praça da República** square and walk up the main street of *Rua da Liberdade* until you can turn right onto R*ua D. Paio Peres Correia*. At the next corner you again turn right, this time onto the *Calçãda D. Paio Peres Correira* where you will find yourself next to the the somber **Igreja de Santiago** church. From here can't help but notice the bell and clock towers aborve the 13th-century **Igreja de Santa Maria do Castelo** church, built on the sight of a former mosque and housing the tomb of Dom Paio Peres Correia.

DELIGHTFUL TAVIRA

Nearby are the ancient ramparts and ruins of town's 13th century **castelo** (castle). The small lanes that cross through this side of town feature several interesting churches and palatial buildings including the

Convento de Nossa Senhora de Graça convent off the quaint **Largo de Postigo** plaza, the **Palácio da Galeria** palace and park on *Calçãda de D. Ana,* and the remarkable Renaissance 16th-century **Igreja da Misericórdia** church near the riverfront.

After returning to the **Praça da República**, you should first stroll down the *Rua José Pires Padinha* and adjacent *Rua do Cais* which are surrounded by a wonderful riverfront garden esplanade. Here you will pass the daily morning fish **mercado** (market) and several good restaurants before reaching the docks where you can see the fishermen unload squid and fish into crates. After a good look around the dockside, you may want to cross the modernized Roman bridge to the other side of town. Here you can see women hanging their laundry out on the panoramic *Rua de Borda de Agua da Asseca* just in front of the riverside. I suggest that you venture inward on the *Rua 5 de Outubro* and turn left to find even more nice plazas and old chuches.

The town of Tavira is close to some fine sandy beaches on the tip of **Ilha de Tavira** island which can be reached during the summer by a 15 minute ferry trip from the town fishing docks or from nearby **Quatro Aguas**. The ride costs about 200$00 roundtrip. Although there are bars, restaurants, and a campsite on the island, you may find that the best accomodations are back on the mainland.

Additional sandy island dune beaches can be reached by rowboat or shuttle service from the approiately named and overbuilt resort area of **Cabanas** and the lovely fortress topped traditional village of **Cacela** to the east and **Pedras D'el Rei (Santa Luzia)** to the west. Long sandy streches of beach can be accessed directly by car without the need for ferry and shuttle service a bit further east of town at **Manta Rota** and **Alagoa**.

MONTE GORDO

Some 22 km away from Tavira on route N-125 east lies the unappealing beach resort town of **Monte Gordo**. This is the first reasonable beach area that Spaniards pass when entering the Algarve, and many of them seem to just settle down here for their vacations among a few older English, Dutch, and German visitors.

The town offers a long sandy beach known as the **Praia de Monte Gordo** and a decent waterview **casino**. For some reason the town's hotels are often packed. The nicest beach in the general area may be found a fw km west at **Praia Verde**.

WHERE TO STAY

HOTEL DOS NAVEGADORES, *Rua Gonçalo Velho, (081) 512-490. Expensive.*

THE ALGARVE 417

A large and modern 3 star hotel with 344 air conditioned rooms with balconies near the beach. Facilities include bar, restaurant, pool, health club, squash, and parking.

HOTEL ALCAZAR, *Rua de Cueta, (081) 512-184. Expensive.*

A modern 4 star hotel a few blocks from the sea which has 95 large air conditioned rooms. Facilities include bar, disco, restaurant, pool, billards, TV, and parking.

VASCO DE GAMA HOTEL, *Ave. Infante Dom Henrique, (081) 423-22. Moderate.*

A good beachfront 3 star hotel with 165 air conditioned rooms. Facilities include bar, disco, restaurant, pool, tennis, watersports facilities, billards, TV, and parking.

HOTEL CASABLANCA INN, *Rua 7, (081) 444-45. Moderate.*

A nice and friendly 3 star hotel with 42 comfortable double rooms near the beach and casino. Facilities include bar, restaurant, pool, sundeck, and TV room.

APARTHOTEL ATLÂNTICO, *Ave. Infante Dom Henrique, (081) 511-040. Moderate.*

A large seafront apartment complex with 88 1 bedroom units that include kitchens and seaview balcony. Facilities include bar, restaurant, shops, and parking.

ALBERGARIA MONTE GORDO, *Ave. Infante Dom Henrique, (081) 421-24. Inexpensive.*

A good and rasonably priced 4 star in near the sea which offers 25 double rooms with private bathrooms, a bar, restaurant, TV room, and nearby parking.

WHERE TO EAT

MOTA, *Praia do Monte Gordo, (081) 426-50. Inexpensive.*

A good and reasonably priced casual outdoor restaurant that offers everything from salads and burgers to fresh caught local seafood. Great for a quick bite.

VILA REAL DE SANTO ANTÓNIO

The cute little border town of **Vila Real de Santo António** *is located 4 km. from Monte Gordo at the end of route N-125 east.* Based on the mouth of the **Guadiana** river, this port city had been devestated by a huge tidal wave and was completely rebuilt by the Marquêsde Pombal in 1774 in less than six months. The town used to serve as the primary border crossing point for excursions to and from **Ayamonte** in Spain by ferry and train but nowadays a more rapid highway and bridge system allows most people with cars to bypass the ferry and avoid town.

There are several interesting old riverfront mansions to look at as well as the **Museu de Manuel Cabanas** museum of wood carvings (closed on Mondays) on the mosaic lined **Praça Marquis de Pombal** square. All that said, the city offers a nice place to spend a few hours wandering around, but an overnight here is unnecessary.

The towns surrounding the Portuguese side of the Guadiana river border are worth a nice day trip. There are boats that take excursions to the quaint town of **Foz de Odeleite** (contact the *Turismo* office on Praça Marquêsde Pombal for booking details and schedules)– lunch included.

You can also drive on route N-122 north up the riverside for 5 km to the fortress town of **Castro Marim** and onward another 31 km or so to the inviting rural village of **Alcoutim**.

WHERE TO STAY

HOTEL GUADIANA, *Ave. de República, 92, (081) 511-482. Moderate.*

A good 2 star hotel with 37 fairly comfortable rooms with private bathrooms in the heart of town. Facilities include bar, restaurant, mini-bars, TV, and parking.

HOTEL APOLO, *Ave. Bomb. Portugueses, (081) 512-448. Moderate.*

A clean and basic 2 star hotel which offers 42 double rooms with private bathrooms. Facilities include bar, restaurant, TV room, direct dial phones, and parking.

WHERE TO EAT

CAVES DO GAUDIANA, *Ave. de República,90, (081) 444-98. Moderate.*

A huge seafood restaurant in an old building on the riverfont which serves well prepared locally caught fish from a vast menu of reasonably priced selections.

PRACTICAL INFORMATION FOR THE ALGARVE

CASINOS
- **Casino do Alvor**, *Praia da Rocha, (82) 231-41*
- **Casino de Vilamoura**, *Vilamoura, (89) 302-997*
- **Casino de Monte Gordo**, *Monte Gordo, (81) 512-224*

CURRENCY EXCHANGE

Most banks throughout the *Algarve* will exchange foreign currency and traveller's checks without hesitation. Private exchange booths, shops, restaurants, and hotel front desks will offer you a rather poor exchange rate. Remember that banking hours are from 8 am until 3 pm from Monday through Friday.

In places like some of the more tourism related areas and big towns you may find a 24 hour ATM or currency exchange machine.

EMERGENCY & USEFUL PHONE NUMBERS
- **Emergency assistance** (S.O.S.), *115*
- **Aljezur Health Center**, *Igreja Nova, (082) 981-13*
- **Lagos Hospital**, *Rua do Castelo, (082) 630-34*
- **Faro Hospital**, *Rua Leão Pinedo, (089) 220-11*
- **Faro International Airport**, *Faro, (089) 818-221*
- **T.A.P. Airlines in Faro**, *Rua D Francisco Gomes, (089) 803-249*
- **Automobile Club of Portugal in Lisbon**, *(01) 942-5095*

MUSEUMS
- **Roman Excavations at Milreu**, *Estoi, (089) 916-20*. A series of unearthed ruins from the 1st century Roman village of Ossonoba. Open by appointment 10 am until 12 pm and 2 pm until 5 pm Tuesday through Sunday. Closed on Mondays and holidays.
- **Infante D. Henrique Archaeological Museum**, *Largo Dom Afonso III, Faro, (089) 822-042*. Contains collections of local archaeological findings, ceramics, paintings, sculptures, furniture, glassware, *azulejos*, and jewelry. Open 9 am until 12 pm and 2 pm until 5 pm Monday through Friday. Closed on Saturdays and Sundays.
- **Regional Ethnography Museum of Faro**, *Rua Pe da Cruz, 4, Faro, (089) 276-10*. Contains collections of paintings, handicrafts, folklore, and scale models of boats. Open 9:30 am until 12:30 pm and 2:30 pm until 4:30 pm Monday hrough Friday. Closed on Saturdays, Sundays, and holidays.
- **Admiral Ortigão Maritime Museum**, *Harbour Master's Office, Faro, (089) 803-601*. Contains exhibits about local fishing, and scale models of famous vessels. Open 10 am until 11 am and 2:30 pm until 4:30 pm daily.
- **José Formosinho Municipal Museum**, *Igreja de Santo António, Rua General Alberto Silveira, Lagos, (082) 762-301*. Contains local prehistoric and Roman artifacts, 16th-century clothing, ceramics, cork carvings, 17th-century embroidery, sacred art, and sculptures. Open 9:30 am until 12:30 pm and 2 pm until 5 pm from Tuesday through Sunday. Closed on Mondays and holidays.
- **Olhão Municipal Museum and Library**, *Largo da Lagoa, 3, Olhão, (089) 705-301*. Contains collections of local fossils, artifacts, handicrafts, and numismatics. Open 2 pm until 6 pm Monday through Friday. Open 10 am until 12 pm and 2 pm until 6 pm on Saturday. Closed on

420 PORTUGAL GUIDE

- **António Bentes Museum of Costumes**, *Rua Dr. José Dias Sancho, 59, São Brás de Alportel, (089) 842-618*. Contains a collection of typical Algarvian customes. Open 10 am until 1 pm and 2 pm until 5:30 pm on Wednesdays only during winter. Open 10 am until 1 pm and 2 pm until 6 pm daily during summer. Closed Thurdays until Tuesday during winter.
- **Municicipal Museum of Archaeology**, *Ruà das Portas de Loulé, 14, Silves, (082) 444-832*. Contains a collection of prehistoric through 17th century archaeological findings. Open 10 am until 12:30 pm and 2:30 pm until 6 pm daily.
- **Roman Ruins of Cerro da Vial**, *Cerro da Vilamoura, Vilamoura, (089) 312-153*. An excavated Roman town and archaeological museum with many artifacts. Open 10 am until 5 pm daily during winter. Open 10 am until 8 pm daily during summer.
- **Manuel Cabanas Municipal Museum**, *Praça Marquêsde Pombal, Vila Real de Santo António, (081) 511-030*. Contains a collection of antique wood engravings. Open 11 am until 12 pm and 3 pm until 7 pm Tuesday through Sunday during winter. Open 4 pm until 8 pm and 9 pm until11 pm Tuesday through Sunday during summer. Closed on Mondays and holidays.

SPORTS & RECREATION

The Algarve has over a dozen world class golf courses (see golf section), as well as several horse riding, sailing, fishing, windsurfing, and tennis centers.

The following is a partial listing of these activities. For further details, please contact any Algarve-based *Turismo* office.

- **Atlantic Diving Club**, *Albufeira, (089) 513-642*
- **Hotel Alfamar Tennis Club**, *Albufeira, (089) 501-351*
- **Hotel Alfamar Windsurfing Club**, *Albufeira, (089) 501-351*
- **Hotel Montechoro Tennis Club**, *Albufeira, (089) 589-423*
- **Hotel Montechoro Windsurfing**, *Albufeira, (089) 589-423*
- **Quinta dos Amigos Horse Club**, *Almancil, (089) 394-536*
- **Fernando dos Santos Stables**, *Alvor, (082) 202-11*
- **Hotel Alvor Praia Tennis Club**, *Alvor, (082) 458-900*
- **Hotel Alvor Praia Windsurfing**, *Alvor, (082) 458-900*
- **Hotel Alvor Praia Fishing**, *Alvor, (082) 458-900*
- **Torralta Waterski Center**, *Alvor, (082) 459-511*
- **Torralta Windsurfing**, *Alvor, (082) 459-511*
- **Algarve Diving Center**, *Armação de Pera, (082) 313-203*
- **Carvoeiro Club Sailing Dept.**, *Carvoeiro, (082) 357-266*
- **Carvoeiro Tennis Club**, *Carvoeiro, (082) 357-847*

- **Ginásio Sailing Clube**, *Doca de Faro-Faro, (089) 823-434*
- **Surfpesca Fishing Ltd.**, *Lagoa, (082) 573-54*
- **Meia Praia Waterski School**, *Meia Praia, (082) 314-910*
- **Capemar Game Fishing Center**, *Portimão, (082) 258-66*
- **West Algarve Horse Center**, *Praia do Burgau, (082) 691-02*
- **Luz Bay Sailing Club**, *Praia da Luz, (082) 789-640*
- **Luz Bay Tennis Club**, *Praia da Luz, (082) 789-640*
- **Luz Bay Windsurfing**, *Praia da Luz, (082) 789-640*
- **Sea Sports Scuba Center**, *Praia da Luz, (082) 789-538*
- **Eurotel Horse Center**, *Tavira, (081) 220-41*
- **Quinta da Lago Horse Center**, *Vale de Lobo, (089) 396-902*
- **Roger Taylor Tennis Center**, *Vale de Lobo, (089) 304-145*
- **Vale de Lobo Sailing Club**, *Vale de Lobo, (089) 394-444*
- **Vale de Lobo Winddsurfing**, *Vale de Lobo, (089) 394-444*
- **Vilamoura Horse Center**, *Vilamoura, (089) 301-577*
- **Vilamoura Sailing Club**, *Vilamoura Marina, (089) 313-933*
- **Vilamoura Tennis Center**, *Vilamoura, (089) 380-088*
- **Vilamoura Marina Yacht Center**, *Vilamoura Marina, (089) 302-925*

TOURIST OFFICES (TURISMOS)
- **Albufeira Tourist Office**, *Rua 5 de Outubro, (089) 512-144*
- **Aljezur Tourist Office**, *Largo do Mercado, (082) 982-29*
- **Armação de PêraTourist Office**, *Ave. Marginal, (082) 312-145*
- **Faro Tourist Office**, *Rua da Misericórdia , 8, (089) 803-667*
- **Faro Tourist Office**, *Faro Airport, (089) 818-582*
- **Lagos Tourist Office**, *Largo MarquêsPombal, (082) 630-31*
- **Loulé Tourist Office**, *Edifício de Castelo, (089) 639-00*
- **Monte Gordo Tourist Office**, *Ave. Marginal, (081) 444-95*
- **Olhão Tourist Office**, *Largo da Lagoa, (089) 713-936*
- **Portimão Tourist Office**, *Largo 1 de Dezembro, (082) 236-95*
- **Praia da Rocha Tourist Office**, *Ave. Marginal, (082) 222-90*
- **Sagres Tourist Office**, *Promontorio de Sagres, (082) 641-25*
- **Silves Tourist Office**, *Rua 25 de Abril, (082) 422-255*
- **Tavira Tourist Office**, *Praça da República, (081) 225-11*
- **Vila Real de S. A. Tourist Office**, *Posta de Turismo, (081) 432-72*

TRANSPORTATION
Almost all of the towns and cities of the Algarve are easily reached by a series of bus and train stations that run from Sagres to Vila Real de Santo António. Many of the depots and stations do not have phone numbers, and may be several km. away from the center of town. You can contact a major station or any local *Turismo* office to get further information, schedules, and current prices. Additional daily air conditioned express

buses from several Algarve cities to Lisbon is offered by RN and other private bus companies.

Please contact any *Turismo*, RN office, or travel agent for details and reservations.
- **Albufeira RN Bus depot**, *Ave. da Liberdade, (089) 543-01*
- **Faro RN Bus depot**, *Avenida da República, no phone*
- **Lagos RN Bus depot**, *Rua Vasco da Gama, (082) 763-014*
- **Albufeira CP Rail station**, *5 km north of town, (089) 571-616*
- **Faro CP Rail station**, *Largo da Estação, (089) 822-769*
- **Lagos CP Rail station**, *just across the bridge, (082) 762-987*
- **Olhão CP Rail station**, *Ave. dos Combatentes, (089) 705-378*
- **Portimão CP Rail station**, *Rua Infante Henrique, (082) 230-56*
- **Silves CP Rail station**, *2 km south of town, (082) 442-310*
- **Tavira CP Rail station**, *Rua da Liberdade, (081) 223-54*
- **Avis Rent a Car in Lagos**, *Largo Portas de Portugal, (081) 763-691*
- **Europcar Renta a Car in Faro**, *Faro Airport, (089) 818-726*
- **Hertz Rent a Car in Albufeira**, *Hotel Tropical, (089) 512-920*

TRAVEL AGENCIES
- **Algarve Marina Tours**, *Vilamoura Marina, (089) 302-772*. A friendly and well-established full service travel agency which can book bus tours, villas, apartments, boat excursions, train and airplane tickets, and other services.
- **RN Tours**, *Ave. 25 de Abril, 210, (089) 554-26*. An Albufeira branch office of a huge national travel company which offers bus tours, reservations, ticketing, and discounts at major hotels in the area.
- **Top Tours**, *Estrada Praia da Rocha, (082) 417-552*. A Praia da Rocha based branch of a good travel agency which can help to book al types of tours, hotels, rental cars, airfare, bus and train tickets, and much more.

TRAIN ROUTES

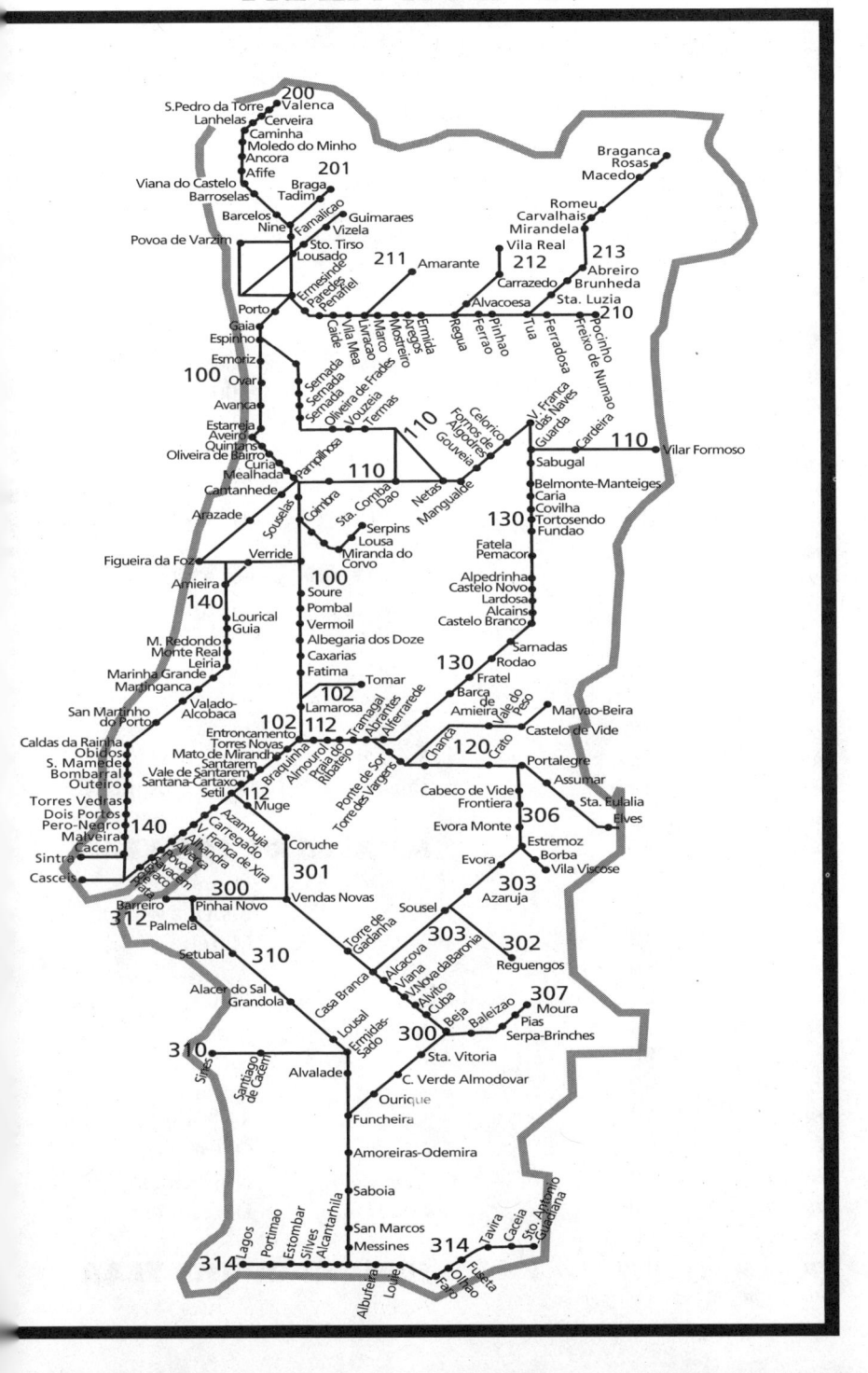

DICTIONARY & USEFUL PHRASES

NUMBERS

zero	0
um, uma	1
dois	2
Três	3
quatro	4
cinco	5
seis	6
sete	7
oito	8
nove	9
dez	10
onze	11
doze	12
treze	13
catorze	14
quinze	15
dezaseis	16
dezassete	17
dezoito	18
dezanove	19
vinte	20
vinte e um	21
vinte e dois	22
trinta	30
quarenta	40
cinquenta	50
sessenta	60
setenta	70
oitenta	80
noventa	90
cem	100
cem e um	101
cem e dois	102
duzentos	200
quinhentos	500
mil	1000
mil e quinhentos	1500
dois mil	2000
um Milhão	1,000,000

DAYS OF THE WEEK

Segunda-feira	Monday
Terça-feira	Tuesday
Quarta-feira	Wednesday
Quinta-feira	Thursday
Sexta-feira	Friday
Sábado	Saturday
Domingo	Sunday

MONTHS OF THE YEAR

Janeiro	January
Fevereiro	February
Março	March
Abril	April
Maio	May
Junho	June
Julho	July
Agosto	August
Setembro	September
Outubro	October
Novembro	November
Dezembro	December

SEASONS OF THE YEAR

Inverno	Winter

DICTIONARY & USEFUL PHRASES 425

Primavera	Spring	*entrada*	entrance
Verão	Summer	*Saída*	exit
Outono	Fall	*aberto*	open
		fechado	closed

COLORS

branco	white
negro	black
azul	blue
verde	green
encarnado	red
amarelo	yellow
prata	silver
ouro	gold

GREETINGS

Olá	hello
como Está ?	how are you?
chamo-me...	my name is..
adeus	good bye
faz favor	please
obrigado	thank you (masculine)
obrigada	thank you (feminine)
muito obrigado	thanks a lot (masculine)
muito obrigada	thanks a lot (feminine)
de nada	you're welcome
desculpe	sorry
com Licença	excuse me
bom dia	good morning
boa tarde	good afternoon
boa noite	good evening
senhora	Mrs.
menina	Ms.
senhor	Mr.
Médico	Dr.
senhoras	women
homens	men

TIME

dia	day
meio-dia	noon
tarde	afternoon
noite	night
meia-noite	midnight
ontem	yesterday
hoje	today
logo a tarde	this afternoon
logo a noite	this evening
Amanhã	tommorow
agora	now
cedo	early
mais tarde	later
velho	old
novo	new
minuto	minute
hora	hour
semana	week
mes	month
ano	year

USEFUL WORDS

sim	yes
Não	no
Está bem	OK
bom	good
mau	bad

Descriptions

pequeno	small
grande	big
menos	less
mais	more
perto	close
longe	far
quente	hot
frio	cold
belo	beautiful

feio	ugly	*sem chumbo*	unleaded gas
este	this		
esse	that	**SERVICES**	
preco	price	*posta da policia*	police station
barato	cheap	*Médico*	doctor
caro	expensive	*hospital*	hospital
		Farmácia	pharmacy
QUERIES		*correio*	post office
quando?	when?	*banco*	bank
como?	how?	*Cãmbio*	exchange
quanto?	how much?	*hotel*	hotel
que?	what?	*restaurante*	restaurant
onde?	where?	*casa de banho*	bathroom
Porquê?	why?	*telefone*	telephone
Não entendo	I don't understand		
		ACCOMMODATIONS	
DIRECTIONS		*quinta*	manor house or estate
esquerda	left		
direita	right	*pousada*	government-owned inn
sempre em frente	directly ahead		
		hotel	hotel
TRANSPORTATION		*pousada de juventude*	hostel
Automóvel	car	*estalagem*	quality inn
autocarro	bus	*residencial*	budget inn
comboio	train	*albergaria*	minor hotels
Avião	airplane	*Pensão*	boarding house
metro	subway	*apartamentos*	apartments
fluvial	ferry	*vila*	villa
taxi	taxi	*campismo*	camp site
Estação	station	*quarto simple*	single room
aeroporto	airport	*quarto duplo*	double room
primeira classe	first class	*quarto com banho*	room with private bath
segunda classe	second class		
ida e volta	round trip	*quarto com dois camas*	room with 2 beds
bilhete	ticket		
bilheteira	ticket office	*air condicionado*	air conditioning
bagagem	luggage	*aquecimento*	heating
estrada	road	*lavandaria*	laundromat
ponte	bridge	*Televisão*	TV
portagem	toll booth	*chave*	key
garagem	garage	*Cãmbio*	exchange
gasolina	gasoline	*gerente*	manager

SPORTS & ENTERTAINMENT

Ténis	tennis
golfe	golf
piscina	pool
bowling	bowling
barcos	boats
canoagem	canoeing
squash	squash
Ténis de mesa	ping pong
equitacão	horse riding
sala de bilhar	billiard room
pesca	fishing
bicicletas	bicycles
Caça	hunting
sauna	sauna
termas	spa
Ginásio	health club
Solário	solarium
casino	casino
cinema	movie theater
Praça de touros	bullfighting ring

SIGHTS

cidade	city
aldeia	village
centro da cidade	city center
rossio	town's main square
Praça	square
largo	plaza
Câmara municipal	town hall
museu	museum
igreja	church
convento	convent
Sé	cathedral
mosteiro	monastery
capela	chapel
claustro	cloister
fonte, chafariz	fountain
pelourinho	pillory
torre	tower
cruz	cross
anta	megalith
castelo	castle
torre de menagem	castle keep
Palácio, Paço	palace
fortaleza	fortress
azulejo	glazed tile
festa	festival
mercado	market
feira	fair
artesanato	handicraft shop
antigo	ancient
floresta	forest
lago	lake
barragem	dam
aqueduto	aqueduct
praia	beach
esplanada	seaview prominade
miradouro	scenic lookout
grutas	caves

BEVERAGES

garrafa	bottle
Café, bica	espresso
Café com leite	coffee with milk
Galão	Café au lait
Chá	tea
leite	milk
sumo	juice
cerveja	beer
vinho tinto	red wine
vinho branco	white wine
agua	water
agua com gas	water with bubbles
agua sem gas	mineral water without bubbles
gelo	ice

FOOD

ementa	menu
empregado	waiter

carta de vinhos	wine list	sobremesa	dessert
conta	the bill	bolo	pastry
pequeno Almoço	breakfast	torta	tart
Almoço	lunch	gelado	ice cream
jantar	dinner	chocolate	chocolate
faca	knife	arroz doce	rice pudding
garfo	fork	pudim flan	flan
colher	spoon	carne	meat
Xícara	cup	bife	steak
prato	plate	lombo	fillet
uma dose	one portion	Leitão	roasted pig
meia dose	half portion	porco	pork
vegitariano	vegetarian	vitela	veal
Pão	bread	pato	duck
mantiega	butter	fiambre	ham
sal	salt	presunto	smoked ham
pimenta	pepper	Chouriço	smoked sausage
piri-piri	a medium hot sauce	tripas	tripe
Açúcar	sugar	borrego	lamb
azeite	olive oil	coelho	rabbit
azeitonas	olives	peru	turkey
vinagre	vinegar	frango	chicken
sopa	soup	peixe	fish
fruta	fruit	bacalhau	cod
salada	green salad	atum	tuna
salada mista	mixed salad	linguado	flounder
ovos	eggs	pescada	hake
ovos mexidos	scrambled eggs	truta	trout
ovos estrelados	fried eggs	robalo	bass
omelete, omoleta	omelet	espadarte	swordfish
bacon	bacon	tamboril	monkfish
hamburguesa	hamburger	cherne	turbot
prego no Pão	steak sandwich	peixe-espada	scabbard fish
batatas fritas	french fries	Salmão	salmon
sande	sandwich	carpa	carp
sande mista	ham and cheese sandwich	sardinhas	sardines
		mariscos	seafood
tosta	grilled sandwich	Camarões	shrimp
Pastéis	filled dumplings	gambas	prawns
Pastéis de queijo	cheese filled fried dumpling	lagosta	lobster
		lagostins	crayfish
Pastéis de carne	meat-filled fried dumpling	caranguejos	crabs
		polvo	octopus

DICTIONARY & USEFUL PHRASES

lulas	squid	assado	roasted
vieiras	scallops	fumado	smoked
Amêijoas	cockles	cozido	boiled
ostras	oysters	frito	fried
Mexilhões	mussels	estufado	stewed
legumes	vegatables	nas brasas	braised
arroz	rice	no espeto	on a spit
cebolas	onions	bem passado	well done
pimentos	peppers	Médio	medium done
batatas	potatoes	mal passado	rare
cenouras	carrots		
espinafres	spinach		

COMMON QUESTIONS

congumelos	mushrooms
pepino	cucumber
alho	garlic
Feijão	beans
alface	lettuce
frutas	fruits
laranja	orange
bananas	bananas
Limão	lemon
Melão	melon
melancia	watermelon
morango	strawberry
Ananás	pineapple
cerejas	cherries
pera	pear
Pêssego	peach
uvas	grapes
Maça	apple
ameixas	plums
tangerina	tangerine
toranja	grapefruit
queijo	cheese
queijo de cabra	goat cheese
queijo de ovelha	sheep cheese
queijo de vaca	cow cheese
quiejo da serra	sheep cheese

Fala Inglês?
  Do you speak English?
Onde é a Turismo?
  Where is the tourist office?
Como Sé chama?
  What is your name?
Como Está ?
  How are you?
Que horas São?
  What time is it?
Pode ajuda-me?
  Can you please help me?
Pode indicar-me a....?
  Can you direct me to.......?
Qual é a estrada para....?
  Which is the road towards....?
Onde é a parragem do autocarro?
  Where is the bus stop?
Onde é a casa de banho?
  Where are the bathrooms?
Quanto custa?
  How much does it cost?
Como Sé chama isto?
  What is this called?
Aceitam Cartão credito?
  Do you take credit cards?
Aceitam travelers checks?
  Do you accept travelers checks?

COOKING METHODS

grelhado	grilled
no forno	oven baked

Tem quartos livres?
>Are there any rooms available?

Qual o Número de telefone?
>What is the phone number?

Qual o Endereço?
>What is the address?

Quando abrem?
>When do you open?

Quando fecham?
>When do you close?

Quando fica pronto?
>When will it be ready?

Onde é a Estação de ?
>Where is the train station?

A que horas sai o autocão?
>What time does the bus leave?

Quando parte o ultimo comboio?
>When does the last train depart?

Por favor, chama-me um taxi?
>Can you please call a taxi for me?

INDEX

Abrantes 344
Accidents and emergencies 65
Accommodations 73, 81
Adegas Tipicas: see Fado
Afife 284
Afonso Henriques I (King/Dom) 19
Afonso III (King/Dom) 19, 300
Aguardente 133
Aguas Radium 324
Agueda 235
Agueda (Rio) 235
Airlines to Portugal 30
Airlines in Portugal 34
Airports 136
Albergarias 76
Albufeira 399
Alcácer do Sal 194
Alcobaça 214
Aldeamento Vilara 87
Aldeia de Serra 318, 354
Algar Seco 397
Algarve Region 378
Alentejo 12, 334, 167
Alezur 380
Aljustrel 219
Almancil 406
Almeida 326
Almeirim 341
Almograve 196
Almourol 343
Alpiarça 341
Alpedrinha 327
Alporchinos 398
Alvão (Parque Natural) 309
Alvito 368
Alvor 389

Alter do Chão 349
Amal 309
Amarante 265
Ambulances 65
Antiques 104
Apartment Rentals 75
Areias de São João 402
Armação de Pera 398
Arraiolos 365
Arraiolos Tapesteries 365
Arruda das Pisões 212
Artisans 104, 105
Atouguia da Baleia 208
AutoEurope 38
Automobile Clube of Portugal (ACP) 36
Aveiro 236
Aveiro (Ria de) 236, 238
Azambuja 339
Azeitão 188
Azeitão Wines 190; see also Wines
Azenhas do Mar 179
Azoia 178
Azulejos 104, 163, 176, 214, 232, 352

Bairrada Wines 81, 129, 232; see also Wines
Banks 62
Barcelos 278
Barragem de Crestuma 263
Barragem de Paradela 300
Barragem de Miranda 306
Bars: see regional and city chapters
Baskets 104
Batalha 218
Beaches: see under specific name

(Praia...)
Beckford, William 179
Beer 121
Beira Alta 12, 201, 298
Beira Baixa 12, 298
Beira Litoral 12, 201
Beja 370
Belmonte 322
Berlenga Grande 208
Bernardes, António de Olivera 360
Berrões 305
Bicycles 111
Boitac, Diogo 321
Bombarral 206
Bom Jesus 276
Borba 351
Braga 274
Bragança 303
Bragança, Duke of 20, 273
Brazil 20
Buarcos 226
Buçaco 20, 81, 232
Buccaco: see Buçaco
Bucelas Wine 131; see also Wines
Bullfights 111
Burgau 384
Burgundy, Henry of 19
Buses in Portugal 47
Business Hours 63
Byron, Lord 179

Cabeço da Neve 315
Cabo Carvoeiro 208
Cabo da Roca 178
Cabo de São Vicente 382
Cabo Espichel 192
Cabral, Pedro 19, 381
Cadaval 206
Caetano, Marcel 21
Cafes 121
Caldas da Rainha 212
Caldas de Manteigas 318
Caldas de Monchique 394
Caminha 287
Camões, Luís de 179
Camping 79
Caparica 186

Car Races 113
Car Rental 35
Caramulinho 315
Caramulo 315
Carrapateira 380
Carcavelos 168
Carcavelos Wines 131; see also Wines
Carlos I (King/Dom) 21
Carris 292
Cartaxo 338
Carthaginians 18
Carvalhelhos 300
Carvoeiro 39
Cascais 172
Casinos 169, 226, 260, 270, 403, 416
Castelo Branco 328
Castelo de Bode 223
Castelo de Vide 345
Castelo Melhor 326
Castelo Mendo 326
Castelo Rodrigo 326
Castillians 18
Castro Loboreiro 292
Castro, Inês de 231
Cávado (Rio) 278
Celorico da Beira 325
Celorico de Basto 266
Celtics 18
Celt-Iberians 18
Centum Cellas 322
Ceramics 104, 163, 176, 214, 232, 352
Cerro da Alagoa 402
Cerro da Piedade 402
Cerro da Vial 403
Cervejarias 124; see also Cuisine of Portugal
Cetobriga 194
Chaves 301
Christianity 19, 219
Churrascarias 124; see also Cuisine of Portugal
Citânias 18, 277
Citânia de Briteiros 277
Climate 24
Côa (Rio) 324

Coimbra 227
Colares 179
Colares Wines 130; see also Wines
Columbus, Christopher 19, 381
Confeitarias 124; see also Cuisine of Portugal
Conimbriga 227
Constância 342
Consulates 23, 64
Cortes 19
Costa da Caparica 187
Costa de Prata region 201-244
Costa Lisboa region 167-200
Costa Nova 237
Costa Verde region 258-297
Cova de Iria 219
Covao do Boi 318
Covilhã 318
Coudelaria de Alter Real 349
CP Rail 38
Crafts and Handicrafts 104
Crato 349
Credit Cards 63
Crime 64
Crusaders 19
Curia 234
Currency 62
Currency Exchange 62, 164
Cuisine 120-124
Customs and Immigration (Portugal) 22
Customs and Immigration (North America) 25

Dão Wine 128
Dias, Bartolomeu 19, 381
Dictionary/Phrase guide 424430
Dinis I, (King/Dom) 19
Directory Assistance 71
Disabled, Travel for the 67
Discoveries, Age of 19, 386
Driving in Portugal 35
Doctors 65
Dornelas 300
Dornes 223
Douro (Rio) 245, 261, 310
Douro Wine 127; see also Wine

Duty Free Shopping 103

Earthquake of 1775 20
Eating Out 120
Electricity 64
Elvas 350
Embassies 23, 64
Emergencies 64
Ericeira 185
Ermelo 309
Espinho 258
Esposende 280
Espumante Wines: see Wines
Estalagens 74
Estoi 412
Estoril 168
Estremadura 14, 201, 258
Estremoz 355
Eurail Passes 40
European Economic Community (EEC) 21
Évora 354-365
Évora Monte 356

Fão 280
Fado 64, 148
Farm Houses: see Quintas
Faro 408
Farol 412
Fátima 219
Feiras Novas 284
Fernandes, Vasco 312
Ferragudo 393
Ferries 42, 138
Festivals, Major 99
Figueira da Foz 224
Fishing 113
Flea Markets 156
Fortresses 201, 201, 226
Fundão 327
Funiculars: see regional and city chapters
Furadouro 238

Gardens: see regional and city chapters
Gama, Vasco de 19, 381

Geography of Portugal 11
Gilão (Rio) 413
Golegã 342
Golf Courses 114
Gondomar 263
Gouveia 317
Grão Vasco: see Fernandes, Vasco
Grand Prix Races 113
Guarda 320
Guimarães 271
Guincho 177
Gulbenkian, Calouste 159
Gulbenkian Foundation 159

Health 26, 66, 65
Health Insurance 66
Henriques, Afonso (King/Dom) 19
Henry of Burgundy 19
Henry the Navigator, Prince (Infante Dom) 19, 245, 381
Hiking: see regional and city chapters
History of Portugal 18
Holidays, National 65
Horseback Riding 116
Hospitals 65
Hostels 77
Hotel Albatroz (Extended Review) 84
Hotel Convento de Sao Paulo (Extended Review) 85
Hotel da Lapa (Extended Review) 83
Hotel do Guincho (Extended Review) 92
Hotel Infante de Sagres (Extended Review) 91
Hotel Palacio de Agueda (Extended Review) 86
Hotel Palacio do Bucaco (Extended Review) 81
Hotel Palacio Seteais (Extended Review) 91
Hotels: see Accommodations and regional and city chapters
Hunting 116

Iberians 18
I.C.E.P. 26
Ilhavo 238
Ilha da Armona 412
Ilha da Culatra 412
Ilha de Lomba 223
Ilha Deserta 412
Ilha de Faro 412
Ilha de Tavira 416
Ilha do Pessagueiro 196
Ilhas Berlengas 208
Insurance, Health and Accident 26, 66
Insurance, Car 37
Inquisition, the 20
Iron Age, the 19
Isabel (Queen/Donna) 20, 209
Itineraries, Suggested 51
Infante Dom Henriques: see Henry the Navigator
Inns: see Accommodations and regional and city chapters
Instituto da Vinho e do Vinho: see Wine

Jazz Clubs: see regional and city chapters
Jewish Communties 20, 222, 312
Junot, General 20
João I (King/Dom) 19
João IV (King/Dom) 20
João V (King/Dom) 184
João VI (King/Dom) 20
Josefa de Obidos: see Obidos, Josefa de

Labiados 305
Lagoa Comprida 318
Lagoa de Melides 196
Lagoa de Obidos 211
Lagoa de Santo André 196
Lagos 38
Lamego 310
Lancaster, Phillipa (Filipa) de (Queen/Donna) 19
Language: see Dictionary

Laundry and Dry Cleaning Shops: see regional and city chapters
Leiria 223
Lima (Rio) 284
Lindoso 292
Linhares 325
Lisbon (Lisboa) 134-166
Lomba 263
Lopes, Gregório 222
Lopes, Teixeira 261
Loulé 405
Lourinhã 205
Ludwig, Johann 184
Lusitanians 19
Luso 233
Luz 385

Mafra 184
Magellan, Fernando 19, 381
Mail and Post Offices 68
Malhoa, José 214
Mangualde 316
Manor Houses 74, 81
Manteigas 318
Manuel I (King/Dom) 20
Manuel II (King/Dom) 21, 233
Marialva 326
Marinha Grande 224
Marisqueiras: see Cuisine
Markets: see regional and city chapters
Marranos 20, 222, 312
Marvão 346
Marquês de Pombal 20, 136, 417
Mata do Buçaco 232
Mateus 308
Matosinhos 267
Mealhada 233
Medical Assistance 65
Meia Praia 388
Melgaço 291
Menus: see Cuisine
Mercados 105
Mértola 372
Mesão Frio 263
Methuen, Treaty of 20, 245
Miguel I (King/Dom) 21

Milfontes 196
Milreu 412
Minho (Rio) 288
Mira (Rio) 196
Mira de Aire 218
Miranda do Douro 306
Mirandela 307
Mirobriga 196
Mogodouro 306
Moledo 284
Monasteries: see regional and city chapters
Monção 290
Monchique 394
Mondego (Rio) 227
Money: see Currency
Monsanto 322
Monsaraz 365
Montalegre 300
Montanhas region 298-333
Montechoro 402
Montedor 284
Monte Estoril 170
Monte Foia 394
Monte Gordo 416
Montemor-o-Velho 227
Monte Sameiro 277
Montezinho (Parque Natural) 305
Moors 19, 154
Moscatel de Setúbal Wines: see Wines
Mountain Ranges: see by specific name (Serra ...)
Moura 369
Museums: see regional and city chapters
Movement of the Armed Forces 21

Nabão (Rio) 220
Napoleonic Wars 20, 204, 232, 246
Nazaré 216
National Holidays 65
National Parks: see regional and city chapters
Newspapers 66
New State, the 21
Nightlife 66

Obidos 209
Obidos, Josefa de 211, 214, 273
Odeceixe 378
Oeiras 167
Ofir 280
Olhão 411
Olhos d' Agua 402
Oporto: see Porto
Outeiro da Cortiçāda 212
Ovar 238

Packing for your Trip 24
Palaces: see regional and city chapters
Palacio do Bucaco 81, 232
Palmela 188
Parking 35
Parks: see national parks, regional and city chapters
Passports, Lost or Stolen 67
Pastelarias: see Cuisine
Pedras de'l Rei 416
Pedras Negras 224
Pedro I (King/Dom) 21
Penamacor 323
Pensoes 77
Peniche 206
Peneda-Gerês (Parque Nacional) 292
Penedono 325
Penhas Douradas 317
Peso 291
Peso da Régua 263, 310
Pharmacies 65
Philip I (King/Dom) 20
Philip II (King/Dom) 20
Philippa of Lancaster (Queen/Dona) 19
Phoenicians 18
Physically Challenged, Traveling for the 67
Piedade 215
Pinheiros, Rafeal Bordalo 214
Pisões 371
Planicies region 334-377
Planning for your trip 22
Poco do Inferno 318
Pombaline Architecture 20

Pombal, Marquês de 21
Ponte da Piedade 388
Ponte de Barca 286
Ponte de Lima 284
Portuguese National Tourist Offices 25
Portuguese Nun, The Five Love letters of a 371
Portuguese Trade Commision 26
Port Wine 127, 261; see also Wine
Portalegre 347
Portel 368
Portimão 392
Porto (Oporto) 245-257
Porto Côvo 196
Porto das Barcas 205
Porto de Mós 385
Porto Dinheiro 205
Porto do Mós 218
Porto Novo 204
Portos 292
Provinces of Portugal 12
Post Offices 68
Portucale 19, 245
Pousada do Castello (Extended Review) 88
Pousada dos Loios (Extended Review) 90
Pousadas 73
Póvoa do Varzim 269
Pragança 206
Praia Adraga 179
Praia da Amoreira 380
Praia da Areia Branca 205
Praia da Arrifana 380
Praia da Baleeira 382
Praia da Bordeira 380
Praia da Falésia 402
Praia da Galé 402
Praia da Granja 260
Praia da Mareta 382
Praia da Oura 402
Praia da Rocha 390
Praia das Maçãs 179
Praia de Albufeira 399
Praia de Alvor 389
Praia de Barriga 381

Praia de Beliche 382
Praia de Consolacão 208
Praia de Dona Ana 388
Praia de Esmoriz 260
Praia de Faro 411
Praia d'el Rei 211
Praia de Luz 385
Praia de Mira 238
Praia de Monte Clerigo 380
Praia de Monte Gordo 416
Praia de Odeceixe 378
Praia de Peniche 208
Praia de São Rafael 402
Praia de Vagueira 238
Praia de Vieira 224
Praia do Amado 380
Praia do Balaia 402
Praia do Baleal 208
Praia do Camilo 388
Praia do Carvoeiro 397
Praia do Castelejo 381
Praia do Castelo 402
Praia do Cortico 211
Praia do Estoril 168
Praia do Guincho 177
Praia do Ingrina 382
Praia do Martinal 382
Praia do Peniche 208
Praia do Salema 384
Praia do Pinhao 388
Praia do São Sebastiao 185
Praia do Sul 185
Praia do Tamariz 168
Praia do Vau 390
Praia dos Pescadores 399
Praia dos Três Irmaos 389
Praia Grande 179
Praia Maria Luisa 402
Praia Marina 398
Praia Norte 202, 216
Praia Nova 216
Praia Pequena 179
Praia São Bernadino 208
Praia Senhora da Rocha 398
Praia Torralta 389
Praia Velha 224
Praia Verde 416

Proclaimation of the Republic 21
Pulo do Lobo 370

Quarteira 403
Quatro Aguas 416
Queluz 181
Quinta da Corticada (Extended Review) 94
Quinta da Lomba (Extended Review) 97
Quinta do Caracol (Extended Review) 96
Quinta Horta da Moura (Extended Review) 95
Quintas 73, 81

Radio in Portugal 69
Rail Europe 42
Railroads in Portugal 38
Raposeria Wine 311; see also Wine
Rates 270
Redondo 353
Régio, José 268
Reguengos de Monsaraz 367
Regions of Portugal 12
Religion in Portugal 20
Remédios 208
Residencials 76
Restaurants: see Cuisine
Revolution, the 1910 21
Revolution, the 1974 21
Ribatejo 258, 334
Rio Maior 211
RN Bus Lines 47
Roads in Portugal 35
Roman Roads and Ruins 18, 194, 227, 280, 292, 417
Romans 18
Romarias: see Festivals
Rosé Wines: see Wines

Sabugal 324
Sabugueiro 318
Sado (Rio) 194
Sagres 381
Salazar, Dr. António de Oliveira 21
Salema 384

Salvaterra de Magos 340
Santa Maria da Feira 260
Santarém 336
Santa Rita 204
Santiago do Cacém 195
Santo Estevao 339
São Jacinto 238
São João de Estoril 168
São Martinho do Porto 215
São Pedro de Estoril 168
São Pedro de Muel 224
São Pedro de Sintra 183
São Pedro do Corval 367
Sebestião I (King/Dom) 20
Seia 318
Serpa 370
Serra da Coroa 305
Serra da Estrêla 118, 316, 317
Serra da Gardunha 327
Serra da Peneda 292
Serra da Pederneira 216
Serra de Aire 218
Serra de Caramulo 315
Serra de El-Rei 208
Serra de Grandôla 195
Serra de Mogadouro 306
Serra de Monchique 395
Serra de Montejunto 206
Serra de Montezinho 305
Serra de Ossa 354
Serra de Sao Mamede 346
Serra de Sintra 179
Serra do Amarela 292
Serra do Barroso 300
Serra do Gerês 292
Serra do Lurro 188
Serra do Marão 265
Serra dos Candeeiros 218
Serra do Soajo 292
Sesimbra 190
Setúbal 192
Shopping 103
Silves 395
Sintra 179
Soajo 292
Soares, Mário (President of Portugal) 21

Soccer 118
Solar do Vinho do Porto 153, 252; see also Wine
Sortelha 324
Sousa-Cardoso, António 265
Spas: see by specific name (Termas...)
Spain, Portugal's wars with 19, 20
Speed limits: see Driving
Sports & Recreation 111-119
Stamps and Postage: see Mail
Store Hours 63
Student ID Cards 69
Swabians 18
Swimming: see Sports & Recreation
Synagogues: see Jewish Communities

Tâmega (Rio) 266, 301
T.A.P. Airlines 30
Tascas: see Cuisine
Tavira 413
Taxis: see regional and city chapters
Tejo (Rio) 154, 343
Telephones in Portugal 69
Telephone calls to North America 70
Television in Portugal 71
Tennis: see Sports & Recreation
Termas das Caldas de Monchique 394
Termas do Curia 234
Termas do Peso 291
Termas do Vale dos Cucos 202
Termas do Vimeiro 204
Time Zone Changes 66
Tipping in Portugal 71
Tordesillas, Treaty of 20
Tomar 220
Torres Novas 223
Torres Vedras 201
Tourém 292
Tourist Offices in North America: see Portuguese National Tourist Board
Tourist Offices (Turismos) 72
Tour Operators, Suggested 28
Tours through Portugal 151, 255
Trains 38

Trancoso 325
Tax 103, 124
Tax Free for Tourists 103; see also
  Shopping
Trás-o-Montes 298
Travel Agenices in Portugal: see
  regional and city chapters
Travel Agencies in North America 27
Travelers Checks 63; see also
  regional and city chapters
Trip Cancellation and Interruption
  Insurance 26
Tróia 194
Turismo de Habitação 74; see also
  regional and city chapters

Valença do Minho 289
Vagueira 238
Vale do Lobo 406
Vasco de Gama: see Gama, Vasco de
Vasco Fernandes: see Fernandes,
  Vasco
Vaz, António 312
Viana do Alentejo 368
Viana do Castelo 281
Vicente, Gil 271
Vila da Ponte 300
Vila do Bispo 381
Vila do Conde 268
Vila Franca de Xira 186
Vila Fresca de Azeitão 189
Vilamoura 403
Vila Noguiera de Azeitão 188
Vila Nova de Cerveira 288
Vila Nova de Gaia 261
Vila Nova de Milfontes 196
Vila Nova de Ourém 223
Vila Praia de Ancora 284
Vilar de Mouros 287
Vila Real 308
Vila Real de Santo António 417
Vilarinho Seco 300
Vila Viçosa 352
Villa Rentals 75
Vimeiro 204
Vinho Verde Wine 126; see Wines
Vineyards: see Wines

Viriatus, Chief 18
Viseu 312
Visigoths 18
Visas 22
Vista Alegre 237
Viveiro 300

Walled Cities: see by specific name
  and by regional and city chapters
Water Skiing: see Sports &
  Recreation
Watersports: see Sports &
  Recreation and by regional and
  city chapters
Wellington, General 20, 204, 232,
  246
What to Pack 24
When to Visit Portugal 23
Windsurfing: see Sports & Recreation
Wines 125-133
World War I 21
World War II 21

Yachts: see Sports & Recreation
Youth Hostels 78

Zambujeira do Mar 196
Zeive 305
Zêzere (Rio) 223, 318

FROM THE PUBLISHER

Our goal is to provide you with a guide book that is second to none. Please remember, however, that things do change: phone numbers, prices, addresses, quality of food served, value, etc. Should you come across any new information, we'd appreciate hearing from you. No item is too small for us, so if you have any recommendations or suggested changes, please write to the author care of Open Road.

The address is:

Ron Charles
c/o Open Road Publishing
P.O. Box 11249
Cleveland Park Station
Washington, DC 20008

EUROPEAN TRAVEL CONSULTANTS

Your Specialists in Unique European Travel

We are North America's leading specialty tour operator for all of the castles, pousadas, quintas, manor houses, condos, apartments, villas, bed and breakfast inns, seaside resorts, spas, and hotels which are listed in this book. We have no minimum or maximum stay requirements, and most service charges are deductable from your final payment.

Call us directly for special wholesale prices on your airfare, rental cars, train passes, travel insurance, guides, and prepaid accommodations. We offer a staff of leading travel experts who have all visited hundreds of towns and villages throughout Portugal and several other exciting southern European nations.

All of our clients receive prompt and courteous service, lots of free advice, and assistance with all your booking needs. Let us work together with you to organize and reserve the best vacation imaginable. Please call our Portugal custom vacation department for information and brochures at:

(800) 585-8085

Toll free 24-hour brochure request hotline from the U.S.A. and Canada.

We offer travel agent, group, senior citizen, and student specials.

TRAVEL NOTES

TRAVEL NOTES

TRAVEL NOTES

TRAVEL NOTES

TRAVEL NOTES

YOUR PASSPORT TO GREAT TRAVEL! FROM OPEN ROAD PUBLISHING

THE CLASSIC CENTRAL AMERICA GUIDES

COSTA RICA GUIDE by Paul Glassman, 5th Ed. Glassman's classic travel guide to Costa Rica remains the standard against which all others must be judged. Discover great accommodations, reliable restaurants, pristine beaches, and incredible diving, fishing, and other water sports. Revised and updated. **$14.95**

BELIZE GUIDE by Paul Glassman, 6th Ed. This guide has quickly become the book of choice for Belize travelers. Perhaps the finest spot for Caribbean scuba diving and sport fishing, Belize's picture-perfect palm trees, Mayan ruins, tropical forests, uncrowded beaches, and fantastic water sports have made it one of the most popular Caribbean travel destinations. Revised and updated. **$13.95**

HONDURAS & BAY ISLANDS GUIDE by J.P. Panet with Leah Hart and Paul Glassman, 2nd Ed. Open Road's superior series of Central America travel guides continues with the revised look at this beautiful land. **$13.95**

GUATEMALA GUIDE by Paul Glassman, 9th Ed. Glassman's treatment of colorful Guatemala remains the single best source in print. **$16.95**

OTHER TITLES OF INTEREST

PARIS GUIDE by Robert F. Howe & Diane Huntley. Discover the romantic sights and sounds of the City of Light with two American travel writers living in Paris. Great hotel and restaurant suggestions, including tips on wine selection, plus nearby excursions. **$12.95**

FRANCE GUIDE by Robert F. Howe & Diane Huntley. The best of France, from Paris to Strasbourg, Brittany to Provence. Extensive wine and cuisine dictionary, plus terrific choices for hotels, restaurants, and fun things to do. **$16.95**

CHINA GUIDE by Ruth Lor Malloy, 8th Ed. The classic guide to China, 704 pages long, written by the premier China travel specialist. Malloy brings you more destinations and more great ways to enjoy traveling to China than ever before. From the Silk Road to the Forbidden City and everything in between, you won't want to visit China without this indispensable guide. **$17.95**

HONG KONG & MACAU GUIDE by Ruth Lor Malloy & Linda Malloy. The definitive guide to Asia's most dynamic cities. **$13.95**

PLEASE USE ORDER FORM ON NEXT PAGE

ORDER FORM

Name and Address: _____
_____
_____ Zip Code: _____

Quantity	Title	Price

Total Before Shipping _____

Shipping/Handling _____

TOTAL _____

    Orders must include price of book <u>plus</u> shipping and handling. For shipping and handling, please add $3.00 for the first book, and $1.00 for each book thereafter.
    Ask about our discounts for special order bulk purchases.

<u>ORDER FROM:</u> **OPEN ROAD PUBLISHING**
P.O. Box 11249, Cleveland Park Station, Washington, D.C. 20008